The Road to Ruins

The
Road
to Ruins

IAN GRAHAM

UNIVERSITY OF NEW MEXICO PRESS
ALBUQUERQUE

© 2010 by the University of New Mexico Press
All rights reserved. Published 2010

First paperbound printing, 2012
Paperbound ISBN: 978-0-8263-4755-8

18 17 16 15 14 13 12   1 2 3 4 5 6 7

Library of Congress Cataloging-in-Publication Data
Graham, Ian, 1923–
    The road to ruins / Ian Graham.
        p. cm.
    Includes bibliographical references.
    ISBN 978-0-8263-4754-1 (cloth : alk. paper)
    1. Graham, Ian, 1923– 2. Mayas—Antiquities. 3. Archaeologists—Great Britain—
Biography. 4. Archaeologists—Central America—Biography. 5. Maya architecture.
6. Inscriptions, Mayan. 7. Central America—Antiquities. I. Title.
    F1435.G7 2010
    930.1092--dc22
    [B]

                                2010002156

Design and composition: Deborah Flynn Post
All photographs were taken by Ian Graham unless otherwise noted.

Contents

Part I — Preclassic

CHAPTER 1

The Road to Ruins

"What *am* I doing in Mexico?" I asked myself, on emerging from the crowded streets of Matamoros in my ancient car. Ahead of me lay a featureless plain cut in two by a potholed highway running dead straight to the horizon. On either side was endless scrub, and an occasional cow, horse, or donkey—any of which might suddenly dash suicidally into the road.

And yet, a mere three weeks earlier I had left New York City with a very different destination in mind: Los Angeles. In fact, a skeleton map of the route to L.A. that I had intended to follow was still taped to the windshield. And to Los Angeles I was still resolved to go, since the main reason for coming to the United States had been to bring over from England a rare and dashing vintage car and sell it to a movie mogul for a vast sum. One of them, I felt sure, would pay a king's ransom to possess it.

The matter of my straying from the planned route could be blamed on an invitation that reached me just before I left Manhattan: it was to the Maryland Hunt Cup and Ball. There, among other pleasures, I could expect to see a dear friend—reason enough, I thought, for a slight detour. But then the event was so enjoyable that it made me reconsider my priorities; for here was I, visiting the United States for the first time in my life, and in possession of a fast and reliable car, so wouldn't it be perverse not to do some sightseeing in the South?

By easy stages, then, I passed through Virginia and down to Georgia, turned west, tarried awhile in New Orleans and Natchez, visited Dallas and Houston, and then drove to see the King Ranch. It was near the King Ranch that I saw, fatefully, a large sign: "Last Gas Before Mexico!"

"Mexico..." I mumbled to myself, "well, that's an idea I hadn't thought of. I'll just have a look at it, from across the Río Grande." Soon, on an impulse, I was driving across a bridge to the Mexican side, unaware that Jack Kerouac's Dean Moriarty and Sal Paradise had done the same thing a few years earlier—"On the Road to Mexico."

Two days later I was gliding into Mexico City. I have no recollection of what was uppermost in my thoughts just then, apart from disappointment that neither of the two people I knew in Mexico was to be found. As far as I can remember, nothing more than idle curiosity engaged my mind, and certainly I had no specific plans, because like most Englishmen I was completely ignorant about this country. And yet, because I had engaged in, and then abandoned, one previous career (physics), and had made little progress in another (photography), and was currently unemployed, I was on the alert for some opportunity to earn a living pleasantly—or as Dean Moriarty said, speaking to Marylou, it was "necessary now... to begin thinking of specific worklife plans." Never, though, did it cross my mind to look for them in Mexico.

1.1 My mother and myself, 1924. Photo by W. Dennis Moss and in possession of the author.

And yet, most unexpectedly, it was in Mexico that by happy accident I picked up a trail that would lead me into a field of activity completely new to me, Maya archaeology; and now I can state positively that never in the fifty years that I've spent tilling that field have I regretted doing so. On the contrary, I can think of no other occupation that would have been half as rewarding.

Serendipity is too weak a word to account for my entry into this field. A whole chain of pleasant events were responsible. To begin with, I chose my parents well. My mother, Meriel Bathurst, was a woman of notable beauty, intelligence, and sensibility. Born into a rich, aristocratic family and given a good private education, she continued as a married woman to grow in human sympathy and spirituality without losing her sense of humor, modesty, or readiness to do menial work. It was she who gave me my formal education up to the age of eight and a half, but alas, when I was eleven, death suddenly deprived our family of her love and guiding hand.

Her own mother was a Tory of the old school, and as such felt an affinity with the humblest country people, including the homeless (for whom she established a shelter in London), but for the urban poor she had little regard, and of course avoided undue familiarity with the middle class.[1] Yet the social status of her own paternal forebears, three generations back, appears to have been modest, or even obscure, but her Scottish grandfather by his own efforts and intelligence made his mark in politics and then became editor of the *Morning Post*. This was Britain's oldest national daily paper, and rival of *The Times* of London.

His son Algernon Borthwick (my great-grandfather) served initially as the paper's Paris correspondent, then as editor, and finally in 1870 he became its proprietor. In 1895 he was given a peerage, and as Lord Glenesk became Britain's first "Press Baron." As was only fitting, he became the master of three impressive mansions, one in London, another next to Balmoral, and a third in Cannes. (My grandmother once revealed that in Cannes she had learned to roller-skate, coached by the composer Rimsky-Korsakov.)

Had he not died young, my great-uncle Oliver would have succeeded his father as owner and director of the paper. He was forward-looking, and had already imported American presses, but as it was, control of it passed to my grandmother in 1908. Under her guidance the paper's Tory and Unionist politics continued unchanged, with my grandmother vetting every editorial with eagle eye. But so conservative was she that advertisers were not permitted to incorporate graphic material in their ads, with the natural consequence that they tended to place them elsewhere. And although her brother had put up a fine new building, Number 1, Aldwych, strangely it contained no reference library—so the *Post*'s journalists had to use a public library, half a mile away. Almost unbelievably, the art critic at one time was a bedridden invalid, who in writing his pieces was obliged to depend upon opinions aired by friends sitting at his bedside.

An old hand at the paper once explained that the fortunes of the paper in the early part of the last century had been to some extent founded on an "Upstairs-Downstairs" principle. "When owners of great houses advertised for a butler, footmen, cooks, valets or maids, they chose the *Morning Post* as their medium. We were the sort of paper that butlers ironed before laying us alongside the breakfast dishes."[2]

Then, after the First World War, with shutters going up on many great country houses, the turnover in butlers and lady's maids declined, and with it the paper's circulation. By the early twenties it was losing so much money that a majority interest was sold to two rich conservative dukes, and my grandmother's income was diminished.

Her husband, my grandfather, was the seventh Earl Bathurst, a quiet and benevolent man whose interests lay mainly in fox hunting and running his huge estate at Cirencester,[3] though he did have scholarly interests, too. One of his achievements was the very fine and hefty illustrated catalog of the family pictures that he compiled and had printed. If one can believe the pseudonymous depiction of him as the lord of "Fleeceborough" in Richard Jefferies' *Hodge and His Masters*,[4] his benevolence as a landlord included toleration of arrears of rent from his tenants in bad farming years. (Perhaps revenue from the coal beds he owned in Derbyshire allowed him to treat his farming tenants indulgently during the agricultural depression of the 1890s.)

As a fox hunter he was master of his own hunt, and since its kennels were not far from the mansion, I used to hear, early each morning while staying there, a joyful chorus from the hounds as they gobbled their breakfast of biscuits and horse meat. The breeding of those hounds was another matter of great interest to my grandfather, and a book of his on that subject is, I believe, well regarded by those in the know.

My father was the youngest son of the Duke of Montrose. In common with the younger sons of most landed families, he was expected to make his own way upon leaving school without financial help. In my father's case, he couldn't have expected much help from his father anyway, since he had virtually no money (I suspect my great-grandmother and her son of having frittered much of it away in their passion for horse racing[5]).

Among the few careers that were then considered suitable for young men in my father's circumstances were the army, the navy, or the church. My father chose the navy, entering it as a cadet at the age of thirteen and retiring in 1919 as a commander. He was a tall, handsome man with blue eyes, a bridge to his nose, and some curl to the hair at the sides of his head. By nature he was gentle, quite intelligent though not intellectual, blessed with charm, and always true. His musical tastes centered on Harry Lauder songs, such as *Roamin' in the Gloamin*, some of which he occasionally could be persuaded to sing to entertain his friends. While golf, shooting, and fishing were his favorite recreations, mixed farming became his *metier*.

He and my mother met just as the Great War broke out, and in 1916, passionately in love, they married. The fact that my father was not in a position to offer any financial contribution beyond his naval pay had at first been an obstacle in negotiations over the marriage settlement, so I think the impasse may have been broken by my grandmother's decision to provide from her own pocket most of the extremely lopsided settlement that was arranged, rather than from Bathurst trust funds. She approved of my father and saw how determined her daughter was to marry him.

On leaving the navy after the war, my father worked briefly for an engineering firm in Glasgow before buying a small farm in the village of Campsey Ash in east Suffolk, the purchase of which consumed about a quarter of the marriage settlement. The house is late Elizabethan, and as my brother has suggested, the name it bore for centuries, "Park House," may indicate that it was built in a deer park as a hunting lodge, its first owner having been, perhaps, a rich man whose actual residence would

1.2 Graham family at Brodick Castle in 1938. Left to right: Brother Robin, Archbishop of Canterbury (Cosmo Gordon Lang), Uncle Jim Montrose (Duke of Montrose), self, Aunt Nelly, sister Lilias, Uncle Malise. Photo in possession of the author.

have been far grander. But my mother, considering that name too grandiose, renamed it Chantry Farm, for she chose to see, with some imagination, a wall of old flint masonry adjoining the house as somehow associated with a chantry of the abbey that did once exist in the village about a mile away.

My father took to farming with a will, and was helped by my mother. For about the next ten years she was responsible for the chickens, managing the incubators, washing the eggs, grading them by size, and packing them for shipment. Sometimes she even cut firewood. A farm manager, or "bailiff" as he was called, was engaged to oversee the other farming activities, which included milk production, cereals, sugar beets, apples, and other crops that were tried, such as black currants—all of this on a farm of only 160 acres. With the bailiff overseeing the work, my father was able to take a job away from home to augment the family income, initially at a sugar beet factory in Ipswich, then at a grain-milling company near London.

Description of the comfortable life that we enjoyed at Chantry Farm when I was young may seem incompatible with the debts that for many years my father was struggling to eliminate. Evidently he and my mother were determined to maintain as many as possible of the amenities they were accustomed to (mercifully, though, these were far simpler than the pompous protocol of footmen with powdered wigs that my father remembered from his boyhood home). But supporting even our modest level of comfort required in those days a considerable staff.

The first sound that I would hear upon waking up, at least on weekdays, came from the gravel on the drive being scratched by the garden boy with a wire rake. Then, in winter, a maid would come into the bedroom I shared with my younger brother, Robin, bringing a can of hot water for our washbasins. Breakfast, at eight, was abundant, with several dishes to choose from: perhaps haddock or kedgeree, or scrambled eggs and bacon. My father always started breakfast with porridge, which he ate from a wooden bowl while slowly perambulating round the table—a Scottish custom possibly engendered by ancient memories of the danger of being stabbed in the back by one's neighbor while seated at table.

In the kitchen, one found Lily, the redoubtable cook, and in the scullery and pantry, the scullery maid and a "tweeny" (or "between maid") whose duties lay in the bedrooms and living rooms as well as in the dining room. Then, my sisters had a governess, and when we were small there was a nanny, and until my brother was about six, a nursery maid as well. Outside, there was a gardener and his boy, and the carpenter/chauffeur/handyman. The gardener was always referred to as Smith, and the carpenter as Peck, but to me he was always Mr. Peck, since I revered him as a mentor in carpentry and mechanics, engrossing topics for me from an early age.

Many were the mornings I spent following him about as he worked. My godmother, Dorothy Johnstone (known to us as "Johnny"), who was unusually gifted in carpentry and mechanics herself, noticed my interest and gave me on my fifth birthday a set of small tools. For a workbench I selected a deep windowsill in the day-nursery, which in time became so gouged and cut that it had to be covered over with plywood (as it still is). So to avoid further damage a small addition to the bicycle shed was built to serve as my "workshop."

But it was electricity that I found most fascinating. When I was about five my father had the acetylene lighting at Chantry Farm replaced by 60-volt D.C. electric lighting, the current being supplied by thirty large glass accumulators. These were charged each morning by a dynamo run by a very noisy single-cylinder engine, operated, of course, by Mr. Peck, under the supervision of his small apprentice. When I was about seven or eight, my sister Lilias was given an album, entitled *The Perfect Schoolgirl*, which contained among other things pages for confessions from the owner's friends. She put to me the questions suggested in it, the first two of which were: "What is your idea of perfect happiness?" and "What is your idea of true misery?" The answer I gave to the first was "Lots and lots of bulbs, wire, and everything electric," and to the second, "Electricity never invented. Second thoughts, rice pudding."

Always on the lookout for mechanical as well as electrical novelties, I remember finding a treasure trove after the gravel-surfaced public road at the end of our front driveway had been asphalted for the first time, for there, abandoned by the wayside, lay a wire-reinforced flexible tube some six or eight feet long. Thinking it might come in useful sometime (a conservationist principle I'd learned from Mr. Peck—and now continue to blame for the piles of potentially reusable objects currently in my workshop), I dragged it, helped by Margaret, the younger of my two sisters, to the place outside the garden where rubbish was burned. Finding myself unable, for the moment, to think of any immediate use for this trophy, I picked up one end and baptized it by peeing into it; but when I invited my sister to follow suit she had to confess her inability to do so. This, I suppose, was my first inkling of sexual dimorphism.

1.3 A story by the young author,
reflecting an early love of mechanics.

1.4 Philip de László's
portrait of my mother,
1935.

If I had spent any time at all hanging about the farmyard, I would surely have been less ignorant about mammalian physiology and reproductive processes. But then, a few years later, my much-loved uncle, Ralph Bathurst, took me to watch my grandfather's team of oxen plowing a field at Cirencester—these being the last of their kind in Britain, and the plowman the last who knew how to call his commands with the intonation they understood.

On that day I must have asked Ralph what was the difference between bulls and oxen—a matter that he seemed unwilling to explain but must have mentioned to my father, for on the very next day, he called me into his study and then spoke mysteriously, and perhaps a little awkwardly, about heifers and cows, bullocks, bulls, and oxen. Alas, I was quite unable to discern the slightest relevance of this to my concerns.

Until the age of nearly nine I was educated entirely by my mother—as my brother would be, too—following a system of home education which had an emphasis on drawing with the proper tools. How she managed this is a mystery, in view of other responsibilities she had taken on, such as visiting distressed families in the poorest part of Ipswich on behalf of the Council for Social Service; work for Call to Renewal, a program of the Mothers' Union of the Church of England; and presidency of PNEU (Parents' National Educational Union). There were speaking engagements, gardening and household chores, and frequent attendance, often twice a week, at Holy Communion at churches that she liked. These might lie some distance away, for she had become an ardent Anglo-Catholic and was admitted to the Community of the Resurrection at Mirfield. Mr. Peck was sometimes available to drive her to her destinations (for she herself never learned to drive), but often she bicycled or traveled by train.

Although modest and gentle, my mother showed very early that she knew her own mind, a trait she exhibited when only five. Queen Victoria, three years before her death, had asked my grandmother to bring my mother and her little brother, Allen, for her to see—this because the Scottish estate of my Borthwick great-grandparents adjoined Balmoral.

In my grandmother's account, "I led Meriel, and Mrs. Grant took Allen, and we were shown into the drawing room by an Indian servant, to whom Meriel at once lost her heart. The Queen sat near a table about the centre of the room and facing the door, and the children marched up to her and each gave her a big kiss quite fearlessly, which delighted her. Allen began to look around the room, and was soon talking at the top of his voice about everything. . . . Meanwhile, Meriel held forth to the Queen about Sambos.

"'What does she mean?' Her Majesty asked me. I answered that she meant the Indian servant. 'They would not like to be called Sambos,' said the Queen, 'Sambos are black, and they are not black at all.' 'I call them Sambos,' calmly said Meriel. 'Then you are wrong, my child,' said the Queen. 'They *are* Sambos,' still persisted Meriel, so the Queen gave it up. . . . The Queen then took a lovely French doll dressed in a yellow dress, with a white 'early Victorian' bonnet, which was lying near her chair, and gave it to Meriel. Meriel said thank you, but I heard her murmur 'I like black ones best,' which the Queen fortunately did not hear. . . . Meriel, when she said good-bye, turned her back on the Queen and curtseyed to me, which made Her Majesty laugh heartily."

If my mother had a fault, it lay in her occasional sharp, and very occasionally angry, remarks when someone's words or actions fell too far short of her high standards. Her diaries record her bitter remorse at these lapses and the confession she often made of them to a priest.

In becoming president of PNEU, my mother succeeded the dowager Marchioness of Aberdeen and Temair. This august lady I never met, but her appearance as recorded in photographs is easy to remember, for she was an exact replica of Queen Victoria in her later years, with hair drawn back in a bun and her dumpy frame clad in black taffeta.

Her late husband, the Earl of Aberdeen, had been Viceroy of Ireland, and on leaving that position had been elevated to the rank of marquess, with the option of adding a territorial designation to his title.

His choice for this, "Tara," raised a storm of protest in Ireland, for here was a Scotsman seeking status through a spurious link with the seat of the ancient High Kings of Ireland. Backing down, he chose to call himself instead "Marquess of Aberdeen and Temair." The subtlety of this ploy went undetected—for Temair was simply the more ancient name of Tara.

Upon my mother's taking up her duties as president, we all went up to PNEU's headquarters in the Lake District, where the secretary, Miss Pennythorne, showed us the Christmas card Lady Aberdeen had sent her. It was a photograph of herself looking properly Victorian, with her little dog in her arms. Neatly printed below was: "From the Marchioness of Aberdeen and Temair." Miss Pennythorne told us she had written to thank her, including a comment that she thought little Temair looked perfectly sweet. Thus was the seat of the ancient High Kings of Ireland reduced to a lapdog.

In September 1932, two months short of my ninth birthday, I was sent to a boarding school in Scarborough, which I disliked from the moment I first saw the bleak, barracks-like building. It was a dismal academy, where we never heard any music, one of the masters was especially objectionable, and the food was poor. Since we had to clean our plates, and the sausages often contained large lumps of a translucent, gristly substance, I always had an envelope in my pocket for the surreptitious removal of these, which I would sometimes discover weeks later in my desk or among my socks and underwear in the dormitory drawer allotted to me.

In summertime, Scarborough itself is a pleasant enough seaside town, but oh so depressing in winter, not least while being led through it in crocodile procession, two by two, past boarded-up shops with peeling paint, with a chill, wet wind blowing off the North Sea. An inherent defect of the school from my standpoint was its distance from home, for this deterred my parents from coming to visit more than once, or occasionally twice, in a year. Well, I bore this stoically, but I pitied the little boys who sometimes arrived at this school when as young as six and a half. Poor wretches, they spent much of their first weeks in tears.

During my first term I earned considerable kudos when our English teacher asked us to write an essay. Whether or not the topic of birds had been set I can't remember, but in any case I wrote about swallows, and described one of them returning to its "adobe." The teacher congratulated me in front of the class for knowing this word, so appropriate for a nest made of mud—but I still feel a tinge of shame for not having demurred, since the word I had really meant to write was "abode."

Every September, we went to stay with our grandparents at Cirencester. During the visit that we made just before I went off to school for the first time, Rudyard Kipling, a close friend of my grandmother's, came with his wife to stay. I remember him as short in stature, with a hat (sometimes a straw boater) jammed squarely and well down on his head, and speaking with a trace of American accent—picked up, I suppose, from his American wife and the years he spent in Vermont. But what struck me most on first meeting him were his eyebrows, for they curled into thick rolls, and I remember thinking that as a writer he could conveniently stow a pen or pencil in them, should he wish to. I was to find him very companionable when occasionally we went on walks together. His love of children was poignant, since he had encouraged his frail only son to join the army in World War I, and lost him in it.

On this occasion, he showed me his new pocketknife, a very fat one containing twenty-five implements, all made of the newly introduced stainless steel, and naturally, I was unable to conceal my admiration of it. Very kindly he managed to obtain another, and sent it to me on the eve of my reluctant departure for the dread school (where, of course, it gave me tremendous status in the dorm). Naturally, I wrote to thank him—though not very promptly, I fear.

1.5 My letter to Rudyard Kipling, 1932.

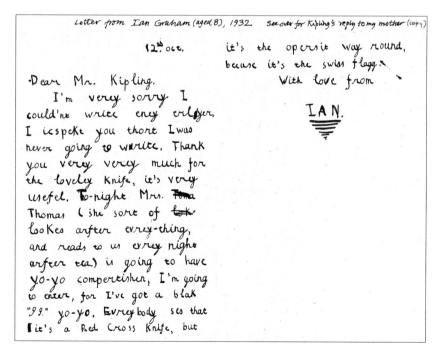

At home during the next holidays, my mother showed me a letter she'd received from Kipling, and according to my reading of it, he remarked on my interest in electricity—or so, for decades, I thought. But recently this letter came to light, and now I find I was mistaken. He is sending her the letter I had written thanking him for that knife: "My dear, the enclosed is yours—not mine—for inclusion in the family archives. What I like is its 'eclecticism.' [So he wasn't writing about electricity at all!] Bits of it are Chaucer's own spelling; bits are Esquimaux, such as 'icspekt,' &c. but all the same, it's a perfectly good letter & says what it means."

1.6 Mr. Kipling's reply.

Later, he was kind enough to write two or three more letters to me at school, but unfortunately not one of these survives. But I do remember very clearly the last one I had from him, for instead of being written with brown ink in his spidery script, it was typed. "I have just bought a Remington Noiseless typewriter, and am not very good at working it yet," he wrote, or something to that effect. The text was embellished with carets and emendations, some of them perhaps deliberate—put in simply to amuse. He described the new water softener that had been installed at Batemans, his home in Sussex, knowing of my interest in plumbing, and told me about piglets that had been born. How I wish I had kept that letter!

My Bathurst grandmother's conservative outlook was reflected in the car she used. It was a huge Daimler limousine of immense height, purchased in 1910 and maintained thereafter in pristine condition, with just one concession to modernity, the replacement of its acetylene headlamps with electric ones. The speedometer had an extra needle that recorded the highest speed attained during a journey. This, my grandmother seldom failed to inspect on alighting from it, to make sure that the chauffeur had not exceeded twenty-five miles per hour. (But once, when she was not on board and I was sitting in front, next to Hanman, the chauffeur, he got it up to nearly fifty on the flat.)

At the outbreak of war, the car was laid up for later use, but when, following my grandfather's death, my grandmother moved out of the mansion to make way for the next generation, the car was sold to a scrapyard for £5. That broke my heart. If I had known what its fate would be, I'd have saved up my sixpences and pennies to purchase it. A dozen years later, however, my undimmed admiration of that beautiful and silently running car was partly responsible for my purchase of that very different one, also thirty years old, which eventually took me to Mexico.

The garage, or coach house, at Cirencester also contained a magnificent coach, which like the car showed a small touch of modernization before being retired: in this case an electric bell under the coachman's seat, powered by a Leclanché cell. There was also a victoria, and a Bath chair, which we used to pull each other about in. Sadly, all of these and the car, too, disappeared soon after the war ended.

To my grandmother, airplanes, of course, were anathema. But in 1910 her patriotic instincts overcame her abhorrence of speed in general, and aviation in particular. This was owing to her discovery that unlike the French, the Germans, and the Poles, the British armed forces were not in possession of a single flying machine. (In fact, her concern is likely to have been fostered by Kipling, who was president of the Aerial League of the British Empire at that time.[6]) So she ordered, in the name of the *Morning Post*, the construction by a French firm of a dirigible 340 feet long, with a gondola large

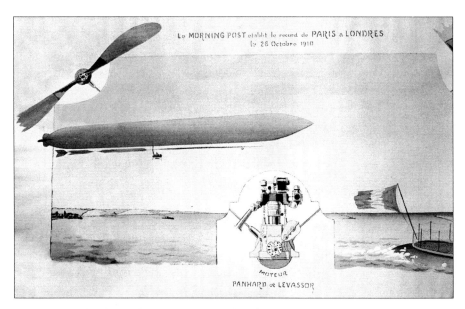

*1.7 My grandmother's airship, its construction ordered by her
for the British Army on behalf of the newspaper she owned.*

enough for twenty passengers, although it may never have flown with more than ten.
This was sometimes called *The National Airship* (contributions toward its construction
having been solicited), and sometimes *The Morning Post*.[7]

So on the tenth of October, 1910, Monsieur Capazza,[8] the Sicilian pilot, started the two
135-horsepower Panhard engines, and as the *Morning Post* told it,

> The screws began to revolve, and, as she got under way, M. Capazza swept
> round her helm with a force and agility that was marvelous when it is
> remembered that he was suffering from the effects of a motor accident that
> had injured his hands and left knee.

The flight to Farnborough was accomplished safely at an average speed of 35 miles per
hour, an alarming velocity by my grandmother's standards, but of course she was not on
board—not she!

Alas, the manufacturers had failed to tell the British Army officers concerned
that the gondola was now slung some two feet lower than originally planned, with the
unfortunate result that while it was being conducted into the hangar built for it, its

fabric caught on a roof girder and quickly deflated, this scene being caught by the *Pathé News* cinematographer. But at least it didn't go up in flames, and was repaired. But I think it a pity that this first passenger-carrying flight across the English Channel has not been recognized as such in any history of aviation that I've seen.

In sharp contrast with his mother, my uncle Allen loved fast cars and planes. He was Member of Parliament for Bristol Central, a keen polo player, flew his own plane, and was a dynamo of activity—in fact I wonder if some hormonal imbalance were responsible, as he could scarcely stand still without jiggling the coins in his pocket. For economy, he used to buy prototypes, these being exempt from the annual and very expensive tests for airworthiness. His first was a Klemm, the existence of which was kept secret from his mother. Then he had an accident, fortunately emerging from it uninjured, but since he was still a director of the *Morning Post*, my grandmother read all about it next day and was not pleased.[9]

Next he bought a Parnall "Elf,"[10] made by a firm in his constituency, and then there came a day when he wrote accepting my parents' invitation for a weekend visit, adding that he would come by air—news that wildly excited me. On that great day, we drove to the RAF airfield at Martlesham Heath, and soon a small biplane appeared, executed a "falling leaf" maneuver to lose altitude, and landed. As my mother had never seen this new plane, she wasn't sure if this was her brother's, but on seeing from across the airfield that the pilot climbing out of it was wearing a flying helmet, but otherwise was dressed for polo and carrying a red bathing suit in one hand, she knew it had to be her brother.

Three days later, of course, we all went to see him leave. His little plane was parked in a hangar beneath the wings of a Vickers "Vimy"—a huge World War I bomber. The Elf was trundled out, and my uncle invited me to climb in for a short flight. Of course I accepted—this had been my dream! He gave me his military overcoat and a flying helmet to wear, and we both climbed in. After the prop had been swung a few times without the engine starting, Uncle Allen climbed out of the cockpit, took a silk handkerchief from his breast pocket, stuffed it in the air-intake as a choke, and with the next swing the engine started.

The flight was extremely exhilarating, if somewhat spoilt by my initial efforts, while banking, to keep my body as nearly upright as the narrow confines of the fuselage allowed, which resulted in disagreeable sideways forces on my stomach. This flight was an unforgettable event in my boyhood, and sometimes, especially when unhappy at school, I would fantasize that Uncle Allen, somehow aware of my unhappiness, would soon be coming in to land on the sports field and whisk me away.

On 11 July 1935, my mother was due to address, with great reluctance, a gathering of the Parents' National Educational Union, of which she was then president, and would do so in London's vast Albert Hall. As an extremely modest person, the very thought of it truly alarmed her, yet she found time to compose a rhymed lamentation on her predicament for my eight-year-old brother, Robin:

How happy is the camel's lot
For I must speak, and he cannot,
He has a strangely ugly face,
Across the desert he must pace,
Men load his hump with burdens sore
And raid his private water-store.
His wrongs are very hard to bear
No wonder he is heard to swear
By grunt, by bubble and by squeak
But, happy beast, he cannot speak.

Ah! how devoutly I could wish
I were the swift and supple fish.
I mop my brow—*he* lingers cool
Within the tranquil, shadowed pool.
He watches with his golden eye
The antics of the heedless fly.
He lurks in waters bright and clear,
The angler's hook his only fear,
Across the stream he darts and plays
But silent, silent all his days.

1.8 My mother, painted in watercolor by my grandmother, 1932.

And Oh! how I could (dumbly) laugh
If I were but the tall giraffe,
Who, at his ease, may roam all day
About the plains of Africay—
May stretch his dappled neck at ease
To gather fruit from tallest trees,
Or amble fifty miles or so
To where the best bananas grow
And never make a sound at all,
But *I* must, to the Albert Hall.[11]

In January 1936 my mother died—as did Rudyard Kipling, on the same day. A miscarriage leading to an infection took her from us while still in her prime. A few days later I was back at the detested school, and I remember, all too well, that for the next few weeks, when lights were turned off in the dorm, I would retreat under the bedclothes to weep.

Some two years later, the school was given a holiday to celebrate the marriage of King George V's youngest son, the Duke of Kent, with the beautiful and charming Princess Marina of Greece. We were taken in two motorcoaches to a lovely expanse of farmland and moor to ramble and picnic. Not long before we were due to leave I picked up a large horseshoe, shed by some carthorse, intending to carry it back as a trophy. Once aboard the bus, and feeling a little tired, I shut my eyes, and then began to be conscious of the changes of pressure on my back as the bus accelerated or slowed down, and the sideways forces on turns. That gave me an idea: I removed the laces from my boots, and having tied them together, suspended the horse-shoe with them from the back of the seat in front of me. Watching its movements, it occurred to me that if its rotations and swings—this way and that—could be recorded somehow, a plot of our journey could be obtained. I'd invented inertial guidance! Of course, I had no notion at all of how to measure those swings and rotations, let alone how to integrate such data. (It has occurred to me since then that the rotations probably owed as much to magnetism as inertia.)

Although that school had a good reputation for preparing boys for competitive entry into "public schools" (or in U.S. usage, private schools), I failed to be stimulated by most of the teaching. In Latin class we learned gender rhymes by rote—useless fragments of which I still remember:

> Abstract nouns in –io call
> Feminina one and all;
> *Bidens* fork and *bidens* sheep
> To the feminine we keep. . .

Similarly, in French there were lists of nouns with different masculine and feminine forms to learn, such as "bouc/chevre" and "singe/genon." Of course, I left school quite unable to speak the language.

Just one teacher (of English literature) did arouse me from torpor. He was a man of rather dashing appearance, still in his prime, and given to wearing suede shoes—which some parents must have looked at askance. Loving the language, he spoke like an actor, and now that I try to recall him, I believe he did rather resemble the actor

Rex Harrison. But the important thing was his active engagement with us, and his ability to keep us alert with his passion for the subject. I still remember a few scraps of his imaginative approach. One was his asking us to decide which of two ways of posing the same question was the more expressive or atmospheric, and to give our reasons:

First, Keats's: "O what can ail thee, knight-at-arms,
  Alone and palely loitering?"

Or another: "Oh what is the matter with you, young man,
  Just hanging about by yourself?"

Gradually, I became lazier at school. My father must have been disappointed to read in my school reports the dreary litany: "Could do better if he tried." The headmaster had wanted me to try for a scholarship at Winchester, and when this challenge failed to buck me up, my father promised that if I obtained one, he would put the money saved to my credit. Even this incentive failed, so I sat the ordinary Winchester entrance exam, and passed it well enough to be put in the bottom class of the Middle Division of the school.

CHAPTER 2

Winchester

I n sending me to Winchester College my father had followed the advice of a former
headmaster of the school, Dr. Montagu John Rendall, who long ago had retired to
what once had been the gatehouse of Butley Abbey and now was the only surviving portion. This was only a few miles from our home. Rendall was a man of imposing
aspect, with a prominent nose and large moustache, and a preference for sporting a silk
kerchief pulled through a gold ring in place of a necktie. His pronouncements, usually
preceded by "Ah. . . ," were delivered in pedantic and often archaic phraseology, but
mostly with a twinkle in his eye.

On a later visit I realized that his spacious living room had been formed centuries earlier by building walls of stone and flint to close off both ends of a great
vaulted Gothic archway, dating from the early 1300s. It was a most impressive chamber. Looking around, I noticed an oaken doorway of recent construction that had a
hinged circular opening, around which ran a beautifully carved inscription in Greek
lettering: STOMA AETHEROS. I'd learned enough Greek to read this as "Voice of
the Ether," and sure enough, this little trapdoor, when opened, revealed a loudspeaker,
while behind the door itself was a chamber almost filled with racks of glowing vacuum tubes, coils, and connecting cables, these forming a radio receiver using the new
superheterodyne system, specially built by BBC engineers and installed for him as a
governor of the corporation.

Previously, my parents had intended to send me to Wellington College, but as
a result of their visit to Rendall they were persuaded in favor of Winchester (for my
father had no school loyalty to consider, having been a naval cadet aboard the HMS
Britannia, a floating wooden hulk moored in the river Dart, where existence must

indeed have been stark in winter). Also present that day were two Winchester masters, Harry Altham and Spencer Humby. Altham became a housemaster at Winchester, and I always regretted not being in his house, for he was most likeable, and in it I would find three or four boys who might have become my close friends.

Instead, I was entrusted to the tender care of one Horace Arthur Jackson, known as "the Jacker," a small man with a bristly moustache, little eyes set in puckered lids, and a lumbering gait, whose general appearance was that of a grumpy gnome. Another peculiarity was his diction: he chewed his words, so they emerged with most vowels and diphthongs reduced to "oy." As a housemaster, his principal goal seemed to be the accumulation of as many sporting trophies as possible for display on the mantelpiece in the dining hall—although for himself he did also collect blue-and-white Worcester china.

In my mother's copious diaries, which fill a whole suitcase, I found that during a visit to us in 1934 a Wykehamist cousin of ours (that is, Winchester alumnus) had described Harry Altham as one of the nicest people at the school; but as for the Jacker, he "hadn't much use for him." Hearing this was enough for my mother to suggest sending me instead to Altham's house, but in keeping with her policy of not interfering in what my father might regard as his domain, she didn't insist.[1] My father worshipped her, but couldn't, I think, help feeling a little inferior to her in matters of sensibility and intellect. So in certain areas my mother trod delicately: for example, she gave up reading difficult religious or philosophical books while they were traveling together on trains, so that he wouldn't feel isolated while her mind browsed on higher ground.

At Winchester, each new boy—or "man," for in the school's usage we were all men, even at thirteen—each new "man," then, was delivered into the care of another boy of one year's seniority, who for two weeks would guide him each day to his appointed place and was charged with teaching him the peculiar vocabulary in use by the boys, known as "notions." When those two weeks were up, the new "men" became servants of the prefects, but I don't remember the service being onerous. One duty that fell to us on Sundays was actually enjoyable: we had to prepare delicacies for the prefects' tea, which usually included tinned asparagus tips rolled up in thinly cut bread and butter. Their manufacture required skill, and many were the rolls we rejected as substandard; but naturally none was wasted.

The prefects were allowed to punish junior boys by giving them a limited tanning with a cane, but in my experience I saw very little abuse of this power, although sometimes this must have occurred. Much worse, I thought, was the repeated bullying of a few unfortunates.

Unlike Etonians, we had no private studies—merely desks arranged round the periphery of a large room, with partitions between desks. So we were open to the general clamor and inspection by the other boys, and as we all slept in dormitories, we never had any privacy. Perhaps years of living like this, higgledy-piggledy together, was effective in knocking the rough corners off our awkward characters, and socialized us, but in my view five years of this regime was excessive and tended to grind off our peculiarities, leaving some of us a bit dull, like pebbles on a beach.

While at Winchester, my drawing pastimes from earlier home-schooling days took the form of fanciful machinery and automobiles. We were not allowed radios, but I did manage to build a one-tube receiver from a design published in *Wireless World*. Just as I got it to work for the first time the Jacker made an unexpected entrance in the hall. Guiltily I took off the headphones, expecting reproof and perhaps punishment, but to my astonishment he seemed almost pleased—perhaps at finding that this lazy boy had actually *done* something! There and then he gave me permission to keep the set.

I'm sure he never thought of the concession he had just granted as transferable, but transfer it I did. I turned it over to the house captain of cricket in return for his promise never again to make me play in a game I loathed—and feared, since I had sometimes been placed at a position in the field known as "short leg." This was on the batsman's left, about thirty-five feet away, where a powerful stroke might give one no more than a quarter of a second to estimate the ball's trajectory and then take suitable evasive action. I'd read that amongst those killed by cricket balls had been Alfred Lyttleton, renowned as the best all-round athlete at the turn of the last century, and thought it quite likely he had been in just in that position on the field when he received the fatal blow.

In the summer following my second year at Winchester my godmother, Dorothy Johnston (who, as noted earlier, liked to be called "Johnny"), kindly suggested taking me to the Lucerne music festival. She had just bought a new Ford 8, which at £100 was the least expensive car ever available in England, and in this we set off, bowling along at 40 miles per hour for three long days, stopping only for picnics or quick looks at a cathedral or two. Upon arrival in Lucerne, we went to the festival ticket office to pick up tickets, and there heard alarming news about the political situation—for we were in the third week of August 1939. Wisely, Johnny decided to turn for home immediately, before we'd heard even one concert. The disappointment was tremendous, but of course she'd made the only possible decision.

By the end of that month my father had been recalled into the navy, and about three days later left for the Azores to serve as a consular official, his main duty being that of providing ship's captains with whatever intelligence there was about the location of U-boats. Before leaving, he managed to arrange for my brother to move in with old family friends; I was sent to my grandparents in Gloucestershire; and my sisters went off to join the women's Auxiliary Territorial Service. Then, having arranged for all the contents of our house to be put in storage, he made it available for housing about fifty children evacuated from the east end of London. How he did all this in those few days I cannot imagine.

I reached Cirencester on the second of September; war was declared next morning, and later on that fateful day I was surprised to see my grandfather in the library with the telephone receiver pressed to his ear—as I'd never before seen or heard of him using that instrument.

"What's that—evacuees?" he was saying, "No, no, can't have any of them here. What? Kent children? No, Viola, surely you know that I sold the house in Kent some time ago. No connection with Kent anymore."

He was talking to his daughter-in-law, my uncle Allen's wife, who had just been appointed evacuee officer for Gloucestershire, responsible for finding hosts for the flood of children being evacuated there from London. But then my aunt explained that these Kent children were not from the county of Kent at all, but were instead the two small children of the Duke of Kent, the youngest brother of the king, and his beautiful and charming duchess.

The next day they arrived, accompanied by two nannies (one of them rather alarming, I thought), and were installed in the nurseries on the top floor. George was four, and Alexandra nearly three—the prettiest and most endearing little girl imaginable. I lost my heart to her at once.

A day or two later I went to the appointed office in Cirencester to collect my gas mask, and was just stowing it away in my bedroom, not far from the nursery, when Alexandra came toddling along. To entertain her, I put it on, producing shrieks of laughter, and then she ran off to tell her brother what she'd seen. Soon the senior nurse came striding in to inquire what I had meant by frightening her little Royal Highness with that horrible thing? I felt I had to tell my grandmother that the children didn't appear to have been provided with these possibly useful accessories, so she took them into town to be fitted with the special children's model in blue and red rubber, with Mickey Mouse ears.

A milestone of little interest to anyone but myself was reached that autumn: it was somehow decided that I was now old enough to have dinner downstairs with my grandparents. This meant changing into a dinner jacket, dress shirt with a stiff, starched front, wing collar, and bow tie. How I hated that rig! It was especially tiresome on the days when I'd just bicycled seven miles from Pinbury at the other end of the park, this being a modest Elizabethan house set in an enchanting dell, with a stream below. For my grandparents, it had served as a kind of Petit Trianon, whither they could retire after the rigors of the London social season and enjoy the simple life. They would bring from the mansion a skeleton staff of, I suppose, the valet (functioning also as butler), my grandmother's lady's maid, the cook, a "tweeny," and a housemaid or two. There, my grandfather spent much of his time writing (perhaps his book on the breeding of foxhounds), setting type and printing from it, and my grandmother in painting and making silk embroidery, at both of which arts she excelled.[2]

Pinbury was now rented to the poet John Masefield, and my grandmother had arranged that I should mow its lawns and do other small jobs, for which Masefield paid me the handsome wage of two shillings—enough to buy twelve Mars Bars. I remember very well the experience of bicycling back through the woods as daylight faded; it was highly atmospheric, and while passing under the opaque foliage of a long, vaulted nave of beeches, even spooky. But I seldom had time to pay attention to that, for usually I would cut my departure fine and have to pedal furiously, returning quite out of breath and with no more than fifteen minutes for bathing and wrestling with recalcitrant studs, cufflinks, and bow tie, and then race downstairs before the gong sounded.

The service of dinner was supervised by Smart, the butler, dressed in black, aided by William, my grandfather's valet (distinguished by a waistcoat with horizontal blue and yellow stripes), and two footmen, "James" and "Frederick" (names borne ex officio, to save my grandmother the trouble of remembering new names when one of them was replaced).

After dinner we moved into the library, where my grandmother would light her cigarette by holding its tip over the tall glass chimney of an oil lamp. Oh yes, there was electricity, but it was given only a subsidiary role in lighting that room. When the time came to retire, we would each take a silver bedroom candlestick provided with a snuffer, light it, and solemnly proceed upstairs, protecting the flame with one hand. My father, thinking this ceremony unnecessarily hazardous, managed to find silver-plated candlesticks of very similar appearance, with built-in batteries and flamelike bulbs. These lit up when raised and went out when set down. But of course this novelty was rejected by my grandmother out of hand.

For her, electricity held insidious dangers. Since the street nearest to the mansion lay less than a hundred yards away, a connection with the public electricity supply would have been simple, but any such plan was anathema to her, since communal electricity smacked of socialism. So the two 25-horsepower horizontal gas engines remained in service, one of them huffing away quietly all morning while charging a 200-volt bank of lead-acid batteries. Of course, those slow-running horizontal engines with huge flywheels, and the producer-gas plant that fueled them, were for me a source of never-failing interest and pleasure.

About a year later, my father returned from the Azores and was appointed to the Kyle of Lochalsh, on the west coast of Scotland. This large, sheltered body of water had been established as a mine-laying base, the principal one in the country, and for this reason and others, a very large area of northwestern Scotland had been put off-limits to all but residents—and the families of officers based there. So our holidays from school were delightful. The Isle of Skye was a five-minute ferry ride away, and occasionally we all crossed over to spend a night or two in a cottage near Loch Corruisk. One side of the loch lies at the foot of a high and nearly vertical rock cliff, where, on a small ledge, a golden eagle had its nest. To me, the loch itself was depressing, for the sun's rays scarcely reached it, but my father keenly enjoyed wet-fly fishing there.

The people of Skye are *sui generis*, and astonishingly, the bureaucrats of Whitehall seemed willing to make allowances for their highly individual character, for the rationing of food and clothing, strictly enforced in the rest of the country, was here a dead letter, nor was the blackout observed. Of course, Skye was well beyond the range of German bombers, but to visitors from the south, drilled to be constantly on the alert for the smallest ray of light escaping from a house, shamelessly blazing windows made one feel very uncomfortable. But on the other hand, eggs and cream, scarce elsewhere, were readily available, and so was tweed from the Outer Isles.

One day as I was bicycling through moorland, I came upon a tent pitched some yards from the road. It was shaped like a fat sausage bisected horizontally. A man was standing near it, so I stopped to chat with him. He was a "tinkler," as itinerant tinkers are called in Scotland. When he told me that he'd had such a successful year that he was taking a few months off, I told him I was sorry, as I'd have liked to learn some of the tricks of his trade (although I hope I was tactful enough not to use quite those words).

"Well," he said, "I could show you how to make something simple, like a mug," and with that invited me into the tent. In it there were two beds, on one of which his "auld woman" was resting, and between them a massive accumulation of objects. My new friend reached under his bed and pulled out a box of tools and a stake, this being a narrow, T-shaped anvil, the vertical portion of which he then drove some way into the ground. Next he produced a piece of tinplate and a pair of tinsnips (or shears); but these had a pivot so slack that I doubted it could cut anything. Of course I was mistaken, for by exerting a contrary, twisting pressure as well as a squeezing force to the handles with one hand, and at the same time a steadying thumb-pressure on the pivot with the other, the blades were brought together firmly enough to slice through tin.

Next, he showed me how, by leaving the snips slack-jawed, he could turn up the edges of tinplate into a right-angle bend. This allowed him to form joints, by linking two such bent-up edges and turning them over more by hammering to form a joint like tightly clasped hands, which could then be soldered. The cylinder that he made by this method was then joined to a disk in the same way, and the upper edge of the emerging mug was skillfully rolled over. Finally, it was given a handle and also rolled edges; then he gave me the finished mug, which I still treasure as an object lesson in the resourceful use of primitive tools. As I was about to leave, he asked if he could buy my bicycle, so I was truly sorry at being unable to oblige him, since it wasn't mine.

My most cherished and enduring memories of Scotland, though, are of visits we made to Brodick, on the Isle of Arran, the whole of which belonged to my aunt Molly, the wife of my father's eldest brother, the Duke of Montrose. A lady of impressive proportions, she had a downright, somewhat imperious manner. I sometimes found her rather alarming, but she could also show a lively sense of fun. My uncle, by contrast, was extremely open and friendly. Poor man, he was left almost totally deaf by an ear infection suffered in his teens, but that didn't stop him a few years later from signing up as a deck hand on a barque bound for Australia. The experience led him to devote much of his life to organizations connected with ships and the sea. I believe he was responsible for creation of the RNR (Royal Naval Reserve), and he also submitted to the Admiralty his design for a new class of vessel, an aircraft carrier. I am told that the first one subsequently built closely resembled his design, except for the addition of elevators to bring aircraft up from a lower deck.

Uncle Jim was a large and strong man, with a voice to match, but being deaf he couldn't adjust its volume to the situation, and occasionally he committed thunderous gaffes—but was readily forgiven by anyone who knew him. On being told afterwards of one that he'd made, he would laugh uproariously at his own mistake if it was a harmless one. Perhaps as a result of his deafness, he was very much an extravert. Practical jokes appealed to him, and when the Archbishop of Canterbury (the Rev. Cosmo Gordon Lang) came to stay at Brodick Castle, Uncle Jim gave him a whoopee cushion to sit on. At fourteen, I almost choked while trying to contain my laughter.

My brother and I were always given the room at the top of the castle's lofty tower. It had a parapet on which there stood a superb telescope removed from a World War I German battleship; it had three rotating eyepieces of different powers and was mounted on a heavy iron pedestal. If, while lying in bed in the morning, I wondered whether it was time to get up for breakfast, I could go out and read the time from the town hall clock in Ardrossan, fourteen miles away across the Firth of Clyde.

Our room was also equipped with a Davy fire-escape apparatus. This consisted of a long cord with a sling to pass under the armpits before launching oneself from the parapet; the cord would then be paid out at a steady rate through a mechanism attached to the wall. One evening I thought I'd test it. All went well until I found myself slowly descending past the windows of my aunt's bedroom, just as she was changing for dinner. On this occasion her sense of humor failed her.

Often I'd get up early enough to go out with the boatman to catch mackerel, which I would then take up to the castle for breakfast—and weren't they delicious! Then we might go out with guns for grouse or blackcock, shooting over dogs; these were champion pointers, delightful to watch as they worked. To my surprise, I also enjoyed deer stalking, but presumably Fraser, the stalker, had instructions to bring me up only to a stag with a crumpled antler or some other defect. Well, that didn't matter. I wasn't interested in trophies, and I knew that defective animals had to be culled.

The greatest pleasure Arran could offer, though, was its beauty. Goat Fell and the panoramic view gained from its top (weather permitting); the sheep on grassland near the shore, seen against the evening light; the wonderful gardens at the castle, largely created by my aunt—those are a few of the scenes I remember with affection. There was even one pleasure to enjoy during our crossing back to the mainland: the cranks, connecting rods, valve gear, oiling mechanism, and so forth of the paddle steamer's engine, all brightly painted, polished, and fully visible from the lower deck. Two that I remember were the *Glen Sannox* and the *Queen Mary* (probably named after Mary, Queen of Scots). Then one day I noticed that a newly painted "two" in Roman numerals had been added to that steamer's name on its bow and stern. How come, I wondered?

The Cunard Steamship Company had always chosen names for its ships ending in -*ia*, such as *Mauretania* and *Berengaria*. Then, in the late 1920s, construction began on what would be the world's largest liner—referred to before launching only by its shipyard number, 534. Completion was delayed by the ensuing period of financial depression, but by 1934 it was nearly ready for launching, and the company's chairman, Sir Percy Bates, went to see the king, to inquire whether the queen would be graciously pleased to launch this great vessel (which Cunard's board had already decided to name *Victoria*). As we learned from Dawson Bates, his son, who was also in the Jacker's house, the king replied that he was quite sure the queen would gladly consent to do so.

"And what name do you propose to give this great liner?"

"We thought it only appropriate that it should bear the name of Britain's greatest queen."

"Her Majesty will certainly feel honored by the choice you have made."

So it came about that our poor little paddle steamer became Queen Mary II (and now, in the twenty-first century, remembered as the first Queen Mary the Second).

I don't believe my father was by nature endowed with spiritual propensities, but out of undying loyalty and affection for my mother he did what he could to further the affairs of the Church of England, such as taking an active part in having a church built in a newly developed area of Ipswich, and later serving for some years as a church commissioner, with meetings at Lambeth Palace. Accordingly, he took pains to have me properly instructed in the faith prior to Confirmation. This took the form of weekly visits to a canon of the church, who by virtue of a position in Winchester Cathedral lived in a charming little house in the cathedral close. He was a quiet man of about fifty, with black hair and an ascetic appearance. I have to confess that I didn't take in a word of the instruction I received, and my unreceptiveness must have been a disappointment for this holy man.

But when, in the college chapel, we in the choir turned to face the altar to say the Creed, and a few boys of Anglo-Catholic persuasion crossed themselves at certain passages, as my mother used to, I did so, too—inconspicuously with one finger against my trouser leg. This I did only as a mark of remembrance, and as a kind of hopeless magical gesture.

I have not forgotten the perplexity with which I accepted, after her death, her beautiful crucifix of ivory and ebony. I think I was expected to hang it on the wall behind my bed, but this was something I couldn't bring myself to do. Unable to resolve the conflict, I hid it, shamefully, in a closet used for medicines and toys. I had not been brave enough to give it to my sister Lilias, as this would have required my confession of unbelief. Some time later she must have found it there and been distressed at my careless disposal of it.

Following those fruitless sessions of religious instruction, I often went exploring in the cathedral, a magnificent building of largely Norman origin. In the course of many visits I'd found my way up various narrow spiral stairways into the space between the vaulted stone ceiling of the nave and the pitched roof above, and then up into the belfry, for in those days nothing was locked. What with these explorations, examination of memorial tablets, and listening to the great organ and the choir, many were the hours I whiled away there.

But it was singing in the school chapel choir that provided the greatest pleasure during my time at Winchester. The chapel itself was a glorious structure, the organ good, and the choirmasters unexcelled. In my time, they were George Dyson, later president of the Royal College of Music; then Sidney Watson, who would move on to New College, Oxford; and Robert Irving, whose flouting of convention by wearing green suede shoes and blue-framed glasses which set off his red hair I much admired—as I did for his having once played variations on the *Rhapsody in Blue* as an organ voluntary in chapel. He later became conductor of the Royal Ballet, and then of the New York City Ballet—and a racehorse owner, too. (Later, in New York City, I had the pleasure of visiting him sometimes.) The musical experience I had at Winchester has proved indelible, and I would still travel far for an opportunity to take part in singing a verse anthem by Pelham Humphrey, or Samuel Wesley's "Blessed Be the God and Father."

Among the masters there were several I particularly admired. One was Eric James, later high master of Manchester Grammar School; another was Eric Emmett, author of books on mathematical and logical puzzles—and I became very fond of his wife Aileen, too. Then there was Mr. Brown, whom I respected for his teaching, although his personality fitted his name while also matching his brown suits. (Poor man, the nickname we gave him was "Dungy Brown.") But he taught us celestial navigation—perhaps on his own initiative, and once he had us calculate how fast each man, according to his weight, had to run upstairs to his top-floor classroom to generate one horsepower.

Another whom I greatly admired was Spencer Humby, whom my parents had met at Dr. Rendall's, nearly ten years earlier. Physics was his subject, and appropriately he looked quite like another Spencer (Tracy)—when playing the role of Edison in the film featuring him.

Spencer Humby did his best to encourage me to study, without much success. My fixed purpose, unfortunately, was to attend as few lectures in the week as possible, and in this reprehensible quest I was aided by two factors: first, I was the only boy in the top science form who was not studying for an Oxford or Cambridge scholarship; and then, the ordinary school exams had been abolished in the interest of wartime paper economy.

Of course, I can't forget that one of the other physics teachers, in the course of describing and defining units of force, energy, power, work, etc., also introduced us to a fundamental unit new to physics, that of negative work, a sort of anti-erg. In my honor he named it a "Graham."

One prescient action of Humby's deserves a mention. He lent me a short report written by Watson Watt, Bainbridge Bell, and J. F. Hurd of the Slough Research Station, published in 1933.[3] Their investigation of the ionosphere by means of pulsed radio transmissions displayed on a cathode-ray tube led to the development of radar research in Britain, and Humby, aware of this, must have hoped that in the future I might find a place in that effort—as eventually I did.

But at school I wasn't entirely idle. For one thing, I was doing some experiments in FM radio (then a recent invention, not yet in public service), which I worked up into a paper submitted for the school's Senior Science Prize; this I was awarded, but only jointly with another boy, because I'd failed to produce the necessary paper on a chemistry topic. Another active pursuit was construction of a wind tunnel, which I hoped would enable me to take *schlieren* photographs showing the flow of air over an aerofoil (aviation being another interest of mine). I was quite taken with photography, accumulating various cameras and spending many an hour developing and printing photos in the school's darkroom. And then, I was also engaged in highly extracurricular activities, making bombs, a mortar, and a folding pistol.

It was my father who first gave me a taste for explosions. In cutting up felled or fallen trees for firewood, he often had trouble splitting the forks of oak trees in the ordinary way, with an iron wedge and sledgehammer, because of their convoluted grain. So he would bore a hole in the recalcitrant wood, put into it a mixture of potassium chlorate and sugar, along with a length of "slowmatch" fuse, and seal the charge with clay, well tamped into the hole. When he'd lit the fuse, we all ran, and were usually rewarded by a very satisfactory explosion that sent shards of firewood flying in all directions.

At Winchester, I employed the same explosive and fuse in making pipe bombs, just for fun, out of ordinary two-inch plumber's iron pipe. I had the pipe threaded at either end to receive plugs, then drilled a three-sixteenths-inch hole for the fuse. On firing, the prototype disappointingly split lengthways along the seam; so for the succeeding bombs I taped a loosely fitting iron ring around its middle, which caused the tube on explosion to rend into two jagged halves, with one of them usually flying off with a satisfactory whine.

Next, in collusion with another boy, I made a trench mortar. The barrel was identical to that of the pipe bomb, but of course plugged at one end only. Instead of

2.1 My wind tunnel, built at Winchester College.

the high-explosive mixture, we used blasting powder, obtained from an obliging gun dealer in town; supports for the barrel were simple legs of bent fencewire. As we set out from the house for the first trial of our weapon, we had the misfortune of finding the Jacker walking in the same direction. Turning to me he asked, "What have you got in that tin, boy?"

"Hypo," I replied, and soon turned off in the direction of the school's darkroom, leaving my co-conspirator, who had the mortar concealed under his raincoat, alone with him; but fortunately in the Jacker's eyes he was a less suspicious character than me. The tin I was carrying had contained blasting powder and lead projectiles, these cast in the school's handicrafts workshop from "tuppence-worth" (two-pennyworth) each of lead. We fired them with great satisfaction from the neighboring hills, where, on return to earth, they buried themselves in the turf too deeply for recovery.

My pistol had (or rather, has—since I still have it) a barrel of copper tubing of quarter-inch internal diameter, so that it could use .22 ammunition "borrowed" from the rifle range. Of course, being a loose fit in that barrel, the bullets rattled down it and emerged without spin and perhaps slightly inclined one way or another, so one was lucky to hit a tin can at ten paces. My pistol's strong point, however, was the way it could be folded and carried in a trouser pocket on Sunday walks by the river. Our Sunday rig was morning coat, striped trousers, and top hat—those precious hats sometimes suffering the indignity of being launched on the river like Pooh-sticks. Then it was very tempting to take a shot at them with the pistol as they floated by, but explaining bullet holes in one's hat would have been difficult.

One of the boys in my house took to setting off far less powerful, but equally alarming explosions, once with the unfortunate matron of the house as victim. Nitrogen iodide, a substance easy to make in the chemistry lab, lies inert as long as its little crystals are damp, but when allowed to dry out, they explode at the slightest jolt. So this boy slipped wet crystals on the tray loaded with glasses of milk and cookies that the matron would be distributing as usual during the evening study period. The explosion caused no damage beyond a little spilt milk, but the poor lady experienced a shock she didn't deserve. (Use of this substance to provoke harmless fright in a college setting has, by the way, a surprising antiquity. William Stukeley, a pioneer antiquary famous for his excavations at Stonehenge and Avebury, wrote that in 1705, while at Corpus Christi College, Cambridge University, "I often prepared the *pulvis fulminans* & sometime surprised the whole College with a sudden explosion. I cur'd a lad once of an ague with it by a fright.")[4]

As prefects, we were given fire-watching duty once or twice a week. This involved patrolling the streets at night with a view to reporting any fires caused by incendiary bombs, and during my patrols I sometimes used the opportunity to attempt to climb into one or another of the boys' houses. On succeeding, I would leave at once, for this was solely an exercise in entering without breaking. Wykehamists, according to one informant, seem to have gained a reputation for expertise in various minor criminal arts, for he told me that army officers captured by the Germans during the war felt encouraged if they found officers from the Rifle Brigade in the camp, because these tended to be Wykehamists, who might be expected to have experience in forging documents, picking locks, etc.

The question of why some of us engaged in these rule-breaking activities is worth raising, though I have no good answer. A plausible factor, of course, was the remand-home atmosphere that challenged us to break the stifling rules. (For example, I spent much fruitless thought trying to devise a collapsible and easily concealed straw boater, which would make furtive expeditions to the cinema much less liable to detection.) Perhaps, also, because we were now nominally "men" (in Winchester College usage), some of us had an unconscious urge to show that in fact we were still boys, who might be expected to get up to mischief.

One or two boys were, in fact, bent on destruction, for motives I don't understand at all. During my years at the school, one burned down a cricket pavilion and another wanted to blow up the headmaster's car—without knowing, perhaps, that he was following the example of Lord Byron, who while at Harrow School tried to blow up the headmaster's house. In my case, I simply wanted to test my abilities when pitted against adult rules, and to get a thrill from the adventure.

One Saturday in my fourth year, a group of us, including some prefects, gave ourselves a leisurely lunch at a restaurant, with plenteous consumption of wine and other illicit beverages, including crème de menthe and who knows what other liqueurs. Then we went on to sample the beer and cider at two or three pubs. Somehow news of our doings reached Horace Arthur Jackson that evening. I was sent for, and asked to give an account of them. In keeping with schoolboy ethics I gave a somewhat modified version, in order to protect the prefects involved. But on interviewing another of our group, the Jacker detected inconsistencies in my account and sent for me again. Luckily he accepted my Mark II version of our exploits, and my friend Bertie Booth, a prefect, escaped undetected.

But of course I was sent to the headmaster to be caned for lying. I took the precaution of putting on my rowing shorts, the nether portion of which was lined with chamois leather, before donning my trousers. This proved to be a quite unnecessary precaution, since the headmaster, a sanctimonious person who had lately taken holy orders (and would become a bishop in record time) had a predictably feeble wrist action.

In the summer term of my last year, Mr. Jackson, with a heavy heart, I am sure, was obliged to make me Senior Prefect of the house, for lack of a better candidate. The row of silver sporting trophies on the mantelpiece had already been shrinking in the previous year or two, but during my regime there came a moment when, if I remember right, not one remained. Then there appeared upon it a very small silver cup for madrigal singing, won by a group that I led. To the Jacker, this may have seemed an even more offensive symbol of decadence in the house than an empty shelf.

The annual cricket match between Winchester and Eton takes place in July, alternately at one school and then the other. Normally it is a great social occasion, drawing a mass of parents. But in 1942 it was decreed that in view of the wartime gasoline shortage, no parent, nor any boy not on the team, was to attend the game, which was to be played at Eton that year. Then a letter arrived from my aunt Nelly, who was a Lady-in-Waiting to the queen. If, she suggested, my brother Robin and I would be going to Eton for the match, she might be able to arrange for us to have lunch with the king and queen.

I went to see the headmaster about this, and his face brightened on learning that two of his boys would thus be honored. Then his expression became clouded, perhaps on recollecting the last time we were face to face—or to fundament. "I would need to see that letter," he said.

I returned to my desk, and tore the letter into pieces. Then I reassembled them with gummed paper, omitting just one fragment—the one bearing the phrase indicating uncertainty: "might be able." I took this document to the headmaster, explaining that I'd torn the letter up and thrown it away, but had retrieved it just in time (lying once again). The headmaster (known to us as "Mothy") was so dazzled by the heading, "Buckingham Palace," embossed on the paper in red, that he dropped his guard and immediately offered to drive us to Windsor Castle himself in his Ford V8. When the day came, he did so; but the drive was rather alarming, because someone had told him that his car's gasoline consumption was lowest at thirty-three miles per hour, so he maintained that speed all the way, even across intersections.

On that day there were, I think, eighteen people to lunch at the castle, including Air Marshal Lord Trenchard, the famous commander of the Royal Flying Corps in the First World War. All of them, however, were courtiers, so Robin and I were the only guests. The king and queen sat facing one another across the middle of the table, and I was placed at the queen's right hand. She was delightful to talk to, but her conversation didn't keep me from quickly scanning the menu card set before us. It promised veal cutlets in aspic, ham, and tongue, and other delights that never came our way at school, least of all in those days of strict rationing.

Since the queen was served first, my turn was last. And then, after a time, the footman offered a second helping to the queen, but she declined it, and so did the princesses. Chatting by then with my other neighbor, I was surreptitiously following the progress of the platter, since I realized that unless someone else took a second helping, I would have to refuse, too, or I'd be holding up the proceedings unduly. No one, it seemed, was either hungry or greedy, so when at last the platter reached me, I, too, declined it. "Oh, come on!" said the queen, and seizing the serving implements, bundled a large second helping onto my plate. I loved her ever after!

Of the conversation that day I remember almost nothing, except that the king questioned me about Wykehamist "notions" (the school's traditional alternative vocabulary), and asked for an example.

"Well, Sir, a baker is a cushion."

"So if I want a loaf of bread, do I go to a cushion?"

"Actually, Sir, no, it's the other way round; you would sit on the baker."

2.2 *Canon Horace Wilkinson, my mentor in workshop practice. In 1900, and as a joke, he had equipped his Model 1 Benz to be ready for any contingency. In possession of the author, by Canon H. R. Wilkinson, Melton Grove, Woodbridge, Suffolk.*

Having enjoyed the hospitality of their majesties at Windsor Castle, I couldn't help recalling a strange experience I'd had some four years earlier, while visiting the Reverend Horace Wilkinson, a retired canon in the Church of England who with his wife lived at Melton, about six miles from our home.[5] A kindly, enthusiastic and humorous man, he was also an extremely skilful craftsman, often making use of his skills to entertain and please the young. I still have—and treasure—a most ingenious and beautifully made Morse-code set he made for me. "Wilks" (as we children called him) also allowed himself some small eccentricities. When his wife chided him for his habit of blowing on his soup to cool it, he made an exquisite little pair of bellows perhaps four inches long and studded with tiny brass nails. These the parlor-maid was instructed to set in front of his place at table whenever soup was to be served.

I loved visiting him, and evidently showed so much interest in his workshop that he offered to give me instruction in workshop practice. So during the school holidays I would bicycle over every week or two to learn more about soldering, brazing, and lathe work. One day, when I may have been about fourteen, I was preparing to mount my bike to go home after one of these sessions, when Wilks called out, "Oh, Ian, I have something I'd like to show you! Do come in—it's in the drawing-room."

Approaching the grand piano, he stooped down and pulled out a box from beneath it. It was about eighteen inches each way, and made, I think, of mahogany. Opening the lid, he extracted from it a human head, more or less complete with shrinked skin and hair. "This is the head of Oliver Cromwell," he announced.[6]

Well, I had never seen a dead person, or any part of one, so I was too horrified to inspect this ghastly object closely, and Wilks soon put it back in its box. Of course, as soon as I was home I told of this unsettling experience, causing my sisters to exclaim:

"But he was an ancestor of ours! That's why Mummy's middle name was Olivia, and there was Great-Uncle Oliver, and Grandmummy's middle name was Frances, after the daughter of Cromwell we are descended from!"

When a little older, I realized I'd missed an extraordinary opportunity: I should have clasped the head to my breast, planted a tender kiss on the shriveled brow, and exclaimed—"Revered ancestor, at last!" But unfortunately there would be no second opportunity, because within a year or so Wilks died, and his son, on inheriting the head, and believing that a decent burial was long overdue, presented it to Sidney Sussex College of Cambridge University—Cromwell's college as an undergraduate.

There, many years later, I looked for a plaque marking its last resting place, and found a very small one indicating that near that spot the head now lay. I was puzzled by the vagueness of the indication, until it occurred to me that perhaps the college authorities feared vandalism by Irish republican extremists, who might wish to avenge themselves with pickaxe or bomb on those pathetic remains. Certainly, during my

Dublin days I had been told such awful tales of the atrocities committed by Cromwell against defenseless civilians that I never dreamed of disclosing any kinship with him; thus it was a relief to find a book recently written by an Irishman, and published in Ireland, which claims that those stories were false and just partisan propaganda.

Toward the end of his life, Cromwell decided that his position as Lord Protector of the Commonwealth should become hereditary, so after his death (from what was termed "tertiary bastard ague") he was accorded fully royal funerary rites. Not only was he to lie in state while his soul passed through purgatory, but his effigy would also have to stand in state while his soul ascended into heaven. Then his embalmed remains were laid to rest in Westminster Abbey.

His son, Richard, did, in fact, succeed him, but for lack of character and ability he soon was ousted and the monarchy restored. Then, in a shameful vote, which even the royalist Samuel Pepys deplored in his diary, the House of Commons resolved that Cromwell (along with two of his generals) should be exhumed and hanged in public. Their tombs were broken into and their coffins hauled away amid jeers, to pass the night in Holborn, reputedly in a tavern. Next day, the three corpses were strung up on triple gallows at Tyburn, near Marble Arch, and at nightfall cut down and beheaded. The bodies were thrown into a pit, and the heads, impaled upon iron spikes mounted on oaken poles, were fixed to a parapet of Westminster Hall. And there they remained as salutary warnings to passers-by until at least 1684.

Eventually Cromwell's head fell to earth and was picked up by a sentry before coming into the hands of a showman, who died in 1738. The identity of the next owner is unclear, but by the 1820s it had been sold to an ancestor of Canon Wilkinson. About a century later, the Canon made it available for study by Karl Pearson and G. M. Morant, two forensic anatomists of the highest repute. After making a thorough examination, which included comparison of the head with most of the known Cromwell portraits, busts, and death masks, they pronounced themselves certain of its authenticity.[7]

Following this personal discovery of our ancestry, I became sufficiently interested in genealogy to work up a family tree—but not one of conventional arboreal shape, for I thought the most logical design, and the least wasteful of paper, would be egocentric, with myself in the middle of expanding circles of generations, until, coming to the tenth generation, there would be an outer ring of 1,024 ancestors surrounding me. As I'd put my father to the left of me, and my mother to the right, Oliver Cromwell, being at the head of the all-female line of descent would be stationed—if one thinks of each generation's circle as a clock face—at about forty seconds after the hour, while James Graham, the great Marquess of Montrose, whom Cromwell had executed, would stand at the head of the all-male line at the hour itself, separated from Cromwell only by Mrs. Cromwell. This relationship should give genealogical enthusiasts a rare *frisson*!

As for my own feelings about the matter, I've sometimes wondered whether the uncertainty I've always felt about my position in the spectrum between democrat and royalist, or between classical and romantic, may owe something to those contrary traditions in my family.

CHAPTER 3

Cambridge

In September 1942 I went up to Trinity College, Cambridge, as a freshman, and called on a scholar named Dr. Patrick Duff, who had agreed to be my tutor, and as such would nominally become responsible for my moral welfare. He was a quiet and scholarly man, but seldom did I ever see him again. Then I enrolled in the Natural Sciences tripos, choosing courses in physics, electronics, and crystallography—this last because no previous knowledge of it was called for, so in this subject, at least, I might be on an equal footing with most of the other students.

The rooms assigned to me (to share with a school acquaintance) were on the fourth floor of Nevile's Court, built in the seventeenth century. This is a small quadrangle in classical style, built out from the back of Trinity's Great Court. Its three ranges are built of fine limestone: two, facing one another across a grassy court, contain chambers for undergraduates and professors, and beyond them, closing the quadrangle, stands Sir Christopher Wren's beautiful library. All three of these ranges stand over spacious arcades.

Our paneled rooms were certainly handsome, and my bedroom had a view over the neighboring New Court. Less satisfactory was the situation of the toilets, as these were on the other side of our court, so if taken short in the middle of a rainy or icy night, a degree of hardihood was needed to descend all those stairs, cross the court in the dark, and then return. I confess that often my solution was to open the window and pee out of it, down to a lead roof two floors below.

Every morning we were woken up at seven by the "bed-maker" (or "bedder") a cheerful, middle-aged woman who made us cups of early morning tea, and later would make our beds and clean up our rooms. She had another duty, and that was to report if any of her young gentlemen were missing from their beds, since a curfew was permanently in force. At 11 p.m. the great wooden doors of Trinity were closed, although for the next hour one could still be let in through a wicket door in one of them—for a fine of one penny. If one arrived after midnight, various recourses were available. The Bishop's Gate could be climbed quickly, but the drop was deep, so this route was inadvisable for those unsteady on their feet. Or you could try leaping across a channel in the Backs, behind the College, but the leap to dry land could only be accomplished from the top bar of iron railings that ran alongside; here again, sobriety was obviously required, although a failed leap resulted in nothing worse than a wetting. Farther round there is an elaborate wrought-iron gate, fitted with spiked extensions at either side to keep intruders out, but in fact, climbing round it was fairly easy, even with a bicycle hooked over one's arm.

The shortest and quickest route, however, was one commenced by stepping on the windowsill of a barber's shop in Trinity Street, behind which the college bathrooms were located.[1] From the barber's sill you clambered up, made a short traverse, and dropped down into the bathroom precinct. But in my time, the barber complained that no sooner had he repainted his windows than the traffic of undergraduate night birds ruined the paintwork of his windowsill, so the College sensibly installed a brass plate on the sill where student feet would tread, and this the barber kept brightly polished.

But if, perchance, you were returning at dawn from a night out in London, the only recourse was to wait until the gates opened at seven, slip in when the porters weren't looking, hurry to one's stairway and creep up until you spotted the bedder entering another set of rooms, then fly up on tiptoes and leap into bed fully dressed, ready to yawn and groan when she came in and pulled the curtains back.

In those days, the Cambridge Night Climbers Society, although officially disapproved of, was still actively engaged in urban mountaineering, its chief aim being the decoration of steeples and other inaccessible places with unsuitable trophies. (The society has since been rigorously banned.) Among its members, the highest status was accorded to those who had braved the frightening leap from one parapet to another across Senate House Passage, far above its stone pavement. Fortunately I never felt the slightest temptation to join in these activities, but I was mildly interested in mastering the preliminary test that members hoping to join the society had to pass. That wasn't dangerous at all.

It was administered beneath the Wren Library. The front of the library is supported not only by columns, but also by two massive L-shaped piers, into which are incorporated three engaged columns and a basal molding running all the way round, about ten inches from the ground. To pass the test one had to circumnavigate the pier, first clockwise and using only the left arm, then with only the right arm, and then the same counterclockwise, without stepping on the ground; in other words, you had to support yourself with your feet on the sloping molding, which on damp days tended to be slippery. Various extremely awkward postures were called for, such as raising a leg to the horizontal so as to hook your foot round a corner in order to get a fingerhold on the next anchorage. In fact, one artificial aid had been provided: a sort of *piton* (actually the slightly protruding head of a nail) that had been driven into the masonry to make passage across the broad north face possible. (I notice that with the society's demise, the nail has been removed.)

One day while I was practicing, and stuck in an awkward posture, a man who may have been in his mid-forties came up and exclaimed: "You're doing it all wrong, all wrong. I'll just run up and put on my plimsolls [aka sneakers]—then I'll show you how to do it." He trotted up a nearby stairway, and I deduced from the neatly painted list of residents on that stairway that this was the famous Professor Littlewood, author of "Littlewood's Law of Miracles,"[2] among other works, and collaborator with an equally famous mathematician, G. H. Hardy. On returning, Littlewood nimbly demonstrated the technique, and with a "there, you see how to do it?" he trotted off.

For other exercise I went on with rowing, which I had started at Winchester as soon as I was free from the dreadful threat of cricket. After all, it did seem sensible to take one's exercise sitting down. Races over the short stretch of "rowable" river were not unduly exhausting; but oh dear, races on the River Cam were a very different matter. So inadequate was my stamina that after five minutes of rowing I'd be wondering whether I could pull the oar through the water even one more stroke—and yet I would *have* to keep going for another four or five minutes. Just to go through the motions slackly was impossible, as the boat would be badly upset.

Weeks before each race I would start dreading it, and now I wonder why I didn't give up rowing immediately. As it was, I stayed in the College's second boat, although during the Lent term, when two of the first crew were chosen for the University boat, I was temporarily placed in the first boat. But I've no recollection of notable victories.

If I've delayed mentioning progress in my studies, it's because I am ashamed of how little of it there was. During that last year at Winchester I had wasted my time without understanding how inadequately prepared I was going to find myself at Cambridge. I knew I'd face a great challenge, so it was with feelings of anticipation mixed with dread that I walked down a narrow alley to the Cavendish Laboratory. The building, with its vaguely classical stone façade, was for me a sacred place, haunted by the ghosts of J. J. Thompson, Ernest Rutherford, J. D. Cockcroft, and many other famous physicists, for it was, at the time, widely regarded as the world's foremost center of research in physics.

I soon discovered that many of its brightest stars had mysteriously disappeared—some, as we now know, had gone to the United States to work on the newly created Manhattan Project, others were nearer at hand, working on radar and other secret research. But Professor N. Feather was still teaching, and he was to give the course I would take. I remember the relief I felt as he began his lecture something like this:

"Electricity owes its name to the Greek word 'eelectron,' meaning amber, for the Greeks discovered that when rubbed with a cloth, amber attracted small, light objects, such as pieces of thread. That is why this mysterious attractive force was called electrical."

"Oh, good," I said to myself, "he's starting at the beginning, and I'll be able to catch up as we go along." But by the end of the lecture we were deep into wave mechanics, and I was lost. Really there was no hope of catching up; for one thing, the kind of mathematics required was far beyond my grasp.

If I'd been more mature I would just have left Cambridge and enrolled in one of the military services. After all, there was a war on—one just then at a desperate juncture. In retrospect I feel ashamed of my failure to do so, while taking just a little comfort from the fact that I did absorb a good knowledge of a subject that would prove militarily useful—electronics.

A topic that had engaged my interest while still at Winchester, and now even more at Cambridge, was the reproduction of recorded music. Of the three components involved—pickups, amplifiers, and loudspeakers—it seemed to me that pickups were most in need of improvement, the underlying cause of their poor performance being rather obvious. A 78 rpm record demanded a lot from any pickup: its needle had to follow one groove without jumping to another, even on discs that were warped, as they often were from having been left in the sun, or on those with holes not concentric with the grooves. Thus, to steer a head made heavy by the magnet in it, the needle had to be stiffly mounted.[3]

The inevitable and unfortunate consequence of this stiffness was that at certain frequency, or pitch, resonance occurred; for the needle in its stiffly flexible mounting was analogous to a table knife with its handle held down tightly on the edge of a table: twang the blade and it will vibrate at a certain frequency, or musical note. For this reason the response of all pickups—that is, the level of electrical output derived from wiggles in the groove—was not uniform for all pitches; some were favored more than others.

My idea was to free the needle responsible for the pickup's electrical (and musical) output from the chore of steering the head along its allotted groove; this would be done by delegating the steering to another component. Thus, in my design, the needle could be given so small a centering force that its resonant frequency would be far below the musical scale. Well then, how could the head with such a floppy needle follow a single groove? My solution lay in provision of a little velvet pad to take care of guidance; this would be wide enough to cover about ten grooves, so there would be no possibility of the head itself picking up vibrations from the record's grooves. These replaceable pads would also perform the useful function of cleaning the record.

I still think this pickup could have been developed into a commercially successful design, but by the time I was free to continue work on it in 1947, 33 rpm vinyl records and piezo-electric pickups were making shellac 78s obsolete.

As for social life, I made some amusing but not notably intellectual friends, and joined an undergraduate club with premises just across the street from Trinity. I have no recollection, though, of having met—except casually at lectures—any female undergraduates. In fact, I had scarcely met any girls whatsoever, and so must have been pretty awkward with any that I did meet. But soon I was to become friendly with a young woman two or three years older than myself, who was not a student.

I had arrived in Cambridge on a recently purchased motorcycle, a 1932 Panther of very modest performance. Then I learned that the Regional Commissioner for Civil Defense was Jock Cranbroke, a Suffolk neighbor, and that his office needed part-time volunteer dispatch-riders in addition to the full-time salaried ones already working there. Of course they would receive gasoline coupons for their work, so I applied for enrollment as a volunteer, and was accepted.

That is how I met Diana Stuart-Wortley, one of the full-time riders. She was tall, beautiful, and dashing, and soon I became enthralled by her. Then she had an accident on the way to London, but brushing off any injuries or possible damage to her motor-cycle, insisted on continuing to London to deliver her satchel of papers to the Home Office. My admiration soared when, next day, I saw her picture on the front page of the *Daily Mirror*, with the headline "The courage of Lady Diana."

Diana had a flat in Green Street, close to Trinity, and I often spent evenings with her, occasionally staying for the night on her sofa, in yearning propinquity. But never did I attempt what I could only have done clumsily—try for an embrace, and then a kiss—because I knew she was in love with a brave and handsome fighter pilot, and for all I know, may secretly have been engaged to him. But there came a day when Diana left on a run to London, and would be spending the night there—and shortly afterwards I was also sent off to London with a dispatch. So the thought of taking her to a nightclub seized me, even though I'd never entered such a place in my life. There was another difficulty: I didn't even know where she would be staying, but I thought I might obtain that information from her father, who, as she had once told me, was often to be found at the Cavendish Hotel, in Jermyn Street.

The Cavendish was then a landmark in the social landscape of the gentry, also for a select band of American habitués. It had been established just before the first World War in a large and rambling house that had belonged to the Comte de Paris, with the initial expense having been borne largely (it was said) by King Edward VII as a way of securing the livelihood of Rosa Lewis, who had been one of his cooks—and a beautiful cook, too.[4] By now, of course, she was no longer young, but still full of spirit, and devoted to the upper classes. The clientele consisted partly of respectable rural gentry, who felt very much at home in the large bedrooms containing excellent furniture, all a bit run-down; and partly of the dissolute offspring of similar background. The latter were charged absurdly low rates; in fact, their elders were subsidizing them unwittingly, because Rosa was sure their parents must be keeping them on too short a leash.

It was quite late when I arrived at the hotel, and an air raid was in progress, with heavy firing from the guns in Hyde Park. Rosa was sitting at a large table in the front hall, chatting with a few guests while dispensing champagne—her usual occupation, as I would learn. Her white hair was neatly waved, hot curling-tongs having been applied to it in the morning as another part of her daily routine. I told her I had a note to leave for Diana's father, Lord Wharncliffe, and inquired where I should put it. "Well, dear," she replied, "his bedroom is number forty-three, and his sitting-room forty-four. You can take it up and leave it there."

After some exploration of the labyrinthine passageways, I found number forty-four, and since no light was showing under the door I opened it and switched on the light—and there, to my dismay, I found his lordship in bed. I apologized profusely and hastily explained, as I turned the light off again, that I was only wanting to leave a message. "No, no, turn the light on, and come in." He got up and put on a dressing-gown. "Have a drink!" And there, on a table, stood a bottle of champagne with its cork drawn, but still full. So we settled down and drank it up. Meanwhile he gave me a Sullivan and Powell "Large Sub-Rosa" cigarette, such a fat, delicious, and beautifully made cigarette that from that moment I scarcely ever smoked any other kind; and when the makers of them went out of business about thirty years later, I stopped smoking altogether. But that open bottle of champagne remains a mystery: I could well believe that he was expecting a visitor, quite possibly a lady who might have abandoned her visit because of the air raid, but why had he drawn the cork?

Once or twice I went with Diana for a weekend at her parents' home, an austere stone mansion in Yorkshire's bleak Brontë country. I soon found unexpected activity in the stable block, and was quite surprised by its nature: Diana's mother had set up a little factory for making electrical cables for airborne radio and radar equipment as a contribution to the war effort. Another surprise awaited me in the men's room near the front door: an inverted tumbler placed over the soap. I had the temerity to inquire of Diana's father the reason for this.

"Why, to stop the rats eating it, of course!"

Happily, Diana remained a lifelong friend, but I wouldn't see her again before her marriage (though it wasn't to the fighter pilot).

My time at Cambridge ended all too soon when exam results were made known, and I was summoned for an interview before a committee of three people, headed by the author C. P. Snow. Unsurprisingly, they showed no mercy, and I went forthwith to the local Labor Exchange and applied to join the navy. I was given a physical, and then the day's intake were sat down to take a couple of tests. One of them was the very same test that the biology master at Winchester had given us, just for the fun of it. This was the Cattell Matrix Test, which was timed and open-ended, meaning that even Einstein might not have succeeded in completing all the items correctly in the time allowed; and to maintain its validity, its distribution was supposed to be closely restricted.

My original score had been reasonable, but because on that occasion the correct answers had been explained to us afterwards, this time I was able to race through the test and get practically all of them right. We remained seated for half an hour or so while information of various kinds was exchanged, then a door was half-opened and two men peered in at me. Oh dear, I thought; if they think I'm some kind of a genius, I might be put into Naval Intelligence—and then be doomed to another humiliating debacle when they discover I am nothing of the kind!

Well, I needn't have worried; all too soon I would find myself swabbing out toilets—or "heads," as I learned to call them in naval parlance.

CHAPTER 4

The Navy

When at last they came, my call-up papers instructed me to report at a naval intake center at Skegness, on the Lincolnshire coast. Before the war, this establishment had been a Butlin's Holiday Camp, the mid-thirties creation of a Canadian entrepreneur, Billy Butlin, who built several of these "camps" to provide inexpensive holidays with healthy fun and games by the seaside for working folk and their families. But according to rumor, the site of this camp had been reclaimed from the North Sea—as was easy to believe on arrival there in early November, with soggy ground under our feet.

There were four enormous buildings, the size of aircraft hangars, named Windsor, York, Gloucester, and Kent in honor of the Royal Dukes. The vast dining hall, and the smaller spaces originally provided for bingo and other innocent pastimes, still retained their heaving and grotesque modeled plasterwork, brilliant in red and gold. Our sleeping quarters were small, vaguely Swiss-style chalets, each provided with a 300-watt electric convection heater, which in winter was far from adequate.

The first thing you were likely to discover on returning at night to your chalet was the disappearance of the lightbulb, and then that the bedclothes were decidedly damp. The curious thing about the bulb was that it invariably disappeared if you left it in the light fitting, but if you removed it and stowed it under the pillow on leaving the chalet, it would still be there when you got back. As that was the standard place to hide a bulb, there must have been some mysterious, unspoken tabu against taking it from its hiding place.

At Skegness we were kitted out with sailor suits, the dark blue collars of which we bleached immediately with chlorine to give the impression of long service in the tropics, and many of us indulged in amateur tailoring of our upper garments, known as "jumpers," to eliminate inelegant floppiness at the solar plexus. This ticklish operation I never did attempt, for if done too radically, the jumper couldn't be removed without one of your mates helping to pull it off. (We were jealous of Canadian sailors who were allowed to have zip-fasteners down one side of their jumpers!)

Of our new clothing it was the navy blue jersey that I found to be the most useful in the long run. These long-sleeved sweaters, reputedly knitted from wool from sheep native to the Island of Jersey, have proved to be astonishingly hard-wearing; mine, at least, shows little sign of its intermittent but still continuing use for more than sixty years.

We did a lot of square-bashing, and learned "bends and 'itches"—knots, to the landlubber; but mostly we just came down with terrible coughs and colds and laryngitis. Many of the lads had left home for the first time, and it was distressing to see how much they missed their mums. But our group was lucky to be under the watchful care of a dear old Irishman, Chief Petty Officer O'Neil, a kindhearted and grandfatherly man with small, twinkling eyes set in his large head.

My modest knowledge of electronics was duly noted at some level, and a month later I and some others were drafted to Walthamstow Technical College, in east London, for official training in that subject. We were all billeted in private houses, and I found myself directed, together with a lanky, red-haired Yorkshireman named Holdsworth, to a miserable row house of the kind built for lowest-category workers a century earlier. It was now occupied by a railway shunter who, we soon discovered, had taken to sleeping every night under his Morrison shelter, this being a heavy steel table designed to serve as a table by day, but an in-house personal air-raid shelter by night.

I was somewhat taken aback, however, when our host indicated the bed that Holdsworth and I were to share; it was not much wider than a single bed! Fortunately the mattress had developed an unexpected longitudinal ridge, so that the two of us tended to roll apart, and I was not exposed at too-close quarters to my bedmate's perfume of carbolic soap. Now, Holdsworth was an excellent fellow, but the arrangement did seem a little unorthodox, and perhaps not in accordance with the strict letter of naval regulations; so after a few days I entered a mild complaint, which produced amusing reactions of official horror. Fortunately I soon discovered that a Suffolk neighbor's retired nanny lived nearby, and that she was willing to take me in as a lodger. All of a sudden my living conditions improved enormously.

After a month in Walthamstow we were sent off to a hutted camp in Lancashire (appropriately named HMS *Ariel*) to learn about an actual radar set. This was ASV Mark II, the initials standing for "Airborne (detection of) Surface Vessels." This set had proved such a success that it had been manufactured in large numbers, not only in England but also in the United States, Canada, and Australia. Since we were being trained as radar mechanics, at a certain stage the instructor began introducing faults into the ten or twelve sets provided for instruction, which we first had to diagnose and then restore to working order. When the day came for our final exam, we trooped into the lab and switched on our sets, but it was an ill-chosen fault that had been introduced, because in a minute smoke began to issue from each of the sets.

The nautical protocols and rigmarole that were in force at this plywood-and-tarpaper frigate seemed at first ridiculous. When our day's instruction was over, some of us might decide to take a bus to Warrington to see a movie, or spend the evening in a pub, but were we permitted just to walk out of the gate when ready to go? Oh no, one waited for the imaginary Liberty Boat to take us ashore. This sailed at stated times. Then, once the phantom vessel was securely moored alongside, and the ship's bell had tolled the time in nautical code, a petty officer would bellow "Liberty men, fall in!" We then shuffled into two lines and marched through the gates, left-right, left-right, and made for the bus stop. It did eventually dawn on us, though, that these and other seeming absurdities might indeed help to make transition to real shipboard life a little easier.

We also had to sleep in our canvas hammocks, which were very narrow and confining. More than once I must unconsciously have allowed a leg to dangle over the side, and then by simply turning over in my sleep suddenly found myself dumped on the deck. (You see? Not the floor!) In the morning we awoke to cries of "Wakey, wakey, rise and shine, the sun's burnin' yer eyes out! Show a leg there!" Then it was lash up and stow; our hammocks had to be rolled, and then laced up into a long sausage in very particular fashion; but it was no longer required of us to pile them up against the "ship's" sides to give extra protection against shrapnel.

While at *Ariel*, I received a letter from a certain Lord Crawford inviting me to visit him in Wigan, for one of my aunts had told him I was lying at anchor not far away. So I borrowed a bicycle and eventually, following instructions, pedaled laboriously to Wigan and then up a street that was lined—as this was Sunday—with miners squatting on the curbstones. (I soon learned that because the coal seams here were so shallow, the wretched miners had to squat as they worked with picks at the coal-face—and post-mortems would show them to have developed squatting facets in their knee joints.)

At the appointed rendezvous, there stood Lord Crawford dressed in Home Guard uniform. He then led me along a short driveway to Haigh Hall, a large and somewhat austere gray granite mansion of classical design (though built, surprisingly, in about 1850). I was welcomed by Mary, his wife, and given sherry; then we sat down to lunch in the breakfast room.

The table was laid with a plastic cloth, silver cutlery, plastic salt and pepper, and a tremendous seventeenth-century silver-gilt tankard as a centerpiece. The worn steel blades of the knives had been polished so many thousands of times in the Kent knife-polishing machine that they now resembled clock-spring, and I found that whenever I exerted any force in cutting through the rather tough portion of the weekly meat ration that my hosts were generously sharing with me, the knife blade might suddenly twist and flip gravy and peas with considerable velocity to one side or the other.

So began my long and greatly valued friendship with David and Mary Crawford and their family. David's ancestors, the Lindsays, had been powerful players in ancient Scottish history, and great collectors of books. Then prosperity deserted them, and according to legend, pages were ripped out of some of their ancient books to use for wrapping butter. But in the late eighteenth century an ancestor married into the family that owned not only Haigh Hall (then a decaying Elizabethan pile), but also the extensive coal and iron-ore beds underlying the property. When the value of these soared with the Industrial Revolution, the Lindsay bridegroom managed them to such good effect that their son, who even as a schoolboy had developed a passion for early printed books and fifteenth-century Italian paintings, was able to start collecting while still at Eton, even buying a Duccio (or near-Duccio) crucifixion for £300 (which sold for a million or more in the 1970s).

Before long, the Elizabethan house was pulled down and a new one built in its stead, and this, it is no exaggeration to say, was designed primarily as a picture gallery and library, with living quarters fitted in. The coal and iron business was to flourish throughout the nineteenth century, and as three or four succeeding generations of Crawford earls became learned antiquarians, they focused their book collecting on several well-defined fields, in which their collections became pre-eminent. David himself was immensely knowledgeable, and owed his chairmanship of various bodies—such as the British Museum trustees, and those of the National Arts Collection Fund and the National Gallery—to his deep knowledge and love of the arts, his commitment to seeing them through rocky wartime and postwar years, and his understanding of the convoluted politics controlling those fields.

I came back for an overnight visit two or three weeks later, and was then taken on a more leisurely tour round the house. There were two enormous libraries full of books, and I remember boxes of Lutheran tracts, large holdings of Napoleonic material, and a printed catalogue of the library itself that occupied at least a yard of shelf space.

On the walls of the stairwell two enormous canvases were hanging, Benjamin West's *Bringing Down the Tables of the Law* and a huge Fuseli. There were wonderful Dutch paintings, and among objects at the other end of the scale I remember a barrel organ with a list, handwritten in sepia ink and pasted in the lid, of the tunes it could play, one of them being "A concerto by Mr. Bach." The tour finished in the basement, which had been air-conditioned to provide wartime storage for objects evacuated from the British Museum for safety, including Sir Christopher Wren's large wooden model of Saint Paul's cathedral.

Next morning I would notice in the hall a pile of at least ten letters ready for mailing that David must have written late the previous evening, in a rapid and almost illegible hand. I was awestruck by his diligence in maintaining such a quantity of correspondence, both official and personal, though I may not have been alone in finding his rapid script quite difficult to decipher.

Once my training at HMS *Ariel* was complete, I was promoted to Leading Radio Mechanic, and had to exchange my jolly sailor suit for a dreadful garment of thick serge with a red badge on the arm, white shirt, black tie, and a little peaked cap, giving me the appearance of a chauffeur; and then I was appointed to a naval stores unit in a small boot-making town in Leicestershire.

From this boring job I was set free none too soon, and sent to Portsmouth for officer training. A welcome development this, but of my time there I remember little except for the effort I made, helped by my father, to secure appointment to a very fine new cruiser, HMS *Superb*, which was to be commanded by Captain Geoff Robson, a close friend of his. I had managed to persuade a ship's radar officer to let me study the circuit diagrams and operating manuals of Naval Set 277, a microwave radar with which *Superb* was fitted, but to no avail; I seem to have been immutably allotted to the Fleet Air Arm (Naval Aviation, in U.S. terms).

So I was posted to a Fleet Air Arm shore base in the Isle of Man, where newly qualified pilots practiced landings on aircraft carriers. That, of course, was a terrifying procedure in a stormy sea, when the carrier's deck might be heaving up and down as much as fifty feet. Some of the pilots had been at sea for some time, and were now ashore for recuperation, a few of them with really bad cases of "the shakes." But the strongest impression remaining with me was the shock I experienced when at the bar one day before lunch I heard one officer say to another,

"You've heard that Tommy bought it this morning?"

"Oh no—too bad."

And nothing more. But gradually I came to understand that hugging and indulging in lamentations would do nothing for their own equanimity and devil-may-care attitude.

I was not to stay long at this establishment, because one day, like a bolt from the blue, there came a quite unexpected appointment to the Telecommunications Research

Establishment at Malvern—commonly known as TRE. This was the lineal descendant of the world's first radar research station (or possibly the second, for I'm not sure when its German equivalent was established). That first lab, set up in 1935 at Orfordness on the Suffolk coast, was soon moved to more commodious quarters at Bawdsey, a few miles distant. (My family home was about ten miles away, and I remember, from when I was a boy, hearing discussions among neighbors about the death rays supposedly being developed there). But when war broke out, Bawdsey was much too close to Germany for comfort, and after a short spell in Scotland, it settled in Malvern, in the West Country—where, under another name, similar research continues.

I was eager to know more of TRE's history, and learned that because of Bawdsey's proximity to Germany, the staff and all the equipment were hurriedly evacuated two days before the declaration of war. They were rehoused, for reasons difficult to imagine, in Dundee, where the arriving scientists discovered to their dismay that in the building allotted to them the only electricity available was D.C. (direct current). Since this was quite useless for their purposes, a heavy cable had to be slung across the street, and across rooftops, to the nearest source of A.C. Whitehall had also blundered badly in other ways: the place was too remote from manufacturers of electronic equipment, from the various ministries in Whitehall that were concerned, and from universities. Moreover there was no suitable airfield from which flight trials could be conducted, and even if there had been, the fabled fogs of that coast would seriously have hampered operations.

About six months later, another bungled migration took place, this time to farmland on cliffs overlooking the English Channel at Worth Maltravers, near Swanage. The site was good, but nothing had been built when the staff arrived, and two of the most prominent scientists found themselves at first in an unheated hut in the middle of a field, far from electricity. And again, the only airfield in the vicinity was unsuitable. But after much wasted time, TRE grew and prospered there, and marvelous research was done.

Then in 1943, a daring and successful combined paratroop and naval raid was made on a German radar station at Bruneval, across the Channel—and suddenly the likelihood of the Germans organizing a return match at Worth Maltravers brought about a hasty evacuation. Almost all the removal vans in the country were commandeered to transport everything to Malvern College, a prep school, whose unfortunate headmaster had been given short notice for finding alternative accommodation.

Malvern, in Worcestershire, was a particularly desirable location because of its situation on the flanks of a prominent hill in otherwise flattish country, so that long-range tests on aircraft targets were possible from equipment mounted within the campus. Of course, the arrival all at once of several thousand people caused serious problems of accommodation to begin with, but by the time I arrived, all such difficulties were long past, and I was lucky enough to be given a room in the Abbey Hotel, which was occupied mostly by TRE people, although a few elderly ladies had clung onto their rooms. I remember one of those old ladies asking me, after I had been there several months, "Why do you always go down to work wearing that black suit with brass buttons?" Indeed, I sometimes wondered about that myself.

One entered TRE through a portal in the neo-Gothic administration building, and there, a little below, lay the cricket pitch, which had been declared sacred turf and strictly off-limits. To one side stood the cricket pavilion, by then converted into a canteen, or cafeteria, and round about were the former boys' houses, a bit shabby, as might be expected. Ours abounded in names and observations crudely carved in the woodwork.

The project I was to help with was in House 2, near the canteen. I was to assist E. K. Williams in the development of a set called Rebecca Mark IV. It would be a particularly interesting challenge, since this would be the first British equipment to make exclusive use of American miniaturized components. These would allow it to be fitted into a relatively small cylindrical canister, so that it could be pressurized to keep out humidity. Previously, almost all British airborne equipment had been so bulky and heavy that their innards had to be distributed between as many as ten different boxes, interconnected with cables. The cables themselves were heavy, and often sources of malfunction.

Rebecca was the airborne and bigger member of the Rebecca-Eureka "duo." Its function was to transmit radio pulses on a particular frequency that would trigger Eureka, a portable, battery-operated set on the ground, causing it to respond on the same frequency. The response would show up on Rebecca's screen, where its distance and bearing from the aircraft would be indicated. Eureka was designed to be given to partisan groups to make it possible for supplies, or a parachuting agent, to be dropped close to them; or to be placed by advance guards in the drop-zone prior to a paratroop operation. Rebecca was also used with BABS (Beam-Approach Blind-landing System).

Williams, or "E. K." as he was known—to distinguish him from the locally famous Frederick C. Williams, or "F. C."—was a man approaching forty, with humorous eyes, a barely perceptible stutter, and a distinctive habit of drawing back the corners of his mouth and sucking in breath as a way of expressing slight doubt about something he had done or said, or something that had gone wrong. I think we got on very well together. When I arrived he had designed Rebecca's circuitry some months earlier, and tested it in breadboard form—that is, with the components screwed down on a metal chassis, or even a wooden base, without much attention to layout. Then

TRE's excellent drawing office and workshops had produced a prototype of the specified shape and size.

A contract for production had recently been signed with EMI, and the fabrication of a preproduction model had begun at their factory in Hayes, southwest London. The navy had provided me with a little van, and quite often I drove in it with E. K. to EMI's head offices, where we could admire the large oil painting by Francis Barraud of the famous dog listening to the gramophone—entitled *His Master's Voice*. The dog had actually been Edison's, but for use by EMI's predecessor, the Gramophone Company, Barraud had painted a turntable over the phonograph cylinder.

There we discussed any problems that had arisen, and when the set was working adequately we took it to Malvern for further tests. I do remember feeling rather pleased with myself for remedying a few defects; one of them, for example, was a matter of the screen blacking out briefly whenever the range setting was changed. But serious testing only began when we received the first production model and then flew it in trials.

Although the duties of my appointment had never been made very clear to me, certainly an important one was testing the Mark IV as installed in various aircraft of the Fleet Air Arm and the RAF This was something I was keenly looking forward to.

When TRE moved to Malvern, the construction of an airfield for TRE's exclusive use was immediately begun at Defford, about twelve miles away. Most of the flying was done by the RAF, but an independent Naval Section was also created, under the command of Lieut.-Commander P. H. Hudson, a regular officer. Henry was a modest and delightful person, and so young-looking for a man of that rank that once, while wearing civilian clothes, he was refused a drink at a bar! Not that he was a drinker: in fact he never had anything stronger than a "shandy" (beer and ginger ale, half-and-half) when he was due to fly. His skill as a pilot was exceptional, and the great knowledge he had acquired of aeronautical engineering would have qualified him anywhere as a test pilot. If anything went wrong in the air, he knew what to do.

I had several experiences with pilots of far less skill. Once, in the Isle of Man, I went up in an Avro Anson, an old twin-engined six-seat feeder-liner. The flaps and the undercarriage were operated manually by the person in the right-hand seat, which was me. When we came in to land, the pilot asked me to lower the undercarriage, which I did successfully, but when he asked for twenty degrees of flaps I couldn't get more than ten, however hard I pumped the lever. We came in on the approach, but the plane just floated some twenty feet up for the whole length of the runway. We made another circuit, with me pumping harder than ever, with the same result. Then I heard the pilot say, "I'll get this bloody bus down somehow, this time!"

After another circuit we hit the beginning of the runway, bounced up into the air, bounced again, and then I noticed a BABS Blind Approach van at the other end of the runway, from which a mechanic was just departing, pushing his bicycle. Seeing us careering towards the van, he started running with his bike in one direction, then turned and with it ran in the other direction, before throwing it down and running for his life. A moment later we hit the van with our starboard wing, which broke off, and we came to rest in a wheat field near a stone wall.

In fact, there had been nothing amiss with the plane. It was simply that the pilot hadn't bothered to read the Pilot's Notes for this aircraft, and flew it as if it were an Airspeed Oxford, a rather similar but faster plane with a higher landing speed and equipped with flaps operated by high-pressure hydraulics. So at the speed we were going, the Anson's feeble flaps couldn't prevail against the slipstream.

Later, I was involved in another encounter with a BABS van. I was to do some tests in a Lincoln bomber, a bigger version of the famous Lancaster. Henry Hudson came aboard, too, just for the experience, and chose to lie in the bomb-aimer's position in the nose. I was seated with the Rebecca scope at the navigator's desk, which faced sideways, behind and below the pilot. When we had finished our mission and were returning to Defford, I glanced at the airspeed indicator in front of me and saw that we were going no more than 85 knots. That made me think we must be on the point of landing, since I knew that this plane fell out of the sky at 85, or did when loaded. Yet the altimeter indicated 1,000 feet. I looked out of the window, and yes, that was about our height. What should I do? Call up the pilot and say, "I say, old chap, d'you know we're only doing 85?" I would get a short answer, I thought, so I kept quiet.

A few minutes later, we really were coming in on the approach when CRASH!!— we had wiped off our underbelly radome and the scanner in it on a BABS van stationed at the beginning of the runway. Fortunately, the main wheels had passed on either side of it, but we did lose our tail wheel. Meanwhile, Henry, in the nose, had seen the van pass a few inches beneath his face as he lay prone in the nose, and was clearly in a bad way when he emerged. So what was the explanation? As far as I could understand, the pilot simply got into a daze, and was only half-awake as we landed.

Occasionally, though, an apparently inevitable crash was avoided at the last moment, as happened one afternoon when I had been testing equipment in a Wellington bomber. As we were preparing to land at Defford, it was found that the wheels wouldn't come down, nor would the flaps (once again). But in the end, all was well, and I can safely say that it was through my personal intervention that a damaging belly landing was avoided, though modesty prevents me from taking much credit for it. The problem this time was traced to a shortage of hydraulic fluid, presumably caused by a leak. What, then, was my heroic role in bringing the aircraft safely to earth? Well, I did no more than replenish the fluid, and was able to do so because, unlike the aircrew, I had been free to indulge in a couple of beers with my lunch—with nervousness perhaps contributing something to my ministrations.[1]

For me, the greatest delight was flying in Mosquitoes, the greyhounds of the skies. Development of this aircraft was begun in 1939 by the De Havilland Aircraft Company, not in response to an Air Ministry specification, as was usual, but as a private venture. As such, it had no priority under wartime conditions in ordering made-to-measure items from other manufacturers, such as the hydraulic system. So De Havilland, which also made Oxfords, had to make do with hydraulics designed for those modest feeder-liners. It was a weakness; but otherwise, the Mosquito was a truly extraordinary machine. It was as fast as a Spitfire, and as a pathfinder for bomber forces it could fly at 35,000 feet about as fast as the German fighters (until the Heinkel jet appeared). As a bomber it could carry a 1,500-pound bomb at 350 mph, whereas the B-17, or Flying Fortress, weighed down by five gun turrets, each weighing about 6,000 pounds, plus their gunners, only carried one 4,000-pound bomb and was 80 mph slower. Yet the Mosquito was constructed entirely of laminated wood![2]

Henry Hood occasionally treated me to some exciting aerobatics in the Mosquito—loops, barrel rolls, and so forth. Only once did we have a bad moment flying the Mozzie—to use its familiar name—and that was while taking off. We were about two feet up, when suddenly I noticed that the starboard propeller was windmilling. This was alarming, because the Mosquito has the very high single-engine safety speed of about 135 knots unloaded (that is, the minimum speed at which it can climb on one engine). Having not yet reached that speed, we would be unable to climb; but if Henry had aborted the landing immediately we might still have been doing about 50 knots on reaching the end of the runway. Luckily the engine restarted, on its own accord.

The head of TRE's Group 33, which embraced all research on interrogators and responders such as Rebecca/Eureka, was John Pringle, who before the war had been a researcher on animal and insect locomotion at Cambridge. One day, after the war had ended, he asked me whether I could do him a favor sometime by catching a considerable number of houseflies, anesthetizing them, performing "halterectomies" on them, and then observing how they flew. Halteres, he explained, are club-shaped appendages that stick out each side of a fly's thorax.[3] Nobody had yet identified their function—a topic that had been discussed since the early eighteenth century—but it was known that they vibrate up and down while the fly is airborne.

Pringle had the idea that since the bulbous ends of them swing in arcs of a circle, they might generate gyroscopic forces detectable by the fly if it yawed in flight, thus enabling it to control the yawing. To test his theory, he provided me with a small bottle of chloroform, a magnifying glass, and a scalpel, and I went to work. I confess that an undue number of my patients died on the operating table, probably from excess of chloroform, but the survivors, after a reasonable post-operative period for recuperation, did seem, when released, to yaw a little more than the average fly, and this I reported to John.

I soon forgot all about this diversion, but then, about thirty years later, I was told that vibrating (rather than rotating) gyroscopes were being used in ballistic missiles, for they are smaller and can't tumble, as gyroscopes do. But it was only in the nineties that I heard from a Bawdsey pioneer, the late Hanbury Brown, that soon after the war John Pringle had published a paper in a scientific journal on his haltere research, for which Hanbury, as I learned on looking it up, had provided highly sophisticated instrumentation. So it does seem probable that this element of missile instrumentation really is based on John's research. Whether or not this is the case, I found in his paper a phrase that made me feel proud: "Preliminary experiments," he wrote, "suggested that they do [control yawing]." I take that to be an acknowledgement of my distinguished contribution to his research, and to missile technology!

Early in 1946 a naval establishment called HMS Duke, down the hill from Malvern College, was closed, and shortly afterwards all TRE offices and labs housed in College buildings were moved down to this empty camp, and the College came back in September. But many of the temporary buildings put up by TRE remained occupied, and my small naval section, consisting of me and two Leading Radio Mechanics, had only to move a short distance from House 2 to a hut beside it. (When the school boys arrived, I would sometimes spot a few of them behind my hut, smoking.)

The cricket pavilion that had become a cafeteria remained open for a time, and one day during that period, while I was enjoying my "bangers" (sausages) and mash, I overheard some extraordinary conversation among people sitting near me, whose faces (but not names) I knew. They were talking about "computers," a word that, so far as I knew, referred only to people, usually women, employed to operate calculating machines. But here these men were speculating about whether or not computers would eventually be able to heal themselves when sick, or reproduce themselves, and I believe I heard something about them perhaps acquiring intelligence comparable to that of humans.

Naturally, I asked one of my senior acquaintances at the earliest opportunity what this conversation could have been about, and he explained. I had read a little about Babbage and his Universal Calculating Engine, and about Vannevar Bush's Differential Engine, but had not, of course, heard the slightest whisper about the now famous code-breaking Colossus at Bletchley Park, nor about Eckert and Mauchlay's computer in Philadelphia. The latter was a very powerful machine, but its lack of one element does deny it full parentage of what we now understand as a computer, and that was a dynamic random access memory, or DRAM.

In the United States, RCA had tried for two years to make a memory of this kind of work, using a specially adapted cathode ray tube on the face of which a pattern of electrical charges could be written—and then read, these representing the zeros and ones of binary arithmetic. However, the technique employed in their "Selectron" for controlling the beam by means of a mosaic of "gates" proved unworkable. But where they failed, TRE's resident circuit genius, F. C. Williams succeeded, and his Williams Tube, also electrostatic, was patented in 1946.

Williams was something of a one-man think-tank, or wizard, who was able to find solutions to many electronic problems. A time-base, for example, is a circuit that generates the steadily rising voltage needed to sweep a spot vertically up the cathode ray tube screen, with radar echoes being shown as horizontal deflections. The time dimension thus extends up the screen, with any momentary vertical position of the spot corresponding to the distance of the object causing the echo. Ideally the spot should move up the screen at an absolutely steady pace, so that yards or meters or miles printed on it would be evenly spaced, but generating an absolutely steady rise in voltage is not easily done. F. C.'s "sanatron" circuit, however, was much better than any previous design (the name derives from TRE slang, "sanitary" denoting excellence, as in, "That doesn't look to me like a very sanitary circuit!"). He followed that with the "phantastron," a time-base so closely linear that it was used successfully in apparatus used for surveying.

Another achievement of his was the lock-follow system used in microwave Airborne Interception (AI) radars. Once an enemy aircraft had been detected by the night fighter, the antenna would lock onto it and keep track of it.

F. C. left TRE in 1946 and was appointed professor of electrical engineering at Manchester University, where he helped design the Manchester Mark 1 computer, which of course contained a Williams tube. The design was developed into a commercial model by Ferranti (also of Manchester), and this was to be, in 1949, the world's first electronic computer to be put on the market. For this achievement, F. C. was knighted. The Williams tube was also a vital component in the IBM 701 Defense Calculator, which came into use along the "Dew Line" in 1953. But the tube suddenly became obsolete with the development of ferric oxide memories.

A fascinating expedition that E. K. and I made was to an exhibition of captured German technical equipment (open only to technical and service people) at the Royal Aircraft Establishment at Farnborough. The material was simply laid out on the floor of a huge hangar, and I don't remember there being much labeling—if any. There were some entirely unfamiliar items, such as dielectric lenses, various beautifully made components, and a German magnetron.[4]

The cavity magnetron must have been the most important invention of the war. It is a small device that can generate enormous power at microwave frequencies (and today there's one at the heart of every microwave oven). There had been earlier attempts to develop magnetrons, but the first really successful one was the work of Randall and Boot at Birmingham University, working under a naval contract. They first ran it successfully in April 1940, and within about eighteen months radars built around magnetrons were being incorporated in operational equipment.

Airborne microwave radars had great potential for guiding bombers at night because of their ability to pick up and display identifiable rivers and cities. But because the crash of an aircraft carrying this equipment might allow the enemy to retrieve this chunky and almost indestructible component, and discover its secret, use of it over Germany was for some time prohibited by Churchill. Then this restriction was relaxed, and soon a bomber did crash in shallow water off Rotterdam; its magnetron was retrieved and sent to the Telefunken works in Berlin to be copied.

It was one of these copies we saw. It had had one of its flat copper cheeks removed in order to display its insides, and what we saw made some of us chuckle. Cavity magnetrons have a central cylindrical space containing the cathode, and surrounding it there are six or eight smaller cavities, which act as resonators, rather as a bottle does when you blow across its top. But its full power can only be obtained when all the cavities are exactly in step, without rogue overtones. A technique was developed at TRE of including little brass straps that connect alternate cavities together, which were then tuned by bending them. The straps of the Telefunken magnetron showed no signs of having been bent, and we imagined the Germans exclaiming, on first looking inside the Rotterdam magnetron, "Oh those stupid British, they cannot even make their straps straight!"

In 1946, it was announced that a new international body, the Provisional International Civil Aviation Organization, or PICAO, would hold meetings in London. TRE's scientists would be able to make valuable contributions in several fields: navigation, collision avoidance, blind-approach systems, etc. We put up a Rebecca stand at the meetings, but as might have been anticipated, it attracted little attention. However, I began to think about a role for secondary radar (i.e., Rebecca/Eureka-type systems) for navigation. It could indicate an aircraft's distance from a known beacon, so that if one could only incorporate into the beacon some method of indicating its bearing, too, then a pilot would know his location.

Of course there were several factors I never thought of, such as possible swamping of the beacon by heavy traffic. But in my innocence I put in long evenings in our hut constructing the "Graham Navigator."[5] There were lots of spare items lying around from which I could help myself freely and adapt as required; but I confess to having helped myself to one fairly expensive item from the stores, a 24-volt rotary converter for providing high voltage D.C. for the airborne unit. In doing so, I knew I was abusing an enlightened policy adopted by the Ministry of Supply, which had eliminated a lot of bureaucratic rigmarole in the interests of efficiency: thus, you just helped yourself from the stores, rather than applying in triplicate for what you wanted and then having to wait an age for it.

I did progress as far as setting up my transmitter and flying the airborne unit. Signals were received and responded to, but there would still have been an enormous amount of work to do, and regarding one crucial element of the circuitry, I soon realized that I couldn't design it without help. In any case, the whole enterprise was in vain, since in July 1947 my demobilization papers arrived, and I had to bid Malvern a sad farewell.

CHAPTER 5

Dublin

As I stepped out from the demobilization center, smartly dressed in the new "civvy suit" given me by a grateful nation, I couldn't help wondering what the future held for me. It wasn't a matter that I'd thought about much beforehand, beyond knowing that I had no hope of returning at once to Cambridge University; nor would my chances for the coming academic year be much better. And for the following year, who knew? Thousands who had served in the armed forces much longer than I had would rightly be accorded priority, and for all I knew, the university might well have lost all interest in my return—ever.

I went back to Malvern to collect my possessions, and there in a bookshop ran into Douglas Naylor, whom I'd met during my first year in the navy. Doug told me he would soon be going to Dublin University (better known as Trinity College, Dublin, or TCD) and suggested that I do the same. This seemed a good idea, so I adopted it at once, and having borrowed his copy of the College calendar, I wrote to a tutor listed there as a physicist.

Less than a week later I was pleasantly surprised to receive word of my acceptance. I consulted the calendar again, and finding "Beginning of Term, 30 September" printed in heavy Gothic type, I set off for Dublin by train and ferry on about the twenty-fifth, marveling at my good fortune. A tiny doubt, however, did nag me: so extraordinarily easy had my acceptance at short notice been that I couldn't help wondering whether I'd made it quite clear that I was applying for the current year. So perhaps I was showing up a year early?

I found Dr. Gregg's office, knocked at the door, entered, and introduced myself. "But what are you doing here *now*?" he asked. My worst fear seemed to be confirmed—until he explained that the operative date in the calendar was "Lectures commence" (inconspicuously printed in italics) three weeks away. So off I went to Galway for an unexpected holiday.

My first impression of Dublin was a mixture of delight and dismay. The splendid Georgian street architecture was indeed a delight, as were the shops abounding in butter, chocolates, and other delicacies strictly rationed in Britain; but this was quickly tempered by the abject and all-too-obvious poverty of many children in those streets, especially when wintry cold arrived. Few of the poor little beggars had shoes, and their feet and legs were red and swollen with cold. I bought one little boy a pair of shoes, only to have a bystander tell me that I was wasting my money; his father would sell them. Another unhappy memory from my first year at TCD (although trivial in comparison) was my daily commute by crowded tram or bus, for on wet winter days it meant having to endure the smell of unwashed clothes and old, damp tweed impregnated with the smoke of tobacco and peat fires.

On the other hand, there was laughter everywhere, a sound rarely heard in England, even after the war was over. Life in England would remain grim for two more years at least, for in view of general malnutrition in continental Europe the government kept food rations as short as ever. For example, the weekly portion of butter was just two ounces, whereas in Ireland there was no rationing at all. When, a little later, I made an excursion to Belfast, the traveler in front of me at the Ulster Customs inspection was carrying a violin case. The Inspector insisted on removing the instrument from its case, and then peering closely into the f-holes. He passed it, and after he had checked my bag, I couldn't resist asking:

"Pardon me, Inspector, I'd love to know what you thought might be concealed inside that violin?"

"Oh, ye nivver know," he replied. "It moight have contained a paound of botter!"

For my first year at Trinity, I'd been allotted rooms in a boarding house pleasantly situated in the suburbs. One house, almost opposite, was considerably larger and better maintained than the rest and belonged, I was told, to a successful mattress manufacturer. Not long before, this man had bought an uninhabited island off the south coast of Ireland, and had been criticized in the newspapers for introducing foxes to destroy the rabbit population. Furthermore, he made himself the object of ridicule by regarding as valid some document the vendor had given him, according to which any owner of the island had the right to assume the title of "The Prince of Thomond."

One day, while at my lodgings, I saw a gig draw up at that house. It was driven by a man distinguished not only by a long gray beard, but also, as later I learned, by the ancient and wonderful title that he bore, the MacGillicuddy of the Reeks. He had come to solicit from Mr. Malone a donation to some good cause. He rang the doorbell, a maid appeared, and he asked her,

"Is Mr. Malone at home?"

"His Hoighness is in the gaarden," the maid replied.

"Then," the august visitor replied in measured and sepulchral tones, "he can bloody well stay there."

Trinity College was founded in the reign of Queen Elizabeth I. In my day, it still had an overwhelmingly Protestant student body, most of them from the "Nurrh," and many of them the offspring of families prosperous from the linen trade. There were also those who (like me, I admit) accepted it as second-best, as did one lad who told me he had chosen Trinity "because I couldn't get into Sheffield"—by no means a distinguished seat of learning in those days. I did wonder whether he deserved to be at Trinity . . . For my part, I was quite content during my years at TCD, though a little disappointed in just one respect. For me, a great attraction of Trinity had been the presence of E. T. S. Walton as professor of physics, for he had shared with J. D. Cockcroft a Nobel Prize for splitting atoms for the first time with artificially accelerated particles. But I soon found that by this stage of his life Walton was spending most of his time devising ingenious demonstrations for pre-med students—as a result of which some wag suggested that he'd only held the atom while Cockcroft split it.

I can't claim to have worked particularly hard at Trinity, but I did get by. Among other activities, I put some effort into contributing to a voluntary series of evening lectures given by science students, for the best of which a silver medal was awarded annually. I gave three talks: one, which cost me a lot of research, was an attempt to describe the underlying principles and the basic anatomy of the atomic bomb—a very difficult undertaking in view of the secrecy surrounding it in those early days. Another covered electronic aids to aerial navigation, with the hyperbolic system of wartime "Gee" and post-war "Loran" demonstrated mechanically by means of pulleys and differential gears mounted behind a large map of Ireland. Threads emerging from three holes (representing transmitters) were tied to a small model plane, any movement of which by a member of the audience I was able to plot backstage. The third was a ridiculous attempt to construct a sonic analog of radar, just for fun (unfortunately I failed to make it work). As the competition wasn't strong, I won medals for the first two talks.

One nonacademic activity that I had hoped to enjoy in Dublin was singing, and I did join a not particularly inspiring chorus. Then by some lucky chance I met an engaging young British couple then living in Dublin, Michael and Elizabeth Morrow, both of whom dressed in vaguely Elizabethan clothes and wrote exclusively with quill pens in ink the color of dried blood. These were habits one could scarcely regard as affectations, for they tried to live and think as Elizabethans, the better to interpret the music of that time.

In England, music from the sixteenth century and earlier was just then beginning to be appreciated, thanks to Arnold Dolmetsch and his gifted family, but in Ireland, those having the slightest interest in that kind of music could perhaps have been numbered with the fingers of one hand. So, in the hope of generating interest in it, the Morrows were looking for a few musicians willing to be conducted by them into this unfamiliar field.

Now, my musical gifts are modest, but in Dublin at that time so scarce were singers of classical music of any kind that when someone mentioned my name to the Morrows as a possible singer, they tried me out from sheer desperation. I'm told that the quality of my voice is pleasant enough, but it's untrained and blessed with neither power nor great range. The most I can say for myself is that I sing accurately in tune, but on the other hand, I'm far from an accomplished sight-reader. So my first experience of making music with the Morrows was challenging, to say the least. I remember the other four singers and I were gathered around Elizabeth, seated with her cello, and were expected to sing from a single sheet of manuscript placed on the stand in front of her, each of us craning forward to decipher the little brown dots with ragged stems representing the notes, while trying not to get in the way of her bow.

A week later, evidently, they still hadn't found a more competent singer, for I was invited to another session. In the meantime, I'd found a wonderful and recently published book, *The Historical Anthology of Music*, compiled by A. T. Davison and W. Apel. I bought the first of the two volumes, which covers a period ending about 1600. It contained material that looked exciting, and even if really too large and heavy for the Morrow's flimsy music stand, it was at least far easier to read than that awful manuscript. But by the following week Michael, nervously stepping into the twentieth century, had found a way to have some pages of it mimeographed.

We gave just one public concert, in the theatre of Trinity College. By this time, Michael had found a harpsichordist, John Beckett, who, with his wire-rimmed spectacles with tiny lenses, looked exactly like Schubert as he bent his heavy frame over the keyboard. One item in our concert was a piece we'd never even rehearsed! Another was a *Caccia* written in the late fourteenth century by Girólamo da Firenze, in which a hunter is described as he sallies forth at dawn with his hunting dogs and companions. He encourages them to beat the bushes, to be on the lookout, and then "Ayo! Ayo!"—he spots a hind, and the dog "Carbón" has got it in his jaws and is holding on.

This was supposed to be followed by a *ritornello*, but the rapid runs in it were more than we could manage (and it was years before I realized that it was meant to be sung quite slowly, as a sort of recap of the day's sport as the hunters dawdled home).

Before long, I must have been quietly dropped from the group as more gifted singers were found, and lost touch with it, but I was glad to find, a few years later, that the Morrows had returned to London and formed a group called *Musica Reservata*, which was to make several LP records. Forty years on, a CD of their music is still in the catalog, and Michael is remembered as an important pioneer in the early music field; but alas, he was hemophiliac, and died in middle age.

There was another extracurricular activity to which I devoted a good deal of time, perhaps more fruitfully. That was making items of scientific apparatus. A few years ago, I was surprised and pleased to receive a letter from David Pepper, now sadly deceased, whom I remember well as a young chemistry professor. In it he told me, among other things, that in his lectures he was still demonstrating an instrument I'd made in 1950, the "Dipole Moment Machine," although now I cannot remember anything about it at all.

Other members of the faculty I remember with admiration and affection were David Webb, a naturalist of enormous learning and charm, and two chemists, even though chemistry was not my best subject. These were David Pepper and Tony Werner, whom I will refer to more later. But as chemistry was something of a mystery to me, I remember also an instructor named Bell, simply because of the little mnemonics he provided—all too necessary in those days, when the direction that chemical reactions would take had usually to be learned by rote, for the nature of the chemical bond was poorly understood. One of his rhymes was this:

Auntie Jane gave Baby Sue
A dose of $HgCl_2$.
Babe Sue's in Heaven now,
And Auntie Jane is wondering how
That extra atom of Cl
Made such a diff'rence to Calomel!

An unforgettable member of the history faculty was Doctor R. B. MacDowell (whose given name I never knew). The first aspect of him that a stranger would notice might well be the many layers of clothing he wore, which in fact might start with pajamas, over which various shirts and light sweaters had been pulled, then a jacket and overcoat, and, topping all this off, a woolen scarf and a hat pulled well down on his head. He spoke in a rapid, high-pitched voice, and almost any question one might pose to him concerning a minor episode in the history of the Abbey Theatre, or an event in Irish politics in the eighteenth or nineteenth century, would be answered by a rush of information, delivered in his high-pitched and distinctive northern Irish accent.

In about 1980 I revisited Ireland, hoping to add to the information I already had about Lord Kingsborough, the eccentric and extravagant compiler of nine elephant folio volumes on Mexican antiquities, who died tragically in 1837. Thinking that MacDowell might be able to give me some useful references about his family, I invited him and David Webb to dinner. We had an excellent and bibulous dinner, and good talk. Afterwards, a little tipsy from all the whisky I had drunk, I accompanied him back to the College, and only when I was about to bid him good-night did I remember that I had failed to ask him about Kingsborough. So I posed my question and "Oh yes," he replied immediately, "there's a book, *The Kings, Earls of Kingston*, by R. D. King-Harmon, privately printed, 1959. Good-night." He seldom failed to produce the goods.

It was through him, I believe, that I met "The Pope" O'Mahony, unlikely as that may seem, for their political orientations were polar opposites. O'Mahony (baptised Eioan, but seldom, I think, called that) was a fervent Irish nationalist. He had trained as a lawyer, and is said to have defended in English courts those IRA members who had conducted a campaign of putting bombs in English mailboxes on the eve of World War II. This legal work he did gratis. To continue doing such *pro bono* work, he had to sell the small margarine factory in Cork that he had inherited, but the money received for that would also run out in time.

Widely respected in Dublin, he also cut an unmistakable figure—short, with a round head, and dressed in traditional legal clothing (that is, striped trousers and a black jacket—the latter, in his case, liberally spotted with egg and other food stains). In my Dublin days, he either lived far out of town or else no longer had a fixed abode, for on learning that I had a sofa comfortable enough to sleep on, he would occasionally knock on the door of my rooms in College and ask if he might spend the night on it.

Lest he might suppose I was a Unionist, I made some show of Scottish-Nationalist sympathies, having learned the basics from my uncle Jim Montrose, who had espoused that cause (at the cost of having to leave the conservative Carlton Club). In reality, I had no strong views on the matter, but my posture seems to have satisfied O'Mahony, for he invited me one evening to accompany him to a weekly gathering at McDaid's Bar, in a street off Grafton Street. There I found a wonderful collection of eccentrics.

Among them was an early enthusiast for three-dimensional films, and a man who knew by heart, and readily sang, every known ballad describing the sinking by the British of shiploads of Irish widows and orphans. There was a reputed expert in black magic, and a housepainter dressed in paint-spattered dungarees whose superb command of freshly minted abuse distinguished him from the others even more than did his clothing. When time was nearly up at the bar, large, gray, Kraft paper bags were filled with bottles of Guinness, and we took the number 15 streetcar to Dalkey. Dismounting from it, we walked to a substantial house belonging to this master of invective, who had evidently prospered by working very hard with his paintbrush. As the party grew, a tall, thin, and lugubrious man with raw and prominent wristbones sticking out from his too-short sleeves took up his post as doorkeeper, slumped in an easy chair opposite the door, where he was kept supplied with bottles of Guinness. Only occasionally did he find it necessary to get up and deny entry to someone or throw out someone else.

His name, I learned, was Sean Daly. He was a street-sweeper, and a Communist who had taught himself Russian in order to read Lenin in the original. While imprisoned for some offense, he had reportedly shared a cell with a condemned man who was allowed neither paper nor pencil to write his reminiscences. So to preserve them, Sean was said to have memorized them, to write down later.

The party warmed up. From the bar, our host began directing golden streams of abuse at almost anyone who caught his attention, but these were so funny that the recipients didn't seem to mind. (In retrospect, I do lament that tape recorders were not yet available, for his wonderfully original objurgations, perhaps never matched before or since, ought to have been preserved for their poetic beauty.)

At one point, I found myself talking to Sean O'Sullivan, president of the Royal Hibernian Academy. He was holding, close against his ribs, a soup-plate laden with potato crisps, and was swaying noticeably. Then losing his balance, he tripped over his own feet and fell flat on his back, lying there with his chest covered with potato crisps. "Somebody pushed me! You pushed me!" (pointing at me, but no one paid any attention). How the party ended, I no longer recall, but I did learn the name of our host. It was Brendan Behan, a name that meant nothing to me at the time.

I was to catch sight of him again before long. One evening, I was treating myself to a solitary meal at Jammet's, then Dublin's best restaurant, while reading a novel. Then a contretemps at the door caught my attention: the manager was refusing admittance to Behan, who eventually left, delivering a well-crafted parting insult. But about ten minutes later I saw him being seated at a table not far from mine, accompanied by "The Pope" O'Mahony. Presumably, they had met in the street by chance, and soon agreed to dine together at Jammet's for their mutual benefit. Behan would get his revenge, since no matter who was accompanying him, O'Mahony would be welcome; and as for the latter, he would get an excellent dinner at Behan's expense.

Absorbed in my book, I didn't see O'Mahony leave, presumably called away by some other engagement. By now, it was getting late, and the waiters were beginning to clear the tables. I saw Behan take a ten-shilling note from his wallet, put it on the table as a tip, and lean back in his chair, rocking on its back legs. The waiter came over to remove the salt and pepper and remaining cutlery. He came back for the flower vase, and finally, wanting to remove the tablecloth, started to slide his hand over it to take the tip. But then,

"Oh no, ye don't!" cried Behan, slapping him on the wrist, "Jest now you wouldn't let me in, so I'm foining yer ten shillings!"

After I'd graduated from Dublin and was living in London, I happened to see a notice in the *Sunday Times* of a new production at the Theatre Royal, Stratford, in east London: it was a play called *The Hostage*, by Brendan Behan. Like a fool, I allowed some boringly conventional entertainment to prevent my attending the opening night. What a mistake—it must have been a wild occasion!

As for one of his friends, I had an interesting encounter with him at about that time. I was walking through Soho, in London, with a TCD friend, David Leary, when we literally bumped into a man on the crowded pavement. Looking up, I recognized the gaunt and gangling figure of Sean Daly.

"Sean!" David exclaimed, "What are you doing here?"

"Oi'm warking at a cancer hospital," he replied.

"Oh, er, and what's your job there?"

"Weell, one of me duties is to measure the carrpses for their coffuns; and sometoimes Oi takes a disloike to 'em; so Oi takes a fooot off the measures, and they have to breeaak something to get 'em in!"

My social life in Ireland, however, was by no means confined to these milieux. I was lucky enough to meet, or receive introductions to, many hospitable people, some of whom invited me repeatedly to their homes for a weekend. Kilruddery, in County Meath, became almost a second home, and I spent several weekends at Birr Castle, as a guest of the Rosses. This ancient castle in the very middle of Ireland, which still bears the scars of cannon balls fired during a siege in Cromwellian times, is nowadays surrounded by superb plantings of trees and shrubs, largely the work of Ann Rosse, whose father was a famous gardener. The interior décor was also largely hers, although to my taste its sumptuousness—patterned, flamingo-colored flock wallpaper, for instance— was a bit excessive for an old castle; but then, not for nothing was she sister of the stage designer Oliver Messel.

The most extraordinary feature of this place, though, was the abandoned telescope in the grounds, once known as "The Leviathon of Parsonstown" (Birr's former name). It was constructed by William Parsons, third Earl of Rosse, a most distinguished astronomer—as his son would also be. Its mirror of speculum metal, six feet in diameter, was successfully cast and ground by Rosse on the premises, after he had found a method of avoiding the formation of stress-cracks during the cooling of large discs. Since these cracks were caused by the perimeter cooling faster than the center, Rosse's solution was to incorporate straps radiating from the center, to conduct heat away from it more rapidly.

The mirror was mounted at the bottom of a fifty-five-foot-long wooden barrel, constructed of oaken staves and iron hoops, with a basket at the top for the observer. The whole thing was mounted on a giant cast-iron universal joint at the center-point between two massive, parallel walls aligned with the meridian, within the confines of which the telescope could be maneuvered by means of ropes and pulleys in a full semicircle between north and south, and by perhaps ten degrees either way, east and west. The rotation of the earth was relied upon for the remainder of that arc.

Started in 1828 and completed eighteen years later, this telescope remained the largest in the world for seventy years, during which time very important work was done with it, such as research on nebulae, and Rosse's measurement for the first time of the temperature of the moon. When finally abandoned, the telescope's historic mirror was removed to the Science Museum in London. Even the great iron universal joint at its foot has to be admired, since it was cast by the Countess. An iron foundry was set up in the outbuilding where the mirror had been ground, and there Lady Rosse made not only this massive casting, but also the very large and elegant ornamental entrance gates for the castle.

When I used to visit Birr, those two great walls were hung with ivy, and the barrel lay on the ground between them. Of course this feature could never be mistaken for a folly, as sham "Gothick" ruins may be, but as an element in the landscape visible from the castle it had a monumental and mysterious quality, outdoing in this respect any other relic that I've seen in a nobleman's pleasure-grounds. (Now, I'm told, the telescope has been restored to working order with a glass mirror as a tourist attraction.)

During one weekend there, four of us drove to visit a rather distant house in County Meath and the two old ladies who lived there. I forget the name of the house, but the last name of the two old ladies was Chapman. They received us graciously at their tea-table, and when Ann Rosse commented that the décor of the house was an unusually intact example of turn-of-the-century taste, we were told that, yes, nothing at all had been changed since Father left, and we were shown a watercolor of the interior done at that time.

"Oh, but wait a minute, his hat is shown on the stand; I'll go and get it to complete the scene."

So where had Father gone? He'd run off with the governess, a Miss Lawrence, who would bear him several sons, one of them with the initials T. E.

The doings of that brilliant and hedonist coterie of undergraduates who enlivened the scene at Oxford in the late 1920s have, of course, been chronicled abundantly by themselves and others—most amusingly in the novels of Evelyn Waugh. My host, Michael, Lord Rosse, was of that Oxford vintage and set, although he himself wrote nothing about those times, becoming instead a pillar of the Irish Georgian Society. Sometimes, though, I encountered other leading lights from that long-gone generation as fellow guests at Birr. Once, on arriving for the weekend on a drizzly Friday afternoon, I found Michael with two or three guests returning from a walk. One of them was a large man of stately presence, clad in a raincoat the likes of which I had never seen: a voluminous, pale gray, transparent plastic affair, brought from America. Its wearer had a most impressive head, the upper and lower portions being large—one might even say bulbous—but seeming to narrow at ear level. His courteous greeting was delivered in a friendly, resonant voice, tinged with an accent that I couldn't identify; I dare say it was originally idiosyncratic, and then consciously exaggerated. In fact, his speech was modulated into a slight sing-song, and I soon noticed that many of his remarks ended with an intriguing upward inflection, as if questioning, or suggesting something unspoken.

This was Harold Acton, who has also described his time at Oxford in *Memoirs of an Aesthete*. I learned that he lived in Florence, and had spent some years in Peking before the war. During this weekend, he described amusingly, but with unconcealed chagrin, the recent seizure and burning by the Customs at Folkestone of the entire edition of his book on Grand Duke Gian Gastone, the last of the Medici. (Later, he published a bowdlerised version.)

He invited me to call on him when next in Florence, and when the opportunity arose in about 1952 I did so. He was living at the great house purchased by his parents, Villa La Pietra, on the road to Bologna. I was shown the extraordinary garden with its open-air theater and topiary statues, the ceiling within the villa painted by Tiepolo—and exhibit number 3, the parents. They were terrible. His mother was an immensely rich Chicagoan who carefully concealed her charm, if she had any; while his father. . . well, he was descended from an English Acton of about four generations back, but his other ancestors were all Italian and his total experience of England, according to Harold, amounted to one week; yet he referred to Italians as "wogs." Poor Harold told me that he still hadn't been entrusted with a key to the villa, even at the age of about forty-five. Then he telephoned, suggesting I accompany him to lunch at

I Tatti with Bernard Berenson, the great art historian (and authenticator of pictures for the dealer Duveen). How could I refuse such an invitation?

With the passage of more than fifty years, few actual memories of much substance have survived, even of that rare occasion, but Berenson's appearance I do remember, and his large and wonderful painting by Simone Martini; also the garden. I remember, too, a ridiculous discussion provoked by my mentioning a new but apparently short-lived craze of balloon-hopping, which had been featured not long before in *Life* magazine. Apparently, aficionados of this pastime, when harnessed with a hydrogen balloon capable of supporting about two-thirds of their weight, were able to make mighty jumps with gentle landings. Jokingly, Berenson suggested at once that this sport would have been ideal for his late wife, whose greatly increased weight and weakened legs had reduced her mobility. There followed, of course, speculation about how she might have been rescued, should a gust of wind have lodged her in a tree.

In 1985, well over thirty years later, I came across a sheet of headed notepaper from the hotel where I'd been staying, upon which I had scribbled, when back from lunch at I Tatti, what I remembered of the conversation at table. Reading it, I was appalled—not at the conversation, but at the fearful reduction in power of recall that I had evidently suffered since then. No longer, as I told Harold, would I have been able to remember one fourth as much—and now, after another two decades, very little indeed!

I typed out a transcript of this document and sent it off to him as a reminder of that day, hoping he might correct any mistakes I'd made, out of unfamiliarity with the people or matters referred to. And this he was kind enough to do.

I'll not print this report in its entirety, but on the other hand I've restored the parts of speech missing from my original "telegraphic" notation. As lunch began, there was talk of Paul Cadmus, Emerald Cunard, and Alice Astor. Then Harold, speaking of reviewers of Berenson's *Sketches for an Autobiography*, described one of them, Peter Quennell. His poetic genius having dried up at sixteen, Harold said, he was now writing competently but not brilliantly, and rehashing earlier work, his *Gibbon*, for example. Now a dried-up little man, he used to be good-looking and admired himself in mirrors; he also used a little powder and shaved his chest, but cared only for the ladies. Bernard Berenson (B. B.) related how a sensible girl had gone crazy for him at sight. He looked feminine, and people used to stop and stare. (In his letter, Harold expressed his hope that I didn't intend to publish those remarks about Quennell, since he was then still alive, and ultra-sensitive—adding that "he still writes better than most of us." But now of course he has long gone to his reward.)

Discussion then turned to Osbert Sitwell's posthumous book (mentioned in connection with some spiteful reviewer) and to the question of whether one will mind criticism beyond the grave. B. B. says he is sure he won't mind; having used this world as a springboard, he will float away out of it. Harold, though, thinks he will know what is being said. I mention *Enoch Soames*, and discussion of Beerbohm's *Seven Men* follows. Harold holds that the accumulation of detail in Proust was not equaled by Max. His caricatures will continue to be enjoyed, but his writings not read.

Now the talk was of André Gide (a close friend of Berenson's). Harold criticized him for denying that he was homosexual (as, of course, Harold was) and for decrying pederasty. (Harold's later comment was that Gide's *Corydon* provided ample proof of his insincerity in this regard, but he thought it possible Gide had tried to conceal his true proclivities from B. B., who was fundamentally puritanical). Berenson calls him a self-made man without Ecole Normale education, and since he doesn't know what has been said, he says it again; but then, true artists don't know the work of others.

Harold tells us he's writing about the Abbé Celestino Galeani, but who's heard of him? Everybody, says B. B., everybody but those young men whose horizons are bounded by T. S. Eliot to the West, George Moore to the East, Gert Stein to the South—who to the North? Sean O'Failoin?—he's not bad. The Irish have easy use of language, but when it comes to W. B. Yeats. . . . Harold says Eliot was a plagiarist, borrowing from La Fourgue in his early work.

Now Edward Hulton was mentioned (he was the publisher of *Picture Post* and *Lilliput* magazines). Harold had heard that B. B. had been rude to Mrs. Hulton. On the contrary, said B. B., he had been charmed, but wouldn't have minded being rude to Hulton. He thought his father must have had something to do with horses—a groom perhaps. (It was rumored that Hulton was not the son of his legal father—a matter of importance concerning his inheritance of a title.) Harold, however, thought he really was the son, but born out of wedlock.

Of Oscar Wilde, B. B. knew him before he got coarse, and says he looked wonderful. With him he was "humble and penitent," and often penniless. *Dorian Gray* was written quickly, for £100. "Will you tell me what you think of it?" he asked B. B., "here's the first copy from the press." The next day, B. B. told him he thought it "awful." Wilde agreed (or so I thought he said). Harold gave his opinion that *Dorian Gray* read better in other languages, saying that translations were good only when there was something wrong with the use of language in the original.

My last note on this table-talk records Berenson as telling us that when young he had beautiful long hair, but at thirty, barbers told him he was losing it. He tried every remedy, and Consuelo Vanderbilt, Duchess of Marlborough, attempted to preserve it by rubbing his head with garlic. London experts, however, recommended simply leaving it, so he did.

The summer-long vacations provided for in university calendars must constitute an important element in undergraduate education, or they wouldn't be so long (unless it's just to suit the professors). Yet I could find no general agreement as to the approved way of spending them. For myself, I did some traveling abroad, such as taking the Orient Express to Istanbul in 1948.

This, my first independent venture abroad, was a wonderful experience, although it soon became clear that the name of the train service, as restarted after the war, was laughably inappropriate, since the journey took four days. Furthermore, the cars were laboriously reshuffled on reaching the Yugoslav border, in what seemed to be deliberate, class-conscious policy. The first- and second-class cars were now at the front of the train (to give us maximum inhalation of smoke from the locomotive), lower-class ones in the middle, and the restaurant car at the tail end, so that any hungry exploiters of the proletariat were from then on required to rub shoulders all too intimately with their victims in the jam-packed corridors of the intervening cars—even perhaps to downtread them lightly here and there.

After enduring those four long days, I felt abundantly rewarded when at last Istanbul came in sight. Since then, I have sampled four ways of approaching that wonderful city from the west—by boat, train, car, and plane—and now know that the slowly unfolding views of its domes, minarets, and ancient walls which greet those coming up the Bosphorus by boat are the most delightful; but in those distant days, long before the City of Istanbul sprawled out of control, arrival by train was almost as marvelous.

I did endure one unsatisfactory night in what proved to be a bedbug-infested flophouse in which old men spent their time playing *trictrac* (a sort of backgammon), before finding slightly more agreeable quarters, and in my wanderings became enchanted with the streets devoted to particular trades: plumbers, coffin-makers, barbers, etc. Then on a visit to the Kahrie Jami, the former Byzantine church famous for its mosaics, I found it a hive of restoration activity. This was being carried out by the University of Pennsylvania, and having scraped up an acquaintance with one of the restorers (whose last name was Wales), I was privileged to watch this work close at hand.

CHAPTER 6

A Widening World

All these had been wonderful adventures, but romance had yet to come my way. In fact I was still a virgin, though not totally innocent—for at Winchester, those who didn't fall asleep immediately at lights-out might occasionally hear tiptoeing on the creaky floorboards of the dorm. But now, thinking that a more complete experience of the joys of sex was long overdue, I screwed up my courage, one evening in London, and approached a prostitute in Bond Street. The experience was dreadful, and I have banished any recollection of it.

But now I had developed a crush on Sibilla, the merry and extremely pretty daughter of Dublin University's professor of Italian—though well aware that she found me unexciting, and perhaps boring. I did, however, form a real friendship with her brother, Riccardo—possibly enhanced by an element of *arriére pensé*. For established practice at that time was that brother and sister were given tickets by their parents in alternate years to spend the summer with their large extended family in Naples, and at the height of my infatuation, I learned that it would be Sibilla's turn to go south that year. So I devised a plan: I would offer Riccardo a free ride to Naples in my tiny Austin Eight. He accepted, we both had fun, and he arranged that I should stay with his generous Uncle Achille.

One evening, Zio Achille asked us what plans we had for the evening, and as we had none, he suggested the casino. Inwardly I groaned, for as far as I was concerned, gambling was not only expensive but also extremely boring—but of course I made no objection. Then, as we set out, Zio Achille asked if we had our passports? *Passports*! Was there really a law in Italy prohibiting minors from gambling?

We walked two or three blocks and came to the entrance of a large, rather run-down apartment building, and rang the bell. We were taken up to a room where a rouged and blowsy woman greeted us and received the entrace fee, kindly paid by Zio Achille. Slowly it dawned on me that this was no gambling den, but a whorehouse—but it wasn't until later that Riccardo explained the source of my misunderstanding: *casinoó* in Italian means a house of ill-fame, whereas an English-language gambling den is a *casino*.

We waited in a stuffy room of Edwardian décor, while Zio Achille engaged *Madame* with banter. Then it was my turn. Very nervously I was ushered into a small chamber, to be greeted by a very pretty and charming girl called Gioia. She quickly sensed my innocence, and made the encounter truly enjoyable. I would have been happy to see her again, but I learned there was no possibility of doing so, because the casinos, then government regulated, circulated the girls to obviate attachments—as well as ensuring they received regular medical checkups. (But a few years later, a female senator of little understanding managed to abolish the state-run casinos, with predictable results.)

Those long vacations also allowed me to attend a number of social events of an entirely different kind: debutante balls. A few of these were now splendid enough for duchesses to appear once more in tiaras that had been dusted off, after languishing in bank vaults for a decade. I had started going to such affairs in London while the war was still in progress, almost all of them being held in a notably stuffy hall, number 23, Knightsbridge. Though never one to cut much of a figure on the dance floor, being constitutionally unable to distinguish between a foxtrot and a quickstep, I found those entertainments quite enjoyable, and soon I became less awkward with girls.

Among those I remember during the war were two or three who, in answer to my inquiries about their war work, told me they were at Bletchley Park. I did think it a little odd that not one of them seemed to know what she was doing there (later, of course, it would be revealed as the center of wartime code-breaking). Another detail that may seem strange today is that while I was walking back up Knightsbridge in the still of the wee hours, I used to hear the sound of crickets in the houses I passed. If crickets still survive in that area, which seems unlikely, their small sounds would never compete with today's ceaseless roar of traffic.

Perhaps I should mention that during those long vacations I actually did a little reading. But I'm convinced that my most rewarding and educative vacation time was spent with the family of David and Mary Crawford. As I've mentioned, I began visiting Haigh Hall, near Wigan, during my naval service. Indeed, I celebrated VE-Day with the Crawfords. David had invited me to accompany him and Mary on that day to Manchester, to see Dame Sybil Thorndyke and Ralph Richardson in a performance of

Peer Gynt. When news of the German surrender came, David went down to the cellar and brought up a bottle of rum, one of the few remaining from the numerous bottles presented to one of his ancestors on his relinquishing his post as governor of Jamaica, toward the end of the eighteenth century. Since the rum was reputed to have been the oldest available at that time, its age cannot have been far short of two centuries by then. We toasted peace with this venerable spirit, finding it colorless, still strong and smooth, but almost devoid of flavor. Then we went off to enjoy a superb performance of the play.

Another play I saw with David, some years later, was at an early Edinburgh Festival, this city being known, of course, as "The Athens of the North." Mary was away somewhere, so David arranged for us to stay at the Roseberys' great house just across the Forth bridge. The play was Shakespeare's *Timon of Athens*. When the curtain went up, we saw an Athens painted in drab browns, grays, and greens, provoking a man seated behind us to comment, in the "ahfully refeened" accent of the town, "No wonder they call it the Aydenborough of the Sa-outh!"

But we greatly enjoyed the play, and then climbed into Lady Rosebery's Bentley, which she had parked right in front of the theatre. As she accelerated away I caught sight of two theatre-goers leaping for their lives. "Silly fools," she hissed. "Can't they see I haven't got my lights on?" We sped off, but as soon as we reached her husband's park, she braked sharply for a pheasant crossing the drive.

David was to remain a kind and inspiring friend for the remainder of his life. So many were the long visits that I made to Haigh Hall, and later to Balcarres, the old Lindsay castle in Fife, that I came to be treated almost as an honorary member of the family. And Patrick (his and Mary's second son, who was about three years younger than I) would become my closest friend—and now a man I've greatly missed since his untimely death in 1986.

But when World War II ended, the one close acquaintance of mine who was unable to look forward to the future with much excitement was David himself, for now he was faced with the arduous and emotionally painful task of emptying Haigh Hall of its vast and valuable collections, prior to selling the estate. There were great sales of books and other treasures, and several of the specialist collections were given, or sent on permanent loan, to other libraries. David did, however, manage to retain the heart of the picture collection and that of the "Bibliotheca Lindesiana"—and installed them at Balcarres, together with a wonderful miscellany of furniture and treasures of every kind.

I mention this because some of the treasures in the house certainly did play a part in that supposedly educative process of university "Long Vacations" each summer. There was such a huge variety of marvelous objects to examine. In the library there were about two hundred *incunabulae*—books printed before AD 1500, most of them with pages so crisp and white, and printed with ink so black, that one could easily believe they were fresh off the press. It was indeed a rare privilege to be able to withdraw any one of them carefully from the shelf, open it correctly as instructed, and attempt to read it.

One of my favorites was Bartholemew Glanville's *De Proprietatibus Rerum* (an edition in English, dated 1494). This was really an early encyclopedia, starting with theology and ending with music and weights and measures. For the author, music was a mystery, and the topic of "sesquialter" obliged him to confess: "These wordes ben in themselves depe and full mystyk: and darke to onderstondynge, but to them that ben wyse and cunnynge in Ars metrik and in Musik they ben more clerer than moche lyghte, and ben darke and alle unbeknown to theym whyche ben uncunninge and have noo useage in Ars metrik."

In another delightful chapter describing the usual members of a household, the duties of the "nourisshe" (or nurse) are listed. "Nourysshe hath ye name of nourys-shinge for she is ordeyned to nourysshe & fede ye childe. . . . As the moder ye nouryce is glad yf the childe be glad. . . . Yf he weep they kysse him . . . and lyfteth hym up now on her sholders, now on her hondes, now on her knees and lappes. . . . And she chaweth mete in her mouth, and maketh it redy to the toothless chylde, that he may the easyler swalowe the meete." (A later edition, though, has this note: "but if ye nourysshe have stinking breath, it is better she should not chaw the meat.")

There was so much else besides: seals, coins, an extraordinary microscope of the early nineteenth century, and a particularly fascinating find, the unsorted papers of David's uncle, who had been British ambassador to the Sublime Porte when the embassy was moved to Ankara—and later, ambassador to the United States.

For a time I was even considering a career in art history, and bought myself a copy of Crowe and Cavalcaselle's *History of Painting*. But in time I had to admit that nature had not endowed me with a good enough iconic memory to prosper in that field. (Unfortunately, I have labored under that same impediment in the study of Maya writing.)

These visits were to continue fairly regularly until I left for America, and even then didn't cease altogether. Nor were they devoid of adventure, for I remember that during one visit we learned that a farm vehicle, cutting across the park, had suddenly come to a halt as one wheel sank through the grass. When it had been hauled away, the vertical shaft of a disused mine was revealed, and the now rotten wooden baulks that long ago had been placed to cover it. The shaft was thirty or forty feet deep, but naturally, Patrick and I wanted to investigate an opening that seemed to exist at the bottom on one side. So we found a rope, tied one end to a tree, then tossed up for who was to go down first. Patrick won, and swarmed down the rope, but then had to report that no horizontal passage seemed to exist.

But then, when he tried to climb out, he found himself unable to do so, and we soon realized that carbon monoxide had somehow settled in the shaft. I ran off and shouted for Tom, his younger brother, to help find a garden hose. He soon found one, and lowered one end to Patrick; and since it was unnecessarily long, cut off (with some difficulty) the excess length to make it easier to inhale fresh air from it. And then, after about ten minutes, Patrick regained enough strength to climb out.

One of the unexpected resources of Balcarres proved to be the cellar. Since the house had not been used for at least fifty years, it contained some unexpected treasures: not only red wine, but gin and liqueurs. There was a bottle of London gin, square in shape, and with typography on its label clearly dating it to Regency times. David opened it, and we found it to have a strong juniper flavor, like Dutch gin, so that when, a few years later, Gilbeys celebrated its bicentenary, claiming in advertisements that its product had not changed in all that time, we had grounds for disbelief.

I believe it was in the mid-1950s that Baron Philippe de Rothschild rented Cortachy Castle from the Ogilvies; this was not far from Balcarres. News of certain arrangements made by these new tenants soon spread among the neighbors, such as the fact that they'd brought their own sheets and towels from France, evidently doubting that such items were yet in general use among the barbarous Scots. They had also brought their chef (an understandable precaution) and arranged for a small plane to deliver meat from France once a week. But since that part of the east coast of Scotland is subject to frequent fogs, there came a day when the plane couldn't land, and the chef, gravely doubting, had to venture to Perth to see what the butcher could offer. The result of this visit was a change in routine: in the future, the plane would fly to Perth weekly to bring meat from there to their house in France.

It was while I was staying at Balcarres that David and Mary invited the de Rothschilds to lunch. As it happened, Pauline was away, so Philippe came alone, and there were just the four of us. As we sat down at the table, David turned to Philippe and asked,

"What may I give you to drink; there's red wine, or perhaps cider?"

Philippe glanced at the anonymous decanter, and replied,

"Oh, I think I will try a little cider. . . "

"Oh come now," said David, "this wine's from your part of the world, you know; are you sure you wouldn't like to try it?"

Feeling a little pressure, he agreed to. I didn't know what this wine was, but naturally, when Philippe raised his glass, I was watching his expression. No anticipation of pleasure showed on his face; if anything, it showed doubt, even dread. But then, on bringing the glass closer to his nose, he looked startled, reflected for a moment, sniffed again, and took a sip. His face became—it's not too much to say—transformed by an expression of beatitude.

"*Could* this be Mouton 1870?"

"Yes, as a matter of fact it is."

"Why, this is *extraordinary*! You know, at Mouton there is a library of all the vintages of Mouton. But ever since I have been grown up, there has been no Mouton 1870—too many people had begged to sample it."

A pause allowed us to savor the implications of this statement. And then:

"I arrive at this determination by the process of elimination."

Then, at Harvard, about twenty years later, I attended the Christmas dinner of an undergraduate society of which I'm an associate member. I was seated at one end of the long table, and on my right sat an undergraduate, Liz Segal, who was already in close conversation with the student on her other side; on my left, there were two middle-aged associate members deeply engaged in a discussion about wine. So I was left to twiddle my thumbs. But then my neighbor, noticing my isolation, kindly turned to me and asked, "And what is the most extraordinary experience you have had in the field of fine wines?"

At first, this question left me at a loss, but then that lunch at Balcarres came to mind. I described it, and my contribution went down pretty well, I believe. By this time, Liz was also listening to our conversation, and when the wine lovers had had their say, she chipped in with, "Why, Mr. Graham, this is amazing! Last Sunday I was watching the *Today Show* on TV, and the guest was Baron de Rothschild. He was asked the same question, and after thinking about it a moment, he answered, 'Well, I remember that twenty years ago, in Scotland...' and he told the same story that you've just been telling."

(My unspoken reaction to this was, oh dear, they are going to think that I watched the same program, and for this occasion, appropriated the story to myself. Well, at least they will have to give me credit for the bit about the sheets and towels, and the butcher's shop in Perth!)

CHAPTER 7

London in the 1950s

By springtime in 1951, graduation from TCD was approaching, and with it, the need to find a job; but I dithered, failing to send off a single application for employment. Then a letter from Tony Werner dropped into my letterbox. Until the previous year, Tony had been a professor of chemistry at TCD, and had suffered the misfortune of trying to teach me chemistry. Still, we'd become friends, and now, most opportunely, he was writing to tell me about a three-year research position I might consider applying for.

He had now taken up a position at the conservation laboratory of the National Gallery in London. The gallery's trustees, he explained, had been criticized in the press over the condition of certain pictures in their charge, and had responded by bringing over an American restorer. But unfortunately this man committed serious blunders while working on two important pictures, one of them attributable to his ignorance of elementary chemistry.

This picture was Bellini's *The Madonna of the Meadows*, a work painted on a wooden panel prepared with a thick coating of gesso, and the condition to be remedied was incipient separation of the paint layer from the gesso. As a first step, then, layers of Japanese mulberry paper had been pasted over the surface, using as adhesive a kind of varnish easy to remove with a certain solvent when the work was finished, followed by a layer of linen. Together, they would ensure the integrity of the paint layer during treatment.

The painting was then turned face-down, and the wooden panel carefully ground away until the gesso priming was revealed. This in turn was scraped away with even greater care until the paint layer itself was reached. Now one could see the painting from behind!

Word of this unusual opportunity spread, and with distinguished visitors begging to see it, the decision was made to leave it as it was for about a month to accommodate those who would be coming from a distance. The rough surface of the newly revealed paint dulled the image, but its appearance could be brightened up by moistening it with refined naphtha (kerosene); but then, to avoid doing this repeatedly, it was decided to give it a thin coat of varnish instead. On resuming the restoration process a month later, this would be removed before laying a new ground of gesso on it; and then finally a new wooden panel.

Only at this point was the restorer's blunder revealed, for the paint layer was now lying sandwiched between two layers of varnish with similar solubilities. As a result, when the time came to remove that rear coating of varnish, the unfortunate man found himself playing billiards with tiny paint fragments floating in a sticky sea. Well, the painting now looks none the worse for the trauma it suffered, but that restorer left under a cloud.

This and one or two other unfortunate occurrences prompted the trustees to develop a program of basic scientific studies relating to conservation problems. One that needed no research concerned the lack of climate control in the storage galleries, for despite the installation each winter of electrically heated tea-urns left boiling away with their lids off, the air sometimes became so dry on frosty mornings that one could occasionally be startled by a sound like a shot. An old hand would then explain, "Oh, that's just the Crivelli altarpiece shrinking in the dry air."

An early move by the trustees was to persuade the Nuffield Foundation to finance three-year fellowships for a chemist and a physicist, with the possibility of a renewed appointment. Well, when offered this opportunity I couldn't very well ignore it—and what more pleasing place to work in could there be than the National Gallery? So I made the necessary application, and to my surprise was given the job. The stipend was not princely—£500 per annum—but in those days that was enough to survive on, even in London.

Scientific tests of limited scope were already being done routinely at the gallery. The lab was equipped with good X-ray equipment, and a very competent young technician was there to carry out, among other procedures, microscopic examination of tiny samples taken from paintings. But that was all.

The director of the lab was Dr. Ian Rawlins, a tall man with a slight hesitation in his speech, which I suspect he used sometimes as a way of clinching his argument in discussions with those lacking a scientific background. He would stutter, "It's all a m-m-matter of p–p-π-by-two." Incomprehension would preclude further discussion.

So in the autumn of 1953 I took a small flat in Mayfair and reported for work. On the chemistry side, Tony was in charge, supervising the researches of John Mills, my new colleague. John and I got along very well, and I was glad to see him gain distinction for his work at the gallery during the many years he worked there, eventually as director of the greatly enlarged scientific department.

The quarters occupied by our little group had been constructed within one enormous chamber, which must once have been a storage gallery. In it, a small chemical lab had been built for John, equipped with a handsome teak bench upon which, emblematically as it were, a stand with six test-tubes had been placed. But under Tony's guidance, more specialized equipment was obtained, and John was soon at work on the chemistry of dammar (a resin employed in varnishes), using the new analytical technique of chromatography.

My own objectives were twofold. One was to study the action of the organic solvents commonly used by conservators in removing old varnish from oil paintings; and the other, to investigate and quantify the reflective property of varnishes.

Varnishes have been responsible for widespread damage to Old Masters. The worst of them was so-called "Gallery Varnish," made with linseed oil and a resin, either mastic or one called copal (from its Aztec name, *copalli*). This, unfortunately, had been adopted at the National Gallery because of a defect in the previously used varnishes made with mastic resin in a solvent, namely their tendency to develop a cloudy "bloom." Historically, this had been most troublesome in Britain and industrial cities such as Dresden—but oddly, not in the exceptionally smoky city of St. Petersburg. Already, in 1843, a campaign at the National Gallery of cleaning paintings with varnish that bloomed caused such an outcry that an investigatory commission was formed. It was one of its members, the famous scientist Michael Faraday, who grasped the true cause of the trouble: the deposition of ammonium sulfate from coal smoke in the atmosphere—whereas the smoke in St. Petersburg came from wood fires.

It was known at the time that varnishes made with mastic or copal in linseed oil tended to yellow, but initially, perhaps, this was tolerated as a part of "Old Master glow." But in time it may totally obscure a painting—and, even worse, become hard and insoluble, making its removal difficult. Furthermore, its outer surface shrinks, causing it to curl and crack.

To remove a copal varnish, the strong solvent acetone has to be used, together with other moderating liquids. So a matter of great concern while doing this was the possibility that the linseed-oil-based medium of the paint itself would also be softened by the solvent and perhaps damaged.

When linseed oil dries, its long molecules bond with each other in the course of time, forming a sort of submicroscopic sponge (a process called polymerization). Within this sponge, other molecules not yet completely bonded remain entrapped, and it is owing to their lubricating effect that the dried film retains any flexibility. But in time, as polymerization continues, the varnish coat becomes stiffer, curls and cracks, and may begin to pull away from the canvas.

Another reason for removing yellowed varnish is that by dulling some colors it can unbalance a picture. A prime example in the National Gallery's collection was Giorgione's *Adoration of the Kings*. The right-hand side of the oblong painting is filled with a crowd that has come to adore, while the other shows only Mary, Joseph, and the Babe—a lop-sided composition. But in the course of several visits to the studio while it was being cleaned, I saw balance being restored as the brilliant blue and gold was revealed in the cloaks worn by Mary and Joseph.[1]

My job, then, was to investigate the effect of solvents on old varnish and paint. For my experiments I was given a free hand with the Wiggins Collection. These were oil paintings, mostly poor copies of old masters, that had been bought by the Wiggins Company, dealers in picture frames. Many masterpieces on exhibition in the gallery now have frames from this source, but the paintings formerly in those frames were of little value—except to us, for they were genuinely old, and done with materials and techniques similar to those used in the paintings they were copied from.

So a number of these were obtained for our use as guinea pigs, and were left leaning against a wall in our lab for me to stick scissors into and cut out samples. (More than once in those days I awoke in the middle of the night with a horrible doubt. Since the X-ray lab adjoined ours, genuine masterpieces to be X-rayed were sometimes propped up near to Wigginses, and the nightmare thought that woke me up was: Oh no! Is it *possible* that by mistake I cut a piece out of one of these? I would sweat with horror and be unable to go back to sleep.)

Obviously, one way of determining how much of the original medium a particular solvent mixture would remove from a tiny sample of ancient paint or varnish would be by weighing it. For such specimens, a microbalance would be needed—preferably one allowing a series of readings to be taken in quick succession as the solvents dried out. But as purchase of such an instrument was not possible, I decided to make one of my own design.

Rawlings then managed to obtain permission for me to make it in the workshops of the Government Chemist's Department, then located in Aldwych, next to the Law Courts. What I made was a balance having only a single pan for the specimen, and none for weights. This pan was suspended from one end of a little girder about four inches long, constructed of very slender glass members, while the other end was attached to the center of a length of phosphor-bronze ribbon, which served as its only support. One end of the ribbon was fixed to a bracket, and the other to the calibrated dial of an old surveyor's transit. Readings of a specimen's weight were taken by turning the dial until torsion of the ribbon brought the beam level, as indicated by an optical system. As readings could be made very quickly, I regarded this microbalance as rather a success, and published a short article on it in a technical journal.[2]

With this balance I obtained some useful data on such things as the effect of mixed solvents on samples of ancient paint, or the leaching out of the original paint medium during the removal of old varnish.

One day, as I entered the Government Chemist's Lab, I heard a loud noise of hammering in a lab across the entrance hall, with a small circle of people watching. Out of curiosity I went in to see what was going on, and observed what appeared to be a simple operation: an attempt to open a tin can of about a half-gallon capacity with hammer and cold chisel—but the metal's resistance to this attack showed it to be extraordinarily thick.

A bystander told me that this had been one of a considerable number of cans of beef stew that had been cached in the Arctic by Sir John Franklin upon abandoning his second attempt at finding the Northwest Passage. As is well known, his third expedition in 1845 ended disastrously, with loss of the entire crew. Not until fourteen years later would a fifth search party find the remains of both vessels and the stores, and bring back some of the latter for deposit in the Imperial War Museum in London.

As the stew had been canned well over a century earlier, the Tin Research Council became interested in the existing condition of the stew. It petitioned the museum to give it one can for research purposes, and this had been delivered to the Government Chemist's Lab for analysis. When at last the lid was off, we all had a sniff at the contents. The smell was at least faintly appetizing.

A sample was then sent over to the pathology lab for analysis, but then one of those present, who had his dog with him, agreed to it being fed a good helping of stew. Next morning, the dog was reported to be in good spirits, and as the lab had found nothing wrong with the stew, we heated some and made a meal of it. What a pity, though, that we didn't have one of those almost contemporary nineteenth-century bottles of Red Constancia from the Balcarres cellar to wash it down with!

Some years later, the frozen remains of two of Franklin's sailors were found under a thin layer of ice. Published photographs showed, even through the ice, the white tunics striped in blue that they were wearing. But when I happened to mention this meal of beef stew to Professor van der Merwe, then Harvard's professor of archaeological science, he told me that the sailors may have suffered from lead poisoning from the solder used in the manufacture of those cans, and that analysis of the stable isotopes of lead in the solder indicated that it came from Cornish mines, as would be expected in Britain.

I was pleased to find that we, in the lab, had a good contact with the small band of restorers. One of them, Norman Bromelle, often came to see us, occasionally to ask for help. On one occasion he requested me to make a gadget for introducing adhesive between the paint layer and the wooden panel of a Botticelli tondo, or circular painting, since for decades it had been necessary to keep this masterpiece lying face-upward because the paint layer was in danger of detachment. The gadget I made (or perhaps it could be dignified by the term "apparatus") was a tin-plate box of about five-by-six inches, like a large sardine can, except for the top being of glass, and the bottom left open. Wires for an electric heating coil came through the side, as did a thermometer. Also soldered into one side was a short piece of quarter-inch tube. The final touch was a rim of sponge rubber around the edge of the open side.

Having delivered this device to Norman, I watched him lay microcrystalline wax on the portion of the painting to be treated, and then place the device over it. Next, a current was sent through the heating coil to melt the wax (while watching the thermometer). As it melted, suction was applied to the tube to draw out air from between the loose paint and the panel, so that when the suction was released, the molten wax would flow through the cracks and under the paint layer. It was a simple and effective technique, and once this treatment had been given to the whole painting, it became possible to display it.

Another frequent visitor was Herbert Lank, the young assistant to the chief restorer, Helmuth Ruhemann. Herbert once revealed that he had been charged by his boss with the duty of giving him a wake-up call every working day at a certain hour from a pay phone. In those days, the British model had two buttons to press, labeled "A" and "B." You inserted two pennies, dialed the number, and when the person you were calling answered, you pressed button A, whereupon the pennies dropped into their receptacle and one's own voice could now be heard by the respondent. Failing any response, you pressed button B and got your money back. Under Ruhemann's regime, Herbert had to go out to the nearest pay phone at the appointed early hour and dial his number. On hearing him reply, he would press button B and get his pennies back—thus saving Ruhemann the expense of purchasing an alarm clock.

The raison d'être for the other investigation I was supposed to undertake (that regarding the reflective qualities of varnishes) was founded in the fact that certain picture restorers were known for the excellence of the varnish they applied, while others were criticized for using varnish that looked rubbery, or too shiny, or was undesirable for some other hard-to-define characteristic. So I began making an optical apparatus that would record how light was scattered from a varnished surface, but my three years at the lab came to an end before I had perfected the instrument. I was offered another three-year fellowship at the gallery, but I had decided by then that spending my life in a laboratory would be too confining and declined the offer.

I had not been working at the gallery for very long before I found that renting that Mayfair flat was too expensive, so when my six months' lease of it ended, I joined Patrick Lindsay and another friend in renting the painter Derek Hill's house during his absence abroad. His bijou dwelling in Hampstead was delightful, and we had fun entertaining. Once, upon someone's recommendation, we had the guitarist Julian Bream to dinner. He can have been only eighteen or nineteen then, and was doing his military service at Woolwich as an ordinary soldier. But his commanding officer, aware of his extraordinary virtuosity, very sensibly allowed him to spend nights away from barracks so that he could perform at venues quite far from London. To get himself to these engagements he'd bought a tiny secondhand van, formerly owned by a fishmonger—as was obvious from the ancient and fishlike smell in its rear compartment. Julian's speech was delightfully and unabashedly cockney, and he astonished us by revealing that he'd only recently resolved an uncertainty as to the career he should follow when demobilized: should he perhaps abandon the guitar in favor of cricket—pronounced cri'et, with a good cockney glottal stop. How fortunate that he didn't!

When Derek was due to return, Patrick Lindsay and I moved into a mews flat behind Sloane Street. One feature quite out of keeping with our modest establishment (two tiny bedrooms, a kitchen/dining room/lounge, and tiny bathroom) was the car that was parked outside it—for Patrick had recently bought a huge 1934 Rolls-Royce Phantom II open touring car of a striking pale blue color; and it was not long before I, following his example, became the owner of a very nice little 1925 sports coupé from the same manufacturer.

One might conclude from our possession of these chariots that we were a couple of exhibitionist toffs, but Patrick was no exhibitionist. He was a dashing sportsman, and courted danger on the motor-racing track and in the air, engaging in these activities only to please himself, not to impress others. Well, yes, occasionally he would put

7.1 *My first car, with precious if endangered passengers.*

on a little swagger, just for fun . . . As for myself, no one could call me dashing, and I bought the Rolls-Royce out of sheer love of its beautiful engineering, and the crafts-manship of the bodywork by Hooper's. But to some extent, perhaps, I may have been trying to keep up with my flatmate.

Patrick was invited to all of the grandest debutante balls during the "Social Sea-son" of spring and early summer, and a few of his hostesses, dimly aware of me as his flatmate, kindly invited me, too. (The laundering of white waistcoats and those dreadful starched shirts and collars became a significant item in our budget.) Balls held during the week were mostly given in London hotels, but weekend engagements were invari-ably held in some stately home in the country. It was these I enjoyed most, because of the often-splendid interiors, lavish dresses—and sometimes even tiaras, which were just emerging again from safe-deposits. (Once, on her way to a ball at Wilton, the Duchess of Buccleuch was involved in a car accident and suffered a cut across her forehead. She told Cecil Beaton of her concern about a possible scar, but he quickly comforted her: "But my dear, how *fortunate*—just on the tiara line!"[3])

The extent to which I really enjoyed these entertainments, though, is another matter. Certainly, I met and made friends with a number of interesting and attractive young ladies; but I was unsure of myself, and never made much of a mark, being a

7.2 The Rolls in Naples, 1956.

stranger in London society. I had spent none of my youth there, and still knew very few people of my age, or their parents.

I do, however, remember one early visit to London with my family to attend the wedding of a relative, when I was about eight. The reception was held in some large and stately hall. At one point I got separated from my family, and found myself jammed among strangers and able to see nothing but the press of bodies and, above, the decorative plasterwork of the ceiling. Then a second cousin spotted me and took me in tow. Soon, we were confronted by a large expanse of gray silk, this encasing an exceptionally large body. Looking up, I saw a dark-complexioned man holding a champagne glass and regarding us with a benevolent expression.

"You know," he said, "I am strictly forbidden by my religion to drink alcohol; but *fortunately* I am so extremely holy that each time I do so, a miracle takes place, and it turns into water in my mouth."

This was the Aga Khan!

As for contact with the opposite sex, I'd certainly had much less than most young men of similar social background, for as children and teenagers in a rural area where well-off families were few, my brother and I seldom had an opportunity to meet girls—and of course familiarity with village girls was out of the question.

Then again, I wasn't a good dancer—tolerably light on my feet perhaps, but as I'd never been taught to dance, I had difficulty in distinguishing between quickstep and foxtrot. And at weekend house-parties I again found myself at a disadvantage, since I hadn't seen even one of the great American musicals (out of snobbish prejudice, I'm afraid) and was therefore unable to sing or even mutter the lyrics along with my partner, whether dancing or simply with friends listening to recordings. In fact, it wasn't until the year 2000 that I actually attended a musical—a superbly mounted *Oklahoma*, in London—and loved it.

Then another explanation of my social disability was disclosed to me by one of my dancing partners. She had just been dancing with Lucian Freud, a young painter who would of course become famous, but just then he was often seen at dances like these (where he met his first wife, Lady Caroline Blackwood). My name had come up, and he revealed to her his diagnosis of my condition. It was narcissism. How marvelous, I thought, that he'd inherited from his grandfather that extraordinary ability to diagnose the psychological problems of people he had never met, as in the famous case of Little Hans!

If one only had the luck to find them, London provided some unusual entertainments. One that I remember well was the annual dinner of the Shikar Club, to which Patrick took me as a guest three or four times. Members of this club, all of them men who had hunted Big Game in distant lands, gathered every second Wednesday of December at a large dining room in the Savoy Hotel, as I believe they still do.

There'd be a maharaja or two, princes from Nepal, wardens of game parks who were back in the home country on furlough, colonels, lairds, and adventurers. Started by a Scotsman, Frank Wallace, and later run by his son, the club apparently lay dormant for 364 days in the year—except that one of the Wallaces must have seen to the annual printing of the list of members, among other chores. This booklet listed where and when each member had hunted. One would find entries such as "Blenkinsop, Lieut.-Col. Horace, Baluchistan '29, Upper Limpopo '32."

The president was a man now greatly missed—the heroic and impossibly handsome commando leader, Colonel Lord Lovat, VC, known as "Shimi" to his friends. As president, it fell to him to break the news of any member's demise during the past year, and for this sad duty he could always produce the perfect "envoi," such as this for an adventurous but recently deceased peer of the realm: "May his feet tread lightly on the Elysian fields as once they trod on the plains of Chinese Turkestan!"

Then some member would deliver a report of his activities. One year, it fell to Air-Vice-Marshall Sir James Grey to report on his search for Really Big Game: the Loch Ness Monster, no less. He proved to be a man who had not entirely discarded his prep school lingo.

"First," he said, "first I want to thank the Army who were terribly decent, for they lent us a jolly good lorry; and then the RAF who let us use an absolutely wizard searchlight. Now, I expect you'll all understand that when you're trying to get in contact with any kind of wild and elusive animal, the way to approach it [now lowering his voice] is through its *stomach*; because once you know what it eats, then you're halfway to making contact with it. Well now, I have to be careful about how much I reveal to you, but I think—yes, I think my committee would allow me to tell you—that we *believe* we do know what the Loch Ness Monster eats."

Voice from one of the tables:

"Could the speaker tell us then what he thinks it does eat?"

"Oh... well... I'm rather sorry you asked me that question, because I thought I'd made it clear that my committee and I are still analyzing our data but, well, I think... we think it is *fish*!"

Poor man, he must have heard some ill-concealed titters from the audience!

Early in the 1950s an astonishing annual event in the musical world began right in our rural Suffolk landscape, only twelve miles from my home. This was the Aldeburgh Festival, the creation of Benjamin Britten and Peter Pears, who had settled in a tiny house on the sea-front at Aldeburgh, separated from winter storms only by a shingle beach. Their view of this beach was quite picturesque, with working fishermen's open boats drawn up on it, also a number of old bathing machines, these still attached by cables to the rusted-up winches that once had hauled them (and the modest Victorian bathers inside) back out of the water. Now they were rented out as changing rooms at sixpence an hour.

At the beginning of one of the early festivals, a small vessel of the Royal Navy dropped anchor about a quarter of a mile offshore, and soon was dressed overall with pennants and lightbulbs that glittered festively at night. It became known that this was a hydrographic survey vessel, and that the skipper had had singing lessons from Peter Pears.

A few days later, Britten performed a Mozart piano concerto, conducting it from the piano, and in the interval I greeted the elderly but sprightly dowager Countess of Cranbrook, whose daughter-in-law had played a considerable part in organizing the festival. She'd heard, she told me, that the skipper of the vessel would be giving a party on board his ship after the concert, and she was rather indignant that she herself had not been invited—and gleefully suggested organizing a boarding party. So on emerging from the hall after the concert I helped her find a boatman willing to oblige. She also rounded up about five other "refusés," one of them being John Francis, Britain's premier flautist. Then she took off her shoes and stockings, rolled up her skirts, paddled a little way into the water, and we heaved her over the gunwales into the boat.

It was a magical evening. The sea was one I'd never seen the like of before: flat calm, and the water itself full of plankton, so that the boat's wake became a golden carpet, and a foot dipped into the water came out twinkling with little stars. An apparently huge, ruddy moon had risen some way from the horizon, and there was a yacht at anchor with its riding light reflected in the water.

We came alongside and, led by Lady Cranbrook, successfully boarded the vessel. The skipper yielded to our invasion with good grace and gave orders for more drinks and *cippolata* sausages to be brought up. Still leaving little pools of water where we stood, we joined in the merry party.

The time came when the invited guests thought they should bid good-night to their gracious host. They descended the companionway, boarded their boat, and cast off. Having had, perhaps, one drink too many, I went to the rail and started singing "Come away, fellow sailors, come away, your anchors be weighing" from Purcell's *Dido and Aeneas*. Peter Pears quickly joined in from the boat, and our duet continued for two or three bars, until I felt confident that he knew the words and music well enough to continue on his own!

This was what I used to think of as my "Walter Mitty" story, until I remembered that Mitty's amazing feats were all imaginary. So my duet with Peter Pears could more properly be called my George Plimpton feat.

I was, however, still looking for some kind of long-term employment, and also for a stop-gap occupation of a remunerative kind. Then, remembering that friends of mine had praised a few photographs I'd taken of their children, it occurred to me to capitalize on this modest success. So I bought a small, British-type trailer caravan, and began fitting it out as a combined darkroom and bedroom. I would seek engagements from the owners of stately homes known to be blessed with young children, and in soliciting their custom would mention that I would arrive with my mobile darkroom-cum-bedroom, so that I wouldn't seem to be imposing myself on their hospitality—while doubting that, if offered, I'd ever refuse it. Of course, the fact that the photo lab would be Rolls-Royce-drawn might also give the impression of long-established artistic and commercial success. But somehow, the conversion of the trailer was never completed, and I sold it.

Instead, I took up architectural photography. I heard that Batsfords, well-known publishers of books on architecture and related subjects, was planning to produce a lavishly illustrated book on Italian cathedrals. They seemed confident about going ahead with this book, but pending the signature of various agreements they were unable to put me under contract.

Taking a chance, I offered to do the work "on spec." As I would need to buy a medium-format stand-camera designed for such work (that is, with perspective control), I hastened to a veritable Aladdin's cave of used photographic equipment then to be found in Holborn, not far from the British Museum. There, I inquired of the owner's son what equipment of this kind they could offer, but had to reject the first one he produced as too battered. Didn't they have anything rather better? He thought for a moment, seemed to recollect something, and disappeared into the back premises—to reappear with a complete and most beautiful set of equipment, which I bought for £100.

Armed, then, with this and the list of views specified by Batsfords, I set off. All went well, the trip was very enjoyable, and the photographs came out satisfactorily. The only disappointment was that by then a decision had been made to cancel the book.

In the long run, however, this apparently fruitless expenditure of time and money proved to be nothing of the kind, for that camera had by then become valuable. It is made of teak; all the metal parts (even the little springs inside the shutter) are gold-plated; it has a full set of lenses; everything fits into a custom-made, alligator-skin case with a purple velvet lining and gold-plated locks, from which little gold-plated keys

7.3 *The author's gold-plated Adams camera. Photo by Ben Fash.*

still hang; and with it came a tripod of hickory and gold-plated brass. It was obvious, too, that the camera had never been used.

The manufacturer's name was Adams, and the London telephone directory led me, camera case in hand, to their shop, where I asked an elderly, white-whiskered man with little granny-glasses who was standing behind the counter if he could tell me anything about it.

"Oh, of course I can," he said, and practically burst into tears at the sight of it. This, he said, was made for an Argentinian millionaire in about 1925, who had specified the gold-plating as being the best protection against deterioration in the tropics. But he was quite unable to explain why it had remained in England, unused. What made the sight of it so sad for him was that Adams had recently been bought by what he called a "tin-pot" manufacturer of flashguns, and the very last camera that this famous old company would ever make was right there on the floor, crated and ready for shipment to somewhere in the tropics. Later, though, I realized that the lenses of this camera were no match for modern ones.

Before long, I managed to get some commissions from Weidenfeld and Nicolson, publishers of art books as well as general literature. The first of these was to photograph in color a full-length portrait hanging in Apsley House, the mansion bought by the government from my mother's family after the Battle of Waterloo, for presentation to the Duke of Wellington.

I would have to take this photo from across a dining-room table, and perched on a stepladder with my head only an inch or so beneath dangling crystal pendants of a vast chandelier. When in position, I arranged a black cloth over my head in order to focus the image on the ground-glass screen, but in the act of removing it caught sight of crystal pendants swinging sideways. Heavens! Was the chandelier swinging, or were the stepladder and I falling over sideways? My instinct was to grab the pendants—but mercifully didn't. Some of the pendants were indeed swinging, but the chandelier as a whole remained motionless. Still, it had been an alarming moment.

Next, I was entrusted with the lion's share of the photography for a coffee-table book entitled *Great Palaces*, and other commissions would follow, including one edited by Sir Mortimer Wheeler.[4]

While still in Dublin I had been smitten by a coup de foudre one evening on seeing a most beautiful and sweet-looking girl at a ball during Horse-Show Week. As I can still remember, her blond hair and striking beauty were set off by a dress with a pleated and bouffant skirt of some gauzy material shading from gray to pink.

Contriving an introduction, I found she was a dancer in the Royal Ballet, and the daughter of a retired and amusingly eccentric naval commander living in Kensington. So on moving to London, I used to give her dinner from time to time, and of course

7.4 A surreptitious photo at Covent Garden.

began attending ballets at Covent Garden, where eventually she was given quite important solo roles, such as the Lilac Fairy in *Sleeping Beauty*.

Well, the outcome of our acquaintance was nothing more than friendship, but I did become enamored of the atmosphere at Covent Garden and ballet's more obvious attractions, though I never developed much technical knowledge or any real understanding of this art, in spite of having read various books and magazine articles about it. But from them I did become aware of the lamentable fact that several famous ballets from early in the century had been lost beyond any possibility of revival for the simple reason that, whereas the movements of individual dancers could be recorded by a written notation such as Laban, to record the movements of an entire *corps de ballet* and other soloists by any graphic technique was not feasible.[5] For example, Pavlova's only complete ballet had proved impossible to reconstruct, even by the combined efforts of those who had danced it.

Then one day, scanning a photographic magazine, I saw an advertisement for a newly introduced 16mm movie camera, the Auricon Super 1200. This camera recorded photographic image and optical sound in "single-system," that is, with picture and soundtrack on the same film, rather than separately, and it had a magazine capacity sufficient for 33 minutes' running time. These cameras, it seemed to me, would solve the problem. Four of them, embedded within the front of the balcony and remotely controlled for starting, stopping, and lens aperture, could cover a whole evening's program without reloading.

As I would obviously have to clear this plan with the performers' unions, I made an appointment first with that of the musicians. There, I was told flatly that a recording fee would have to be paid. This would certainly be a problem, but perhaps the Covent Garden Ballet itself might help with negotiations.

And then: Actors Equity—would they also demand recording fees? They didn't, but instead came up with a different, quite unexpected (and I think ridiculous) objection. The use of a movie camera, they claimed, would be unfair to the *audience*. How so? Because the dancers would be playing to the camera, thereby failing to give the spectators their full money's worth!

The obvious solution, of course, was to do any filming for archival purposes at dress rehearsals, where one camera attended by a cameraman would suffice. But by then I was beginning to arrange for my departure for the States, and abandoned the project. So this was another false start.

CHAPTER 8

New York City

B y June 1957 my self-imposed deadline for departure was imminent, so I booked a berth in the liner *United States* for passage to New York, and delivered the car for shipment by a later sailing.

This great flagship of U.S. Lines was a most unusual vessel. It had been designed for service, not only as a liner, but also for possible military use in case of war, when high speed would be important. For decades, its top speed was kept secret, and daring estimates were made that perhaps it could reach 37 knots; but now a credible source has stated that during sea trials this leviathan achieved the astonishing speed of 43 knots, propelled by machinery of 250,000 horsepower! In passenger service, though, she was run only a little faster than the *Queen Elizabeth*.[1]

In some other respects, too, that liner was unique. As every passenger was soon informed, the only piece of wood in the entire ship was the butcher's block, thereby banishing fear of shipboard fire. A less positive feature was the strong impression— aided by gray-green décor—of being confined within a giant filing cabinet. So in spite of its remarkable qualities, it was not a vessel likely to claim one's affection.

The passage was calm. Then the skyline of New York City came into view, fully living up to its reputation. But I can't forget my surprise on first setting foot on the dockside, primed with expectations of modernity that the sight of skyscrapers had engendered—only to be confronted by two ancient but magnificent Mack trucks of about World War I vintage. Their rear wheels were driven by massive chains and their radiators positioned, like Renaults of that period, behind the engine, with the bulldog mascot in front.

Of course I was full of excitement, but my immediate movements were limited, since I knew that my dear friend Ruthie Pratt, who had offered me a bed for my first few nights in town, wouldn't be at home until later. So once the immigration formalities had been completed, I tagged along with two Italian shipmates whose first priority was to go as pilgrims to a small museum on Staten Island dedicated to the memory of a certain Antonio Meucci, recognized by them as the true inventor of the telephone (as the U.S. Congress would also do in 2002).

After ten days spent as Ruthie's guest I began to feel more at home in this marvelous city, and when the Rolls arrived some days later we drove in it to see something of Long Island, visiting her uncle in Syosset on the way. Ruthie, though, was no stranger to the car, having accompanied me in it to Positano a year earlier.

Then I moved into the YMCA on West Twenty-Third Street as a temporary perch. But what about the car? Fortunately, a most generous American friend had offered to house it in his garage on the Upper East Side, so it was only a matter of gaining access to that garage. Arriving there, I found it was guarded by a stout and friendly character called Sammy who seemed to sit all day long in its open doorway, chatting with passersby. His only concern about my car was the possibility that a drop of oil might descend from it to sully the spotless red composition floor. So I carefully laid a carpet of newspapers beneath it whenever I brought it in, and no complaint was ever made. Of course, this very kind invitation wasn't open-ended, and I must confess to abusing this friend's generosity by leaving the car there rather longer than he'd bargained for; but at last I found a reasonably priced garage near a not-too-distant railroad station on a commuter rail line.

After a couple of weeks at that "Y" I moved, just for the sake of comparison, to the one in a less ancient building on West Sixty-Fourth Street, an experience that unexpectedly proved handy in table-talk about twenty-five years later. I'd been invited to have lunch at Le Cirque—a very grand restaurant—in a party of about a dozen, and had been enjoying conversation with the lady sitting on my right. When the time came for a general switch, I found that the man seated on my left was Lord Spencer (whose formidable wife, Raine, was sitting across the table, keeping her eye on things). I had once briefly met Spencer's terrible old father, Jack, a notably boorish character, but I'd heard his successor spoken of with sympathy. I also knew that thanks to doctors in Germany he had lately made a better recovery than expected from some mysterious and prostrating infection in the head.

But now, how was I to initiate the conversation? Ah, yes of course, I have it, and turning to him inquired,

"Lord Spencer, have you been here in New York before?"

"Well, yes, as a matter of fact I have," he replied, "it was a number of years ago, whilst I was doing my military service. On that occasion, I stayed at the YMCA."

Well—now we were away! We discussed the relative merits of those two YMCAs, their gymnasia, the food, and so on. I thought it very sweet of him to reply as he did.

Of course, the Y had been no more than a temporary haven, and I soon moved into a flat on First Avenue, shared with a new acquaintance. Unfortunately, we disagreed about most things, so it was a stroke of luck when I ran into Quentin Keynes. Quentin was a traveler and serious book collector, and I'd first heard of him when he and my friend Patrick Lindsay went off to southwest Africa to look for, and if possible photograph, the giant sable antelope. Now, since his previous flatmate had left, Quentin invited me to take his place in the set of rooms he had within a house on East Forty-Third Street. I grabbed at the chance.

His rooms, and those of a few other men who were also lodged in the house, seemed to represent, for New York, an unusual arrangement. (Only once did a young woman, Sarah Rothschild, brave her way into this cohort of male lodgers.) The house belonged to a charming widow of proper Bostonian stock. She had four sons, the youngest being about fourteen, so to help pay for their education she was taking in these lodgers, reserving for herself the second floor. We all used the front door, reached by a stone stairway, or "stoop." The door into Quentin's room and mine led directly off the front hall, the floor above was occupied by Mrs. Walker, and other denizens of the house occupied the two higher floors. Locks and keys, as I remember, played no part in our lives; even the front door was left unlocked for much of the time.

The street-level floor, or semibasement, was occupied by a telephone answering service called "The Belles." It was run by two friendly and mountainously fat ladies who had built up a clientele consisting almost entirely of theater people. Large, autographed photographs of stars decorated the walls, and you were likely to hear one of them taking a message from some actor or theatrical luminary, while the other might be enunciating, "Mr. Tennessee Williams' residence?"

Of course, their presence in the basement contributed usefully to Mrs. Walker's finances, but then I found that it conferred another benefit. Many years earlier these ladies had been involved in running a "numbers game"—an illegal form of gambling conducted by telephone—so the excellent relations they had with the underworld rendered this particular house immune from the attentions of burglars, and made it unnecessary to lock the front door—until some thief of a different stripe found he could make off with packages on the hall table that had been delivered from stores.

Incidentally, these two ladies were just then gaining much wider recognition as the inspiration for a very successful musical comedy, *The Bells Are Ringing*.

In the autumn of that year, a friend invited me to Southampton, Long Island, for a weekend, so I drove there in the Rolls. Having parked it in the street the next day, I returned to find a man looking at it admiringly. We chatted, and he told me he was the proud owner of a Bugatti Tipo 35, a racing car famous for its exploits on European circuits in the 1930s; also that he kept it at his weekend place just outside the town. Then he suggested that as he'd be racing it at the Bridgehampton track the following weekend, perhaps I'd like to accompany him. I agreed, and arrangements were made for meeting.

Only then did I learn the name of my host. He was Charles Addams, the great *New Yorker* cartoonist.[2] A week later, then, back in Southampton, I was driven a mile or two out of town to a rather desolate area, perhaps a quarter of a mile from the seashore, and was shown into the former stables of a large "cottage" (this term, along the New England coast, applies to fine wooden mansions of a dozen rooms or more). This one had been swept away some years earlier by a hurricane, with only the brick-built stables surviving.

This was a U-shaped building, its two wings containing loose boxes, and presumably a tack room. Most of the original partitions remained, with the spaces in one wing adapted as kitchen, bathroom, and perhaps a storeroom, while on the other side slight alterations had turned them into bedrooms, with walls of vertical and much kicked and chewed wooden boards surmounted by iron bars. The connecting element, formerly the carriage house, was now the living room, its concrete floor concealed beneath a smooth red finish. In the middle of it stood a large and comfortable settee; but at one end of this I was astonished to see, projecting nearly three feet out of the floor, the upper part of a huge cast-iron valve, operable by means of an iron handwheel two feet in diameter—this, presumably to control the draining of floodwater through buried pipes. For a moment, on recollecting stories I'd heard about him, I had a vision of Addams seized by a fit of his legendary madness, fiendishly rotating this great wheel to flood the surrounding land.

Concerning this legend, Wilfred Sheed wrote in a posthumous volume of Addams's cartoons, "The story was that every year or so Charles Addams would grow weary of tapdancing around the brink of insanity and slip over the edge for a breather, finally submitting a cartoon so blood-curdling that he had to be put in restraints. . . . Nothing could have made the Charlie I knew happier than such stories. . . . He had his apartment fitted out with an embalming table here, a headsman's axe there, and bats, skulls and other cheery bricabrac." By now, his name has lost those fictitious undertones, no longer conjuring up images of gloom, impending threat, and ghastly imagination. But in any case, his appearance, as I remember it, suggested none of these: he was tall, with a large head, large ears, a rather heavy nose, and eyes that were good-natured and twinkling. He seemed a sweet man.

The Bugatti started up with a healthy roar, and Addams put on a soft leather helmet. As we entered the streets of Southampton they resounded not only with the roar of its exhaust and the whine of its supercharger, but at traffic lights there came a hideous grating and clanking from a gearbox apparently on the point of exploding into flying gearteeth and shards of gearbox. I could only suppose that the Bugatti was a recent purchase, for it does take time to master a "crash" gearbox (that is, one lacking synchromesh), especially when changing to a lower gear—and some are more ornery than others. But I did wonder about possible terror among any of the bystanders who believed in those reputed episodes of madness; they would have fled on recognizing the helmeted maniac at the wheel of this outrageously noisy vehicle.

In early December, I heard from a spy (her aunt) that the girl I had been hopelessly enamored of for many months seemed to have cooled towards her then-favorite beau— thereby giving my hopes a cautious boost; also that a small dance at Christmastime was planned. But no invitation to it arrived, and my spirits sagged once more. Christmas Day itself was a blank in my calendar, but an item in the *Tribune* on Christmas Eve suggested a way of spending the morning usefully. The Goldwater hospital on Welfare Island (now Roosevelt Island) was appealing for volunteers to help bring wheelchair-bound inmates from their wards to the hospital chapel.

That morning, then, I took a bus across the Queensboro bridge, a steel lattice structure that steps on Welfare Island on its way across the East River to Queens. The hospital was for the seriously incapacitated who had no friend or relative able to look after them. The last man I wheeled back to his ward after the Christmas service was a black from Virginia, whose name I no longer remember, though I visited him later a few times. He had been a waiter, until suddenly he lost all use of his arms and legs; his case, he told me, baffled the doctors. Lying there, day after day, with no one interested in talking to him, and no one to turn the pages of a book, he still contrived to keep his mind going by making up little jingles, some of which he proudly recited to me.

On leaving Goldwater, I went to investigate a vast and obviously abandoned building standing by itself at the southern extremity of the island. Finding the door unlocked, I went in and saw at once that it had been a hospital—the notorious Bellevue Hospital, in fact, a dismal institution in its later days. None of the bedsteads seemed to have been removed; paper plates and prescriptions lay scattered on the dusty floors; and suddenly it occurred to me that the occasional homeless man or drunken bum

8.1 The abandoned Bellevue Hospital.

might have availed himself of those beds—and could even have expired there without anyone knowing. At that very moment, I caught sight, through a doorway, of a man apparently lying on the floor, although the only part of him I could see was a leg. With my heart in my mouth I tiptoed through that doorway—to find just an artificial leg still shod with a shoe.

I ended the afternoon by climbing up the girders of the bridge, trusting that for lack of traffic that day no cop would catch me. I hasten to add that although unhappy, I had no thought of suicide; I was just feeling wild.

A few months before this, I'd found employment as assistant to a fashion photographer, Virginia Thoren. She was of Swedish origin, and had a studio in a loft on East Twenty-Fifth Street. Photography of EMBA mink coats was her mainstay, and I was engaged to replace her former assistant, a Japanese man, who'd left to set up on his own. Virginia was a very nice person, and her kindly disposition was never better displayed than it was one day when, in midmorning, she expressed her concern that no one had called me up with birthday greetings. Taken by surprise, and slow off the mark as usual, I hadn't managed to blurt out that this was not in fact my birthday before she'd begun announcing plans for a birthday celebration for me, that very evening. So it came about that I and some dozen Scandinavians, mostly women, would take our seats that evening around a table in the parish hall of the Swedish Lutheran church. The dinner consisted of a delicious *fiske grateng*, a berry pie—and then a lilting rendition of "Happy Birthday to You"! It was so sweet of her!

Later, I found the explanation of this unexpected celebration: that particular day had been marked in her engagement book as the birthday of her former assistant. Of course, when my actual birthday did come round, I certainly wasn't expecting any of my friends to telephone their greetings, but just in case, I had to call anyone who conceivably might to abstain from doing so.

When I had applied for a Green Card at the U.S. consulate in London, I was informed that unless the applicant could demonstrate a certain level of wealth, it would be necessary to have someone quite well off as a sponsor (I never discovered how much the generous sponsor stood to lose in a worst-case scenario). Fortunately, one of the American regulars at the Cavendish Hotel very kindly offered to fill that role: he was a Virginian named Sam Small. Two or three weeks after I'd begun working for Virginia Thoren, Sam telephoned and invited me to join him for a cruise in the Caribbean on his uncle's yacht, with a couple of dozen other friends.

The offer was tempting indeed, but could only be refused. Of course, I asked him about his uncle's yacht, since I couldn't imagine there were many yachts large enough to accommodate so many passengers. Well, the vessel that his uncle, General

John Franklin, would be using as his yacht on this occasion was the liner *United States*! Apparently it was due for a refit at Newport News, Virginia, and as Franklin was chairman of the board of U.S. Lines, he had the splendid idea of taking a somewhat indirect route from New York City to Newport News. Lest any busybody shareholders should take an interest in a small band of socialites going up the gangway, departure from the pier in New York was set for 3 a.m.

In the spring of 1958, my boss announced that she would soon be taking a month's holiday, and I in turn told her of my plan to leave within a couple of months for California. We agreed to part, and did so on the best of terms. Needing short-term employment, I then went round to the Society of American Magazine Photographers to see what temporary jobs might be available, and there I found one on the list that sounded very interesting. The famous photographer Irving Penn needed extra help for the next three weeks—and to my astonishment I landed the job.

His studios were on about the sixth and seventh floors of a large building on West Fortieth Street, overlooking Bryant Park. The upper floor contained the fashion studio and darkroom, while beneath it was another studio equipped with a kitchen, since photographing food formed an important part of the business (another profitable sideline was photographing the Rheingold Girl of the Year, for a brewery that long ago ceased to exist).

At that time Penn had a Belgian assistant, Robert Bresson (a young man soon to make a name for himself as an independent photographer). If, for instance, the program for the morning was shooting a lemon meringue pie prepared from General Foods' frozen version, the manufacturer's representative would arrive with a dozen boxes of it, and start preparing them at intervals of, perhaps, ten minutes. As soon as the first one was delivered, its meringue topping freshly puffed up and temptingly bronzed, Robert would start experimenting with the lighting, the background, and the camera angle; and as soon as the pie began to wilt under the lights and lose its fresh-from-the-oven appeal, it would be whisked away for pie number two to take its place. At last, Robert would decide that he'd done his best, and Penn would appear, summoned by a bell. He would throw the black cloth over his head, inspect minutely the image on the ground-glass screen, murmur approval to Robert, who would then introduce a loaded dark-slide, cock the shutter, withdraw the slide, and hand Penn the cable release. Penn then made the exposure (and then, as often as not, joined us in eating the latest pie).

In describing this routine I don't mean to denigrate Penn's part in the production of superb advertising photographs of food; what I've described was the result of the careful training he imparted to a gifted student. Understandably, though, he never in my brief experience allowed an assistant to actuate the shutter, presumably to avoid any possible doubt or dispute concerning copyright.

So what was I hired to do? A decade earlier, Penn's wife, Lisa Fonssegrives, had been the preeminent photographic model in New York. Then she retired, but had recently told her husband she was interested in resuming her career. So he'd taken a number of photographs for her to use as publicity. But there was a problem. Although her figure was unchanged, the torrid steam-heat of New York interiors in those days had taken a toll on her skin, which was now creased with tiny wrinkles. My job, then, was to make prints of the best negatives, contriving to show the eyes, eyebrows, nostrils, and mouth in reasonably strong contrast, while holding back details of the flesh surrounding them. It was a task rather beyond my capabilities, and I don't like to think of the large number of sheets of 11-by-14-inch Ilford Multigrade paper that I consumed in this effort. How Penn regarded my efforts I can't remember—a fact that suggests good nature.

My year in New York City went by quickly, speeded by many delightful entertainments. I was taken to a wonderful production of *Don Giovanni* at the old Metropolitan Opera House; went to Birdland several times; enjoyed interesting dinner parties; and of course explored Manhattan. Once I walked all the way up to The Cloisters, and another time down to Battery Park. Occasionally, I would walk up to a lively bar on 126th Street, simply because this was refreshingly unlike those dismal midtown saloons. The latter were invariably long, narrow, and dark as Hades, whereas this one was circular and brightly lit so that conversation and badinage could be general, and any patron's particularly colorful necktie could be admired to full effect by all.

Of surprise to me were the apparently rigid conventions of the Upper East Side. By scanning the society magazines I gained the impression that a high proportion of young men were married at the age of twenty-three to nineteen-year-old brides. (I also suspected that because I was thirty-five and single, some thought I must be gay.) Clothing also seemed to be narrowly prescribed by magazines, as I first noticed when out of curiosity I visited Vassar Collage, for there I found the young ladies in virtual uniform of short hair, regulation raincoat, white socks, and penny loafers.

This impression of conformity in clothing was reinforced a couple of years later when I accompanied my friend Susan Stein to a dance at River House, the invitation to which suggested "fancy costume" as an option. As sack dresses were just coming into vogue, we decided to follow fashion. I bought two used sacks from a Puerto Rican grocery store for ten cents each, got going with needle and thread, and made Susan a nifty sack dress, on the posterior of which I painted "Saks 5th Avenue." For myself I tailored a pair of shorts that proclaimed behind "Saks 34th Street" (a branch that closed long ago); the message in front, printed in heavy type, read "California Pink Beans." On arrival, we were a little disappointed to find no one else in costume, but I think we relished our singularity and danced with all the more *brio*.

Of evenings at the theater, one was unforgettable. I had been invited by my very kind friends, Minny and Jim Fosburgh, to a performance at the Belasco Theater of Noel Coward's *Present Laughter*, with Coward himself playing opposite Eva Gabor. (This

8.2 Susan Stein and I in our fashionable grocery store
"Saks" dresses, on our way to the River House dance.

production had been introduced at short notice late in January, near the end of a run of *Nude with Violin*, which had been doing badly.) The performance was superb, but our enjoyment of it was marred by the fact that every time some line produced uproarious laughter, we'd hear, two or three seconds later, loud and apparently derisive hoots. Each time, this "ha–ha–ha" came like a dash of cold water in the face.

Afterwards, we went round to see Coward in his dressing room. Once the preliminary embraces, and the "darling Noels" and the "darling Minnies" and "dearest Jims" were over, and I'd been introduced (and Coward had removed a front hairpiece, for him an unprecedented adornment, but necessary for the youthful part he was playing), Minnie spoke up and assured him that the production was superb, and his performance most amusing and truly memorable.

"But dear Noel, weren't you dreadfully upset by that awful laughter—it was so *chilling!*"

"Oh *no*, darling, that didn't upset me in the slightest. It was dear Johnny Ray; you know how dreadfully deaf he is; so he brings someone with him to repeat the lines into his hearing aid!"

(It may now be necessary to explain that Johnny Ray was the first pop singer to cause members of the audience to lose control and fall about in the aisles.)

Another evening's events persist in my memory because of the unexpected turn they took. I had met a young married woman named Jane Goodrich (that was her maiden name; I never met her husband, whose surname, Poniatowski, naturally made him a claimant to the Polish throne). More interesting to me was the fascination she professed concerning the possibilities of balloons, an interest I shared to some extent.

Shortly before the queen's coronation in 1953 I had fantasized about the possibility of putting up a captive balloon somewhere along the route the procession would follow: it would provide a wonderful vantage point for press photography. At that time, the only use for balloons in the public imagination was the wartime one of forming a barrage of captive balloons to deter low-flying bombers. As for the passenger-carrying potential of balloons, that had been forgotten—except by one man, a Frenchman named Dollfuss, who actually owned one and sometimes ascended in it.

Then, some years later, I was challenged by my friend Nell Dunn, shortly before her marriage, to arrange for herself and her spouse to depart from their wedding reception at the Ritz Hotel by balloon. The very idea of a free flight was, of course, unthinkable—that could have dumped them in the North Sea—so the departure would have to be by captive balloon. I therefore planned the ascent to take place at the eastern end of Green Park, next to the Ritz, and its descent at its western extremity near Hyde Park Corner. But how would the balloon be towed from takeoff to the landing point? By a dray horse borrowed from the nearby Watney's Brewery.

As I planned it, the "balloon" would consist, in fact, of eight or nine rubber balloons of the kind employed to lift meteorological sondes into the stratosphere. These would be contained within a net, and if one were to burst—an extremely unlikely event—that would be of little consequence. I therefore purchased ten from a manufacturer in Lancashire, for seven shillings and sixpence each. Next, I went to a basket maker in a village near my home and explained what I wanted. This was at a time when a tax had recently been imposed on nonindustrial purchases, and the old fellow looked at me shrewdly and commented, "If you wuz to call that a weed-baasket, you woont have to pay noo parchase-tax!" So, in time, the world's largest weed-basket was duly delivered.

Next, I visited an official of the Ministry of Civil Aviation, a man whose mustache and language indicated an RAF background.

"Oh, jolly good show," he exclaimed, "bang on, more power to your elbow!"

But he did warn me that I'd also have to obtain permission from the administration of the Royal Parks, of which Green Park is one. There, I'm sorry to say, my balloonatic fantasy was deflated. It was explained to me that on that day various persons, undoubtedly including a number of elderly ladies, would be sure to have paid a penny each for the hire of a folding deck chair, and any equestrian and aeronautical activities would interfere with their peaceful repose in them.

So in New York, with balloons in mind, I went round to see Jane again, in the expectation of more talk about them—only to find that a new technological wonder was now occupying her thoughts. She'd just met three young scientists from Brooklyn who had found a way of persuading two different chemical substances to bond, which under ordinary circumstances had never shown any inclination to do so. This discovery might open up a wonderful world of compounds previously undreamed of.

The key to producing these unions was the use of exceedingly loud noise. The normally shy or independently minded molecules would be so badly shaken they would clasp each other in terror, and bond permanently. (Of course, they explained this in rather more technical terms.) But the crucial element of their technology was a new way of generating shock waves in a tube by means of some technique that wasn't revealed to us. Jane was ecstatic, and exclaimed, "You know who would really be excited about this? Salvador Dalí! Let's go and tell him!"

But it was getting late, so I agreed to drive round to pick her up next evening; then we'd go on to the Saint Regis Hotel, where Dalí lived and usually held court of an evening.

When, next evening, we entered the Dalí Bar, there he was, sitting with his back to a wall he had painted with his signature Chilean or Peruvian desert scene: there were lines meeting at the vanishing point on the horizon, cactuses, and a few skeletons of quite large animals adding interest to the scene. Dalí's right hand was resting on a black cane topped by some exotic silver emblem, and on his left there sat a young lady—beautiful and very blonde. She was introduced to us, but I didn't catch her name. We were invited to draw up chairs.

When Jane introduced the topic of "megaphonic catalysis," as one might call it, Dalí's waxed and upturned mustache twitched with excitement.

"Oh, but tonight I feel verry scientific! Heere (extracting from his pocket a small photo), heere is photo of my painting, titled 'The destroction of matter.'"

It showed part of a spiral and some broken lines diverging as they crossed a dark background.

"And heere is recent clipping from *New York Times*, announcing in fact the destroction of matter, photographed for first time!"

(The images were quite similar, the one in the *Times* showing the tracks of elementary particles passing through a photographic emulsion in a magnetic field, but having searched unsuccessfully in that newspaper's index for any mention of the destruction of matter, I'm a bit dubious about the primacy of Dalí's version.)

I stole another glance at Dalí's beautiful companion, noticing that her cheeks were very pink, but also oddly shiny, as if varnished. The fact that she also remained perfectly silent and expressionless made me wonder whether perhaps she had refrained from speech and smiling for fear of cracking the varnish. But then, suddenly, during a lapse in the conversation, she stretched out her right arm and made a claw of her fingers.

"Tonight, I feel vi-o-lent!" she announced, and relapsed once more into silence. So, as it was getting late, we left the bar, but when Dalí caught sight of the Rolls-Royce, he immediately suggested going for a spin through Central Park in it, and this we did, to Dalí's evident delight.

Forty years later, I opened a copy of *Vanity Fair*, and there found an article about the young and beautiful actress Uma Thurman. It told also something of the interesting career of her mother, Nena; how, while still at her Swedish high school, she was recruited by a fashion photographer to become a photographic model; of her move to New York City and greater fame; and of how, as she told a *Vanity Fair* reporter, "Salvador Dalí and I became great buddies. I would sit around at the Saint Regis Hotel with him and meet weird people." I wonder, then, how Jane and I rated on her scale of weirdness?

But I was glad to hear from friends of hers that despite a subsequent marriage with Timothy Leary (a *guru* and dyed-in-the-wool weirdo), she has survived as a delightful person.

CHAPTER 9

Mexico and L.A.

With arrival of the month of May, I knew it was time to tear myself away from New York, and pursue my original purpose in bringing the car to the United States: selling it in Los Angeles. This car, I thought, ought to attract more interest in California than in the East, since that was the land of convertibles (not that this particular specimen could ever be converted from open touring car into a truly weatherproof conveyance, as its side screens were missing). But scarcely had I marked on a map the highways I had chosen for my drive to California before I was persuaded to make one little detour to attend the Maryland Hunt Cup and Ball, where I'd find some of my friends.

I would also learn that, as in moral conduct, once one deviates from the straight and narrow path, it's all too easy to stray farther afield—in my case to Washington, D.C., and then Gordonsville, Virginia, and Charleston, South Carolina, until I was alarmed to find that I had strayed two miles over Georgia's southern boundary and into Florida. Here a sharp change of course was called for, and I headed west. Further pleasant experiences awaited me in Louisiana and Natchez, Mississippi, and then, for no good reason, I steered for Dallas and Houston.

I must tell what happened to me in Houston. On my first day there, having hitched the car to a parking meter and gone off on some errand, I found on returning a man of Germanic appearance—hair cut short and flat on top, rolls of fat on back of neck, cigar in hand—who commented approvingly on the car, and told me that he'd once been a collector of old cars himself, but had since switched to collecting horse-drawn vehicles. He asked me where I had come from, and when I told him he exclaimed, "Well, you must be pretty exhausted. Why don't you go and take it easy for a few days on the Gulf Coast?"

I suppose I explained that this plan hadn't occurred to me.

"Well, look," said Mr. Pabst, "I have a house down near Galveston. Tell you what, you come home with me, I'll give you the keys and some sheets and towels, you buy yourself some groceries, then stay down there as long as you like! You just drive down to Galveston, get on to the beach, head south along it for six miles, and there you are. No mistaking it, there's no other house anywhere near."

Having accepted his extraordinary offer and collected the keys, I drove the fifty miles down to Galveston, bought food supplies, and drove down the beach as instructed. The house, about a hundred yards back from the sea, even had stables, as well as a garage under the house. The beach was sandy and shelved gradually into the water— the water being actually hot, about 85 degrees. I stayed for three days, dealing with an oil leak from the engine, taking it easy, writing letters; and then I returned to Houston to thank Mr. Pabst of the Pabst Lumber Company for his extraordinary hospitality.

9.1 Ian Graham: a formidable vaquero, *in Maryland. Photo in possession of the author.*

9.2 *The Rolls approaches the Mexican border.*

I decided to allow myself one more detour—to the King Ranch. On the strength of having once met someone connected with it, I drove in, only to find my contact was away. I took the tour, and found myself suitably impressed. But I missed seeing any work with cows: the season for that was over, having ended "when the flies got bad."

It was then that I passed a gas station with a fateful sign, "Last Gas Before Mexico."

"Mexico . . . " I said to myself, "now that's an idea."

So it came about that on June 12 I crossed the bridge from Brownsville to Matamoros. I remember nothing of the town, so busy was I coping with the traffic and the pullulating humanity and solicitous persons eager to help tourists. Then at last I was clear of town, driving through uninteresting country along a straight and poorly surfaced road.

I soon discovered dangers in driving along this road. It came from horses, which would suddenly spring out of a thicket, and from cattle grazing by the roadside, one of which, without warning, might suddenly chase another into the road. The resulting corpses along the road were being cleaned up by vultures and dogs.

In time, distant mountains would fringe the plain; then I saw several table mountains—or what looked like them—and later a volcanic plug. In the burning heat I was glad to see a gray column of rain, and enjoyed passing through a retreating fringe of it, where the air smelt of myrtle and hay.

Next day, with the landscape becoming mountainous, I took a steep little road up to Ciudad Santos, a very old Huastecan Indian village. Here many of the houses were of stone, whereas in the valley nearly all had been of mud-brick. Women were weaving elaborate costumes, but I was so busy with the camera that I didn't have time to look closely. The impression I retained was of elaborate headgear (a cloth worn almost like a turban) and a brightly colored overskirt, or apron.

On arrival in Mexico City I made a wonderfully lucky choice of hotel, the Génève. The rooms were scrupulously clean: every day the chambermaids wiped over the doorknobs, chair arms and toilet seats with cloths moistened with alcohol, yet the room rate was just 28 pesos per day—less than $2.50. But having come so far, I did regret having failed, before starting on this excursion, to collect the names of a few contacts in Mexico, just in case I should find myself there unexpectedly. Before I left New York, Sarah Rothschild had suggested accompanying me, and swinging through Mexico on the way to Los Angeles—because, she said, her mother and the painter Niko Ghika would be passing through there on their way round the world, and it would be such fun to surprise them there. But I'd turned down the idea, being dead-set on going straight to L.A.

As it was, only two names did occur to me, Leila Noble and Dorothy Norman, neither of whom proved to be in the country. I sat down and racked my brains; then a name came floating in, that of a British painter of whom Teddy Millington-Drake, an English painter, had spoken: Bridget Tichenor. I looked up her telephone number, and when I called her she immediately invited me to a small party being given that evening. Afterwards we went to a nightclub, El Eco. The entrance was through a wide, black door pivoted in the middle, and into a white-painted passage about twenty-five feet high, a strange and imposing space. The room itself was vast, its walls covered with enlargements of sketches and doodles done on paper napkins, these being the work of Henry Moore when at this club one evening. He had crumpled these up and tossed them away—but of course they were retrieved by the manager—doing so perhaps on all fours.

Bridget then invited me to a dinner party she was to give the next evening. On entering her house, whom should I see through a doorway as I went to hang up my coat but Sarah Rothschild—or so I thought at first, for actually it was her mother, with Ghika. A strange coincidence.

When seated at table, one of my neighbors was a lady named Carmen García-Pimentel, and when I told her that I'd been that day to the Museo Nacional (the old one, on Calle de Moneda) and had been impressed by the pieces of Maya sculpture on exhibition, she agreed enthusiastically, and went on to tell me of an expedition that she and her husband, Luis, who was sitting across the table, had recently made to some ruins called Yaxchilan—a place practically impossible to get to, she said. They had taken some movie film there, and she invited me to come and see it at their house, next evening.

Next morning, however, Montezuma struck a crippling blow. But I was determined to see Luis and Carmen's film of that expedition, so I stayed in bed until almost 10 p.m., filling myself with Entero-Vioform, and then, still feeling very frail, set off by taxi. Alas, the driver had no index or map of streets, and we drove all over town for an hour and a quarter before abandoning the search. The driver demanded two hours' pay for his efforts, and I went back to bed effing, feeling furious, frustrated, and physically feeble.

One drizzly day, well over thirty years later, I was working at the ruins of Toniná, near Ocosingo in Chiapas, when four tourists arrived—a woman with two grown daughters, and a man. We got into conversation, and I suggested that having come so far they really shouldn't miss the opportunity of visiting Yaxchilan, since it would be easy to go there from Ocosingo by light plane.

"Oh," the lady replied, "we were to have gone there today, but couldn't because of the weather. But actually, I've been there once already, in 1959."

I thought for a moment before replying,

"Forgive me, but are you sure that wasn't in 1958?"

"Well," she replied, "Yes . . . I believe you are right. But how could you possibly know?"

"Because I believe you must be Carmen García-Pimentel!"

In Mexico, almost everybody uses the *segundo apellido* (their mother's surname added to their father's) in any context of the slightest formality. So I had been struck by the fact that Ignacio Bernal, then the director of INAH (the National Institute of Anthropology and History) invariably cited his name, as author or official, simply as Ignacio Bernal, and I did vaguely wonder what his segundo apellido might be. Then one day, consulting a biographical dictionary, his name caught my eye, and there it was: García-Pimentel. So Carmen's husband was Bernal's nephew, and now I could understand how that young couple came to be among the very few who had visited Yaxchilan at that time.

A day or two later I drove with Bridget to Tepoztlan. The toll road took us up into the clouds, and out again to reveal a glorious view over a flatter region which melts into distant mountains. We climbed up to a temple—the first temple of the very many that I was to visit in the future.

Mexico was beginning to exert its charm, and I wonder at my ignorance about it, particularly regarding the Mayas: how could it be that I had never even heard of the Maya civilization? I went to various bookshops, to see what they could offer on that topic, and soon realized that, unless I'd had very bad luck in my search, there didn't seem to be any well-illustrated and readily available book that dealt in a fairly comprehensive way with the architecture, sculpture, and lesser artifacts of the Mayas. Of course, there was Sylvanus Morley's book, *The Ancient Maya*, published only a dozen years earlier and containing plenty of photographs, but these were in black and white. Now, in the late fifties we were entering the era of coffee-table books, large quarto volumes with splendidly reproduced color photographs.

I began to wonder: could I not, perhaps, come back after I had sold the Rolls, and travel about taking photographs for such a book? Photographically, at least, I felt capable of taking on this task, and began to dream about it.

9.3 From Mexico to California.

To begin with, I made some inquiries about the feasibility of visiting Yaxchilan, but was advised to give up any such crazy notion. Didn't I know that it lay in a part of Mexico that was a wilderness inhabited by savages? This metropolitan opinion did remind me of what I had heard Italians say, even in Rome, about the south of their own country. In that case, at least, I had been able to satisfy myself that the truth was different.

The cash supply was now running low, so I tore myself away from Mexico City and drove to San Blas. There I visited a neighboring bay, modestly described in a brochure as "the second most beautiful bay in the world." I had to visit that! Well, it was a disappointment: the bay was quite nice, but the water was full of palm-frond trash and dead fish, and there were no waves.

I drove northward along the coast, and 140 miles beyond Mazatlán came to Culiacán, where the road crossed a river that had been canalized into a wide, cement-bottomed sluice. But since the water was about two feet deep, a nearby railroad bridge seemed to offer a better alternative. I tried fruitlessly to obtain information about train schedules, but did manage to cross the bridge without any awkward confrontation.

Three miles from Guaymas I found Miramar, a bay that I would indeed place high in a world listing of bays; at any rate, it was there I had one of the most enjoyable baths of my life. The water was still but clear, and as the light faded with approaching night, the mountains surrounding that lovely bay retreated into silhouette. A three-quarter moon was shining and the sky became full of stars. I floated and lazed for a long time, thinking of how hot and parched I had been not long before.

Next day, I reached the border town of Nogales. Having gone through the border, I went to change my few remaining pesos, and on returning to the car, found a small crowd round it. Someone, in pressing to look inside, had leaned against one of the adjustable windshield extensions hard enough to crack the glass, which I had only recently had replaced in Mexico City. That really annoyed me, and then I noticed a cop tying on a parking ticket, when it wasn't at all obvious that parking there was forbidden.

Very foolishly I got into an argument with him instead of just driving away; with my foreign license plate I would never have heard any more about it. Idiotically, I cast the ticket with a theatrical gesture at the cop's feet. He arrested me at once as a litter-bug, climbed into the car, and told me to drive with him to the police station.

My name was taken, alien registration card shown, and available cash displayed. My pesos had yielded only twenty-four dollars.

"Are you employed?"

"No."

"Is this all the money you have?"

"Yes, for the moment it is."

"So, what are you going to do when this money's spent?"

"Well, sell something, I suppose."

I was thinking of a camera, or something of the kind. And there, of course, glittering through the window of the Station House stood another saleable asset, the Rolls-Royce.

"Do you have a peddler's license?"

"Excuse me, are you joking?"

"I certainly am not; and I'm thinking we may have to keep you here as a vagrant."

"Really? Do vagrants usually travel in their own Rolls-Royces?"

No answer.

So I was to be cast into the slammer, but first I was allowed to drive the car across the road to a parking garage. That reduced my resources to twenty-three dollars. The jail was quite a large room of cubic shape, two-thirds of which was occupied by a smaller steel cube containing two cells with barred doors, both equipped with a seatless toilet and a camp-bed with rather dirty blankets folded upon it. On a mattress on top of the steel box lay an insouciant, cross-eyed Mexican youth who was in for fifteen days for speeding and not having a muffler on his car. Endless streams of his young friends came by to chat and give him cigarettes through the bars.

The captain granted my request for a clean blanket, and I was served a hamburger and coffee. Later, I was taken to be arraigned by the part-time judge, whose normal occupation was running, or perhaps owning, a small supermarket. I was charged with two offenses: a parking violation, and "dumping or depositing trash, garbage, or odoriferous matter upon the highway."

Back in jail, we were joined late that evening by a drunken bum, who kept shaking my hand and assuring me that we were all friends behind bars—and also in front of them, no doubt. Just then it occurred to me that the jersey shirt I was wearing was of appropriate design: red and white horizontal stripes!

Next morning I was tried. In my defense, I submitted that a parking ticket could not be regarded as either trash or garbage, any more than a hundred-dollar bill could be, and as for the suggestion that it was odoriferous, I rejected it as far-fetched. But the subtlety of my argument was lost on the judge, and I was fined ten dollars for the parking, and fifty dollars for the garbage-dumping—this causing a sharp intake of breath on my part. But then, having no evidence of a previous record, the judge suspended that part of the sentence. So off I went, heading for San Diego with thirteen dollars in my pocket. I made a detour back into Mexican soil to fill up with Mexolina, a sulfurous-smelling gasoline that cost only twelve cents a gallon—half the price of gas in the States. Of course, with an octane rating of fifty-five, any postwar car would have choked on this stuff, but to the old Rolls it was mother's milk.

That night I slept pleasurably in the desert, and by dint of repeatedly accelerating to seventy miles per hour, and then coasting with the engine switched off, I reached San Diego with some gasoline and a few dollars to spare. And then, after suffering an annoying delay in San Diego, waiting for money that I had asked my New York bank to send telegraphically, I was on the last leg of my long journey to Los Angeles.

Once there, and mindful that my primary objective was to sell the car, I drove round to the offices of *Road and Track* magazine in Venice. I asked the editor, John Bond, whether he would be interested in featuring the Rolls in the "Salon" section of the magazine; and if so, would he like to do the road test immediately?

"*Road* test!" he exclaimed, "What do you mean, road test?"

"Well, you publish those acceleration curves, and handling and other data; don't you obtain them by road testing?"

"Oh, dear me, no. No owner would allow his car to be tested."

"Well, *I* will. I've often run the car flat-out, with no apparent harm."

So the Rolls was the first, and perhaps only, vintage car ever to be road-tested for that feature.

Next, I enrolled in a *Concours d'élégance* at the Blarney Castle restaurant. That was a bad mistake. The judging was geared to American standards of over-restoration, with penalties for the tiniest scratches (no allowance at all for honorable scratches earned on the road); also for not having all the tools fitted into specially made trays, and for not being equipped with flares and reflective triangles in case of breakdown at night. Those rarities, sound mechanical condition and real elegance, were ignored. The Rolls came in almost bottom, behind an MG TD.

The third stratagem of my sales campaign was to go round to the *Los Angeles Times* offices and put in a classified ad for the car. Next morning I was relaxing by the pocket-handkerchief-size pool of a mini-motel in Santa Monica when the owner came over to tell me I was wanted on the telephone.

"Me! On the telephone? That's impossible, nobody knows I'm here."

"Well, someone really is asking to speak to you."

I went to his office and picked up the phone.

"Hello, is that Ian Graham?"

"Yes, that's me."

"This is Coco Morton, you may remember we met at Stanway a couple of years ago."

"Yes, of *course*! But how on *earth* did you track me down to this motel?"

"Oh, because your photo is in the *L.A. Times* today."

"*What!*"

Then I remembered that as I returned to the car after placing the ad, and was climbing in to drive away, a man came up and asked me about it. When he also inquired where I had just come from, I told him flippantly, oh, from Mexico, via jail in Nogales. Only now did I realize that he must have been an *L.A. Times* reporter, and had taken a photo without my noticing. I was described as "gliding into town from the lock-up in Nogales, Arizona."

Having seen the photo and recognized the car, Coco called the *Times* and managed to persuade the classified ad department to reveal my address. So it was that I found myself driving up the Pasadena Freeway to have lunch with that most hospitable family. Coco and Jane immediately invited me to stay with them in their beautiful house, and I fear that I abused their hospitality to the extent of staying for two months, and had a tremendously enjoyable time as their guest.

9.4 Modest
announcement
of my arrival in
Los Angeles.

PART 2   **Los Angele**

VOL. LXXVII   Times Classified Advertising Number, MAdison 9-4411   SUNDAY MORNING, JULY

RUBBERNECK BUS — Ian Graham, touring Briton, causes necks to crane in town with his 1927 Rolls-Royce Torpedo, only three of which ever were produced. After 10,000 miles of open-air touring, he was jailed in Nogales, Ariz., for parking ticket. Graham said Lawrence of Arabia once drove the car.
Times photo

BY THE WAY...with
BILL HENRY

To almost anyone who watched the telecast of President Eisenhower's appearance before the Canadian Parliament and then carefully read the text of his speech in The Times it must have been plain that this was an extraordinary and unusual type of international meeting in these days of widespread hostility, suspicion and misunderstanding. Too bad the whole world can't talk in a similar atmosphere.

FRIENDSHIP—Those who only read the Eisenhower speech and missed the opening words of Prime Minis-

Angelenos Rubberneck
at Rolls-Royce Hot Rod

Vintage 1927 Model Owned by Briton
Once Was Driven by Lawrence of Arabia

In a city long accustomed to offbeat motorcars, Ian Graham caused heads to turn yesterday.

Mr. Graham, 33, an Englishman with a nose sunburned from 10,000 miles of open air touring, glided noiselessly into town from

$300,000 Hall
Dedicated hv

9.5 California girls.

Then on finding that one of my New York friends, Susan Stein, was in L.A. at her father's house in Beverly Hills, I called her, and was invited up—and "up" was the operative word, for I hadn't realized how far up those hill houses were to be found, for smog had limited one's view to the lowest level of foothills.

On entering the house, I was taken by Susan to a large room with correspondingly large windows—and to my astonishment they revealed stunning views, right to the horizon of the Pacific Ocean. How could this be? Susan had to explain that when the house was built for her father, smog had been a rarity, but later, with it obscuring the view most of the time, he'd engaged a professional photographer with a large-format camera to come up on a clear day, photograph the views from each window, and fit enlargements of them on the exterior of each window!

But alas, my good friend Susan had not long to live.

Another acquaintance of mine from New York days was the actress Liliane Montevecchi. Hearing she was filming in Hollywood, I called her up, and was invited to lunch at the MGM commissary. Afterwards, she took me to the set where Audrey Hepburn was to play Rima in *Green Mansions*.

And this was where, for the very first time, I found myself in a rain forest. There were trees ranging from low palms up to forest giants, which looked as if they might soar hundreds of feet, but lesser trees of all sizes made their crowns invisible. Great vines looped down, and through the leaf-strewn forest floor a babbling rivulet made its way. Of course, I had no inkling that I was fated to spend years in forests closely resembling this—except for the abundance of mosquitoes and lack of air conditioning.

In another studio I was shown the tree that Rima would climb, seeking refuge from her pursuers—in vain, of course, as they would set fire to it. But, as Liliane told me, the producers were worried that in some markets the audience might find the incineration of this fairy-like, bewitching creature unbearable; so an alternative version of the final scene would be shot, in which Rima would find the tree to be hollow, enabling her to slip down inside it, and survive . . .

So much was I enjoying life as a guest of the Mortons that my need to sell the car rather slipped my mind. In any case, I couldn't consider driving it around with a large For Sale sign taped on the windshield—it would be so demeaning for the car. But at last I forced myself to do just that, and immediately a buyer presented himself. I have to say, he was not the ideal buyer, as he clearly had no real appreciation of vintage cars. He was a football player who played end for the Rams, weighed 230 pounds, and could do the high hurdles in thirteen seconds (if I remember correctly). But his thighs were so thick that he could barely squeeze between seat and steering wheel; even more inconvenient was his inability to work the pedals one at a time without taking his shoes off. I had also been a little worried about a professional athlete buying an expensive car near the end of his career, but I needn't have worried: he'd married a Beechnut heiress.

The sum I got for the car was not vast, but at least it was about four times what I had paid for it, and besides, it had played a crucial role in finding me a new career. A small fraction of the proceeds was then spent on the purchase of a second-hand Studebaker, and in this I drove back to New York, via San Francisco, Yosemite, and Chicago, visiting the usual attractions along the way. Then I sold it and sailed for England on the liner *Queen Mary*.

Part II — Early Classic

CHAPTER 10

1959

Introduction to the Maya World

As soon as I was back in England, I applied for a Readers Card at the British Museum Library, and in that superb and much lamented Reading Room (closed thirty years later when a new library was built) I began to study whatever I could find about the Maya and the terrain they occupied.

As I knew nothing of bibliographies, the books I selected must have been a mixed lot. Some did describe explorations in that area, and others, early excavations in those ruined cities. But I soon realized that the quality of such works covered a very wide range. Some were of lasting value (those of John Lloyd Stephens, to begin with), but I did dip into others that I never for a moment should have taken seriously.

Among these was *Quest for the Lost City*, by Dana and Ginger Lamb. This work, I thought, might be a helpful guide for a neophyte intending to brave the unknown terrors of the jungle. But then, some of the exploits described by this couple in the opening pages did set me wondering about authenticity—such as their claim to have started out from California with only a few dollars, and later to have made, with just a *machete* and no previous experience, the beautiful dugout canoe they illustrate. But I'll return to other aspects of their behavior in a later chapter.

In the British Museum itself I found my way to the Maudslay Room, where original and beautiful sculptures were on display, from sites I'd barely heard of, such as Copán and Yaxchilan. Then, brashly entering the Department of Ethnography's offices, I found other splendid casts. One was of the very large Ixkun Stela 1, and another of the mosaic sculpture from the Lower Temple of the Jaguars at Chichén Itzá—this one painted in colors that supposedly matched those still visible on the original.

On enquiring about these, I was told they'd been made in the 1890s for someone named Alfred Maudslay, and I was directed to the museum's library to see other fruits of his work—the big and beautifully illustrated archaeology volumes published in the series *Biologia Centrali-Americana*. They were an inspiration, and for me later, a model.

So with notebooks full of a strange mixture of authentic information and rubbish, I flew to New York, and from there to Mexico City, where for several days I stayed at the Hotel Génève again, while gathering other information. Brashly, I also went to see Ignacio Bernal, then director of INAH (the Instituto Nacional de Antropología e Historia), just to ask permission to take photographs with a tripod in archaeological zones, as required by INAH. Bernal quickly dictated a letter stating that *desde luego* I had permission to do so. Now I found myself confronted by one of the innumerable difficulties that a beginner faces with any foreign language: what did this mean? I looked up both words in the dictionary, and it looked as if they meant, as I'd suspected, "from then." But from *when*? Only later did I learn that it means "of course!"

Next morning, having taken an early bus, I reached Oaxaca before dark, and was able to make out in the distance the hilltop ruins of Monte Albán. I decided immediately to walk there early next morning. I dragged myself out of bed at about 4 a.m. and set out, having taken care on the previous evening to identify a street going in the right direction. With good luck I found the road, and reached the ruins just before sunrise. Then the first rays of the sun made the dew on the grassy plaza glisten like silver, and on it, long shadows were cast by three donkeys grazing there. The sight was magical, and I was ready to leave by the time the first tourist buses arrived.

I moved on to the ruins of Mitla, not far distant. There, I found lodging in the house of a Mr. Frissel, the *panjandrum* of the place, who not only kept guest lodgings but also had a private museum. I have to say that I found him a man of very definite opinions, and extremely unattractive. Asked where I was heading, I told him, Chiapas and Guatemala.

"A foolish plan, young man. That area's dangerous. We see many people who tell us they are going that way, and they never come back." That didn't sound at all encouraging, but of course one could think of quite another explanation for the phenomenon. Undaunted, then, I took a bus to San Cristóbal de las Casas, and on arrival went straight to Na Bolom, the former convent which Frans Blom and his wife, Trudi Duby, had adapted as their house and as a center where students and interested travelers could congregate (Na Bolom, "the House of the Jaguar" in Maya, being a pun on Blom, and Maya for "tiger").

There were bedrooms available, and a superb library, for Frans, or "Don Pancho" as one learned to call him, had been in the early 1930s the director of the Middle

American Research Institute of Tulane University, after making remarkable explorations of the Maya area in the late 1920s. Trudi, the energetic, forceful, and proudly communistic daughter of a Swiss Lutheran pastor, had met Frans in the Lacandón jungle in the 1940s, when his career had foundered and he was drinking too much. She took him in hand, and by the time I knew him he was courteous and kind, as I'm sure he always had been, and glad to share his knowledge, but just a little quiet.

Frans really came to life only when Trudi had departed on some journey—usually taking a group of paying guests on a horseback trek that might last several days. That first night, after dinner, Don Pancho would sit beside a blazing log fire in a great armchair carved and painted with emblems of his work, and tell us tales of his travels. With his handsome Nordic features and shock of white hair, he could have been a mariner recounting his voyages to Greenland centuries ago, and that is how I like to remember him. But then one wouldn't see him again until Trudi had returned, to confiscate the bottles he had smuggled in.

As any visitor would be, I was enchanted by the beauty of the town and of the hills and forests around it, but most of all by the Tzeltal and Tzotzil Mayas from the surrounding area who came into town with merchandise. The men, wearing the extraordinary costumes distinctive of their villages, were especially striking. I was to become a regular visitor to Na Bolom for many years, although my sojourns in the house tended to be brief because I found Trudi's hectoring ways and her sometimes baseless prejudices rather irritating—however much I admired her for her passionate crusade to protect the Lacandón Mayas and the rain forest that was their world.

Before I left, on that first visit, Don Pancho wrote a fulsome note recommending me to the authorities at Copán, and with extraordinary kindness presented me with a sleeping bag of the mummy-type that zips up to the neck. Then, after reaching Palenque by bus, I made a quick sweep round the Yucatán Peninsula, taking in Palenque, Uxmal, Chichén Itzá, Cozumel, and Chetumal, before drawing breath in British Honduras.

There, in Belize City, I took a room in the Palace Hotel, a dilapidated four-story wooden structure set back from the street. Dismal though it was, I soon realized that its bar, a separate building close to the sidewalk, had to be the social center of Belizean *bon-viveurs*—men mostly of a skeptical but cheerful tendency. Soon, I was chatting amicably with a gent, red of hair and face, with a small beard and a British accent.

As my new acquaintance, Jim Currie, denied being encumbered by employment, I quickly identified him as one of the dying breed of "remittance men"—that is, sons who have embarrassed their prosperous families to such a degree that their fathers at last find

1959

129

it necessary, in the interests of tranquil family life, to inform their wayward offspring, not that their monthly allowances would end, but that they would have to pick them up at a bank in some distant British Colony, the choice of which would be theirs.

Next day, returning to rehydrate myself after touring the town, I found Jim there again, and now he suggested my accompanying him on a cruise in his motor yacht. On seeing it, I marveled at the generous remittances he must be receiving, for this had been the *Doris*. He had bought it from the immensely rich tobacco heiress, Doris Duke, and renamed it *Pamela*, though the cutlery, engraved with the yacht's original name, remained in use. But eventually I learned that Jim was not a remittance man at all, but had his own fortune, and was living in Belize just because it suited him.

We made for Ambergris Cay, where we fished and swam. Through the crystal-clear water I spotted below us a peculiar object on the clean, sandy bottom, where the water was about fifteen feet deep. It proved to be a pile of cannon balls, rusted together, presumably while in a barrel that fell overboard; no trace of that remained, of course. That evening, Jim recited an amusing if indelicate verse about women's anatomy, the author of which I immediately recognized from its highly distinctive style as that of A. P. Herbert, a distinguished author, lawyer, playwright, sailor, and Member of Parliament. This was later confirmed by Herbert's son John, who had been at school with me.

Then I ran into a young woman I'd known in England, who had married and now was living in Belize City with her husband. She invited me to dine and spend a night at their house, and that evening she played for me an LP of two Mozart sonatas for piano and violin (K 301 and 304). I had never heard either of these before, and was overwhelmed—not only by the wonderful music, leaping and confident at first, then introspective in minor mode—but also by Nathan Milstein's performance. I played the disc again before going to bed, and arose very early next morning to play it once more before leaving, for never before had I been so deeply affected by chamber music.

Now I took a bus to the Guatemalan border, crossed it, and flew to Guatemala City, where I found an excellent cheap hotel, the Centro-America. For a dollar-fifty per diem one got a bed (sometimes sharing the room) and three skimpy meals, to be consumed with compulsory television. I spent a few days visiting the museum of archaeology and looking around the city, and then left by bus for Copán.

My map showed a road going to Zacapa, and from there through Jocotán and Camotán to Copán, and I supposed that where there were roads, there would certainly be, if not a bus service, then at least a little traffic, and a good chance of getting a ride. So at Jocotán I set off in the afternoon, carrying a camera bag containing a Hasselblad

1000, a small canvas grip with spare shirt, a jersey, my 1931 Leica, shaving gear, and odds and ends, and under my arm the mummy bag wrapped in a ground sheet. Stupidly, I equipped myself with only a small bottle of water and very little to eat.

I walked and walked, looking back at intervals hoping to see a cloud of dust heralding the approach of some vehicle, but none came. As the sun was close to setting, I chose a small space close to the river and among pines for my "camp." After a failed attempt to climb down to the river for a badly needed bath before having a snack, I slept fitfully, bitten by ants attracted by a cookie I'd reserved for breakfast.

Awakened early by a thin drizzle, I went on my way, and for some inexplicable reason, never approached one of the few *campesino* dwellings along the way to ask for a tortilla and a cup of coffee. It grew hotter and hotter, until by midafternoon I took to waiting in the shade of a tree until a cloud hid the sun; then I would hurry on, keeping an eye on the cloud and the next tree. Eventually the road began to climb, and I to feel exceedingly weary, until at last I reached the frontier, and nine miles farther on, the town. Thank heaven the Pensión Welchez had a vacant room. I bought Coca-Colas, and lay trembling with exhaustion on my bed.

Of course, I was thrilled by the ruins of Copán, and spent two or three enjoyable days among them. Uppermost in my mind, though, was the question of getting back to Zacapa; I just couldn't face walking all the way there again. Then I heard the sound of a plane overhead, and saw a twin-engined Beechcraft circling lower and preparing to land at the grass airstrip close to the ruins. My spirits rose; perhaps there would be a chance of flying out in it.

The plane came in a little short, hitting the barbed wire fence. As it taxied up I could see torn canvas underneath, near the tail, and a dangling metal strut. A man, looking rather pale (who, I learned later, had been engaged as copilot and interpreter), jumped out and quickly disappeared. When the owner emerged from his plane, he was obviously an American, and full of years. I asked him if he needed assistance, and he agreed that he did; so I carried out repairs to the plane after going to the village and buying a pair of blue jeans as a source of material to repair the torn fabric, a curved needle, strong thread, and adhesive tape. After wiggling that strut off, doing some clumsy stitchery, and applying the tape to it, I certified the plane as airworthy (since I felt sure the fuselage had strength enough without that strut).

Lunch, now? We found a *comedor*, and my new friend stipulated just some potatoes and an egg, his stomach wasn't too good. Well, where had he come from?

"From Buffalo, New York. I've a factory up there. Used to make refrigerators, but business turned bad and now we make men's sock suspenders. . . . Perhaps we'll have

1959

to close down altogether, soon. But the plane—it's been a good little plane, but I guess I'll have to sell it, so I thought I'd make one more trip."

"Well, uh, may I ask which way you'll be going from here?"

"Heading home."

"In that case, I wonder if perhaps you'd be so kind as to give me a ride to Guatemala City? I *would* be grateful."

"How high is that?"

"About four or five thousand feet, I think."

"That's rather high: you see, my heart's not too good."

On returning to the plane, he checked the oil with a dipstick. "Hello, wonder where the oil's gone in this engine. Well, never mind, I've got some more."

I took him on a tour of the ruins for an hour or two, which seemed to interest him, before popping my question. "Well, Sir," I asked, "I'm wondering if you really could save me a very long walk by flying me to Guatemala?"

"I'll tell you another problem, young man: only got one parachute!"

Later, in Tikal, I heard that this brave old fellow had at least got that far on his way home.

As it was, I managed to get a ride in a jeep to Zacapa. And there, having decided to visit Quiriguá, I took the train. An old German doctor, a long-time resident of Mexico who had given me several useful pieces of advice, did give me one piece that unfortunately was mistaken. For some reason he told me that, if going to Quiriguá, I should leave the train, not at Quiriguá station, but at Los Amates. So that is what I did, arriving at about midnight. A man who was also leaving the train offered me hospitality for the night, but for no good reason, I felt distrustful and refused. I decided instead to sleep out in the open, near the railway line, and having selected a spot, I deployed my ground sheet, arranging my camera bag under it, with its shoulder strap extended towards the middle, where I would be lying on it, to eliminate furtive removal of same. I then lay down in the mummy bag, zipped it up to the neck, and fell asleep.

I had a nightmare: I was tied to the railroad track; my arms were tied, too, immobilizing them, and a train was approaching! I partially awoke and managed to sit up, to be dazzled by the approaching train's headlight. Then I woke up completely, and ahhh! I was beside the track and not on it, and my arms were bound only by the sleeping bag. With a clatter and roar the train passed by, and I went back to sleep.

But in the morning, my camera bag had disappeared. On collapsing after that fright I must have fallen back to one side, no longer lying upon the shoulder strap. Adios, Hasselblad! But I still had my old Leica in the canvas grip. Economically, I had suffered a blow, but I'd already come to the conclusion that this trip could serve only for reconnaissance. Taking serious color photos would need better equipment and a planned set of subjects.

From Quiriguá, then infested by mosquitoes (and one of only two places from which I have ever fled on that account), I took the evening train back to Guatemala—certainly a cooler ride, but I would miss seeing the landscape.

A day or two later I flew by Guatemala's Aviateca Airlines to Cobán, the flourishing center of coffee production in the highlands. Catching sight of Cobán's landing field on the approach, I was alarmed by its shortness, but I found it had an ingenious, and perhaps unique feature. Flat terrain is scarce at Cobán, so at what must usually be the upwind end, the strip ran up a graded hill with a flat top, and that was where the terminal was sited. Similarly on takeoff, descent down this chute provided rapid acceleration, and a short takeoff run. Quite exciting!

From Cobán I took a bus down to Sebol. This, I was told, was neither village nor town, but a ranch at the head of navigation of the Río de la Pasión, and that from there, quite large boats constructed of sheet metal plied the river, carrying passengers and beer and other merchandise bound for Flores.

The bus was full, but there was just room for me, standing in the doorway. Before boarding it I'd noticed that the front tire on that side had suffered a hernia, with a bulge of pink innertube protruding. On a stretch of concrete paving in San Pedro Carchá, the only town we went through, I could hear the little "flap-flap" this protuberance made each time it hit the cement paving.

Miraculously, we arrived, but to bad news: the regular beer-transporting boat had just left, and wouldn't be back and ready to leave again for a fortnight. But no sooner had I decided to return by bus (tire hernia permitting) and then fly instead from Cobán to Flores—than word came of several trees having been blown down across the road since we came down it. Was there another way out? Apparently not.

The prospect of spending two weeks in Sebol had little appeal, but hearing of a petroleum geologists' camp nearby, I went there hoping to find some solution.

The two or three buildings of the Union Oil Company's geologists' camp were of match-boarding, painted white and roofed with corrugated iron. I entered one, and found two young men lying on camp beds in minimal attire, one of them holding a short air gun. I thought it prudent to inquire whether I might enter, but he gave me a friendly welcome.

"Why the gun?" I asked.

"Oh, just shooting rats."

And quite soon the false ceiling of cloth stretched across the partitions of this hut was dimpled by the feet of a rat passing overhead, and then—bang!

"Missed, darn it!"

How any rat that fell to his gun would be disposed of remained a mystery.

Another interesting character in that hut was Sam Bonis, whom I would often meet in the future. Having married and settled in Guatemala City, he became the leading expert on the country's volcanic geology, and it was he who now gave me a useful suggestion. I might consider walking, or perhaps hitchhiking, to a village called Raxujá. I could spend a night there and then walk to the Standard Oil of Ohio (or Sohio) Company's site at Chinajá, where, since drilling was in progress, I'd have a good chance of cadging a flight to Flores. So I did walk to Raxujá (ten miles along a muddy road), but then postponed any idea of going on immediately upon hearing rumors that ancient ruins had been found in the vicinity.

The search for them that I made with a guide was exhausting and fruitless, but we did find a cave, littered with ancient and undisturbed pottery. Then we looked into a vast hole about three hundred feet deep, at the bottom of which a substantial river flowed. On the walk back to Raxujá next day, we saw *faisán* and *perdiz* (birds I would later relish as rare treats in Petén camplife), and tracks of wild pig, deer, and jaguar. We passed limestone rocks naturally broken and weathered into grotesque shapes, and outcrops all shivered into roughly equal pieces—crazy patterns, still in place like a finished jigsaw puzzle, with edges softened by weathering to resemble a perfect "rusticated" wall.

On return to Raxujá (nowadays spelled "Raxruja"), I found two highland Maya who were hoping for employment at Chinajá, and they agreed to accompany me and to carry one of my bags in exchange for two dollars and something to eat along the way. We set out next morning, but all we had to follow were deep ruts left by the bulldozer that had smashed its way through the forest to Chinajá about two years before to construct the airfield. This must have been done in the rainy season, because the ruts were over a foot deep; but now they were overgrown with grass and other vegetation, causing me to fall several times into the well-concealed ruts.

It was said to be seven leagues, or twenty-eight kilometers, to Chinajá (the Petén league being roughly the distance a mule and driver cover in one hour). I was close to collapse when at last we arrived at about 6 p.m. On asking at the geologists' and drillers' quarters whether they could possibly give me a meal and somewhere to sleep, I was hospitably received, given a lemonade, and taken to a magnificent shower room. Never before had I been enjoying a shower so much, when suddenly my pleasure turned to gall.

Two men came in and started showering, and I heard one say, "Can you believe it, yet another tourist has arrived! What can we do about this? They keep coming. If only they understood what it costs to house a person here for a day; it's about three hundred dollars now, isn't it?"

I dried quickly, and crept out.

But then I realized, soon enough, that the man was joking. Three hundred dollars may well have been the cost per person, per day, averaged for the whole camp and including fixed costs, but the addition of one person would make very little difference. Above all, I doubted whether they'd *ever* had a tourist drop in before! Everyone I met, in fact, was friendly, and next morning, when a De Havilland Beaver came in to take one man to Sayaxché and another to Flores, I was offered the fourth seat.

On landing at Sayaxché, the pilot taxied off the strip, and immediately one wheel sank into mud up to its axle. Flores, or anywhere else, was out of the question for the moment, so I gave the pilot my heartiest thanks and decided to become acquainted with Sayaxché.

There was quite a decent little lodging there, largely patronized, as I soon found, by prosperous amateur fishermen and jaguar hunters. Then I engaged a boatman to take me upriver to a settlement on the riverbank called El Seibal, where I was lucky enough to find a man willing to take me along a three-mile track to the ruins of the same name. (A Guatemalan archaeologist has pontificated that only the spelling "Ceibal" conforms with the Royal Spanish Academy's rules of orthography—thereby displaying his ignorance of the word's origins, which are not Peninsular, but Carib. Even old Webster guessed that!)

And there I found the superb and beautifully preserved Stela 10, still standing erect and scarcely weathered after more than a millennium. Countless trees must have fallen to the left and right of it, but miraculously it had remained intact. When I look at the photograph that I took then of the stela, this vision of a monument from the past, framed by the fronds of *corozo* palms and other trees, gives me a shiver of pleasure; but it was a vision that necessarily vanished in 1965, when the plaza of the ruins had to be cleared as a preliminary to archaeological research.

From Sayaxché, I got a lift in a boat going up the Arroyo Subín; then jumped on a four-wheel-drive truck going to Flores, this being one of the two motor vehicles then existing in Petén, and a vital link in the carriage of the beer brought downriver from Sebol.

Flores, the administrative capital of Petén, is a tiny island, which then was still skirted by a grassy foreshore, where horse races round the island were occasionally held on Sundays. Most of the houses were roofed with corrugated iron, each piece no more than

1959

135

10.1 Seibal Stela 10, beautifully preserved.

about three feet long, because all of them had been imported from British Honduras, and that was the maximum length possible for loading on mules. Much of this good old heavy-gauge galvanized iron remains in place, some of it one hundred years old by now, I'm sure.

In those days there was a wooden walkway supported on piles connecting Flores with San Benito on the opposite shore, or mainland, but most of the traffic was by canoe, as some of it still is; but there was a difference: in those days, all the canoes were dugouts, propelled by *canalete*, a long oar which serves also as punting pole. There were also a few extremely large canoas hollowed out from ceiba trees, used for carrying heavy merchandise, such as sand or rocks.

With cars unknown in the streets of Flores, grass grew picturesquely between the cobblestones, and the whitewashed eighteenth-century church on the highest point was agreeably unpretentious. (Its façade was soon to be modernized in the most hideous fashion, and later revamped again, this time into a stately, twin-belfry, pseudocolonial reincarnation. But this was definitely an improvement on the "moderne" version.)

Unfortunately, little or nothing has since been done to preserve the more interesting buildings. One of these was the Hotel Cambranes. As a hotel, it left absolutely *everything* to be desired, except the room rent, which was twenty-five cents, and there was little to choose between it and the rival Casa Blanca—for the same price). I used to dread having to spend a night in Flores. But the Cambranes, the only three-story building on the island, its balconies enclosed by crudely fretted balustrades, was at least a picturesque old pile which could (and should) have been saved, instead of being replaced by a graceless concrete motor-tire store.

From Flores I went, of course, to Tikal, where the University of Pennsylvania's bold and ambitious project was in its early stages. The few tourists then visiting the site were accommodated in a large, palm-thatched building adjacent to the archaeologists' living quarters and dining hall, where they enjoyed the privilege of sitting at the same long table as the archaeologists, eating the same food, and partaking in the general conversation. Water was scarce, but peanut butter abundant—because some generous tourist, told that the contentment of the field director, Bill Coe, depended on a constant supply of this delicacy, had endowed a permanent supply of it.

Rum was also available, and I heard of (but didn't witness) an after-dinner venture by Coe and Linton Satterthwaite, a veteran not only of the Piedras Negras project in the thirties, but also of the Lafayette squadron of the Royal Flying Corps in the First World War. They attempted to gain sufficient speed on the airfield in the expedition's jeep to take off. Perhaps it did become airborne for a second, thanks to a hump in the runway, but a second later crash-landed, fortunately without injury to pilot or passenger.

1959

On return from Tikal, I went over to British Honduras and the ruins of Benque Viejo; then came back to Fallabón on the Guatemalan side (its name being derived from "Fireburn" after a long-ago conflagration, with spelling based on Creole pronunciation and Spanish orthography; later, its name was changed to Melchor de Mencos). There I engaged an *arriero*, or mule driver, named Manuel Morfín to take me first to the ruins of Naranjo, and then to those of Yaxhá. This would be my first "expedition" into the jungle with a guide and a cargo mule.

We set out next day along an open lumber road, or "truck pass," a Belizean loggers' term that Peteneros would adapt as *trocopas*. A five-hour slog brought us at last to a clearing near a small pond, or *aguada*. This spot, known as Chunhuitz, was a seasonal camping spot for chicleros, and there we spent the night. Suddenly I caught sight of Manuel climbing a tree, with climbing irons strapped to his legs, like those of telephone linesmen. When up some twenty feet, he hacked away at its branches with his machete. I couldn't imagine what he was doing. But when down again, he explained that this tree was a *ramón*, or breadnut, and that its leaves and bark were, in his words, like ham and eggs to mules and horses—provided they've been raised on this diet. I admit that on setting out I hadn't even thought about the question of fodder for the mules. I assumed there'd be grass.

Manuel was extremely deaf, but often sang, the first line of one of his songs being *Te quiero, mula*. But if the animals, on deciding to run away at 4:30 in the morning, were relying on his deafness, they were soon disappointed on finding a *tranca* (barrier) put up by Manuel the previous evening across the trail.

10.2 *Digging a pit in a dry* aguada, *looking for water, Holmul, Guatemala. (PM # 2004.15.1.0669)*

The next day, we had five and a half hours of very heavy travel through two long stretches of *bajo*, these being low-lying areas of sticky black mud—but my spirits were kept up by thoughts of the river and the orange trees above the ruins that Manuel had spoken of. But on arrival, I found the river was only a stagnant pool, and on immersing myself in it, the minnows bit me as fiercely as mosquitoes—and these were now joined by other flies called *chaquistes*, with bites that are even more painful and leave much redder spots. These we had to endure until dark.

On visiting the ruins next day, I was in for another surprise: there was a platform crowned by a building containing three narrow but very tall vaulted chambers. Well, I knew just enough to realize this wasn't Naranjo, but instead Holmul, as I remembered from an illustration I'd seen. The architecture was certainly very interesting, but I hadn't counted on such a long excursion—the real Naranjo being much closer to Fallabón—and here, the only stela was plain; and as I would discover on visiting the real Naranjo, there was no orange tree there at all, and in any case, the local name for *that* site was "Manantial." So I suppose he guessed that Naranjo was just another name for Holmul, since there, an actual orange tree does grow (or did).

Next day, then, another long walk. Yaxhá was reached in eight or nine hours, and there we found shelter for the night in a deserted chiclero camp. While I was enjoying a delightful swim in the lake, Manuel shot a hen faisán for our dinner. Next morning I climbed the main pyramid and was rewarded by an extraordinary panorama from its top, with yellow ground-orchids in the foreground and the lake's green water down below (Yaxhá, the site's original Maya name, means "green water"). About one-third of the vaulted chamber was still standing, and in it I spotted two graffiti, one a puzzling, but almost unmistakable representation of a sailing ship of European aspect, complete with rudder, the other an ingenious doodle of a pair of ducks, one inverted, drawn with a single line in a symmetrical design. (Many years later I learned that there had been a Spanish settlement nearby in the eighteenth century.[1]) Then in the ruins we found some of the stelae. This, then, was my baptism in jungle travel, and a most interesting experience it was, although rather testing for a neophyte. Next day I returned to Fallabón, and from there took the five-dollar Aviateca flight back to Sayaxché.

During my earlier sojourn in Sayaxché, I had learned that visiting Yaxchilan was not a total impossibility—though success couldn't be guaranteed. I found the idea of going there quite exciting, as this had been the source of the beautiful lintels I'd seen in the British Museum, and besides, there were temples and other sculptures to admire.

I broached the subject with Julio Godoy, the young owner of the hotel. He said he could take me in his boat as far as Agua Azul—the old, and by then largely abandoned,

1959

139

10.3 *Aguateca, Structure I.*

headquarters of a mahogany concession on the Mexican side of the Usumacinta River. There, Julio told me, I might with luck find a boatman to take me the rest of the way to Yaxchilan; and that on return to Agua Azul, I might possibly find at the landing strip there a plane that could take me to Tenosique.

My immediate plans, however, suddenly changed when I went into a tiny general store in the corner of a house in Sayaxché to buy a soft drink. Chatting with the owner in my halting Spanish, I told him of my interest in Maya ruins. In that case, he said, he could show me some that he had found while out shooting wild game.

"When could we go?"

"Tomorrow, if you like."

The rainy season was beginning, and that day it rained most of the time. In Don Oscar's small dugout fitted with an outboard motor, we went up the tributary that flows into the Pasión at Sayaxché; then navigated the length of a lake; and at its southern extremity entered a narrow and quite shallow *arroyo*, or creek. Finally, on reaching the foot of an escarpment, we came to a pool fed by a spring. Here we left the boat, climbed the steep slope of the escarpment, and came upon a great chasm running along it, a by-product of the geological upheaval that had created the escarpment. At its narrowest, the width of the chasm was about ten feet, at which point it was spanned by a bridge—partly of natural origin, it seemed, but also unmistakably improved by the hand of man.

Crossing this, we came to mounds, none of them very impressive, but almost immediately we came upon a small stela, its lower portion partially engulfed in the roots of a large tree, its upper portion showing a man in elaborate dress, and some hieroglyphs, all of this being adorned with philodendron. For me, this was a Eureka moment! I was almost sure that neither the site nor the stela were known to archaeologists. Other carved stelae were lying in the plaza, some face-up and eroded in varying degrees, but an investigation with my fingers of the underside of one of them seemed to indicate well preserved sculpture on that side. (Later, I would be warned against doing this, as a snake might be there.)

This was the site now known as Aguateca. But with rain starting again we didn't tarry. I had already decided to come back in the following year and undertake some amateur (and, of course, illegal) investigations of the site myself.

It was time to return to Mexico, and the most direct route, if not the easiest, would be by going down the Pasión River and into the great river Usumacinta.

I entered into negotiations with Julio, and a fare of twenty-four dollars was agreed upon for transport one way to Agua Azul, a former mahogany camp on the Mexican side of the river—and then we set off. In later years, by which time Don Julio had gained experience and prospered, he confessed to having miscalculated badly, suffering a loss on this venture.

What I found at Agua Azul was a big warehouse constructed of heavy boards, with Don José Rivera in charge of it. He lived in a hut behind, looked after by his cook—a Lacandón girl. A few men of undetermined function lounged about. Two of them, though, were persuaded by Don José to take me to Yaxchilan and back, and he explained that my arrival was well timed, because in four days time a light plane would be coming in to take him and the Lacandona to Tenosique, and there would be room in it for me.

So I was taken to Yaxchilan in a *cayuco*, the smallest size of dugout. Going downstream, the *canaletes* served mainly to steer the boat, and we tended to stay near the banks, but in places where the current swirls round to reverse the flow, we swung away nearer the middle of the river. At one point, the bowman, to my astonishment, suddenly dived overboard, and emerging, climbed in again. He explained that he had just missed catching a turtle. All the sodden *peso* bills in his pocket had to be removed, to dry in the bottom of the boat.

1959

10.4 Macaw on fallen Yaxchilan monument.

Owing to the silence of our progress, we saw animals that could never be seen from a powered boat. At one point we spotted a barba amarilla *(Bothrops Atrox)*, the most dangerous snake found in those forests. Rufino aimed his .22 rifle and fired, but missed, or possibly grazed it. The snake immediately took to the water, swimming towards us with its head raised. I imagined it climbing into the boat, and made ready to dive overboard. But he fired another shot, and hit it—a wonderful achievement for a marksman with muscles trembling from hard work, and firing from a standing position in a wobbly canoe.

On arrival, I was taken to see Miguel de la Cruz, the senior of two brothers who shared the duties of guarding the site. I signed a visitors' book (containing perhaps thirty names), and was invited to hang my hammock in a hut containing twenty or thirty immature *guacamayas* (scarlet macaws). Miguel moved these up beyond a partition to make hammock-room for me. (So Miguel, I regret to say, was a pioneer in the business of stealing fledglings from their nests and raising them for sale.)

Next morning, I chose a particularly tame one, and having perched it on my wrist, carried it up to the great temple, Structure 33. Once there, I placed it on the large, moss-covered human head of stone that had broken off the seated figure lying outside the temple—and took a photograph that pleased me at first, until I realized how improbable the scene was, and then how deplorable was the trade in macaws—a matter I'll mention again.

The experience of seeing Yaxchilan in romantic but apparently terminal abandon (as Carmen García had described it two years earlier) provided me with another impulse toward some kind of involvement in the field of archaeology. But ten years would pass before I came back to this particular site.

The return journey to Agua Azul required tremendous stamina on the part of my two boatmen, as well as knowledge of reverse eddies. This river flows very fast, in some places at around five miles per hour, and in crossing from the upstream limit of a reverse eddy to one on the other side, the cayuco would be carried back one or two hundred yards. But on many stretches, there were no reverse eddies, so that hard poling along the banks against the current was the only recourse.

Back in Agua Azul, I was very pleased to see the plane come in next morning, and doubly so to arrive safely in Tenosique; and then, finding no compelling reason to tarry there I took the next train to Palenque. There I would spend two days, enraptured by the ruins, for nowhere else in my limited experience of Mesoamerica had I seen such beautiful and well-preserved architecture, or bas-relief sculpture and modeled stucco of such quality—all of this in a landscape of great beauty.

1959

11.1 *A wayside shrine in Chiapas.*

CHAPTER 11

Chiapas and the Pasión River

I n February of the following year I returned to Mexico, full of eager anticipation, and lost no time in setting off by bus for Chiapas. My destination once again was San Cristóbal de las Casas, and in particular, Na Bolom, the home of Frans and Trudi Blom. Once there, I spent a few days exploring the town, and then on their advice visited three Tzotzil Maya towns, Chamula, Zinacantán, and Huistán. Actually, these are neither towns nor villages, but rather the administrative, religious, and ceremonial hubs of large, well-populated areas, the hills and valleys of which are studded with rancherías (small groups of houses), while the centers themselves have few permanent residents.

With Lent approaching, Trudi and Frans were recommending their visitors to attend the Carnaval ceremonies at these highland Maya towns. As I would learn, these are no Shrove Tuesday affairs, for they may last several days. I visited two of them, both visually extraordinary but difficult to comprehend—especially the one at Chamula, where elements of pre-Columbian New Year ceremonies have survived, while sidetracking the Christian component. In the following year I was to visit a third carnaval, that of Tenejapa, a Tzeltal Maya community, where the festivities continue well into Lent.

Chamula is only a few miles from San Cristóbal, and because its Shrove Tuesday fire-running ceremony is the most spectacular, it draws the largest crowds of tourists—which nowadays the Chamulas do their best to limit.[1] Basically, the Festival of Games, as the Chamulas call it, is a winter solstice festival, dedicated to the sun and Christ (or the Sun/Christ, born to Moon/Virgin Mary). None of it takes place in the church. The focus of the celebration is on the five "primeval" days: four of chaos and expectation, culminating in the Firewalk (or run) over a track covered with burning thatch, this being the Path of God, representing the path of Sun/Christ across the sky, representing also the first ascent of the Sun/Christ to the zenith and into the heavens, to purge evil at noon on the fourth day. The fifth day (the first of Lent) is known to the Tzotzils as "Fish-Eating Wednesday."

In the midst of the vast crowd in this largely open site (permanent buildings being few), one finds a ceremony led by men named as *Pasiones*, two for each of Chamula's three *barrios*, or districts—one incoming, the other outgoing in each of them. They wear white turbans and two-piece outfits resembling red pyjamas. Dualistically, they represent both the Sun/Christ and the ethnic and political forces that would destroy Chamula.

The most striking participants are the *maashes* (monkeys) dressed in white trousers and extraordinary braided uniforms with cut-away tailcoats embellished with red piping—a uniform said to have been inspired by the Emperor Maximilian's troops—whereas their hats of howler-monkey fur strangely resemble the ceremonial "bearskin" helmets of the Brigade of Guards in London—if you ignore the multi-colored ribbons attached to the crown. Carrying small mirrors to flash about, they symbolize evil survivors of an earlier epoch of abandon. Gradually a great crush of maashes and other men holding tall bamboo flagpoles and incense-burners gathers near the church.

A broad runway leading from the west end of the church to three large wooden crosses standing about a hundred yards away has been strewn with old thatch from houses in the village. Then, all at once, men come running with firebrands to set it alight. Disregarding the initial flames, young maashes and older men in black woolen *chamarras* start running along the burning track in bare feet, some carrying birches with which to keep intruders and photographers off the sacred runway. They continue to run up and down until the last glowing embers are extinguished—in a ritual supposedly derived from a pre-Columbian New Year ceremony of stamping out sin from the old year. Homemade rockets are fired, launched from the hand, and the fiesta continues.

At Huistán, a small town near the junction of highways leading to Comitán and Palenque, respectively, the carnaval was completely different, its main event being based on Spanish *corridas* (horse races). Here, the normal male headgear is a straw hat, wide-brimmed but very shallow, and worn at a rakish angle inspired by the halo of the patron saint's statue in the church, which long ago got bent. But for the fiesta, the *alféreces* (officers in the community) arrayed themselves in black hats, festive red or white jackets with very short tails, and trousers bordered with embroidery—the elders among them also wearing red and blue bandannas. Then, mounted on horseback with

11.2 Chamula: the fire run.

11.3 The fire run at Chamula.

11.4 The fire run at Chamula.

*11.5 The fire run
at Chamula.*

*11.6 Huistán Holy Week: A pause for
prayer before the start.*

*11.7 Huistán
musician/dancer
with whited
legs and
breech-clout.*

sheepskin saddles, they careered endlessly around a circuit, stopping only to pray in front of the church while kissing their thumbs and refreshing themselves in the saddle with another cigarette and a shot of chicha, a fermented beverage, before careering off again.

Near the church, a musical background was contributed by one man with a penny-whistle and two with large drums. Here and there were small parties of young boys known as *tan-chacs*, bare-chested, wearing breech-clouts and painted white all over, including their heads. Other boys playing harmonicas had handkerchiefs tied from the forehead to hang over their faces. Their dance step was: one, two, pause, one, two; on one, shuffle one foot forward, two, stamp other heel on ground; then take next step with same foot on one. A number of men wore brown or white masks with red noses, white horsehair beards and mustaches, and black cloaks temporarily sewn into tight trousers, with various baubles hanging from them; these were called *negros*, and traditionally represented Jews. There were falsetto yelps of "how!" descending in pitch, but even these were sometimes drowned by popular music blasted from phonograph discs so worn that little but scratchy surface noise could be heard—but this was none of their doing; instead it was deliberate interference by the adjacent shopkeeping ladino population (dominant Spanish speakers of mixed ancestry).

The horse race seemed to go on until the last participant capable of staying in the saddle gave up or fell off. It was certainly a picturesque event, if limited in appeal,

11.9 A pause in the Huistán Carnaval.

but a few years later it was brought to a sudden end when an evangelical missionary, undoubtedly aided by the ladinos, managed to get hold of all the costumes and
burned them.

Of the three carnavales I attended, the most fascinating was certainly that of Tenejapa,
a center of the Tzeltal-speaking Mayas, which I visited in the following year. When
Trudi learned of my interest in going there, she engaged a guide for me, and at about
four in the morning he and I set off on horseback in total darkness. I couldn't believe
this would be possible, but my mare showed at once that she could make out quite well
where she was stepping along the rough track.

11.10 The road to Tenejapa.

As it became light, I began to perceive that the highland country we were passing through, some six thousand feet above sea level, was well covered with oaks and pines, and drained by sparkling streams. Then at dawn, the low-lying mist in the valley we were entering suddenly became a silver sea below us as the first rays of sun facing us fell upon it. Now and then we passed men heavily laden with produce they were carrying to market in San Cristóbal, followed by their wives. Some men bore towering backpacks constructed of saplings and loaded with pottery vessels of their own making, while the women were burdened with calla lillies and other flowers they had grown.

At last, after six hours' riding, we came to a high ridge providing a view steeply down into a valley below. We gazed down on square houses with roofs of wooden shingles, neatly arranged on its flat, grassy bottom, but now in the square in front of the church there was obvious excitement—a procession was forming of men dressed in red uniforms and carrying huge red banners. The sound of trumpets and occasional drum-beats floated up. The scene was far beyond anything I had imagined, and for a moment I wondered whether I hadn't somehow strayed into Shangri-La.

After descending to the plaza by a steep zigzag path, my guide sought help in finding me accommodation from the *secretario*, a man of mixed Maya and ladino ancestry, while strongly resembling the actor Raymond Massey. He kindly invited me to spend the night in his own house, and ordered fresh *juncio* (pine needles) to be spread on the floor on my side of a curtain dividing the room. There I was to sleep quite well for two nights, with the secretario himself, another man, four children, and a parrot on the other side of the curtain.

11.11 My guide's accidente de tránsito, 1960, Chiapas, Mexico.

11.12 Early morning over Tenejapa.

11.13 Tenejapa: The procession of the "bulls."

When settled in, I went out and immediately came upon a man all but hidden in a framework of wood covered with rush matting, with an opening for his head in front, bull's horns attached on either side, and its tail behind. The bull-man, dancing ceaselessly on bare feet, was leading a procession, while small boys with string lariats laughingly tried to lasso the horns. Other men of apparent seniority called *wotwotse* (the name has stuck in my memory!) or *nailes*—I am not sure which—carried batons ingeniously embellished with curled shavings pared from the baton and still attached to it. One of their functions seemed to be settling disputes. Among other participants in this carnaval were female impersonators known as *maruches*, but just what their function was I failed to determine.

The procession circled round the square, crossed it diagonally in both directions, and then broke into a run, together with bearers of large red flags fluttering from poles serrated at the top. Another similar procession then appeared, differing from the first only by coming from high rather than low Tenejapa, and this one made for a second grassy square in front of the ruins of an earlier church. Later, there appeared at the rear of this procession a weird-looking man called a *cantador*, with various skins and other accessories hung about him, and carrying in one hand a dried-up and poorly stuffed *comadreja*, or some other low-slung, burrowing animal, while in the other he held a wooden-shafted iron spud. Over and over again he was chanting a short and lugubrious dirge.

On two sides of this grassy square the wives of certain officials, perhaps nailes, were squatting with bowls, bottles of *chicha* (corn beer) and gourds. The weird old man then addressed each woman in turn, and made a shallow cut in the turf in front of her with his spud. Then, taking a few gourd seeds out of a pouch, he placed them in the cut, as if sowing them. Often he would bring the comadreja down and make it appear to be digging the seeds up again in dumbshow. A good deal of banter accompanied all this. Each woman would then

11.14 Tenejapa: The bulls sally forth for Carnaval.

11.15 Tenejapa: Boys trying to lasso bulls by the horns.

11.16 Tenejapa: "Bull" and retinue.

give him a small glass of chicha and take possession of those seeds, which I suppose her husband would later plant in a corner of his *milpa* (corn field) to ensure a fruitful harvest.

On a later visit to Tenejapa, I came across another little ceremony being conducted around a table set up behind a house. The table had been covered with squash seeds, and a man standing by it was playing a beaten-up brass trumpet. In a leisurely way some kind of blessing of the seeds was being conducted—probably these were the seeds to be used for the ritual just described. Rashly I volunteered to take over the trumpet; but could I play it? The combination of my limited ability as a trumpeter and the oddity of the mouthpiece resulted in no more than embarrassing squawks. I began to fear that I was endangering the next year's maize or squash harvest, but fortunately this debacle resulted in nothing but good-natured laughter.

Although Tenejapa has a large church with a tiled floor, there had been, I was told, no resident priest there for decades. But at least during carnaval, a great deal of private worship was going on. As the Indians have no use for pews, there were none—contact with the ground being more fitting, in their view. Near the altar, a few men

11.17 Carnaval scene at Tenejapa.

were lying prostrate, with lighted candles stuck on the floor in front of them, while they prayed and fingered rosaries.

A much larger number of women were sitting on the floor with their legs doubled under them, each of them surrounded by her children and a mass of lighted candles. Each woman was chanting in a high, seemingly falsetto voice, with impressive breath control, for some were sustaining their chants for almost a minute without drawing breath. But often these were interrupted by sobs—or sobbing reproofs which I imagined might translate as "San Pegro, I washed your shirt in spring water and made many offerings to you, and what did you send me? A rheumatism that's crippling my husband"—or something of the kind. (Highland Maya speakers, finding the "dr" in *Pedro* hard to pronounce, substituting "gr.")

Every incantation, sustained on one high note, closed by dropping a third, then up to the leading note, perhaps an element of Catholic plainsong chant that somehow has survived. The sound of all those women chanting like this at any pitch that suited them, punctuated with sobs and resonating in the uncarpeted and unfurnished church, was one of the strangest I've ever heard.

Before returning to Tenejapa at carnaval time the following year, I equipped myself with a Bell and Howell Filmo 16-mm movie camera and an Uher reel-to-reel tape recorder. No one objected to their use in this or the following year. But then the construction a few years later of a road brought in rapidly increasing numbers of tourists, and the Tenejapans found the constant barrage of Instamatics objectionable. Filming then became impossible.

For various reasons, my films remained unedited for many years, but now at last a 30-minute DVD has been put together from them by my friend Eames Demetrios, thereby assuring that some record of these extraordinary festivals will survive.

Some years later I witnessed another religious festival in the Maya highlands—one of quite another kind, but impressive in its own way. This was at Comalapa, a small and prosperous town about twenty miles northwest of Guatemala City. It had a population of both Mayas and ladinos. The Maya men wore thick *delanteros* (aprons) of woven wool, and the women, white *huipiles* with a red band across the shoulders, and those with babies carried them under the huipil.

The occasion was the feast day of the church's patron saint, St. John the Baptist. The church is a very fine one with a white-painted stucco façade on which prancing tigers and armorial devices are picked out in color, and to one side stands a solid but elegant belfry. When I arrived, the wooden statue of St. John was waiting on a litter outside. He was holding a card neatly painted with *Mi Nombre es Juan*, with an alarm clock at his feet. I entered the church, where a priest with a French accent was delivering a sermon full of warnings about Protestants. The church contained a large number of wooden saints, also a fine group of wooden horsemen on sturdy beasts, and a gaggle of sickly-looking priests with expressions and gestures that managed to be both unctuous and ecstatic. I couldn't inspect the altar closely, but it seemed to be of silver, and very fine.

With the sermon and singing over, some women came out and knelt before St. John, tending censers, while others holding gaudy wands knelt around him. Then the alarm clock on the saint's litter went off, and middle-aged acolytes in red cassocks and white surplices came out holding a silver and partly gilt cross and two silver standards, all three very fine. They were followed by *cofrades* in black cloaks, bearing superb silver staffs. The band formed up, the bearers of the saint's litter raised it, swaying him from side to side, and the procession moved off at a slow and solemn pace. An oboe-like *chirimía* in front played what may have been a Maya tune, accompanied by two drummers, while the procession behind the litter included a small brass band playing Guatemalan waltzes and popular tunes. The procession made a circuit of the streets, stopping twice at shrines, and returned to the church. The Santo was then borne backwards into the church, and three fire balloons were let off from the church steps. The whole ceremony was very soberly conducted.

11.18 Splendid church furnishings in Comalapa, Guatemala.

A year later, I returned to Comalapa to witness the ceremony again. This time, as the saint was not waiting outside, I asked a bystander whether he would be appearing.

"*Sí, sí, esta vez, él viene en avión!*" (Yes, he's coming by plane, this time!)—and sure enough, out of the church, borne on men's shoulders, came a homemade airplane, with St. John standing in the cockpit with his alarm clock, and "PANAMERICAN" painted on the plane's fuselage.

As I have never had an opportunity since then of visiting Comalapa, I do wonder whether that fine silver altar, the cross, and the standards—and the ceremonies—have survived the turmoils that were soon to ravage the highlands. I hope so, but one can no longer be sure.

One of the principal objectives I had for my wanderings in Guatemala in the spring of 1961 had been Aguateca. Accordingly, I made my way to Sayaxché, and found a boatman of Belizean origin who was willing to take me there for an overnight stay. Lightly equipped with sleeping gear and simple food supplies, we made our way up the Arroyo Petexbatún in a cayuco propelled by a single long paddle, or canalete, then down the length of the lagoon of the same name, and finally up a narrow stream, the Arroyo Aguateca. Midway up this stream we were blessed with a lovely sight: four jabiru storks standing at a distance of about thirty feet—which, of course, never would have stayed if we'd had an outboard motor. These birds are perhaps four feet tall, their feathers white, with crimson bands round their long necks, black heads, and long, straight beaks. I have seen them again only twice: once when six of them flew right over me at Seibal, and again when I spotted two of them standing in their nests, high up in a tree on the riverbank.

The arroyo ended at a small lagoon about a hundred yards across. It had a bottom of sulfurous mud, but a little spring of drinkable water was found close to the most suitable camping spot. As night approached, I hung my hammock, but was puzzled by my boatman choosing to sleep in his cayuco—until I discovered that he was a Carib black from southern British Honduras, for I had been told that Caribs never really feel at home on land. For my part, I chose to sling my hammock between two trees at some distance from the boat, and did it badly, having had no practice. Twice I had to dismount and make adjustments to the ropes by flashlight before slumber became possible. I did then fall asleep; but in the middle of the night I was woken up by fierce roaring—from jaguars, I was sure—and close at hand! How long I remained frozen with foreboding I can't remember, but anyone familiar with those jungles will have guessed that these frightful sounds came in fact from the most innocuous of creatures, howler monkeys.

On this visit I did no more than explore the site a little to get a better idea of its size, took a few photographs, and then returned next morning to Sayaxché.

Returning to Mexico once again in 1962, intent on exploring Maya country, I was once again drawn to San Cristóbal and Na Bolom at Carnaval time—as if by a magnet. Then, in time for the fiestas, there also arrived two young European women, Nina Georges-Picot and her friend Irene, both of them charming and intelligent, and I

11.19 Pierre Ivanoff
and his cook at
Sayaxché.

did wonder whether I could persuade them to accompany me to my next objective, Aguateca. Irene, unfortunately, had other plans for some onward journey by herself, but Nina, whose mother was none other than Natasha Gelman's friend Nadia, gladly agreed to come along with me to Sayaxché, with a view to going on to Aguateca. So we mounted a bus and rattled off to Guatemala, braving the perils of rockfalls on the still unfinished highway near the border at La Mesilla, and then, scarcely pausing in Guatemala City, flew up to Sayaxché.

There, we encountered a tall Frenchman of Russian origin, named Pierre Ivanoff, and had lunch with him. He told us stories of his explorations on the Río Orinoco and his travels in the Far East, including the Island of Nias, near Sumatra, where he witnessed a remarkable festival that included displays by men dressed in ancient armor. He seemed an amusing fellow, and a tough traveler. Then he said something about some ruins called Dos Pilas, talk of which I'd already heard.

For the moment, though, I was concentrating on Aguateca, and as I could hardly wait to raise up the fallen stela that seemed likely to have a reasonably well-preserved underside, Nina and I went in search of a jack. In this I was helped by Don Oscar Guzmán, who had, of course, first introduced me to the site. He gave us valuable advice about victualing the expedition, and found us not only another worker, Trinidad Montalbán, but also an ancient lumberman's jack with which to raise the stela. It was made of blacksmith's ironwork and baulks of some heavy wood, and must have weighed about two hundred pounds.

Trinidad was a man of predominantly Maya ancestry, short and stocky and no longer young, but still of immense strength, as he would demonstrate on reaching our camp by heaving that jack onto his back and slogging up the steep path to the ruins with it—these lying some two hundred feet above the lake. I also engaged a black Carib boatman named Cayetano.

We set off on a lovely day, but wind made the lake choppy, and low water level made passage up the arroyo difficult, but we did arrive, and made our camp. Then we did some mapping of the site, cleaned moss and lichen off the monuments, before turning our attention to the fallen Stela 7. Between its underside and the ground there were places where one could thrust one's fingers in to ascertain whether or not that face of the stela was sculptured, and in this case there was carving that felt crisp and well preserved. (Later, I would learn that we'd been slightly incautious; one should first rootle under the monument with a stick to chase off any coral snake that might be lurking there; these are small, and have no folding fangs, so fingertips are about the only part of the body they can bite.) Then we tackled the difficult task of raising that stela, and accomplished it without mishap.

The sculptured surface showed little sign of weathering, but unfortunately, a stratum in the rock less then an inch below that surface was weak, and in fact a cleavage plane, so a considerable area had split off. Some had evidently done so after the monument had fallen, as the fragments were found lying in their original position that it had while standing. We were therefore careful not to disturb them, in the hope of obtaining some epoxy resin at Tikal with which to cement them back in place.

Nina had to return after about ten days, and I went on to Tikal, where Ed Shook, the director of the project there, very kindly gave me not only epoxy, but also some latex emulsion with which to make a mold of the sculptured surface. I returned to the site, this time accompanied only by Cayetano, and attached some fragments (not very successfully, since the stone was still too damp), and applied a coat of latex—which dried extremely slowly for the same reason. As several coats of latex would be needed, the days went by and I became worried about my supply of cash. I could replenish it at Barclay's Bank in Belize City, but getting there would involve an Aviateca flight from Sayaxché to Flores, then one to Fallabón, followed by a bus ride to Belize.

Rashly, I had applied another coat on the morning of our last day, and our departure would have to be at first light of dawn if I were to catch the 9 a.m. flight from Sayaxché. By late afternoon the mold was still tacky, so I decided not to peel it from the stone until a very early hour next morning (in retrospect I realize that this was not a well-considered plan, as the latex was unlikely to dry at all in the humid night air).

So at about 4 a.m. I set off up the trail by the light of my flashlight—which to my dismay was growing dim. I pulled the mold off the stone, but before I had gone very far, the flashlight was no longer casting a beam, but just glowing. Since I still had

11.20 Aguateca Stela 3, my first discovery of a previously unknown monument.

to cross the chasm over the remains of the ancient Maya bridge, I was reduced to proceeding on all fours, with the rolled-up mold across my back, simply feeling my way along the path that had been cleared by machete. I was in danger, of course, not only of tumbling into the chasm, but also of encountering a snake, since snakes tend to emerge from their lairs at night. Well, I did get down safely, and soon we were on our way, but not quite soon enough, for just as we were nearing Sayaxché we heard the plane take off. But with the help of a loan from Don Oscar, I reached Belize City three days later.

In Belize, anyone with an appreciation of language is likely to pick up nuggets of linguistic delight in the city's streets and markets, although full appreciation of them does require some familiarity with creole pronunciation. I used to listen spell-bound, though with only partial comprehension, to conversations in public places. Nothing that I heard, however, matches the crown-jewel of an argument—the very epitome of dialectic—collected in the central market by my old friend Joya Hairs: there, a ding-dong dispute between two ladies of very substantial build and heads tied in kerchiefs, was triumphantly ended by one of them when she proclaimed in a loud voice, "I would call you a bastard, on'y you donn favor a lovv-chile!"

Just twelve words for a double-barrelled insult!

I returned to Flores, and there met Ben Reina, an anthropologist from the University of Pennsylvania's museum. He invited me to go with him to the little town of San Andrés on the lakeshore to the west, where he was doing research—for here there were still a few Mayas speaking the Itzá version of the Maya language. (One of nearly thirty Maya languages that are still spoken, this one may also have been spoken by some Yucatec rulers before the Spanish Conquest.) We stopped on the way for a swim under a glorious sunset, and then were most surprised to see a canoa approaching under sail. The sail was clearly homemade with a gaff rig, well set, and the boat was carrying one man, a dog, and some merchandise. Ben had never seen a sailboat on the lake, and neither have I, in the forty years since then.

From San Andrés we went along the shore to San José, where the Itzá language and tradition was, and still is, preserved more strongly among its population of about one hundred families. As this was the Wednesday of Easter week, the service of Tinieblas (or Tenebrae) was to be held.

In the church there were two near life-sized Christs on crosses, one of them black, and to the left of the altar, three jawless skulls in a niche (relics, as Ben explained, of spiritual men of ancient times). Another Christ, dressed in purple, was standing, and as the congregation watched, a man combed His hair painstakingly, and changed His clothes to robes of white—a very lengthy procedure.

After another long wait, female prayer makers arrived. Twelve candles were lit, and reciting of the Lord's Prayer began, with much use of the rosary, and pauses to ring a bell and extinguish one candle each time. Unfortunately, the dramatic effect of this was spoilt by some difficulty in turning off the electric light. Then, this figure of Christ was blindfolded with a white cloth and conducted to a small prison cell, constructed of canes and garnished with greenery, at the west end of the church. This was the signal for all—especially children—to bang on pews and doors with their fists; there was also hammering from outside on the doors, which had been closed all the while.

Returning to Sayaxché, I found a great deal of activity centered around a large canoa that was being loaded with numerous boxes. Four of the men proved to be students and staff members of the Peabody Museum project at Altar de Sacrificios, ruins far downstream near the confluence of the Pasión and Salinas rivers. Then, falling into conversation with one of those four Americans, I learned that he was the project's field director, Ledyard Smith, and a most affable man he was. He, in turn, spotting my unorthodox and travel-stained possessions, politely asked where I'd been. I explained, and then, to my astonishment, he invited me to join them for a quick visit to their site at any time, or straight away, adding that the boat would be returning to Sayaxché next day. Gladly agreeing, I ran to the nearby Godoy hotel to leave my possessions there, and was ready to take the seat assigned to me in the boat—a box of two dozen canned hams.

It was a long journey on a placid river, with only a few dwellings on its banks. I caught sight of one very large fish, perhaps a shook, and several turtles. On arrival, there was a steep bank to scramble up to reach a row of neatly constructed cabins, a kitchen and comedor (dining room), and a lab. Two or three graduate students were there, among them Dick Adams and John Graham, and since this was Easter, Ledyard had other guests, Ed Shook, Aubrey Trik, and Adolfo Molina Orantes and his son. (Adolfo, a charming man, had been the Carnegie Institution's lawyer in Guatemala.) It was a merry party, and the day I spent there was instructive. Ledyard then most kindly told me that if ever it suited me to return for a day or two, I'd be welcomed.

John Graham, whose specialty was epigraphy, decided to accompany me to Sayaxché, since he wanted to visit that recently discovered site, Dos Pilas, as reports told of many inscriptions there. So when back in Sayaxché we found a boatman, and as a guide Lisandro Flores, the discoverer of those ruins. After an hour's boatride up the Petexbatún River—the same that leads to Aguateca—we landed, and then had a stiff two-hour walk to the site, where we found a *champa* and two small spring-fed pools of cool water. But someone had made a terrible mess of the plaza, where every tree in it had been felled. This had been the work, Lisandro said, of a certain Don Pedro—by which, as we would learn, he meant Pierre Ivanoff.

Next day, John spent most of his time studying the hieroglyphic stairways, while I roamed, looking for sculptures. Several of them were magnificent, including one set in a niche high up at the end of a mound. I was intrigued by this, because it seemed to have been broken in an unusual way, with two straight fissures meeting at an obtuse angle. But with so much else to see, and the plaza rendered almost impenetrable by the trees that Ivanoff's men had felled, reconnoitering was difficult. (I was told later that Ivanoff's motive for having those trees cut was to make the site visible in aerial photographs—his brainwave method of establishing the site's location!)

I resolved to start work on the sculptures at this site as soon as I had an adequate record of Aguateca's monuments—and in fact did return, but not until February 1966, and then I went straight to that broken stela, hoping to work out its history. Perhaps it had originally been erected in the central plaza, but then had somehow been broken. (But how? Were trees already growing in the plaza that might have damaged it in falling?)

One may suppose that the huge effort—unique as far as I know—of repairing and re-erecting a monument of that size indicates its outstanding importance. But for the ancients to set it up again in the plaza was really not possible, because the shaft was broken obliquely upward from the subject's heels at an angle of about fifteen degrees; and the substantial piece broken off may well have shattered into several fragments, for unless it had, why would a replacement have been made (as it was) from a thinner tablet?

So I supposed that a decision was taken to re-erect it in a niche in a building high above ground, where the edges of that heavy but damaged shaft could be gripped on both sides by masonry. A problem still remained: all but the heels of the figure were missing from both feet. The solution adopted by the ancient restoration team was to first cut a new slab tailored to fill the missing portion of the shaft, and then to carve more deeply into the original shaft to fashion new feet where his knees had been. Strangely, they made no attempt to slim down what had been thighs into credible lower legs, for as they are, the legs look grossly swollen. But this rehabilitation of a broken monument by the ancient Maya is fascinating, and to my knowledge unique.

As new monuments came to light in future years, I would return to Dos Pilas several times, but even so, one large and beautifully preserved stela had been spirited away—and then recovered. How did this happen? Well, one day, a customs inspector at Puerto Barrios, Guatemala's Caribbean port, was about to pass a crate of saw-cut marble sheets, closely packed, when he noticed sponge rubber protruding between some of the sheets—a quite unnecessary padding for mechanically sawed sheets of

11.21 Turning a stela at Dos Pilas. Photo by Otis Imboden, who tried to get a photo with a maximum number of sweat bees on Ian's back, but was thwarted by a photo engineer who touched them all out in the similar print published in George and Gene Stuart's Mysterious Maya, *p. 30. National Geographic Society. Photo by Otis Imboden, courtesy of George Stuart.*

stone bound together. Opening the crate, he found sections of a Maya stela that had been sliced into seven pieces, each of which had then been thinned. Of its origin there is no doubt—it came from Dos Pilas, but even so, one of the component slices managed to disappear before the others reached the National Museum—but at least a photograph of it survives.

Archaeologically, the drainage basin of the Río de la Pasión, from Seibal downriver to Altar de Sacrificios at the river's confluence with the Salinas, is notable for a number of other ceremonial centers, most of them on its south side. One of the smaller ones is La Amelia, first reported in 1937 by the Carnegie archaeologists, Ledyard Smith, Harry Pollock, and Edwin Shook. (What amorous encounter, or what tragedy, lay behind the name "La Amelia" is unknown.) But here they found a sizable acropolis, with a ceremonial stairway on its south side. Six of its blocks were carved with recumbent figures and hieroglyphs, and at one end of the stairway stood the lower portion of a well-preserved stela, the upper four-fifths of which were lying in front, having broken off cleanly long ago.

In the 1960s, Ed Shook visited La Amelia again, and found to his dismay that the upper portion of the stela had disappeared. To preserve the surviving portion he had it transported to Sayaxché; it portrays a charming recumbent jaguar looking back over its shoulder. Now, I must confess to having forgotten the various odysseys of the two halves, but essentially they came into the collection of Ernest Erikson, a Swedish wood-pulp magnate, and upon his death came into the Folkens Museum of Ethnography in Stockholm. I seem to remember playing some small part in having the whole monument repatriated to Guatemala.

In 1968 I visited the site myself, and having become familiar with patterns of monument placement in Pasión River sites, I was able to recognize this "stela" as, in fact, one of the pair of wall panels that often flank hieroglyphic stairways in that region. There was, however, no sign of the other one here, so I set my men to digging where I thought it ought to be, and there it was, broken long ago into dozens of fragments by a falling tree. (But what wonders this discovery did to my reputation: I clearly had paranormal sensibilities in high degree.)[2]

I decided to have all the pieces carried to the riverbank, two and a half miles away. The largest one had to be slung from a pole heroically borne on the shoulders of my two strongest men, with much encouragement and frequent rest stops. Then we took them upriver by boat to Sayaxché, where I spent a week in a storage shed of the Godoy Hotel rebuilding the panel with epoxy resin. In the end, I was surprised and delighted at finding that few fragments were missing, save for one large piece in the upper left-hand corner. Naturally, I intended to return to the site and dig deeper for it,

*11.22 La Amelia,
Panel 2—broken
centuries ago, now
reconstructed from
thirty fragments—
before breaks
were filled.*

but never did, so that task remains for someone else in the future. I filled in the cracks with plaster, and planted the restored panel at the east end of the *alcaldía*, where the morning sun would show the relief to good effect and keep it free from mold, but for some reason, a later *alcalde* most unfortunately replanted it, facing north!

Another interesting experience on the Río de la Pasión awaited me in May 1967. While in Sebol, at the head of navigation of the river, a man named Tomás de la Cruz (unrelated to my friends, the de la Cruzes of Yaxchilan) told me of carved stones that he'd seen at Tres Islas. From Sebol, he said, these three islets lie about one-quarter of the way downriver to Sayaxché, and he was willing to guide me there. Our trip down the river was more difficult than I'd expected, for we had to pass some thirty rapids before reaching our destination, the river being exceptionally low at the time—but we arrived safely and camped on the riverbank.

We found the stelae lying close to a bluff overlooking the river's west bank. There were three, or more precisely, two and a half, and they were clearly Early Classic and quite well preserved. But looking about, I was astonished at seeing no sign of any mounds nearby. When I mentioned this later to Juan Pederson, a nice old Danish lumberman, he explained this.

"Oh, yes," he said, "I remember Don Fulano de Tal [i.e., "someone"] telling me that he had found them quite far away in the jungle, so he hauled them to the river bank with his oxen."

Not an impossible explanation; but it was demolished when, a year later, I found an unworked ball of jade buried next to the butt of one stela, and then, cached in the setting of another, a pair of bowls, one placed as a lid on top of the other, which held a large number of obsidian bladelets.

I spent three days digging out the stela fragments, then drawing and photographing them. In the meantime, an excellent Kekchi Maya of my acquaintance, Don Lolo Kilkan, arrived by prior arrangement with his son to take me back to Sebol (they had fine classical given names, Eliodoro [or Lolo] and Miltiades). I went out spearfishing with them one evening. Miltiades had a homemade acetylene headlamp which worked quite well, but while seated behind him in the boat it was alarming to see smoke and occasional flames apparently issuing from the top of his head.

A year later, I left Sayaxché with Polo Linga and another man for a return visit to Tres Islas. Even with our fast aluminum launch the journey took us five hours; the straight-line distance is not great, but the sweeping meanders in the river must add more than fifty percent to it. At the camp site on the riverbank we propped up our shaky old champa; and then I set the men to building a considerably larger one for friends of mine, the Hempsteads, who would be going downriver to spend a day or two as guests of Ledyard Smith at Seibal.

While the champa was under construction, a boat pulled in, and out of it stepped a gnome-like man with such a large Mexican straw hat that he looked like a mushroom. Suspended by a webbing belt, a large revolver swung close to the gaiters encasing his ankles—and he was also carrying a twelve-gauge shotgun in a canvas case. He didn't introduce himself, but eventually I found out that he was Carl Mechel, an Austrian engineer working for the Guatemalan Recursos Hidráulicos in connection with a Mexican project for damming the Usumacinta River. He had a camp a little way up the river, and he told me he would return the next day to help with raising the big stela if I would lend him five gallons of gasoline.

The next afternoon, Mechel returned with three men, and with their help we managed to turn the top half of Stela 2 on its back, and, with much more trouble, raised the lower portion to about 45 degrees, to facilitate photography. Next day, Mechel came again and we raised the butt of Stela 1. Then I started throwing rocks under it to prop it up at the desired angle of about sixty degrees, and did so with such haste that I threw in one rock before I had removed my hand from the last one, and squashed the fourth finger of my left hand. Mechel had a first-aid kit in his launch, and kindly attended to it.

The Hempsteads arrived, and I believe enjoyed their visit. But some time later I heard that Mechel had denounced me to the officer commanding an army unit in Sayaxché as a looter. He said I had arranged the fragments of Stela 1 in the hope of selling them, and the other stelae, too, to wealthy Cobán coffee growers. When next I encountered him (in Sayaxché) I called him the equivalent of a bloody liar, or worse, and insisted he go with me to the army officer and substantiate his claims.

Nothing more came of all that, but then I discovered that without telling anyone he had removed the two halves of Stela 1 to Santa Elena, and had erected them up in the yard of a high school. He had set the upper half in a concrete base, thereby rendering about five inches of the sculptured surface invisible (and perhaps inextricable without damage), while the lower half was set into another concrete base—upside down! Thus, ten inches altogether of sculptured surface were buried in concrete, but the plain base of the stela stood up proudly for all to admire.

I expressed my annoyance and contempt for this wretch so plainly that a *petenero* who had once traveled with Mechel in his boat to Sayaxché told me that as they approached the landing on that occasion, he caught sight of me on the landing and quickly told his boatman to turn into the mouth of the Arroyo Petexbatún, to avoid that dangerous man, Graham!

Turning back once again to my notebook for the year 1960, I find, among descriptions of various travels in Yucatán and Guatemala, a page revealing that I was dreaming of building a little tourist lodge in Sayaxché, with estimates of the cost of construction and furnishing. This plan was soon given up, to be replaced eventually by one that took several years to bear fruit: the construction of a modest house on the shores of Lake Petén Itzá to serve as my base for work in the whole Maya area.

When the time came to return home, I made my way to New York City, and there booked a tourist-class berth on the RMS *Queen Elisabeth*. As folklore had it, the two main concerns of the Cunard Line—apart from making a profit—were safety at sea and isolation of the classes. To this end, the long corridors running from one end of the cabin decks to the other on both sides had elegant gates of slender wooden members that reached down to about fifteen inches from the floor (or deck, as any sailor would call it). It was therefore possible to crawl under them, if necessary, while in the event of a real emergency they could easily be smashed down.

There came an evening when, as I sat in the tourist-class saloon, two beautiful and well-dressed young ladies appeared and politely inquired if they might seat themselves at my table. We chatted awhile, had drinks, and then they invited me to join them next evening for the "fancy dress" evening in the first-class restaurant—an invitation that I couldn't refuse. (I presume the purser had ushered them through the gates to go slumming on the lower decks!)

But what to wear? As it happened, I had with me a white dinner jacket and two pieces of potentially useful photographic lighting equipment. One was a dished reflector with a universally jointed clamp to allow adjustment of its orientation, and the other, an aluminum reflector that could be packed flat: it was circular, with a segment of ninety degrees cut out, and two little catches to maintain it in conical form when required. So I decided to insert the flat reflector under my jacket and across my chest, like a breastplate, and to wear the dish as headgear, with its adjustable clamp above suggesting a radio antenna. And then, the substantial beard I'd grown while in the jungle may have added something to the general oddity.

Next, I'd have to reconnoiter the route to the appointed rendezvous, so I went to the nearest gate, and with a quick look behind me to make sure I was unobserved, launched myself forward on the deck, slid under the gate, got back on my feet, and sauntered off, unconcerned, to establish the location of the first-class restaurant.

That evening, I showered, changed, and carried my props plus two sheets of paper to the gate on the appropriate deck. I pushed the breastplate and helmet under one side of the gate, and to avoid soiling my shirt spread the paper beside it and repeated the sliding maneuver on it, and then, gathering up my props, sauntered casually off to the appointed rendezvous.

I greatly enjoyed the company of the girls, who were obviously sisters. Then the time came for those in costume to parade before the judge. Well, I won first prize, and was conducted up to the captain to receive it. A bearded man himself, he stared at me and asked rather sharply, "Where have you come from?" for very likely he hadn't observed any young and bearded first-class passenger on this voyage. I was on the point of gibbering and trying to explain, when I rallied and announced, "Planet X-17." With a wry smile he handed me the prize, an alarm clock embellished with the crest of the Cunard Steamship Line. It was a good one, and until recently worked when required.

And who were the girls? By a strange coincidence they were the daughters of Nathan Milstein, whose recorded performance of Mozart sonatas had so enchanted me not long before. [3]

CHAPTER 12

Natasha

T he reader may understand my enthusiasm for returning to England, knowing that for several months I had traveled with just two shirts worn alternately, a single pair of trousers, and a pair of boots (but no socks!). At some point a feeling stole over me that perhaps the time had come for a short break in Mexico City, where I would enjoy a long, hot bath, a change into clean clothing I had left there in a suitcase—and perhaps enjoy some social life. Then, on looking through an address book, I was reminded of an introduction given me by my friend Nina Georges-Picot and her mother, Nadia, the wife of the French ambassador to the United Nations. This introduction was to Natasha Gelman[1] in Mexico City.

On calling her number, I was told she was at her house in Cuernavaca, and then, on reaching her there, she kindly suggested my coming at once for a visit, an invitation I accepted with enthusiasm. My hostess proved to be tall, blonde, and about forty, with wide cheekbones, a commanding manner, and impulsive generosity—for when, in answer to her inquiries, I'd given her a very brief account of my travels, she exclaimed, "Well, you must be quite ready for some relaxation. Why don't you go down to Acapulco for a while?"

"Acapulco? That sounds delightful, but why do you suggest that place in particular?"

"Oh, because I have a house there. It's fully staffed, so just go there—I'll tell them you're coming—and stay for a week or two. Oh, and there's a Jeepster outside. I believe its gas tank is full, so take it!"

This was an astonishing replay of Mr. Pabst's impulsive generosity in Houston. But as a person always open to a good offer, I promptly equipped myself with a copy of

War and Peace and drove off. The house proved to be perhaps the finest in Acapulco, built about a hundred feet above the ocean, and with a garden leading down to its private beach. I stayed for a week, just reading and swimming. The only time that I ventured out to a public beach, I found it to be strewn with TWA air-hostesses. I managed to strike up a conversation with one of the more attractive ones, and after an hour or so of pleasant chat, invited her up to the "schloss" for a drink in the evening. She came, but with hair curlers. Well, perhaps they were professionally required after a swim.

On my return to Cuernavaca, Natasha asked me whether I now felt refreshed, and if so, what my future travel plans were.

"Well," I said, "There *is* one place I'd really love to visit, although I doubt whether getting there would be possible, and that's Bonampak."

"Bonampak!" she cried, "That's a wonderful idea. Let's organize a trip there. We'll ask Nadia Georges-Picot to join us, and Trudi Blom can make the practical arrangements. And your contribution can be taking photographs."

"Oh!" I exclaimed, "well of course, I can't imagine anything more exciting, but there's just one difficulty: my Hasselblad was stolen recently."

"No problem at all! Jacques, my husband, has lots of cameras. Come, choose some," she said, taking me to a cupboard and opening it. I chose a Contax, a Rollei for color slides, and one of the new "electric-eye" Bell and Howell 16-mm movie cameras.

Wondering who this extraordinary woman could be, I gradually learned that because her mother, a Czechoslavakian, had been a well-known provider of specialized hostess services in Mexico City, Natasha had met many interesting and wealthy men. With one of them, Serge Rubinstein, she was to live for a time in New York City. He was a well-known (and in fact notorious) operator on Wall Street. Though long dead, he is still remembered because, years after he and Natasha had parted, he was found strangled in his Fifth Avenue house (the former Bache residence). The murder remains unsolved.

Jacques Gelman, the man she married, was also of Russian-Jewish origin. After spending some time working in the film industry in Germany, he had migrated to Mexico, and there married Natasha. Having a great interest in theater, and particularly vaudeville, he often went to back-street theaters in the barrios of the city. Then one evening (according to the story I was told), he returned from one of these and described to Natasha the brilliant performance by a young comedian that he'd just witnessed.

"That young man could have a great career if only he had a good manager," he declared, "and, you know, I believe that's work that I myself could do. But of course, one needs money to launch any such career. . . "

To this Natasha is said to have replied, "Jacques, if you're really sure of this man's talent, don't forget I still have the emerald necklace that Serge gave me. We could sell that. Do you think it would bring enough money?"

Apparently it did, and the comedian signed a life contract. His name was Mario Moreno, better known as Cantinflas. Jacques produced his films, and when *Round the World in 80 Days* was made, he ended up with the rights to the Spanish-language version.

On finding themselves in a position to collect paintings, they formed one of the world's greatest collections of Picasso, Diego Rivera, and School of Paris paintings. When Jacques died, Natasha went to live in New York, managing to bring the collection with her, and at her death in 1989 at the age of eighty-six, she left most of it to the Metropolitan Museum, where it now fills two galleries. (But I must say, I was disappointed that not one of the French paintings went to a Mexican national collection).

Now plans for our expedition advanced. Natasha's telephone call to Nadia in New York was answered by a great rattling of r's. From where I sat it sounded like distant machine-gun fire, but Natasha interpreted the reply as positive. She would come. Trudi Blom, in telegraphing her agreement, forewarned us of just one difficulty: a party of senators had hired all but one of the horses she had hoped to provide for the leg of our trip between the landing strip at El Cedro and Lacanhá.

When Nadia arrived, she was wearing tennis shoes and carrying a Russian Easter cake in a plastic bag. We flew to Tuxtla Gutierrez and transferred to a Cessna, which took us to El Cedro, a former chiclero camp in the jungle where some Lacandón Mayas now lived. The debris from preparation of parrot soup lay around, so I gathered up the feathers, and finding a patch of burned soil, arranged them to spell "Bonampak," and panned the movie camera along to create the title of my film.

Trudi then arrived with the hammocks and food supplies, and the three of us agreed that, for two good reasons, Nadia should have the horse. One was that her sneakers were unsuitable for walking through the jungle, and the other arose from a story she had told us that dated from the time when her husband was *en poste* in Venezuela: visiting a hacienda, they were shown a splendid stallion but were told it had become uncontrollable, even by their best riders, and was going to be put down. But Nadia begged for a chance to ride it; she mounted, they galloped off, and when she dismounted upon returning, the stallion nuzzled her affectionately. So now, of course,

12.1 *A Lacandón girl at Lacanha, Chiapas.*

she would have to ride the horse, and would be led by a guide, while we would take a more direct route that involved crossing a river. This we could do by walking or crawling along a tree that had been felled across it to serve as a bridge.

The three of us and our guides had already reached the campsite and begun hanging the hammocks when something like machine-gun fire was heard, and there was Nadia. She burst forth with an almost incomprehensible tirade in a mixture of languages, but I understood that the horrse in herr opinion was a rreject from the equine rrace, the guide was an imbecile, and as for the saddle, rreally it was a surrvival of medieval instrruments of torrturre. Fortunately, none of this was understood by the poor guide.

12.2 *Natasha Gelman, burdened with large backpack, and Lacandón at El Cedro, Chiapas.*

The hammocks Trudi had brought were U.S. Army Korean War surplus. Their design was an ingenious combination of hammock, mosquito net, and waterproof roof, with provision, even, of a cloth hanging loosely beneath the hammock itself to prevent mosquitoes from poking their noses through it. The delicate-looking nylon netting connecting the perimeter of the hammock to the waterproofed "roof" was provided with a zip-fastener on one side.

Hammock-time arrived, and Natasha successfully climbed into her unfamiliar cocoon, but when Nadia tried, she was thrown out, landing in a heap on the ground. Trudi and I rushed to her aid, and soon she made a second attempt. This was no more successful, so I offered her my hammock, and soon she was safely ensconced within in it. Trudi also retired into hers.

I undressed, retaining only skimpy briefs, and being confident of mastering any hammock, launched myself into the one that had been Nadia's—and found myself thrown against the netting on the far side. Concerned about rupturing it and bringing down Trudi's wrath upon my head, I attempted to reduce the pressure against the netting by kicking the leg I had been standing on out horizontally, as a counterpoise. There I lay, laughing helplessly. The ladies scrambled to unzip their hammocks and

12.3 *Trudi Blom and Bor, a Lacandón guide.*

come to my assistance, and one of them took hold of my leg like a pump handle and lowered it to the ground so that I could put my weight on it.

Inspection of the hammock revealed that one of Trudi's volunteers had restrung the *manos*—the set of cords connecting the suspension rope to the row of eyelets in the hammock—knowing that they should be graduated in length, but had graduated them in the wrong direction, so that the hammock was convex rather than concave. So I slept on the ground that night.

Next morning, an hour's walk brought us to the ruins, guided by Bor and Chankin Viejo, senior members of the Lacandón community. The façade of the temple was covered entirely with a kind of long grass, and the mural paintings within looked only whitish at first glance, but when moistened by spraying kerosene with a Flit gun, the colors became quite vivid. This effect was due to a layer of calcium carbonate that had been deposited in the course of centuries by water seeping through the masonry of the roof, picking up calcium salts from it, and then, when mixed with carbon dioxide from the air, being deposited as calcium carbonate. The layer itself was quite

12.4 Bor, with homegrown cigar.

12.5 Bonampak: The Temple of Wall Paintings in 1961.

transparent, but because its surface was crystalline, it refracted light in just the way a ground-glass screen does. But as kerosene, or naphtha, has a refractive index similar to that of the carbonate, its microcrystalline surface, when wetted with it, allows light to pass through without dispersion.

A few years later, spraying the murals was prohibited. I can well believe that ordinary kerosene does contain impurities harmful to the paint layer, but I wonder whether the UNESCO experts who were called in ever thought of permitting the use of purified naphtha for a limited period, instead of rushing into ill-considered measures that rendered the murals no more than ghostly shadows of their former state. (Fortunately, recent work has somehow made the murals much more visible.)

For the return journey to El Cedro, Nadia insisted on walking, so Natasha went off on the horse. Our march was uneventful, but when Natasha arrived at El Cedro, she, too, came out with forceful exclamations.

"Oh my God, this reminds me of that *Italian*, twenty years ago! I feel as if I had lost my veerginity to an elephahnt!"

Trudi looked scandalized, and asked me, sotto voce, "Who is this woman who can talk like that? Either she is from the high aristocracy, or else from the gutter!"

I resumed my travels in Yucatan, eventually gravitating to Puerto Juárez, on the Caribbean coast, whence a ferry to Cozumel was said to leave every so often. There was indeed a boat of curious appearance lying at anchor, with a high stern-castle

12.6 Portrait of Natasha Gelman by Diego Rivera, 1943. Oil on canvas, 45 x 60 in. Photo by the author.

like that of a galleon. Nothing moved until mid-afternoon, when several Mayas appeared out of the bush, one of them with two pigs. Helped by another, he hoisted the pigs into a rowing boat, lifting them by the ears and tail, against their strenuous objections, and took them out to the "galleon." Loading them onto this was another noisy business.

Soon, other hopeful passengers appeared out of the bush, and I joined them in boarding the good ship *Cisne* (Swan). Learning that we would not arrive till morning, I claimed a space on the deck by stretching out on it. Darkness fell, and silence eventually reigned—except for a snoring sound. I had seen an enormous turtle lying upside down on deck, so I asked the Maya next to me if it was the turtle making that noise. He didn't think it was, so I went to investigate, flashlight in hand, and there in the prow its beam fell on an extremely large and almost naked human belly, slowly rising and falling in slumber. It was the skipper's.

Then the skipper awoke and moved to the tiny wheelhouse, which he could reach into rather than enter, and fired up the diesel engine. This caused tremendous shuddering of the whole vessel. The cause of this wasn't hard to determine: the engine had three cylinders, but two of them had low compression. To limit the vibration of the engine on its mountings, balks of timber had been jammed between hull and cylinder block.

Cruising speed with the engine in this condition, but assisted by a ragged sail, seemed to be about three knots, and since the current of about two knots was running against us, we didn't arrive until 11 a.m.

Luckily, on landing in Cozumel, I chose, of the two hotels, the right one. This was the Mayalum, owned by an Englishman named Ilya Chamberlain and his American wife. She was an excellent cook, and Ilya an unusual and amusing fellow. He told me he was a member of the Birmingham family that had produced not only screws, bolts, and other hardware, but also two notable politicians, Austen and Neville Chamberlain. He himself claimed to have been an infant-prodigy violinist, and to have played in concerts conducted by Sir John Barbirolli, and he showed me a photograph of himself aged about eight, dressed in velvet shorts and a shirt with a lace jabot, holding a violin. But, as he told me, he had soon given up the instrument, and when, at my urging, he did produce a neglected violin with two strings remaining, the sound he produced was excruciating. But I don't doubt his story.[2]

Music remained very much a part of hotel life; waiters were chosen largely for their ability to sing, and guests were given instruments with which to accompany them after dinner—these being objects to be scraped or struck. My favorite was an unusual percussion instrument: the lower jaw of a mule, painted in bright zigzag colors, and retaining a full set of teeth loosely set in their sockets. One grasped one side of the jaw, then hit the other side with a fist, causing vibrations—like those in a tuning fork—and with them, great rattlings of teeth.

Then I went with the Chamberlains on an expedition to Tulum by boat. Apart from a lighthouse keeper, who lived not far from the ruins, there was not a soul living anywhere near. I found it easy to imagine that I was John Lloyd Stephens (and, of course, I was scarcely better informed about the place than he had been).

I had also become interested in the southern portion of the Territory (as it then was) of Quintana Roo, so after leaving Cozumel, I flew down to Chetumal. My *especial* goal was Xpuhil, where a building with three steep-sided and elegant towers had been examined in the 1930s. But when I questioned people in Mérida who might be expected to know how to reach the place, I received only discouragement. A hopeless quest, I was told.

Then I discovered that a truck did make occasional runs to Xpuhil, along a recently opened *brecha*—that is, a track cleared of trees but not improved in any other way. The truck lurched about, sometimes slowing to a crawl in order to climb an outcrop of rock. I stood the whole way, gripping the front edge of the cargo pan, while conscious of being in the line of fire of a gun held between the knees of a man sitting in the cabin.

At a small settlement named Km 71, (now Nicolás Bravo) we stopped for something to eat, but having spotted an interesting tower about three or four hundred yards away on the south side of the road, I went to investigate. There were two towers with interior stairways and some mosaic decoration remaining on one of them, and an intriguing tunnel led into the heart of the building. I would have to come back to investigate it. But for now, it was on to Xpuhil, which I recognized as similar in some ways to the Km 71 building.

A year later, I did return to Km 71, arriving after dark. When I asked someone where I could hang my hammock, he suggested the alcaldía. I was a little anxious about theft of my belongings in its open patio, but as I was then traveling with some camping equipment, I was able to arrange an alarm system of strings, which if kicked by a night intruder would cause two cooking pots to crash noisily to the ground.

Hardly had I gone to sleep before the alarm went off. I sat up and cried out challengingly, *"Quién es usted?"*

"Pues, yo le pregunto la misma cosa—I ask you the same question: who are you? For I am the mayor, and I want to know why you have come here."

When I explained that I'd come to examine the ruins, he replied that, according to report, I had been here before.

"Yes, but only for twenty minutes."

He considered this.

"Twenty minutes is a long time to be looking at any ruin . . . "

In later years, I have occasionally been reminded of this opinion. But we came to an agreement. A policeman would accompany me during my investigations. He was produced, and off we went. I soon discovered that he came from the deserts of Sonora and was scared stiff of the forest; and although the nearest house was no more than fifty yards away, he evidently felt so extremely nervous that while I was clambering rather perilously round one of the towers with a tape measure, he fired two shots with his revolver at imaginary predators in the undergrowth. Having climbed down, I then disappeared into a hole to investigate what turned out to be quite an interesting labyrinth, and on emerging, found that he had made off for the safety of "downtown."

When back in Mérida, I went off one day by bus to visit the ruins of Sayil, equipped with the Austrian-type rucksack that Natasha had passed on to me, complete with groundsheet and sleeping bag. The driver put me down at the beginning of a well-trodden path, which in a mile or so brought me to those splendid ruins. I admired the palace and a few other buildings, and then went to see the guardian. I found he was still dependent on a pre-Columbian *chultun* for his supply of water—this being a bottle-shaped excavation dug into soft stone to form an underground reservoir, with a circular paved area around its mouth as a catchment area.

I asked him if it were feasible to go on to Labná?

"Well, yes, but it's quite far . . . "

"Are there any turns I should take?"

"No, just follow the most trodden track."

So off I went, but before long came to a fork and was quite unable to decide which was the more traveled path. I tossed up, but on meeting a man a mile or two along the way, I learned that of course I'd made the wrong choice. I marched back and along the other track—and then on and on, for miles, before meeting another human being. He told me to take the next turning to the left. The midday sun was blazing down, my water bottle was now empty, and soon I was feeling desperately thirsty. I was also becoming aware that because I had lately spent several days in and out of Caribbean waters, the previously hardened soles of my feet had peeled off, and big blisters were forming within my boots.

Passing a row of beehives arranged under a corrugated roof, I decided to rest awhile in its shade, and then noticed a black cloud obscuring the sun. Soon there was thunder, and mercifully it began to rain. I had some aluminum foil in my bag (for use as a reflector when photographing small objects) so I formed it into a gutter to direct water into my empty bottle. The clouds retreated and I marched on, refreshed—but then thought it prudent to abandon the search for Labná and find my way back to the highway. This, fortunately, I succeeded in doing, but it was a very long walk on tender feet, and on reaching the road, I just collapsed—done in. But I still had just enough energy to set up my camera on my small tripod to take a picture of myself in a state of utter exhaustion.

So I learned a lesson: never wander off alone in sparsely populated Yucatán. Of course, I should have known that without having to learn it the hard way.

Now it was time to return home, but there was a problem. My money was almost exhausted, and by the time I'd flown from Mérida to New Orleans, not enough

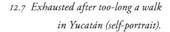

12.7 *Exhausted after too-long a walk in Yucatán (self-portrait).*

remained for the flight to New York. Fortunately, the British consul there agreed to cash a check, enabling me to fly onward to familiar territory. But now I would have to conjure up more cash for crossing the Atlantic, or else wait patiently for a transfer from my bank in London.

The next evening, friends invited me to accompany them to a Gallo jug party (guests would bring quart bottles of Gallo wine as a contribution to the merriment). There, I found myself talking to a bearded poet named Samuel Menashe, who told me he would be leaving for England by sea in three days' time, courtesy of a Greek ship-owner's wife who liked to support the arts.

"Oh! aren't you lucky! I wish I could find such a wonderful sponsor."

Two days later, Samuel was on the phone.

"You still want to go to England? Yes? Well, you can go instead of me, free. I have decided, you see, that my soul is not yet quite ready for the *crise* of experiencing Europe. So listen: just take the train to Philadelphia, find your way to the Richmond docks, and look for the SS *Atalanti*. Then, just give your name as Samuel Menashe."

I followed his advice, was greeted and taken on board, and signed on as honorary assistant cabin-boy—for the vessel was not registered for carrying passengers. The cabin assigned to me, however, was the owner's, on the top deck and paneled in mahogany. The SS *Atalanti* was a "Liberty Ship," product of a wartime mass-production line in which the vessels were constructed in two halves that were then welded together. Our cargo consisted of junked cars that had been compressed into blocks hardly larger than a coffin, but here at one corner might be a swoop of fender, and there a squashed steering wheel. I could almost believe that if a charmed magical fluid could be found to dunk them in, they would slowly swell and regain their original lineaments, like Japanese dried flowers. But instead, their destiny was Wolfsburg, where they would be melted down and turned into Volkswagens.

We cast off, and were on our way. At the appointed hour I went below for the evening meal. The captain knew only a few words of English, but "Sparks," the radio operator, spoke it well. The food was not appetizing. Breakfast next morning consisted of cornflakes served with "filled milk" (condensed milk fortified with hydrogenated fat) and hot water. Then there were thick slabs of bacon, warmed enough to make the fat translucent. Practically every dish was anointed with olive oil, vintage in the worst sense, for I wouldn't have been surprised to hear that one of the fuel tanks had been cleaned out and filled with olive oil some years earlier.

On we chugged at about nine or ten knots. Then the weather deteriorated. The wind rose, and by about nine in the evening on the third day I left my cabin to look outside, and had to use all my strength to open a forward-facing door—and then was somewhat alarmed on making out in the dark the shadowy figures of the first mate and another sailor attending to a lifeboat. That was when I remembered that under extreme conditions Liberty Ships had been known to come unstitched in the middle.

But next morning, we were still chugging along as usual and on the ninth day arrived in Rotterdam. Now the skipper, with Sparks translating, very kindly invited me to accompany them to their next port of call, in West Africa. I thanked him with many an *efkaristó*, but declined his invitation. Only later did it occur to me that if the SS *Atalanti* had, in fact, split asunder in the storm, then I, whose name was neither registered in Philadelphia on the ship's muster roll, nor likely to be remembered by Samuel Menashe, would simply have vanished mysteriously from the face of the earth . . .

I crossed to Harwich on the ferry and reached home. Having developed my films and made enlargements in a bathroom converted into a darkroom, I was reasonably satisfied with the resulting photographs—even quite pleased with some. Color transparencies, of course, were lacking, but now my enthusiasm for making a second photographic expedition in the following year to obtain these slides began to wane as the excitement of searching for previously unknown sites increased. As for the text to accompany the photographs, I had rashly decided I might write it myself, and I did in fact produce about half of it before setting it aside. But on reading that text a few years later I was so appalled at having got almost everything wrong that I tore it up immediately, for if published it would have been a lifelong source of embarrassment.

CHAPTER 13

Travel in Petén

Those few travelers now living who haunted the Department of Petén forty or fifty years ago must surely remember how deep were the initial impressions it left on them—for better or worse—as there was little that corresponded with the average visitor's normal life. But then, after a season or two of wandering in those jungles (prudently accompanied by an old hand), most of its strange and occasionally alarming sights and sounds would have become familiar, save, perhaps, for a few of the less common that might be disturbing. There's a night bird, for example, with a call that sounds so much like the cry of a lost traveler that on first hearing it I could not get back to sleep—only to be told in the morning that it was just the cry of a certain hawk. On the other hand, there were real dangers I failed to recognize until years later. So now I'll try to describe some impressions that a novice might have on first venturing into the jungle—or *monte*, as the locals call it.

To begin with, anyone leaving Guatemala City in the early 1960s bent on exploring those uncharted jungles was almost obliged to fly directly to Flores, the administrative capital of the province, for there was no road connecting the two. But from Flores, flights did depart for a number of destinations within the province, most of them centers of activity in lumber or chicle—the raw material of chewing gum. But with few exceptions, tourists flew on to the great ruins of Tikal, to spend a night or two at the Jungle Lodge before returning to the capital. Those with other agendas, or simply looking for adventure, could fly from Flores to other airfields such as Poptún or Sayaxché, perhaps to fish, or study wildlife, or just see how people lived in that remote region.

Imagine, then, that you're flying, one fine morning, from the capital to Flores in one of those doughty DC-3 Dakotas. After clearing the mountainous backbone of

Guatemala and descending to about a thousand feet (the usual altitude for flying over the lowlands), you'd first of all be impressed by the immensity of the forest, and then by the total absence of roads. In fact the forest, disappearing into a distant and hazy horizon, could easily be mistaken for a great green ocean ruffled by small waves—save during seasons when patches of purple, blue, or bright yellow appear, which one soon understood to be blossoms on the crowns of trees.

The presence of humans, on the other hand, was hard to detect. On my first flight over Petén, starting from an oil company's airstrip close to the southern border of Petén, to Sayaxché on the Río de la Pasión, I spotted not a single dwelling, though on later flights, coming up from the capital on the usual airline route, two or three settlements might be seen, each far removed from any other, each consisting of a pond, a church, and from about forty to a hundred houses. And yet, apart from quite large and almost trackless areas in its southwest and northwest, Petén was not trackless at all, and roughly one-tenth of its twenty-two thousand inhabitants earned their living by working in its forests.

With a total absence of roads, there were of course no cars, either, but in fact one chicle contractor did own a Power Wagon, and another an ancient truck. (The remains of a pioneering Model T Ford could also be admired in La Libertad where it had come to rest long ago, the glass in its headlamps now violet from decades of exposure to the blazing sun, but how or why its long-departed owner ever brought it there is a mystery.) The doughty old truck, however, did play a vital role in Petén life, for by forcing its way through narrow necks of forest that interrupt a chain of savannas, it regularly delivered to Flores all the beer and other supplies brought down the Pasión River by boat from Sebol—then the terminus of a road down from the highlands.

The primary means of long-distance travel had therefore to be by air. Aviateca, the national airline, had a fleet of some eight or ten aircraft, most of them Dakotas, which served about a dozen grass landing strips within Petén, and perhaps as many more in the rest of the country, where roads of a kind certainly did exist. Fares were low: $11.88 from the capital to any airfield in Petén, and $5 for hops within that district.

In Petén, the primary function of this network was to serve the chicle industry, the biggest employer there, for its product, solid blocks of raw chewing gum wrapped in sacking and each weighing about thirty-five pounds, had by law to be taken to the capital (instead of being sent to Mexico or British Honduras), and it was much cheaper to transport them from the jungle by air than by mule train.

Passengers and cargo traveled together in these planes. Since they were former U.S. Air Force planes adapted for paratroop use, the seats were hinged to the sides of the fuselage, so when not needed for passengers they could be unlatched from the floor, then swung up and secured out of the way. Thus, bedsteads, fifty-gallon oil drums, corrugated iron, sacks of cement, sawn lumber—almost any kind of cargo could be accommodated alongside the passengers—and was.

Imagine, then, that you're going to Petén for the first time in those days. After an interesting flight starting at 7 a.m., you've landed on the gravel strip at Flores airport. The terminal is a corrugated iron structure with a *comedor* (restaurant) behind it, run improbably by El Checo, who was in fact a Czech. The airport is actually in Santa Elena, a small settlement on the south shore of Laguna Petén-Itzá, while Flores itself, the island capital of Petén, lies across the water nearly half a mile away.

Perhaps you've come with the idea of following up a story you heard at a dinner party in Guatemala City: a geologist working for an oil company had described a sort of causeway he had come across in the forest. It seemed to be S-shaped in plan, with four stone statues of monkeys set up along it. He said it lay some fifteen miles north of Santo Toribio, a tiny settlement between Poptún and Fallabón, but suggested that it shouldn't be too hard to find if one could just get hold of Chema, a chiclero based there who is easy to recognize since part of his nose is missing.

You've brought with you from Guatemala City a whole lot of provisions, and these, packed in cardboard boxes, have been checked through to Santo Toribio, for Aviateca has a flight there on Thursdays. But your geologist acquaintance, on perceiving your interest in actually looking for this feature, has strongly recommended your finding a chiclero obliging enough to draw up a list of essential equipment to purchase in Flores before going any farther afield.

But first you have breakfast at El Checo's, and he kindly volunteers to provide just such a list of things you'll need, having dabbled in the chicle business himself at one time. Here's his list: a hammock of blue-jean complete with manos (the strings for attaching the row of little eyelets at both ends of the hammock to the ropes) and the rope itself, about eight yards of quarter-inch hemp (or thinner nylon), a *pabellón* (a box-shaped mosquito net with sleeves provided with drawstrings at either end for the hammock ropes to pass through), a sleeping bag (or else a thick blanket converted into one by plying needle and thread), a towel, a *bolsa ahulada* (locally made rubberized sugar sack, useful for keeping hammock, bedding, and towel in while on the move), a groundsheet of plastic, a *comal* for heating tortillas over the campfire (in a pinch, a flattened forty-pound lard tin would do), an empty gallon can, or plastic *galón*, pots and pans, detergent, matches, and, as firelighters, some spills of resinous pine, a flashlight, a hurricane lamp, and for it a bottle of kerosene.

In addition to the dry goods brought up from the capital, some vegetables, black beans, bouillon cubes, lard, salt, prunes, and eggs; also a small amount of bread and five or ten pounds of "Torti-ya," a useful, if not particularly delicious, instant *tortilla* flour—and by the way, it was important to obtain a smooth, rectangular piece of wooden board and some plastic film cut into a circle, two items necessary for shaping the *masa* made from Torti-ya into discs ready to be baked into tortillas on the comal. Oh, and a cloth to wrap the tortillas in, to keep them warm.

Of course, you're already in possession of stout walking boots, a compass, 100-foot measuring tape, notebook, camera, pens, mosquito repellent, soap, towel, aspirin, toilet paper, Band-aids, water canteen, and water-purifying tablets; and then if Chema has a .22 rifle or a 20-gauge gun, you should buy some ammunition. What about government permission to make an archaeological investigation? What an absurd idea! No one would ever ask to see such a thing, or imagine that it might be required.

How fortunate that it's only Tuesday, so there'll be time for all this shopping. But now, some lodging for the night must be found. Presumably it will be in Flores, and it appears there are two ways of reaching the island, either by dugout canoe, or else by walking nearly half a mile along the shore to the west, and then crossing to the island by means of a wooden trestle causeway, strictly reserved for pedestrian use.

Flores is quaint and attractive. Many houses have carved or fretted wooden balconies and shutters, and a few have elegantly molded lintels over their doorways. The roofs are mostly of corrugated iron, painted red and composed of sheets no more than three feet long, the reason for which is explained: they had to be cut to this length for transport on muleback from Belize. The streets are cobbled, with grass growing between the stones. Walking up to the church, one finds a pleasant, if undistinguished, whitewashed building fronting a little park adorned with an elegant bandstand (and a tiny building nearby proclaims itself as headquarters of the Flores Philharmonic Society).

Looking for a hotel, you are directed to a lower street, and find a wonderfully eccentric three-story wooden edifice, with decorative fretted balusters—the Hotel Cambranes. It looks promising, and you peek inside. But Ohmigod, the "sanitary" facilities—beyond one's worst imaginings! Well then, how about the competition, the Casa Blanca? This is a simple construction of white-painted boards with a corrugated iron roof, on the very edge of the water. The facilities are marginally less awful, so you check in there, but fail to pass a restful night on account of the comings and goings of guests who shake the building with their heavy tread, and all the hawking and spitting that can be heard through thin partitions.

As for the comedores (restaurants) in Flores, one tended to find hunger fading as the dishes were served. Better, then, to walk back to El Checo's table at the *campo de aviación*.

It's Thursday, and the plane from Guatemala lands, taxies back, and then with a roar and blizzard of dust swings halfway round to park, close to the terminal.

13.1 *Flores, Petén, before road traffic reached it,*
with Hotel Cambranes in center.

Passengers emerge, cargo handlers get busy, and a man climbs a ladder onto the wing carrying a hand-operated pump and hose, unscrews a plate on the upper surface of the wing, and inserts the pump. The other end of the hose is already in a fifty-gallon drum, and the man starts pumping.

"What!" you ask, wonderingly, "can refueling be necessary after only an hour's flight from the capital?" No: he's pumping gasoline *out* of the wing tank to add to the local reserve supply.

Passengers for Santo Toribio and Poptún are not called, for the plane is scheduled to go in the opposite direction first, to Paso Caballos. It returns two hours later. Cargo is unloaded, other cargo loaded, and then a comical voice announces over a cracked loudspeaker "Santo Tor-r-ribio y Pop-Pop-Poptún!"

Having no faith in seatbelts, all the men have taken the precaution of purchasing *octavos* (one-eighth-liter flasks) of raw spirits to keep their own spirits up during the flight. Because of the noise, and a certain tension, there's no conversation while in the air. On approaching the landing field, the pilot lowers the flaps and the plane pitches to a nose-down attitude, causing a clatter of empty octavos as they skitter forward along the wooden floorboards. There's a bump, and the plane rolls to a stop. The women cross themselves, the doors are opened, steps are wheeled up, and the passengers, relieved to be setting foot once more on solid ground, are greeted by friends.

There's discouraging news: Don Chema has gone hunting, but he's expected to return later in the day, or perhaps tomorrow. No one else seems ever to have heard of that serpentine causeway. In any case, a lodging of some kind will have to be found for one night, at least. The Aviateca agent offers his cargo shed as temporary lodging; so does the owner of the one little *tienda*, or store, in the village—the space he offers being in a thatched hut almost filled with crates of soft drink bottles (mostly empty), lumber, a bicycle lacking its front forks, a box containing a broody hen, and other interesting items. You accept his offer, since meals will be provided, although the alternative proposal of having a corner of the Aviateca shed cleaned out for his sole use did have a certain attraction.

So Arturo, the helpful owner of the tienda, assisted by his son, pushes back and piles up these treasures until there's space enough to hang a hammock, and his wife kindly offers a plate of refried black beans, fried eggs, excellent tortillas, and an orange *refresco* (the color at least is orange). Refreshed, you return to your lodgings to hang your hammock. For a novice, deploying this is not a simple operation. It takes time to get the hang of it, for when properly rigged, the sleeper can repose diagonally across it, making it possible to lie on one's side without undue curvature of the spine. But unless the gradation in length of the little strings of the mano and the hang of the hammock itself are properly adjusted, one's head is either forced uncomfortably upward, or else it has an annoying tendency to flop suddenly over the edge of the hammock.

Then you cut in two the rope you've brought and try hanging the hammock—wondering why you were advised to bring such a long one. The result seems tolerable, although perhaps the manos could do with some tuning. Now for the pabellón. You untie one end of the hammock and thread it through the sleeve at one end of the pabellón, and then, losing your way for a moment among the confusing folds of cloth, find the inner sleeve. You rehang the hammock, only to wonder how the net is to be expanded into boxlike form. Since there are tapes at the corners, what's needed, presumably, is string to attach them to fixed objects such as—in this case—rafters in the roof. You consult your host who confirms this as being often the best system, but not always practicable in the forest. The other method employs two light sticks or bamboos about four feet long to serve as spreaders. But he also tells you it had really been a mistake to cut that long rope in two, because it should run from one end of the hammock to whatever tree seems convenient (or rafter in a room), and having been secured to that, taken back across the hammock to another tree (or rafter), secured to this, and then tied to the other end of the hammock. The horizontal run will serve two purposes:

one can hang one's clothing and a towel over it, and it affords some protection from a branch falling in the night—if not too heavy.

That night, you sleep poorly. The uncertainties of the immediate future may have been partly to blame, but a more likely cause was the novel experience of lying in a hammock of unyielding blue-jean. And then, there'd been strange roaring noises during the night—heaven knows what they were.

But came the dawn, and re-energized by eggs, beans, tortillas, coffee, and the freshness of the morning, you explore the village. The church is a small thatched building with plastered adobe walls and a bell hanging within a miniature belfry at the peak of the west façade. Then you inspect the aguada. As a source of water for drinking or personal hygiene it will never do, since cattle and pigs share its use. But there's said to be a spring not far away. The morning goes slowly; then suddenly Don Chema makes a welcome appearance.

Again, though, there's disappointment. It was not Don Chema who found that causeway, but Chus, his brother-in-law—and he, alas, is no longer alive, having perished when a tree fell on him at night in his hammock. Still, Don Chema knows in what area it was found, and thinks there's a chance of finding it again. The only trouble is, that part of the forest was hit by a whirlwind two years ago, and much of it is now a tangle of fallen trees and secondary growth.

A verbal agreement is reached: $3 a day for Don Chema, $2 for Pepe, the arriero (mule-driver), and $1.50 a day for hire of the mule. When this arrives, its halter is tied to a post, and the pack-saddle put on. This doesn't resemble at all the kind constructed of wood that you've seen in the highlands, for this is a large, flat, double-ended canvas cushion stuffed with dried grass. It is draped across the animal's back and held in place by a cinch, the final tightening of which is achieved by hauling with one foot placed against the animal's flanks, on a rope that's doubled around a hand-carved wooden hook attached to the other end of the cinch.

Before being loaded, the explorer's belongings have had to be repacked in stouter cardboard boxes kindly provided by last night's host (they had contained cans of Nestlé milk for his store). These boxes are larger and stronger, and in any case repacking was necessary to equalize the load on either side of the mule. The boxes—there are now four of them, two large and two small—are loaded into two sacks, the mouths of which are now sewn up with a curved needle threaded with twine.

Don Chema throws a loop of rope over the pack-saddle, and Pepe hoists one sack against the mule's flank, supports it with one hand and his chest, feels beneath the sack for the loop of that rope, and throws it back again so that it now girdles the sack from beneath. Don Chema lifts the other sack, and supporting it likewise with his chest, quickly knots the ropes into a figure-of-eight lashing. Now the bolsa ahulada, the men's hammocks, and a rather heavy but unidentified object wrapped in sacking, are stowed centrally along the animal's back—*de sobornal*, they call it—and a tarpaulin (*trapol*) is thrown over the entire cargo. The whole lot is secured once more with rope passing beneath the corners of the sacks to ensure that the trapol remains in place.

Don Chema thinks the best plan would be to go as far as a campsite named Ramonal today, about four leagues distant (a *legua* being the equivalent of four kilometers, or the distance a mule-train will travel in one hour). The trail we follow for the first two hours is clear, but then we turn off down another that obviously has seen little if any traffic lately. This becomes obvious when we arrive at a large, fallen tree blocking the way. It roots are up against a mass of rocks on the left, so the *deshecho*, or bypass, that the men are starting to cut will have to pass right round the tree's large crown.

When this is completed after more than ten minutes of machete work, Pepe notices that the cargo has tilted a little to one side, so he heaves it back and tightens the cinch (perhaps the mule, in self-protection, had puffed out his ribs while it was first being tightened). Now we are on the march again. The trail goes up a ridge about two hundred feet high, and down again, and the high and shady forest we have been walking through begins to thin out into scrubbier vegetation, with some trees in it thorny and others oddly stunted. The surface of the trail itself has also hardened into waves that are awkward to walk over, and with the reduced shade the heat begins to be oppressive. This terrain Don Chema calls a bajo—low ground that during the rainy season becomes a muddy swamp. The undulating surface of the trail, he explains, was formed by the repeated passage of *muladas* (mule trains) along it while muddy.

This bajo seems endless, but at last we're on higher ground once more, and it's a relief to be walking on a level surface, although there are some bad patches with thin roots exposed—and suddenly you crash to the ground, tripped up by one of these roots. But you get up unhurt, and continue trudging along. Then Don Chema suddenly halts, and tries to indicate to the explorer something he has spotted high up in a tree, but even with your sharp eyes you fail to see anything unusual; then Don Chema, who has been carrying his .22 rifle slung over his shoulder, raises it, fires, and a *cojolito* falls to the ground. This is a brown bird somewhat smaller than a turkey, and apparently good to eat. You marvel that anyone can watch where he is stepping, keep on the alert for some overgrown side-turning that it may be necessary to take, and detect birds perched high up in the trees, all at the same time.

There's another ridge to cross, higher than the last and rather tiring, as you're not in good training. But for the next few miles the trail slopes gently downhill, and at last your arrival at Ramonal is announced. You are in a clearing about forty yards across, within which four tired-looking, palm-thatched shelters are standing.

Pepe ties the mule's halter to a tree, and with Don Chema's help lowers the cargo and carries it to one of the huts, which has walls on three sides made of saplings, closely bound together, and a roof of palm fronds. This hut is obviously the kitchen and comedor. At one end is a low and heavily constructed table upon which a thick layer of ashes, small stones, and lime must have been piled, moistened, compacted, and finally patted to a smooth finish. Upon it at the far end there's a horseshoe-shaped construction eight or ten inches high, evidently of the same material. This is the *fogón*, or kitchen fire. Two old machetes lie across the "horseshoe" as supports for cooking vessels, and on the table lies a fan for blowing embers into life. As Don Chema explains, this consists of curly *faisán macho* tail feathers stuck into a discarded metal flashlight, which was then flattened with a heavy blow to serve as a handle for the feathers. Apparently the faisán is another large bird that's good to eat. (Later, you identify this as *Crax Rubra*, and the cojolito as *Penelope*.)

At the other end of the hut is a dining table of some soft wood dressed flat with a machete. Close to its two longer sides, short, forked posts have been driven into the ground as supports for the benches, these having been, like their supports, tree branches, with the difference that the surfaces to sit on have been trimmed flat. Between one corner post of the hut and the trunk of a nearby sapling, there's a horizontal wooden bar about two feet long, lashed at waist height with *bejucos* (vines). Don Chema explains that this is where the *molino* would have been mounted—the corn-grinder for making masa for tortillas—but for this short journey the use of Torti-ya was much simpler.

You look around with some disdain at all the trash strewn about the campsite (or *jato*, as his companions sometimes call it), and begin clearing some of it up for burning—but then out of curiosity you follow Pepe as he goes off down a track carrying the galón. It leads to the aguada, a pool some thirty yards across, in the middle of which a large tree with buttress roots is growing. The surface of the pool is covered with greenish-gray, velvety leaves, apparently floating, which Pepe calls *lechuga*, or lettuce. No, he says, these are not edible, but are welcome as they help reduce evaporation from the pond. A flimsy kind of pier made of sticks lashed together runs out into the water, too rotten for use, but in any case not required now for filling the galón.

The fire is lit and the coffee pot balanced on the two machetes. Lunch consists of coffee, pilchards in tomato sauce, *frijoles refritos* from a can but with onion added, and bread. Tortilla making can wait until evening. Having rested awhile and smoked a thin *Payasos* cigarette, Don Chema does some tidying up and decides which champa we'll use as dormitory. One of them has four walls, having been built for a cook, but a larger, open-sided one seems to be in better condition; even so, he takes the precaution of cutting some forked poles, the lower ends of which he sharpens to a point and thrusts into the ground at an angle, while the forks are trimmed and then jammed against the champa's old posts to reinforce them against the tension of occupied hammocks.

Having emptied the contents of the bolsa ahulada onto your groundsheet, you are contemplating the task of rigging the hammock when Don Chema comes to the rescue. He picks up the groundsheet and carries it, with the other contents of the bolsa, outside, then sweeps the floor with an old broom standing in the corner, the business-end of which is a frond from a palm, which because it serves this purpose so well is called *escoba*, or broom. The groundsheet is laid again, Don Chema hangs the hammock and tests it, and then hangs his own.

Now he draws my attention to a number of little conical pits in the soil around the camp, and explains that these guarantee an absence of fleas—a frequent plague at chicle campgrounds. The pits are flea traps made by curious little bugs known as *cochinitos* (piglets), which excavate them with what seems to be a muscular tail; and then they lie in wait for fleas to tumble in to give them a meal.

Pepe, meanwhile, has unwrapped that mysterious and heavy item that had been loaded on the mule's back, and carries it to the edge of the clearing. It proves to be a pair of telegraph-linesmen's climbing irons of crude blacksmith work. He straps them on his legs and then, with a short rope passed round the tree and tied to his belt, climbs up it, kicking his heels down with each step to make sure the sharp iron point has penetrated the trunk securely, and with each pair of steps pulling himself forward for a moment to flip the rope higher up the tree. On reaching a branch, he cuts it off with his machete, and it lands with a crash. He climbs up to the next branch and cuts that down too. Both of them are big, and apparently sufficient, so he climbs down again.

The explorer is mystified, but that evening, when the mule is tethered on a long rope close to the fallen branches, it starts to tear the bark off them with bared teeth. Don Pepe then explains that this tree is *ramón*—or breadnut—and that its abundance here is responsible for the campsite's name, Ramonal.

As light begins to fail, Don Chema prepares with your help a mess of rice, onion, and corned beef in a pan, placing it when ready near the fogón, removes the old machetes from it, places the comal there instead, adds firewood, and then uses the faisán fan to encourage the fire. Now he makes a masa by adding water to two mugfulls of Torti-ya, and shapes the mixture into golfball-size lumps, placing them in rows on a cloth. Next, he sets the round piece of plastic film on the board we have brought, and taking a ball of masa, places it on the plastic, pats it with his fingers while turning the evolving tortilla and the film beneath it. When satisfied, he takes the edge of the film between his fingers, slides it off the board, and with one quick motion peels the film off the nascent tortilla and deposits it on the hot comal.

While he's preparing the next one, Pepe takes charge of the one already on the comal, moving it about and turning it over when one side is done. As they are produced, the tortillas are stacked within the folded cloth, to keep them warm. The coffee is heated again, and dinner is served.

That Don Chema and Pepe enjoy chatting and exchanging gossip soon becomes obvious. A favorite topic is women and everything concerning them; another concerns frightening encounters with wild beasts. Then, perhaps for your benefit, a few tragedies, accidents, and unexpected deaths from disease are recounted. But you have difficulty understanding more than about one word in every three or four, since *peteneros* tend to omit the last syllable of many words, and if possible the first as well. You also notice that *f*'s and *j*'s can be interchanged, resulting in statements like, *"Ya se jue al fuego de fut"* (he's already gone to the football game); or *j* may not be pronounced at all, as in *"Fan se fe el feres"* (*Juan se fue el jueves*).

You take the opportunity to ask about certain health hazards you've heard of, such as malaria and something called "chiclero ulcer." Naively, you inquire whether this was a stomach ulcer caused by worries about possibly falling from a tree, for wasn't there quite a risk that a chiclero might accidentally cut his own rope?

"Well, yes," Don Chema replies, "that can indeed happen, especially when he's been cutting that zigzag channel in the bark for the sap to flow down, then reaches a branch and has to arrange another safety rope above it.[1] In this awkward maneuver a

13.2 *A chiclero's grave.*
(PM#2004.15.1.0698)

rope may accidentally be cut. But this has nothing to do with the ulcer; that's caused by the bite of a fly, and strangely enough it doesn't seem to affect women working in chiclero camps. So perhaps the flies are not found at ground level."

"Is there a cure for it?"

"Well, there does seem to be now. Two of my *compadres* have been cured by injections. But when I got it, I tried various 'cures,' battery acid and so on. They didn't work. The *mosca* gradually ate away part of my nose, as you can see, but eventually its advance just ended."

He goes on to explain that ears are another favorite target for this infection.

You are horrified, but exhaustion puts an end to further thought about this subject, and you sleep well except for one interruption in the middle of the night when you are startled out of slumber by a loud "craaack!" You feel sure that it came from a tree branch breaking almost overhead, and that you hadn't heard the sound of it actually crashing to the ground. That was worrying, but you are calmed by lack of reaction from your companions. Then slumber claims you again.

Your companions were up at first light, kindling the fire and making tortillas. Breakfast begins with *mosh*, an oatmeal that no Scotsman would dignify with the name of porridge, since it's full of sugar and liquid enough to be drunk out of a mug, but quite agreeable under these circumstances—unless prepared with "instant oatmeal," which results in a goo resembling wallpaper paste.

You and your companions now start preparing for another day's march, and since you now seem quite confident about them, we'll wish you success in your mission and leave you to it.

But what, you may ask, are the principal dangers and sources of discomfort that face travelers in the jungle? Well, as for danger, my own experience of forty-three seasons, each of three or four months, inclines me to suggest that a person in normal good health, with good eyesight and accompanied by an experienced guide, has little to fear—and one can at least discount the possibility of a traffic accident!

Snakes and jaguars, I suppose, are the most commonly imagined sources of trouble. But it is only in the rainy season, a time when vacationing travelers rarely enter the jungle, that snakes are commonly out and about by day. Of those in Petén, the most dangerous are the fer-de-lance, or barba amarilla ("tommygoffs" in Belize), and the *mano de piedra* ("jumping tommygoff" in Belize). I have had few encounters with these; but I should add that I felt safe because I always had in my baggage a kit of anti-venin complete with syringe.

My confidence, however, was shaken when a man working for Richard Adams at the ruins of Río Azul was bitten in the leg. He was given *Antivenin* and taken

13.3 *"Barba amarilla"* (Bothrops nummifera), *a snake quite easy to miss on the trail.*

13.4 *Don Polo, the one-legged chiclero, at Ixcanrío.*

as quickly as possible to the hospital in Flores, where several more shots of the same were injected. But then he was found to have internal hemorrhage (possibly provoked by a pre-existing ulcer); he was flown to the best hospital in Guatemala City, where his heart briefly stopped beating—but fortunately was restarted. He made a good recovery, but lost that leg.

So, to state the obvious, it's always wise to watch where you are stepping, or even sitting, while in the jungle. When recruiting men for my first visit to the ruins of Machaquilá, I was told an absurd but cautionary tale when one of the men I'd hired suggested I take on a man nicknamed "Mala Suerte" (bad luck). I objected to the very idea of having such a man in the team.

"Oh, it's not that he brings bad luck; it's just that he had a bit of it. You see, he went out into the bush early one morning to squat, but carelessly did so right on top of a barba amarilla, and was bitten in the buttock. Well, he had his machete, and quickly cut off a slice of it. It bled tremendously, but he's OK now, except that he does sit rather lopsided."

As for the mano de piedra, its venom is said to be rather less potent, but this serpent has a nasty way of launching itself at you from its normal coiled-up state. If it misses, though, it's unable to jump again at once. The only time I've actually seen an attack by one was during a visit to the ruins of La Pasadita, while accompanied by a journalist from the London *Daily Telegraph*.[2] I had just been telling him about this snake, and reassuring him about the rarity of its attacks, when one did launch itself—but fortunately missed. (With true British phlegm, he made no mention of this incident in the book he wrote.)

Rattlesnakes seem to be rare in Petén, although common in Yucatán and northern Belize. One of the few times I've seen one was when I had engaged three young men at Chichén Itzá to open a trail for me to a seldom visited structure. They were making good progress, but then came to a halt. One of them lit a cigarette. How strange! But then one of the others pointed to a shrub just ahead, and in it lay a rattlesnake, coiled

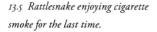

13.5 *Rattlesnake enjoying cigarette smoke for the last time.*

but with its head raised. As I got my camera ready, the smoker cut a long, slender stick, slit one end with his machete, and into the slit inserted the still glowing stub of his cigarette. He pushed it slowly through the slender branches of the shrub until it was only inches from the snake's head, so that the smoke drifted toward it. Within seconds the snake fainted, and was then killed by a slash of the machete. So smoking really can injure your health—if you're a *cascabel*.

If jaguars are now less aggressive than once they were (as old accounts seem to suggest), they have greater reason to fear humans, having been hunted so aggressively. Amateur sportsmen hunted them as trophies; so did ordinary petenero hunters for their pelts (in the 1970s I twice came across the skeleton of a spider monkey tied to a stake as bait for jaguars). And in those days there was a blue Land Rover with Belizean plates that used to cruise along the road between Flores and the Belize border, blowing its horn as it passed houses along the way. Anyone with a jaguar hide to sell knew what that driver's trade was. But at last, even the good people of Munich became persuaded of the impropriety of flaunting their coats of jaguar pelts, and this trade seems to have diminished.

Today, even in the relatively settled and cultivated parts of Petén, these beautiful creatures survive. Not long ago, I was looking for a small cave that I had seen many years earlier near the village of Colpetén; it contained a stalagmite set up on a masonry plinth like a stela. Upon entering one cave, I saw immediately that it was not the one I was looking for, but did notice a gentle flow of cool air coming out of a hole in the cave's wall; this opening was about three feet in diameter and a few feet above the floor. Just below it, there was a flat surface that would make entry through this hole quite easy, and I was already kneeling on it with a view to entering when I noticed dried blood on it. I seemed to be kneeling on Lady Jaguar's dining-room table, an impertinence she might resent, so I quickly got down.

In the open, however, I don't believe jaguars are dangerous. One evening I arrived at Tikal, and finding there was no room at the Jaguar Inn, I hung my hammock in its grounds. I hadn't long retired into it before someone came out to tell me that a jaguar was nosing around the kitchen door, looking for scraps. I stayed in my hammock, not out of bravado, but simply because I am convinced of their harmlessness when away from their lairs with cubs in them. I directed my flashlight briefly toward the kitchen door and did see yellow reflections from its eyes—the only glimpse of a jaguar that I've ever had in Petén.

Insects can certainly be a nuisance, and some unfortunate individuals seem to attract them and suffer from them more than others. But one of the most objectionable of all these little creatures makes no distinction between its victims, and that's the fly that begets the beef worm, or *colmoyote*.[3] This burrows into the skin and anchors itself there with three rows of little spikes, so that ejecting it by squeezing is almost impossible. There is, however, a foolproof method of killing it. This you can do by asphyxiating it in its burrow with surgical tape, or by applying to it a blob of chicle or manax sap on a scrap of paper—for when dead it is easy to expel. The one thing not to do is to scratch it, as this may cause a streptococcal infection difficult to deal with without medical attention.

The life cycle of this grub is quite unusual. Its progenitor, a botfly, is so timid that it hasn't the courage to deposit its grub directly on a warm-blooded animal—a necessity for the grub's nourishment and incubation. Instead, it captures a mosquito in midair, quickly transfers the sticky grub to its captive, then releases it. Once released, the mosquito thinks, "Good grief! What a frightening experience! I need a drink"— and hastening to find the nearest human being, dog, or other warm-blooded animal, takes a good swig of blood, and rubs off the grub, which crawls away in search of an inviting pore to worm its way into.

The worst of many experiences I've had with colmoyotes began one morning while I was working alone at the ruins of Seibal. I got out of bed, and in passing my hand across my forehead found it was strangely soft and puffy. Looking in the mirror, I saw that above a sharp dividing line the upper portion was obviously swollen with liquid. As the day progressed, the dividing line moved slowly downward, and by next morning had reached the eye sockets and swollen them so much that I was only able to look downward. Of course, I wondered what would happen if this liquid, whatever it might be, penetrated into the brain. Water on the brain, at least!

Then, wondering if a colmoyote might be the culprit, I felt all over my scalp and found a spot on top that did seem suspicious, for perhaps the scalp's high rate of blood circulation might cause this exaggerated reaction. But how to get rid of it?

13.6 Scolopendra, *a four-inch-long visitor to my hammock, but it failed to use its powerful sting this time.*

Fortunately, I was in a well-equipped camp, and thus able to find two mirrors. One of these I lay flat on a table, where it was now within my restricted field of vision; then, with one hand holding the other mirror just above my head and the other hand wielding nail-scissors, I snipped away at hair in the region of the likely source of trouble until that was accessible enough for a gob of chicle resin to be applied; and soon the swelling disappeared.

It is advisable, then, to wear a hat, or tie a bandana on one's head: not only to avoid colmoyotes in the scalp, but also to prevent the sharp hooks of a *bayal* palm catching in your hair—especially when riding or traveling in an open truck.

Lately, however, those tiresome colmoyotes have been less in evidence. How so? Well, on the outskirts of the city of Tuxtla Gutierrez, Chiapas, there's a factory building identified by a large sign, Fábrica de Gusanos (Worm Factory). There, colmoyotes are bred by the million, sterilized by radiation, and packed into cardboard boxes with little holes punched in them. These are then distributed over the jungle from aircraft, and eventually the flies hatch and get busy with mating—ineffectually. Of course, this expensive program is not aimed at improving the well-being of humans, but rather that of cattle, because hides blemished by colmoyote holes fetch a lower price.

As for the chiclero ulcer that disfigured Chema's nose, the chances of catching this are slight, and treatment of the Mexican and Central American variety of this affliction is now much more effective than it was more than thirty years ago. In 1962 I myself developed a patch of this ulcer on the back of my upper arm, perhaps from a bite received at night while my arm was in contact with the pabellón netting as I slept in my hammock. The doctor in Flores who made the diagnosis recommended a course of twelve injections of Repodral, a compound of antimony. I disliked the idea of these: for one thing I hate injections, and for another, compounds of antimony are toxic. So in view of the slow growth of the affected area—which looked like wet salame—I decided to do nothing about it until back in England.

Once there, I made for the London School of Tropical Hygiene, a prime center of research and treatment in this field, and explained the nature of my affliction to a nurse or receptionist at the entrance, feeling a touch of pride at my interesting condition.

"Have you been referred here by your personal physician?" she asked.

"Well, no—because I have no personal physician."

"Then we're very sorry, we cannot attend to you."

So, with my tail between my legs, I retreated, wondering what I should do next. By extraordinary good fortune, someone recommended consultation with Dr. Sir Philip Manson-Barr, in Harley Street. But while grateful for the advice, I was also apprehensive of the fees this consultation would incur, Harley Street being the location of the most famous and expensive doctors, and this one, having been knighted, must be extremely famous and expensive. But seeing no alternative, I made an appointment.

Entering his consulting room, I found at his desk a stout and genial man of about seventy-five.

"Well, what can I do for you, young fella?" he asked.

"I think I have a touch of leishmaniasis."

"*Ooh*, how interesting, let's have a look." I rolled up my sleeve.

"Ah, *lovely*; haven't seen any of this for thirty years. Got some wonderful stuff for it . . . Only trouble is, getting old . . . can't remember what it's called. Well, like to see the little devils?"

"All right," I replied.

Sir Philip then took a metal scraper from a cabinet, pulled out a Bunsen burner attached by a long rubber tube to a gas outlet—obviously to sterilize the scraper; but, slapping his pockets, found no matches to light it with.

"Got a match?" he inquired, and then answered his own question in the form of a dreadful schoolboy insult that he must have remembered from the age of about eight (though kindly reversed it): "Yes, your bottom and my face!"

Somehow he managed to ignite the burner, sterilized the scraper, stained the specimen, and then pulled out of a cabinet an ancient brass microscope liberally corroded by verdigris. He focused it and let me see the little devils. They resembled jellyfish, but presumably were single-celled organisms.

All this activity restored to his memory the name of the ointment to be topically applied. It was "Ichthiol," and my own memory may have embellished his description of its principal ingredient, which I recall as a product of fossilized fish mined from rocky outcrops in some South Pacific island. These were then packed in discarded buffalo horns, and collected every few months by traders passing by in windjammers.

Sir Philip then told me there were three varieties of leishmaniasis: the Mediterranean, which usually clears up spontaneously; the Mexican (mine), which very occasionally does; and the Brazilian, which never does, and is always fatal unless treated. Then he did something rather naughty by showing me an 8-by-10-inch close-up photo of someone with an advanced case of the Brazilian variety—pure horror, nothing but black bubbles, with three recesses corresponding to eyes and mouth.

Then he went on to tell me his son was interested in this disease and had identified its vector, a tree rat.

"Brazilian government very grateful; sent along a gold medal. I sent it back, explaining that it wasn't me who did this work, but my boy. Trouble was, we never saw it again!"

Once I had started exploring in Petén, I had a great many things to learn (some of which I never quite mastered, even after more than forty seasons in the field). One early practical problem concerned those cardboard boxes loaded on horses or mules. Nestlé and Pears soap boxes were of good, strong cardboard, able to withstand most collisions with trees without serious damage. Experienced and well-disposed mules take account of the width of their burden, and seldom run them into trees, but many are less clever, or considerate. *"Líbrese mula!"* the arriero shouts in vain, following such a collision. By the mid-1960s, though, boxes from the grocer or supermarket became increasingly flimsy, so I brought down from Boston two fiber suitcases made for carrying commercial samples. These proved durable, but I soon realized that one of them was too wide, for it chafed against the mule's hindquarters, and had to be retired. The other has remained in use for thirty seasons, carrying cooking equipment, reinforced to some extent by the steel comal (griddle) that I'd had custom-made to fit in it.

Photographs taken during Carnegie Institution expeditions into the Maya lowlands during the 1920s and '30s include scenes of camp life, a few of them showing boxes of distinctive appearance arranged on shelves in camp. As they had obviously been made for use on beasts of burden, I longed to obtain a few of these—but had no hope of doing so. Then, one evening, a group of Peabody Museum archaeologists active in a different field held a little celebration in their office, where the largest item of furniture was a huge old glass-fronted display cabinet, some seven or eight feet tall. A toast was proposed, and in tilting back my head to drain the last drop in it, what should I espy on top but three of those old boxes! I made off with them in a hurry, and held another little celebration.

Painted on them were the names and destinations of several well-known archaeologists active before the First World War, among them E. H. Thompson and Alfred Kidder, so they were themselves antiquities, made of what appears to be compressed, resin-impregnated paper, and with corners reinforced by sturdy iron fittings. They are still in good condition and remain in use.

13.7 Chiboj spider.

CHAPTER 14

Kinal, Río Azul, and Yaxhá

In about 1950 the Guatemalan Congress passed petroleum laws regulating exploration for oil and gas. By its terms, the "District" (as it then was) of Petén was
divided into about twenty concessions, one of which, a large, uninhabited tract in
its northeastern corner, was granted to the Sun Oil Company of Philadelphia.

As soon as scouting parties had made some examination of the terrain, Sun's
bulldozer, starting from Belize (then British Honduras), crossed the border and began
forcing its way northward through high forest until, at a point some twenty miles
south of the Mexican border, it swung to the west, reaching at last two small but deep
lakes—a location known as Dos Lagunas. There, a very long and well-surfaced runway was built, and then a splendid camp, with dormitories that even had electrically
heated clothes closets. With everything now coming in by air, the bulldozed track was
abandoned, but eventually local enterprise opened a muddy track southward through
the jungle to connect Dos Lagunas with Uaxactún—in the dry season at least—and
then with Tikal, already linked by road to Flores.

When, in 1961, Sun's field geologists found ruins about six miles west of the British
Honduran border, and eight south of the Mexican, the project director, John Gatling,
invited me to spend a few days there, kindly providing transportation of everything
that I needed, including water. Although not extensive, the site had impressively high
exterior walls—quite fortress-like, I thought, although never describing them as such,
for it was common knowledge at the time that the ancient Maya were a uniquely peace-
able people, with no need of fortresses. But now that that romantic and improbable
view of the Maya has been discarded, talk of a fortress no longer seems absurd.

Searching for a name to give it, I hit on a word I found in the Motul Maya dictionary: Kinal. Derived from *kin*, or sun, it means *"Lo que calienta"*—that which heats (petroleum in this case, of course). In my brief published account of this site, I reproduced a graffito, access to which had been revealed on the inside of a thick masonry wall by some crazy looter. He had simply attacked and penetrated the wall, but hadn't despaired on finding that the chamber within had been filled up in ancient times with rocks, as the first step before building an upper story. At considerable risk of being crushed by falling rocks, he removed a considerable amount of this fill before giving up.

14.1 Anatolio López Pérez and his furry companion.

One of my men, however, had, on his own initiative, started hauling out more of this rock-fill, paying no attention to my warnings of obvious danger. It was an insane operation, but it did reveal most of that large graffito, which included one hieroglyph and part of a bent-over human figure. (I did not, at that time, immediately recognize that initial breach of the wall as an early example of the greedy and destructive mania for looting that was soon to spread across the Maya lowlands.)

Three years later, when Sun's geologists found a substantial ruined city about five miles northwest of Kinal, John Gatling invited Dick Adams—then a graduate student at Harvard—to spend a couple of days studying this other site, which was given the name Río Azul.

Nearly twenty years later, in April 1981, Bruce Dahlin, a member of the Brigham Young University team working at Mirador, told me of rumors that tombs with painted walls were being opened up by looters at ruins somewhere east of Dos Lagunas, at a place called Las Gardemias (in fact, a corruption of "Gardenias"). So without losing time, I set off with Anatolio López Pérez, the exceptionally intelligent man who had succeeded Abelardo Ventura as my principal Petén guide. On the way there we heard of other ruins at a little ranch called Corozal, about seven miles south of Dos Lagunas. So next morning, Anatolio and I, accompanied by our informant, drew up at the ranch and found an obviously tipsy youth named Carlos, who immediately produced a bottle of *chumpiate* (rot-gut corn-based liquor) and offered it all round. He took a long swig, as did his friend Jorge, who looked like a city dweller—plump and unaccustomed to physical labor. Carlos then volunteered to show us round the ruins, but first he had to explain something.

"These ruins, you know, are being excavated. This little property is my uncle's, and he's allowing us to work here. You'll understand that we have to charge you a fee for admittance."

Sure enough, there were numerous trenches and a small pile of intact monochrome plates, which the excavator impulsively thrust into my hands as a gift. As we went round, Carlos earnestly sought my advice as to where precisely he should dig next, while Jorge more than once strayed off the path and had to be retrieved. There were a few stelae in terrible condition, but also one that was carved with hieroglyphic inscriptions on all four sides, and much better preserved. I was allowed to take photos, but had to pay twenty dollars for the privilege. (In Dos Lagunas, next day, I was told that Jorge was the son of a colonel who had been murdered, and that he himself had become such an alcoholic that he could no longer live in the capital. Now he was married to the nurse in Dos Lagunas, an older woman who was not, unfortunately, especially well favored by nature.)

Pursuing our way to Dos Lagunas, Anatolio and I at last found a guide to Las Gardemias. Previous inquiries had been answered by unconvincing professions of ignorance about the site, but eventually a wall-eyed and devil-may-care Mexican agreed to guide us there. We drove some way down Sun's old bulldozed track, but it was so muddy that we decided to return, hire two cargo mules for our equipment, and walk to the site. Now we heard disquieting rumors of men recently seen at Las Gardemias, since they were unlikely to be as friendly as Carlos and Jorge. But there was no one there. Campfires were long dead, and the tremendous trenches slicing into high mounds seemed to be a few months old.

Two or three of the very tall pyramids in the central group had some elements of architecture showing. They were impressive, and one of them had an inscription high up in modeled stucco, this confirming my suspicion that this site had to be the Río Azul of Adams and Gatling. At least seven apparently rich tombs had been found there, and sacked. One seemed to have collapsed during excavation, but its contents had been dug out of it, presumably in search of jades. Never before or since, I'm glad to say, have I seen such a spread of beautiful but smashed polychrome vessels as I saw there, scattered on the ground.

Then our guide appeared to find (quite by chance, of course!) yet another deeply trenched pyramid. I scrambled into the narrow cut—so neatly executed that I suspect it was the work of men trained at Tikal for legitimate excavation—and on walking forward some yards found a hole in its floor. I knelt and thrust my head down into the

*14.2 Río Azul: inscription painted at
the head of a great tomb.*

impenetrably dark interior; but on switching on my flashlight, I nearly pitched head-
first into the hole out of sheer astonishment, for the immaculate white walls of the huge
burial chamber were covered in designs painted in orange and brown, and there at the
center of the apse-like end was an inscription so clear that I could read its date even
with my head poked upside-down through the hole in the tomb's roof.

Clearly, this had to be reported as soon as possible, so we loaded up the mules
and walked the eight leagues back to Dos Lagunas. That was on the Tuesday of Easter
week. Next day, Anatolio and I drove to Flores, and on Thursday I flew to Guatemala
City to report our discovery to Rafael (Rafa) Morales, director of the Museo Nacional
de Arqueología y Etnografía. I urged him to establish guards there as soon as possible.
And then, since there was nothing else constructive that I could do over Easter weekend, I betook myself to Antigua, and witnessed there for the first time the splendid
solemnity of the public processions down the many streets carpeted with flowers and
dyed sawdust, skilfully laid for the occasion in elaborate designs.

Returning to Guatemala City on the evening of Easter Day, I was astonished to
learn that Rafa had already left for Río Azul by road, and had taken with him several
men—money for all this having been provided immediately by the Asociación Tikal.

He had assembled his *posse* in Flores, including in it two Hacienda policemen, and lost no time in making for Río Azul, taking Anatolio with him as guide.

An unwelcome surprise awaited them. Looters (four of them, apparently) had returned. There was an exchange of gunfire, but no one was badly hurt. (I really regretted that not even one of the looters had been wounded just enough to be captured and tell tales.) Rafa's men then began constructing a camp, and I returned to the site from Antigua on Wednesday of that week. Over the next four days I mapped the main structures of the site, while others investigated trenches, finding another painted tomb—and then in one champa of the looters' camp, an extraordinary discovery among the discarded flashlight batteries and other rubbish: two tiny, fitting fragments of an exquisitely carved cedar-wood bowl, the extreme fineness of which could only be appreciated fully by examining it with a magnifying glass. But how could anyone have been so *careless* as to abandon such a treasure—and what had happened to the rest of it?

On being told of these discoveries, Dick Adams applied for permission to mount an expedition, and was granted it. His team's work resulted in many valuable discoveries of various kinds, including six looted tombs with hieroglyphs painted on the walls; but the expedition was terminated in its third season by an outbreak of a fever resembling malaria, yet resisting normal treatments for it.

In the course of this expedition, one tomb was found that the looters had missed. When excavated, a jar with handles and a cap was found among its furnishings. Attempts to remove that cap were initially unsuccessful—until it was twisted. Then it came off, and to general astonishment it proved to have a screw cap—or more precisely, a locking flange cap, the like of which has never been found, before or since, on a pre-Columbian jar anywhere in the Americas.

My colleague David Stuart, then scarcely twenty years of age, studied the hieroglyphs painted on this vessel and identified it as "the deceased person's drinking vessel for a fruit-flavored chocolate drink." Inspection inside it having revealed a deposit of some kind, this was carefully scraped out, and a sample of it sent to the laboratories of the Hershey Chocolate Company. Analysis duly confirmed the presence of chocolate! This was a remarkable and important confirmation of the syllabic reading of Maya glyphs, the validity of which had at that time yet to be recognized by some epigraphers.

Now that I have recounted something of those later excitements in Sun Oil's old concession (long since abandoned after drilling a dry hole), I must wind back to the mid-1960s. As I've mentioned, on taking up my amateur study of Maya sculpture and inscriptions in Petén, I confined it at first to ruins located in the Sayaxché area, largely because that was where I happened to have been dropped off that time by Standard Oil of Ohio's plane. And then the various interesting ruins easily accessible from there by canoe were to keep me busy, on and off, for several seasons. One determining factor in all this was undoubtedly the Godoy Hotel in Sayaxché—a modest establishment, but the most agreeable in the Petén of those days, with visiting fishermen and jaguar hunters accounting largely for its prosperity and good service.

But then, upon recalling my first and very brief visit to Yaxhá, and having examined since then the splendid photographs that Teobert Maler had taken of its monuments sixty years earlier, I'd become interested in having a closer look at that site. I'd also noticed, during a flight from Melchor de Mencos to Flores, a body of water of a most unusual shape—it was almost square. And later, I found this feature did show as a white square on Cartografía's 1:50,000 map of the area, based on aerial photographs. A close look also seemed to show another feature: a small group of mounds nearby, possibly connected to Yaxhá by a *sacbe* (causeway). So in 1966 I flew to Melchor and engaged Abelardo Ventura and another man for a little expedition to Yaxhá.

14.3 Abelardo Ventura, faithful guide, and Gigante at Holmul.

By then there was a road (of a kind) and a bus service between Melchor and Flores, so with Abelardo's cherished dog Gigante perched upon the roof with our kit, we had an easy drive to the turnoff to the ruins. How we transported our baggage to the lake, three miles away, I forget; perhaps we got help from a passing mule and its owner. Then, near the narrow neck of dry land separating twin lagunas (Yaxhá and, just east of it, Sacnab), we found an old shed, perhaps a fisherman's, and made ourselves at home in it.

I'd heard tell of illicit excavations at one of the islands near the west end of Laguna Yaxhá, and as it was a cloudless day, I decided that we'd paddle out there in a small and ancient dugout beached near the hut—presumably a fisherman's. It was in terrible condition. Since one end had evidently rotted away entirely, or perhaps been damaged beyond repair, it had been sawn off and replaced by a flattened-out canister of a kind that one saw in markets containing forty pounds of lard. Then, at the end that now was indisputably the prow, the heartwood had rotted, so the resulting hole, four or five inches in diameter, had been filled by forcing into it a foot-long log of suitable size, wrapped in sacking. There was just one seat near the middle, this being a board jammed in athwartships. The paddle had also seen better days.

Though I was a little worried about the scant freeboard, with the three of us and Gigante in this tiny vessel, we reached the island safely and inspected the interesting Postclassic temple standing at the island's rocky highest point, and the pits dug by looters. Then I noticed a broad and sharply defined band of black cloud rising from the west, and then a breeze blowing from that quarter. I gave orders for immediate departure, and asked Abelardo to cut a *penca*, or stem, of *guano* palm, thinking it might keep my notebook dry in case of rain.

We set off, the wind rose, the black mantle of cloud obscured the sun, and it began to rain. Now worried about our safety, I held up the palm branch as a sail, and for a time we sped along, but then Gigante, in trying to shelter himself from the rain, somehow caused the thwart to collapse, and I fell backward with my legs in the air. No longer could I hold up the guano sail, and I was becoming quite anxious as waves built up. Although the west wind was blowing us directly towards our hut, I ordered Abelardo to steer for the south shore of the lake, which was much closer. He paid no heed. Having repeated the order to no better effect, I added the threat that unless he steered to the nearer shore I would dock his wages.

"What does that matter to me, as I'm going to die!" was his mournful reply.

Now there was lightning and thunder, with the interval between them diminished to a fraction of a second. After one dazzling and deafening strike I noticed dead fish floating by, and thought—and still think—that it was a miracle that we, the only objects projecting from the water, had not attracted the lightning.

14.4 My photograph and drawing of Yaxhá Stela 13.

At the ruins next day, I did inspect the square body of water, and decided it must have been dug by the Mayas (odd, when the lake was quite near), and inspected the little causeway, but what pleases me most is having photographed Stela 13.

This is a well-preserved monument broken cleanly into four parts of roughly equal size. The only existing record of it had been a poor photograph taken in 1932, so it was lucky I took another—and also drew it—because on my next visit to those ruins one of those pieces had disappeared. Then we set off on foot in search of the tentatively identified reservoir. The *fotomapa* showed it to be little more than three miles away from the ruins at a bearing of three degrees east of north, so we had no trouble finding it.

The reservoir's banks were substantial, for a cross-section of the west side showed it to be fifteen feet above the surrounding and only slightly inclined terrain. The banks must have been built up from soil excavated from its center, and the source of water became apparent on reaching a wide gap at the west end of its south bank, where there were clear signs of a seasonal arroyo emptying into it. (My notes on the reservoir's dimensions are confusing, but it was about one hundred yards square.)

Then we went in search of the putative sacbe that the fotomapa seemed to show not far from the reservoir's southwest corner, in soil where the vegetation tended towards that of a bajo (swamp). We had no trouble finding it, though most of it was much less

14.5 Abelardo Ventura, Gigante, and an ocelot at Holmul, Guatemala.

than a meter high. We followed it to its termination at a compact group of mounds, the tallest of them being about fifteen meters high. From its orientation, the beginning of the sacbe was surely in Yaxhá proper, but frankly, this little investigation produced little useful information, save for the fact that a reservoir or fish pond had been created just where the need for one cannot have been crucial.

CHAPTER 15

El Mirador

Having done all that I could at Kinal, I boarded a plane at Dos Lagunas to take me back to Flores, and as usual during such flights, occupied my time by scanning the landscape from the window beside me. Luckily, I was seated on the starboard side—otherwise I would never have spotted a most unusual lump projecting from an almost flat horizon.

"Good heavens!" I thought. "What could that be?"

A high and isolated hill? Surely not. A Maya pyramid? No, again; it was much too large—bearing in mind that it might still be twenty miles away. But whatever it was, it would certainly be worth investigation. So, as soon as I was back in the capital I hastened to the Dirección de Cartografía offices to see if it appeared on any map—and found there was no map showing anything at all in that area.[1]

One of the staff, however, told me that the whole of Petén had recently been photographed from the air by the Hunting Aero Survey Company, and that the man I should see was Ingeniero Raúl Lee Silva. He proved to be most helpful—as he would be on many later occasions when I came to bother him. He pulled out numerous folders of aerial photographs covering an area from about fifteen to thirty-five miles west of Dos Lagunas, and some ten miles from north to south. I studied pair after pair of these photos through a stereoscope without finding anything unusual, until, on selecting another pair to look at—good grief! I jerked my head back instinctively from the stereoscope as two great virtual needles threatened to poke my eyes out!

Aerial photos made for cartographic purposes are taken at regular intervals along straight-line flight paths—intervals that are quite large in relation to the altitude. Thus, when looked at through a stereoscope, the relief is greatly exaggerated—hence the startling impression I received. A second look left me in no doubt that these were artificially constructed mounds, and that between them they had composed that lump on the horizon I had seen from afar. There were other less gigantic mounds to be seen, and causeways, too, these showing up very clearly, radiating from the site across the low, swampy areas known as bajos. Stupidly, I failed to trace those features immediately onto transparent film, but I did work out the approximate distance and bearing at which these monster mounds lay from the nearest settlement accessible by air from Flores, this being Carmelita, a center of chiclero activity.

Naturally, I was anxious to visit that amazing site, but decided to wait awhile before doing so. I felt it would be wise to gain a lot more experience of travel in those vast forests before plunging into them in the naïve hope of finding my way to a site of unknown name, and about which I knew nothing at all except its distance and bearing from Carmelita.[2]

On the basis of that information alone, it would obviously be quite impracticable to set out from Carmelita and try to blaze a trail with eyes glued to compass in the hopes of eventually bumping into one or the other of the huge mounds. Nowadays, of course, one would rely on GPS navigation, but that technology still lay far in the future.

As I saw it, the forest was like a vast, uncharted ocean. True, there existed the equivalent of some navigational "buoys," or islands, in the form of chiclero *parajes* or *jatos* (camps), but these were not marked on any chart, nor would they be easy to identify unless one's guide knew them. And besides, the names of campsites do change in the course of time. So the only recourse lay in something resembling the mariner's dead reckoning.

And so, having decided to test the idea before steering for the big ruins, I made a trial trip in another part of Petén. My procedure was as follows: In a notebook small enough to fit in a shirt pocket, I wrote the numerals 0 to 9, and then 0 to 9 again repeatedly, in a column down the left-hand margins of many pages. Then, supposing we set off at 8:46, I would enter "8:4" before the first "6" on the page, and record on that line the compass bearing of the initial direction of travel. This would be updated every minute if the bearing changed. At 8:50 I would add the "5," and at 9:00 add the "9:0." For a compass, I used the unbeatable liquid-damped, prismatic model that the British army had used for at least almost a century. I used these also for surveying, since they could be read, hand-held, to better than one degree (far superior to any other compass I have tried), but for use on the trail, I noted the direction of travel only to the nearest five degrees. If our course remained unchanged in one minute, I merely added a vertical stroke beneath the last reading, since time could not be wasted for a fuller notation, owing to the importance of keeping up steady progress. Accordingly, I always had to hurry to catch up to my men after I'd stopped to take a reading and enter it in the log. I also timed and noted any delay the minute it occurred. Then I developed symbols to note physical features, such as slopes ahead or to left or right, escarpments, bajos, stream beds crossed, aguadas (little ponds), mounds large (X) or small (x), and so forth.

In camp that evening, I would plot these readings on graph paper, at a scale of 2 mm per minute, which represented a scale roughly equal to 1:40,000. Then, on return to Guatemala City, I would tape transparent film over the stereo-pairs of aerial photos of the areas we'd been through, and examine them with the stereo viewer. On that film I'd mark any topographical features of the kind that I might have seen on the trail. Since the aerial photos were also at about 1:40,000, I would then attempt to find congruities between the features apparent in the photos and those noted on the plot of the trail.

More often than not, sufficient matches were obtained to rectify my plot to good agreement with the photos—as also with the natural features shown on published maps based on those photos, although these were at 1:50,000. But this system did fail completely in karst terrain, where the multiplicity of little hills and the absence of streams usually made it impossible to match anything.

As a rule, I plotted both outward and return journeys; the outward, to monitor the general direction of travel; and the return, to obtain a more accurate plot, because on the outward journey, there would be many delays while *desvios* (detours) were cut around trees that had fallen across the path, or halts for straightening the loads on mules, or for some other reason. And then sometimes there were completely new paths to open, these being impossible to plot while this was going on at a snail's pace, so I usually left measurement of them for the return journey.

Another advance I had made upon the previous year's expedition technology may be worth mentioning: this was an early version of "Graham's Victualing Tables." These were meant to help me estimate the quantity of provisions of various kinds needed for a given number of men for a given number of days. For example, one pound of flour plus one-fifth of an ounce of baking powder and some lard would provide flour tortillas sufficient for four meals per man, or more if an equivalent amount of rice were brought. Figures for sugar, beans, coffee, etc., were also arrived at—although some of them proved a little unreliable (ditto, supplies of cigarettes!). Their reliability did depend on the cook employed, and I soon learned to keep a sharp eye on the cooking fat if near a river, because extravagant amounts of it tended to be used for frying fish unless one doled it out personally.

So in 1962, emboldened by trials of GPS (Graham's Positioning System) and GVT (the Victualing tables of the same genius), I decided that the time had come to go in search of those enormous mounds—though I would soon realize how ignorant I still was of jungle know-how in general. Be that as it may, on the fifth of March, I boarded, in Guatemala City, an Aviateca DC-3 flight bound for Flores, Petén, bringing with me camping equipment and food supplies for two and a half weeks; and then from Flores took another flight to Carmelita. There I found a wide, grass landing field, on one side of which was a large *bodega* (warehouse) built of sawed lumber, with corrugated iron for a roof, where blocks of chicle were accumulated for shipment; next to it was the Aviateca office. An aguada at the near end of the field was dry. The houses, ramshackle thatched huts with walls of poles lashed together, were grouped near the bodega, and on the other side of the field there were a few more. One house of the main group, differing from them only by being larger, was proudly pointed out to me as the cinema, where a 16-mm film was shown once a week during the chicle season—provided the electric generator obliged by starting. There were also two tiny shops selling warm Coca-Cola and other sticky drinks, cigarettes, matches, flashlight batteries, lamp oil, cord, files (for sharpening machetes), halters, and other useful items. On the far side of the landing field, a stagnant stream provided water for washing, but since the surrounding forest had been cut back for several hundred yards all around to provide pastures for mules and a few head of cattle, the general impression of Carmelita that I received was bleak. Of course, it was the dry season—the off-season for chicle work— so not much activity could be expected there. The chicleros would all be living it up in the bars and brothels of Flores or Guatemala City.

For passing the night, I found a dreadfully dirty hut in someone's backyard where I could sling my hammock, also a comedor where chicken-foot soup was available, accompanied by tortillas so hard that they must have been leftovers from the previous day. But when it came to recruiting a guide and mule-driver, I had better luck. Carmen Domínguez and Carmen Guillén looked as if they might be intelligent and reliable men, and this they proved to be. When I tried to explain where I wanted to go—a site with huge pyramids, and with causeways radiating from it—Carmen Domínguez told me that within the past year he had taken a gringo couple to those very ruins: the camp near them was known as El Infierno. On returning to the States, the husband had written an article for a newspaper describing their expedition, and had sent him a copy.

When Carmen came back with it, I found it was from the Akron, Ohio, *Sunday Beacon-Journal* of 22 January 1961. In it the author described how he and his wife had ventured on this quest after seeing an aerial photograph of ruins with causeways radiating from them; this had been shown to him by an oilman friend of theirs who was working in Petén. Well, as an ambitious though utterly green explorer myself, I confess to having felt a little crestfallen at this news, but soon consoled myself with the thought that in such a big site this couple would surely have missed several features, so I shouldn't cancel the trip.

Owing to my inexperience, loading the mules took an age; the boxes were of very unequal weight, and I had omitted to bring a comal for cooking the tortillas, and a few other items. Still, we were off in good time to reach the small lagoon of Calabazal for the night. Two more days brought us to Las Ruinas, where I was shown a structure with a roof-comb embellished with modeled stucco figures of monkeys and other creatures, already somewhat damaged by senseless blows from machetes. These I remembered having seen illustrated in a book, where the site was called La Muralla.

Another two days' walk brought us to El Infierno. Shortly before reaching it we were skirting the edge of an apparently large but shallow lagoon with trees growing in it: these, I was told, were *palo tinte*, or logwood, the source of dye that attracted many buccaneers to the Yucatán Peninsula in the eighteenth and early nineteenth centuries. But when we had ascended a slope up to the ruins, a row of three tall pyramids seemed familiar, and I suddenly remembered having seen a photograph of them, later identified as being at a site named Naachtún. And yet, it had been to this very site that Carmen had brought the couple from Ohio. I was obliged to conclude that while their enterprise and energy had been praiseworthy, less so was the inclusion in that article of a photograph of the explorer's wife leaning against a low wall, with a caption describing it as the retaining wall of one of the causeways. For at Naachtún there was no such causeway.

I sat down to plot the previous day's trail. At La Muralla, I had become a little concerned because we were well to the east of the huge site, according to my reckoning. I found that from La Muralla our course had at first trended northeast, and then bore even more toward the east. Next day, then, we backtracked to a camp with the improbable name of La Balalaika, and from there reopened an overgrown trail to the west that brought us to El Sireno, where we joined an open trail leading to El Danto, and then to a camp named El Mirador. This name ("the lookout") sounded promising, and indeed, both Carmens confirmed that the camp owed its name to tall mounds.[3]

Soon we were passing mounds of various sizes, some of them six or eight meters in height, and came at last to a small aguada. Fortunately there was water in it (on subsequent visits it was usually dry), and in it were quite a number of *huilín*, small fish resembling catfish—and perhaps that is what they were, immature catfish. (As this aguada and many others like it dry up seasonally, I can only suppose that birds are responsible for renewing the stock by dropping eggs from fish they have caught in permanent streams.) A day or two later, one of the Carmens knelt by the edge, ruffled the surface of the water to attract the fishes' attention, and then cut at them with the blunt edge of his machete. In this way he made a useful contribution to dinner.

We made camp in a clearing near the aguada, and while Domínguez was busy cutting ramón for the mule (for we'd brought just one), and Guillén was making tortillas, I wandered off to look at an unusual grassy patch visible from the campsite. And there, set up in the middle of it, was a small cross of sapote wood, and on it was nailed a neatly cut piece of cedar wood trimmed to the shape of a heart. It bore a touching inscription that must have been carved with a very sharp pocket-knife:

PATRISIO GOMEZ FALLECIO EL 21 DE FEBRERO DE 1929 DE EDAD DE 11 AÑOS

Evidently, that patch of grass had been weeded by visiting chicleros ever since.

There was still enough time for a quick look at one of the really big mounds. I remember that we hadn't gone far, with my two companions leading the way, when I became aware of increasing darkness, and was thinking that a thundercloud must have obscured the sun; but then we came up against the foot of a mound. Neither to left nor right could I discern the corners of this mound, and then, with astonishment, I realized that it had

15.1 Wooden memorial tablet for Patrisio Gomes near the ruins of Mirador.

been the looming mass of this colossal mound, soaring up through the trees, that had dimmed the light by blotting out a large portion of the sky.

Next morning I began a compass-and-tape survey. I started, of course, with the big mound, which, as it stood by itself on flat ground, made it all the more impressive, for this showed it to be entirely man-made. Its base measured 125 by 110 meters. Now to measure its height: my primitive method relied on a hand-level, a pocket instrument containing a spirit-level by means of which objects exactly level with the eye can be identified. My elementary procedure was to first cut a straight stick to a length of 1.5 meters, and then, resting the instrument on top of the stick and keeping the bubble centered, swing the instrument a little to one side or the other while looking ahead, until some stone, or perhaps root, is found at exactly that level. Now, keeping one's eye fixed on that stone (or root), start climbing up until the measuring stick can be planted next to that chosen mark. Then say to oneself "one." Repeat procedure till one reaches the top, keeping count of these units. Finally, to obtain total height, multiply number of these units by 1.5 meters, add any portion of a 1.5-meter unit of height remaining at the summit, and there you have it!

The figure I obtained for this mound was 55 meters. Since this is exactly the height quoted in reports published after extensive research and professional surveying had been carried out in later years at Mirador, I have always wondered whether my unreliable measurement had been taken on trust, or whether, by astonishing luck, I'd actually arrived at the correct estimate! I say this because I have always found it quite difficult to concentrate on keeping a reliable count of the 1.5-meter units while climbing up a steep and often loose surface without letting one's eye stray from the chosen mark, while at the same time avoiding a stumble or other misadventure, such as grabbing a spiny palm to retain one's balance.

The view from the top of that mound was stupendous—indeed, a view indelibly imprinted in my mind. The most noticeable feature, of course, was the other great pyramid, standing several hundred meters away to the south, and just as tall. There were others to left and right and in between, some very large by ordinary standards, but in this setting almost puny. The causeways traversing the bajos also showed up plainly, an effect that puzzled me when I went to investigate them later, because in each case the surface stood little more than a meter above the surrounding terrain. Then I noticed that the trees growing on them were taller than the usual stunted growth in bajos; so the built-up roadbed must have provided more favorable conditions for growth.

Also visible from that high viewpoint were distant ruins apparently lying at the far ends of two of the causeways, one to the south, the other to the southeast. These I hadn't spotted in my examination of the aerial photos at Cartografía, as they were outside the area that I examined.

15.2 Mirador causeway.

Now I was faced with the formidable task of mapping these ruins. I had the Carmens cut me a network of straight but narrow *brechitas*, or lines of sight, with sharp bends where necessary. Sticks impaling numbered scraps of paper were set up at the bends, and when the distance between them was longer than my tape, others would be set up between them, as necessary. Once the distance and bearing between all of these had been measured with tape and compass, then the location of such features as corners of mounds relative to the nearest numbered stick could be measured.

This procedure differed in no respect from the method I'd used at Kinal. Any competent surveyor would now expect me to describe the plotting of these sticks (properly dignified as "stakes") on graph paper to verify a satisfactory "closure" of each loop of the survey network, before going on to plot features such as corners of structures or stairways. I must now confess that in this instance I took the risk of postponing any such plotting until after my return from this journey, the main reason being my failure to bring with me any suitable board to serve as a drafting table. All I could do for the moment was sketch the mounds, identifying each feature as it was measured with the number of the "shot." And because it's convenient, when writing up one's notes, to be able to refer to a specific structure by a name or number, I started bestowing upon the larger structures the names of my more cherished girlfriends—until the supply of them ran out.

As the survey proceeded I became disappointed at the lack of standing architecture among these ruins. In fact, I was unable to find more than one small area of masonry in the entire site, that being on the big, southern mound. I tried to think of an explanation for the unusually ruinous state of everything, and wondered if I might have found it upon examining a specimen of mortar from that patch of surviving masonry, for I detected in it a significant admixture of mud. Could, then, the poor quality of mortar have been responsible for such widespread collapse? Or was the noticeably poor quality of the local stone to blame?

Later, though, I began to suspect another explanation: perhaps the whole abandoned city was older than all others hitherto known in the Maya lowlands. This rash speculation was prompted by the peculiar conformation of the tallest temples at Mirador. They were unlike any that I knew of in the Maya area (with two exceptions) in that each of them stood on a high terrace, flanked by a pair of lesser pyramids built on the same terrace, but standing farther forward—an arrangement known as "triadic."[4] It was rather an adventurous theory for an amateur to propose, and on my return from Mirador I tried it out on some of my acquaintances, without receiving much encouragement.

As soon as the stores of essential foodstuffs had diminished to a three-day supply, we struck camp and headed back to Carmelita. The return journey to Flores was uneventful, and I went on by air to Guatemala City. There, I hastened to Cartografía, to spend the better part of a day studying aerial photographs. I studied the images of Mirador, of the causeways, and of the two sites they seemed to lead to. I also attempted to identify features (streambeds, aguadas, etc.) noted in my plot of the trail with those apparent in the aerial photos.

With that done, I flew back to Petén, this time to Sayaxché, with the idea of availing myself of Ledyard Smith's kind invitation to spend a few days downriver at the Peabody Museum's camp at Altar de Sacrificios. And there on the riverbank was Ledyard, supervising the loading of food supplies and other material. He was as hospitable as ever, and the three days I spent at his camp were not only restful and enjoyable, but also instructive. I learned a good deal in conversations with him, the graduate students, and some guests—Ed Shook and Aubrey Trik from the Tikal project, and Adolfo ("Fito") Molina,[5] whom I shall return to later.

Naturally, I took the opportunity during that weekend to plot my survey data from Mirador. This worked out well enough, apart from one unwelcome discovery— the very thing, in fact, that I had feared the plot might show. For in the middle of my map there proved to be a large, blank area into which I had never penetrated, and where, for all I knew, another large pyramid might lurk, as yet unmapped. At this point, I remember Ed Shook asking me at what scale I was plotting this plan.

"40 mm per 100 feet," I replied.

"Oh, but that will never do!" he exclaimed.

I explained that the only tape I possessed was marked in feet, whereas my graph paper was millimetric; and that, really, there was no problem, because the scale could easily be adjusted photographically.

By the fifth of April I was back at Carmelita, and three days later the two Carmens and I settled into a camp called Los Camarones, through which we had passed before, about two hours before reaching La Muralla. I halted there because comparison of my trail plot and the aerial photos indicated that the ruins at the end of the causeway running out from Mirador in a southeasterly direction ought to lie about two kilometers west of it.

We spent a whole day, and then part of the next, hunting for those ruins. My notes record that, most uncharacteristically, I then swarmed up a *liana*, Tarzan-like, to the lower branches of a tree, and having reached the top, was able to spot the ruins and take a compass reading on them. So we found them, and I spent three days mapping them, plus one more on the return journey. (When back in England, I contrived, with the help of the Motul Maya dictionary, to devise a name for these ruins: Nakbe, meaning "by the causeway.")

Then we went on to Mirador, mapped the large structure that I had missed, and improved the plan in other ways. Altogether, this rough plan had taken eleven days of compass-and-tape work to produce. Yet this poor specimen had to serve Brigham Young University's Mirador Project, some years later, for two whole seasons, owing to certain difficulties arising from their computerized survey system—and also the particular surveyor they had hired to operate it.

While preparing brief reports for publication on these two sites, I studied the aerial photographs in greater detail, so as to produce a map of the area in which bajos would be indicated by stippling, and the causeways (sacbes) traversing them would also be shown. It was while doing this that I noticed two more very prominent mounds set close together. One seemed to be pyramidal, and the other, about 100 meters to the east, was a very long mound oriented north and south. Together, the mounds resembled the bar and dot of the Maya hieroglyph for "six." Since I had no opportunity of visiting this site, nor another one lying at the end of a causeway to the south of Mirador, I labeled these two simply as "Y" and "Z" respectively.

The "Z" ruins, visible toward the south from Mirador, should be easy to find, I thought, since they lay only about nine miles from Carmelita, and seemed to be near a chicle camp known as Tintal. So on March 5 1966, I set out to find "Y," the "bar-and dot" ruins. Carmen Domínguez, one of the two Carmens, agreed to come with me again, with the *proviso* that he be allowed to make a quick trip first to his rancho to lock up. But when he appeared next morning, plainly stupefied with rum, I found another arriero, Ricardo Cus by name. A Kekchi from Senahu, he told me he knew all the trails in the area we were heading for.

We set out in a heavy rainstorm, and passed a miserably cold and wet night at Calabazal, where the champa roof leaked, and water ran down my hammock cord from the tree it was tied to. Next day, the weather improved, and we camped for the night at Lechugal, bothered there only by fleas, for evidently a party of chicleros had left there just ten days earlier, and the poor fleas were starving. Next morning we backtracked to the stony bed of a small, dry arroyo that crossed the trail. While studying Cartografía's aerial photos in Guatemala, I'd made a note that by following this, downstream to the west, to the point where another arroyo joins it, and then walking due north, we ought to hit the ruins.

This we did, and in due course ran slap into the long north-south mound that formed the "bar" of the Maya "numeral six" in the aerial photos. Ricardo was impressed, and I certainly never expected to hit the bull's eye so exactly. Then, after a quick look round, we continued north (cutting our way, of course) until we met an east-west trail that Ricardo knew of, going through campsites known as La Muerta (because a cook had died there) and Güiro (named for a calabash tree). I decided to make camp at Güiro, as there was a good clearing there already, and water, too; so I decided on "Güiro" as a provisional name for this site—better than "La Muerta," anyway. We spent two days surveying the ruins, and then set off heading west and then south, and reached Tintal camp, and once there, had no doubt whatever that this was site "Z."

(Later, in 1968, I found my way to another large mound, west of Tintal and locally known as La Florida, this one being largely of natural formation. Mistakenly, perhaps, I never returned to study it.)

I distributed copies of the maps I had made of the area between Carmelita and the northern border of Petén to various interested colleagues, and was therefore quite surprised, a few years later, to see a TV program about the "search" for "Wakna." This was a new name replacing my admittedly makeshift "Güiro" (but fated to be replaced, or perhaps improved by receiving another name, Wakahtal).

I was duly impressed—of course, by the potent collaboration that had been arranged, involving the California Institute of Technology, NASA (with its side-looking radar), Huntsville, Uncle Tom Cobley and All—linked of course by satellite communication. Thus assisted, these pioneers did succeed in "discovering" my old Güiro. I wonder how much this circus had cost: at least five thousand times more than my trusty old war-surplus compass, I suspect.

Since few readers of my report were likely to have access to stereo-viewers suitable for use with the 8-by-8-inch aerial stereophotos of Mirador that I had obtained from Cartografía, I cobbled up a simple apparatus employing half-silvered mirrors that provided a virtual stereo image of the site and surrounding area on a horizontal board. Then, having covered this board with a layer of plastilene, I was able to model it to correspond with the 3-D aerial image of the site. Finally, I made the forested areas on higher ground more distinct from the bajo areas by pricking them all over with a sharp point. My photograph of this is reproduced on page 42 of the report. But this, certainly, was not a technique that I expected anyone to copy!

CHAPTER 16

Afghanistan

On returning to England early in September 1962, much later in the season than usual, I was looking forward to spending a certain amount of time lazing about. But that illusion vanished even before I'd unpacked my bags, for my old friend Patrick Lindsay—now long lost to us, unfortunately—had left a series of messages, each more frantic than the last. Where in the name of Heaven was I?

I had agreed to join him on an adventure that did at first sound a little audacious: helping him drive a *maharaja's* 1932 Rolls-Royce from India to England, by way of Afghanistan—the car being one that had seen little use in recent years. But no departure date had been settled when I left for Guatemala.

The roots of this plan went back to Patrick and Amabel Lindsay's honeymoon. They had spent it at the Rambagh Palace, Jaipur, as guests of the maharaja and *maharanee*, known to their friends as Jai and Aisha. Patrick's passion for cars had taken him to the garages at the back of the palace, where, like most Indian princes, Jai (as I learned to call him) kept a stable of cars, each of which was dedicated to some specialized purpose: ornate limousines for state occasions, touring cars, *purdah* cars with windows of darkened glass, and cars for tiger hunting. Most of them were Rolls-Royces, with bodywork made to order.

One of these vehicles in particular had attracted Patrick's attention. It was a 1932 Rolls-Royce Phantom II touring car. Its sides were painted maroon, and the fenders, wheel-discs, and upper surface of the hood were of unpainted polished aluminum. The only discordant detail was the instrument panel, faced as it was with pink celluloid containing fish-scales or some other sparkly ingredient. According to its owner, the car's use in recent years had been mostly in first gear, in processions behind elephants. Indeed, the odometer confirmed its limited use: only twelve thousand miles in thirty-five years.

When the time came for the newlyweds to return home, Patrick plucked up courage to ask his host if there were a chance of him selling him the car?

"Oh no, no, Patrick," he replied, "I cannot sell it to you . . . . No, I will give it to you!"

From that point the idea of driving it back to England grew in Patrick's mind, and he decided that I should accompany him.[1] Patrick was a superb driver and pilot—he even flew his own Spitfire—but he was not a mechanic, and as an old friend he knew that I had driven my somewhat similar Phantom I to Naples and back, and then from New York to Los Angeles by a somewhat indirect route. He also knew that I had some knowledge of the mechanism of those cars, and—most important—I could handle the gears. Rolls-Royce gearboxes were marvels, but like other cars at the time they lacked synchromesh, so the modern driver, unpracticed in this forgotten art, makes horrible and potentially expensive noises when attempting to change gear, whereas those experienced in the art do so without the slightest noise or jerk.

Patrick, of course, had never forgotten his plan of driving the car to England, but for about ten years his work at Christies had kept him too busy to put it into effect. Then he saw—or made—an opportunity, and shipped off six new tires to Jaipur; and that, as far as I can remember, was the extent of his advance preparations, apart from alerting the Jaipurs of our approximate arrival date. But as he had had no way of getting in touch with me in the Guatemalan jungles, I found myself when back in London and weary from traveling, having to race about getting travel permits, a phial of Chlorodyne,[2] suitable clothes, and so forth, and join Patrick at Heathrow airport two days later. We flew to Delhi, and then on a feeder airline to Jaipur, I myself zombified by then from much travel and inability to sleep on that long flight.

At some time in those past ten years, the fortunes of Indian princes had been drastically reduced. The Rambagh Palace had been turned into a hotel, and the Jaipurs were now living in a comfortable house that previously had housed their British agent. The next day we visited the garages behind the palace to inspect the car, which had already had its new tires fitted. I raised the hood to obtain some impression of past maintenance, but Patrick hissed that as a guest of the maharajah, this was not suitable behavior. So I asked the "garage-wallah" about the oil.

"Oh, engine-oil verry clean, verry clean engine-oil!"

"Well, I really would like you to change it before we leave."

"Verry well, sahib."

Aisha was sure we wouldn't get farther than ten miles before it broke down, but she was too pessimistic, for it ran a good 140 miles without that happening. I diagnosed fuel starvation, and dismantled one fuel pipe, cleaned it, and the engine started again, but after a few miles, stopped again. This procedure was repeated, until at last I found that cotton-waste had somehow found its way into the main fuel line between tank and pump.

Between Agra and Delhi a new problem arose: overheating. I made various attempts to clean out the cooling system, with only partial success, so in Delhi I took the car to a garage equipped with a hydraulic lift to work on that problem, and also change the oil—for I'd lost all confidence in the work of Jai's garage-hand. But try as I might, I could not loosen the drain plug in the oil pan. So instead, I loosened the aluminum plate in which it was set by removing twelve small bolts. I pried it away from its gasket—then there was a considerable pause before oil, or rather, the thickest imaginable black goo, began to ooze out. Yes, the oil had been topped up in the past, but clearly never *changed*. I wondered how much sludge had accumulated and hardened in the crankshaft oilways, and how soon a main bearing or big-end would fail.

16.1 The Rolls stuck in soft sand in Afghanistan.

16.2 *Traffic jam in Afghanistan.*

Once more on the road, and shortly after leaving Lahore, we encountered a tributary of the Indus. It was about a hundred yards wide and two feet, six inches deep, so we had to recruit a number of locals to help us push the car to the other bank. On dry land again, I would have liked to drain all the oil (and water, presumably) from the pan, including remnants of sludge, there and then, but couldn't because we did not have enough oil to refill it—and were told not to expect any for the next twenty-five miles. But that was not a matter of concern: Rolls-Royce bearing loads are very low, and an oil/water emulsion would suffice.

The Khyber Pass presented no difficulties, nor did a terrible stretch of road leading to Kabul. There, our host for two nights, the Indian ambassador, insisted that the only way through Afghanistan into Iran was along the asphalt road through Kandahar, which had been built under U.S. auspices. That route sounded very boring, for we'd brought with us a copy of Robert Byron's *The Road to Oxiana*, and were anxious to see the northern regions.

From conversations haltingly conducted with various people, taking a northern route did seem feasible. We needed permits to travel through that area, but these were obtained in Kabul without difficulty. Thereafter, two matters of concern remained.

One was the availability of gasoline; so to be on the safe side we hoisted a fifty-gallon drum on the backseat and had it filled. Indeed, for the entire distance from Kabul to the Iranian border we never encountered a single gas station or pump, yet that drum proved to be unnecessary, for in every small town someone could provide us with fuel: he would have a large galvanized tank of it somewhere at the back of his house, and would shuttle to and fro with a tin pitcher and funnel.

Then there was the route to consider. At that time, the notion of a northern highway connecting Kabul to Herat with a tunnel through an eleven-thousand-foot mountain was no more than a twinkle in the eye of Russian military planners. We would have to make our way along rough tracks, but had confidence in Rolls-Royce craftsmanship and our new tires. Our highest priority in planning our route beyond Kabul was a visit to the great cave-monastery of Bamiyan—the world's greatest Graeco-Buddhist monument—and we were assured that it was accessible by a road that ran along the banks of a stream in an open valley.

16.3 A Kuchi nomad boy on migration with his family in Afghanistan.

16.4 Kuchi child.

We had, however, obtained a large-scale map, and on it traced another route, a minor road running through the Hadjigak Pass, eleven thousand feet above sea level. Thinking this route might be more interesting, we took it, and were glad we did, for the views were splendid. It was fascinating to see caravans of Kuchi nomads with camels and donkeys moving down to warmer regions for the winter. Shortly before the top of the pass we came upon a broken-down bus and had no difficulty towing it to the top, with the weight of the extra gasoline over the back axle greatly assisting traction.

Many descriptions and photographs of Bamiyan have been published, but none could do it justice. The beauty of the place was unforgettable, for there stood the great Buddha, 160 feet high, carved out of rock within a niche. Its walls were once covered with polychrome paintings, some of them still visible above the Buddha's head, and to see them close at hand there was an interior stairway leading to the top of it. There were actually two Buddhas in niches, but out of ignorance we failed to see the other.

Even the least imaginative visitor must have conjured up some vision of the hundreds of cells, passageways and stairs dug into the mudstone cliff, as they were more than a thousand years ago, when that labyrinth was occupied by monks: one could almost see the Buddhist pennants and hear blasts of great horns. These must have been one of the world's greatest-ever monuments to piety—just as they became, conversely, a most dreadful monument to religious intolerance when the faces of the Buddhas were sliced off by Muslims in the eleventh century. This shocked me more powerfully than any other hate-driven destruction of religious art that I had seen. Worse was to come, of course, when the Taliban finished the task by destroying the statues completely. That act of barbarism defies description.

Next, we drove thirty miles west to see the lakes of Band-i-Ameer. These were formed over thousands of years by mineral deposits from water seeping out of the nearby rock face. The buildup of these deposits formed natural dams, elevating the lakes far enough above the surrounding terrain to make possible the construction of primitive vertical turbines for powering a grain mill.

The road north from Bamiyan continues through a narrow and steep-sided ravine. At the bottom of this chasm is fertile soil, and beside the road runs a stream, the Daria Qanduz. At intervals, some of the water is canalized at a lesser gradient for irrigation of the tiny plots, and every so often the road crosses one of these ducts. These bridges may be only a foot high, but to a long car they present a problem, as there is no possibility of leaving the road and finding an alternative course. When faced with the worst of these bridges we decided there was nothing for it but to jump it.

16.5 Bamiyan, before its destruction.

*16.6 A mud-brick fort that Patrick Lindsay
and I passed in central Afghanistan.*

I backed up for more than a quarter of a mile, then accelerated at full power. On hitting the bridge there was a jarring crash, with the front wheels briefly leaving the ground; then I found the car had ceased to steer, skidding instead to a halt. We got out, fearing severe damage to the wheels, for they had wire spokes like those of bicycles (but much thicker). However, they were intact. Looking under the car, I could see that the bridge had caught the car's soft underbelly, which was protected against dust by a tray of light aluminum. The hump of the bridge had broken through this tray and caught the two brake-cable levers, forcing them backward, where they were detained by the crumpled metal of the tray. A few well-directed blows freed them, and we were on our way.

At last, we emerged from that extraordinary gorge and made our way to Pul-i-Kumri. Our next trial was a long stretch of desert. The gravel track we had been following suddenly disappeared beneath sand and was replaced by three faint tracks: to the left, to the right, and straight on. We chose the middle way, hoping it would lead us to Mazar-i-Sharif.

All went well for a time until we strayed from the barely distinguishable beaten track, and we found ourselves stuck in soft sand. Attempts to rock the car free were futile. We had some water and a little food, but the situation was certainly worrisome, as we hadn't seen any other vehicle in this desert. At long last a small cloud of dust appeared, far off. As it approached we could discern within the dust an Afghan bus— that is, a stake-sided truck with boards arranged transversely as benches, and the driver's cabin gorgeously and imaginatively decorated with scenes of a Nirvana well-populated with sloe-eyed maidens, fabulous winged beasts, and sparkling streams.

The driver halted and the passengers, all of them men, poured out. They were very willing to help, but could we get them all to heave on the rope at the same time? Having picked up a smattering of Pashto, we did our best to render into the vernacular "one, two, three, heave!" It worked.

Our helpers had only to bring us a little closer to the bus before a tow-line could be hitched to it, and we were pulled from the sand. We thanked all concerned profusely and inquired if a few of them might like to complete their journey by Rolls, in case a little help should be needed farther on. Volunteers readily appeared and we reached Mazar-i-Sharif. The next day we halted at Balkh to see the remains of what has been claimed as the world's most ancient city. Now, all one can see are eroded mud-brick walls, although these are still impressive.

Our course now lay to the west, and for much of the route we were within a parched desert, with faint outlines of distant mountains to the south, sometimes visible through a hot, purplish haze. Yet here and there, astonishingly, there was cultivation, made possible by moisture persisting beneath the sand. Occasionally, we came upon informal markets where magnificent, bearded men wearing striped gowns were selling melons and black wool from the fat-tailed sheep we saw on the hillsides. The men weighed their merchandize with balances, using stones as weights.

On we went, to Maimena and the Murghab River. There were woods, and more cultivation. We became excited upon spotting on our map a notation, Gin Factory. Could it be that here, perhaps because of a different religious affiliation, alcohol was legal? The thought of gin and tonic spurred us on, but the only gin we found was a cotton gin, for now we were in cotton country.

It is a pleasure to recollect the friendliness we encountered, and the willingness of most Afghans to try to communicate with strangers. The car, of course, was a source of wonderment wherever we went, but neither adult nor child ever touched it; they would do no more than make stroking or patting motions without touching the metal. Later, in Iran, bystanders would demonstrate their greater familiarity with cars by leaving handprints on the polished radiator while kicking a tire or two and exclaiming, "Ah, Ford . . . "

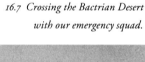

16.7 Crossing the Bactrian Desert
with our emergency squad.

16.8 Kuchi nomad.

Before we left London we had debated whether to buy revolvers, since the image of ferocious Afghans keeping British and Russian forces at bay in the nineteenth century dominated our imaginations. To our surprise we found them to be as peace-loving and well-mannered as any people—but then we were unaware of having chanced upon the brief Golden Age of modern Afghanistan, a time when music was heard in the streets and women could show their faces, and even sit as deputies in the national parliament.

Patrick and I derived enormous pleasure from our escapade. A more enjoyable motoring adventure could scarcely be imagined. So it became especially painful to read of the catastrophes that later befell this unlucky people.

We drove on to Herat, crossed the border to Mashhad, stopped to admire the great minaret at Gumbad-i-Kavus, and reached Teheran. There we turned south, because Patrick couldn't spare the time to drive all the way back to England, and in any case both of us had some familiarity with most of that route, save for the portion in eastern Turkey. So we went on to Isfahan, admiring there the Chehel Sutun Palace and the Great Mosque, then to Persepolis, and finally to Abadan, where we consigned the car for shipment to England—and then flew back home.

CHAPTER 17

Machaquilá

In the 1960s vast areas of Petén remained unpenetrated by modern exploration, and it was on these areas that I focused my attention, seeking leads from groups such as the chicleros and oil companies who ventured deeper into the uncharted regions than others. I've mentioned in passing the valuable contributions to Maya archaeology made by two oilmen working in Petén, who more than any others went out of their way to report ruins found in their concessions. These were Larry Vinson of Esso and John Gatling of Sun Oil. Vinson himself wrote up and published the first, if necessarily brief, report on a previously unknown site, Aguateca;[1] while John Gatling encouraged others, myself among them, with active support. So by 1961, with my new interest in recording ruins as an enthusiastic amateur (for that's all I was), I had learned to value oil company geologists as sources of information. They were, after all, the first educated people to penetrate in any numbers into almost all regions of Petén, and as such would be likely to mark on their maps, and even perhaps report to the authorities (as required), any ruins with visible monuments or standing buildings.

A few well-educated men had indeed been sent by the chewing-gum companies to Petén quite early in the century, but they themselves rarely ventured far into the forest or off its main trails. However, the chicleros, native men working for the chewing gum companies, came to be the predominant informants as to the whereabouts of previously unknown archaeological sites, and often served as guides to the few who would tromp about the jungle. By the 1920s, archaeologists of the Carnegie Institution of Washington, led by Sylvanus Morley, had already taken advantage of the information that chicleros and their bosses could contribute to their own efforts in that area. Naturally, they concentrated on the area easiest to travel in, that being the northeastern quadrant of the province, where the best chicle was found. *Caminos de área* were maintained (these being tracks for mule trains wide enough for two mules to walk side-by-side, and generally free of low branches), although going could still be very difficult in swampy bajos during the rainy season. The remainder of that vast lowland plain was to remain almost trackless and archaeologically *terra incognita* for another quarter of a century.

With Kinal behind me, the next oil company whose local headquarters I visited in Guatemala City was Signal, but Lloyd Miller, its representative, told me—from across a vast and astonishing mahogany desk, deeply carved with designs found on a Maya vase in the American Museum of Natural History—that his crews had not encountered any ruins of note.

Then I moved on to the offices of the Union Oil Company, in whose camp at Sebol, two years earlier, I had met Sam Bonis. In these offices, I had the good fortune to encounter the Costa Rican brothers Escalante, who told me that a short distance downstream from a camp of theirs, on the left bank of the Río Machaquilá, they had found extensive ruins.

They showed me a carved block of stone they had found among those ruins and had brought back by helicopter (the stone was serving that day as a doorstop). The stone was fine-grained and hard, and the beautifully carved hieroglyphs had survived in mint condition. The Escalantes told me they had also seen several fallen stelae among those ruins, and a partially preserved building of excellent masonry.

A map of the company's concession was produced, showing it to comprise a large part of southeastern Petén. On it was marked a long brecha, or wide track, which their crews had cut from near Poptún, the principal settlement in that area, heading northwest until it reached the nearby Río Machaquilá. From there, the brecha followed the river, mostly following its right, or northern, bank; this was because two or three streams entered it from the south, and these, while narrow, were too deep for laden mules to cross. Thus, it was possible to bypass those tributaries by crossing to the right bank at one of the few wide shallows where the river, flowing over rock, was fordable—as long as the river was not in spate.

The river's course thereafter inclined to the southwest, and the brecha ended at the company's "Campamento Final," near which, on a hilltop, they had opened a helicopter landing patch. The camp was also near the point where the river's course divides, to unite once more several kilometers downstream. During the dry season, the western branch carried all the water, but it was on the left bank of the seasonally dry branch that the ruins lay. They also gave me the names of two of the men who had worked for them, both residents of Poptún.

At that time, no published map of that area showed anything but the river, but what would that matter, I thought, with guides available and a trail unlikely to be badly overgrown? So, wasting no time, I bought provisions, caught the next Aviateca DC-3 to Poptún, and was soon conferring with one of the men whose names I'd been given, Pablo Paredes, a tall, slim, brown-haired man of calm demeanor, perhaps in his middle thirties. All was arranged expeditiously. The other Union Oil employee, Enrique, would also join us; Jaime, of mixed east Indian and Mexican blood (but a British Honduran subject) would come as cook (wearing a bluc visor that gave him the appearance of a clerk or a bygone Wimbledon tennis star); and the arriero, or mule driver, would be Brígido, a reserved and taciturn man.

17.1 Pablo Paredes and I, washed but still exhausted, on our return from Machaquilá.

On Thursday, the eighteenth of May, 1961 (the year before my trips to El Mirador and Afghanistan), we set out on horseback through pine-studded savanna, reaching the edge of the rain forest just two hours later. From there, the horses were sent back, and we and the cargo mule walked on, and in half an hour arrived at a very large spring, the source of the Arroyo Concomá. This we followed for one and a half hours before reaching the village of that name, and found it populated exclusively by Kekchi Mayas. One very poor house in the village into which I poked my head contained only two objects worth more than about twenty-five cents, the corn grinder and an axe, while the washing line seemed to display a collection of rags, rather than clothes. But the house we stayed in, that of José, was much larger and better furnished.

At 2 a.m. the women of the house arose and started grinding corn and making tortillas. Here, they were using ashes instead of lime for softening the corn, and because tortillas made of masa prepared in this way were said to last a week, instead of two days, I bought a supply. For the hospitality we had received, though, our host would not accept a penny.

Setting out early next day, we arrived within half an hour close enough to the Río Machaquilá to hear it, but when, a little farther on, we came to its bed, it was dry, for this river, over much of its course, runs underground during the dry season. It wasn't until we reached our next camping place, Machaca, that we saw the water again.

On the following day, after two or three hours' walk, we came to a small spring, and then noticed that we had lost the Union Company's marks on trees, and were on a chiclero trail. We blundered on, although conscious of going in the wrong direction, until we came to a range of precipitous cliffs and difficult passes, and finally into a natural amphitheater with vertical rock walls. It may have been terrain similar to this that caused Hernan Cortés such difficulties in this area when, in 1525, he was heading for Honduras, having passed through what is now Flores. In any case, we turned back at once to that small spring and camped there, having endured a difficult day, with no more than three leagues gained in the right direction. But we dined well, the men having bagged two birds.

The next day, three hours of easy walking on a clear trail through groves of *corozal* palms (with opposed, rather than fan-like, fronds) brought us again to the big river and a chicle camp, established by men from Concomá, but there was no one there—all of them being out working just then. Fish and birds were being smoked on a rack of sticks over the fire, and upon a heavier grill of poles over dying embers below, and covered with palm leaves, were roasted pieces of wild pig. We helped ourselves to a piece of pig, leaving twenty-five cents for it, as a snack before going on our way. I also took the opportunity of having a refreshing bath in the blue-green, milky water of the river.

Soon, we found a good trail, and followed it for three and a half hours, and then camped by the river, where I found a little sandbank to laze upon in the sun. The men caught *machaca*, (the bony but tasty fish after which the river is named), and we roasted a faisán.

In the morning, the men had upset stomachs, from which, this time, I was spared (having suffered one on the first day out). We followed the river, passing numerous waterfalls and cascades up to three meters high. Eventually we made camp in a pokey place near a stagnant pool, and from there for the next four days, we commuted to the ruins, six kilometers away. Although a campsite nearer the ruins would have eliminated some, or nearly all, of the two and a half hours of walking each day, there had been no certainty of finding water along the seasonally dry branch of the river.

The ruins were more exciting than anything—short of Bonampak—that I could have hoped to find. With only one exception, the stelae had been erected along two sides of a plaza, and almost all had fallen face-down; this gave me hope that their sculptured faces would be well preserved. There was also a large altar supported on four cylindrical supports and now covered by a thick mat of leaf mold, rootlets, and moss. Two buildings, at least, were constructed of most beautifully cut stone blocks—and in all my wanderings since then I have not seen finer. The fact that one of these buildings retained a portion of its roof vault was also interesting, because the prevailing opinion at the time was that the Maya of southern Petén did not construct vaulted roofs.

This little expedition had been made simply as a reconnaissance, bringing enough food for only a few days' sojourn at the site. So I decided to limit my activities to mapping it, using compass and tape. With the long commute from our camp, the survey took four days. Then we packed up for the return journey, which was accomplished without incident, although rain made the track very sticky and slippery in places, and I slipped more than I usually did because the heel of one boot had come off—with the other threatening to follow suit.

The four men and I, and one mule, had been away for twelve days on this trip, and the total expenses amounted to about $150. On reflecting that the same sum of money could have been spent on a single evening at the El Morocco nightclub in New York, this did seem a bargain.

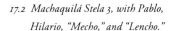

17.2 Machaquilá Stela 3, with Pablo, Hilario, "Mecho," and "Lencho."

Now I would have to lay my plans for a longer sojourn at those ruins in the following year—ruins that I decided to name simply "Machaquilá." I thought it would be worth trying to make latex molds of all the well-preserved sculpture, and estimated that this might take three weeks of work at the site, and about twenty gallons of latex. I then had the idea of requesting the British Museum, which had not been active in the Maya area for some time, to make a grant for its purchase, and for them to undertake the production of casts from the resulting molds. On this one occasion I did ask David Crawford, then the chairman of the trustees, if he would consider my application kindly. But I doubt if the success of this application can be attributed entirely to his advocacy, for the other trustees were far from being cyphers.

If the stelae were to be molded, then they would have to be raised up on edge, so hydraulic jacks would be needed. These, Ledyard Smith of the Peabody Museum very kindly agreed to lend me when the season's work at Altar de Sacrificios had ended.

Money in my bank account being another necessity, I persuaded Weidenfeld and Nicolson, the publishers, to commission me to take about half of the photographs for a coffee-table book entitled *Great Royal Palaces*. Doing this entailed work at Hampton Court, Holyrood House, Stockholm, Copenhagen, and other palaces (including the palace of Monaco, which strictly speaking is not royal at all). Since I had been a playmate of Prince Rainier at Brodick when we were boys, I had the temerity, upon arrival, to telephone the private quarters with the idea of renewing our acquaintance—and was rewarded with an invitation to accompany Nanny to the theater, which I did with pleasure.

That photographic commission was barely profitable, but what else could an almost unknown photographer expect? Then suddenly my problem was solved in a most unexpected way: my grandmother decided to pass on to her grandchildren the proceeds from selling the remainder of the lease on her corner house in Belgrave Square (which then became the Portuguese Embassy). My portion, about eight thousand pounds, made possible several years' work in Guatemala, for which I shall always be grateful.

My ambitions for field work in the following year, 1962, were not centered exclusively on Machaquilá. Far from it; there was work I was anxious to do in northern Petén, and I knew from experience that water in that area dries up so early in the dry season that work cannot be contemplated any later than March. The same considerations didn't apply to Machaquilá, especially since I had been assured that a few large pools of water remained in the river's dry branch near the ruins throughout the dry season.

So I arrived in Poptún on about the twenty-third of May. Pablo Paredes was awaiting my arrival and had persuaded his young brother-in-law, Hilario, a cheerful and intelligent young man, to join us. Six months earlier, Hurricane Hattie had caused terrible devastation in British Honduras, especially in Belize City, noted for having an elevation of about one meter above sea level. Naturally, the newspapers reported nothing about the area around Poptún, so I was relieved to hear in Poptún that damage farther west was unlikely to be serious.

Early in the morning of 26 May we began loading the miscellaneous sacks, cases, and tubs of latex. Thinking that these seemed too much for three mules, I offered to hire another, but Lencho, the arriero (whose proper name was Lorenzo), seemed satisfied with the awkward, top-heavy loads. No sooner had we left than a mule put a foot on a weak board in a bridge and fell, with one leg down the hole. We hastened to unload him, and extricated him unhurt and quite calm; but he was very reluctant to cross bridges after that. In the savanna, we saw a lot of trees blown down by wind—here, surprisingly, from the west. The first stretch of high forest was also in a mess, but farther on it was perfectly clear.

At Concomá, everything was as before, and José invited us to stay once more in his house, volunteering, moreover, to come with us to the ruins. As dusk fell, I lit the Coleman lamp, and José played one of his two homemade violins, which had one

*17.3 José at Concomá, playing his homemade fiddle,
the night before leaving for Machaquilá.*

string of nylon, the others being fiber from corozo palm. He knew only one tune, really, but it was nicely played, soft and soothing. His little boy, only one and a half years old, began dancing—never having seen anyone dance, as we were told. There was quite a squash at night, with about twelve adults and a few children sleeping in the house.

We decided to pursue the course taken the year before as far as Machaca, but then—instead of following the river, which makes a great arc to the north—we would follow a more direct route that had been opened before the hurricane. Pablo, Hilario, and three others then set out with axes to clear the trail to the next campsite. On the following day, we decided that the men would go out to clear the trail, but camp would not be broken until a campsite named Corozal had been reached. Meanwhile I lay guiltily in my hammock, reading *Lord Jim* and dozing, conscious of my uselessness with an ax. Soon after breakfast, a mule standing nearby started violently, and there was a shrill scream. We rushed to see what was up. There were crashing noises in the tangled mess where trees had fallen, and then I saw that it was a tapir with a young one (the scream, I believe, having come from a mule). All I could really see was a gray back, taller than any pig. Then there was a huge splash, and I caught sight of what looked like a small hippo, and a smaller one, swimming underwater.

I now learned that chicleros had cleared the trail to Corozal soon after the hurricane, but then a lesser storm hit, the effects of which we were now clearing up. With the three extra men I had recruited at Concomá, we would soon run short of staples, and unless the going became easier, I would certainly run out of money for their wages.

On the fourth day I sent José back to Poptún to buy twenty-five pounds of flour, two of lard, and five of rice. On the fifth, I went to watch the men working, and did a little amateur wielding of the machete myself. In one place a tamarind tree had fallen across the narrow defile between two hills, leaving no possibility of a detour. There was nothing for it but to cut with axes through the tough, fibrous wood in two places so that a section could be rolled away (chain saws being then unknown in Poptún). About three-quarters of our trail was now completely new, and I found that returning from the progress made in two and a half hours took me fifteen minutes. But then, in the evening, José trotted back with fresh supplies, plus two very welcome pineapples.

We moved on to a campsite by a pool in the otherwise dry riverbed. Then I noticed the mules making purposefully for the riverbank and, hearing heavy splashing, went to investigate. They were swimming to one end of the pool, scrambling out, and ambling off down the dry bed of the river. I caught one, but the bay *mula* and the *macho* ran ahead of me. I called Lencho, who managed to catch those crafty beasts.

In the evening we erected two great beams at either side of the plastic shelter, for hammocks to be slung from it, like a dormitory. When the time came to retire, a great

17.4 Lencho and his pack mule, struggling through the storm damage on the way to Machaquilá.

deal of adjustment was needed, causing laughter, José in particular getting a lot of fun out of such things.

On the seventh day, I sent a man off to hire another mule, and bring in a *quintal* (one hundred pounds) of maize, because the Concomá lads feel weak on a diet of flour tortillas. I gave him also a letter to mail to John Gatling, requesting a loan of one hundred dollars so as to be sure of being able to pay the men's wages, since I had decided that I was by no means going to give up and waste the effort we had already made.

That night, I overheard the men talking in their hammocks about the stelae at Machaquilá. Lencho said something about the writing on them not being understood, whereupon Pablo put in, "Oh, but don Juan can read it; he's not a mere geologist—*they* can't read it; but he's an *arch*-geologist!" (I only wished I could!).

Next day, when the Concomá lad returned from Poptún with the mule and provisions, I accompanied him to the place where the men were working. I carried a bucket of water for them (because the jerrycan had been filled with the flour). What a strain that was, walking six kilometers along a partially cleared track without stumbling!

On the tenth day, Lencho and I had a tremendous battle to prevent the mules landing on the east side of the pool, intending to run for home. The three of them swam about for a long time, probing for soft spots in our defenses, while we retaliated with blows from branches. Eventually, tired out with swimming, the wretches retreated. Poor Lencho was worried and depressed by the mules. He felt for them, was more withdrawn than ever, and would scarcely eat.

I noted that the chiclero ulcer on my arm (leishmaniasis caught from an insect bite at Aguateca) was growing in size quite noticeably. Pablo went off to find a *varrillo*, or Santa Maria tree. He told me its resin had cured the ulcer he had in just the same place, but unfortunately in my case, it didn't.

Following an afternoon storm, Lencho announced that the mules had run away, but wouldn't get farther than Corozal, where he had erected a *tranca*, or barrier, and on the following day he brought them back—looking quite unrepentant, so we loaded them up and moved on for a two-and-a-half-hour advance. I feared that since José was unlikely to return until the following day, we'd be rather short of food in the meantime, but to my surprise and pleasure, whoops announced his arrival with a mule, plus Pedro Ik, and all the things I had ordered, including a forty-pound lard tin for cooking the maize in, and a grinder. He really was an excellent fellow. Everyone was very cheerful, and the sheer numbers of us, nine, made it a party. In addition, he had brought a bird (*mancolola* or *tinamou*) for supper.

After supper, Mecho entertained us with accounts of extraordinary experiences. First, there was that day in 1953 when he was at Paxcamán, a settlement past which the road now runs from Flores to the junction of roads leading to Tikal and the Belize border. The village is arranged around an aguada, and on that day, the water suddenly started draining out of it, forming a whirlpool. The earth shook, trees fell and were sucked down, and the aguada became quite empty. The noise of this occurrence was heard in Flores, Mecho said. Later, when it rained, the aguada filled again. (I went to Paxcamán later and heard some confirmation of the story.)

Geologists consider seismic activity in Petén as highly unlikely, but I have heard another story, possibly dating from the same time, of heavy tremors at a place about twenty kilometers northwest of Paxcamán, which is still known as El Temblor ("The Earthquake"); a small Early Classic site is found there.

The interest aroused by this story encouraged Mecho to tell us another of his experiences. This concerned his encounter with a *sisimit* near the Río Chiquibul. This stout, furry beast strikes such fear into you that your gun drops from your nerveless fingers. Ingeniously, its feet are attached back-to-front, so that trackers never find it. While it usually walks on four legs, it is capable of standing on only two (the hind legs, presumably). Also known as La Peluda, it is the subject of many folktales.

17.5 José of Concomá.

From general conversation, I collected some indications of possible value in weather forecasting. Signs that it is going to rain: a tree falling; a wet frog falling on you; hearing a call, "quo-quo-quo-quo" from a small, black bird; a plague of little flies; a tilted moon; much heat.

Signs that it is not going to rain: none that anyone could suggest.

Since we were, by then, scarcely halfway to our destination, I'll spare the reader further details of the journey. Of course, the mules managed to run away again—twice, in fact! What they need to keep them contented is a mare as madriña (godmother). But these poor beasts were also hungry; they were used to grass, and some of them to ramón (breadnut), which was scarce. A mule was then sent to Poptún, to bring in another load of maize, and also from there, letters were mailed for me. One was to Pat Culbert requesting him to lend me a hundred dollars and send it to Poptún, and another to my bank in London asking them to telegraph money to me in Guatemala, so that I could repay his loan and John Gatling's.

A few hundred yards short of our destination, the fates—furious that in the face of all their contrivings we had got this far, and thus all the more determined to thwart our plans—made their desperate last bid to keep us out. Across the narrow passage between the steep riverbank and a vertical rock wall at the foot of a hill, they threw down a great tree, its roots up against the rock, its branches in the water. It was a *chechem negro*, notorious for its highly caustic sap. Cutting it with an axe carries a high risk of droplets of sap causing burns on the skin—and far more serious trouble if those droplets get in the eye. Somehow, though, the boys won through.

Thursday, 21 June: The longed-for day—the twenty-seventh of this appalling journey. We were finally at the ruins, and I thought, how lucky I was to have Pablo in charge, and such a willing crew of men.

Now they set about sweeping the campsite clean, as Pablo said they used to do when working for Union Oil (to reveal any snakes), and in the afternoon we started cleaning up the plaza. We also cut away the tree that was holding Stela 4 in its embrace. Next day, Pablo and two lads went off to the heliport to look for carved stones left there by the oilmen, like the one I had seen at Union's office, and they came back to report finding one resembling it, and two others, smaller and broken. They had brought them down to the trail, where the Concomá boys would be able to load them on their mule when leaving.

When, later, an account of my journey to Machaquilá was published, I heard from Linton Satterthwaite, a veteran archaeologist at the University of Pennsylvania, that someone at Union Oil had offered him a flight to El Final for a quick look at the ruins. He took the flight, but for some reason his excursion from there to the ruins had not been practicable.

Those Concomá boys would not, however, be leaving until two days later, because I would need their help in raising the very heavy Stela 10. Moving heavy monoliths with inadequate lifting gear is a most alarming (and in fact dangerous) job, and I was then relying more on manpower than I ever would later, when I had devised a better technique. At one point, I needed a stone to put under the jack, and José was just putting one in place when Pablo cried out, "It's got a nose and mouth!" And so it had: a face with eyes closed, almost in full relief, with a tenon at the back (it is now in the National Museum).

Great quantities of fish and birds were being smoked that evening for the Concomá contingent to take home, and at 6 a.m. they left, with Pablo accompanying them to where the heliport stones lay, to supervise the packing and loading of them. Then he returned, and we would pick up the stones at Concomá on our way home.

We spent fifteen days at the ruins, almost entirely engaged in turning stelae or fragments thereof, washing them, applying coats of latex, and photographing them as soon as the latex was removed—because then the carved surface would be spotlessly clean. But because all of the stones were damp through and through, the latex molds never dried on them completely. So I had a hut built, with walls of palm fronds, and shelving inside. A fire was kept going within, and the molds were laid on the shelves to dry out completely. Palm roofs were also built over various stelae and fires kept going under them in an attempt to speed the drying of latex on sodden stone.

After ten days at the ruins, Mecho, the cook, gave notice ("Mecho" was the familiar abbreviation for Nemesio, I discovered, just as Lencho is for Lorenzo). We were not, he said, *conforme*, and there was a good deal of truth in that, but I knew that cooking was not his real profession. All this was the result of a mild reproof I gave him the night before for taking it into his head not to make coffee, but instead, *atol* (a thick, maize-based beverage), and I'd been very tired and looking forward to coffee. But things were smoothed over.

Not that there was much left to cook, anyway. The salt supply had now come to an end—a serious problem. But two days later I was surprised to find my beans salted; a little cache of salt, twisted up in plastic film, had been found in Pedro Ik's empty palm shelter. There wasn't much, but I thought it a propitious moment to ask if the men would stay one more day—on double pay? They agreed to, and I spent the time turning the stelae back face-down and doing other odd jobs.

Next morning, the river had risen considerably because of rain in the night. We packed up and left, feeling weak and exhausted before we started. For much of the day

17.6 Mecho, "el mago de la cocina"
(the kitchen wizard).

we were walking through mud, or with water up to the ankles, but somehow we managed to stagger through to La Cuchara in eight and a quarter hours, without stopping. Next day, after some delay occasioned by Lencho's need to mend one of his boots, the sole of which had come off in the muddy bajo, we set off at 8:15. At La Machaca it was obvious we would have trouble crossing the river farther up, and there at the crossing Pablo and Hilario were awaiting us to help carry the cargo over.

Pablo, in fact, carried nearly all of it across, walking on a tree trunk, which was about fifteen feet above the water. Then again, farther on, we had to cross again, and there it was more difficult, partly because much of the only suitable tree trunk was underwater and slippery, and more important, there wasn't a good place for the mules to enter the water. Pablo, in the river, pulled at the rope of the mula, and she dived in and disappeared completely underwater, reappearing about three seconds later with upper lip drawn up, the nostrils clamped shut into two slits, and showing pink gum. She swam successfully to the other side, but the girth had broken and the packsaddle was floating downstream. One way and another, crossing that river took nearly two hours.

Lucky now with the weather, we reached Corozal at 6:30, extremely tired. We had excellent faisan, but only one tortilla each. The last day's march was uneventful. We stopped for the stones at Concomá, but received the bad news that the horse had become so tired and weak that the stones had had to be abandoned. Perhaps they were left by the side of the trail in one of the areas that were underwater when we trudged back, so that we missed them. In any case, we made it back to Poptún with food supplies amounting to a little pepper and some baking powder.

Early in 1968, having returned for some reason to southeastern Petén, I took the opportunity to call on Pablo and his family, and was glad to find it had increased. Then he told me that in December 1966 a crazy Italian named Alberto Bixler had come to see him, with the proposal that Pablo accompany him on a voyage in his rubber boat down the River Machaquilá to the ruins of the same name. Pablo, of course, drew his

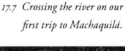

17.7 *Crossing the river on our first trip to Machaquilá.*

attention to the serious and almost insoluble difficulties of the undertaking, but Bixler was not to be deterred. After all, he was a north Italian!

I have forgotten where Pablo said they embarked, but it was probably a few kilometers up the road, where the road to Flores crosses the river. As the expedition supplies were unpacked, Pablo was perplexed at seeing no materials for preparing tortillas, or porridge, or even spaghetti. Not even dry biscuits were in evidence. He commented on this, and was curtly informed that the modern explorer had no need for those bulky provisions: he was sustained by Nu-V bars, vitaminized and mineralized chocolate-covered peanut brittle bars, weighing one and a half ounces each. For some reason, Alberto had also brought some condensed milk. (I suspect that these bars were no more than the long-established Guatemalan candy, Manibarras.)

Pablo soon found that whenever he suggested some course of action, such as lashing their belongings to the boat before attempting to shoot rapids, Alberto became angry, saying, "You may know how to use a machete, but you don't know anything about seamanship. I do!"

They came to a substantial waterfall about halfway to the ruins, where Pablo couldn't abstain from recommending a portage. He was sharply put in his place. They flew over the fall and overturned, losing their boots, machete, hammocks, and almost all the Nu-V bars. Pablo did save his *xalbec*[2] (woven shoulder bag), which contained the compass I had given him.

Boarding their vessel once more, they arrived at Campamento Final. From something the Skipper said, Pablo perceived that his original aim had been to bring out a carved stone, so he told him that they had now arrived at the ruins. Bixler (or Lisi, which may have been his patronymic) became angry, but was at last persuaded that it would be more prudent to start at once down the trail leading to Poptún. Pablo contrived sandals of bark kept in place with *bejucos* (vines). They had nothing to eat but uncooked inflorescences of *pacaya*, which indeed are tasty when cooked and added to scrambled eggs, but pretty indigestible raw. Nevertheless, they managed to reach Poptún in seven days, their feet swollen and full of thorns, their clothing torn, and their bodies thin as rails.

The genesis of this remarkable adventure can be traced to a conversation I had at Tikal, about eighteen months earlier, with Dr. Robert Dyson, who was then director of the University Museum of the University of Pennsylvania. He asked me whether I could produce some contribution for their magazine, *Expedition*, and my suggestion was an account of my second round-trip to Machaquilá. The topic was approved, and an article quite similar to the account given here was published in the magazine, with illustrations. Imagine, then, my surprise on seeing in a New York bookstore, some three years later, a volume entitled *Machaquilá: Through the Maya Jungle to the Lost City,* by Albert Lisi (New York City, 1968). There it all was, Nu-V bars and a great deal more! Parts of the book are hilarious. He enters Guatemala from Chiapas, and in Quesaltenango notes a curious feature of Guatemalan table etiquette.

"When someone left the table he would say either *Muchas Gracias* (many thanks) or *Boñ por Véchio* (good in behalf of old age: a trilingual phrase of French, Spanish and northern Italian dialect. How it came about is a moot question)" (p. 52).

Of course, what Lisi misheard was, *"buen provecho!"* meaning (as I like to translate it), "Much good may it do you!"

And then of a mule, Lisi said: "I say she, because I think of a mule as female. Actually, they are neuter, the get of a horse and a donkey, and cannot reproduce. But if you look closely at one they appear female" (p. 90).

I imagine that, if he had looked closely at more than one mule, and perhaps happened upon a daydreaming *macho*, he might have been quite surprised.

There was rare excitement, too, when they reached the jungle.

"Then the *saraguate* [howler monkey] suddenly dropped to the ground fifty feet to our right and with a loud, tigerish shriek, started to charge. . . . It was up to me. I threw my pistol out and fired twice into the ground ahead of it. The *saraguate* stopped twenty feet away, completely surprised. Then it clawed the ground, gave a last roar and ran back to its tree" (p. 94).

I find it interesting that Pablo remembered his name as "Bixler." That was hardly a name he could have imagined; yet it sounds like a possible north Italian surname (a well-known one is Traxler). Did Lisi, then, with his hopes of helping himself to a piece of Maya sculpture, think it prudent to travel under an assumed name?

These adventures, foolhardy and unproductive as they were, I should not have troubled to mention were it not for the vile imputations that the wretch made against Pablo. A man whose character I had ample occasion to judge, and whose calm good sense under difficult conditions I greatly admired—a man, in fact, whom I regarded as the salt of the earth—is painted by this idiotic jackanapes as disloyal and treacherous. And in his desperation, Lisi had promised to reward Pablo with a rifle—but, of course, did not keep his word.

Well, I did draw the attention of his publishers to the absurdity of that book (perhaps I should have written a scathing review of this book, instead). But in any case, I was rewarded by a wonderful explosion of abuse from the author—one I wouldn't have missed for worlds. Dated New York City, 21 November 1969, it runs:

"Mr. Graham—One of the chief reasons for the retarded advance of civilization are [is?] people like you. Luckily, for those of us who genuinely and in innocence care for humanity, science and Art, there are still men like myself around to deodorize the sheepfold. Progress depends on generosity, sharing.

"I dislike and try to avoid people who are pretentious and hypocritical. You on the other hand, Mr. Graham, have chosen to deliberately run into me, without knowing my character. A foolish move. I don't think you know that I am a Northern Italian, or what that implies, but I think you can understand this. I am a Teobert Maler, with teeth [I was quite unaware that don Teoberto lacked them!]. A lesson is in order, if only for justice . . . etc."

Enclosed was a typed document for me to have "signed and witnessed by one of my superiors," in which I was to confess that my accusation was false. Failure to do so would bring down upon me the full weight of the Law.

But that was the last I heard of him . . .

CHAPTER 18

Seibal, Caves, and Codices

While visiting Tikal in 1963 I had the good fortune to meet Bob Wauchope, a field archaeologist with great experience in the Maya area, and at that time director of Tulane University's Middle American Research Institute. By happy coincidence he sat down for dinner next to me at the common dining table of the Tikal Project's camp; we chatted amicably, and on rising from the table he invited me to sample the Scotch whisky that usually, as he told me, accompanied him on his travels.

Bob was a plump and genial man, and a few sips of whisky gave me the courage to tell him of discoveries I'd made in the course of my amateur explorations, mentioning Aguateca, Mirador, and Machaquilá. I believe he had seen my article on Aguateca in the *Illustrated London News*, and I asked him if there were some other journal that might accept a more detailed account of these other sites. But his suggestion was that instead I should work up descriptions of them and send them to him; then perhaps he would be able make a recommendation.

On returning home, I got down to work, using the very large table at which my father, uncles, aunts, and my own sisters had learned their early lessons, and I was hoping that while working at it I could educate myself in a different field—the technique of drawing Maya monuments. Those I had drawn for the Aguateca article were by no means satisfactory. For one thing, I had tried to restore missing areas, showing them either with broken lines, or with clumsily applied watercolor shading—only to realize that any attempt at replacement of missing areas was a mistake. There were also questions of line weight and scale that needed further thought.

I took the work of Professor William R. Coe, director of the Tikal Project, as a model. He had made a great advance on previous work by stippling the plain, recessed background areas of relief sculptures, thereby making them easier to "read." He also drew every sculpture at the fixed scale of 1:12. His drawings were based on photographs taken at night by electric light, several shots being taken, with light falling from a different direction in each one. This technique was feasible at Tikal where a mobile generator was available, and also sufficient manpower to move heavy pieces of sculpture about. But I, lacking these facilities in the jungle, would have to find some other technique.

I made my drawings on Canson tracing paper: excellent material, but correction of a line drawn in India ink required possibly destructive scraping with a razor blade and/or use of white paint. To make corrections easier, I drew at a large scale, but then ran into the problem of producing a thick line, for I believe I knew nothing of stylo-type pens, such as Rapidograph points of 0.6 mm or more—or at any rate didn't possess them. I did make one drawing entirely with a brush, but only at the cost of enormous labor.

Then there was the matter of producing a print for reproduction. I began photographing my drawings on that precious two-and-a-quarter-by-three-and-a-quarter-inch plate camera, but with the emulsions available on glass plates of that size it was difficult to obtain sufficient contrast to insure strong black lines, while avoiding general grayness of background and ghosts of corrections. But then I discovered that close contact between tracing paper and white backing paper helped in obtaining good contrast, and to secure it I went to the trouble of building a large and quite primitive vacuum easel.

I usually worked on these drawings and maps after dinner, and on two occasions at least, when my father came in to bid me good-night, he asked, a little wistfully, "I hope they are paying you for this work."

I had to tell him no. His forbearance was noble, for he must have been worried about a son who had bought a Rolls-Royce, and before long a second one, while earning very little and obviously running down the few thousand pounds, intended as capital, that his grandmother had given him. My stepmother was more direct: she hinted that I was on the road to ruin (an expression I have remembered!), and tried hard to persuade me to look for a job as a schoolmaster. She was sure I could find one.

At this point, I received a completely unexpected—and indeed astonishing—offer from Professor Gordon Willey, the Bowditch professor of archaeology at Harvard. He was writing to tell me of the museum's decision that after the current work at Altar de Sacrificios had ended, they would begin a few seasons of excavation at the ruins of Seibal—the Guatemalan government's permission for this having already been granted. A surveyor was therefore needed to map the site, starting early in 1965 during the museum's last season at Altar—so that a map of at least the central area would be

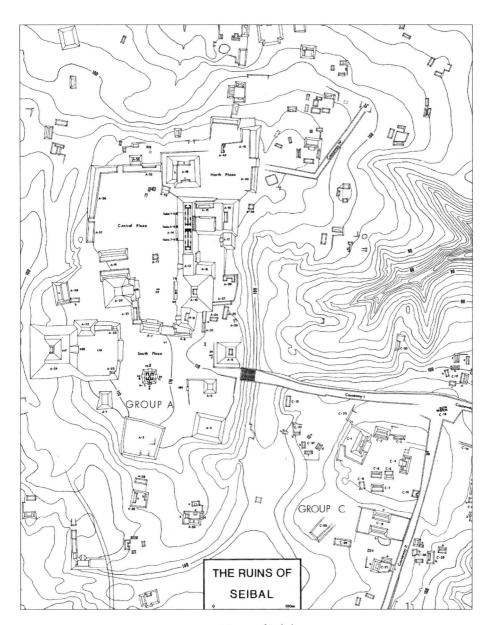

18.1 My map of Seibal.

available in provisional form when their work began in the following year. There would be a stipend. Was I interested?

Of course I was interested, and greatly flattered—but also apprehensive, given my almost complete lack of qualifications. However, I wrote to him accepting the offer.

As already mentioned, the little money that I had earned in the previous few years came from photography, and now the publishers Weidenfeld and Nicolson commissioned me to do all the photography for a coffee-table book to be called *Splendours of the East*, covering palaces, temples, tombs, and so forth between Iraq and Japan. Fortunately, the end of my Splendours tour would coincide perfectly with the start of the season at Altar de Sacrificios, since the plan was to establish a camp for me at Seibal with equipment and supplies brought from Altar soon after the season there had begun.

The general editor appointed for this book was Sir Mortimer Wheeler, an archaeologist who had gained great distinction for work in both India and Britain. And just at that time he was much in the public eye as a participant in a television program called *Animal, Vegetable or Mineral* (a similar program produced by the Museum of the University of Pennsylvania was called *What in the World?*).

Sir Mortimer had *presence*; he was tall, with a shock of hair the color of tobacco stains, wit, and a reputation with the ladies. But having watched him on television I came to think of him privately—and perhaps priggishly—as a prominent vulgarian. And in meetings held at the publishers to plan the book and my itinerary, I believe I wasn't the only one irritated by his determination to get his way—or at least put in his ten cents' worth—in discussions outside his area of expertise, such as southeast Asia.

To write the text of this book, various appropriate experts were engaged, but from none of them did I receive any guidance as to what buildings, or what details, should be photographed. The budget allowed for just two days at each site, the first of which I would spend mostly in scouting subjects and viewpoints with pictorial possibilities, and noting the times of day when they were well lit; and next day, weather permitting, I would photograph them in color and black-and-white.

All went well, except for a minor setback at Borobodur, in Java. A small temple near it attracted me, but a poster on flimsy paper proclaiming "Ganjang Malaysia!" (Smash Malaysia!) had been affixed with adhesive tape to the side of it I wanted to photograph. I asked the man who sold entrance tickets if that could be removed while I took photos. He said no. I turned to other subjects, but when I was about to leave, the local office of Rent-a-crowd, which had evidently been summoned to deal with an ill-disguised agent for the Malaysian enemy, had rallied round, with an army officer in charge. I was accused of having tried to tear the poster down, proof of which was that one corner had come unstuck. I was taken away and then flown under escort to

Jakarta. By then I was becoming apprehensive of being cast into some hellhole, but thank heaven I was cast into nothing worse than a room in the Intercontinental Hotel, with a soldier squatting outside my door.

Since I was held *incommunicado* with the phone cut off, and nothing seemed to have happened in the course of two or three days, I felt that the next move was up to me. At Angkor I had shared a hired car with a young woman who was a counselor at the Dutch Embassy in Jakarta. I wrote a brief SOS note addressed to her, and opened the unlocked door of my room, just ajar. The soldier had taken to walking up and down the corridor, and the moment came when I saw a man who looked British turning into the elevator area, while the guard was nearly at the other end of the corridor. I burst out full speed, and thrust my message in the startled man's hands.

"I'm being kept under guard in room so-and-so—*please* deliver this!" and then ran back to my room—and a very angry guard.

I learned later that the man worked for Shell Oil, and was understandably cautious about serving as a go-between in any delicate matter. So in fact he returned to his room, read the message, tore it into pieces, and flushed them down the toilet. Then he made contact somehow with my Dutch acquaintance, and she, having diplomatic status and therefore not at risk, came to see me. She reported on my situation to the British embassy, and I was soon released.

Having completed my work in Japan, I flew to Los Angeles, and stayed several days with the Mortons. I bought a copy of Breed and Hosmer's manual of surveying, much of which I knew could be ignored, since it was relevant only to surveys of land worth thousands of dollars per square foot. For the work I was to do, centimeter accuracy was unnecessary. But there was still a great deal to learn.

Even so, time could be spared for visiting the newly opened Disneyland. For me, the most amusing presentation was the Jungle River Ride. A boat with a fringed awning set off downriver (actually running on underwater rails), and at the opportune moment a guide shouted, "Look out! There it is! The man-eating hippopotamus!"

The skipper fired, and slowly the stricken beast subsided into the water, which was now turning red with its blood. Then, thankfully, we passed into calmer waters, gliding by a Khmer temple, with the statue of a Boddhisatva and a huge spider's web in front. As the photograph I took of this came out well, I made an eleven-by-fourteen enlargement and submitted it as a joke with the other prints for possible publication in *Splendours of the East*.

"Ah! Wonderful photo, this one," exclaimed Sir Mortimer, "we'll certainly use it. Pity it's not in color, though; it would have been just right for the jacket."

Later, I quietly withdrew it.

18.2 Ledyard Smith, Gordon Willey, Timothy Fisk, and Carleton Coon canoeing from Altar de Sacrificios to Seibal, 1963.

18.3 Ledyard Smith at the ruins of Seibal.

But that was later, for I went straight from Los Angeles to Guatemala City, and there joined members of the Altar de Sacrificios team. We flew to Sayaxché, and made the long journey down the placid Río de la Pasión in a very large dugout. Besides Gordon Willey and the field director, Ledyard Smith, there were four graduate students and one visitor, Professor Carleton Coon, an amusing man of strong and independent character, noted for his sometimes outrageous opinions delivered in a rasping voice. Ledyard, I already knew slightly from previous visits to Altar. A modest man, he was an extremely competent field archaeologist and had a friendly, often chuckling, way of talking. I became very fond of him and his wife, Betty. Gordon introduced me to the surveyor's transit that I would be using. It was a veteran of many campaigns, beginning with Panama '08. Of course, I had never seen a transit before, but study of Breed and Hosmer enabled me to comment favorably on one or two of its features, in the hope of allaying any doubts Gordon might have as to my competence.

Next day, Gordon, Ledyard, Carl, and the student allotted to stay with me at Seibal for some days as an assistant, embarked once more, heading back upriver to Seibal. Halfway there a dreadful realization hit me: I had forgotten to bring the transit! A Freudian slip, if ever there was one. But in fact, the lack of it was of no importance, since my first task was to lay out north-south and east-west lines of stakes using compass and tape, and the transit could be sent with the next boatload of supplies.

My colleague and I lived in a tent until thatched huts and a comedor, or mess hall, had been built. The latter was supposed to be an exact copy of the one at Altar de

Sacrificios, but it certainly looked smaller to me—and so it proved to be, the explanation becoming apparent when I happened to find on the ground a fragment of measuring tape bearing the numeral "95." So the first meter or so of the builder's tape had broken off.

After about two weeks, my first colleague departed as planned and a young graduate student, Gair Tourtellot, came to assist me. He was to gain experience on the job before starting to survey the area surrounding the central zone that had been assigned to me. But I'm afraid I taught him a surveying technique of which neither Breed nor Hosmer would ever have approved. The standard technique called for bearings between one stake set in the ground and another to be observed by means of the transit in both directions, forward and backward (i.e., on the reciprocal), and for distances between them to be measured with a steel tape. But where ravines had to be crossed—and at Seibal there are several with very steep sides—orthodox measurements of distance would require the laborious process of "chaining"—working one's way down a slope so steep that footholds would often be insecure, and then measuring one short distance after another using a tape held horizontally and plumb line. But even on the

18.4 Ledyard and me at Seibal.

flat I'm afraid I often roamed quite far from the nearest stake, setting up the transit on the basis of stadia rod measurements for distance, and setting the compass dial at the reciprocal of the shot to it from the preceding station.

Even with these shortcuts I found it difficult to complete the map on time, and until recently I have comforted my guilty conscience with the reflection that no one in my lifetime would ever detect the inaccuracies. But now, I'm not so sure. The latest GPS system is so extraordinarily accurate that someone with a real grudge against me could easily destroy my reputation as a surveyor with one morning's work. But in any case, there still remained the difficult task of drafting the map neatly. This I did in Cambridge and it took a long time; quite how long I can't remember.

During my brief stay at the Peabody's Altar de Sacrificios camp (following my first visit to Mirador), I happened to chat with one of the workmen named Trinidad Betancourt. He was a tall, thin black from British Honduras, now living in La Libertad. His sister, Doña Maria, was also working at Altar as cook for the archaeologists' camp.

18.5 Seibal, Peabody Museum camp, February 1968.

As Don Trin had formerly been a chiclero, I asked him whether he'd ever come across any *reyes* or *reinas*, using the terms (kings and queens) that were commonly used by Peteneros for stelae.

"Yes," he said, "I did find one a few years ago while working chicle at a camp called La Pailita."

"Oh, really? How interesting! About how tall was it?"

"Well, perhaps about fifteen meters."

Fifteen *meters!*—a figure well beyond the bounds of possibility. But Don Trin seemed a man of sober judgment, so I told him I'd very much like to see this fabulous monument, should the opportunity arise.

In 1965, when the museum had left Altar to start anew at Seibal, most of the workforce was retained, including the Betancourts, so I arranged with Don Trin that we would go in search of this great rey as soon as the Peabody's season closed at the end of March.

So when the time came, Don Trin and I set off in an old Jeep, driven by a youth who unfortunately had been resting all morning in a bar. But taking into consideration the steering wheel's backlash of one whole turn, and a consequent violent wheel wobble occurring at 10 mph, he was doing quite well until all of a sudden, about eight miles short of La Libertad, he suddenly fell asleep, and it became my turn to drive. But we did reach La Libertad.

There, we hired a cargo mule and a young man to lead it, and I persuaded the owner of that famed power wagon to drive Don Trin and me to San Pablo, a settlement of just a few houses about fifteen miles away. After passing through extensive savannas, we came to a track through a horrible tangle of what had been high forest until about ten years earlier, when a frightful conflagration raged for months in northwestern Petén, destroying hundreds of square miles of forest. But now this track had been cleared as far as San Pablo. Ramón, who had set off with the pack mule before dawn, duly caught up with us, the truck went back, and we three went on, reaching Laguna San Diego in another four hours.

Next day, we reached a camping spot some ten miles away to the north, where previous visitors, finding the aguada completely dry, had dug two pits in it about eighteen inches deep, into which water the color of coffee with milk in it had seeped. By then a metallic sheen had formed on its surface, but by boiling it and allowing it to settle, a drinkable fluid was obtained.

By this time I'd learned from Don Trin that the rey was housed within a cave. He and Ramón then went off early in search of it, while I stayed behind, writing letters and reading—interrupted only briefly by the arrival of a herd of about a dozen *jabalí*, looking for water. Finding none, they ambled off, snapping their jaws as if to show their annoyance.

Next morning, after walking for about an hour, the men began casting about, confused by a number of recent *picados* (trails lightly marked), and then went off separately. Feeling the heat (for the weather was scorching that spring), I began to doubt the very existence of the cave—to say nothing of the fabled rey—and sat down to rest and read for a while. When the men returned, neither of them had managed to find the cave, as was not too surprising, since this was an area of karst formations: that is, innumerable hillocks, all quite similar.

After a rest and a snack of hot soup and cheese, the search was resumed, and soon the two men were back to report the discovery of another cave containing abundant sherds of pottery, but no rey. Now they suggested moving on to a different camp, La Pailita, in order to find another cave that would help orient them in their search for the rey. So we moved on. It was a two-and-a-half-hour walk, and on arrival we found an equally poor supply of water, and a group of *shateros* (gatherers of *shate* grass) to share it with. After lunch I began digging a test-pit in this other cave.

18.6 La Pailita: drawing water from a hole dug the previous evening in the dried-up aguada.

Next morning, the men continued searching—and I digging—but a few hours later they returned triumphantly, having found our rey only about half a mile away. On seeing that this cave was up a steep slope and invisible from below, I was now able to understand Don Trin's difficulty in finding it, as also his description of it as being fifteen meters high!

The first glimpse of the rey himself was unforgettable, for in the murky light that penetrated beyond and below the lip of the cave we saw, seated just in front of a thick stalagmite/stalactite column, a life-size figure, eerily green from a coating of mold. Large fragments of polychrome pottery vessels, some of them halves of vessels, lay scattered on the floor to one side—evidence, I felt, that this cave and the statue in it had remained forgotten and undefiled since the very last time Mayas had come to make their offerings, perhaps a thousand years earlier.

Constructed of stones and mortar, and finished with a smooth coating of plaster, the figure was seated upon a "throne" that appeared to be an offshoot of the stalagmite. Capped by a disc of limestone, he held an ax in his right hand, an unmistakable emblem of *Chahk*, the rain god. A large boulder behind and to one side of him had an upward-gazing mask of plaster applied to it.

This lightly provisioned trip had been undertaken simply for reconnaissance, so we packed up next morning before dawn, with the intention of coming back better provisioned in the following year, when water might also be less scarce. But now the men told me to my dismay that they intended to walk all the way back to La Libertad in one day! I really doubted that I could do that, passing through that savanna in broiling heat; but with astonishing good fortune we found in San Pablo a truck belonging to the United Nations Food and Agriculture Organization, in which I was given a ride for those last fifteen miles.

In the following year I had just begun planning a return visit to La Pailita to make a more thorough investigation of this unique shrine, when I was given extremely depressing news: vandals had destroyed the statue. Well, I suppose I was lucky to have obtained *some* record of it, by the skin of my teeth. Since then, nothing resembling this statue of Chahk in a cave has been found.

In general, my interest in caves had been slight, as few inscriptions have been found in them. But after La Pailita, I was intrigued by the description someone gave me of a huge cave system through which a substantial tributary flowed into the headwaters of the Río de la Pasión. My informant described evidence of ancient occupation in these caves, and told me that I should start from Raxujá (Raxrujá)—that same small settlement I had passed through on my way to the Sohio camp, back in 1959. From there, it seemed, I should follow that tributary, the Río San Simón, upstream.

18.7 *Chahk in his cave at La Pailita, perhaps*
the only photo of it in existance.

Arriving at Raxujá, I found a man whose milpa was near the caves and therefore knew them well. This was Santiago Genovés, a thin man with curly black hair, a heavy smoker, and also rather wily—in fact, as well as in appearance. He recruited two others for the expedition: Pedro, a Kekchi, evidently a humorist in his own circle though otherwise quiet (but notable also for his ability to go through thick bush almost like a tapir); and then Hilario, from southeastern Guatemala, a slow, amiable, bumbling, and self-deprecating man. "No tengo valor, yo no sirvo," he sometimes said, and I found he would agree to almost anything that I said; though when I surprised him with the unlikely theory that lack of salt could cause cramps, the nearest to agreement he could manage was, "Es probable que es cierto!"

A house was found where I could hang my hammock for the night. But this little settlement was the most miserable and obviously disease-ridden I'd ever seen. Children were crying everywhere, and messes on the dirt road running through it were evidence of widespread diarrhea; so I was especially careful to receive my tortilla at meals directly from my hostess's comal (but in vain, for some days later I developed amebic dysentery, the cure for which in those days required hospitalization).

Following the river upstream, we arrived at an entrance to the caves after walking for three and a half hours. This entrance (for there were others) was spectacular, since it resembled in some respects an atrium. In a high and otherwise irregular rocky outcrop, there was a recess—its floor fairly level and its walls roughly approximating one-quarter of a sphere, perhaps fifty feet across, with the entrance to the cave in the middle. There were also two or three recesses at floor level on either side of the entrance, possibly natural, but I was inclined to consider them man-made. In front of each of these was a low semicircular wall of dry-laid stones, perhaps three feet high. (I must add that this description relies entirely on memory, but its general aspect was certainly as described.)

At first, I thought they must be pens for keeping animals, but I couldn't understand why such pens should be necessary. Then I found a report that at Chan Kom, in Yucatán, shaman priests were so scrupulous in the preparation of offerings to the gods that the chickens to be offered had been kept isolated for a certain length of time before being sacrificed. So just possibly these enclosures could have served, with nets stretched across, as special coops for sacrificial virgin-birds, conveniently situated near the place of ritual sacrifice in the caves.

I really don't have much confidence in this explanation, but the only other one I could imagine is equally speculative, and was suggested by a passage in Henry Chapman Mercer's book, *The Hill Caves of Yucatan*. He describes a technique of hunting in which a blind is constructed, then grains of maize are scattered on the ground nearby. The hunter enters his blind (here, in one of these recesses) with a blowgun, and when doves or other birds of interest come to feed on them, he shoots. The still air in the cave mouth would obviously provide ideal conditions for blowgun shooting, since the accuracy of this weapon of low muzzle velocity is prejudiced by the slightest crosswind.

On entering the cave, I remember finding quite an extensive area of flat soil off to the left, in which I found a whistle-figurine of a "fat-man," half-buried. On descending, I found a tunnel leading to the southeast, and straight ahead, a three-foot-wide sacbe, or ceremonial pathway, forty-three feet long and raised between twelve and eighteen inches from a base of soil. It seemed to lead to a pool of water.

The various curving and branching passages and halls were too complicated to record in a brief visit, but the largest hall was colossal—as spacious, I reckoned, as any church in Guatemala City. Here and there were objects such as bark-beaters and manos for use with metates left propped against walls of the cave, but now cemented to them by translucent calcite deposits. Then there was a natural tunnel about seventy feet long and of triangular section, the entrance to which had once been blocked up with rough, dry-laid masonry. In this an opening had been made, large enough to crawl through. Two stalagmite columns within the passage almost blocked one's way, and at the blind end of it was a natural chamber eight feet long by two and a half wide, with a natural constriction eight feet from its end that was only two feet wide. This, too, had once been walled up.

The chamber had contained a burial, but practically all of it contents had been removed, except for two slabs at the far end, placed almost like pillows. By sieving the soil I recovered no more than two milk-teeth, an adult incisor, fragments of bone, four little pottery beads, two small, red-painted shell necklace ornaments—and one uncertainly identified gall stone.

What struck me as the most unusual feature of this cave, however, was a group of stalactites near the entrance to this part of the cave system. They had grown horizontally! As an explanation of this phenomenon, I can only suggest that a prevailing current of air from one direction has caused more rapid evaporation—and thus of lime deposition—on one side of a budding stalactite than on the other. As some of these were about four feet long and thick as a thigh, they looked unstable, and I had to spend some time choosing a sleeping area that was suitably level and not directly under one of these, in case it should break off in an earthquake. And as it happened, on reaching Coban two days after leaving the cave, there was a strong tremor!

With the biennial International Congress of Americanists due to take place in Spain in the spring of 1965, several of my new colleagues who were planning to attend it encouraged me to join them, among them Eric Thompson, Gordon Willey, Harry Pollock, and in particular, Ledyard Smith. The meetings were to be held in three cities: first in Barcelona, then Madrid, and finally Seville. Some forgotten engagement kept me from the Barcelona sessions, but I came for the other two. They were very enjoyable, and I met there for the first time several colleagues whose work was known to me.

At Madrid, of course, we all looked forward to seeing the Museo de América. This had been founded in 1941, and a large building had been erected for it, but years had passed without any artifacts being installed in it. The exciting news for the congresistas was that the building would now be opened for the first time, just for us to see the Madrid Codex, one of the only three pre-Columbian Maya manuscripts then known to exist.

This late pre-Conquest manuscript had long ago been divided into two halves that ended up in separate collections, one being known as the Troano, and the other as the Cortesianus. When it was realized that they were two parts of one codex and had eventually been brought together, the two were known first as the "Tro-Cortesianus," and then simply as the Codex Madrid.

We gathered outside the Museo's large brick building, and at the appointed hour were admitted into the spacious entrance hall. There we were detained for a considerable time by two or three officials who had lengthy greetings to convey, accounts of the museum's creation to relate, tributes to worthy personages to render, and so forth—until all of us, I believe, were becoming impatient. Then at last we were released, and like a stampede, tore up the stairway to a large gallery where the Codex was displayed.

As one of the first to enter the gallery, I glanced first at one half of the Codex, which was sandwiched between two sheets of glass mounted in an iron frame. Iron rods welded to the ends of this frame were pivoted in a substantial wrought-iron framework, allowing rotation of the frame so that both sides of it could be examined.

Then I saw that the other half was lying on the floor, surrounded by a wooden frame but unprotected by glass. I never discovered how long it had lain like this, exposed to dust and sunlight coming through the extensive glazing in the roof. Of course, those congresistas most interested in it squatted around it in excitement, pointing out to each other various interesting details. But I became concerned that someone might in his enthusiasm stab carelessly with a finger against the surface of the codex itself; or that a pair of spectacles might fall on it from someone's nose. But as an absolute nonentity, I could scarcely call for this or that congresista to back off a little, or restrain fingers pointed too enthusiastically at some detail, so I went over to Gordon Willey to ask if perhaps he would call for everyone to back off. Gordon, however, was never one to exercise authority, so I simply continued clucking round the codex like an anxious hen.

Then CRAASH!! tinkle tinkle. . . In consternation, we saw that an unfortunate priest had quite innocently rotated the framed and mounted half of the codex, unaware that the glass had not been secured in its frame! We stood there, some with heads bowed and hands on forehead, in Grecian attitudes of grief. Someone went off to summon the director, and soon busy footsteps were heard. On arrival, Pilar Fernández summed up the situation in a flash and took immediate action. She grabbed one end of the codex and started pulling it up.

"¡Déjelo, déjelo!"—I shouted. She paid no attention, and then a henchman came over to reprove me for reacting hysterically. (Did he think I was afraid of injury from flying shards of glass?) Gathering the wretched codex over her arm as one might a small rug, she marched off. Fifteen minutes later we were informed that the codex had suffered no damage.

CHAPTER 19

A Glimpse at Glyphs

It was John Graham, I believe, who first told me about the work of a Soviet epigrapher named Yuri Knorozov. John, a graduate student at Berkeley at the time (and unrelated to me), told me there was a good chance that the key to reading Maya hieroglyphs had at last been found—while showing obvious excitement at the prospect. This was in the early 1960s, at ruins on the Pasión River called Altar de Sacrificios, where the Peabody Museum of Harvard University was in the middle of a three- or four-year investigation of the site, under Gordon Willey's direction. John's function there was to study the inscriptions.

Maya script was by then one of the world's last undeciphered scripts of major importance, and undoubtedly the most important in the New World, for the texts surviving from other pre-Columbian culture areas are generally much shorter, less abundant, and unlikely to yield much information.

The study of Maya writing had for decades been in the doldrums—dead in the water, as sailors say. Some progress had been made on other pre-Hispanic Mexican texts, but as for that of the ancient Mayas, whose culture area still embraces a vast region stretching from Yucatán down to El Salvador and half of Honduras, that was resisting decipherment, despite the availability of abundant texts for study.

In this field, little progress had been made (with a few notable exceptions) until late in the nineteenth century, when two brilliant German scholars, Paul Schellhas and Ernst Förstemann, made seminal contributions. The name of another great scholar, Eduard Seler, is often—and rightly—coupled with theirs in recognition of his truly outstanding work, but his contributions in the narrow field of decipherment were few.

19.1 Yuri Knorosov, with me.

Schellhas is remembered for having identified the figures and name-glyphs of deities, for these were the first noncalendrical glyphs to be identified. But unfortunately he became discouraged about the prospects of further advances in decipherment, and abandoned this field for the remainder of his long life.

Ernst Förstemann was less easily discouraged. He was librarian of the royal library in Dresden, and as such had in his charge the most valuable of the three surviving pre-Hispanic Maya manuscripts, all of which were written on bark-fiber paper and illustrated in colored inks—this one being known as the Dresden Codex. By the 1880s, Förstemann had worked out the Maya vigesimal system (that is, arithmetic of base 20), while also identifying correctly some hieroglyphs and deity names. Encouraged by these achievements, he went on to study the inscription on the Temple of the Cross at Palenque, and managed to establish the chronology of certain events recorded on it—in outline, and of course without being able to suggest what kind of events these were.

Those early scholars had little material to work with, their most fruitful sources being those three Maya manuscripts, all of late date. There was, however, something else: a handwritten record of Bishop Diego de Landa's questioning of a bilingual and literate Yucatec Maya, in the mid-sixteenth century. The bishop quizzed him orally about the Maya alphabet: first of all, what was the equivalent in Spanish of *ah, beh, se* (*a, b, c*), and the other letters of the alphabet (as pronounced in Spanish, of course). A scribe was at hand to set down answers given by the Maya, some of whom, when their Spanish failed them, made little explanatory drawings instead. But these answers impressed no one; indeed, some of the answers must have struck those present as quite absurd. For *beh*, the Maya informant drew a pair of feet, and for *sheh* (in those days one of two forms of the letter *x*, as used in Spanish), he drew a person vomiting.

Clearly, this interview had been a waste of time; that was obvious. But fortunately the questions and the spoken or sketched answers were preserved, and when Knorozov studied the written report about 350 years later, he guessed at once that de Landa's informant was thinking *syllabically*, rather than alphabetically. He was enabled to make this leap of understanding by virtue of having studied both linguistics and many of the writing systems that have come into use in various parts of the world. So he was well aware that some scripts were indeed syllabic, rather than alphabetic.

With this preparation he was able to throw an entirely new light on Maya writing: that it was syllabic—in other words, composed largely of consonant-vowel pairs. For it's now well established that in Maya writing, a single sign usually represents a consonant-vowel pair, such as *beh*, and this is a word that in Maya does mean *road*. But as an object of this kind was difficult for the Mayan informant to explain in a word or two, he chose instead to draw feet, as the parts of the human body most closely connected with roads. And as for *sheh*, well, this does simply mean *vomit* in Maya.

Yuri Knorozov then went on to offer readings of other hieroglyphs (or simply "glyphs"). Since most Maya words are of the form consonant-vowel-consonant, he proposed that these were expressed in writing as two consonant-vowel pairs, with the vowel of the second pair kept silent when read aloud; also that Maya rules of spelling required the vowel of that second consonant-vowel pair to match that of the initial pair; thus "kak" would be expressed by *ka-k[a]*. When published in Russian in the mid-1950s, Knorozov's work attracted little if any notice outside the USSR until an English translation was made by Sophie Coe, the wife of Professor Michael D. Coe, who had recognized its importance. This was published in 1958.

But even then, his readings were rejected by most scholars active in this field; the script *had* to be ideographic—meaning that the glyphs represented *ideas*, rather than vowels and consonants. But in judging the reaction of Western archaeologists to Knorozov's article, the opening paragraph of his paper should also be taken into account, for this disparaged Western "imperialist" academics in no uncertain terms: as poor wretches, who with their terrible disability were unable to match the glorious achievements of Marxist-Leninst dialectic, etc, etc.

Had they been more familiar with Soviet publications they might have interpreted this introductory paragraph for what it almost certainly was: stock boilerplate inserted by some party hack. But Western archaeologists, unaccustomed to reading Soviet journals, and failing to recognize such insertions as what they were, took the opinions to be Knorozov's own.

Among these critics, the most severe was J. Eric S. Thompson, a deservedly celebrated English scholar who had given long and extremely valuable service to archaeology with the Carnegie Institution of Washington. He had indeed recognized some grammatical structure in Maya writing, and the fact that "affixes" could sometimes represent syllables—affixes being minor graphic elements in the composition of hieroglyphs (for these are generally composites of several elements joined together in one "glyph-block"). So Knorozov's proposal that Maya writing was largely phonetic was quite unacceptable to him—as it was at first to most other respected scholars. Certainly, Knorozov made mistakes, but today his early work is recognized as fundamental—though even now, when the phonetic decipherment of innumerable texts might seem to have validated his initial breakthrough, loyal Thompsonians pop up from time to time to express their disagreement.[1]

The most astonishing three years in the history of Maya studies were certainly those in the late 1950s. For in that short span of time we would see the publication of not just one, but three crucial contributions to decipherment of Maya writing by three different scholars, working independently—if we overlook the fact Knorozov had actually published his work three years earlier in Russian (the years before the English translation appeared don't count, of course!).

19.2 Sir Eric Thompson.

The second of the three discoveries I've mentioned showed that the inscriptions contain historical matter—a notion scarcely considered previously. This was the work of Heinrich Berlin, who was born in the eponymous city in 1915, and had emigrated to Mexico at the age of twenty to escape Nazi persecution. Within five years of settling in Mexico he was working with others at the ruins of Palenque. With the passage of only three more years, he would publish an article on Palenque inscriptions.

His fertile brain produced many publications, but two of them stand out. One of these describes what he called "emblem glyphs"—a term that he chose as not being too specific (and on that account it remains in use). These glyphs, described by him in 1958, form a group that he found particularly intriguing, for they incorporate two relatively constant affixes and one principal element, or "main sign," that is variable.

On investigating the distribution of these various forms of main sign, Berlin noticed that each was predominant at a particular site, a finding that led him to conclude, tentatively, that such glyphs might represent the names of each site. His caution was wise, for although the general significance he proposed for these glyphs has held good, he himself would draw attention to a slight problem. This was the occasional presence of the same emblem glyphs at two sites. (And later, at the great Maya city of Copán in the south, no less than four were found together, suggesting some kind of quadripartite division of political authority in that south-central region of Maya lands.)

In the following year, Berlin produced another paper of even greater importance. The Mexican archaeologist Alberto Ruz had just discovered the famous interior stairway leading down from the top of the lofty Temple of the Inscriptions at Palenque to ground level. That stairway had been filled up with rubble in antiquity, and its entrance concealed under a pavement of heavy stone slabs. But when at last Ruz and his men had worked their way down to ground level, their efforts were amply rewarded by finding there a tomb chamber, or crypt, containing a magnificent sarcophagus. On its sides were images of nine individuals, carved in low relief, each accompanied by name glyphs that are recorded elsewhere in the site—and not as deities. This observation of Berlin's strongly suggested the notation of personal names— a pioneering decipherment.

Over the next twenty-five years, Berlin was to publish more than fifty articles on Maya epigraphy and Latin American art history, before his death at the age of seventy-three.

The third of these remarkable pioneers was also of Russian birth, though almost entirely North American in upbringing. This was Tatiana Proskouriakoff. She was born in Tomsk, Siberia, in 1909, and known by her family and friends as "Tania." Her

19.3 The staff of the Carnegie Institution, ca. 1946. Left to right, top row: L. E. Lawrence, Tatiana Proskouriakoff. Middle row: F. Richardson, unknown, A. Menassalian. Bottom row: A. V. Kidder, F. Scholes, J. E. S. Thompson. Print from Corpus of Maya Hieroglyphic Inscriptions archive, Peabody Museum, Harvard University.

mother was a physician, and the daughter of a general; her father a scientist, as his own father had been. With the outbreak of the First World War, her father was sent as a chemist to Philadelphia to supervise the production of explosives for export to Russia—bringing with him his wife and two small daughters.

When the war ended, the family decided to stay put. In 1930, Tania graduated in architecture from Pennsylvania State College, but soon found, in the depths of the Depression, that employment was hard to find. On one occasion, though, she took on a small job at the University Museum of the University of Pennsylvania: it involved copying drawings at scales suitable for needlepoint. By extremely good fortune, this little work of hers came to the notice of Linton Satterthwaite, a notable Maya archaeologist (of whom I have fond memories). Quickly appreciating Tania's potential in his field, he invited her to join the museum's 1936 expedition to the great ruins of Piedras

Negras, in the unpopulated northwest corner of Guatemala; on the Mexican side however, it lies not far from Palenque, an ancient city of great historical importance and blessed by the survival of several beautiful buildings and sculptures.

Following this heaven-sent introduction into the field of archaeology, Tania paid a visit to Palenque, and on seeing there the elegant Temple of the Sun, she knew that she had found her vocation. For the following season Tania was engaged once more for work at Piedras Negras, with expenses paid but without salary; but in the following year, with the Depression still continuing, Satterthwaite threatened to "fire" her (while, I imagine, characteristically screwing up one side of his face), because he couldn't agree to go on employing her without salary. But while at Piedras Negras, Tania had taken the opportunity to investigate and measure the remains of the site's acropolis, and with these data made a reconstruction drawing of it.

On her return to Philadelphia, this drawing was shown to Sylvanus G. Morley, the director of the well-funded Carnegie Institution of Washington's Division of Historical Research. Morley encouraged her to produce more drawings of this kind, and the eventual outcome of her work was a salaried position—and in 1943, promotion to membership of the CIW staff. Then finally, with the CIW's withdrawal from archaeology, she joined the Peabody Museum of Harvard University as a research associate.

Now free to turn her attention to any topic that intrigued her, Tania chose to study Maya hieroglyphic writing. This, in fact, had been the topic of the first paper she ever published (in 1944), and within a very short time she produced another, quite modest in presentation but of surpassing importance. This was entitled "Historical Implications of a Pattern of Dates at Piedras Negras, Guatemala." At one blow, this freed the study of Maya writing from a lengthy stagnation—one that was attributable to the generally accepted notion that Maya monumental inscriptions contained nothing but astronomical matter.

At this point, I'd also like to mention David H. Kelley, a Canadian and first-class epigrapher, who was, with Michael Coe, the first of Knorozov's supporters in the Western world. Kelley, it seems, was undeterred by errors of a kind that any scholar might make while working in total isolation—as Knorozov had been. Then, in 1966, he read a paper at a meeting in Mexico City in which he presented a decipherment that effectively combined the contributions of Knorozov, Berlin, and Proskouriakoff with some of his own, by reading phonetically from inscriptions at Chichén Itzá the word "Kakupakal," and presenting this as a personal name. No one had previously identified a name in Maya texts, but this one appears fourteen times in Chichén Itzá inscriptions. He also presented documentary evidence in texts from colonial Yucatán that support this reading as a name.

To this brief account of the early years following the enlightenment that all Maya epigraphers owe to Knorosov, I must add a sad and inexplicable coda. For within a few years of proposing syllabic values for graphemes (written hieroglyphic signs), Knorosov went off in another direction, reading them as entire words—an astonishing volte-face. Almost no one followed him, except a student of his, Galina Yershova.

Here, it may be appropriate to consider where persons interested in studying the monumental inscriptions of the Maya could, at that time, find suitable grist for their mill; that is, published photos or renderings of them. The answer is quite simple. There were two principal sources, both of them as reliable as could possibly be expected at the time. One was a set of four large-format volumes, accompanied by one of text. This was the work of an Englishman named Alfred Maudslay, based on expeditions he made in the 1880s, and published soon after in an unexpected publication series, the sixty-five-volume *Biologia Centrali-Americana*.

This vast and extraordinary publication is one of the greatest privately conceived and financed compendia of scientific importance ever published. Its begetters were two friends, Frederick D. Godman and Osbert Salvin, both naturalists. Godman was wealthy enough to sponsor all the fieldwork done for them by a host of specialist collectors, as well as the highly qualified draftsmen responsible for the innumerable illustrations that fill those volumes.

The fact that Maudslay's work appeared as a five-volume appendix to a publication series dedicated to natural history simply reflects two things: Maudslay's longstanding friendship with both Godman and Salvin, and Godman's enormous generosity—together with his understanding of the importance of Maudslay's work. He also knew how important it was to have the excellent photographs reproduced in large format. Maudslay had taken the trouble to master the art of photography, so it was fortunate that he began his work just when the development of photography had brought clarity of image (in the hands of experts) to a level that would not be surpassed for another century. And a second happy coincidence was recent improvement in the technique of reproducing photographs in books.

The other important recorder of Maya inscriptions was a German named Teobert Maler. A tireless explorer of Maya sites, he did most of his work between 1885 and 1910. Like Maudslay, he had mastered photography and used a large-format camera. Initially, he had supported his work by selling prints, until commissioned by the Peabody Museum of Harvard University to continue working under its sponsorship. So, between them, Maudslay and Maler managed to record a very large number of monuments at ruins widely scattered over the Maya area.

The expeditions of those two pioneers, both of them centered on recording Maya inscriptions, were followed by others mounted by the Carnegie Institution, and also by various universities, most of them primarily interested in excavations. But alas, the high standard of photography established by those two pioneers was not maintained, as explained in greater detail elsewhere in this book. And in any case, the general acceptance of mistaken notions concerning the content of Maya inscriptions led to a slump of interest in them, and the laborious procedures of recording them with care were given up.

And then, as an outcome of the terrible First World War, academic interest in pre-Columbian research declined. So it was fortunate that before the war broke out, Sylvanus Griswold Morley had ignited in the governing body of the Carnegie Institution of Washington a small but promising spark of interest in the study of the Maya and their script. Peace, therefore, had not long been established before Morley was fanning this ember into flame, and a new department of the CIW was born, eventually to be termed its Division of Historical Research. This was based in Cambridge, about two hundred yards from the Peabody Museum, and its principal focus was on excavating Maya ruins (and in some cases, restoring them). Other related studies were pursued, including that of Maya writing.

In the 1920s, Morley himself had been the most enthusiastic researcher in this field, but it seems that by the following decade he had concluded—despondently, one imagines—that the subject matter recorded in Maya hieroglyphic texts might well be so arcane as to be devoid of any interest. Perhaps it just described relations between the gods in outer space, or their conflicts, and who, today, would really care about such matters?

Morley's discouragement was understandable, especially as he was fully engaged just then in writing and editing the four large volumes, plus one of illustrations, entitled *The Inscriptions of Petén*. This was a tremendous work reporting the CIW's explorations at many sites in the Maya area in the course of many years; but the inscriptions found at all these sites receive little attention beyond citation of each one's date in the Maya calendar.

Eventually, in 1958, the CIW closed down its Division of Historical Research. Its closure is said to have been precipitated by a redirection of the institution's priorities triggered by the launching of Sputnik, although I suspect that Morley's death and the retirement of the division's director, Alfred Kidder, may also have been important factors.

But though in the doldrums, research into Maya epigraphy had by no means come to an end. For J. Eric Thompson was soldiering on at his home in England. He and his wife, Florence, had settled in Essex, and as this was no great distance from my family's home in Suffolk, they were sometimes kind enough to invite me for an overnight visit. This was generous, for I can't have been a very stimulating partner in discussions concerning the subtler points of hieroglyphic writing, in view of my total inability to comprehend its systematics as envisioned by Eric. The only solid contributions he ever had from me were a few photos or drawings of monuments I'd found.

Eric was probably the last person to have a first-class grip on the whole range of studies concerning the Maya. Today, of course, no one could possibly have such complete mastery, so huge is the body of available information, and so many its specialized branches. Eric was very diligent in publishing his work, and I believe he was a generous colleague, but understandably he was upset when much of the vast conceptual structure concerning the Maya that he'd built up in his brilliant mind was challenged— and finally, in the opinion of most epigraphers, rejected as woven out of gossamer. My heart bled for him, and I found myself making excuses for the occasional ungenerous remark he might make about some triumphant protagonist of this "new wave" of phonetic decipherment.

Well, I was floundering already in the whirlpools of Eric's vision of the Maya universe, so when this great wave of phonetic interpretation came at me from another direction I could scarcely keep my head above water. After all, I'd never pretended to be anything but a bushwhacker outfitted with camera, compass, pencil, some grains of common sense, and an instinct for self-preservation. But the reports I was beginning to hear of progress in this new direction did persuade me to consider prolonging the short-term engagement I had originally contemplated for this pursuit, if only some method of replenishing my diminishing resources could be found.

CHAPTER 20

Río San Pedro

Even before I had returned to Guatemala, early in 1965, I had become seriously concerned about the surge of looting in Petén. At several sites I had found the sliced-up remains of previously undamaged monuments—and later, advertisements in art magazines for splendid Maya monuments of unknown origin. So on hearing of recent looting at ruins on the Río San Pedro, I decided to go and see for myself what damage had been done in that seldom visited area.

The San Pedro runs from east to west across northern Petén, then crosses the Mexican border and empties into the Río Usumacinta. Thirty years earlier, there had been a substantial center of the chicle business at a place on its banks called Paso Caballos—its name marking the point farthest downriver where the fording of horses was possible. Fifty miles farther downriver there was a ranch called El Naranjo, and then, near the Mexican border, a small sawmill. There were no other settlements, and as far as I knew, the entire drainage of this river was archaeologically terra incognita.

That chicle establishment far upriver had been created in the 1920s by the Chicle Development Company. This company built a large house for offices and staff accommodation, installed an electric light plant, and constructed a capacious concrete water tank, with a corrugated-iron roof provided with gutters draining into the tank beneath it. This tank was really a necessity, because the river water, in percolating through the beds of gypsum rock that predominate upstream on its right bank, picks up enough calcium sulfate to give it a bad taste, while also rendering it useless for cooking beans—an even more important effect, for beans just don't soften in hard water.

Then the company had had to dredge a channel through rapids halfway down the river, and again through a heavy deposit of mussel shells, before they were able to convey their chicle by boat to Tenosique, on the first stage of its journey to the

*20.1 Awkward passage up a tributary
of the Río San Pedro.*

factory in Chicago. Apart from these obstructions—both of them quite difficult to pass in a small boat—the river flows calmly. Some ten years later, the Guatemalan government prohibited the exportation of raw chicle via Mexico for economic reasons, and a landing field was made at Paso. From then on, the chicle was flown to Guatemala City in Ford Trimotors—and the lighting plant, screened house, and water tank were abandoned.

On hearing reports of looting at ruins near that ranch down the river, I decided to examine the damage myself. I would need a boat, but on making inquiries at Paso, I was told there was only one, a large dugout canoe belonging to the Guardia Rural, or police.

So in Flores I went to see the governor of Petén, who readily prepared for me a letter of authorization addressed to the owner of the ranch. Then I spoke to the captain of the Guardia, who was equally obliging and gave me written permission to make use of the boat. Next, I went to Sayaxché, where I persuaded Polo Linga, a very experienced boatman of my acquaintance, to accompany me on this trip, bringing his outboard motor, and I found a *boga* (bow-man) named Guillermo. And lastly, I hired a station wagon to take us to Flores, where I purchased food supplies and a fifty-gallon drum of gasoline.

Next morning we departed on the twice-weekly flight to Paso, having paid the ridiculously low freight charge of seven dollars for the cargo and five dollars each for us. The Guardia received us cordially, and we were invited to sling our hammocks in their quarters (the former company house), which was reached by a long flight of masonry steps, the top one inscribed with the date of its construction, 1924.

We set off early next morning, with the sun glaring red through the smoke of forest fires. Down this fifty-mile stretch, the river was in places a hundred yards wide and showed no obvious signs of current. There were abundant waterbirds to admire, and orchids on overhanging branches, but not a single habitation. We found the dredged passage at the rapids still marked by poles driven in forty years earlier, and at last arrived at El Naranjo, at an elbow in the river. Having secured the boat, we walked up a long slope, where about twenty mules were grazing. There was a row of men sitting on a bench in front of the house, silently staring—an unprepossessing bunch, I thought. One of them looked like the archetype of all Mexican bandits, with long sideburns and a thin moustache.

We learned that the *patrón* was absent, but I was allotted half of a chicken house to hang my hammock in, and Polo and Guillermo were given a palm-thatched, open-sided shelter, or *galera*. On the other side of the river, we saw fires smoldering and sometimes flaring up—set, I was told, by alligator hunters to drive their quarries out

RÍO SAN PEDRO

295

of reedy swamps known as *civales*. Those fires, we heard, had spread to high forest, and were evidently extensive, judging by the reddened sun we had seen when leaving Paso.

A tall, slim woman with an intelligent look, Doña Marta, agreed to cook for us (her Mexican husband, Moisés Alpuch, also tall and handsome, was a chicle contractor on a small scale, and a man who would do me a service some years later). Then we were shown a spring near the riverbank, where cooler but still somewhat limey water flowed.

My lodgings had walls of poles set fairly close together, but not close enough to exclude the largest of my nocturnal visitors, a huge toad, which woke me up by knocking something over. The more numerous visitors were big, tan-colored cockroaches, which attacked the victuals in force, eating their way through polyethylene bags; in the morning I threw a boxful of them to the chickens, to their delight. A large sow was sleeping immediately outside my walls, in fact reclining against them, she and her litter contributing strange sounds to the midnight music of my gallinaceous neighbors.

In the morning I learned that the sideburns belonged to the nominal guardian of the ruins, but if that was really his position, I was puzzled, for I was fairly sure that of all the archaeological sites in Petén, only Tikal and Seibal had guards. Anyway, he did show me round part of the site. The center of it was not far from the ranch house, and yet every single tree had been cut down within the one square kilometer occupied by the ranch. Since it was illegal to fell trees within an archaeological site, here was the first sign of the rancher's contempt for the law.

The best preserved stela had evidently been lying face-down until turned by the looters, who used two fragments of a carved altar as props to make it easier to saw the stela's butt off. But when the hardness of the stone thwarted them, they drilled a row of holes with the idea of splitting it off. (In 1971, Ed Shook told me that a young acquaintance of his, the son of a member of the Consejo del Estado, had flown up to El Naranjo in someone's private plane, and found looters at work boring holes in a stela, while the guardia looked on, all quite happy and joking.) Finding themselves still frustrated, they turned to cutting off the inscription: they tried sawing first, and then chiseling—with predictable results. Then I went to examine the large pyramid behind this stela, and found that its rear portion had been totally demolished by the looters.

Next, the so-called guardian of the ruins showed me a stela that was now almost hidden beneath a tree recently felled, and kindly cleared enough of it away to make it visible. It was only moderately weathered, and had evidently been in four roughly equal pieces, though one of them was now missing. Polo built a scaffold and ladder to enable me to photograph that, and also the large stela. Then I drew and photographed most of the other sculpture.

20.2 Aviateca DC-3 minutes after crash landing at "Lacandón" airstrip, 1961.

Since I had only brought enough food for four days, it was now time to start mapping the site, with Polo's assistance. The area must have been partially cleared in the previous year, but there were still many piles of recently cut brush making the job more difficult. But, oh, it was *hot*! In April, when skies are clear and the air is still, Petén can be almost too hot for work even to be contemplated, let alone engaged in; but there at El Naranjo, in a treeless expanse, it was a furnace. It was pointless to speculate about the shade temperature, for shade there was none. Then I noticed that the bubble in the glass tube of my K&E hand-level was becoming smaller and smaller as the heat expanded the spirit in it—until it burst! It was only by taking quick dips in the pool at the spring that Polo and I were able to go on working.

On the fourth day, the patrón of the ranch returned. He was a Mexican from Campeche named Manuel Dehesa Morales. I gave him the governor's letter and went back to work. And then, just as Polo and I had come across a large altar that we hadn't previously noticed, several men appeared with flaming torches, setting fire to all the brush, and this, dry as tinder, burst into roaring flames. Polo and I had to run for our lives.

Not a word had Dehesa said to me about the imminent torching. I sought him out and cursed him with unconcealed fury, using the worst epithet I could conjure up, *pendejo cabronal!* It was lucky, I suppose, that he didn't retaliate with a slash of his machete, but perhaps he remembered the governor's letter and abstained. But in any case, I took him to be not so much a choleric type as a cold and calculating wretch.

I stalked about in a vile temper for most of the afternoon, and while gazing at smoldering waste, uttered my views of Dehesa to a man I encountered, who turned out to be his brother! He told me Dehesa had yet to buy the land, and only applied for it; also that he was now primarily in the chicle business and had cleared a landing field some twenty-five miles to the southwest. (And there, two Lacandón couples had settled, apparently the last of scattered colonies that more than a century ago still existed in Guatemalan territory. The landing field soon came to be called "Lacandón," and a few years later the DC-3 in which I was traveling came in there to pick up chicle, but crashed and slid off into undergrowth. The plane was a write-off, but fortunately there were no serious injuries, and in no time the two Lacandón men were grinning down from on top of the vine-draped fuselage as the passengers scrambled to leave it.)[1]

The journey back upriver was uneventful, and the scheduled DC-3 carried us back to Flores. I reported my findings to the governor, and then, back in the capital, did so again to David Vela, the editor of *El Imparcial*, the one serious newspaper in the country. He requested a written account, and this I delivered, along with a rough drawing of the three surviving pieces of the stela that had been under the fallen tree. I also hinted strongly that Dehesa was responsible for the looting—or was at least complicit: for how could he not be? Vela, a member of the board supervising the National Institute of Anthropology and History, translated and published the article, which in later years he would refer to as the first published notice of the looting that was beginning to imperil Guatemala's archaeological heritage—along with that of most other countries.

Believing those ruins to be unknown, I delved in a Maya dictionary and cooked up a name, "Ocoltún," meaning "stolen stone"—or so I hoped, and as such it appears on some maps. But then I learned that in fact the site had already been mentioned in a published report written by Ed Shook, of the Carnegie Institution. During World War II, he had been appointed to supervise the extraction of rubber from trees growing wild in Petén, and while doing this work had traveled down the river and made a brief inspection of the ruins, giving them the name "La Florida." This name of course, supersedes Ocoltún. Fortunately, Shook had also photographed that stela broken into four fragments, while all four of them were still in situ.

In retrospect, I wonder if there may have been an additional reason for Dehesa's hostile attitude. For there were ruins of far greater importance of which I knew

20.3 *El Perú Stela 34 was first sawed into blocks; then the carved front surface of each was sawed off, to be reassembled for sale. I retrieved what I could of the discarded lateral inscriptions, one of which can be seen here.*

nothing—and wouldn't for some years—situated upstream a few miles below Paso Caballos, and these were being plundered at that very time, in an operation based downriver in Tenosique—or so I believe. Without the slightest doubt, Dehesa was involved, and it would have been inconvenient for him, to say the least, to have me around witnessing the arrival of a boatload of "merchandise."

By the time I did hear about those ruins, five years later, a landing field had been cleared at El Naranjo ranch for a weekly service by Aviateca. I had flown in there primarily to take a second look at La Florida, but then Moisés Alpuch told me about El Perú—as those other ruins had been named, for no obvious reason. Three months earlier, as he told me, he had taken Sally Christie, a graduate student at the University of Pennsylvania, to see them.[2] She was traveling with her husband and young son, but they had found the walking very hard, halting often to rest, and in the end had been able to spend less than an hour at the ruins. She may well have been planning to return for a more serious study, but then she, her husband Robert, and the child went to Belize for a weekend at Ambergris Cay. The plane they chartered crashed and they all perished.

So then Moisés dropped me at La Guacamaya on the right bank of the San Pedro, about four miles downstream from Paso. Five years earlier, this spot had been uninhabited, but now a young man from Tabasco named Antonio Cabrera had chosen to settle there with his family, probably because of a freshwater pond that lies about half a mile in from the riverbank. He had been there for more than a year, and obviously was very poor. The only structure he'd managed to build was an open-sided galera, through which pigs and chickens wandered. The two older boys looked unhealthy, with distended stomachs and brownish hair that should have been black. Everything they needed had to be sent for from Paso Caballos, and came at exorbitant price, so I persuaded Antonio to trust me to send directly by Aviateca various groceries and a protein supplement (produced by a brewery as a by-product), instead of paying him cash for his services.

Then I watched as they took an afternoon siesta, two adults and three children piling into one huge, homemade hammock. At night, they retired into a homemade bed consisting of two sacks sewn together and stretched across a wooden frame. Antonio's wife had a perfect Maya profile, and I remember her best for her tortillas: they were the finest I'd ever eaten.

In the morning, two-year-old Manuel came up shyly and kissed my hand as a greeting. Then after a quick breakfast we set off. In about an hour we came to an escarpment, up which an oil company had bulldozed a track, ascending it diagonally. We followed that, and almost the first feature I saw was something very unusual, a square subterranean chamber, originally vaulted from two, or just conceivably four sides (the vaults had fallen)—this, in a flat extension of the plaza.

The stelae were a grisly sight. Nearly all of them had been sawn or deliberately broken. All the damage seemed to have been done within the previous four or five years, except for one early stela with a beautifully preserved sculptured surface, for this one, judging by its fresh appearance, could only have been smashed up recently—and most destructively, perhaps with the back of an axe, and certainly without use of a saw. I was able to fit a few fragments together, but most of them seem to have been carried away, and as these can hardly have been reunited into anything saleable, I imagine they were junked.

By mid-afternoon it began to rain, so we started back, but Antonio, who lacked experience in the bush, went off in the wrong direction, until I checked my compass. Then we came upon some *coche de monte* (collared peccary). Antonio shot one in the leg, his dogs attacked it, and one pig managed to get a dog's hind leg into his jaws. There were frightful squeals, until Antonio managed to put his foot on the throat of the pig, and the

20.4 *Pigs on a plane: a noisy load for an Avro Anson in Chiapas.*

badly bitten dog was freed. It was still a job to kill the pig, which managed to go on snapping its jaws fiercely.

The dog limped home on three legs, and was recovering remarkably well until it was given the customary hair-of-the-dog treatment: that is, poulticing with a gravy made from the liver of the pig that bit it. Next day, though, it was improving. When back at the ruins that day, I made a sketch plan of the site's center, and then awaited the arrival of Moisés to take me back to El Naranjo.

The sky was threatening as we left, and soon the rain began and became a cloudburst. The surface of the river became white with rebounding raindrops and splashes until the rain settled down to a drizzle. The poor boatman, Ernesto (known to his friends, for some reason, as "Borracha") had no raingear and soon was obviously feeling extremely cold. I was wet through in spite of having a raincoat and being half-covered by a plastic sheet. By the time we reached Pénjamo (a camping spot), Ernesto could bear the cold no longer, and as it had stopped raining, brought the boat to shore in order to find something else to wear. I lent him a dry but sweaty shirt, and got out a groundsheet from my baggage to drape him with.

Soon, it grew dark, and the riverscape became one huge Rohrschach blot, slowly changing shape, with the boat heading towards the narrowest part of the blot. Flashes of light from *cocayos* on the banks (these are luminous flying beetles) appeared as two synchronous flashes, each one above its reflection.

Then we reached the rapids. The first one saw of them was a faint streak across the black of the river, then a rushing sound could be heard above the noise of the outboard. After three of these rapids had been negotiated, we swung round two grassy promontories on the right-hand side, keeping very close to them. In the beams of two flashlights (both quite weak) I could make out very little; certainly not the entrance to the Chicle Development Company canal, which I remembered having to pole through, from an earlier visit in the dry season. But now, with the motor shut off, Moisés and Ernesto were controlling the boat with poles as it surged and swung about, shouting to each other, *"Pegadito, pegadito! Abrese, no hay pena; por atrás! Con este puto foco no se mira nada; cambia su lado!"* and finally, *"Ya pasamos, por gracia de Dios!"* ("Now we are through, thank God!")

There remained one more rapid, its passage made more confusing and weird by a cloud of vapor that hung over it and caught the sweeping flashlight beams.

Half an hour later we came to El Caribe, a camp on the right bank where Moisés had chicleros working. The sound of the motor woke them up, and soon they were emerging from their pabellones and giving us coffee. With considerable satisfaction we also absorbed some heat from the *fogón* (a cooking fire set on a surface of ashes and lime mounted on a table). The chicleros were a picturesque band of men in the lamplight, and when the cook emerged from her chrysalis, she proved to be a Maya-speaking woman from Yucatán. But how different her manner was from that of her "sisters" in her homeland; she was joking and teasing with great assurance and in a very loud voice.

We reached El Naranjo at about 11 p.m., and I climbed into my hammock around midnight, extremely glad to be out of damp clothes.

It wasn't until April 1973 that I returned to El Perú. On this occasion, the Aviateca flight to Paso Caballos called first at El Naranjo, and as the plane approached the runway, I saw that something was going on in the East Plaza of the La Florida ruins. So while the unloading and loading of cargo was in progress, I ran down and discovered that—of all things—a sawmill was being set up there! A deep trench had been dug near Stela 9 for the sliding carriage on which trunks were to be guided through the saw, and logs were already being piled up nearby. Impotent fury overcame me: how could such senseless barbarities be permitted?

On landing at Paso Caballos, I arranged to be taken down the river to La Guacamaya on the following day, and for a mule to be sent there for our use. The boat passage would be provided by Don Valentín García, who was firm about departure at 4 a.m. because he would be transporting pigs to a place farther downriver, and pigs cannot stand heat. Once, he told me, he had been taking pigs on a long journey, and several died. "The lard," he said, "melted, and they drowned in it."

So we were up at 3:45 a.m. There was no sign of life elsewhere, however, and it was not until seven that we departed.

I had a camp made near the ruins, and we spent ten days there. The only changes I noticed were two small acts of senseless vandalism. On my previous visit, I had epoxyed together some fragments of a beautiful pectoral ornament and part of a belt, the red paint on it still bright (these were among the fragments of the recently smashed up stela, mentioned above). Now it had been broken into pieces again, and on the cheeks of the belt mask had been scratched: "R. Aguilar, *ruinero*," and on the pectoral, "Ian Graham, *estelero*."

Rubén Aguilar had been with me on that earlier visit; but I was greatly surprised at seeing my own name, since to the best of my knowledge no Petenero in those days knew my actual first name, for I was always "Don Juan." The other vandalic act was worse: prominent among the adornments of the towering headdress of Stela 18 was a grotesque mask. This was carved in full relief, so that although it was shown in profile, the full set of teeth and the palate could be seen from a suitable angle. This had been deliberately smashed. (Only slightly mitigating this loss were photos I'd taken of both damaged items on my previous visit.)

Later, I figured out who was responsible. In the capital, I had met a charming Guatemalan lady who had opened an excellent restaurant on the Avenida Reforma. Her Argentinian husband I had met only once, but I noticed after a time that he was seldom to be seen, and I learned why: he now spent most of his time jaguar hunting along the Río San Pedro; and, significantly, on the one occasion on which I ran into him in Petén, he was accompanied by Manuel Dehesa. I was also told that he had developed a serious drug habit. Perhaps he eventually pulled himself together, but of his responsibility for this senseless vandalism I have no doubt, since he did indeed know my proper given name.

Among the tasks I tackled during this sojourn at El Perú was an attempt to recon-stitute one of the many sawn-up stelae. To begin with, its top, carved with quite badly eroded glyphs, had been sawed off and left alone, as having no interest. The rest of the shaft had then been cut into blocks, and the carved surface sliced off each of them. I

20.5 El Perú Stela 39, reconstructed on paper, as planned for the "Monument to the Unknown Looter."

thought I would be able to reassemble at least those blocks bearing the inscriptions on their sides, as these could be matched, but was much less confident about solving the huge jigsaw puzzle of all the other blocks that had one plain surface (the back) and five sawn surfaces. Still, I was anxious to do this if possible, because if successful, I might be able to identify it with the restored sculptured surface displayed in some museum, by comparing both the dimensions of the latter and the pattern of the saw cuts in it with those of the reassembled blocks. In this way, a precise provenience for the museum piece would be established, and the texts on the face of monument completed by those on the sides.

The task, I thought, should be feasible if one studied the angle of the saw cuts (for they were seldom cut exactly at right angles to the surface), and also the exact dimensions of each cut face of each block. Any hollows or striations in the stone cut through by the saw would help identify a match. With these clues, it might be possible to match up all the mating surfaces. The strenuous part of this task was the physical labor of heaving heavy blocks about and trying them for fit, with the attendant danger of hernias and squashed fingers.

At last the job was done, and I looked for some nearby vantage point from which to take a photograph—a general view showing the assembled blocks. There was only one small mound, no more than eighteen inches high. I was about to step on it when I saw that in fact it was a heap of sawn fragments, now covered with leaves. What I found was scarcely believable, for there, jumbled up in a heap, lay the rectangular fragments of carved surface that had been cut with so much labor from that stela! But the rectangles of carved surface no longer existed as such; they had all broken into smaller pieces.

The whole thing was mysterious and most depressing, for of course it presented me with the far more challenging puzzle of fitting all of these small fragments back onto the same blocks of stone from which each one of them been cut. The fact that the carved surface was badly eroded made this jigsaw puzzle much more difficult. But at last I had almost all of them in place—with one curious exception: for just one block, I could not identify a single fragment cut from it.

This anomaly was puzzling, but a possible explanation occurred to me: perhaps the carved surface from that one block had been sent off to the promoter of this whole wretched enterprise as a sample, and he, upon receiving it in his comfortable air-conditioned headquarters, perhaps in Tenosique's Hotel Rome, would have sent back the message, "This is worthless. Junk it."

My labors had largely been in vain, but not entirely. The inscriptions on the sides were recorded, and we do know, in outline, what kind of scene had been carved on the front, for it showed unmistakably two men with "flap-staffs" facing each other.

On later visits to El Perú, I made use of the same technique to "reconstruct" other stelae. In the plaza there was one unusually large mass of cubes of stone, and this I was able to sort out and recompose into two stelae, originally set up side-by-side in a row of three (the third stela having been too badly damaged to interest the looters). This done, it was easy to determine where the reconstructed monuments had come to rest. One was in the Kimbell Museum, in Fort Worth, Texas, and the other in the Cleveland Museum of Art, Ohio.[3]

But in both of these, the lower register of the stela was missing—as a close inspection of the Cleveland stela would lead anyone to conclude, for there are otherwise inexplicable lumps in relief at the bottom, these in fact being edges of the earth-monster mask that had been below it. At the site, I noted that the now shaven butt of that stela, still lying there, showed that the sculptured surface on the basal register had been removed as four slices, the height of each being about twice its width. So when an FBI agent I met during the Hollinshead case showed me photographs taken by him in 1971 of a carved limestone panel cut just like that in the home of a Mr. Andrews of San Diego, California, it was easy to identify it positively as the lower register of the Cleveland stela.

Because the FBI photograph was not very sharp, I needed a better one to make a composite of the whole monument for publication. With this in view, I called on Mr. Andrews (the founder and owner of the now defunct Pacific Southwest Airlines) and politely asked if I might photograph his antique panel.

"No, you cannot," he replied.

"But sir, you may not be aware that the slices of your panel are wrongly assembled; won't you allow me to show you how they should go?"

"No thank you," he replied, and closed the door in my face.

I also put together the remains of another large monument, Stela 39, both on paper and photographically. The fact that both its front and back had been carved, with the whole of one sawn off, but only certain blocks sawn from the other, made the task a little easier. The areas missing from this side show that a pectoral ornament and belt, presumably rich in detail, had been cut from the subject's waist and thighs, as had two areas on either side of the principal figure's legs—these, presumably, bearing images of either prisoners or dwarfs. But the basal register—a fine monster mask with little seated figures within the eye sockets—was left intact.

On Wednesday, 18 April 1984, I summed up in my notebook the work I had just done at El Perú: the mapping, sufficient for my purposes, and all the sculpture in the main plaza recorded.

The biggest job was posed by Stela 38, for some of its sawn blocks lay in a pit. These had to be winched out—save only the butt, which was too big and still partly buried. These pieces compose the back and sides of the lower portion, below an old fracture, of a fine stela, the entire front of which had been sliced off and removed. Now at least I have the exact pattern of cuts, and could recognize it quickly. The upper fragment of the stela lay face-down, so the back is quite eroded, but the lower half is well preserved. One mystery remains: In front of this stela there's a looter's pit, and near it lie fragments of a circular altar with an inscription on its rim. Also nearby are altar supports in the form of grotesque heads, and cut fragments which seem to indicate there having been a third one. All this goes to suggest that the said altar once rested on those supports in front of the imposing stela, 3.3 m tall; and that the looters moved it to look for a cache beneath. Then what can be the explanation for the wide and thick slab of stone lying half-buried in that pit? It looks as if it had been there before the digging. On one edge there seems to be the top, or more likely the bottom of a glyph panel, as if it were a stela butt. Then, where is the rest of the stela? I am also perplexed by the apparently missing blocks of the stela that stood in the centre of the plaza. This wretched piece seems to have been attacked with hammer and chisel before being neatly sliced (evidently by a better equipped band of looters).

"This year," as I noted in my diary,

we encountered variable weather, but at least there were no insect plagues as in other years—one year chiggers, another *colmoyotes*, another ticks. But the heat became intolerable. Already exhausted when I arrived here, I gradually lost all energy as the air became more oppressive, heavy with moisture and smoke, and perfectly still. I had to force myself to drag my bones about. Then one afternoon. . . it began to cloud over, thunder was heard in the distance & a few drops of rain fell. It wasn't until we had dined & taken to our hammocks that the rain became heavy, and then lightning flashed and thunder began to crash. For lack of a trench under the eaves of our *champa*, water was threatening to sweep into it, so we began furiously digging a trench with trowels, and using a machete to cut roots. The rain became so torrential that at intervals I had to stop excavating and throw water out of the trench with the trowel. Then the storm passed right over us, with the sharp crack lacking the resonance of more distant thunder; and only then I did remember it was Friday the 13th, and wondered whether a tree would fall on us. What did fall was hail in lumps the size of sugar cubes. What a sight I must have been in those flashes of lightning, as I worked stark naked and not even wearing boots (no point in getting them wet).

The next day was beautifully cool, my energy returned, and nearly three more weeks of useful work were accomplished before returning to Guatemala City. And there, on collecting a packet of mail forwarded from the Peabody Museum, I found among its varied contents a torn scrap of paper bearing the legend: "You're invited State Dinner at White House, May 18th."

Well, good heavens, what was this? Surely, there had to be some mistake. But having no reason to remain in Guatemala, I flew back to Cambridge—to discover that no mistake had been made. So as a first step I had my dinner jacket dry-cleaned, then took the train to Washington, D.C., found a room at a modest hotel near the old Willard Hotel, and at the appointed hour presented myself at the door of the White House.

Perhaps I went to the wrong door, but it certainly wasn't flung open invitingly, and gradually it occurred to me that perhaps guests invited to state dinners don't usually arrive on foot! But in the end I was admitted, and during the cocktail period mooched about, not knowing a soul, though I did recognize Rock Hudson. Then at last we all trooped into a vast dining hall, accompanied by music played by the orchestra of the Marine Corps Women's Band. Shown to my seat, I found I was placed between the Indian ambassador's wife, who spoke not a word of English, and Selwa Roosevelt, known as "Lucky," the wife of Archibald Roosevelt. Now I could understand how I had been included in the guest list, for I'd met her a couple of times with my old friend Ruthie Pratt, and Lucky was now the president's chief of protocol.

When dessert was served, it took the form of individual cactuses growing out of a "soil" of chocolate mousse in little plastic flowerpots, with tiny slivers of coconut serving as prickles. Lucky then told me confidentially that at the last minute before the service of dinner, she had gone down to the kitchen to check that everything was ready—and noticed to her horror that sitting on the chocolate mousse at the foot of each cactus was a little Mexican asleep under his large sombrero! She had them removed at once!

Then followed lengthy orations by President Reagan and by his guest of honor, the president of Mexico, Miguel de la Madrid, and then at long last we all arose from our tables. Then Lucky seized me and dragged me aside, announcing that she would introduce me to the president. As this was the last thing I wanted, and I couldn't imagine why he should be interested, I demurred and hung back, but in vain, and soon I was hustled into the Presence. Lucky introduced me as an archaeologist, and Reagan, who had just returned from China, responded by expressing his amazement at the antiquities he'd been shown in China.

Well, my knowledge of China and its antiquities was shamefully inadequate, so in attempting to keep up my side of the conversation, I mentioned an extraordinary Chinese film that our revered professor of Chinese archaeology, the late K. C. Chang, had shown us at the Peabody Museum. It followed various stages in the excavation of a tomb dating from the time of the Warring States, about 400 B.C. The climax came when the lid from a great stone sarcophagus was raised, and proved to be full of pink jelly. Sleeves were rolled up, arms plunged into the jelly, and out of it was lifted a well-preserved body. This was laid on a table, such jelly as still adhered was swabbed off, and there lay a female corpse in an extraordinarily good state of preservation. A calf was pinched and showed elasticity; then a knee was raised and, amazingly, it doubled up without resistance.

"Do you know," Mr. Reagan asked me, "what—ah—this jelly was made of?"

"I'm sorry, Mr. President," I replied, "I'm unable to answer your question, because the magnetic sound track of our print of the film had been wiped out."

"Oh—ah—I'm sorry to hear that, because I'm thinking—ah—that if it can do that—ah—for the dead, then I'd like to sleep on it!"

At this point someone, to my great relief, tactfully stepped in to turn the conversation to some less morbid topic. But then I noticed that at my side there was a diminutive young woman busy with pencil and notepad—and sure enough, the Style Section of the *Washington Post* carried next morning an accurate version of our conversation under the headline, "Toasts and Jelly at Reagan's Dinner for de la Madrid."

On returning to El Perú in 1998 for about the fifth time, one of my aims had been to make preliminary plans for the reconstruction and re-erection of Stela 39. The task would be challenging: first a concrete foundation would have to be prepared, and then two tall and substantial poles erected with a beam secured across the top. A chain-hoist hanging from this would enable each block in turn to be raised and then lowered into its proper place and secured there with mortar. Nevertheless, I thought the task would be well worth the trouble.

How impressive this "Monument to the Unknown Looter" would be, with the entire sculptured surface sliced clean off one side, and the other partially preserved, save for glaring rectangular gaps; and then, the undamaged monster mask below would show the high quality of what had been lost. But alas! I found on arrival that some ignorant and forever cursed looter and vandal had hacked off part of that mask not long before, destroying its value and gaining absolutely nothing for himself by doing so.

From the tourist's point of view, the ruins of El Perú in their present state offer few attractions—merely the discarded remains of once-great monuments that are beginning to hide their injuries under mantles of moss; and shapeless mounds revealing no finished masonry. My projected monument would at least have provided an educative focal point, and an image suitable for distribution on postcards.

So far, I have not succeeded in positively identifying any of the missing pieces of this particular stela. In Stockholm, however, there is a large stela fragment which may well correspond with the portion above the fracture of this stela. This fracture would have occurred long ago, presumably when the stela was knocked down by a falling tree. If this identification is correct, then what, I wonder, happened to the lower portion?

The locations at that time of monuments or fragments identified as coming from El Perú were these:

> In Mexico: Oaxaca
> Puebla
> In the U.S: Cleveland
> Fort Worth
> Chicago (a fragment recently returned to Guatemala)
> Dallas (an altar, tentatively identified)
> In Europe: Paris
> Stockholm (tentatively identified)
> Zurich
> Brussels, later transferred to Budapest.

If the Dallas altar really is from El Perú, then very likely it was a table altar, formerly supported on those sculptured legs next to Stela 39. In her brief notes, Sally Christie mentioned "a beautiful large altar stone. One side had just been cut with a chain saw. Probably left because they heard we were coming. They must be organized and well financed to afford saws like that." Although I am sure she was mistaken in supposing that a chainsaw had been used, rather than the usual two-man, crosscut saw, this report may be significant. When I arrived, three months later, that altar had disappeared from the site (for I cannot believe I failed to notice it); and later I was told that the arrival at El Naranjo of an altar had been the cause of considerable amazement. Then in 1981 my friend Don Chofo, of Laguna Perdida, told me he had seen the altar before it was looted, and identified the looter as a certain Miguel Mazariegos, of El Martillo, downstream from the ranch. He likewise described the astonishment caused by the objects brought out, including "an altar showing an Indian standing on steps." This does sound like the altar sold by John Stokes of Palisades, New York, to the Dallas Museum.

The Zurich piece was identified only on the basis of style. It consisted of the belt and thighs of a ruler carved in characteristic El Perú style, with three rows of Oliva shell "tinklers" shown in almost full relief. (An auction catalogue shows that it was later sent to Hamburg for sale.)

The Brussels piece I happened to see from the sidewalk, while looking through the windows of an art gallery, the owner of which I later came to regard as one of Europe's principal importers of plundered Maya antiquities. Its odd, polygonal shape was intriguing, so I went in to have a look, and on recognizing its El Perú style, took out a sheet of paper and started to draw it. The proprietor, correctly suspecting me of being an enemy agent, came over and said, "I will allow you two minutes to sketch this piece."

Back in my office at the Peabody Museum, I had no difficulty identifying it as having been cut from Stela 37. This monument had never been completed by the Maya, and its polygonal shape could be accounted for, partly by avoidance of an area left for a planned inscription, but not yet carved and left rough, and partly by a break subsequently suffered by the shaft.

Whether this piece belonged to the gallery owner, or had been sent to him by Everett Rassiga for sale on consignment, I do not know. But a subsequent encounter with this piece rather suggests the latter. I had been told that because of the prohibition against the sale of such antiquities imposed by UNESCO in the early seventies, Rassiga had negotiated exchanges with Iron Curtain countries. Thus, in exchange for a Maya sculpture, he would receive some item originating within those countries that *could* be sold legally in the United States.

When, therefore, I happened to be in Budapest some years later for an entirely different reason, I inquired at the Néprajzi Múzeum whether there were any Maya pieces in their collections. It was August, and most of the staff were on vacation, but a most obliging employee allowed me to search in the storage area, and there I found, inserted on edge in a rack with plywood partitions, a limestone panel, smoothly sawn on one side. I pulled it out, and it was the piece I had last seen in Brussels.

El Perú is a very large site. I cannot claim to have mapped it all, but the mapping I have done (with the help during one season of my former colleague Peter Mathews) shows it to be one of the largest in Petén. But just ten minutes of wandering in the main plaza revealed the magnitude of destruction wrought by the looters, and made me lament bitterly that archaeologists had not been the first to find those ruins.

I once made the acquaintance of a dear old Englishman, Moysey Adams, who had worked for the Chicle Development Company in the 1920s. During that time, he established a seasonal camp up the Río San Juan, not far from El Perú. He still had a map that he had made of the area, and gave it to me; it showed that his men had never penetrated into the vicinity of El Perú. Chicleros of later times would certainly have been aware of the site, but with the exception of Ed Shook, inquisitive archaeologists never reached that area—and Ed was not told of it.

If, fruitlessly, one attempts to place the blame for the great disaster that the sack of El Perú truly was, who should bear the blame? Collectors and dealers and their field workers must certainly bear much of it, but the primary responsibility, as I see it, rests on another person—someone I can identify only as "ancestor" in a genealogical tree of culpability—yet a person who, just by himself, could have, and should have, prevented this particular disaster from occurring. How so? Well, that bulldozed track we followed up the escarpment on my first visit—where was it going? As the marks of its passage show, it went right through the center of the ruins, where the driver could not have failed to notice the tall mounds, and probably the stelae, too. The bulldozer was surely not just going for a Sunday afternoon stroll, but instead preparing a track for the vehicles of geophysicists to use, so it must have borne some traffic during exploration of the area. But did that oil company (Citgo, formerly Cities Service) report their discovery, as required under the terms of their concession? Apparently not.

One curious anecdote concerning a monument from this sadly plundered site may be worth telling for intrinsic interest. This had its origin in January 1980, when I found a note in my diary, while on my way to Mexico, reminding me to try getting in touch with a lady named Dolores Olmedo (known to her friends as "Lola"), among whose countless possessions there was rumored to be a fine Maya stela. Boldly I called her up, and to my pleasant surprise was invited to come and see it.

She was living, I found, near Xochimilco, in a house built by its *cacique* (chief) in the sixteenth century, within a large, walled enclosure containing lawns, ponds, swans, flamingoes, and macaws, among other creatures. The house itself was filled with paintings by Diego Rivera—as was hardly surprising for a lady who was widely known to have been his mistress, but it seems she had also bought some herself, perhaps to keep the price up.

One also hears that a relationship that she once had with Miguel Aleman had also been beneficial, for when Mexico City's old railway station was demolished, she somehow ended up with some of the real estate, which must have been a comfort in her declining years. Also whispered was a possible connection with the drug world.

The stela was in the dining room, overlooking a long, marble-topped table surrounded by twenty ornate chairs. It was almost four meters tall, and proclaimed to me its origin as El Perú, or some other site not far from there. It had been cut into horizontal slices and (presumably) reassembled right there, in the dining room.

It was going to be difficult to draw the whole thing in one morning, even with the help of the tall stepladder that the staff obligingly produced. In fact, using that ladder was quite hazardous, as the floorboards were rotten on one side of the stela. On climbing to the top step, I attempted to achieve some stability by grasping the stela's deep relief, and in doing so got my hands dirty (to be avoided when intending to draw). Even so, I was afraid that the ladder and I might keel over and crash down on the marble table.

During that morning, when Madame Olmedo came in to see me, I found a dumpy figure in a bouffant black silk dress. I took note of her pale skin, retroussé nose, and a hairline that began, like Queen Elizabeth I's or that of Italian Rennaissance ladies, far back on the head; in Madame Olmedo's case, a facelift or two may have played a part.

I would have until nearly three o'clock—the usual luncheon hour—to work. But when the maids laid the table, they put two places, and I'd seen no family member or likely guest in the house. I began to worry, having heard some tale of Diego Rivera's daughter Ruth, whose husband was arrested on charges of involvement in the drug trade. Fearing that her husband's associates would bribe the prison guards to poison him to keep him quiet, Ruth decided to bring all his meals to him herself, and these she arranged to obtain from Lola Olmedo's kitchen.

But he would die anyway—and later I learned that her husband, who won fame as a rider in the Olympic games, and was a friend of both Aleman and Olmedo, was caught with a large amount of cocaine in the Paris airport—but died of poison before trial.

So it struck me, as a fantasy, that perhaps she might know of me as a notorious troublemaker in the Maya antiquities market, and therefore invite me to a Borgian feast. (But fortunately I made my getaway in time!)

CHAPTER 21

Operación Rescate

It was the growth of European railroad and steamship services in the 1820s that first enabled collectors, national or individual, to carry off massive monuments removed from sites in the eastern Mediterranean with which to embellish their well-appointed halls. Rivalry among the great powers in acquiring such sculpture would become intense, with agents of France, England, Bavaria, and Prussia cruising the eastern Mediterranean in search of fine specimens—a race in which France emerged triumphant with the Venus de Milo.

Although interrupted for a time by World War I, the trade in heavy antiquities began again soon after peace had been restored, for by 25 March 1924, the well-known Paris dealer René Gimpel noted in his diary: "A specialist in Egyptian art has told me that he is waiting for a large Egyptian statue. To get it out of Egypt it was cut into 46 pieces. This happens every day."

Forty years later, this lamentable business began to afflict the Maya area, too, with ill-gotten trophies being openly advertised in European and American art magazines. But in spite of having learned something of the workings of this trade, I could never imagine that a Maya stela might appear in a department store; yet that is just what confronted me in 1966, on entering the Los Angeles branch of May's.

The stela happened to be one with which I was quite familiar: Stela 8 from Naranjo, Guatemala. There it stood, displayed as the centerpiece of an exhibition of Latin-American crafts, textiles, pre-Columbian ceramic vessels, modern imitations of them, etc. Peering through the greenery surrounding the stela I could see that it had been thinned, thereby losing the hieroglyphic inscription on its back.

When asked the price, a salesman told me it was valued at sixty thousand dollars, but was not for sale. In other words, it belonged to Mr. Morton D. May of St. Louis, Missouri, himself. (When I contacted Mr. May and suggested that he return it to Guatemala, he declared that he'd smash the stela rather than do so. Not for nothing was he known to his friends as "Buster May.")

I informed the Guatemalan government that the stela was in May's possession, but before any action could be taken, May had loaned this jewel of his collection to the St. Louis Art Museum. There was an exchange of letters, in which the title to it was restored to Guatemala, and in a gesture of goodwill, the government allowed it to remain on display in the art museum.

Naranjo is a large site in the Department of Petén, located—conveniently for looters—only eight miles from the Belize border. Fortunately, Teobert Maler, while working for the Peabody Museum early in the twentieth century, had made an excellent record of the monuments. His photographs are superb, but unavoidably his coverage was incomplete, and with the passage of fifty years, a more detailed record of the site and its monuments was badly needed.

When I was engaged by the Guttman Foundation to make a pilot study as a trial run before launching the Corpus, I chose Naranjo as one of the two sites for this trial, partly because of its easy accessibility, and also because a more complete record of its sculpture would certainly be useful. I had in fact briefly visited those ruins in 1959, finding them overgrown but not noticeably disturbed. Since then, I'd heard rumors of looters working there, but on returning to the site ten years later I was horrified to see the extent of the damage. Whether this had been the work of a single group or of various predators at different times I couldn't determine, but the fact that between them they had tried a number of absurd and damaging methods of reducing large sculptures to portable fragments showed a total lack of experience, or even common sense.

My decision to revisit Naranjo was timely, because the report I delivered to the Guatemalan Institute of Anthropology and History (IDAEH) aroused great concern, as it did at the National Museum of Archaeology and Ethnology. Neither institution, however, had sufficient funds to do anything about the situation until board members of the Asociación Tikal came to the rescue, having decided to extend their reach for the first time beyond Tikal itself (the asociación being a nongovernmental organization created primarily to supply some of Tikal's needs).

The director of the National Museum of Archaeology and Ethnology, Rafael Morales Fernández, lost no time in joining me at Naranjo, and we began planning the removal of those monuments that appeared to be in greatest danger. We hired a

*21.1 The aguada at Naranjo, three days before
our departure, March 1969.*

four-wheel-drive truck, ropes, winches, boards along which heavy stones could be winched up into a truck bed, and so on; and we rented a small field on the outskirts of Melchor de Mencos as a temporary storage area, and had it fenced in with barbed wire.

As most of the stelae had already fallen, one concern of ours was that by removing any stela to safety, knowledge of its original location would be lost. This was a matter of importance because the Maya often buried offerings of some kind in front of a monument's butt. So before leaving the capital, I'd had a one-inch-diameter bronze bar cut into pieces about one-and-a-half inches long, bringing also a set of punches, 0 to 9. Before removing a stela, then, we would punch its number onto one of those short pieces of bar, and bury it where the stela had been. This would enable any future archaeologist interested in knowing the exact setting of a stela that we had removed to find it with a metal detector.

We made good progress, but then Don Rafa had to return to the museum, and I had other expeditions planned. We were both worried about the security of the monuments we had assembled, and on returning a month or two later, I was alarmed at finding a small and well-preserved stela, newly discovered (and later numbered 41) lying in the street near the center of the town! In time, all these stelae, fragmentary or entire, were removed to a fenced area near the Flores airport, just behind the offices of FYDEP (the government agency responsible for Petén). There, unfortunately, they would remain for several years, and I began to suspect that some, at least, of the fragments had disappeared. But another two or three years would pass before I found the explanation.

While in Poptún, "a little bird" told me that various fragments of a stela of middling size, confiscated by the army from looters and of unknown origin, were still in the military compound. On asking to see it, I was referred from one officer to another, and eventually to a colonel, who proved not to be the arrogant and dismissive kind of colonel I'd expected, but instead, a calm and friendly person, willing to help.

He did, however, warn me of one difficulty: the fragments were in a small shed that also contained sticks of dynamite. Now, I knew that dynamite of recent manufacture was perfectly safe to handle; but these sticks were ancient, and I was advised to handle them with great caution. There must have been about forty of them, scattered about the floor, so I very delicately moved just enough of them to allow me to reach the back of the hut where the stela fragments were, and then began carrying them out one by one. It would have been easy to lose one's balance, carrying those heavy slabs of stone, but fortunately that didn't happen.

21.2 1973: Bridge on brecha *cut into Ucanal, which
comes in handy for transporting monuments to safety.*

Now: what to do with them? As I had epoxy paste with me, I suggested to the colonel that I cement the fragments together, attach them to a concrete pillar, and set up the restored monument on the dividing strip of the straight two-lane road that had been constructed inside the army base, up and down which platoons were marched daily. They could salute it, I thought, with an "Eyes, right!" on marching past. The colonel agreed, and I attached the stela (which had lost its butt) to the concrete post he provided and set it up as suggested. Because it had been thinned by the looters before it was broken, these operations were not too difficult.

Some years later, I passed the military base and noticed that the stela was no longer there. I had to ask several people before I learned its fate. The terrible period of military government, guerrillas, and repression had arrived, and the Poptún base now contained units of Kaibiles. These were the most fearsome soldiers in the army, trained to be tough and brutal. Rumor had it that on training exercises they were forced to eat dogs for survival.

Rashly, perhaps, under the circumstances, I approached a young lieutenant and asked if he knew what had happened to the stela. "Oh, it's now in the *parquesito de los Kaibiles*"—their little park. When I asked if I could go and see it, he replied that I'd need the permission of an officer of captain's rank or above. On obtaining this, I drove with him about half a mile into the pine woods to a clearing in a dell at the foot of a hill. This was the sacred grove of the elite military group. In the middle was a truncated pyramid of masonry surmounted by a flagpole and bearing an inscription cast in bronze (the Oath of the Kaibiles, by which they swore to strive ever toward improvement of their strength and capabilities, to pay no heed to heat or cold, hunger or thirst, etc.) From it ran radial pathways, edged with white-painted stones, each of them ending at a circular pathway, also edged with stones and defining the sacred space. In a move, perhaps, to petition succor from the ancient gods, fragments of Stelae 4, 28, and 35 of Naranjo, now painted white, had been placed at intervals round the circular path, just where the "spokes" met it. These had certainly been in the FYDEP compound, near the Flores airport. Another pathway led to a cement "stela" portraying the legendary figure of Kaibil, surrounded by fanciful hieroglyphs, and at the northernmost spoke stood the stela from the dynamite hut, also painted white.

I wonder what went on in this grove, thirty years ago. Did Kaibiles go there to examine their souls, or come *en masse* to celebrate mystic rites? I imagined them assembled by the light of the moon to reaffirm their oath and make a sacrificial offering, the nature of which I dared not imagine—all this to an accompaniment of Wagner played by a military marimba trio.

But I also have great satisfaction in reporting that *Operación Rescate* may be credited with transporting several fine sculptures to the National Museum of Anthropology and Ethnography in Guatemala City, while many others, entire or fragmentary, were deposited in the overflowing storage facilities at Tikal, much of this through the efforts of my friend, the late Rafa Morales.[1]

22.1 *Huey helicopter landing next to table altar
at Machaquilá.*

CHAPTER 22

Back to Machaquilá

E arly in 1969 the French archaeologist Henri Lehmann tracked me down in Guatemala City to ask a favor. He was organizing a great Maya exhibition that would open in the following year at the Petit Palais in Paris, and explained that he had obtained permission to transport a monument from Petén for exhibition there.[1] So now he was hoping I could suggest a stela suitable for this purpose.

As it happened, I had just come from Tamarindito, a site perched on the same upthrust ridge as Aguateca, where I'd started making a rough plan of the site and recording its monuments. Among these was a stela that I found lying face-down, with half of it still partly buried and therefore well preserved. In one sense the fact that it was broken into four pieces was regrettable, but from the aspect of removing it to safety— even via Paris—its breakage would certainly make matters easier.

By happy coincidence, the Dirección de Cartografía had in the previous year set up a Shoran distance-measuring station in the very plaza where the stela lay, choosing that spot for its height and clear view to the horizon; and to bring in the Shoran equipment and its antenna tower by helicopter, the plaza had been bushed as a helipad. So nothing could be more convenient, and as soon as Lehmann and the Guatemalan Institute of Anthropology and History had approved the plan, I returned with a couple of men to clear the helipad again, and with that done, I made the necessary arrangements with the Fuerza Aerea.

The Huey helicopter arrived punctually in Sayaxché. Captain Urrutia, the pilot, looked to me like the best type of World War II fighter pilot: tall, with curly black hair, he moved with quick and athletic assurance. With a ready grin, sparkling eye, and a devil-may-care look, you could be sure that he cut a devastating swath among the girls.

We flew up to Tamarindito, where three men awaited us to help load the stela fragments for their flight to Sayaxché, two pieces at a time. There, the four pieces were boxed and consigned to the capital by DC-3. For once, things went exactly as planned, but I must say—despite the wise maxim, *de mortuis nihil nisi bonum*—Lehmann's reputation for parsimony was fully confirmed, for he never offered to reimburse me for any of the expenses of this expedition, though he did reward me with a fish dinner in a restaurant that left him six dollars out of pocket—for the two of us. Nor did he bother to attribute to me the drawing of the stela that was reproduced in the exhibition catalog.

At the conclusion of the Seibal project in the following year, Gordon Willey and Ledyard Smith had already expressed concern about leaving the tall, slender, and still intact Stela 3 at the site, for fear that looters would break it in pieces and make off with them. Arrangements were therefore made with the relevant authorities for the stela to be transported, first by helicopter and then by DC-3, to Guatemala City, where it would be set up in the National Museum—as would the Tamarindito stela upon its return from France.

Stela 3 was fourteen feet tall, so there was no possibility of its fitting inside the helicopter's fuselage; Ledyard therefore had it wrapped elaborately, and then by some means established exactly where its center of gravity lay. Nylon ropes were then bound tightly around it at that point, knotting them at one side to form a loop for suspension. When the helicopter arrived at Sayaxché, the pilot (Captain Urrutia again) came over by jeep to familiarize himself with the situation.

He approved the setup, and that afternoon a whine and rhythmic flapping sound was heard, and the helicopter was soon hovering above the stela. A crewman jumped out and attached the hook at the end of a cable hanging from the belly of the machine onto the loop of rope, then hauled himself in. The engine screamed, and the Huey slowly climbed away. We all breathed a great sigh of relief.

It was not until next day that we heard how close to destruction the stela had come. With the helicopter whisking it through the air at about 80 miles per hour, the slipstream made it rotate. There was, indeed, a swivel joint between hook and cable, but this was not designed to swivel under a heavy load. Inevitably, then, the cable started to coil upon itself, becoming shorter with every revolution, and before long the stela would be banging against the runners and damaging them. Urrutia told me later that he already had his hand on the jettison lever, when—by the greatest of good fortune—he spotted a swampy area, and descended to rest the stela lightly upon it. The cable then untwisted, the flight was resumed, and Sayaxché was reached before the cable had become dangerously coiled again.

22.2 The author making a rubbing of Seibal, Stela 3.
Photo by Gordon R. Willey.

About a month later I was lodged at the Godoy Hotel in Sayaxché when who should appear there but Colonel Casasola, the promotor of FYDEP (the Petén development organization), accompanied by aides. He had come to escort President Méndez Montenegro and the minister of foreign relations to the inauguration of a nearby sawmill, and on learning that they might go on to Seibal, I offered my services as guide. My offer was curtly rejected.

"Oh, no thanks—the director of the Instituto de Antropología is coming."

(Knowing that he was scheduled to be in France, I doubted this.) Then David Vela, editor of the newspaper *El Imparcial* and member of the Instituto de Antropología's governing board, arrived and asked if I would provide this very service—thereby giving me, I must admit, a moment of *schadenfreude*. But on reaching Seibal, the president showed little interest in the ruins, unlike the minister of foreign relations, Emilio Arenales Catalán, who was much more lively and enthusiastic.

About two years later, Arenales called me to his office to discuss a project. In the following year it would be Guatemala's turn to hold the presidency of the United Nations General Assembly, and he could now reveal that he'd been named for that important post. Then he told me that with it came the privilege of mounting an exhibition of Guatemalan antiquities in the Metropolitan Museum in New York, and his ambition was to exhibit some fine examples of Maya monuments—but not, if possible, any of those that had long been exhibited in the National Museum. Perhaps I could make some suggestions—adding that he'd be able to secure the cooperation of the army in transporting any such monuments.

My recommendation was quickly made: Machaquilá. Here were monuments entirely unknown to the world, some of them almost as fresh as when first carved. The fact that some were broken into two or three pieces would make loading much easier, and the eventual cementing of them together would be simple. The only difficulty about this plan was preparation of the helicopter landing patch.

Arenales approved the plan. My decision not to consider walking in to the site from Poptún, as before, in order to cut that patch may have been influenced somewhat by my unhappy memories of the last time I did so. More persuasive, however, was my reasoning, first, that the site lay closer to the mouth of the river than to Poptún; second, that hurricane damage to the forest would be less serious that far west; and third, that the drop in elevation from the ruins to the mouth of the Río Machaquilá, as read from maps, didn't seem to suggest serious difficulty with waterfalls.

So a mid-sized dugout canoe with outboard motor was hired in Sayaxché, along with its *motorista* and four general workers (woodsmen all, as then went without saying). With food supplies, camping gear, a drum of gasoline, and axes all loaded in the boat, we set off upriver in early June 1968. On reaching Rancho Santa Amelia at the

22.3 *Hauling the canoe up over the rapids on the way to Machaquilá.*

mouth of the Santa Amelia River (which is actually the same river as the Machaquilá), we stopped for the night with my old acquaintance, Don Felix Kilcan. Shortly after setting off in the morning, we noticed an interesting relic: a mahogany log, sawn at both ends and lying on the bottom of the shallow river. It must have lain there for at least sixty years, ever since the days when the Hamet Mahogany Company was working in the area and floating its logs down the Pasión and Usumacinta rivers, to be caught by a chain across the river near Tenosique. A small proportion of logs always sank, and I'm told that even after decades underwater they are still worth money. But just then, of course, we couldn't consider trying to tow it away!

Soon, we began encountering obstacles. One was a tree at least a foot thick that had fallen across the river, its upper edge about an inch underwater. One of the men took his shoes off and, standing on it with his feet apart, swung his axe to cut it between his feet, with diminishing effect as the axe had an increasing depth of water to splash through first, but he did sever it.

Then there were rapids. The motor could not be used, for fear of damaging the propeller, but with all of us in the water, pushing, most of them were soon overcome. There were certainly more cascades and waterfalls than I had bargained for, and passage through a few of these entailed closely fought struggles.

22.4 *A dangerous*
moment on the way
to Machaquilá.

For the worst waterfall, which may have been about four feet high and rather narrow, with a flow that was thunderous, we unloaded everything on the bank. With long ropes attached to the bow, three of the lads were pulling for all their might from shore above the falls, sometimes securing the ropes around trees for a brief rest. Meanwhile, the rest of us were up to our waists in the swift current, trying to push the stern up—and sometimes finding it hard to remain upright ourselves. Our great fear was that the canoa might crack when halfway up, balanced on the rocky ledge, for they are not constructed to resist extreme bending forces amidships, and might break in two.

But we were lucky. In two days we arrived at El Final and made camp at the ruins. So, now to prepare the landing patch. I'd been given no guidance regarding the size it should have, but someone had told me it should be the size of a basketball court—but then, I had no idea of how big that was, either! In any case, we went to work in an area of the plaza adjacent to the table altar, this being free of really large trees, and then we cut up and dragged away the trees as they were felled. That done, we broke camp and returned to Sayaxché without incident. From there I sent a message reporting readiness of the landing patch, and moved to Poptún, where a helicopter coming from Guatemala would have to land in order to refuel.

I waited, but no instructions were forthcoming. A second message was similarly ignored. I then went up to the capital, but it wasn't until nearly three weeks after my first report of readiness had been sent that I managed to get in touch with Major Fuentes, who said, "Fine, then, tomorrow you can leave with Captain Morales as pilot, or on Friday."

But next morning at 7 a.m. the captain telephoned to say he had *catarrh*. Well, could he, I asked, find a substitute?

Nothing more was heard for the moment; then I was told that departure was planned for Monday. Come Monday, President Johnson's visit brought everything to a halt. So on Tuesday I delivered by hand a written ultimatum to Arenales, a similar verbal message to Colonel Batres, chief of public relations of the army, and another to the minister of defense: either they would provide a helicopter on the morrow, or I would leave for England.

This ultimatum produced results. Departure was set for 8:30 a.m. But when that hour came, the pilot, Rosales by name, appeared without his baggage, and went off to get it. Then Colonel Fuentes appeared, and as Rosales was still missing, I indicated my disappointment (or something of the kind) at this delay. A new pilot was promised, and as it turned out, this was Urrutia again, with a calm, undemonstrative copilot of Kekchi origin from Senahu.

We left at 10:15, landed at Poptún to refuel—allowing me, conveniently, to collect the bags I had left there—and then went on to Sayaxché. I engaged Antonio Kilcan and another experienced man, and asked Don Oscar to recruit ten other men for the next morning; then I went to the nearby sawmill to order sawn lumber.

Next day, with some of the men on board, along with camping equipment and provisions, we took off and set a compass course for the ruins. The landing patch was not hard to find, with the very visible dry bed of the river nearby as a guide, but I felt real fear as we approached the patch for landing. How it had shrunk! Indeed, as we came in, I was alarmed to see the blades chopping leaves and twigs from the trees, because I knew that if just the tip of a blade were to break off, the resulting imbalance could cause a disaster. But we settled down intact, and Urrutia simply sucked a breath in noisily with the corners of his mouth retracted, while flapping his right hand up-and-down sideways from the wrist three times. The Huey was unloaded, the men cut down and cleared away a few more trees, and Urrutia went back to Sayaxché for the night.

By the time the helicopter returned next morning, we had further enlarged the patch, and had moved two of the smaller stela fragments into position for loading. This time the lieutenant was piloting it, and Urrutia sat in the copilot's seat. He looked rather pale, and asked for a drink of water.

In Sayaxché, later, I heard that on returning there, Urrutia had downed a couple of drinks, and then offered rides to some girls. Apparently he threw the machine about in frightening maneuvers—one person even telling me he had looped-the-loop, but I'm not sure if that's possible in a helicopter! After another drink or two, he took out his revolver and shot out the bulbs of several streetlights (which hadn't functioned for years, anyway). He was then locked up for a while, so his pallor next morning was understandable.

The rest of the operation proceeded without a hitch. Urrutia was flying again, and on one trip, while wandering about the site, he discovered two fallen stelae that I had failed to notice (numbers 18 and 19, the first of these, a fine one—and stolen since then, of course). The stelae were loaded without boxing them up, as none was carved on more than one face. It was a considerable struggle, however, loading the thick and heavy Stela 13, even with all the men heaving and pushing to slide it up the sloping boards that we had put in place. When back in Sayaxché, crates were constructed from the boards I had ordered for each of the sculptures and any fragments of them. We brought out four stelae in all, and these were transported to the capital on a military plane, and then forwarded to New York City for exhibition.

When, in succeeding years, I ran into Captain Urrutia from time to time, he always waved gaily, or stopped to chat, perhaps reminiscing about our three stela-removing operations. But then I heard he had died as the result of a quite unnecessary accident. Like other military pilots, he was sometimes seconded for service with Aviateca, flying their dear old DC-3s to Petén, and on one occasion, having landed at Flores, he was being waved by ground crew to the parking space. But the waved instruction given him to turn put a wheel into a deep ditch overgrown with weeds; a propeller hit the ground, broke off, and, cutting through the cabin, severed Urrutia's legs. He died a few hours later. He was a brilliant pilot, and the loss of him must have been a grievous blow to the air force. As for myself, I miss the cheery encounters that I had with him, and remain immensely grateful for the services he rendered archaeology now so long ago.

As for the stelae we took out: upon their return from New York, three were set up permanently in the National Museum of Archaeology and Ethnography in Guatemala City, near other Maya monuments displayed there. But I did wonder what had become of the fourth. This was the heaviest and the least beautiful of the four, but it was highly unusual in having the head of the Sun God projecting from the top of the otherwise rectangular shaft; furthermore, the main feature carved on the front was a huge *Ajaw* glyph with the significant element represented, not by the usual abstract design, but by an anthropomorphic figure.

I made several inquiries concerning the whereabouts of this stela without success. Had it been spirited away in Sayaxché, before being loaded on the plane for the city? I could scarcely believe that. Or had it somehow "missed" the plane to New York, or been mislaid on the return journey? No one could tell me, and it wasn't until 1998 that at last I found it. All this time, the stela had been lying in the basement of the National Museum in Guatemala City, in its original, but unlabeled, crate.

Before turning to other topics, I have some remarks to make about that forest in southeastern Petén, the setting of those struggles I have described. Extending, east to west, from Concomá to the Pasión River, and from the Machaquilá River southward almost to the line dividing Petén from Alta Verapaz, this forest of three thousand square miles had been almost uninhabited when on separate occasions I first traversed each of its bounds.

Half a century earlier, lumbermen had penetrated a little way into its western fringe, but the only reminder that we saw of their presence had been that sunken log. Geologists, too, had passed through, only to become discouraged by their tests, and departed, leaving scarcely a sign of their passage. Chicleros had lately penetrated its northern fringe, mostly coming in from across the river, but the chicle in this region is not of good quality (although adequate for bubblegum), and in any case, natural chicle was already beginning to lose its market share to a synthetic product. So I cherished a hope that the forest might remain untouched—for it was an Eden.

I gained this impression most strongly during our journey upriver, during intermissions between our encounters with storm damage. In the river we found pools almost black with dense congregations of machaca fish. When someone threw in a hook without bait, the fish were so ignorant that one of them would take it at once. We found large turtles, as many as six or seven in some pools, lazily swimming about. (Merely for sport, we spent some time diving in and trying to catch one, without success.) And we saw an otter, now a rare, if not extinct, creature in these forests.

One day, as we were eating breakfast, a group of spider monkeys came by. These, of course, have been not only teased, but all too often shot for the sale value of the baby clinging to its mother's back. In fact, one of my men, to my great annoyance, did shoot a monkey during our long journey to Machaquilá in 1961. For two days the pitiful baby distressed us with its cries, especially at night. When another troop of monkeys came by, we released the baby, but its cries were probably too weak to have been heard by them, and in any case, the chances of it being adopted were negligible.

But this particular little family of *micos* that visited us at breakfasttime may never have seen humans before, because instead of throwing things at us, or shaking the branches, or trying to defecate on us (as they sometimes do, mostly missing their target

22.5 *A baby spider monkey fallen*
from its nest.

because they have yet to discover the principle of ranging shots), these seemed only to be intrigued by us. Two of them climbed down to perhaps twenty-five feet above our heads, watched us for a while, and deciding, perhaps, that we were not very interesting creatures that didn't move, they took a brief nap and then swung away.

If the fauna in this forest were living in a state of nature, so too were the flora; we saw not a single stump of a felled tree, nor zigzag cuts in the bark of *chicosapotes*, or other marks of tools on wood. In fact, I can state with certainty that there cannot have been humans within thirty miles, because we passed not one campsite on the riverbanks.

In May 1975, I wrote a proposal for the establishment of a Machaquilá National Park, of roughly the same area as the Tikal National Park. It would extend thirty kilometers east-west, with the ruins situated five kilometers from its western extremity (so as to embrace as much high forest as possible). A friend undertook to present this proposal to the appropriate member of the Guatemalan government, as I expect she did; but nothing more was heard of it. A few years later, by which time a logging road had been bulldozed into it, running from near Poptún in a west-southwest direction, an entity called the Cooperativa Agrícola Integral Fraternidad La Machaca was soliciting a much larger tract for its own purposes.

Then in 1989 a better opportunity arose, during the closing years of Vinicio Cerezo's presidency. Legislation was being prepared for the creation of various parks and reserves in Guatemala. Edna Nuñez de Rodas, then the director of the (Guatemalan) National Institute of Anthropology and History (IDAEH), asked me for suggestions, and I gave her a modified version of my earlier proposal. But by then, creation of such a park was politically much more difficult, as many of the *parcelas* (rectangular lots) into which much of Petén had been arbitrarily divided were already occupied, if not by the titular holders, then by Kekchi settlers. Although the latter may have lacked legal rights to the land, they would be almost as difficult to eject as rightful *parcelarios*.

The act creating these parks did indeed establish a Machaquilá Reserve. Its area was roughly equivalent to the one I had proposed, but unfortunately it was L-shaped, and therefore less compact. But the real disappointment was its low status: no provision at all was made for surveying and marking its boundaries, or for maintaining it inviolate, as far as I could tell. So within a few years the only species of wildlife to be found in that reserve were inedible.

Part III — Late Classic

CHAPTER 23

The Corpus Program

Reviews of my Tulane volume had been favorable, even encouraging, but I still had to consider how much more work of this kind I'd be able to do. For by 1968 I had spent about three-quarters of the money my grandmother had given me (frittering it away, in her opinion, as she regarded with horror anything to do with Mexico or Central America). It was therefore depressing to reflect that I might be limited to just two more seasons in the field—all the more so in view of offers chicleros had made to take me to sites said to contain monuments.

As for these, I had no way of knowing whether or not they had already been recorded by archaeologists—or at least mentioned by them in passing. But this didn't seem to be a matter of great importance, since further study of any site could certainly prove useful; even the confusion and waste of time I've described earlier concerning the ruins of Naranjo tend to prove that point.

The *Mapa Preliminar de Petén*, published in 1959, shows few geographical landmarks: some tributaries of the Pasión River, a few lakes, and about a dozen permanent settlements—but, of course, no roads, as there were none. I knew it would be fruitless to estimate how many other ancient sites there might be, but I was sure there would be enough to keep me busy for several more seasons, or even a lifetime, and now that I was competing against looters, the need to reach them before they did was more urgent than ever.

At about that time, the potential importance of engaging in another laborious and cash-consuming venture began working its way into my fantasies for the future. For I was beginning to suspect that much of the existing record of Maya inscriptions was not as thorough as it might be. To verify this suspicion, I made copies of published illustrations of some texts at two very different sites. One was Chichén Itzá, which had been the object of intensive research in the 1920s. The other, a very small site in Petén called La Amelia, located near the Río de la Pasión, had been examined only briefly in the 1930s by archaeologists of the Carnegie Institution of Washington.

Off I went, then, armed with these copies, and on arrival at one site and then the other, I stood in front of the relevant sculptures and drew their inscriptions at dusk, illuminating them by flashlight, with its beam aimed at raking angles to the surface of the stone, and from various directions in turn. Sure enough, I found that I'd recorded many details invisible in the published illustrations.

So it was with some excitement (mixed with doubt and foreboding) that I considered the implications of this little trial, suggesting as it did the need for a large proportion of all Maya sculpture previously published to be recorded again more carefully, with both field drawings and photography done with better lighting. But the chances of ever accomplishing this for more than a small portion of known inscriptions seemed remote—and then, how many more inscriptions lay waiting to be unearthed?

As for the existing photographic record of Maya monuments, superb work had been done in the 1880s by Alfred Maudslay, and between 1895 and 1910 by Teobert Maler, the two great pioneers of Maya exploration, but in the work of their successors one could see only a sad decline in quality. Ironically, this can be blamed on technical progress on two fronts. One was the introduction in 1898 of roll films (and film packs), together with film-processing labs in every city. Unfortunately, these improvements were regarded as dispensing with the need for trained expedition photographers.

Previously, such a photographer would have developed his pictures during the evening of the very day he took them, so that any unsuccessful shots could be repeated on the morrow. Now, with George Eastman's invention of the roll film ("You press the button and we do the rest"), trained expedition photographers began to be regarded as unnecessary, their place being taken by inexperienced members of the crew who saw no reason to develop their negatives on the spot.

Then there was the issue of judging exposure times. This would remain a matter of guesswork until the 1930s, when photoelectric exposure meters became available. One only has to examine the photographic files of expeditions mounted before the introduction of these instruments to find instances in which a careless photographer had taken several shots of the same subject without even trying a range of exposures. I realize that following development, negatives wildly under- or overexposed may have been discarded, but one may wonder whether corrected exposed shots exist of those taken? Similarly, several shots of the same subject may be found, all of them ruined by failure to check the focus between exposures.

Nor is there much evidence of attention being paid to the way subjects were lit. Neither Maudslay nor Maler had the benefit of artificial light for their generally well-lit photos (except for Maler's masterly use of magnesium powder or tape); instead, by observing at what time of day the natural lighting was most propitious for a particular shot—and sometimes by having a shading tree cut down—and then promptly developing their negatives after exposure to check their quality, they both achieved wonders. These two factors, in my view, were largely responsible for the record of Maya inscriptions made in the first half of the twentieth century being poor, as compared with those of the 1880s and 1890s.

But there was another factor in this decline: the general abandonment of mold-making. If the rationale for this was economic, then it was hardly sustainable, for the cost of making papier-mâché molds was insignificant, as was that of their transportation and storage.

All this added up to a considerable loss of irreplaceable information during the interwar years, especially regarding those limestone sculptures that carry subsidiary inscriptions, for these are always smaller in format and only lightly incised, often with a depth of less than one-tenth of an inch. Many stelae that fell to the ground long ago were found with their incised inscriptions well preserved, even though they'd lain for centuries face-down or under a protective layer of soil. But as soon as archaeologists (or other curious folk) had unearthed them and left them exposed for a few decades to tropical rain and the destructive action of lichen and moss, those inscriptions soon became illegible, or nearly so. Yet these often contain interesting information, such as the sculptor's name (first identified as such by my former young colleague, David Stuart) and the fact that sometimes several named sculptors had been employed on a single large monument.

Molds, in the absence of good photographs, could have saved them. Those of papier-mâché, neither expensive nor difficult to make, have long been used by archaeologists in Mesopotamia and other parts of the world, and in the Maya area by Maudslay for all sculptures save those in full relief. But alas! In the one region of the American continent where they would have been most valuable, the making of molds of any kind has never been routine in twentieth-century archaeological practice, except for a few made more recently with an excellent latex product that became available in the 1950s.

But during the second period of great explorations in the Maya lowlands, beginning in the 1920s, there was another reason for the negligent way in which Maya inscriptions were recorded—just the fading hopes of ever being able to read them. By 1930, even Sylvanus Griswold Morley, the greatest booster of Maya research in general in the years between the two World Wars, and once its most enthusiastic epigrapher, had essentially given up hope of deciphering Maya writing. Never was this loss of interest better displayed than in a photograph taken in 1932 at a vast and newly discovered ruined city named Calakmul, in the wilds of southern Campeche. Stela 52, a very large, heavy, and intact monument, had been found. The fact that it was laying face-down suggested that its sculptured face might be well preserved, and so it proved to be. Men equipped with long and heavy poles to use as levers were brought to the scene. They began levering one side of it up, and by the time their exertions had raised that side about eighteen inches, an intact inscription running down that side became visible. So the ideal moment for photographing and drawing this text had now come. Wooden chocks could have been put under that raised edge to prevent it falling back, and make it possible to wash, photograph, and draw the hieroglyphic text at leisure—and give the men a rest. Unfortunately none of this was on the program. One photo was indeed taken, but the purpose of this appears to have been simply to show the process of levering up this heavy monolith.

So, as my colleague Simon Martin once pointed out to me, the only record of the sides that we have from this expedition is a photo of men straining at the levers, with just glimpses of a few isolated but well-preserved glyphs visible between their legs!

About thirty years later, looters came to cut the main body of the stela into blocks of a size suitable for transport. Having cut it into smaller slabs, they sawed off the edges that carried those hieroglyphic texts. Fortunately, the large slabs they were carrying off were confiscated, and the reconstituted stela can now be admired in the Mexican National Museum of Archaeology—but stripped of the hieroglyphic texts that formerly ran down both its sides.

So, to the gradual erosion of Maya history and religion recorded in texts on stone, there now was added a sudden destruction of it, fueled by greed.[2]

Unexpectedly, a hint of possible future support for my work was relayed to me by Bob Wauchope. In March 1966, he had received a letter from Dr. William R. Coe of the University of Pennsylvania, then director of the Tikal Project, which read in part as follows: "Ian Graham stopped by Tikal in early February and we had a long talk. The enclosed 'proposal' was the result. Ian gave a copy to Gordon Willey at Seibal. I saw Gordon later at Tikal along with Ledyard [Smith]. Gordon was interested and indicated willingness to provide $800 towards the total, provided we here, and hopefully Tulane, would contribute equal sums. I have checked here and am assured that we can contribute our share. . . . Gordon suggested at this stage that the 'committee' be kept very small and that I act as chairman. I don't clearly remember the suggested composition of this committee . . . but of course it included yourself."

The proposal was that I engage in compiling an inventory of archaeological sites in Petén, using oil company as well as archaeological records. "It would be enough if detail and accuracy were set, say, at Maler's level: decent photographs of monuments and exposed architecture; Brunton [compass]-and-tape over-all site maps; plans, profiles and elevations on a rectified basis of exposed architecture; possibly surface-collection of sherds. . . . The extended program might also include thorough recording of Petén sculpture." In a fuller version of the latter part of this proposal, set out in two single-spaced pages of typescript dated 2 February 1966, Coe added that this was "a program suggested to me by Ranneft a few years ago." (Ranneft was an admiral in the Royal Netherlands Navy, who in his retirement made great efforts to find the "key" to Maya script. Writing to me on 2 June 1963, he quoted an opinion expressed by Eric Thompson in a letter to him: "There is really a great need for someone to visit Maya sites and re-photograph such texts with modern means of artificial light—we need light coming from more than one direction.")

Unfortunately, Bob Wauchope had to reply that because his budget for the next year had yet to be approved, he was unable to contribute that eight hundred dollars. Thereupon, the scheme seems to have been abandoned. But in retrospect I am not sorry, in view of the low priority that the recording of sculpture would have been given—or rather, the extraneous activities that were suggested.

Then, less than two years later, a letter from Eric hinted mysteriously at the possibility of support coming from some other quarter, and sure enough, a letter dated 13 March 1968 reached me in Guatemala City. It came—like a bolt from the blue—from a Mr. Edgar H. Brenner, a Washington, D.C., lawyer, and the gist of it was an invitation to accept a research grant from the Stella and Charles Guttman Foundation to work up a program aimed at recording all known Maya inscriptions. I soon learned that Mr. Brenner ("Ed" to his friends) was a nephew of Mr. Guttman and a director of his uncle's foundation.

This seemed almost too good to be true, but I sent off my enthusiastic acceptance on 3 April. Soon, when back in Petén, I began thinking about such matters as the appropriate scope of this work: should carved monuments lacking inscriptions be included, what about sculptural fragments, and inscribed objects of bone or jade, and what about a standardized nomenclature for monuments and their texts? I jotted down these and a few other such topics in my field notebook.

What, then, had been the genesis of this bold plan? It turned out that some five years earlier Ed Brenner had visited Yucatán, and had come to wonder how it could be that the Maya script had not yet been deciphered. Then he put his finger on a crucial impediment facing would-be decipherers—the scarcity of reliable source material—and began working up a proposal for the creation of a publication series that would fill this large informational gap. As a Yale graduate himself, he enlisted the help of a Yale professor, Michael Coe, in editing his proposal.

When finished, he showed it to William D. Rogers, a partner of his at the well-known Washington law firm of Arnold and Porter. Rogers responded enthusiastically, and since he was also president of the Center for Inter-American Relations, in New York City, he had little difficulty in persuading the center's director, Tod Catlin, to assemble an advisory committee to administer the Guttman Foundation's preliminary grant. Initially the committee consisted of Coe, Tatiana Proskouriakoff (of the Peabody Museum of Harvard), Floyd Lounsbury (a linguist and epigrapher at Yale), and Gordon Ekholm, curator of Mexican Archaeology at the American Museum of Natural History. Others were added later.

As envisaged by Ed Brenner, the program would begin with a pilot project administered by the foundation—this to be completed in two years. Initially, I was engaged for six months to design the work; that is, to decide what kinds of artifacts would be included in it; how they should be reproduced and at what scale; what should be the format of the volumes; what ancillary information should be provided, such as interpretation of the hieroglyphic texts and images; whether unmapped sites should be surveyed, and if so at what scale. I would also have to list sites known to have hieroglyphic texts and enumerate them, so as to estimate how many volumes of the *Corpus* when completed (if ever!) they would fill—and several other matters.

Later, a period of fieldwork would be carried out at one or two sites, so that all the resulting photographs, field drawings, and text could be assembled as a prototype fascicle. A record would be kept of the time spent on this, so as to provide a basis for estimating roughly the duration of the entire project. All this would be done in the course of my normal, self-supported, and much longer field season.[3]

Owing to the protracted delays that plagued the wafting of Machaquilá stelae by helicopter to Sayaxché (as described in another chapter), I was unable to leave Guatemala until mid-July, rather later than usual, by which time I was badly in need of a vacation; so it was arranged that my employment would start on the first of October, 1968.

In the meantime, I debated where to do the necessary research. I was inclining towards Tulane University, because I felt sure that Bob Wauchope would welcome me, and the Middle American Research Institute's library has outstanding collections of relevant material. The winter climate would also have its attractions. But then I remembered that the Carnegie Institution of Washington's Department of Archaeology had been based in Cambridge, Massachusetts, and that upon its dissolution in 1957, all of its photographic negatives and prints had simply been trundled over to the

Peabody Museum about two hundred yards away, to be incorporated in the already large collections of that museum. So there could be no better resource for my purposes than this.

Emboldened by the presence in the Peabody Museum of Gordon Willey and Ledyard Smith, of whose support I felt confident, I rented an apartment, bought a large card file, and moved into the Museum's Tozzer Library, and there began searching the shelves for publications that illustrated carved stelae, lintels, etc., and then grading the quality of each illustration on a scale of one to ten.

After about a week, I heard that the librarian was wondering just who this person might be, and whether he should be charged by the day or the week for use of the library's valuable resources. She consulted Professor Stephen Williams, the museum's director, who, with Gordon's approval, resolved the problem; for now, to my utter astonishment, I was appointed as "Research Fellow," complete with Harvard I.D. (Years later, and near the end of his life, Gordon Willey, the very distinguished Bowditch Professor of Central American and Mexican Archaeology and Ethnology, confessed to me ruefully and with his usual frankness that he had given only weak support for my appointment.)

There were many decisions to make before launching this study, several of them being crucial. For example, I'd been urged by some colleagues to include commentaries on each hieroglyphic text. I opposed this notion with simple objections: (1) that I was quite incompetent to write them; (2) that the inclusion of commentaries would at least double the cost and physical bulk of the work; and (3) that any commentary would soon become outdated, in view of new approaches to decipherment then being developed.

Among other matters to resolve was that of nomenclature, for it was time to standardize and abbreviate this for convenience in references and tabulations of any kind. Because some site names were inconveniently long, such as Altar de Sacrificios, or Santa Rosa Xtampak, it occurred to me to copy the airline practice of giving each site a three-letter code. This would be followed by a two- or three-letter abbreviation for each of the common classes of sculpture, such as "St." for stela, and "Lnt." for lintel; and finally, a numeral to identify a particular item in this class at that site. Artifacts of a kind rarely encountered, such as an inscribed limestone pot, would fall under "Msc." for miscellaneous. Using this system, Piedras Negras Stela 10 would be referred in print as PNG:St.10, and to this could be added a letter and numeral to specify the column and numerical position in it of a particular hieroglyph.

Soon after deciding to adopt this scheme I happened to visit the University of Pennsylvania, and the University Museum, in Philadelphia. While there I took the opportunity to call on Linton Satterthwaite, whom I'd met at Tikal and greatly respected for his contributions to Mesoamerican archaeology, these having begun thirty-five years earlier at Piedras Negras, in Guatemala. As I might have expected, Linton, a stickler for logic and rigor in all matters, quizzed me at once about my methodology in deriving these abbreviations, and when told of my makeshift approach, exclaimed at once, "Oh, that will never do! Abbreviations must be derived logically!"

I could only reply that the airline system seemed to function quite well, and assumed that when an airport was first established at, say, Antananarivo, then ANT would first have been considered, but on finding this had been assigned to Antwerp, ANR or ARV might been chosen—or even AAA! I was rather dismayed by his objections, until I remembered that Eric Thompson had cheered me up by admitting his inability to digest much of the heavy going in Linton's extraordinary compendium on the Maya calendar. This, I imagine, was something that Linton worked on during slack periods of military service during World War II.

As for the design and content of the *Corpus* volumes, each (except for volume 1, the introduction) would consist of 192 pages and be devoted to sites within one of five general areas, such as Yucatán or Central Lowlands. And to make them less unwieldy, and hasten publication, each would be published in three parts.

An important decision was to publish one photo of each piece at a scale of 1:10, and when necessary another at a larger scale whenever fine detail in a monument might be difficult or impossible to distinguish at the smaller scale. The drawings, though, could be reproduced at any suitable scale.

And then, in order to accommodate all but the very tallest stelae at the standard scale of 1:10, I decided upon a page size of fifteen inches by twelve. Although well aware that this size would be difficult to shelve, I was convinced, and still am, that the advantages of this format outweigh its inconveniences. I also decided not to devote any volumes to the well-known cities of Chichén Itzá, Tikal, Palenque, Copán, and Quiriguá in the early stages of the program because at none of those was there much danger of theft or serious deterioration of the monuments.

Ed Brenner had urged that the *Corpus* be published in loose-leaf form. Apparently this system is convenient in the legal world, in view of the constant accretion of new case law, opinions, precedents, etc. For the *Corpus*, this system would certainly have removed the tiresome constraint of having to gather the material necessary for publication of numbered monuments from a particular site in an order as close to numerical as possible before publishing them. But on the other hand, I could imagine loose-leaf pages being mislaid, or falling out when their punched holes became torn, so I favored the volumes being bound normally. A compromise was reached: no page, or rather, leaf, would carry matter concerning more than one monument, so that a fervent loose-leaf advocate could simply have the binding cut off with a powerful paper cutter, and then have three holes punched in them.

It soon appeared that quite often all the printed matter, photographs, and drawings of the smaller sculptures could be accommodated on just one side of a page, leaving the other wastefully blank. So when a few years had passed without hearing of anyone who'd had the binding of a *Corpus* volume chopped off, I quietly abandoned the loose-leaf facility.

Having completed the inventory, I left for Yucatán in late January with two objectives in mind: pursuing my normal fieldwork, and spending limited periods at two dissimilar sites for estimating the "output" of drawings and photographs per week at both of them. For this, I chose Uxmal and Naranjo.

At Uxmal, a well-known and easily reached Mecca for tourists, I stayed in the Hacienda Hotel (then the only lodging there) and nothing could have been more comfortable or convenient. My objective was to record photographically and in drawings the numerous carved tablets that serve as edging for four low, rectangular platforms in front of the Cementerio complex. These tablets, which constituted a large area of stone reliefs, had never before been registered in their entirety, but they were indeed easy to work on. I made my drawings after dark, using controlled electric light, current for it being provided by a tiny gasoline-powered generator.

Having finished that task, I recorded sculpture at various sites in Quintana Roo, Campeche, and Tabasco as part of my normal activity, and then flew to Guatemala. A further flight by DC-3 took me to Melchor de Mencos, in Petén. From there, Naranjo lies about twelve miles away along a former logging road. I had, of course, been there before, and this time I took with me Don Abelardo Ventura, an old and reliable acquaintance, together with his cargo mule. There, I set to work recording monuments and making a new plan of the site—until the aguada dried up completely a month later.

On my return to Guatemala City, I suddenly felt weak, and on looking in the mirror realized that I had hepatitis. I placed myself in the hands of a Guatemalan doctor who was, conveniently, a son-in-law of Alfred Kidder, the renowned archaeologist who had headed the Carnegie Institution's Department of Archaeology for some years. The doctor kindly installed me in a small, private hospital where I could watch each day, through my bedside picture window, the great plumes of smoke being thrown up by Volcán Pacaya, while the nighttime view showed that what was being ejected was not just smoke, but also fountains of large red-hot rocks.

Following this unscheduled delay, I found myself hard-pressed for time, for I was expected to turn in my report by the end of July. But I had a problem: I had planned long before to join friends in the middle of that month at their newly purchased house near Lucca, in Tuscany, and was extremely reluctant to cancel that visit. As the one amenity this house lacked was a swimming pool, I knew there would be children pining for one. So I purchased a portable Sears Roebuck, fifteen-foot-diameter swimming pool and filtration pump—all for $150. With considerable trouble I transported it by bus and taxi to the Italian Line's pier in New York City on the eve of sailing, together with a suitcase.

The suitcase was to be delivered to my cabin, and the swimming pool to the hold, for collection in Genoa. The suitcase contained all the graphic material needed for preparing the required number of copies of my report to the advisory committee. As for the report itself, that remained to be written (perhaps by the poolside!) on a cheap typewriter I would purchase locally. Then, having assembled the material in binders and mounted the photographs, I would airmail them to the members of the advisory committee.

But on entering my cabin—oh woe, no suitcase! The purser having kindly lent me a master key, I entered every single cabin, falling on my knees to look under the bunks, but had no luck. At Algeciras, at Naples, and finally at Genoa, I watched baggage coming down conveyor belts. No suitcase of mine, only despair!

From Lucca, I immediately called Italian Lines in New York—no easy matter, then—and two days later did so again. This time they informed me that my suitcase had been found in the street outside their dockside offices.

"Oh, thank goodness! Then please send it on by air immediately."

"Very well, but it will cost you . . . " (I don't remember how much, but a large sum.)

"Surely not! That suitcase was delivered into your custody, so the responsibility is yours."

They were adamant, so I had to pay. But on return, I took the Italian Line to the small claims court in New York and was awarded my pound of flesh.

When the suitcase arrived, the only missing item was a Rolleicord camera of no great value. So I set to work immediately, typed out my text, assembled copies of it with the specimen pages of illustration, had them bound, and airmailed them off to the committee members—just in time!

My report was accepted, and the Guttman Foundation contributed a further fifty thousand dollars towards future work.

In the following year, Stanton Catlin proposed that an exhibition be mounted at the Center for Inter-American Relations to raise public awareness of Maya hieroglyphic writing to a level equivalent to that enjoyed by the other well-known ancient scripts, and also to celebrate the initiation of the Corpus Program. It would open in late January 1971, close two months later, and then reopen in Cambridge for a similar period. It was felt that the Metropolitan Museum's one-hundredth anniversary exhibition, *Before Cortez*, due to open a little earlier, would prime public interest in this field.

From my point of view, this was almost too much! I had no experience of such work and wasn't all that familiar with the Peabody Museum's holdings; and anyway, I rather resented the prospect of being kept from my proper work—for among other things, I was expected to write the catalog and provide the illustrations. But in fact, I found the experience enjoyable, and some of the challenges I faced were interesting enough.

Steve Williams was keen to put on a good show, and decided that the museum's plastercast of the ten-foot-tall Copán Stela "A" should be included. Nervously, I canted it over a little, and noticed that near its foot the plaster had deteriorated. Our conservator was too heavily engaged in other work to treat it, so I took it upon myself to do the job. Filling the lower six or eight inches of the cast with plaster would certainly strengthen it, but the added weight might rupture its rather thin plaster walls during handling and delivery—especially during the former, for to get it out of the third-floor gallery and onto a truck, a window would first of all have to be removed, then a crane maneuvered to swing it horizontally out of the window and lower it onto the truck bed.

So instead, I made for this job a mixture of plaster of Paris and expanded polystyrene pellets of about two millimeters diameter. This was much lighter, yet quite strong. But when the crane arrived, I couldn't bring myself to witness the cast's removal, and was greatly relieved when it returned from its travels undamaged.

As if by magic, this exhibition would confer on me another boon—this time through the agency of an elderly man, apparently not of Mexican descent, whom I met at a cocktail party in Mexico City. Noticing that I seemed to have no acquaintances among the guests, he kindly engaged me in conversation for some time, in the course of which I told him something of how I passed my time. And then, following a pause, he asked a question—or rather, as he put it, begged a great favor of me, and went on to explain that for many decades he'd had in his possession a collection of ninety-two large-format platinum prints taken by the great archaeological explorer Teobert Maler. Just having these precious rarities in his house had always seemed a privilege, but now—well, the situation in Mexico City was no longer so secure, and he was wondering if I might, as a great favor, be prepared to keep them safe for him until things settled down?

I must confess that I had never yet even seen a platinum print—much less, any prints of Maya ruins in Yucatán made by Maler some eighty years earlier. (Few of them, as eventually I would learn, had even been published as ordinary carbon prints.)

So it was that Señor Boker, the proprietor of a magnificent hardware store founded by his father or grandfather (and still trading there today) delivered this unique collection into my hands for safekeeping in the Peabody Museum, with permission to mount a temporary exhibition of them if interested in doing so—and this indeed I soon did, mounting it for a month in New York City. And then at some point, Señor Boker, sensing my admiration for Teobert Maler's extraordinary life and works, mentioned that he was also in possession of a copy of Maler's memoirs, the original of which seemed to be lost. He added that he would be glad to see some of this material published, if I had any interest in preparing an edition of it. But just then I had no thought of doing anything of that kind, preferring to put all my energy into the Corpus Program.

CHAPTER 24

La Naya

Events in my field season of 1971 were for a few good reasons pleasant to remember; but these were, alas, far outweighed by another that was tragic. One decidedly good event was Eric von Euw's arrival to work for the Corpus Program—as it was now called. That year, I reached Petén in February, and because Eric was not expected to arrive until a month later, I decided to investigate in the meantime a site that I'd heard about in the previous year while at Tikal. There, I'd met Ismael Tercero, one of the Guatemalan students who had been given scholarships by the Ford Foundation to work at Tikal, and he told me of his visit to a site called La Naya, near Laguna del Tigre, a small lagoon southwest of Laguna Yaxhá. There were stelae there, one of which he had photographed—and then buried to ensure its preservation. On this trip he'd been accompanied by one of the Tikal Park Rangers, or guarda-bosques, a man named Pedro Arturo Sierra, and on the basis of his account, I decided that I would try to visit the site myself.

In the following year, then, I obtained permission to take Pedro Arturo with me to La Naya, and set off with him from Flores in the old Volvo I'd bought from Tania Proskouriakoff and driven down from Cambridge. It was the third of March, 1971, when I (as I wrote in my journal three days later)

arrived at El Zapote [on the road from Flores to Melchor de Mencos], hoping to find Braulio López ready to rent his mules. But he hadn't returned. Went on to Km. 50, where a Maya-looking man, Agustín Chan, has two *ramón*-eating cargo horses [*ramón* being an acquired taste]. Settled that he would bring them along to Km. 54, our entry point—but first he asked me if I "bought stones." At Km. 54 a man from the south, with a beaky nose, called Antonio Salas, agreed to come too. Conveniently, he has a thatched porch just large enough to park my car under. We waited an age for Agustín; finally I started to drive back, but then met him plodding along the road. Set off at about 1 p.m. along a trail that is, much of it, a truckpath [logging road] about eight years old. Came to beginning of a *milpa*, then a camp with two poor *champas* by the edge of a delightful little lake, El Tigre, about 150 m in diameter. The boys built me a *champa* of *guano arrimado* [palm fronds resting on a cross beam, from one side only], and I cooked a rice dish with curried corned beef. Felt very happy to be really back on the job, and Pedro the *guadabosque* seemed an exceptionally good fellow. Tall and thin, about 40, responsible-seeming. We then went about preparing our quarters, and I was vaguely aware that Pedro had gone round the side of his *champa* when we heard two shots in quick succession. At first I thought he had shot something (we had been discussing a *cojolito* that was calling), but I realized almost immediately that the shots were too closely spaced, then saw Pedro run back and fall to the ground on his hands and knees. I ran up to him, and saw a bullet hole in his back. I held him, and tried to get an answer, but there was only a ghastly spluttering, and within a minute he was dead.

Agustín called, "It's the *guardia* [police]" and ran off with Antonio in the opposite direction, where I soon joined them. "Impossible," I said, "the guardia wouldn't do that." "Yes, it's the *guardia*," he insisted, "a party of them have come this way recently."

The uppermost thought in my mind was to run out to the highway and get help as soon as possible. I'd taken off my shirt, and had neither money on me nor a flashlight, so I took Agustín's ancient 16-gage, all tied up with string and wire, and crept back to my *champa*, and found the things I needed, including two new shells (but forgetting to take the compass), while keeping as sharp a look-out as possible. When I got back to Agustín, Antonio had left him. The two of us then made off as fast as possible. [I wanted to take the trail back to the car] but Agustín didn't want to, in case gunmen were waiting for us [on the trail]. Accordingly we made our way through the bush.

It had been about 5:45 when the murder occurred, and soon it became dark. We blundered on as quietly as possible, not using the torch, but the sky was overcast, and when, perhaps an hour later, the moon shone through for a moment, we saw we were heading in the wrong direction. There was nothing else to do but sit or lie down until the moon came out again, but it never did; instead, it began to rain at 10 p.m. We had no machete, but managed to break off some *guano* [palm] fronds and make a bit of a shelter, each of us having one frond to lie on, and another over us. But it became extremely cold—and windy, which was worse, and the rain continued. Agustín did sleep for a moment [but mostly] we just lay there shivering convulsively, both of us tormented by cramp in the legs, and feeling utterly miserable, with the appalling murder in our minds.

At 6 [the next day] we started off, with the sky still overcast. However, Agustín suggested that a distant *cojolito* might be the same one we'd heard near camp last night; and I thought I heard a truck in the opposite direction, so we headed that way. After half an hour we came to the trail, and got to the road at about 9. Antonio had preceded us by about five minutes.

Nearby lives a "Comisionado Militar" (who reminded me of Carl Mechel by his loud and rough voice, and something in his appearance). Him, I took with me in the car to Melchor, going first to the military police, and then to the *Guardia Rural*. Hopeless, both of them. I prevailed on a young military lieutenant to radio Poptún for instructions, but in the half-hour I was watching he was unable to get in on the air traffic dealing with such important matters as bulldozers. However he put in a plea of urgency for his call. Finally he suggested I have breakfast in the *comedor* nearby, and afterwards announced that he had informed Poptún, but received no instructions. I wondered whether he hadn't just stopped trying.

The 70-year-old *guardia* lieutenant on the other hand was bureaucratically obstructive. He told me the locality of the murder fell in the Flores district [or municipality] by a few kilometers, and that I'd have to take a letter he had prepared to Flores. I asked whether the judge and the *guardia* couldn't be alerted by radio? No, he said. Again, I insisted that it was important not to lose time. Now the sergeant became angry, and threatened to charge me if I wouldn't cooperate! Nothing for it, then, but drive 90 km to Flores. Went to *guardia* HQ. A soldier was sent to summon judge, but came back with message "Return at 4 p.m." So I went to see him myself. He was rather a charming old man, and explained that his stomach wasn't very well that day, but tomorrow he might be well enough to go to the scene of the crime. I asked if there wasn't some urgency in making his report, so that the body could be removed [since in Guatemala the law insists that the dead be buried within 24 hours], but he said "Oh, we sometimes let two or three days go by. . . " The *guardia* sergeant in Flores, an energetic fellow, was as indignant as I at the careless attitude. I came back in the afternoon (it had been about 12:15 when I got to Flores) and went to the other judge's office. He, the head judge, was angry when he heard the story, and named the mayor to do the job.

Soon after, I met the new captain of the *Guardia* [or rather, Chief of Police]. This man looks like some *jefe* from the time of Porfirio Díaz. Very stout, he has an expressionless *mestizo* face, wears a gray suit, generally with the zip at half-mast. With narrow eyes in that expressionless face, he seemed to watch everything with concentration. He was appalled that my visit to Melchor had been fruitless (and next day went there himself to deliver a blast at that useless lieutenant). [For this, I could hardly fault the captain, whose name was Nicolas Estrada Vallejo, but I soon came to share the almost universal loathing of him. His *apodo*, or nickname, was *Chicote* (whip). He was a monster.]

The posse of police went off at about 3:30, but the mayor and registrar and another official weren't ready until about 5. The mayor walks slowly, explaining that he'd broken his foot in a car crash a few years back. But it certainly didn't help that he was wearing elastic-sided "winkle-pickers" [shoes with exaggeratedly pointed toes], which, when we reached the muddy part of the track, came off at frequent intervals.

The registrar and secretary wanted to stride on ahead. "But you don't know the way," I said. "Oh, we'll follow it somehow; are there any turns to know about?" I did my best to explain.

It soon grew dark, and I swung my lamp back and forth to light [the mayor's] way as well as mine. We made very slow progress; then he tripped and fell, and lay groaning in pain from having landed on his bad hand. He was sure it was broken again. However, a couple of minutes later it was all right and we continued, but now side by side, with him holding my arm. He began to complain of thirst, saying plaintively that I'd promised we would pass a pool of water in an hour, and already we'd been going more than one and a half hours, and no water, so we must have missed it. "No, we'll be there soon," I replied. Later, he began to give up hope of ever arriving, and I had to coax him along.

We got to the lake after rather more than four hours. There lay Pedro exactly as I had left him, and the police group were finishing a meal, having helped themselves liberally to my provisions. I was especially cross that they'd taken all the cigarettes [I had brought for my men].

The required formalities were gone through, and Pedro's papers were found—I had been embarrassed by not knowing his full name, which I now learned was Pedro Arturo Sierra del Valle, related to del Valles of La Libertad [acquaintances of mine]. At about midnight they left, with the corpse tied onto a horse. The *alcalde* considered riding back, but I really thought he should spend the night there. We were now alone, the alcalde, Antonio Salas and I. The *alcalde* complained that the police shouldn't have left us defenseless, in this dangerous spot; he would never be able to sleep here. He proposed to walk out. "You'll never make it," I said; "instead, if you like we'll go back about a kilometer and sleep there." It was a fine night and it wouldn't rain; so that's what we did.

The next day I made my statement at mid-day, and hoped to obtain the services of two police to return with them that same day; but the captain was out (on his visit to Melchor) and I didn't see him until evening, when he readily agreed to provide men. The next morning I left with two police at 7:30, but on arrival at Km. 54, discovered that neither Antonio nor Agustín had returned from Flores, where they, too, had gone to make their statements. Their wives were sure they'd been locked up. Reluctantly, therefore, I had to drive back, leaving the police at Km. 54. I found that Agustín had done his piece, and then taken on some "refreshment." Antonio was finished an hour later, but where was Agustín now? We found him in a bar, very drunk, and got him reluctantly away. We would use Antonio's horses, but I wanted Agustín's dogs to come, to warn us of any prowlers. He was too drunk, but sent his son instead.

We reached the camp at four, and I suggested, rather late, that we go to look at the ruins to see if the looters' work had continued. None of us was sure of the way, and we cast about before approaching them after nightfall. Suddenly we heard a Thunk! . . . We stopped dead, and listened; a minute later, another Thunk!

We crouched, sub-machineguns at the ready. I strained to see a glow of light, as the men couldn't have been excavating in the dark, but there was bright moonlight, so I wasn't sure. We waited, hearing occasional noises, for about five minutes; then one of the police said, "You know, it's the branch of a tree knocking against another tree, in the breeze!"

The next day, we went to the ruins, where we found a horrible mess. At least two stelae had gone, and the one between them was in the process of being removed. The face had been sawn off the upper part, but the saw must have broken or become blunt, because [the looters] had laid the stela down, and had been engaged in hacking the back away with machetes to lighten it.

I made a rough and ready cross of *zapote* wood, held together with wire and epoxy, and set it up where Arturo died.

There were two schools of thought about the murder. According to one, the motive was simply the looters' fear of arrest, and an argument in favor of this view was that when the noise of our activities in setting up camp caused the gunman to investigate, he would probably have paused, concealed behind a large tree just where the path opens onto the camping area, and simply shot the occupant of the nearest champa, which was Pedro.

According to the other view, Pedro was shot because the murderer had a grudge against him. Pedro, the forest ranger, was known to be *malo*—that is to say, a strict enforcer of regulations, and that was the defense presented at trial by the accused, Eduardo Carrillo Donis, who said he became angry when he saw Pedro Arturo, because he had been the cause of his son's death two years earlier, although I never learned the circumstances of that.

Carrillo was that same comisionado militar whom I had taken with me to Melchor, on getting back to the road early in the morning after the murder. He had probably been involved in the looting at La Naya before, since some Maya pots were found in his house wrapped in a shirt. In any case, he was sentenced to twenty years in prison, incommutably.

Later, I learned that another bunch of looters had been caught in the act of despoiling La Naya two years earlier. In January 1969 a lieutenant, a sergeant, and three men of the Guardia Rural surrounded the plaza of the ruins and challenged them. They ran, firing, and the last to flee was shot dead. Of the two who escaped, one was later arrested.

Following that event, Ismael Tercero was sent to estimate the damage and reported that one all-hieroglyphic stela had been made ready for removal—the one he later told me he had buried. Since then, I have twice been back to La Naya: once to map it, and then later to rescue the wretched scraps of sculpture—with the help of Eric von Euw and a U.S. Air Force helicopter. But when, after my first brief examination of the site, I failed to find any obvious sign of a smallish stela having been buried, I hoped to persuade Ismael to come with me to the site and show me the place. But I found that he had fallen into disfavor with the Tikal Project, had left the country, and was living in Los Angeles.

And by curious coincidence, so was the stela, for I found it in the Bowers Museum in Santa Ana, California. Comparison of it with Tercero's photograph (given by him to Linton Satterthwaite, who passed it on to me), showed that the dealer who sold it to the museum, Clive Hollinshead, had improved its appearance by modeling some cement hieroglyphs in the lower left area, where they had weathered away completely. While not very convincing, they were good enough to deceive one "expert" who included them in his commentary on the inscription published in the museum's guide!

The next venture I had in mind was to rescue some small stelae from a site several miles east of the road from Flores to Tikal, and north of a village called El Zapote (this name I would apply to the ruins, too). I'd first heard of this site while in Carmelita on my way back from Tintal, for someone told me that the Guardia had received a tip-off concerning two men who were about to transport a small stela—or rather, the sliced-off front of one, cut in half and loaded on a horse—from Flores to Mexican terrain, passing through Carmelita. In the kind of operation that is all too seldom attempted in Petén, two guardias were sent out to Carmelita by plane, and then, having walked partway down the trail toward Flores, concealed themselves. After some time, along came the horse (renamed Arqueólogo by the men who had hired it), and the guardias sprang out to arrest them. The stela was cleary Early Classic in style, and I managed to learn its origin, a site north of Laguna Macanché.

I went to visit these ruins, which proved to be quite small and on a hilltop, and there I found seven other small stelae, most of them having lost a portion of their carved surfaces to a looter's saw. I made a plan of the site, and photographed and drew all of the stelae except one, one half of which had been crudely hacked off. I supposed this to have been the back, since what I could feel of the underside with my fingers suggested figurative carving on that side, rather than glyphic. Then it began to rain, and at this, the men announced their intention of returning home. We had plenty of food for a longer stay, and money enough to pay them, but it was May 3, the Day of the Cross, and it had rained. For any Maya, this was a call he could not ignore—he'd have to go home and plant his milpa. I offered them double wages, to no avail.

In mid-March 1971, then, I went to see the vice-minister of defense—for in those peaceful days one could wander into the Palacio Nacional and have a reasonable chance of seeing any person in authority that one might wish to see. I asked him whether I could possibly have the use of a Huey helicopter in about a week's time to rescue the stelae at El Zapote. "No problem," he said.

Eric now arrived in Guatemala City, and we flew up to Flores, bought supplies, and with six men and two guardias, one brandishing a submachinegun, we made camp by an aguada at the foot of the hill, then advanced cautiously up to the site. There

24.1 *Eric von Euw preparing fragments
for transfer in helicopter.*

was no one there, but damn it! (as I wrote in my journal), Stela 1 had been destroyed, with only a few carved fragments remaining, or so it seemed. But a day-and-a-half's work by the men with axes and machetes produced a heliport of modest size, and I did manage to find a considerable number of the fragments of Stela 1. Then one of the men shot a brocket deer before we left, making all of them happy at having some meat to take home.

I went back to the capital and was authorized fairly quickly to have the use of a helicopter that happened to be in Petén. So I flew back to Flores, and with Eric drove to El Caoba, the nearest settlement to El Zapote. We engaged six men for next morning, went on to Tikal to request that men be on hand to unload the helicopter, and returned to Flores.

By then, both Eric and I were tired and hungry, but luckily the provisional comedor of the new Hotel Maya Internacional was open, so in we went. I greeted two men sitting at table in the comedor with a polite *Buenas Noches*. To this, one of them replied, *Cara de huevón*—not the most friendly greeting. He said *he* knew who I was, a stela robber, and mentioned Carl Mechel, the tiresome Austrian hydrographer who had accused me of looting at Tres Islas. After addressing me with further pleasantries in a voice thick with drink, he grabbed a fork, got to his feet, and declared his intention of killing me. His companion shouted, "Be careful, he's dangerous!"

I grabbed an empty beer bottle, which, if necessary, I could make more fearful by breaking it, but we managed to escape unharmed, although unfed.

I should not have blamed Eric if, after the murder and now this, he had departed for home immediately, but he took it all in his stride. (The two men, I discovered, were government employees, a draftsman and an agronomist for FYDEP, the organization that ran Petén in those days.)

The helicopter picked us up, and as I directed the pilot to the group of low hills on one of which the ruins lay, I began to worry about spotting our helipad; and when it did appear, it seemed alarmingly small, but we landed without trouble. We loaded the heavier pieces (Stelae 3, 4, and 5, and the larger fragments of Stela 1), and these were sent off to Tikal. Then we wrapped all the small fragments of Stela 1 in newspaper, packed them in cardboard boxes, and a second flight took them, Eric, and me to Tikal. That afternoon I started epoxying the fragments of Stela 1 together, and by the end of the following day it had been reconstructed, with only tiny pieces missing from

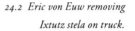

24.2 Eric von Euw removing
Ixtutz stela on truck.

the front surface. To the untutored eye the sculpture is far from beautiful, but it does represent a fine Early Classic *Chahk*.

A month or two later, Eric and I set out to rescue another monument, this time from the ruins of Ucanal—a site discovered in 1914 by R. E. Merwin of the Peabody Museum. For a long time, those ruins were known to very few, the chicle in that part of the forest being of poor quality, so there was little reason to keep trails open. Merwin had reported the Río Mopán as running by the ruins, but it's no longer navigable that far upstream, and it cost us two long searches to find the site. (Nevertheless, a looter did find a solitary and poorly preserved stela at Yaltutú, not far away, and had started cutting that with a power saw.)

Stela 4 at Ucanal is large and unusually thick, and as it was lying with its sculptured face down, this had remained in excellent condition. Recently, however, construction of a new highway passing within three miles of it had begun; settlements would inevitably spring up along the road, and Ucanal and its monuments would become known to "interested parties." And then, the fact that it was broken in two would make its removal a little less daunting for the looters—as also for us!

It was, in fact, so heavy that use of a helicopter to remove it was unthinkable, but since the Guatemalan army had agreed to provide a heavy dump truck when required, I left Eric and Don Abelardo Ventura in charge of a gang of men who would open a long brecha through the forest to the nearest highway, and when the truck arrived, they succeeded in winching the two halves of the stela up into the truck bed.

All these operations, financed principally by CIRMA, were carried out more successfully than I'd ever expected, and Eric certainly proved his worth, as he would in completing other difficult tasks.

CHAPTER 25

The Peabody Museum
and Early Associates

Soon after I'd joined the Peabody Museum, Tatiana Proskouriakoff kindly offered me space in her large semi-basement office, which already had drafting tables placed in front of its two windows—one of them still in use by an artist she employed. (Children and dogs seemed to be very interested in our activities, especially when the windows were open in summertime.) I must acknowledge at once that daily association with her was not just a privilege, but an inspiration. She was a remarkable woman, and one of the first things I noticed about her was the way she used her hands to take hold of any small object that she wanted to inspect: with her wrist drawn up and back, as also her third, fourth, and little fingers, she would hold her thumb and forefinger about half an inch apart, as if preparing to take between them something as delicate as a butterfly's wing. And then, an aspect of her character that I soon noticed: a slight contrarian tendency, especially in response to truisms. But she was very sociable, by no means keeping herself apart. Almost every day she would eat her lunch in the museum's basement smoking room, next to her office, along with a mixed bag of scholars, the museum's deputy director, students, and its lively carpenter.

This room was furnished with about a dozen seats removed from passenger cars of the Boston and Maine Railroad—these having been designed by Earnest Hooton, a noted Harvard physical anthropologist active in the early twentieth century (even so, I found them surprisingly uncomfortable). Since the room was usually filled at lunchtime, I soon became acquainted with most of the staff, which in those days was a tiny fraction of what it is today. Tania did, though, move in there rather too often during the day to smoke a cigarette, and I wondered if perhaps she hadn't taken up smoking in the first place out of contrarian spirit!

But she also had a remarkable capacity for sustained work, no matter how tedious it might be. The best example of this was the task she undertook upon finishing her work on Maya script, for then she figuratively rolled up her sleeves to study and classify a vast collection of fragmented jades and, if possible, find fitting fragments. These, dredged from the Sacred Cenote at Chichén Itzá, had been in storage for eighty years. In Postclassic times, the ancient Maya themselves looted ancestral tombs at Classic Period cities as far distant as Piedras Negras. These would then have passed through traders and into the hands of pilgrims visiting the Sacred Cenote at Chichén Itzá, the prime focus of pilgrimage in the Yucatán Peninsula. There, the jade pieces would have been charged with their purchaser's prayers, then sanctified by placing them on the embers of an incense burner. The jade pieces were then tossed into the waters of the Sacred Cenote, as offerings to the gods. But on hitting the cold water, most of them would have shattered from thermal shock.

When dredged up a century ago, jade fragments that had been lying on sand or gravel had retained their green color, whereas others that lay on organic matter, such as rotten wood, turned black. So the color of a fragment was rarely helpful in trying to match fragments. But Tania's extraordinary visual memory and knowledge of Maya imagery enabled her so often to connect two fragments that share no mating faces at all. Clearly, this same ability also underlay her successes in the field of Maya epigraphy.

25.1 Tatiana Proskouriakoff.

25.2 Federico
Fahsen (Guatemalan
ambassador) holding the
medal of the Order of the
Quetzal, which he had
just presented to Tatiana
Proskouriakoff.

It was of course a tremendous privilege to work for several years in daily contact with her. I found her tendency to disagree stimulating, and never impolite. (The only occasion, to my knowledge, on which she did express mordant opposition was when she arrived in Los Angeles to deliver a paper at a conference, only to discover that it had been organized by a society of antiquities collectors. She turned round and went straight back to the airport.)

On the other hand, she sometimes erred on the side of trustfulness, as when a TV-producer from a newly established MGM documentary-film offshoot arrived to highlight her work on the Chichén Itzá Cenote jades. But then she lost her nerve and asked me to do the talking while being filmed. Of course I demurred on the score of utter ignorance about the jades, but she was adamant. So while waiting for this man and his camera equipment to arrive, I tried first one and then the other of the two beautifully embellished jade noseplugs that were among the pieces she had selected, finding one of them to be a good fit in my nose and the other too loose.

Arriving late, the MGM man turned out to be a highly unattractive individual: grungy, with long, oily hair, his eyes hidden behind tiny dark-blue shades. But by the time his equipment had been set up, a lunch break was called for, so we repaired to the lounge next door.

Restored by sandwiches, we returned to the "studio." While fielding this man's questions it occurred to me to demonstrate a nose plug on camera, but could find only one of them. At the first opportunity I sidled over to Tania and whispered that one of them seemed to be missing.

"Oh, don't worry," she said, "I'm always losing things, but then they turn up."

This one, I'm afraid, never did.

In addition to the privilege of sharing Tania's office, I now had easy access to a resource of the greatest importance for the work I was to do. That was embodied in a long row of filing cabinets filled with mounted photographs of Maya sculpture. It was the largest file of its kind, and I imagine it still is, since I've added a great deal to it, as it's now the crown jewel of the Maya Corpus Program's office.

Credit for the existence of this great resource goes to the Carnegie Institution of Washington's Division of Historical Research. As previously mentioned, this division, mainly concerned with archaeology, had for many years been housed in a wooden building about two hundred yards from the Peabody Museum, so when, in 1958, the CIW most regrettably decided to close it down, all of its archives and photographic negatives and prints were simply trundled over to the Peabody Museum on trolleys. Were there questions of copyright? The Carnegie was much too grand to be concerned with such trifles. This unique archive has of course been of crucial value to the Maya Corpus Program—and the magnet that attracted me to Harvard. The Peabody's own collection of photographs taken by Teobert Maler and others in pre-Carnegie years before the First World War has also been of prime importance.

As for the experienced field archaeologists of that Carnegie division, some of the most active made the same short migration—among them Harry Pollock, Bob Smith, his brother Ledyard, and Tania. So with these in the museum I enjoyed solid support, as I did too from the Bowditch Professor of Mesoamerican Archaeology, Gordon Willey—then a relative newcomer to Maya studies, his early archaeological activities having been in Florida and Peru.

As I've said, my own resources were practically exhausted when the Guttman Foundation stepped in to create the Maya Corpus Program, and when that crucial support came to an end, I turned to the National Endowment for the Humanities. The NEH proved to be a loyal patron, but because their support was solely in the form of matching grants, I still had to rustle up half of what was needed for each three-year grant, and as a stranger in the land, I really had no idea where to turn for that.

But while in Mexico I visited Cuernavaca in the hope of meeting some wealthy American sufficiently interested in Maya archaeology to make a contribution. I was just beginning to fear that I had failed when someone mentioned to me the names of Mr. and Mrs. Murray Vaughan, who had a house in that town as well as others in

Toronto and St. Andrews, New Brunswick. When back in Cambridge, I succeeded in reaching Mrs. Vaughan at St. Andrews on the phone, and announced my name. She immediately launched into rapid chatter, not a word of which I understood. Then it turned out she had mistaken me for the Reverend Mr. Graham, minister of the church there—but if she was voluble, she also proved to be wonderfully impulsive.

With resolution of the misunderstanding, I made my pitch, and she seemed interested; indeed, she sent along a check for a thousand dollars straightaway. Soon, and for the next few years, she made much larger contributions, and of course I visited the Vaughans enjoyably at all three of their homes. Then her husband died, the house in Cuernavaca was given up, and she took to spending lonely winters in Palm Beach, where a fortune hunter soon wooed her, she married him, and the contributions ceased.

Before long, it was agreed that an assistant should be recruited to speed up the work, and Eric von Euw, who was about to receive his Ph.D. in engineering from Lehigh University, presented himself as a candidate, having heard through some mysterious grapevine that I was looking for an assistant. Although he lacked any relevant qualifications beyond fluency in Spanish, I felt confident of his ability to do useful work, and took him on. I'm sure he never considered making a permanent career in this field, but as he had been brought up largely in Argentina and Mexico (though of Swiss and German parentage), the idea of working seasonally in Latin America, and especially in Mexico, appealed to him. Valiantly, he stayed on the job for seven years (for he was very badly paid, I must confess) and endured long spells of work at remote sites.

In 1971, then, Eric joined me in sharing Tatiana Proskouriakoff's office. This was when Tania was steeped in her study of the jades from the Sacred Cenote at Chichén Itzá.

Needing some help in this seven-year project, Tania engaged a talented assistant, Char Solomon, who many years later became her biographer. In addition to assisting Tania and Eric in the jade study, Char was also to enjoy, or endure long spells of, very different work by joining Eric on some of his difficult excursions to remote sites in southern Quintana Roo, where there still remained vast areas of trackless and uninhabited forest.

The most arduous and lonely mission undertaken by Eric and Char must have been the two long periods they spent at Calakmul, a huge site then extremely difficult to reach. It had been visited, in fact, only by lumbermen and looters since the Carnegie Institution of Washington had worked there in 1933. As it happens, one of the particularly valuable acts of Eric and Char at Calakmul was to photograph the damaged remains of the inscribed sides of Stela 52 that have already been mentioned, for at some time following their visit, those sawed-off fragments seem to have vanished, leaving Eric's photos as the only remaining record of them.

If the systematic compilation of data for Corpus fascicles progressed more slowly than forecast in the early 1970s, one explanation of this was my decision to spend a good deal of time visiting various sites hit by looters, in the hope of saving something from the wreckage. But at last, two fascicles were ready for publication. (Here I should confess to some wild optimism that led me to forecast completion of the program within sixteen years, when even sixty may not get us to the halfway mark. But there's a good precedent: James Fowler took five times longer than predicted to finish his great Oxford English Dictionary.)

Volume 1, *Introduction*, presents the three-letter abbreviations, or codes, for site-names and types of monuments (replacing the earlier long-winded descriptive titles), and the symbols to be used on plans; tables of days and months for a complete Maya Calendar Round; and other material. All that remained was to find the money to have it printed.

25.3 *At work in the Maya Corpus office, Room K, in the basement of the Peabody Museum, 1974. Photo by Hillel Burger.*

One day, while walking along New York's Fifth Avenue between Thirty-Ninth and Fortieth Streets, I happened to look up at a large building on its west side that had originally been an S. H. Kress store (and would soon be demolished). To my surprise, Maya hieroglyphs seemed to be represented, rather freely, on a band of carved limestone running along the façade between the second and third floors. So I paid a visit to the offices of the Kress Foundation (a great patron of the arts) to inquire which of the three Kress brothers had been interested in the Maya. The reply that I eventually received was that to the best of anyone's knowledge, none of them had been. But I must have subtly indicated the motive for my inquiry, for the foundation, with great generosity and rare caprice, announced that they would be pleased to defray the costs of printing the first volume. It's a pleasure to express my sincere thanks to them once again. That first volume was published in 1975.

Volume 2, Part 1 appeared at the same time. This presented the first twenty-four stelae of Naranjo, a site which had already, as mentioned above, been badly damaged by looters. The costs of printing this fascicle were defrayed by a number of generous friends.

We were off to a good start—one that marked indelibly a turning point in my own life. Only a few years earlier I had dreaded the future as I then imagined it: the replacement of my rewarding, if often uncomfortable, life in the jungle by one in some dismal office. For I found it difficult to believe that I'd ever find a reasonably congenial and well-paid position in business, or any other employment, knowing how hopelessly unbusinesslike I am; but I tried to persuade myself that, on the other hand, I might discover that leading a settled life, married and with a family, could eventually compensate for the boredom of business.

Now, however, the likelihood of being able to carry on as before was tremendously invigorating. For this opportunity, I was ready to trade off any residual longings for a conventional, domestic life and instead remain single.

26.1 Yaxchilan, Stela 11 in its original location.

CHAPTER 26

Yaxchilan, 1971

Eric had agreed to begin his work for the Corpus by recording a stela we had found at the ruins of Ixtutz, near Poptún, having raised it with our "Lug-all" winch. He would also record the numerous elements of a stone mosaic panel that Merle Greene had unearthed there, not long before.

Then, on 22 May, I set off for Yaxchilan to attempt some emergency architectural repairs to the principal temple. Today, of course, Yaxchilan is a Mecca for lovers of Maya ruins, but until the late 1970s (when a road was built from Palenque to Frontera on the Usumacinta River) any would-be visitors had to choose between two options. From Guatemala, they could travel for two days downriver from Sayaxché, Petén, straight to the ruins—as I had, years earlier; or from the Mexican side, take a light plane from Tenosique, and with some trepidation land on the four-hundred-yard grass strip prepared in the 1960s by Yaxchilan's gruff and somewhat unbalanced guardian, Miguel de la Cruz. (I regret my failure to record his quaint and delightfully misspelled notice announcing a landing fee of 25 pesos. The Americans, he told me, paid up without demur, but as for the French—he shrugged his shoulders in a quite Gallic gesture.)

Before Miguel had made that grass strip, really determined travelers coming from the Mexican side had no choice but to fly in to Agua Azul, an old mahogany station on the river, and then trust to luck in finding a boatman to take them downriver. Evidently, such determination was uncommon, because (as Miguel's tally showed), visitors to that wonderful site were as rare as hen's teeth—to use a favorite expression of Eric Thompson's.[1]

The Mexican government's installation of a resident site guard at Yaxchilan in 1931 has rightly been hailed with approval and relief, for had this not been done, Yaxchilan would undoubtedly have been plundered of its sculpture, just as Piedras Negras was in the 1950s and '60s. I once found, in the Peabody Museum's photographic archives, a photograph of that guard, Ulíses de la Cruz. His stiff thatch of black hair and formidable appearance were to be reproduced almost identically in the person of his elder son, Miguel, who would eventually succeed him in the post (with his younger brother, Juan, as assistant). I made a print of this photograph of their father and gave it to Miguel, whose gruff reaction was, "Ah yes, I was a little younger then; but wait, I never had a revolver like that one; that's very strange!"

Those living in the Usumacinta valley seldom saw photographs of themselves, and mirrors must also have been in short supply, to judge by an experience I had with one of the two men who had so laboriously propelled me in a cayuco from Agua Azul to Yaxchilan and back in 1959. I had photographed this man, Rufino García, as he was resting from his labors in a hammock; then in 1971, having discovered where on the river he was living, I landed and found him, again lounging in his hammock. I gave him the eight-by-ten photo and asked, "Do you recognize this fellow?"

"Yes," he replied after studying it, "but he's dead now."

For a second I thought he meant, philosophically, that the young man he once was no longer existed, having been replaced by the older and perhaps wiser or more cynical man that he now was. But he continued, "I met him once—that's Yon Sosa!"

Yon Sosa and Turcios Lima were the two famous pioneer guerrilla leaders in Guatemala in the early '70s, and Yon Sosa is known to have been active along the river. So I concluded that unless Rufino were the spitting image of Yon Sosa, he couldn't very often have studied his own quite distinctive countenance in a mirror!

Apart from the installation of Ulíses de la Cruz as encargado, and the later nomination of his sons to succeed him, nothing whatever had been done to preserve the ruins. When I first visited them in 1959, an Amercan engineer had placed sheets of tarred corrugated cardboard over various carved lintels that were lying face-up, in an attempt to preserve them from damaging moss or lichen growing on them; it had been a Pemex official, I was told, who could be thanked for this. When I returned ten years later, nothing further had been done to arrest erosion of sculpture. Being better prepared on my second visit, I had brought with me a photograph taken fifty years earlier of Stela 7; in it one could see very clearly the likeness of a squirrel in a cartouche near the lower right-hand corner; but now its outlines were barely discernable.

Two or three of the more important standing buildings, Structures 40, 33, and 19, were also in perilous condition. The first of these had a great cedar tree growing out of its roof at an angle of about 45 degrees, which in a storm could easily crash, pulling a large portion of the vaulted roof with it. Then, the great temple, Structure 33, surely one of the finest of all surviving Maya buildings, was threatened with partial collapse, and Structure 19, the "Labyrinth," also had a big cedar growing from its roof, though the fall of this one didn't seem imminent.

There had, however, been a raid led by an audacious and incompetent ingeniero hired by INAH to bring back sculpture to help fill the halls of the new and splendid National Museum of Anthropology. Some of the lintels that had fallen from their doorways were removed to Mexico City—a justifiable action, from the point of view of conservation. But this man cast megalomaniacal eyes on Stela 11, which still stood proudly in front of its temple, on the highest acropolis of the site—the only stela, of the more than thirty that had remained erect, with its four sculptured sides still well preserved. It was a memorable spot: from beside the stela, a vast panorama of Guatemala lay before one across the river—or did, whenever a few saplings had first been cut down.

But this man—in his pride, his *soberbia*—uprooted the stela, without, of course, finding any necessity for an archaeologist to be present to record the particulars of its setting or to look for buried offerings that might be found there. Then, with what must have been enormous difficulty, he boxed it up and lowered it with ropes and pulleys from a height of about 340 feet down a slipway of sapling trunks to the river's edge. There it was somehow loaded onto three large canoas lashed together and propelled upstream by outboard motors to Agua Azul.

When the plane came back from delivering an earlier load of sculpture (this being one of the ex-Royal Canadian Air Force Avro "Ansons" which in those days were busily transporting coffee, pigs, and other merchandise from the roadless lowlands to San Cristóbal and Villa Hermosa), the pilot would then have been invited to look at the last and greatest trophy that he was to whisk away.

"Caray!" he may have exclaimed, "Surely you're not expecting me to transport that! It's *far* too big and *far* too heavy for this small plane and this short runway!"

So the stela was left on the foreshore, where for several years it remained forgotten, invisible during rainy seasons, because submerged. In time, the protective wooden box made for its removal had rotted away, so canoas coming in to Agua Azul must sometimes have scraped across its face as the waters receded; and when high and dry again, the ladies of Agua Azul quite likely used it as a washboard.

Then Trudi Blom arrived, and at the sight of this, all her fuses blew. "Enough!" she cried, and organized a rescue mission, co-opting as assistant Professor R. E. Franklin, of the Department of Engineering at the University of Michigan, who was then living in retirement in San Cristóbal. By Herculean efforts they managed to return the stela to Yaxchilan in much the manner of its arrival, and then to haul it up the steep, sandy riverbank. Returning it to its original setting would, of course, have been ideal, but for private and unfunded well-wishers the difficulties of doing so were far too great.

YAXCHILAN, 1971

Without, of course, any thought of attempting these particular tasks myself, I wrote to the director of the Mexican Instituto Nacional de Antropología e Historia requesting permission to do three things:

1. Bring in masons and the necessary materials to strengthen one or two endangered buildings. (For this purpose I had requested a thousand dollars from Mr. Landon T. Clay, of Boston, who kindly obliged.)

2. Erect shelters of corrugated *fiberglass* over any stela, lintel, or fragments thereof that were lying unprotected.

3. Build myself a galera, or open-sided thatched shelter, in some discreet corner of the site, to use as my base of operations.

The Director of INAH at that time was Dr. Ignacio Bernal, the most distinguished Mexican archaeologist of his day, an excellent scholar and a man of cosmopolitan outlook, free of the nationalistic prejudices typical of political appointees. (He was, alas, soon to suffer a purgatory of congressional inquisition sparked by a maniac former employee of the Secretariat of Public Education named Julio Cabrera Ruiz, from which he eventually emerged unblemished, but distressed.)

In his reply, Bernal wrote that of course I could—and *should*—do those things; the fiberglass shelters would be ugly, as I myself had suggested, but they were necessary, and of course I needed living quarters while doing this work.

His letter was on official stationery, but there was one thing wrong with it: it was written in English. So I wrote again, asking for a version in Spanish. When this hadn't arrived by the time I reached Guatemala, I telegraphed a reminder, and received my Spanish language permit telegraphically in Guatemala.

With this in hand, I purchased a few sacks of lime and cement, many sheets of corrugated fiberglass, and suitable quantities of provisions, and then engaged Felipe Quixchán, a mason who had worked for the Peabody Museum at Seibal, and two laborers, plus the crew of two (as *motorista* and boga) for a large dugout canoe. Along the way, we added another man to our labor force.

On arrival at Yaxchilan we were greeted enthusiastically by Don Juan, who almost immediately heaved a bag of cement onto his quite narrow shoulders, and almost trotted with it up to Structure 33. He was delighted that after such a long period of neglect, something was going to be done.

His son Luis (or rather, one of his many sons, for the brothers were notably philoprogenitive) was also pleased, but being of a less-active nature, he took the good news sitting down. He had, however, a nice gift for me, a bolsa ahulada that he had made. Such bags are used by anyone going into the forest for keeping hammock, pabellon, and blanket in, and when filled with these they serve as comfortable cushions during truck or boat rides. They are sugar sacks waterproofed with native rubber, and in this case, Luis had adorned it with an inscription in darkened rubber, and an enlarged version of my own signature.

He had once asked me to find him educational books, but the only one I had found in Guatemala City to bring him was a single volume of a Spanish encyclopedia (*Esparragos* to *Francia*). But my dream of a palm-thatched shelter evaporated on being informed of something I hadn't noticed, that guano thatching palms are extremely scarce thereabouts. So I had to make do with a pitched roof of polyethylene, although later, sufficient palm leaves for the purpose were brought from upriver.

Next morning, I went with Luis to look at buildings that might be candidates for emergency repairs, and we soon agreed that the case of Structure 33 was much the most urgent, besides being far more practicable than Structure 40. The carriage of cement, lime, sand, and water up to the level of Structure 33 would be arduous enough, but to the elevation of Structure 40 it would have been three times more exhausting. (When, several years later, INAH's Roberto García Moll undertook consolidation of structures on that high acropolis, two horses named Estela and Dintel were employed to carry up the materials.)

Another reason to dismiss the idea of working up there was that having cut down the tree growing out of the roof, a controlled dismantling of it would have been necessary so as to remove the roots, before it could be rebuilt with mortar. Unless this were done, the roof would soon disintegrate, having previously been held together, to some extent, by the very roots that were threatening to destroy it.

Structure 33 stands at the top of a long stairway leading up to it from the plaza. Rectangular in plan, it is twenty meters wide by five meters deep. Three doorways, each spanned by a beautifully carved lintel, give access to the interior, which has four internal buttresses projecting from the rear wall. The central pair of these once formed a shrine, with a flat roof over it—but this had collapsed long ago. Within this shrine sat a life-size statue of a seated ruler with a huge headdress—until this was broken off by the collapse of that roof. At both ends of the temple, partition walls create small chambers, accessible through a doorway. The vaulted roof of this building soars up into a roof-comb, fretted with apertures, which still show remnants of stucco figures and abundant decorative elements.

But from the left-hand doorway, as you look at it from in front, there ran a crack, gradually widening as it continued up to the top of the roof-comb. The reason for this was quite obvious: at that end, the facing stones had fallen away from the lower portion of the front wall, as they also had from the side and back walls for a distance of three or

26.2 Yaxchilan Structure 33, in need of repairs.

four meters from the corners. From the back wall, which is about one meter thick, only the exterior facing stones had fallen, but at the front, both facing and hearting stones had fallen, leaving only the interior facing stones to bear the load, and these, yielding to the great weight of the roof comb, were now bowed under the weight. The pressure had even caused individual stones to crack, and the wall seemed ready to burst inward at any moment, and bring down the entire end of the temple.

At the other end, it was the rear wall that was in the worst condition, having lost about half of its masonry over a stretch of twenty-two feet from the corner, and the rear corner itself was missing, so that one could easily walk through it. The front corner also gaped in places.

26.3 Yaxchilan: my albañil and crew, closing a gap at one corner of Structure 33.

A nagging doubt of mine was settled on that day when the men brought in a boatload of good coarse sand from about three miles downstream. So, having concluded that repairing those walls in the temple was feasible, and that sand was available, I sent the boat back to Sayaxché to bring enough lime and cement to bring the total to forty sacks of one and eight of the other, and more boxes of foodstuffs that I had left behind—and also, very important, to bring Eric, who would be waiting there.

A week earlier, soon after we had arrived at Yaxchilan, a busybody doctor from Tenosique flew in with Pedro Pech, the encargado of Bonampak, and together they persuaded Miguel that my permiso was not valid; I had brought only a Guatemalan document, they said. Miguel came blustering up (he was really a timid man, lacking in self-confidence, and tried to conceal this weakness with bluster).

"Your document carries no eagle," he said in his forceful voice, "and it has Guatemala printed on it!" (Miguel was almost illiterate.)

"Yes," I replied, "that's because it is a telegram *received* in Guatemala, but here you see printed proof that its *source* was Mexico."

He was impressed by this argument and told me I could proceed. But that night Don Juan came and told me his brother had changed his mind (just like Miguel not to come and tell me himself).

Next day, he avoided me, and went off upriver to the military base at the mouth of the Lacantún River. When he came back, I asked him what had transpired.

"I don't have to tell you," was his gruff reply. But next morning Miguel changed his tune and said I could continue so long as I didn't cut any trees. We went up to the temple together, and he asked why I didn't start at the southeast end, as being more endangered. I explained that it would be difficult to work there because of the barricade of *copo* (fig) roots, but now Miguel was all for cutting them.

Two days later, the colonel from the Lacantún base arrived, an intelligent and apparently sympathetic man. But he told me that it really was necessary to go to Tuxtla Gutierrez and obtain a better document. As luck would have it, a plane was due to come in next day, bound for Comitán, and from there I could take a bus.

But the plane never came, and no one knew when another might. Two days later, two DDT-sprayers arrived, who were to be flown out to Ocosingo the next day, and it did come back. It was an aged Cessna, with a hole in the instrument panel where the airspeed indicator had formerly been—but the pilot was willing to take me. From Ocosingo a bus eventually brought me, after wide detours, to San Cristóbal. There I found a birthday fiesta in progress at the Loughlins, who were renting the poet W. S. Merwin's house. The *mariachi*, the abundance of food and drinks, and the delightful company provided a sudden and refreshing contrast to Yaxchilan.

The following day I took a taxi to Tuxtla, and went first to see the INAH delegate for Chiapas, Duvalier by name, and then telephoned Bernal, who said he would get Ignacio Marquina, the ancient head of INAH's Department of Monumentos Prehispánicos, to send a telegram. Bernal told me that he had originally telegraphed his permission to Tenosique, as I had requested (but unfortunately had forgotten about).

I waited all afternoon and evening for Marquina's reply, making hourly visits to the telegraph office, but nothing came. This was Friday, so at 10:30 p.m. I telephoned Marquina again, who said he had sent the telegram. To whom? To the presidente municipal! So that was the explanation, but an odd one.

I also took the opportunity to ask his permission to dig a stratigraphic test pit between the ball court and Juan de la Cruz's house, which could almost immediately be converted into a latrine, as we had done at Seibal, as "land mines" had rendered that area near the entrance to the ruins of Yaxchilan practically impenetrable. But—

"Oh no," exclaimed Marquina, "we are trying to get away from all that; it belongs to the past. Today we must think in terms of porcelain fittings!"

Thirty years later there was still a total lack of sanitary facilities at Yaxchilan, for either resident staff or tourists.

At nine next morning, nothing was known at the presidente municipal's office about any telegram. A dreadful suspicion then arose, that perhaps he meant the presidente of Ocosingo, the municipality in which Yaxchilan lies. So I telephoned Marquina again, who said this time that the telegram had been sent to Duvalier. At midmorning, I managed to get in touch with the latter, and persuaded him to telephone Marquina himself, and suggested that if successful he might prepare a document certifying that Marquina had given his permission for the work to be done. Not a chance of that! He advised me instead not to do anything at all at Yaxchilan. (I wonder whether, in a strange kind of sympathy, Duvalier was not imagining himself in my shoes, since he would have recoiled in horror at the idea of having to work at such a place.)

In desperation I went to see the governor, whom I found to be a cordial and impressive man, anxious to help, and help he did. Next day he had me flown to Yaxchilan in his own plane, where I was pleased to find that reconstruction had been going on quietly. That was a relief, since several days had been wasted, in the course of which both the food I had brought and the money for the men's wages would otherwise have been consumed fruitlessly.

At the west end of Structure 33 it was necessary to dig down in search of foundations upon which to build up the end wall, and we found them—a row of very large stones.

As elsewhere, we left the replacement of facing stones to some future project, and were careful to keep our masonry from projecting into the space that this facing would need to occupy. I am glad to say that when INAH did at last decide to do something about one of Mexico's greatest jewels, Roberto García Moll, the archaeologist appointed to do it, had no complaints on this score.

Nearly four weeks after leaving Sayaxché for Yaxchilan, we now were ready to return. Miguel had been out after turtle the previous night, so I was unable to bid him good-bye, although this was hardly a cause for lamentation. I had arranged with Luis that he would return Miguel's spade and wooden box, used for mortar, and we were about to cast off when Miguel came blustering to the water's edge:

"Where's my spade?" was all he had to say.

26.4 *Repairing Hieroglyphic Stairway 1 at Yaxchilan, Chiapas, Mexico, ca. 1970.*

Whether or not it was my emergency restoration work at Yaxchilan that reminded INAH of the existence of that ancient city I shall never know, but when I returned there in about March of the following year I found a camp being built under the guidance of a young Mexican archaeologist named Jürgen Brüggemann. I was immediately struck by the fact that he'd had the living and dining room of his camp roofed with steeply pitched corrugated iron, thus insuring torrid heat within it, whereas the palm-thatch roof of the patio was pitched so close to horizontal that it would certainly rot within a season.

Two tall lattice towers of steel had also been brought in, in sections, and between them an antenna had been strung for short wave radio telephony. One of the masts, however, was sited at the very edge of the grass runway, and to this the pilots naturally objected. Brüggemann held firm—until more potent authorities intervened. And then, two enormously heavy 13 kW diesel generators were also brought in. How this was accomplished I never discovered, as I avoided conversation with the man, but I did wonder what use he intended to make of so much power. Then he turned his attention to providing water for the camp. An electrically driven pump was connected to a hose that had its other end in the river. The pump was started, and Brüggemann gazed expectantly at its outlet pipe—but water came there none. The poor fellow was ignorant of an elementary law of physics stating that on our globe, water cannot be sucked up to a height of more than about thirty feet.

While at Yaxchilan I avoided the man; but when, early in the following year, I visited INAH's offices I ran into him by chance, and gave him a cheery "Well, how are things going at Yaxchilan?"

"Terrible," he said, "Terrible. It is impossible to work there. Everyone thinks he knows best—the site guards, the pilots, doctors from Tenosique, the governor of the state, and then there's that Señora Blom who thinks she's the empress of the Usumacinta! But I can tell you one thing: *you* will never be allowed to work there again!"

"Oh well, hey-ho!"

I had come in the hope of introducing myself to the newly appointed director of INAH, Dr. Guillermo Bonfil Batalla, simply to make his acquaintance; but on being ushered into his office I had the surprise of my life upon hearing him say,

"Oh! I'm extremely glad to make your acquaintance. You see, we've had a little trouble with the archaeologist appointed last year to work at Yaxchilan, and have chosen as his successor an excellent and very modest young man named Roberto García Moll. The only difficulty is that he's had no previous experience of the Maya area, so we have been wondering if you would be kind enough accept a joint appointment with him?"

This was a proposal as alarming as it was astonishing, for I had none of the necessary experience, and no matter how *modesto* my joint director might be, I could easily foresee friction arising between us. Fortunately, though, I was able to express my sincere feeling of flattery at his offer, and real regret at my inability to take advantage of it, owing to my unbreakable obligations toward the Maya Corpus Program.

In fact, I did sense, when that season began, a slight initial resentment on Roberto García Moll's part, but before long he must have seen that I had no interest in trespassing on his turf, but instead might relieve him of the task of recording and publishing the monumental sculpture. In fact, we soon established very cordial relations, and I rejoice that he has never ceased keeping a watchful eye on this precious site, even when charged by INAH with more wide-ranging administrative responsibilities.

26.5 Me at Yaxchilan. Photo for National Geographic magazine by Otis Imboden.

26.6 The author at Yaxchilan Structure 5 photographing the hieroglyphic stair at night ca. 1975. Photo by Luis Cuevas.

27.1 My drawing of Lintel 24 from Yaxchilan.

CHAPTER 27

A Sidetrack into Biography

By the late 1960s the flow of looted Maya antiquities into Europe had become so distressing that I made a point of keeping my eyes and ears open for any information on this front (to use a suitable military term!). So I began visiting the showrooms of French, Belgian, and Swiss art dealers, and before long, the galleries of otherwise respectable museums.

Many years later I learned that Australia had introduced a scheme of tax deductions for donors of works of art to public museums, a concession similar to that existing in the United States—and then that a dealer named Leonardo Patterson had been quick off the mark in offering the Aussies a chance to take advantage of it.

Thinking it might be productive, I resolved to make a two-week reconnaissance "down-under." As expected, Patterson had tried to unload some of his fake wall paintings, but these were pathetic productions. But I knew that my long journey would not be fruitless, because the Australian National Gallery of Art in Canberra had purchased (or been given) a very fine stela—well preserved, too, apart from unnecessary damage suffered in the usual process of sawing it into more easily handled blocks.

Accordingly, I wrote to my cousin Kirstie, who was then married to an Australian and living in Sydney, to announce my intention of arriving within a few weeks, and she kindly replied with an offer of accommodation. I did photograph and draw the Canberra stela, but thanks to Kirstie I succumbed to the lure of another sizeable undertaking, unrelated to Maya sculpture.

This began when she asked me whether I'd ever seen the album of watercolors that used to be in her parents' old family home in Scotland.

"No," I replied, "and I've never even heard of it."

"Oh, well it's mine now, so I'll bring it down for you to look at."

The paintings in this album, about fourteen inches wide, were the work of Count Amadeo Preziosi, born, as I would learn, in Malta in 1816. As a young man he was sent by his father, a lawyer, to study law in Paris; but then his father would hear of his son's misstep—one that parents commonly deplore. For his son had strayed into the wrong set, abandoning his studies in favor of art—watercolor painting in particular. With his father threatening to disown him, he moved to Constantinople, where he soon prospered as a painter.

Upon the death of his father, Amadeo visited Malta again, and from there embarked for Sicily with a new sketchbook in hand. After crossing to the toe of Italy, he worked his way slowly northward, painting as he went, through Naples, Rome, Florence, Genoa, and finally through the new Mont Cenis tunnel to Paris. There, he would stay for about two months—until his sketchbook was full.

Preziosi did little to change the world's aesthetic sensibility, but perhaps there's never been a greater technical virtuoso in watercolor painting, in one regard at least: the fact that he never messed up! For mistakes in watercolor painting cannot be corrected.

Every painting in this rectangular album is a double-page spread, and this, of course, means that upon completing one scene, and then intending to begin another, he would have two choices: either to turn over two pages (as any watercolorist in his right mind would do), or else begin the new painting on the back of the right-hand half of the previous one—a procedure too perilous, I imagine, for any other watercolorist to have attempted. As I've indicated, just one mistake dooms a watercolor, and with double-page spreads painted on both sides of each page—a total disaster!

His choice of scenes to paint could also be unusual, for he had something of a journalist's interest in people and street scenes. One scene in this album is an interior view of the city morgue in Paris. This had been built for the purpose of displaying, for a limited time, any bodies that had been fished up from the River Seine, or found dead in the street, so that wives whose husbands had failed to return home could look for them there. The bodies were displayed naked (with a cardboard *cache-sex*) so that their clothes could also be displayed, hung on hooks, to facilitate identification.

Surprisingly, *Murray's Guide to Paris*, a very proper publication, used to recommend visitors who had just "done" Notre Dame to nip round the east end of the cathedral and visit the morgue (until it was rebuilt elsewhere in 1907). Preziosi's view of it shows two toothless hags cackling at the sight of the corpses, along with a couple of cheeky boys.

These watercolors were done soon after the Prussians had left Paris—and before Hausmann had begun revamping the city. The Tuileries is shown roofless and window-less (it would later be demolished), but the gardens are well kept and well patronized, and close inspection reveals details of the latest type of garden hose: this was made up of lengths of rigid tubing with flexible joints at intervals, where pairs of tiny wheels can just be discerned.

"But these watercolors have to be *published*!" I exclaimed to Kirstie. And then I had to fly back to the United States on what was at that time the world's longest nonstop flight, Sydney to Los Angeles—as I had good reason to remember. For I had a window seat, and for about eight hours hadn't wanted to trouble my neighbors by leaving it, until I remembered reading about the incidence of deep-vein thrombosis caused by lengthy immobility. So, apologizing to my two neighbors, I tried to get up, but found that I couldn't. My right leg refused to move. Horrified, I sat back, and then manually hauled that knee up—only to discover that my sock had become cemented to the carpet with chewing gum carelessly discarded on the floor by a former occupant of my seat!

Just one more incident of travel...

A year later, I went back to Sydney with a four-by-five-inch camera and electronic flashes, and successfully photographed all the album's pages. The Preziosi project now began to consume my spare time. I went to Turkey with my camera and photographed a few fine examples of his work there, but then discovered a wonderful trove in Romania. In the early nineteenth century, a Romanian had been installed as king of his country, but then he was found wanting, so it was decided to try an imported king: a Hohenzollern, one from the southern and Catholic branch of the family. This king was well liked and successful, but at the time he was chosen, Romania was technically still under the suzerainty of the Turkish sultan, a status that required him to make, before accepting the crown, ceremonial acknowledgment to the sultan of his dependent status.

It must have been during the new king's visit to Constantinople for just this purpose that Preziosi met him; and perhaps the king told him that he had a new and large country to rule, little of which he had yet seen, and also a palace and a summer residence, both with bare walls. So he would be most grateful if Preziosi would kindly visit his country and paint some views for him to hang on those walls. (This account, of course, is speculative.)

But as Preziosi did go to Romania to paint for the king, I went there, too, and found the commissioned paintings were still in storage at the old summer palace at Sinaia. And there, the administrators very kindly brought them out for me to photo-graph. Next, I found there was a sketchbook of Preziosi's in a Bucharest museum, this containing rapid and lively watercolor sketches of markets and dances. I photographed all of these and several of the actual buildings he painted.

Then I heard of another great trove of Preziosi paintings: this one at the Victoria and Albert Museum in London. These had been collected by an employee of Shell Oil in Turkey, Rodney Seawright, who collected watercolors perceptively and on a large scale. So with the material already in hand, and with the permission given me to photograph the V&A paintings, I could have produced a fine book, with an introductory article that a professor of art history at the University of California at Los Angeles had offered to write. This was none other than Donald Preziosi, a great-grandson of the painter himself! But now for many years I have let the project lapse owing to the pressure of Maya work, and all the effort I put into it may have been in vain.

If I failed to pursue this project with sufficient vigor and persistence, at least I know why this was. Preziosi had made an ill-timed intrusion into my work of recording Maya inscriptions, continuation of which I was beginning to regard as almost a sacred obligation, in view of the absence of any similar program elsewhere.

For I had indeed been postponing for too long another project that came under this rubric, but much closer to my heart and to the central drift of my life. This would be a biography of Alfred Maudslay, whom I've already mentioned as one of the two pioneer nineteenth-century explorers of Maya ruins and recorders of their hieroglyphic texts (the other being Teobert Maler, a German and near contemporary of Maudslay's, and another man of great determination and talent). All Mayanists owe Maudslay a great debt, but owing to his modesty, it was only his work that was known, and little about the man himself.

Maudslay and Maler were both very productive in their own distinctive ways, but lamentably, no one came forward to continue their work. If others had done so, a great deal of important information could have been recorded that now is lost forever. As for the relative contributions of these two great pioneers, these cannot be weighed for value, because of the different paths they trod. But I can say, without fear of diminishing Maler's work, that Maudslay's was in a real sense the "onlie begetter" of the Maya Corpus Program.

When I set out to gather material on Maudslay, I certainly faced an uphill task, for there existed no published biographical material whatsoever. None—not even in reference works such as Who's Who or the Encyclopedia Britannica. But now, with the long delayed and then almost explosive growth of interest in the Maya, Alfred Maudslay (1850–1931) has come to be regarded by archaeologists as the great pioneer of scientific exploration of Maya ruins, for he brought into his work an entirely new level of professionalism.

Born in London in 1850 and a graduate of Cambridge University, Maudslay made a quick visit to Guatemala soon after graduation, where he may have been impressed by the few Mayas still living there, but undoubtedly by the quality of their ancestors' artifacts, as judged by the few Maya sites he had chanced to see. But then, about one-third of a working life later, he laid his plans for a return to Maya territory with admirable foresight. He was already a good photographer, and since he had selected as targets for his work Copán and Quiriguá, two sites with abundant sculpture carved in the round, he must have understood the importance of making plaster casts of them. Proof of this is the very large consignment of plaster of Paris and other necessary material he had shipped out to Guatemala before leaving, and the professional plaster-caster he brought with him.

Making casts of three-dimensional sculptures, such as the huge zoomorphs at Quiriguá, was far from being a simple matter, for only a limited area of sculpture could be molded at one time—for otherwise the rigid mold might be impossible to remove, clamped in place by re-entrant curves. So these were made in numerous more-or-less rectangular pieces, bounded by dykes, each of which had a small conical projection at one end and a similar depression at the other. These served to insure accurate registration of the piece-molds when eventually assembled for the final step that would be taken thousands of miles away: pouring plaster into the assembled molds to make the facsimile.

Each piece-mold had to be carefully wrapped for carriage on muleback to a distant port for shipment to England. Most of them arrived safely, and when casts from them had been made, Maudslay engaged a very gifted artist to make line-drawings of them for publication.

Maudslay's large-format photographs were also triumphantly successful, and by happy coincidence, recent technical progress in reproducing photographs in printed books resulted in quite satisfactory images. And the drawings by Maudslay's artist, Annie Hunter, are superb.

After mounting half a dozen expeditions to Maya regions, Maudslay took up the challenge of translating and publishing, in appropriate style, the great sixteenth-century work of Bernal Díaz, *The Conquest of Mexico*. To this day, the four-volume set is the classic version, and abridged editions, the most widely read.

My hope was that an adequate biography of Maudslay might serve as a useful contribution to the history of Maya archaeology, but for me it would also be a labor of love, since my work has really been a continuation of his initial work, though conducted under less difficult conditions and shirking altogether the making of those definitive casts. As a biographer, of course, I was a complete beginner and had no idea of how to start my research. Then I had rather a good idea. Since Maudslay is an uncommon name with that spelling, why not try the British telephone directories, for perhaps there were living relatives bearing that name. So from my old home in England, I went to the public library in a nearby market town and began working my way through volumes occupying three or four yards of shelf. But fortunately I hadn't looked through more than perhaps eight volumes when I came across a Mrs. Maudslay, with an address in Dorset.

I called her, and found I'd "holed out in one," as golfers say, for not only was she related to Alfred Maudslay by blood, but also by marriage, to his favorite nephew, who eventually became executor of his will. In this capacity he ended up with all the material not mentioned in the will—odds and ends, many of them, but some of great value for my purposes. Mrs. Maudslay immediately invited me to visit her, and offered me every assistance. I made two more visits, in the course of which she gave me very interesting information and also told me to help myself to any document that might serve my purposes.

Some of these I later passed on to the British Museum, but one of them I did, with the family's permission, give to the National Portrait Gallery, in London. This was a "physionotrace" of Alfred Maudslay's grandfather, Henry Maudslay, who was one of the greatest pioneers of the Industrial Revolution. (Physionotraces are profile portraits that were made partly by mechanical means, shortly before the invention of photography. I believe there are only two other images of Henry Maudslay, both small, and neither of them as lifelike as this.)

Completion of this biography during my spare time took a few years and some traveling, including visits to Tonga, Fiji, and Samoa, where Maudslay had spent some years as a colonial administrator. Its completion gave me great satisfaction, for no matter how deserving he and his achievements were, the likelihood of another writer feeling an urge to celebrate them did not seem very great.

CHAPTER 28

Lee Moore

In August 1971, I spent a weekend with friends at their summer cottage in Woods Hole, Massachusetts. Another guest was Denie Weil, a cousin of theirs, and she, on being told how I spent my days, declared that I was just the kind of person that for some time she had been hoping to meet.

Why? Because in April of that year she had gone down to Yucatán alone for a few days, and during the first leg of the return flight, which had a stopover in Miami, she had been seated next to a youngish man, quite snappily dressed, who mentioned that he had once worked in Perú as an exporter of orchids. And then—as he went on to say—he'd found that the exportation of antiquities was even more profitable. And then another discovery: that pursuit of the same trade in Yucatán brought even greater rewards. As a result, he had transferred his operations entirely to that area. And as Denie seemed interested, he described his technique for bringing out large monuments by first sawing them into blocks of convenient size, and then slicing the carved surfaces off (as described in a preceding chapter).

Now, however, he was faced with a real challenge. A modeled stucco façade in deep relief, several meters long, had come to light in situ on a mound somewhere in the Yucatán Peninsula, and he wasn't sure how to remove it or prepare it for shipment. It was with the hope of obtaining advice on these matters that he was now returning to the States.

"But—," Denie had exclaimed, "but this is immoral!"

"Oh, come on now, don't give me this legal stuff!"

"I didn't say illegal, I said immoral!"

And there—abruptly, the conversation ended, and that man left the flight at Miami. But on the second leg of her flight to New York, Denie noticed that her

28.1 *Lee Moore's shameless graffiti at Calakmul.*
Photo by Eric von Euw.

neighbor had left on his seat his copy of *The New Yorker* magazine, and stamped on it was his name and subscription mailing address. So, still feeling indignant, and being a businesslike person, she tore it off and filed it away; and now, on returning home from Woods Hole, she mailed it to me.

"Lee Moore!" I exclaimed to myself on receiving her note. "So that's where the wretch lives: in South Miami Springs!" I had inwardly cursed his name for some time, as information reached me of his looting activities, and with increased fury since my colleague, Eric von Euw, had shown me the photo he took of Moore's impudent graffito, "Recuerdo de Lee H. Moore," on the interior plaster wall of the only building still standing at Calakmul (once one of the most powerful Maya realms, as we have learned from decipherments some years ago). For presumably it was he who was responsible for the dismemberment of some, at least, of the few well-preserved stelae at Calakmul (as described here in Chapter 22).

When Denie Weil had that encounter with him, Moore may have been planning to discuss with someone claiming to be a conservator the technical problems of removing the stucco façade, and then to arrange meetings with dealers, such as Everitt Rassiga in

New York, who might help underwrite this operation. In fact, Rassiga did contribute, or rather invest, in the operation, as did a banker/collector in Philadephia.

What technical advice Moore received I don't know, any more than I know the methods he actually employed to remove this stucco façade, but there's evidence suggesting that another surviving stretch of modeled stucco then existed but fell to pieces during Moore's first attempt at removal. This surviving portion (or most of it) was successfully detached in several sections, somehow smuggled out, and brought to New York. The operation was expensive, reportedly costing about $125,000.

To make a worthwhile profit, the purchase price would have to be about double that; but what collector, in 1970, could be expected to pay so high a price? The likeliest customer, as it must have seemed to Rassiga, would be the Metropolitan Museum; so it was to this museum that the unrestored fragments were taken and laid out on the floor of an empty gallery.

I have been told that just then the museum's lawyer, Dudley Easby, was in Mexico finalizing the loan of some very large pre-Columbian sculptures that would be centerpieces of *Before Cortez*, one of the exhibitions being mounted to celebrate the museum's centenary. There in Mexico City, according to a story for which I cannot vouch, Easby was walking into a meeting when one of the Mexican officials remarked that he was interested to see Mr. Easby carrying that big briefcase.

"My briefcase! How can that interest you?"

"Because," he replied, "there are rumors circulating here that it contains money for the purchase of a Mexican stucco façade!"

Realizing that the success of their long-planned show was jeopardized, the museum packed the pieces up and shipped them to Mexico, where, suitably restored, they now cover an entire wall of the Sala Maya in the National Museum of Anthropology. The result of this extraordinary unilateral action was that Rassiga, the Philadelphian collector, and Moore each lost his entire investment.

In 1973, the *New York Times* decided to run three full-page articles on successive days, describing recent progress in Maya research. It was only the second time in the newspaper's history that such coverage of any topic had been attempted. The author, the late Robert Reinhold, allotted part of one article to my efforts at recording inscriptions, and the rest of it to the equally strenuous efforts of those who cut them up before they have been recorded. (In those days, a gallery touting a piece for sale would proudly describe it as "unrecorded," thereby implying that none of the four countries that between them now constitute the Maya area would have any grounds for reclaiming it.)

Reinhold, warming to his mission, gathered a great deal of pertinent material for these articles, even going so far as to accompany me on a short expedition to the badly plundered ruins of El Perú, in northern Guatemala. Naturally, he also pumped me for whatever background information I had gathered on some of the people I'd named as being engaged in that nefarious trade; so in the case of Lee Moore I told him what I knew about the stucco relief. Moore was both a looter and a runner: that is, he obtained his goods directly from his own operations at archaeological sites in Mexico or Guatemala, shipped them up to Miami, and sold them to bigger dealers—though later, directly to collectors. He was also a "restorer" of painted Maya vases.

So when Reinhold telephoned Moore at his home, having first switched on his tape recorder (taping phone calls is legal in the state of New York so long as *one* of the parties is aware of it!), he started by asking Moore whether he had ever been to Mexico City and was told that, yes, of course he had.

Reinhold: "D'you know about this panel that was sold—or at least offered—to the Metropolitan Museum a few years ago, and then returned to Mexico?"

Moore: "Which one?"

RR: "This great big wall panel."

LM: "What do you want to know about it?"

RR: "Uh, do you know anything about it—about how it got out?"

LM: "Uh—ah, ah—why?"

RR: "Well, it just seems to me a kind of—probably the largest piece that was ever taken out, and I was curious about it."

LM: "Hey this is interesting; why would you ask *me* about it?"

RR: "Well, to tell you the truth, because someone told me you had something to do with it, and I don't know. . . "

LM: "Well, let's leave it at that, that somebody told you I had something to do with it. . . "

After barely suppressed hints about the recognition he felt that he deserved for "saving" this stucco façade, Moore stated that he would really like to see something published presenting his point of view.

RR: "Uh-huh, well, if we do something, it will be as a balanced piece."

LM: "Right, I understand that. But at least, let the people know that it's not people like ourselves—you know, they're putting *down* the art dealers like we are a bunch of bandits; every article that has ever come out since all the stew over the. . . the big wall that started the whole thing, has come out like we were a bunch of Mafia and a bunch of bandits, and we're destroying things for posterity—when actually we're *preserving* them—in the name of art, of course. . . . But, you know, most of the archaeologists, the *greatest* archaeologists that are best known are in our favor. I don't know if I should name their names, you might probably know who they are . . . "

RR: "Michael Coe, are you thinking about?"

LM: "Yes sir, yes sir. And he would back me up all the way. And also Gordon Ekholm would, also. But of course they're being fired upon by some of the people, by name of Stephen Williams. I'm sure you know who he is. And they're the cats who are stirring up all this. And Clemency Coggins, who is not even an accredited archaeologist, she's some woman who wants to blow her head off, that's all. But I could tell you a lot about these things; I could tell you exactly how the big wall came out, probably."

[Later] "Listen, I've got all the photographs of that big wall, in situ, and—you know—of it being taken off. It just so happens that I was going by one day and I took some photos . . . "

Then Moore mentions a fresco:

"I don't know where it is—it's somewhere in the States, or it may be in Europe. But it was in New York, and it was not known that it was part of the [same] building."

RR: "I understand Rassiga had it?"

LM: "Yeah, and that's the one thing that was not sent back to Mexico [and] not included in the return of the wall."

RR: "Then it must be in some private collection?"

LM: "That's right. I haven't seen it anywhere. You might ask Rassiga. . . . If you talk to him you might mention that you understand there's a fresco, but don't tell him where you got your information. He hates my guts."

—and then:

LM: "You know, they [the archaeologists] catalog all that stuff, and you know, people if they're not archaeologists, they say, so what! You know, what difference does it make?"

RR: "Well, if you're seriously interested in Maya culture you want to know how it got there, how it changed, and how the art developed, and these are serious scientific questions."

LM: "Oh yeah, I'm not completely mercenary about this . . . but I can't see some of the things they are screaming about, like information that we're destroying. We don't destroy information at all."

RR: "Oh come on, now—how can you say you don't destroy any information?"

LM: "Like, what are we destroying? We dig a hole in the building, we go into the building, we take up the burial. Now, all burials are basically the same. Now, every-body knows how the Mayans were buried, so they're not going to learn anything new by seeing another Maya burial. They're all placed the same; it's just that different pots come out of different burials."

RR: "I'm not an archaeologist, but I feel they wouldn't agree with you."

LM: "Well, this is the way it's been explained to me by Coe. You know I cite Coe quite a lot because I feel he's the great authority, and he tells me that all the information that they're screaming about doesn't amount to a hill of beans. . . . It means nothing to anyone else, and not even to him, and he's the top archaeologist."

When Reinhold's articles were published, I considered them judicious and well told, but Moore, I fear, must have been quite disappointed at their "unfairness" and their lack of "balance."

Emboldened by the success we'd had in terminating Hollinshead's operations, I soon began to consider which other looter or dealer we might make trouble for or put out of business. Lee Moore was the most obvious target, for there were few looters who, to my knowledge, had done as much damage as he, and nothing could be more satisfactory than putting an end to his depredations.

One consequence of Reinhold's article was that I could no longer consider simply walking into his home, warehouse, or gallery (if he had one) in the hopes of recognizing a piece as coming from a known site—a necessary first step in getting the FBI interested. Instead, Moore would immediately recognize me. That he had me in mind is evident in articles, such as one in the *Miami Herald Sunday Magazine*, in which he contrasted his own noble and public-spirited activities with those of "Graham and his narrow-minded bunch of jerks" who dedicate their lives to numbering and cataloging works of art before hiding them away in basement storage areas where they would remain invisible for ever.

The only strategy I could think of for penetrating his base of operations was to disguise myself and become a member of a bigger group. The opportunity arrived when I was asked by a CBC (Canadian Broadcasting Corporation) arts magazine program to collaborate in a feature on the antiquities trade. I suggested they feature Lee Moore but insisted that my role be an inconspicuous one as grip, or gaffer, or best boy—or whatever the TV equivalent is. Thereupon I shyly scouted three New York City purveyors of toupés, hairpieces, etc., in search of a long-haired, drippy, hippy-type wig. At last I found the source of such articles, at about Fifty-First Street and Second Avenue in Manhattan. They could supply what I wanted, but at a cost of $300, and the wig would take three weeks to make. Unfortunately, both time and money were too short for this, so I was obliged to settle for a ready-made, stick-on moustache.

To complete my disguise I obtained a pair of glasses heavily framed in tortoise-shell, and having oiled my hair with cold cream, parted it in the middle. I looked a total fright, and not the inconspicuous assistant I had meant to resemble. To make matters far worse, the Canadian director insisted on my being the interviewer.

"Impossible!" I cried. "For one thing, there's my obviously English accent; for another, I would probably ask the very questions that would make Moore suspicious at once."

But he was adamant. I then had to think of a pseudonym, and chose "George Bathurst" (borrowing the name of a cousin, for fear that I might otherwise forget it!).

The TV crew and I assembled at a Miami hotel, and Moore and his Peruvian wife kindly offered to come there and guide us to their suburban home. I was the first down when they arrived, so we repaired to the bar, where the conversation soon turned to the impediments they faced in continuing their noble work of making ancient art available to all, despite the undemocratic and restrictive policies of certain elitists.

"And zi vurst of zem," said Mrs. Moore, "is zat Ee-ahn Grajam!" I must have blanched under my makeup.

28.2 Poorly disguised, I interview the looter Lee Moore. Photo in possession of the author.

The Moores lived in a modest house surrounded by a little lawn and a tree or two. We got down to work in their living room. My first slip occurred early on, when one of the crew called out "Ian!" and I looked round, before remembering that fortunately a member of the TV crew, of Scottish origin, was also named Ian.

"Oh, I didn't see where he went," I replied weakly.

The interview was going badly, with Moore unwilling to make any definite statements. And my own general discomfort seemed to grow as the TV lights raised the temperature. Then one of the Canadians came over and suggested in a whisper that I should go to the bathroom. There, to my dismay, I saw that one side of my moustache had come unstuck—and I'd carelesslly neglected to bring the spirit gum! I returned to the living room a more pensive person, with my chin permanently supported by one hand, so that a forefinger could support the drooping half of my moustache.

28.3 A slip of the moustache away from disaster. Photo in possession of the author.

Then, by general agreement, we escaped the heat by moving out of doors. But in passing through the dining room I had noticed that at one side of it, the carpet was covering a long, bulky object. It could only be a stela, I thought, so I would have to have a quick look. Doing so would be risky, since Mrs. Moore remained somewhere in the house, but when the cameraman needed to reload a magazine I went with him, and just had time to throw back a corner of the carpet.

Nothing but lumber met my eye. I wondered: could the Pink Panther have done any better?

I have often reproached myself for not, on camera, theatrically tearing off moustache and glasses, and addressing Moore openly as myself. It would at least have made some dramatic and usable footage. As it was, I suspect that the entire rather expensive outing was a write-off for CBC—an unhappy reflection, and I'm sorry for the producer. For myself, I felt dirty, and as soon as possible I made for the beach and threw myself into cleansing waters.

Before long I was to learn that Moore had known all along that it was I who would be coming, and in disguise—a careless word in my office having been picked up by a graduate student visiting from another university, where his professor was notoriously friendly with Madison Avenue dealers. (Hmm, who could that be?) So I wonder if Moore may not have deliberately stowed his lumber under the dining room carpet, just as a tease. Rather a good one, really!

CHAPTER 29

The MacArthur

O n returning to Cambridge from the field in April 1981, I was astonished to find friends and acquaintances rushing to congratulate me, and had to ask what on earth they were talking about? Then the extraordinary tidings sank in: I'd been given some kind of prize I had never heard of: a "Prize Fellowship" conferred by a foundation named for its donors, John D. and Catherine T. MacArthur—the previous existence of which had been little known. So now, people were asking, "But where have you been all this time? Journalists have gone crazy looking for you!"

Newspaper clippings were shown me, and there, among my three or four months' accumulation of mail, was a large, fat envelope from this Chicago-based foundation, announcing that for the next five years I would receive each month the very healthy sum of about $4,500 (tax-free, too!), and that an additional $10,000 would be directed by the foundation each year to any recognized institution with which I had an affiliation. I rubbed my eyes in disbelief—I could only be dreaming.

Previously, financial support for the Corpus Program had been at best uncertain. In its still fairly short life, the National Endowment for the Humanities had steadfastly awarded it each of the three-year matching grants that I applied for, and I could only hope that Mrs. Vaughan and other generous donors might continue to contribute the necessary sums for the NEH to match. But as neither of these sources could be counted on to continue their support, this "manna" fallen from heaven was going to provide quite unexpected security for the project for a considerable time.

It would also benefit my personal finances, since the terms of the fellowship deliberately refrained from specifying how the money should be spent. One could fly off to Las Vegas or Monte Carlo and blow the whole lot if one chose to, or plunge into the stock market, buy a Maserati, or relapse quietly into idleness on the Isle of Capri. Apparently the foundation was not in the least concerned about what one did with their monthly subventions, yet I'd never heard of any MacArthur Fellows—and by then there were well over one thousand of them—abandoning their work to indulge in idleness or the fleshpots.

In the middle of the 1930s Depression, John MacArthur, the son of a coal miner, had borrowed $2,500, and with it bought a bankrupt insurance company. He started selling "dollar insurance" in Florida—with the beach as his office, or so I've been told; and when this business prospered, he invested in real estate in Florida and Chicago. Having been extremely frugal in spending money on himself, he died forty years later as one of the only two self-made billionaires then in existence.

In 1970, eight years before his death, he had turned over most of his assets to establish the foundation, but during his lifetime it remained inactive, and I believe it was only upon his death that its trustees found how serious a problem they faced (among them was his son Roderick, who, having made his own fortune, set up his own foundation, the "Little Mac"). They would have to decide quickly how to disburse five percent of about $4 billion in support of worthy projects within one fiscal year, not one of which had even been identified. The law mandating such disbursements owed its existence to the vast growth of the Ford Foundation's assets. While no one suspected that particular foundation of any subversive agenda, Congress awoke to the possibility of some foundation with sinister aims amassing potentially dangerous power by retaining all of its income in a cumulative trust.

Just who deserves credit for proposing the solution that was eventually adopted, I can't say—perhaps it was Rod himself—but it was simple: give a lot of it away! Discreet inquiry among leaders of such fields as medicine, academia, social services, the arts, etc., would surely be able to identify a number of individuals engaged in work deserving support but currently not getting enough of it to allow their talents full scope.

Losing no time, the foundation mailed inquiries to a couple of dozen active leaders in various fields, asking each of them to propose a candidate in strict confidence. That, essentially, is how the first "Prize Fellows" were chosen, and how the foundation avoided federal sanctions. Since those early days, it has famously focused on a broad but cohesive field embracing many excellent long-term programs; but the Fellows Program continues.

Later in that unforgettable year, we were told there would be a three-day gathering of those who'd received what the press unfortunately chose to call "Genius Awards." (Most of us were intelligent enough to know that we were not geniuses; as for myself, I could only imagine I was given it for pertinacity.) This gathering would be held in Chicago, where the foundation has its offices, but the meeting would be at some undisclosed address in the outer suburbs. The date announced, mid-January, suited me quite well, as I could go on from there to Guatemala to begin another season in the field. Of course, Chicago can be notoriously cold, but I didn't consider I'd need to burden myself for the rest of my travels in the tropics with winter clothes, since I was sure the building would be warm, if not overheated.

I flew to Chicago, and at the airport met two other Fellows and one Life Fellow—Barbara McClintock, the famous plant geneticist. We climbed into an enormous limousine with darkened-glass windows and were driven away—in what direction I couldn't tell, as frost had glazed the windows. At last we drove into a large estate and drew up at a vaguely eighteenth-century-style French chateau, built by a modestly successful railroad baron, in the midst of a vast expanse of lawns which now looked like Siberian tundra, with every blade of grass thick with ice. Far off, there were a few stunted trees. This proved to be the coldest weather ever recorded in Chicago, and within about three minutes I had to abort my planned reconnaissance of the surroundings, since my wardrobe had been chosen for my next destination, the Petén, in Guatemala.

I remember nothing about our activities on that first evening, but a meeting was announced for late in the afternoon of the next day. We sat down in two rows, and in came Rod MacArthur (in a light-blue, knitted polyester leisure suit), followed by Gerald Freund, newly appointed as director of the Fellows Program, and there were two others whose names and functions I forget. Gerald gave us a bit of background, such as the fact that the total stipend awarded each fellow would be calculated on the basis of age (so, for the first time in my life I felt glad to be on the old side). Then we learned that our stipends would be tax-free (a concession withdrawn by the IRS some years later) and that no annual reports were expected. And then, before moving off for the happy hour, Gerald asked if there were any questions. Most of us, I imagine, felt a new and unfamiliar absence of any nagging problem, but one man, a biologist from a midwestern university, raised his hand.

"I can foresee the possibility," he said, "that someone named as a Fellow might find it inconvenient to take up his or her fellowship at once; so would postponement be an option?"

There was a whispered confabulation among the four officials; then Gerald told us that, at first glance, they could see no fundamental difficulty about this.

"Then, I assume that the total remuneration awarded to such a Fellow would be increased to take account of three factors: first, his increased age, as a basis for calculating his stipend; and second, the extra income accruing to the Foundation by virtue of the delayed drawing-down of capital for paying his stipend; and third, inflation and the falling purchasing power of the dollar."

An embarrassed silence prevailed. Then one of the committee members—it may have been Gerald—mumbled indistinctly and suggested that we move on for the happy hour, as with considerable relief we did. But while walking down a passageway towards the bar, I found myself beside the biologist, who turned to me and asked,

"I forget which university you're at?"

"Harvard," I replied.

"Oh," says he, "I have thorough contempt for that university."

"Really? Tell me, then, is it the faculty you despise, or the student body, or perhaps the campus itself?"

"All of them!"

One Harvard professor, not a Fellow, did proclaim to the press a year or two later his disapproval of the program, maintaining that it was a waste of money since no one really benefited from it. (Sour grapes? For I can't remember him presenting any convincing argument.) It was true that in my own case, I couldn't claim just then to be in desperate need, because funding from a generous donor and matching funds from NEH were in place for another year or two, but I could foresee the possibility of lean years ahead— and the Corpus Program would have to be kept going for decades yet.

Before long, those lean years did arrive—when Mrs. Vaughan could no longer contribute and the Reagan Congress gutted the NEH. Had it not been for the MacArthur money that I'd invested against possible hard times in the future, the program would almost certainly have shut down—perhaps forever. And even while private donors and NEH were still supporting our work, unforeseen and unbudgeted but still very necessary expenditures did sometimes arise, and in those cases, MacArthur money proved a godsend. (There was, however, one fly in the ointment, for not only was I paying my own salary, with a cut of 28 percent for Harvard, but income tax on it, too! But then, the grant was needed to provide my colleague with a salary, as well as financing field-work and publishing costs.)

The professor who uttered this criticism can't have made more than a cursory assessment of the work and background of the other Fellows in our group. One I remember was Elma Lewis, a black woman from South Boston who had founded the National Center of Afro-American Artists. She was then in danger of losing her eyesight. The building she rented to house it had originally been a synagogue serving an area that decades earlier had been largely Jewish; but now, a narrow-minded man living in

Connecticut was doing his best to dislodge her from that building, on supposedly religious grounds. Only by virtue of the money she was receiving as a Fellow was she able to hire lawyers to overcome that man's lawsuit—and for herself to have advanced laser surgery to restore her sight, damaged by diabetes. More than twenty years later, I found the center flourishing, and Elma, in her late eighties, still playing her part on the board of directors.

Then there were those who mocked the fellowship given to a Canadian magician known as "Randi." Of course, the choice did seem absurd. But a little inquiry would have revealed that Randi was facing a legal suit for damages of three-quarters of a million dollars, and who from? The Israeli who famously claimed—and "demonstrated" in regularly staged public shows—his ability to bend spoons by concentrated mental power. Metal spoons might seem unlikely objects to respond to mental powers, but a disappointing proportion of nominally educated persons were ready to suspend their disbelief. Randi, of course, as an expert magician, saw through the legerdemain, and denounced it as nothing more than a cleverly executed trick, which he could perform with equal facility. (He also challenged any possessor of "psychic powers" to perform wonders that he couldn't duplicate himself.) Thereafter, the magician refused to perform whenever Randi was in the audience, and then tried legal action to silence him. This alone, in my view, justified the foundation's backing Randi in his debunking of pseudoscience.

For the next few years, annual gatherings of MacArthur Fellows were held in the Chicago Statler or Hilton hotels, and very enjoyable they were. Talks given by Fellows in small rooms made available for them were often highly interesting; but eventually the sheer number of Fellows made these annual gatherings unwieldy, and they were given up.

Before long, it began to look as if the Corpus Program had a guardian angel bewitching the MacArthur Foundation's selection committee, for Peter Mathews, a recent Ph.D. from Yale whom I'd recruited as assistant, would also be honored with a fellowship. He had joined me when Eric von Euw left after doing yeoman work, some of which I've already described. Peter stayed on for some years before returning to teach at his alma mater in Calgary and later in his native Australia.

The next Maya epigrapher to be named a MacArthur Fellow would be David S. Stuart—at eighteen years of age, the youngest-ever recipient of the award. At that time he hadn't even graduated from high school; but years earlier, at the age of twelve, he had famously revealed to an audience of professional archaeologists his decipherment of a Maya hieroglyph. So, after getting his bachelor's degree, and finishing the coursework for his Ph.D., he, too, joined the Corpus Program, and did produce a superb fascicle on the monuments of Piedras Negras, as well as working toward the publication of a hieroglyphic dictionary.

If the Corpus Program has fared better financially than I could have expected during my fifty years at Harvard, I cannot gloss over the fact that the university itself steadfastly refused to help keep it afloat. Not one penny of salary did I have to thank it for (whereas the program caused substantial amounts of money to flow *into* Harvard's coffers in the form of 28 percent "overheads" on the four three-year grants awarded it by the National Endowment for the Humanities—with me paying some of these matching funds out of my MacArthur award). Although for many of the years from 1983 on the Peabody Museum paid me a regular salary, none of my attempts to get help from that secretive unit of the university, the Development Office, was listened to.

Good fortune, however, had not deserted me. Just as the MacArthur money was running out, I had another astonishing piece of good fortune. In about 1979, my friend Robert Pirie told me about a company then being organized that in his opinion had unusually favorable prospects; and that if I were interested he'd be able to get me some shares "at the float." It was just unfortunate that when the time came, my liquid assets had fallen to about three thousand dollars; still—I decided to plunge most of that on this dark horse.

When trading in this stock began I watched it nervously almost every day. It climbed, and when it had doubled in value I took what I considered to be the very prudent step of selling half of it, thus recuperating my initial cash position. But oh dear, what an unfortunate decision! The shares I sold would now be worth about $15 million—for this was Home Depot! But I still had the other half. . .

Of course, I had to use some of this stock as matching funds for a new NEH grant, just as I had earlier with MacArthur Foundation money—and much of it was contributed before Home Depot's stock had risen very far. Then, when the NEH was gutted by the Reagan Congress, more Home Depot stock had to go, no longer matched by federal grants but at least free of capital gains tax, as they were gifts to an ostensibly nonprofit institution. So now, only a few of those pennies from heaven are still in my hands.

I suppose it was only natural that an area of Mesoamerican field research long abandoned and now revived would not be recognized quickly by university administrators as having relevance in the coursework of students. Deans of the Faculty of Arts and Sciences exercise powerful control in the realm of fund-raising; but perhaps I was not alone in regarding the holder of that position in 1977 as either unimaginative or hidebound, on the basis of an opinion that he enunciated to the director of the Peabody Museum. This was that the Corpus Program "had no place" in the university. What basis, I wonder, *could* he have had for this sweeping judgment, for I'm sure he didn't pick it up from Gordon Willey, the Bowditch Professor of Mesoamerican Archaeology, nor from the director of the Peabody Museum at that time, who ruefully passed this *diktat* on to me. And here I acknowledge gratefully the positive, although admittedly variable, support given the Corpus Program by a succession of Peabody Museum directors. (And apropos that short-sighted dean's diktat, Harvard has since had, for a time, an undergraduate course in Maya hieroglyphic writing, with a substantial enrollment.)

CHAPTER 30

Uxmal

In January 1975, I signed on to take a large group of dentists from Ohio and their wives on a tour of Maya ruins. On arrival in Mexico City from the United States en route to meet the tour, I went, for some reason, to the British Embassy, and while there, picked up an interesting piece of information. The gist of it was that within a few weeks, the queen and the duke of Edinburgh would be visiting Mexico, and then an embassy secretary revealed that the governor of Yucatán would be entertaining the royal guests to a great dinner at Uxmal, in the quadrangle of the Monjas.

"Oh, I'd give anything to be there," I blurted out. "It sounds like a tremendous occasion!"

"Well, it's the governor's party, and not ours," she replied, "so really, we've no say in the matter. Still, perhaps we could put your name forward."

I went on my way, which now led to Puerto Limón, a port on Costa Rica's Pacific coast. There I was to join the tour group; but first we would be visiting the Galapagos Islands. I was relying on that part of the trip to compensate for my anxieties regarding the second part, for after we'd passed through the Panama Canal, I would be shepherding them through the ruins of Quiriguá, Tikal, and two or three sites in Yucatán.

But alas, we never reached the Galapagos, because halfway there, the ship suddenly heeled over in a U-turn. Five minutes later the reason for this unexpected maneuver was disclosed: word had been received that the Ecuadorian government had passed a law restricting landing rights to those arriving in an Ecuadorian bottom (the legal term for a ship, I was told), and our bottom was Greek. So this was a great disappointment.

30.1 *Modern house with stela and façade sculpture imbedded in the wall, near Chichén Itzá, Yucatán Peninsula.*

Once the tour of Maya ruins was over, I went off to do some work at the ruins of Piedras Negras, then returned to Mérida, and on the appointed day took the bus to Uxmal, in the faint hope of finding that by some miracle I had been invited to the festivities. On one score, at least, I felt easy: I had with me, for the first and probably the last time in my career in Mesoamerica, some good clothes: a rather snappy Italian linen suit, brought to impress my flock of tourists. But on arrival at Uxmal, an invited guest showed me his invitation, and what should I see printed on it but Traje Típico as obligatory dress, which meant, for a man, a guayabera—that is to say, a shirt of Cuban or Yucatec style, worn outside the trousers and embellished with sundry pleats and buttons. I'd never possessed such garment, but now, just in case I happened to be invited, I thought I should visit the Hacienda Hotel's shop, and sure enough such things were for sale—but at a quite exorbitant price.

With nothing better to do for the moment, I hung about in the hotel's lobby, reading. Then in came a tall, black-bearded man, carrying a pile of six or seven cardboard boxes imprinted with the Union Jack. Summoning a boy, he handed him one and told him to deliver it to room 14. And then to another, "Take this one, please, to room 29."

"Hmm," I said to myself, "I bet those are guayaberas for the official British guests." Then suddenly I remembered having read in a Mexican newspaper that the foreign secretary, James Callahan, had been obliged to cancel his visit to Mexico because of some domestic political crisis. I leapt to my feet, ambled over to the hotel official and asked him,

"Have you one there for Mr. Callahan?"

"Let me see . . . yes, here you are!"

My problem was solved. I found the shirt to be drip-dry, of best quality synthetic fiber, with French cuffs, a quite unusual profusion of pleats and decorative stitching in front, and it also had a small rectangle of cotton fabric stitched into the fly, upon which a ball-point pen had inscribed "Sr. Callagan."

Things were going my way, for now someone came to tell me, to my astonishment, that indeed there was an invitation to the dinner awaiting me. And then, a little later, I encountered Eric Thompson, who, as the most distinguished British Mayanist, had been bidden by the governor to make a speech at the dinner. When Eric asked where I would be spending the night, I mumbled that I was hoping to catch a bus to Mérida, or get a lift.

"No need to do that," he said, "the room I've been given in the hotel has two beds, so the other's yours."

I was told that the governor had initially invited about two hundred and fifty guests to this dinner; but, poor man, so heavily had he been bombarded with requests for invitations that the number of guests rose eventually to about thirteen hundred. As far as I could see, the service of dinner for so many people was accomplished miraculously, and the food was good. I was astonished that such a large number of portable kitchens, trestle tables, and long tablecloths were available for hire in a city as small as Mérida.

I found myself seated next to an extremely pretty Yucatec maiden wearing a huipil embellished with the finest embroidery, which, as she showed me, was of identical appearance inside and out. Her table manners, very delicate and of the carefully crooked pinky description, contrasted with those of my other neighbor, a manufacturer of string, who on finding in his mouth a piece of gristle or chicken skin, simply moved his knees apart and let the offending morsel fall from his mouth to the ground.

During the previous two years, trenches had been dug in various parts of the ruins for electrical cables; pits for junction boxes and concrete cabins for transformers and switch-gear also sprang up here and there, while within the Monjas quadrangle, lamps were installed in great trenches that had been dug into the terraces for the purpose. These were (and still are) covered over during the day with hinged metal covers, which when stepped on produce a resounding clangor, to the embarrassment of the visitor responsible. None of these installations, of course, was for the benefit of the queen; they were for *Luz y Sonido*—or Sound and Light show.[1]

The spectators would be seated in stands within the Monjas, but the view from there lacked any prominent architectural feature facing them in the middle-distance, owing to the fact that the Palace of the Governor, widely regarded as the most beautiful of all pre-Columbian buildings, unfortunately faces in the wrong direction. Accordingly, the archaeologist César Sáenz was charged with rejuvenating the Templo Mayor, or Gran Pirámide.[2]

Whereas the small temple on top had an elegant and partly intact façade, the flanks of the pyramid on which it stands had deteriorated into rubble. Getting to work, Sáenz cleared away rubble from its foot at the front (the side that would face the spectators seated in the Monjas) and found that the lowermost steps were still in place. Then, with astonishing speed, a great stairway flanked by splendid terraces rose up, with wiring and floodlight fittings built integrally into their corners, as if the Maya had long ago foreseen the need for them.

The Sound and Light installation was not quite complete when the governor gave this great dinner, but a decision was made that for this important occasion the first seven minutes of the program would be shown—though only in black and white, because the color filters had yet to arrive. So, as soon as the meal was over and the speeches delivered, a switch was thrown to start the lighting sequence and soundtrack—and at once the main fuse blew. All was inky blackness, which must have thrown the security men into blind panic. But soon the lights came on again and the show proceeded as planned.

Next, a group of dancers from the Ballet Folklórico de México appeared, some with flaming torches in each hand, and one dancer, I seem to remember, with another torch incorporated in her headdress. They performed a ceremonial dance dedicated to the rain god Chahk. Now, this was in late February, a time of year when rain never, ever, falls in Yucatán; yet so moved was Chahk by the invocation addressed to him in song and dance that a light drizzle began to fall. Some diners reached back and covered their heads with the skirt of the tablecloth behind them; then someone miraculously produced an umbrella (an exotic object at Uxmal) and offered it to the queen, but she, with true noblesse oblige, declined to accept it, and received a rousing cheer from the crowd. Then the rain became heavy, and everyone ran for shelter.

Back in the Hacienda Hotel, I noticed there was a crowd up in a seldom-used balcony above the lobby. I went up to see what was going on, and found there a display of the gifts given by the governor to the queen, and of those the queen had brought for the governor (the late Carlos Loret de Mola). I had a look at them and hung around. Then, to my astonishment, the governor came up and spoke to me. As I was practically unknown at that time in Yucatán, I can only imagine that someone had casually pointed me out as both British and an archaeologist.

"I should not tell you this," the governor told me confidentially, "because I know you are English, but I have recently committed a small theft!"

So saying, he pulled from his pocket a pair of long white gloves!

Next morning, the royal pair made an early start for their drive to Tizimín, where they were to inaugurate a zoo. I was taking it easy, when I noticed that some very English-looking young women were relaxing by the swimming pool. I wandered over and managed to strike up a conversation with one of them, and found that her duties concerned the royal wardrobe. I suggested to her that for a stay as long as this—for they were to spend over three weeks in Mexico—a wardrobe of considerable size must have been brought for Her Majesty.

"Oh yes," she said, and told me how many trunk-fulls there were.

"Well, it must be a headache keeping track of all that; don't you ever find that items get mislaid?"

"It's funny you should mention that," she replied. "Last night Her Majesty could *not* find her white gloves. We hunted for them everywhere, and someone was sent out to the dinner table to look for them there; but they seem to have disappeared altogether."

Of course I kept a discreet silence, while imagining a vitrine in the governor's house where a pair of white gloves would now have a place of honor, perhaps lying next to a handkerchief dropped by the Empress Carlota during her visit to Yucatán, late in 1865...

When describing earlier the steps leading to the formation of the Maya Corpus Program at the Peabody Museum, I mentioned the two short, experimental periods of fieldwork that I carried out at that time, one of them being at Uxmal. The inscriptions that I chose to focus on for that study were the numerous and easily accessible carved blocks in the so-called Cementerio. But any thought of producing a site plan in the

30.2 *Frederick Catherwood's 1844 drawing of
the "Governor's Palace," Uxmal.*

time available was quite out of the question. I did wonder, though, how much time it would take to produce one.

Plans of unknown accuracy had previously been published of some of the principal architectural complexes, and in 1933 a professional surveyor had done some good work covering a small area for Frans Blom, but nothing like a satisfactory plan had ever been made. Obviously, the mantle of scrub forest covering much of the site would make the task of surveying it rather difficult.

Over a century ago, it would have been easier, for when John Lloyd Stephens and Frederick Catherwood visited Uxmal, the hacienda was producing sugar cane and cattle, since sisal (or *henequen*) had yet to develop commercial value. Stephens found that the area surrounding the ruins had lately been cleared for cultivation, revealing, among other things, a wall apparently encircling the ruins. During my 1969 visit, I could scarcely find any vestiges of it, because the peripheral area was then entirely covered in thorny scrub, with the exception of the entry road, the caretaker's house, and the archaeological camp, and in those areas the wall had long since been plundered of all its stone for use in construction of the hacienda, and more recently for highway building. I began to wonder whether anyone would ever undertake a proper survey of those ruins.

Fifteen years later, I thought the time had come to produce a second *Corpus* fascicle on a Yucatec site (to join the one that my colleague, Eric von Euw, had already produced, covering three small but interesting sites in the peninsula). So I decided to take on the challenge of Uxmal. Initially, I thought I might shirk surveying, and instead cobble together a plan from already published sources. But on discovering how inaccurate and how incomplete they were, I decided with considerable reluctance that I would have to get going with transit and stadia rod myself.

At this point, another difficulty became apparent: every working man at Uxmal was employed by the hotels (of which there were three by then)—so there would be no casual workers available to help me. My only recourse would be to drive the ten miles to Santa Elena in the evening to engage one or two men, arise next morning before dawn to drive over and pick them up, and at the end of the day, take them home again. I did this many times, but on other days I did the machete work myself, cutting many of the sight lines and subsidiary paths to the corners of buildings and other features.

This was a most disagreeable occupation. I was accustomed to cutting my way through the forests of Petén, but quite unprepared for the terrible hooked vines at Uxmal, the worst of them called *beeh* and *dziuché*. On at least two occasions, on swinging my machete back, I found my upper arm caught by the needle-sharp hooked barbs of beeh, and then in reaching back behind my head with my left hand to disengage the barb, that arm also became hooked! Thus crucified, flesh had to be torn. There were also flat areas covered with thick and very tall grass, where one could be tripped up and brought crashing to the ground—transit, tripod, and all—by stumbling over a block of stone, or worse, falling into the mouth of a chultun (one of those underground chambers so abundant in the Uxmal area). I had an overwhelming urge to put a match to those grassy areas, but managed to resist it.

Since I was unwilling to spend two hours every day picking up men from Santa Elena, I had to find a way of carrying forward the survey without them. My rather exhausting solution was to carry the following items on one shoulder: tripod (with transit mounted on it), fiberglass stadia rod, machete, and a photographic light stand. I would set up the transit at a suitable spot for shooting back to a previously plotted mark, and afterwards to other features needing to be plotted; then set the light stand over that mark, put up the stadia rod, and tie it to the light stand with a bootlace. This system worked quite well, except that, all too often, having erected the stadia rod and tied it to the light stand—perhaps high up on a mound or terrace—I would return to the transit, get the transit's telescope directed at the rod, and apply my eye to it—just in time to see the rod topple over in a gust of wind.

So it was that in stark contrast with the luxuriousness of my living conditions at Uxmal, my working conditions were dreadful. In that low, scrubby jungle the heat was torrid, obliging me to drink a dozen bottles of sticky *refrescos* each day (no bottled water then being available), and at the end of the day, big patches of salt would show on my shirt. Mapping Uxmal was undoubtedly the most grueling task I have ever under-taken, but I am unashamedly proud of the result. With the surveying done, I made as neat a job as I could of drafting the final plan; and possibly its users will assume that neatness also signifies accuracy. I take comfort in the reflection that until someone else makes another survey, years hence, with electronic "total station" equipment, knowl-edge of all its inaccuracies will be my secret.

From the time when the late Dr. Ignacio Bernal was director of INAH (the Mexican Institute of Anthropology and History), I had no difficulty in obtaining the necessary permission to do the fieldwork necessary for preparing Corpus volumes; on the con-trary, a succession of directors were supportive. But then, in the early 1970s, INAH became concerned that an increasing number of small colleges, many of them from California, were obtaining permission to dig some small site, often in western Mexico, and then would leave without backfilling their trenches. It was ostensibly to pay for cleaning up after them that a 15 percent tax was introduced, applicable to the budgets of all foreign archaeological expeditions. So when presenting my next application for a permit, I suggested to the then-director of INAH, Dr. Bonfil Batalla, that since we had no intention of excavating, we might be excused from paying this tax. He agreed, and no tax was ever levied on us during the next twenty years.

Then in 1993, a Dr. Serra Puche became president of INAH's Consejo de Arqueología, and she insisted that we pay. She was deaf to my pleading that since the Corpus Program was a year-round activity, a 15 percent tax on the annual budget would cripple it; nor was she moved by my plea that since we were recording for posterity an important part of Mexico's national patrimony, and did no excavating at all, some concession would be appropriate.

This lady was also director of the National Museum of Archaeology, and not long after this dispute arose, I had to ask her for something else: permission to take a few photographs of just one sculpture in the museum. After keeping me waiting for half an hour, she emerged—tall on high heels and magnificently attired—and looked down on me as if I were some kind of unattractive worm that had crawled in. But yes, she was willing to authorize the taking of this photo, conditional upon my paying 15 percent of the budget for this operation. So, having taken the photos, which required the use of one roll of film, I handed over to her, with perhaps a trace of arrogant disdain, a full seventy-five cents.

But in connection with the tax on our budget, I had fun drafting a letter in which I announced, *"Ya no voy a trabajar más en México!"* (I'm never going to work in Mexico again). I reminded her that no plan of Uxmal, one of Mexico's most famous national treasures, had previously existed, and pointed out that, for Corpus purposes, a plan of the entire site was not necessary at all. My motive for making one had been simply to render a service to Mexico, but now realized my mistake: I should have carried with me phials in which to collect the sweat and blood I had lost in the process, and then sent 15 percent of both to the Consejo!

Since then, I have had no further trouble on that score!

The history of renovations at Uxmal—which, together with Palenque, constitute the two most beautiful of all Maya cities—has not been a happy one. As both Frederick Catherwood's drawings and aerial photographs taken in 1930 show, its condition was indeed ruinous, although here and there areas of impressively carved mosaic masonry still reared up amidst the rubble. From the outset it was clear that extensive and careful clearing of that rubble would be needed—to be followed by consolidation of the standing masonry. Here and there, intrusive work would also be needed to prevent further decay, such as installing new lintels in doorways that were in danger of collapse.[3]

The Palace of the Governor, however, had remained in remarkably good condition until the middle of the nineteenth century, when it would suffer two episodes of damage. Happily, both of these were made good without loss of authenticity. Early photographs show that by then, virtually all of the facing stones of the façade up to a height of six or seven feet were missing: obviously, they had been prized out for use in constructing the hacienda, for in those days, the main road (or camino real) between Mérida and Campeche ran past the foot of the platform supporting the palace, making that building one of the most convenient sources of dressed stone for loading onto wagons. But in the 1930s, these facing stones were replaced by similar ones collected from elsewhere in the site, all of them being cemented into cavities that were left in the mortar when the original facing stones were removed.

The second loss occurred in the rainy season of 1926, when a large portion of the west façade of the Palace of the Governor became detached and fell to the ground. Fortunately, early photographs of that portion existed, so that it was possible to reassemble the carved elements on the ground by studying the photographs, and then securing each element back into place with mortar.

The Monjas was in much worse condition. A considerable portion of the façade on the western range collapsed in the mid-nineteenth century, and there were losses from the north side, too. The former was reconstituted in the 1930s on the basis of a drawing of the entwined serpents made before it fell by that somewhat imaginative early-nineteenth-century artist, J. F. M. Waldeck; the restoration done on this basis was ingenious, even if somewhat speculative. Many elements freshly carved for the purpose were used for this work, as also on the north façade. But in my view, all these operations were legitimate, in varying degrees.[4]

Today the Monjas can hardly be called a ruin at all: except for the back of the western range, hardly anything suggestive of the hand of time meets the eye. Buildings have been embalmed in new masonry, thus foreclosing the possibility of excavation in the future; but in any case, very little excavation has been carried out anywhere at Uxmal; the great trenches dug for the Sound and Light Show installations were, until recently, almost the only ones ever dug there—and I've been told that they were neither supervised nor used advantageously by archaeologists.

The work of César Sáenz at Uxmal had not ended with the construction of the impressive but hypothetical terraces on the Gran Pirámide; he was to continue the rejuvenation of the great pyramid of the Adivino. Its roof had been reconstructed in the 1930s, as had its western stairway; now he, or perhaps officials at INAH, decided that the masonry cladding of the whole pyramid was too shabby and needed replacement. Large areas of the original masonry still remained in situ, but these were removed on the pretext that they would appear as ugly blots upon the two acres of gleaming new masonry now being installed.

Unfortunately, inadequate steps were taken to attach this "overcoat" to the existing structure. One might have expected Sáenz to take a tip from the ancient Teotihuacanos, who inserted large stone dowels into the existing masonry of the Temple of the Sun before expanding it with another thick layer of masonry (these pegs became very noticeable after that layer had been removed a century ago). So it should have been no surprise when the lack of dowels allowed the new cladding to move and develop fissures. Rainwater soon penetrated those cracks, softening the interior masonry, with the result that expensive repairs had to be undertaken to stabilize the cladding and to a large extent renew it. While I can claim no more than partial possession of the facts, I venture to blame the architect for failing to foresee the instability of the masonry overcoat laid by him over this vast and quite steeply pitched pyramid.

Then there's the matter of overrestoration, and of rebuilding from scratch: these make me wonder sometimes what motive, or psychological imperative, calls for such activity. Are there some people in power who feel uneasy in the presence of partially ruined buildings, seeing them as reminders of the subjugation and harsh treatment suffered by their ancestors at the hands of invaders? Perhaps there are other motives, but whatever these are, the urge to complete does seem to show in the work of several archaeologists working in Mexico. But fortunately there are honorable exceptions, three of whom I'll mention.

Over the years, Uxmal has become less and less a noble ruin, not only in its general appearance, but also in terms of the percentage of original masonry remaining in the major structures. Until recently, the Tortugas building headed the list, for only about 30 percent of its masonry is original. But when, in 1999, after an absence of two years, I returned to Uxmal, I was astonished to see two buildings that had definitely not been there at all on my last visit. They stand at ground level between the Adivino and the Palace of the Governor, and both are shown on my plan of the site as low mounds. But today the visitor sees one of them as a miraculously preserved colonnaded Maya structure, still standing after a whole millennium.

In reality, though, it's a total reconstruction: one that presents an interesting case-study in the formulation of restoration policy. First, it should be said that the young archaeologist responsible for this work did carry out a very careful excavation of the collapsed remains of this building—this in itself a distinctly encouraging novelty—and found good evidence that the building had suffered a sudden and complete collapse, as first became clear when most of the columns were found lying just where they fell, in a row along one side of it.

It became clear that most of its long west side had been constructed as an open colonnade—and once the orderly collapse of this building had been revealed, it must have been very tempting to re-create it. But one crucial difficulty about this plan must have been apparent, namely that such a building had already demonstrated its inherent instability. For in common with all types of vault, the Maya variety exerts an outward pressure on its supports, as do the halves of Old World vaults; the crucial difference between them lies in the Maya vault having its two halves built independently, and the vault depending for its integrity on the stiffness of the roof it supports—unlike the true vault, which can stand alone.

During the construction of their vaults, the Maya had learned to forestall the natural tendency of the half-vaults to topple toward each other by placing horizontal wooden beams to separate the two halves at one or more levels, according to the height of the vault. Then, capstones uniting the half-vaults would be placed, and over them a flat roof of masonry laid with mortar, so that once the mortar had hardened, this solid mass would take over the function of resisting the natural tendency of half-vaults to fall toward each other. In other words, the flat roof would be exerting the necessary stiffness and outward pressure. (The beams, no longer of structural importance, were generally left in place to serve as hangers.)

In this daring structure at Uxmal, the slender columns themselves would of course be quite unable to resist the inevitable tendency of the vault to splay apart, and this almost certainly explains why collapse occurred when the side of the building supported exclusively by columns suddenly blew out, causing most of the roof to fall in the same direction, and with it, most of the other half of the vault. Then, the two ends and the rest of the long back wall would have just slowly disintegrated and become covered by soil and vegetation, until nothing was left to distinguish the remains of this daring structure from more conventional ones. Certainly, I mistook it as such during my survey of Uxmal, as did those looking for columns to use for their own purposes in the nineteenth century.

Obviously aware of the problem, the archaeologist responsible for the reconstruction of this building devised a solution. Metal tie-rods, or braces, would be incorporated. True, for maximum effect, these would have to be placed, inauthentically, at the spring of the vault, rather than higher up, where the Maya always placed them. (I'm also quite sure that horizontal metal rods running longitudinally must have been incorporated within the walls at vault-spring level, to spread the tension exerted by the tie-rods.)

To look even a little authentic, those steel braces had to be concealed within wooden sheathing, but I imagine that drilling a hole down a twelve-foot-long log of chicosapote or palo tinte (logwood) would be almost impossible, hence the use here of some blonde and relatively soft wood of blatently inauthentic color and thickness.

It may be asked, what other option could there be—apart from burying everything again? My suggestion would have been to rebuild the back and side walls to a modest height, and leave the fallen columns where they were. This would have provided a useful demonstration of the limits of Maya building technology, and the consequences of pushing too far beyond them. Or else, first of all construct a secure chain-link fence around the site, then reconstruct the building just as it had been—with, for safety, temporary supporting props that would be removed some months after completion, when the mortar had set. And then wait for it to fall down. What better or more exciting demonstration could there be of an ancient architect's vaulting ambition overreaching itself?[5]

As regards the practice of restoration, I do worry that overrestored and structurally inauthentic buildings such as the one I have described herald a new phase of Disneyfication of archaeological sites in Yucatán. In this state particularly, the desire to maximize revenues from tourism now seems to override any concern for authenticity. In 1993, an agreement was signed at a purely Mexican convention in Tlatelolco, which explicitly rejected any role for tourism in making decisions concerning archaeological conservation. To be consistent, should not a meeting now be called to declare this a dead letter?

But UNESCO's international Charters for the Protection and Management of the Archaeological Heritage may prove more enduring. The Venice Charter of 1964, signed by Mexico, as well as that of Lausanne in 1990, banned the rebuilding of fallen portions of ancient buildings. These charters, and the general philosophy of restoration as developed by European architects and archaeologists, were taken seriously by at least the younger Mexican archaeologists. Augusto Molina Montes summarized these extremely well in a book published in 1975, as did Daniel Schavelzohn in 1990 in a work replete with case studies. And field archaeologists such as Eduardo Matos Moctezuma working in the Templo Mayor in Mexico City, Roberto García Moll at Yaxchilan, and Norberto Gonzalez at Xochicalco, did confine their activities to clearing, excavation, and consolidation.

In recent years, however, a regressive trend has become apparent, especially in Yucatán. These accords are being ignored, even by the younger archaeologists. Can this trend be attributed to pressure from state governors, or perhaps direct financing by them? One cannot deny that archaeologists have an *interest*, as Carlos Margaín pointed out long ago, in undertaking restorations and reconstructions, although many have abstained from doing so.[6] Since Uxmal has been declared by UNESCO a World Heritage Site, it is theoretically possible that the quite unnecessary reconstruction of buildings might result in the cancellation of that nomination, although that does not really seem likely. Or will sense prevail, rebuilding cease, and demolition of those new buildings at Uxmal be ordered? One only has to look at the famous Caracol at Chichén Itzá to be convinced that the Carnegie Institution's deliberate restraint in restoring that building was much wiser.

CHAPTER 31

The Colonel-Bishop

In February 1976, I drove down from Petén to Guatemala City in my Land Rover to have it overhauled and took a room at my favorite hotel, the Panamerican. Exhausted after a long drive, I went to bed early—to be woken from deep sleep at four a.m. by what I slowly realized was an earthquake. Only a faint light prevailed, but there were strange noises, and then I dimly perceived that a large wardrobe was dancing over in my direction—but kindly refrained from tumbling over on my bed. So sleepy was I that when, in less than a minute, the shaking stopped, I said to myself, "Oh, an earthquake, I suppose," and went back to sleep.

Renewed jolts then woke me up completely, and then I realized that for many people—thousands, perhaps—this earthquake might have been devastating. I got up and walked into the Cathedral square to find hundreds of people, huddled and praying or moaning with desperation, their houses having collapsed—and loss of life certain to be heavy.

The full extent of the disaster would not be known for many days, since the death toll had been highest in remote villages, many of them difficult to reach, even under normal conditions. There in the highlands most houses were built of mud-brick and roofed with tiles—the worst type of construction for seismic zones, for its walls are soon shaken to pieces and the roofs fall. The principal cause of death, I've been told, was asphyxiation by mud-brick dust as the occupants lay trapped under fallen roofs. The toll in the end was about forty thousand.

Because bridges were down and many roads blocked by landslides, I had no hope of driving back up to Petén. So I flew there to carry out a mission entrusted to me by the National Geographic Society. Under its aegis, a campaign of excavations at El Mirador was being planned, so a landing ground for helicopters was required—and if possible, one that could be expanded into a strip for short-takeoff planes. My job was to find the best location and arrange for the clearing of it.

I flew to Dos Lagunas, a starting point about the same distance from Mirador as my previous one, Carmelita. But here I had some difficulty in finding an arriero and mules—eventually having to hire one small and elderly animal, and then two others from a woman named Catherine, the daughter of prosperous Californians. Catherine had persuaded her parents that a hotel in Dos Lagunas would be a surefire commercial success, but in fact it was simply a love nest that she and her paramour were building—he being William, a very large Belizean black, who arrayed himself as a West African chieftain, hung about with various mystic cult objects. They had brought in two magnificent oxen, with which to haul the lumber, as well as the two mules, geese, goats, and another Belizean, Al-butt (as they called him, imitating his Belizean accent), who looked after everything. (Unfortunately for the happy pair, Catherine's mother, becoming suspicious, was just then cutting off the flow of funds.)

The man I engaged as arriero was Milian, a thin, lugubrious person who knew the area well, and the combination of his knowledge and my prior study of aerial photographs of the Mirador region resulted in our finding not only a good, flat area of low vegetation for helicopters or short-takeoff planes, but also a good source of water, even in that exceptionally dry year; it was even near enough to the ruins for daily transport of it by mules to the archaeologists' camp to be feasible.

Then I made a quick visit to Washington, D.C., for an Organization of American States party celebrating the opening of an exhibition in which the Corpus Program was featured; and then another quick one, this time to Mexico City with Steve Williams, the Peabody Museum's director. We went to hand over formally to President Luis Echeverría a representative selection of the gold and jade treasures that eighty years earlier had been dredged from the Chichén Itzá cenote—these in exchange for some artifacts from Mexican national collections. Our appointment at the presidential residence, Los Pinos, was for a late hour; even so, we had a long wait for the president to arrive, and when he did, he seemed utterly exhausted but managed to keep going, helped, I think, by some drug. He sat up stiffly, and was impossible to talk to.

On returning to Petén, I made various visits to record newly found stelae, and then, early in Holy Week, drove to the Belizean border town of Fallabón to see my old guide and friend Don Abelardo Ventura, for he had sent me an intriguing message about ruins reported near Holmul. Our visit to that site is described below.

In 1960, the Guatemalan president of the day, General e Ingeniero Manuel Ydígoras Fuentes, arranged for a large car to be flown up to Fallabón in the Fuerza Aerea's Fairchild Packet, nicknamed the Flying Coffin because of its shape.[1] On arrival he climbed into that car and was driven to the British Honduran checkpoint, about half a mile away. When asked for his passport and visa, he pronounced firmly:

"I am the President of Guatemala, and I do not need a visa to enter our national territory," to which Sergeant Neil replied, "I am very sorry, General; if you'd had the proper documents you would have been welcome."

By prior plan, Fallabón was immediately renamed Melchor de Mencos—after a heroic Guatemalan sergeant of long ago—but the British missed the opportunity of bestowing Sergeant Neil's name on Benque Viejo, the little town on their side of the border!

Years later, the Guatemalan government devised a plan for bringing Belize into blessed union with Guatemala through popular support. Improvements of every kind would make Melchor a model town, a magnet for Beliceños, and to administer this plan, Coronel y Obispo Jorge Mario Reyes Porras was appointed—his bishopric being in the Mormon Church.

Reyes was given a generous budget to renovate Melchor. He started by building a powerful radio station. That may have pleased the locals, but not the inhabitants of Flores, since he was using the frequency of the much weaker Radio Petén, about fifty miles away. He improved the streets and the electricity supply, and then set up the "Expendio Popular" on the main street. This was a grocery store, very neat and clean, where the prices were low—as well they might be, since transport of the merchandise was gratis, thanks to the military. (Whether the local merchants ever dared express an opinion about this is doubtful.)

Provisions such as rice and sugar were put up in plastic bags printed with slogans such as *Beliceño, el quetzal es tu símbolo*, plus a map of Belize with a quetzal perched on its northern extremity. The Belizean ladies who shopped there soon learned to bring unmarked bags, in which to repack their purchases before passing through Belizean Customs, which otherwise would confiscate them. But they had trouble with the glass flagons of cooking oil, which had the offensive emblem baked onto the glass. They could be seen scraping away ineffectually with penknife or machete.

Almost every day Reyes would be at the Expendio, fussily arranging his merchandise and making pyramids out of bars of soap and tins of sardines. He was like a child, playing shop. But not everything during his regime was quite so sweet.

What, then, was the news that Don Abelardo wanted to give me? It was that a young colleague of his named Pacay had discovered a stela at a minor site south of Holmul—important ruins that had been excavated by Raymond Merwin of the Peabody Museum in 1912 (and unintentionally visited by me in 1959). Frankly, Merwin's report is not very interesting, and unaccountably fails to include a site plan, but there were standing buildings, and early ceramics of wonderful quality were found in tombs. The fact that no carved monuments had been found there made Pacay's discovery of a stela at an outlying site quite exciting.

The stela proved to be broken and incomplete, although other fragments may have lain buried, but its style proclaimed an early date. I spent two days drawing and photographing the fragments, and gave this site the name "La Sufricaya"—after a species of tree growing there. Many years later, I gave my sparse data on the site to a young Guatemalan archaeologist, Francisco Estrada-Belli, who soon went to work there and showed the site to be much larger and more important than I could ever have guessed.

On leaving La Sufricaya, I went in search of another site discovered by Merwin, my attention having been drawn to it in a roundabout way. Some years earlier, I had been looking through the Peabody Museum's site-by-site index of photographs, and there found one listed as "Sactankiki Stela 12, photo by R. E. Merwin." Well, I knew about the origin of that strange name for a site otherwise known as Seibal, because Teobert Maler related that while visiting Seibal in 1895 he'd heard from a local guide that an aged Lacandón man living in the vicinity had told him (either as a tease, or while in his cups) that Seibal had been the capital city of his ancestors when they still ruled the land, and that in those days that ancient city had borne the proud name of Sactankiki.[2]

But how had this name become attached to the stela photographed by Merwin? Well, while the great fourth centennial celebration of Columbus's voyage was being planned in Spain, another was being organized for the following year in Chicago, and in Guatemala, Federico Arthés, a well-educated French contractor of chicle and timber, had been engaged by the government to collect material from Petén for exhibition in the splendid pavilion that was then being built for Guatemala in Chicago.

Arthés, of course, would have been acquainted with the managers of the Hamet Mahogany Company, then working along the Río de la Pasión in the neighborhood of Seibal, and on hearing from them of this site, and knowing of Gorgonio López as Maudslay's former mold-maker, Arthés engaged him to make molds of some of the stelae there.[3]

Whether it was Arthés or Gorgonio López who painted that exotic name on the back of all the casts is unknown, but they seem to have been exhibited in Chicago under that name. When the exposition closed, they were given to the Peabody Museum of Harvard through the influence of its celebrated Curator, F. W. Putnam, who had been in charge of the centennial's Anthropology Hall. Eventually, all but one of them were passed on by Putnam to other museums, the exception being that of the magnificent Stela 10, which remains in the museum, its back still marked in bold brushstrokes, "Sastanquiqui Stela 10."

But I did find the notation on that catalog card, "Stela 12," very puzzling, as I was sure Merwin never went anywhere near Seibal; and besides, what we know today as Stela 12 was discovered three years after Merwin had left Guatemala. So I looked up Merwin's photograph of it and found it showed an image quite unknown to Mayanists: the lower half of a stela, showing striding legs and a belt ornament that suggested a very early date. This photo had never been published.

I consulted Merwin's 1910 field notes, and these revealed the origin of this monument to be a site not far from Holmul named by him "Seibal Dos," for presumably, in seeking a name for it, he consulted his guide, who probably glanced at the reedy pond nearby and suggested "Cival"—this being the local term for such a pond. But as *petenero* elocution is erratic, treating *be grande* and *be chiquito* (*b* and *v*) as simple alternatives, he probably heard the word as *seibal*, and to differentiate it from the great site on the Río de la Pasión, added *Dos*. Then later, the person who catalogued Merwin's negatives at the Peabody quietly dropped the "Dos" from "Seibal," and then, finding there were eleven known stelae at Seibal, gave this one the number twelve!

Here, I take the opportunity to protest against a Guatemalan professor's edict that the spelling "Seibal," employed by the Peabody Museum for its reports on excavations there, contravenes the Spanish Royal Academy's rules of orthography. He seems unaware of the fact that as *seiba* is a word of Caribbean origin, its spelling falls outside the reach of Old World rules of orthography. (Rightly, Mexico has retained the spelling "Seiba Playa" for its populous seaside town in Campeche.)

Well then, regardless of these confusions, Don Abelardo and I went in search of this site, and with some trouble found it, with a cival close by. Merwin's field notes included the data of his compass-and-tape survey of the site, but frankly, I couldn't make head or tail of them until I had made my own survey; only then could I see sufficient resemblance to be sure that this really was his "Cival." Merwin did note the dimensions of the stela, but by a strange oversight neglected to include its location in his survey notes, so that in the short time available our hunt for it was unsuccessful. Later, I gave my data on Cival and its stela to Francisco Estrada-Belli, and I've been very pleased to hear of exciting discoveries he made there.

On return from this little expedition, we reached Melchor de Mencos on Easter Saturday, where of course I would spend the night at Don Abelardo's house, across the street from the police station. Feeling exhausted from the long walk, I went to bed early, and soon fell asleep. Then shouts and screams—part of a dream at first—became real as I awoke.

My bedroom was on the street side of the house, and looking out of the window, I saw that the police were up to something. I pulled on trousers and shoes and went out to have a look. I saw a tall young man held by two or three policemen with his back to the chain-link fence of the police compound, and the corporal (the police chief there) was punching him in the stomach. The youth was crying out, and two women were screaming. I went up to the corporal, and laying my hand gently on his arm asked him to desist. He spun round and dragged me through the gateway of the police headquarters, swearing at me, then released me and went back to hitting the unfortunate young man.

Don Abelardo then came running over and, grabbing me by the arm, dragged me away, saying that the man was dangerous when drunk and that he (the corporal) was involved in a dispute with the lad over a woman (they had come from the Holy Saturday evening dance). So, from a distance we stood and watched. The young man was eventually released, and the corporal, looking round, caught sight of me and shouted, *"Este puto es la mera mierda, agárrenlo!"* (grab the bastard!).

I was then seized by two policemen and the corporal and dragged into the police quarters. Once out of sight, they began to hit me, and the corporal kicked me hard in the thigh from behind. Then, in front of the door of the prison cell, and while I was still held by the police, the corporal, like the brave man he was, aimed another kick at the vitals from in front. As he was half-drunk and didn't aim well—and I quickly doubled up a little—the kick landed in my stomach, where it hurt badly enough. Then I was thrown into the cell, and we enjoyed an exchange of insults.

Inside the dark and stinking cell, I grabbed the bars of the only window, gasping for air. Then a voice from the darkness asked, "Is that Don Ian?" and identified itself as that of Moisés, who had worked for me a few years earlier at Naranjo. He proved to be a pleasant companion, always merry and often singing. The cell was about four by four and a half meters, and housed five inmates when I arrived. There was no bucket or other sanitary arrangement; one simply peed against the wall, and we were let out once a day after 8 a.m. to the latrine. Those with stomach upsets couldn't always manage the wait, of course.

The floor was littered with food remains and cigarette stubs, and the walls bore stains and designs executed in feces. During my stay, the other cell, which was partly open to ours, was occupied by a poor deranged man who was being kept there to safeguard his family, awaiting transfer to a hospital in Guatemala. He sang long and strange songs, talked all kinds of nonsense in a high poetic voice, reminding me rather of some Guatemalan peasant preacher of evangelical persuasion—and he would laugh to himself, mostly at night. He was not allowed out at all, so that his cell was disgusting beyond description. He had drawn houses and faces on the wall, also using the only medium available.

Drinking water was never provided for any of us; we had to rely on friends or relatives to bring it.

My cellmates were good fellows, and most were there for being drunk. Moisés had been there since Wednesday, waiting for the court to open after the Holy Week recess. Erminio, who came in shortly before me, had hair and ears caked with blood; he had been arrested in his own house, thrown to the ground, and hit on the head twice with a pistol. Its safety catch wasn't properly on, so that it fired, blowing off the tip of the policeman's third finger.

In the morning they brought in the young man who was being beaten up when I came on the scene. His name was Francisco Uc.

Meals were sent over by Don Abelardo, one of them being a portion of the faisán he had shot on our way back. What else was going on I was unable to learn, since no visits were allowed until one had been tried, and the prison is isolated from the street. On Sunday night our community was increased by two drunks, one of them completely insensible, and from him eventually an abundant trickle of urine spread across the floor.

One sinister event began with the appearance of the corporal to ask Francisco Uc if he had any *heridos visibles* (visible wounds). None, he said, except for a bruise on his arm. (One good reason for choosing to punch people in the stomach is that no bruises do result.) He was let out of the cell and went away for a time with the corporal. Until then, he had complained about the blows he had received in the stomach, but now—at least on Monday morning when I asked him—it appeared that he no longer had the slightest recollection of any such blows.

The secretary of the *juzgado* came by on Monday morning to say that everything possible was being done to clear up my case. He seemed a nice man, and it turned out later that on Sunday he had been waiting anxiously for the judge's return, hoping to get the case over at once. At about 3:30 that afternoon I was called before the judge. He was quite elderly, with a dark face and rather hollow eyes behind his spectacles. I couldn't form any opinion regarding his complicity with the police, but decided to tell him my views and suspicions concerning the corporal, and to say that the matter would not end with his decision that day.

It seemed to me later, and others agreed, that the judge was in fact impartial, and working for me against the machinations of the police—and Colonel Reyes. Anyway, he explained that he could not pronounce me innocent for a technical reason: the police had witnesses (other police) who testified to my lawless behavior, whereas I had none—except for Don Abelardo, and I didn't want to involve him. A question I asked myself was, how can a person held incommunicado in jail, and ignorant even of what are the charges against him, ever get hold of any witnesses? I imagine that the percentage of prisoners who are declared not guilty under this system must be close to zero.

The judge had fined me forty-five dollars, but now there was a difficulty over payment, because in Melchor, the customs service is the only office authorized to receive fines, and they were about to close. Next morning, I was full of hope. There was a man who came round to sell water and soft drinks to the prisoners, so I paid him to buy me brushes, a bottle of Pinosol, and five gallons of water. One of the police agreed to extend our latrine time, and we got to work, scrubbing the floor and the walls really clean. Then I stood on the upturned tub and wrote my name as high as I could in pencil: "Ian Graham, Peabody Museum, Harvard University." I sometimes wonder whether it's still there. If alumni have visiting rights, I may go and look someday.

Time, however, pursued its way relentlessly, and I started to make noises about the right of foreign prisoners to make contact with their consulates. Then Don Abelardo appeared and told me I was free to leave, conditional upon a search of my car. Two policemen were just then going through the little containers of curry, black pepper, and baking powder (very suspicious) in my box of provisions, when the judge spotted them and called out that he had never ordered any search of the car. So I was free!

But I had not quite finished with the corporal. I remembered that they had confiscated my flashlight, so I approached him, just as he was playing with a new toy in front of a row of Mayas sitting apprehensively on a bench. His plaything was a bunch of four canes bound together with colored plastic tape and provided with a ring for attachment to his belt. He was testing its flexibility by bending it between his hands, and then making practice shots with it, cuts and forehand drives.

"Corporal," I said to him sweetly, "would you kindly return my flashlight?" He scowled at me and thrashed the cane about, and after a long time, someone came back with it, its battery run down, of course. Then I added,

"You know, corporal, punishment is not a function of the police, but of the courts."

"Deje de joderme!" he shouted at the top of his voice, plainly audible down the street (this might be rendered as "leave me alone!").

I went back to the Juzgado to pay the fine of one of my cellmates, who was finding that his upset stomach made confinement particularly distressing. There I was told that the police had been trying hard to cook up some other serious—and if possible, criminal—charge against me. Having noticed a rotted and broken board in the walls of the jail, they were planning to charge me and another prisoner with damaging it with intent to escape. As it was, the charges in the escrito really made me laugh: for example, "that I threw myself at the police with kicks and blows, thus allowing an arrested man to escape; and that I shouted threats and insults, which out of respect for the court will not be repeated here."

I learned that these police, the Policia Nacional, had been brought in by the colonel, displacing the Policia Militar Ambulante, who were not too abusive. The village was living in terror of this lot, and I heard all sorts of horror stories, not all of which can have been true. What I did pay attention to was a warning against driving to Flores; the colonel, some elderly citizens suggested, could easily radio ahead and create trouble, or even an ambush. So I engaged a driver to take the Land Rover to Flores before dawn, and I went up to Guatemala City on that day's Aviateca flight from Melchor.

On arrival in Guatemala City, I made an appointment for the next morning to see the minister of foreign relations, Adolfo Molina Orantes ("Fito," whom I have mentioned earlier as a friend of both Ledyard Smith and Harry Pollock). He was a charming man, and a man of great good will, but the manner of his death, a little later, still appalls me. He and the vice-president, Enrico Cáceres Lehnhoff, were asked by the Spanish ambassador to come to his embassy to meet with a group of leftist *campesinos*, mostly Maya. One of them, however, brought in and then threw a Molotov cocktail, and most of those in the room were burned to death (though the ambassador did escape with his life).

I told Fito of my misadventures, going so far as to drop my trousers to show him the purple bruises. Fito was appalled, but I sensed that he was in no position to take on ruthless colonels. So I sat down and wrote a strictly factual account of the events of the previous few days, and typed it out. I had several copies made, and delivered them to the offices of the president, the minister of defense, and the chief of police. And when I returned to Petén, I gave one to Colonel Reyes.

He hit the ceiling. I was a subversive element and he was going to throw me out of the country immediately—something he never managed to do. If some people didn't understand his policies, he said, it was because they didn't know the peteneros as well as he did—a doubtful proposition in my case. They were lazy, and for that reason he had ordained that no man of working age could enter a bar before six o'clock in the evening. He had also ordained that no child under fourteen could be seen on the street after 8 p.m.

"Some people call me the New Ubico," he said, thumping his chest, "and I'm proud of the appellation."

(Ubico had been the dictator of Guatemala from 1934 to 1944. He is remembered, among other things, for arranging a great National Exhibition, in which one exhibit was a pair of live Lacandón Mayas in a cage. They soon succumbed to a climate far colder than they'd ever experienced, and died.)

Reyes then became promotor of FYDEP. As such, he had control of forestry policy—as of everything else. He had his son appointed a director (fronting for him) of a large lumber and sawmill company, which was given an expanded area of forest for its operations. I have been told that the large revenues that accrued to Reyes and his son were sent for safekeeping to his brother-in-law, who lived in Miami—but then his brother-in-law decamped, and Reyes never saw the money again. This is a story I can't vouch for, but I hope it's true!

CHAPTER 32

Trade in Antiquities

Throughout my career my preoccupation with the whereabouts of looted monuments led to many unforeseen adventures. Our trip to Bonampak in 1960 had put me on friendly enough terms with Natasha Gelman for her to invite me to dine at the large and comfortable house that she and her husband, Jacques, shared in Mexico City, and then to spend the night there.[1] This was on the Paseo de la Reforma. And on a second overnight visit, a few weeks later, I accompanied her in calling on Josué Sáenz and his wife Jacqueline (or Jacqui, as her friends called her), who at that time were living within walking distance, just around the head of a ravine, at 1777 Paseo de las Palmas.

Sáenz had prospered as a banker and in industry, becoming in fact a World Bank representative, and also president of Mexico's Olympic Committee. After chatting with them for a few minutes, Natasha took me downstairs into a long room that ran out as a low wing toward the street, starting from semi-basement level—as I remember it—and emerging at ground level, for the land sloped downward toward the street.

And there I stood transfixed: Maya stelae, lintels, and other sculptures lined the walls! Until then I had been unaware of any trade in such material, or of the looting that supplied it. Now I do regret that for lack of a camera that day I was unable to photograph the collection; nor could I, with my still very meager knowledge of Maya sculpture, identify even one of those pieces—but one which almost certainly would have been there was a sculptured stone panel discovered by those intrepid adventurers, Dana and Ginger Lamb.

The fact that Maya sculpture had just then become an item of international commerce is easily explained, for with the dollar's purchasing power declining as a result of the

Vietnam War, wealthy people had begun looking for undervalued commodities to invest in, rather than in the stock market, and many were willing to put their money on Primitive Art (as it was then called).

The special attractions of this "commodity" were, first of all, the previous neglect of it by museums and collectors, so that a healthy "upside" in value was almost certain; and then—whether or not the investors in such artifacts actually appreciated them as works of art—they could be kept for a few years to mature in value and then be given to a museum, in exchange for a tax deduction, and in the meantime displayed as trophies. Jay Silberman, a well-known Virginia-based appraiser specializing in this business, would probably value any piece at multiples of the price paid for it a few years earlier, thereby providing donors to a museum with a healthy tax deduction—no small benefit at a time when the top rate of income tax exceeded 50 percent. (It's only fair to state that indeed there were collectors who truly appreciated Maya sculpture and ceramics, and bought them without thought of monetary gain: among these I would name the late Dominique de Menil of New York City, and Samuel Josefowitz of Lausanne, but they and a few others were a small minority.)

By this time, many of the finest treasures to come out of ancient and unguarded sites were being brought by dealers such as Everett Rassiga (a former airline pilot), or runners such as Sosa, straight to that house in the Paseo de las Palmas—and later to their more spacious house in the Desierto de los Leones, on the southern edge of the city. It was Jacqueline rather than her husband who really appreciated pre-Columbian antiquities, and she had excellent taste, for no fewer than twenty-one of the objects exhibited at the Metropolitan Museum's centenary exhibition, *Before Cortés*, were from their collection. But even so, she could sometimes steel herself to part with some of it—such as the six hundred small artifacts she sold to Mrs. Margaret MacDermot, of Dallas, who then presented them to that city's Museum of Fine Arts. By then, the Sáenzes had officially stopped trading because the Mexican government had announced that it was preparing a law making it illegal to buy, sell, or transport archaeological artifacts.

A year later, in 1971, a small exhibition was mounted at the Grolier Club in New York City, the haunt of rare-book collectors. (By chance it opened soon after *The Art of Hieroglyphic Writing*, the Peabody Museum's exhibition which was also held in New York City). There, at the Grolier, one could admire three previously unknown stone panels, beautifully carved with hieroglyphic inscriptions, as well as a large number of ceramic plates and cylindrical vessels, some elegantly painted and others carved or incised with equal virtuosity. No provenience was given for any of these, nor had vessels of such quality ever been exhibited before. And if this were not sufficiently astonishing, there—almost unbelievably—was a Maya codex on bark-fiber paper, which, if authentic (as it is widely, though perhaps not universally, held to be), is only the fourth pre-Columbian Maya codex known to exist.[2]

The display of these remarkable objects, most of them from the Sáenz collection (or warehouse!) created a furor. As for the codex, it was rumored that after receiving it from Sáenz in Mexico City, Michael Coe had passed it on, sandwiched between two pieces of cardboard held together by a rubber band, to a former president of the Grolier Club for him to take to New York (in what may have been this gentleman's first and last engagement as a runner). Then, after the show closed, rumors abounded of attempts to find a buyer for it. But as the result of pressure by the Mexican authorities, it was returned and is now preserved in the Museo Nacional de Antropología.

A full twenty-four years later, in December 1995, I telephoned Sáenz and found him willing to receive me. We had a good chat—largely, of course, about laws governing the possession and trading of antiquities. Then I asked him the question that had really prompted my visit: did he have any photos of those sculptures I had seen in the Paseo de las Palmas thirty-five years earlier? No, he said; but I'm afraid I found something else he told me rather difficult to believe. It was that many of them he'd never paid for, so that when laws governing trade in antiquities began to tighten, he simply returned them to the dealers. Remarkably patient, those dealers!

In the Maya area, the first example of large-scale looting that I myself came across— and certainly one of the most regrettable—was the work of a wretch named Delfino Suarez. A native of Tabasco, he'd had chicle and lumber concessions in the lower regions of the Usumacinta River before devoting himself to the plunder of ancient sculpture. To this end, he established a base on its banks at El Cayo, about nine miles upriver from the great ruins of Piedras Negras, but across the river on the Mexican side. (El Cayo itself is a site that had carved stelae and a fine lintel—instant grist to his mill.) From this base he was able to engage in the dismemberment and removal of Piedras Negras stelae without worrying in the least about interference from Guatemalan authorities, for in those days not a soul was living on Guatemalan territory within fifty miles of that great ruined city.[3]

So he and his men sawed up the fallen stelae and panels with careless abandon into chunks they could drag down to the riverbank, and they did their work in a most destructive manner. Perhaps the most wasteful reduction of a stela was that of Stela 3. As found by Teobert Maler in 1895 it was complete, although broken into two halves and one small fragment, but otherwise the sculptured front was well preserved. The first evidence of looting at that site to reach the archaeological world came in 1963, when this stela's long hieroglyphic inscription, sawed and cracked into about ten pieces, was offered to the Brooklyn Museum. It was purchased, but on discovering

32.1 *Stela reassembled from twenty-one blocks,*
with sculptured surface laid back in place—to the
extent possible.

its identity, the museum very properly yielded title to these pieces to the Guatemalan government (which sensibly sent them as a loan to the Miami Museum of Science). But almost half of Stela 3 has just disappeared. Four pieces remain at the site; and there's one small fragment depicting a lidded vessel that had been shown standing on the ruler's throne, beside his right knee. This came to rest in Mérida, where I found it years later in a modest private collection of half a dozen items kept in a garden shed. On seeing my photo of it, David Stuart, as usual, recognized its provenience.

Stela 2 from the same site, also badly damaged by Suarez and his gang, was bought by the Minneapolis Institute of Arts in 1966. When featured in the museum's *Bulletin*, the institute's director sagely observed in print, "It is remarkably similar to one found at Piedras Negras of exactly [the same] period." Yes, the likeness is uncanny.

I remember very clearly the first time that I ever happened upon the actual scene of a stela's partial dismemberment. That was in 1962 at Dos Pilas, an important Maya city of the Classic period near Sayaxché, Petén. A year or two earlier I'd gone to Sayaxché with the intention of recording the sculpture at that site myself, having just heard of its existence. But then, as already mentioned, I met a Frenchman of Russian ancestry named Pierre Ivanoff, who told me he was working there, so of course I abandoned my own plans of doing so.[4]

This man, an adventurer who could turn on the charm when necessary, had managed to coax a contribution of five hundred dollars from Karl-Heinz Nottebohm, a prominent and upright businessman in Guatemala whose whole family I later came to know and appreciate. This irked me, as I felt I could have made more fruitful use of that money myself!

Ivanoff had rented a merchant's storage shed with barn doors in downtown Sayaxché, where, when not at the site, he could often be seen in full view lying on a mattress amorously entwined with his expedition cook, an attractive young lady of Kekchi and Belizean black parentage. They used to wander about the streets tightly clasped together, raising the eyebrows of Sayaxché's conservative residents; and such was her loyalty to fashion that she braved thorns and biting insects to wear Capri-length pants in the jungle.

Pierre could be entertaining, but undoubtedly he was a rogue, as I would discover; for when at last he'd retreated from Dos Pilas, I hired, as guide and assistant, one of his men, Gonzalo Castellanos, and off we went to that ruined city.

I mapped the central part of the ruins—as well as I could, because Ivanoff had cut down every tree in the plaza, leaving an almost impenetrable tangle and no shade—and then began documenting the stelae. While I was preparing to jack up the large upper fragment of Stela 8, Gonzalo remarked,

"When *el francés* raised this, we could see the writing clearly printed in the soil it had been lying on."

And on jacking it up, this graphic description held good—but I saw to my dismay that a thin slice of the upper portion, carrying the first two rows of glyphs in a most beautifully carved inscription, had expertly been sawed off. This was undoubtedly Ivanoff's work, for Gonzalo's remark showed that he had indeed raised that heavy slab, and I found it interesting that when Ivanoff sent Eric Thompson photographs purporting to include all the stelae he had photographed at Dos Pilas, among them there were none of Stela 8.

At some time in the mid-1960s, I went to see Dr. Gordon Ekholm, curator of American Archaeology at the American Museum of Natural History in New York City. He was a useful contact, since he kept close tabs on Mesoamerican pieces passing through the market. But it was while chatting with Junius Bird, a distinguished naturalist whose office was across the corridor from Gordon's, that I first heard about looting at the extensive ruins of Naranjo. He showed me a letter he'd received from a Colonel C. J. Tippett, of Ocala, Florida. (I had a faint suspicion, on meeting him later, that his colonelcy might have been Southern and honorary.) He had written to tell Bird of a Maya city that he and some colleagues had discovered in Guatemala. It was described as containing many curiously carved slabs of stone, and among his photos was one showing a stela being mercilessly hacked to reduce its weight. Bird wrote back to inform the colonel that it was a registered site called Naranjo which had been known for eighty years, and advised him to leave it alone.

Only a week or two later I happened to visit a friend in her apartment, and there, idly picking up an auction catalog of sporting prints, what should spring to my attention but an item consigned for sale by "Mrs. Elizabeth Whitney Tippett, of Ocala, Florida." And then, as a further coincidence, I ran into Betsey Whitney a week or two later. She was the second wife, and widow, of John Hay ("Jock") Whitney, who had

32.2 Dos Pilas Stela 8, as left by Ivanoff, with Gonzalo Castellanos holding a fragment in place.

been U.S. ambassador in London, and it was there I had come to know and admire both of them. So I asked her if this Mrs. Whitney was in any way related?

"Is she *ever*!" she replied, "She was Jock's first wife. And Ocala was one of his properties. He gave it to her as part of the divorce settlement."

Liz had been a tall and handsome blonde who rode like Jehu but then became intolerably masterful. The settlement, Betsey told me, was far too generous, "but as Jock admitted, 'Yes, it was rather expensive, but it was worth it at the time.'"

Tippett, I learned, had recently held a minor post in the U.S. embassy in Peru; but now his principal marital function was described to me as carrying his wife's handbag. As it happened, I met both of them later at an equestrian event in Massachusetts. She was very large, commanding, and capable on occasion of forceful utterance in stable-yard language, but when I found myself seated at dinner next to her quiet little husband, I was disappointed by my failure to elicit any reminiscences of his adventures in Guatemalan jungles.

The damage at Naranjo was disastrous, and one could see that there had been more than one party working there—or if only one, then its members must have been so new to the job that several different techniques of reducing large stone shafts to portable fragments had been employed experimentally. Some monuments were attacked with chisels, others cut with saws (but the stone there is too hard for ordinary saws); yet others had been heated by setting bonfires on them and then dousing them with water—a technique so effective that thermal shock reduced them to countless shards almost impossible to reunite. And then, an equally grotesque brainwave: in order to snap off the butt of a stela as if it were a bar of chocolate, they (or others) drilled a row of one-inch holes with a gasoline-powered rotary rock drill!

Naturally, I described to archaeologists of my acquaintance the atrocities I'd seen at La Florida, Naranjo, and other sites. They were appalled, but none perhaps was more outraged than Dr. Clemency Coggins, by training an art historian and deeply engaged in many aspects of pre-Columbian studies. At that time, she was associated with the Peabody Museum of Harvard University, and soon decided to air the topic of looting at the 1968 International Congress of Americanists, due to be held in Stuttgart and two other European cities. As a result of her advocacy and the documentation she presented, a resolution was agreed upon by the delegates deploring this kind of vandalism. Encouraged, she expanded this into an important article, "Illicit Traffic in Pre-Columbian Antiquities," published in *Art Journal* in 1969.[5]

UNESCO then formulated a convention banning international trade in antiquities. All countries were invited to ratify it, and the American Society for International Law was beginning to discuss whether, or to what extent, the United States could agree to implement such a law. I was called in to provide background information, and it must have been at one of those meetings that I spoke to a lawyer in the federal government about possible strategies for making life uncomfortable for those involved in this trade.

In the autumn of 1971, Dr. William Bullard of the University of Florida (who previously had been assistant director of the Peabody Museum) called to tell me that Stela 2 from Machaquilá had briefly been exhibited for sale in Florida. For me, this was very interesting news. I'd given some thought to the policy one might follow whenever a Maya sculpture not known to have been in the United States for any length of time might make its debut on the market, for this would raise a ticklish question. On the one hand, it was important to record new pieces while they were accessible; but on the other, any display of interest in such a piece by an academic known to be opposed to the importation of stolen antiquities, and likely to cause trouble for the dealer offering it, might result in that piece going underground. A notable instance of such an occurrence—the disappearance of the Palmer collection—will be touched on later in this chapter. But in this particular case I had already recorded and published the piece, so its disappearance from sight would be of little importance from the point of view of archaeologists.

In the 1970s, there was no federal law prohibiting the importation of plundered antiquities from other countries, nor any bilateral agreement between a country that was a net importer of antiquities and another that (unaware of the fact) was exporting them. But following Bill Bullard's call, I embarked on a lot of telephoning and picked up information from various sources, among them—improbably—the manager of a supermarket in Decatur, Georgia, to whom the Machaquilá stela had been shown while on its way to New York.

It seems that the stela had been bought (from Guatemalan guerrillas, according to one unreliable account) by José Guerra, a Belizean known to be engaged in the local antiquities trade, together with Ed Dwyer, brother-in-law of the owner of the Robinson Lumber Company, then active in Petén. Reportedly, the price was three thousand dollars. It was then sold to the men who shipped the stela to Florida: a Belizean named Jorge Alamilla and two Americans, Johnny Brown Fell of Mobile, Alabama, and his cousin Harry Brown of West Helena, Arkansas, all of them partners in a shrimp-exporting business. While still in fragments, the stela was shipped to Florida concealed in a cargo of shrimp. At this point, presumably, the Los Angeles-based dealer and restorer Clive Hollinshead (British-born, but by then a U.S. citizen) was called in to reconstruct the stela.

Next, Fell and Alamilla bought a 1962 Oldsmobile station wagon, and with the stela in the back, set off for New York City. There, they offered it to the Brooklyn Museum, and to Emmerich (who declared it a masterpiece but wouldn't touch it), then to Leonardo Patterson, who was not interested either but did introduce them to Marjorie Neikrug at her gallery at 224 East Sixty-Eighth Street. While they were trying to persuade her to buy it, the station wagon with the stela in it was towed away for illegal parking.

Their next stop was Milwaukee, where a relative of Alamilla's was city engineer, and there they tried to sell it to Glenn Rittenour, a Methodist clergyman (who later, with obvious reluctance, testified at the trial). Finally, they drove their precious cargo to Los Angeles, where Hollinshead bought it.

How to put this sketchy information to good use was a matter far beyond my competence. But chance came to the rescue—as it sometimes does—for in November of that year I happened to be in Washington, D.C., and one morning called on my old friend Ruthie Pratt, by then married and living there. She remembered it was my birthday, and kindly opened a bottle of Ruinart champagne in celebration. After we'd emptied it, I lurched off downtown and found myself on a sidewalk rubbing shoulders painfully with a rough-hewn customer of granite—the former Post Office, but at that time the FBI headquarters.

"Aha!" I said to myself, "Perhaps they can help me."

I slouched in and asked to see an agent, and in due course found myself sitting at one end of a table, at the other end of which sat a hefty young man now running too fat who looked as if he might have distinguished himself at college on the football field. He asked my name and the date of my birth. But when, on noting it, he failed to wish me a happy birthday, I began to suspect I wasn't facing one of the bureau's sharpest sleuths.

But he invited me to describe my concerns, and this I did for about fifteen minutes, mentioning various rogues in this field, such as Patterson, Hollinshead, and Alfonse Jacobowitz, who traded as "Jax" and with dreadful irony was based in Sylvanus Morley's former home in Yucatán, Hacienda Chenku. When I'd wound up my spiel, my interlocutor, studying his yellow pad, announced,

"Well, what you've told me is very interesting, and I assure you that we'll investigate these matters. Some of the names you've given me sound familiar; this Leonardo Patterson, I've heard *his* name, and this Eyean Graham . . ."

I made a hasty exit!

Later, I was able to talk with an FBI attorney, who gave me crucial information.

"In the absence of any international agreement," he told me, "or specific accord between the U.S. and Guatemala, the only way is to give him a dose of ITSP."

"ITSP, what's that?"

"Interstate Transportation of Stolen Property. But to get a conviction under this federal law you have to prove two things: that the object was transported from one state of the union to another, and that the accused knew the object was stolen."

He sounded encouraging, so I called an old friend, Bokhara Legendre, then living on the West Coast, and asked if she would be kind enough to call on Hollinshead and feign interest in Maya stelae. This she did, convincingly enough to be invited to admire the stela where it lay in his garage-cum-conservation studio. So now we had the evidence of interstate transportation required by the feds before they could swoop. And swoop they did, discovering also from Hollinshead's records that another Machaquilá stela was in the possession of that Harry Brown of Helena, Arkansas, mentioned above (but unlike Stela 2, this one had been murdered by clumsy dismemberment).

The case, *U.S. v. Hollinshead et al.*, was tried in Los Angeles at the end of February 1973. Since I was to serve as a witness, I was excluded from the court and heard none of the courtroom drama. But I was privy to many discussions outside of it.

One of the accused, Ed Dwyer, had turned state's evidence, and a vignette I remember is of him walking the corridors of the courthouse between the U.S. attorney and Bill White of the FBI, with his hands resting on the shoulders of both men. Jorge Alamilla, on the other hand, chose, as a Belizean national, not to show up, and so remains a fugitive from U.S. justice.

There were so many interlocking stories and characters involved in this saga that I failed to make sense of them all. But the name of one witness called by the prosecution, an oilman named Ted Wiener from Dallas (but then living in Palm Springs and Lake Tahoe) did ring a bell. He had financed Hollinshead's purchase of the stela in return for part of the profit, and I remember him also because of an intriguing story I had heard. Some ten years earlier he and two other collectors, John Huston, of Hollywood, and Billy Pearson, the well-known jockey, had gone to Mexico together to loot a site there. This escapade illustrates the spurious pride that some collectors enjoy in discovering a fresh site to loot, and perhaps the kick they get in evading the law—for in this case at least, financial gain could hardly have been a motive.

After an entire day of deliberation, the jury found the accused guilty on both counts. The two stelae were returned to Guatemala, and Stela 2, after disassembly and a more skillful reconstruction, has traveled the world to be exhibited in loan exhibitions. The case was reported widely in the press and had some importance in airing this problem and setting a legal precedent.

The archaeologist David Pendergast, himself a staunch opponent of looters, who had worked for years in Belize at Lamanai and other sites, once witnessed an interesting scene. While at the Belize airport on May 11, 1971, he saw airline employees struggling with two suitcases due to be loaded on a TACA plane bound for Miami, but clearly of extraordinary weight. A customs agent had them opened and found pieces of an Itzimte-like stela, fragmented and wrapped in newspapers. David chanced to visit the airport again next day, and was interested to see that Leonardo Patterson and Marcello Bucchi (a more professional operator), had flown in when things went wrong. Patterson was charged but jumped bail.

Patterson, a Costa Rican black, cut an elegant figure, and at one time gave his New York City address as 40 Sutton Place—a prime location. Once, when on a visit to Lausanne to record two stelae in the collection of the late Samuel Josefowitz, I was to meet him briefly. The doorbell rang, and there was Patterson, slender and elegant in a well-tailored black suit. Later, Josefowitz wrote to tell me that on that occasion Patterson had booked a room for himself, his English girlfriend, and their pet ocelot at the Hotel Beau Rivage, one of the world's most famous hotels, noted for the displaced royalty and dowager queens who were living out their lives there in the lap of luxury. As Patterson had given Sam Josefowitz's name as a reference, the manager called him to confirm its authenticity; and then on the Pattersons' departure had reason to call again—to report that the very costly brocade curtains in their room had been torn to shreds by the ocelot.

Patterson seems to have been regarded by others working the same trade as a beginner, yet only once (to my knowledge) was he actually incarcerated, and that was in Texas, for the theft of turtle eggs. But in what may have been his most profitable venture he quickly exploited Australia's introduction of legislation resembling U.S. income tax codes; that is, tax deductions were now allowed for gifts of works of art to tax-exempt institutions, such as universities and museums. So while dealing with collectors unfamiliar with pre-Columbian art, Patterson was able to dispose of a lot of dreadful junk; even so, some of his "Maya" mural paintings were rejected. Later, I inspected one of these in Boston. It was a perfectly obvious fake, crude in execution, done with impossible pigments, and on closer inspection, the end of a thick nylon filament was sticking out from the mural's surface.

He would surface again in fine fettle with an exhibition in a public museum in Santiago de Compostela, in Galicia, Spain. This bore the splendid title: *O espíritu da América prehispánica: 3,000 años de cultura*. There, a visitor could feast his or her eyes on no less than 724 objects, all of which (presumably) had already been bought from Patterson, or were for sale. I was somewhat dismayed to see that several colleagues who should have known better contributed to the catalogue, for about half of the pieces displayed were crude fakes. Alas, I missed the show, but it received notable coverage (entirely adverse) in the journal *Mexikon, Aktuelle Informationen un Studien zu Mesoamerika* (vol. 19, no. 1, 1997, Schlossberg, Germany).

Prompted by Clemency Coggins's *Art Journal* article, the American Society for International Law formed a panel to investigate the whole topic. Their recommendations, informed by studies of the matter by the now long lamented Professor Paul M. Bator,[6] were instrumental in the drafting and passage of the Pre-Columbian Art Act of 1972. This prohibits the importation of monumental sculpture from ten Latin American countries. Coincidentally, it was shortly after this law went into effect that Machaquilá Stela 2 and the remains of Stela 5 were recovered for Guatemala. This was a landmark case, in which for the first time a foreign government had sued in U.S. courts to recover cultural property.

32.3 Leonardo Patterson's very poor, obviously fake "Maya" mural.

At the same time, concern about international trade in antiquities and art treasures had become the driving force behind the impressively titled "UNESCO Preliminary Draft Convention Concerning the Means of Prohibiting and Preventing the Illicit Import, Export and Transfer of Ownership of Cultural Property." This would develop into the UNESCO Convention ratified in 1971 by virtually every country that found itself exporting archaeological treasures and fine art against its will. But to nobody's surprise it was spurned by some of the principal importers, such as the United States, Switzerland, Belgium, and the United Kingdom (belatedly, the United Kingdom and eventually Switzerland did ratify it, but not the others).

When it came to implementing this convention in the United States, the Subcommittee on Trade of the Committee on Ways and Means of the House of Representatives first held hearings on a bill in August 1976. Formal statements and letters to the chief counsel were sent in by numerous archaeologists, some with illustrations (including my photo of Dos Pilas Stela 8, as left by Ivanoff). A six-page statement declaring their opposition to the bill came, as expected, from the American Association of Dealers in Ancient, Oriental and Primitive Art, and a short one from Edward Merrin, a New York dealer, who ended his submission with a rhetorical question: "Why must we continually make the citizens of the United States suffer when the only other countries that are signatories are iron curtain countries, some of the Arab countries, African countries and Mexico who is increasing their shipment of drugs into the U.S. and are castigating Israel for the attack on Entebbe."

The first bill was voted down, but then a second, modified version, H.R. 5643, was given hearings in May 1977. This time, about a dozen witnesses read statements, and material was submitted by nearly two hundred individuals. Professor Michael D. Coe, of Yale University, who chose to sit at the hearing among the dealers, argued that archaeological treasures would not be properly cared for in their countries of origin, citing "even a major museum in which the roof has fallen in through neglect." This was clearly a reference to the Guatemalan Museum of Archaeology and Ethnology, where indeed the roof of one exhibition hall had recently been renovated, but Coe's version of the problem had been adjusted, for in fact no roof had "fallen in." Builders were called in because water was pouring down the inside walls during heavy rain. Accordingly, the artifacts on exhibition were duly boxed up and removed to the basement (as I witnessed), the roof was rebuilt, and the artifacts installed once again, undamaged.

Then a brilliant but sadly flawed student of Coe's at Yale, David Joralemon, warned the committee against "the hypocritical posturings of American museums who have already amassed vast holdings of world art, or the self-serving statements of third world socialist countries which are blinded by xenophobia and doctrinaire aversion to private property."

As with the previous bill, no action was taken, and hearings on yet another bill, H.R. 3403, were held in September 1979. Under its weakened terms there would be no blanket prohibition of trade in archaeological artifacts, but a foreign country could appeal to the U.S. president for temporary emergency action prohibiting trade in some specific class of material judged to be in jeopardy. And this is now part of U.S. law.

The attitude of Michael D. Coe regarding the collecting of archaeological specimens was puzzling, and entirely opposed to that of his older brother, William (better known as Bill). As both of them had developed an interest in archaeology early in life, they went off together as students to the vast and then neglected ruins of Cobá, in the Yucatán Peninsula, made some useful discoveries there, and jointly published a report on them. Then they engaged in more ambitious excavations at Nohoch Ek in British Honduras—a pioneering choice, because no such minor site had ever been thought worthy of excavation. Again they published their findings as joint authors; but then, brotherly relations came to an end.

According to legend (supported by an archaeologist who was working in the same area at that time) a heated dispute between the Coe brothers arose at Nohoch Ek (and they have avoided each other's company since then). At the site, one of them was at the bottom of a deep stratigraphic pit. Furious, his brother removed the ladder, leaving his sibling unable to climb out and therefore at the mercy of mosquitoes and cold night air until morning. One wonders, could this dispute have concerned the handling of some excavated artifact? Perhaps it would seem unlikely that a painted vessel of the finest quality would be found at such a minor site, but in fact archaeologists did make just such a discovery at another minor site named Buena Vista del Cayo, not far away.

This particular vessel was immediately recognizable as having been made—or at least painted—by an artist working at Naranjo: he is recognized for his individual and very fine hand, using red with orange infill on a white background. Presumably this vase was given by K'ak' Tiliw Chaan Chahk, the ruler of Naranjo, to the lord of Buena Vista as an expression of political alliance: it shows that great ruler seated above the vanquished (and apparently deceased) ruler of Ucanal, an important city about twenty miles to the south. The sociopolitical relations between those two sites could never have been elicited from the vase itself, had it been looted and come through the market. Evidence of this kind, coupled with information provided by texts on stone monuments, has created an understanding of Maya geopolitics undreamed of fifty years ago.

In 1970, the art correspondent for the *Boston Globe* came to see Professor Stephen Williams, director of Harvard's Peabody Museum, to ask him why the museum was selling off its artifacts.

"Selling our artifacts? We're doing nothing of the kind!"

"Well, perhaps you would care to look at this Christie's catalog?"

This was of Northwest Coast ethnographic objects, one of which, a magnificent Haida mask, was illustrated in color on the cover. Neatly painted on its forehead was a number, 1605. Its estimated price was twenty-five thousand dollars (the equivalent of about seventy-five thousand dollars today).

That astute *Globe* art critic, however, suspected that the notation on the forehead was a museum catalog number, and in seeking its source came first to the Peabody Museum of Harvard, knowing perhaps of its outstanding collection of Northwest Coast material.

Steve Williams at once suggested they go downstairs to the catalog room to investigate. There, this mask proved to be part of the first big accession of any kind that the museum had received. That was in 1869, and all of it was from the Northwest Coast. But there in the catalog, loosely inserted between its pages, was a sheet of plain paper on which was scribbled in pencil:

1772—Comb—Tlingit or Haida, rec'd 1869
1786—Rattle—Haida—N.W. Coast 1869
1605—Mask—Alaska—N.W. Coast 1869
Received the above in Exchange
Michael D. Coe [signed by his own hand]
for the following—
Human effigy beating drum—of pottery, purchased in New York 1948 by W.R. Coe & M.D. Coe. Tarascan, provenience unknown.
Pottery vessel (hour-glass form) human face on rim, collected by W.R. Coe & M.D. Coe, July 1949, found by an Indian in a cave near Negroman, Cayo district, British Honduras. Bought from Capt. E.J. Moy, British Honduras. [This was a Lacandón incensario, which I'm told cost them US$20. It has since been discarded by the museum.]

The deal was done while Mike Coe was a student at Harvard, and at that time the director of the Peabody was an easy-going man, with a penchant perhaps for favoring gilded scions of wealthy parents. And then, very generously, Coe turned the mask over to his roommate in Harvard College—a man also destined to achieve distinction in a field of non-European art. He in turn may have given it to his wife, for apparently it was she who trotted down the sidewalk to Christie's to put it up for auction. Here, the mask fetched only seventeen thousand dollars—perhaps because dealers scented something fishy about that numeral and the mask's provenience. Its buyer, however, was a member of the Peabody Museum's Visiting Committee, who most generously restored it to the museum's collection.

Decades later, Coe wrote to me asking permission to reproduce some published drawings of mine. Of course, I granted him this, but couldn't resist suggesting in a postscript that since he had now enjoyed having the rattle, said to be the finest of its kind, for nearly half a century, then perhaps he might consider donating it to the Peabody Museum—and thereby obtain a large tax deduction. Answer came there none; but could he have failed to recognize this as a shot across his bow?[7]

Unquestionably, Michael Coe has made important contributions in our field, most of them originating in his study. For example, he and his Russian-speaking wife, Sophie, were responsible (as already related) for drawing attention to the seminal but previously ignored work of the Russian scholar, Yuri Knorozov, who had provided a crucial insight in the decipherment of Maya writing. Then in the late 1960s, when beautifully

32.4 A smoking gun note of Michael Coe's trading exploits.

painted pottery vessels began to appear in the market, dug from tombs by looters, Coe was to play a prominent role in emphasizing their potential importance and value. Many were cylindrical vases, others plates and jars, with only a tiny proportion surviving in good condition. The result was sudden excitement in the antiquities market, and that, of course, galvanized the looters to search for more of them. Thousands of "dry trenches" must have been dug before the looters determined which regions yielded vessels of the highest value, northeastern Petén being one of them.

Some of the jars had designs painted in a band around their rims, and it was Michael Coe who pioneered the study of these. Although glyph-like, they had been dismissed as merely decorative, but by demonstrating that there was a standard sequence to them, Coe argued persuasively that they must be hieroglyphs. And then, following Eric Thompson, who had connected a scene painted on a cylindrical jar with a passage in a post-Conquest manuscript, Coe went on to identify many scenes on similar jars as illustrations of Maya creation stories. Later, he and Peter Furst explained some previously puzzling scenes painted on a number of Maya vessels; these were revealed as portraying the administration of psychotropic or intoxicating fluids, such as balché, to high-ranking persons by means of enemas.[8]

Such scenes have illuminated facets of Maya courtly life that never would have been represented on monumental sculpture, and for archaeologists to abstain from studying them simply because their provenience was tainted would do nothing to discourage looting—so long as they themselves refrain from authenticating such merchandise. More pertinent is the problem of overconfident restoration of painted vases, as this can destroy their credibility as evidence of the past. Dicey Taylor, a pupil of Coe's, demonstrated this convincingly in 1978.[9]

I remember the excitement caused by the discovery at Altar de Sacrificios of a beautifully painted cylindrical vase depicting a jaguar-masked dancer wearing jaguar tights, with other figures. More than twenty years later, Stephen Houston and David Stuart proposed convincingly that here the jaguar was the dancer's "co-essence," with a glyph reading "way" expressing relationship between living and supernatural entities.[10] As this was one of the earliest and finest of Maya vessels to come out of the ground painted with a narrative scene, I was allowed to make a "roll-out" photo of it, using homemade equipment. I had already done another of the famous Fenton vase[11] in the British Museum which was found nearly a century ago.

The modern technique of making roll-outs was developed, I believe, by Royal Dutch/Shell, perhaps for recording strata revealed in drill-cores. It has since been used to very good effect by Justin Kerr, a New York City photographer, who has published roll-outs of thousands of painted vessels (almost all of which have arisen, of course, from a different underworld). (Recently we met for the first time, and I told him of the

simple apparatus I had constructed forty years earlier to make two roll-outs: one was of the Fenton Vase, and the other, a fine one from Altar de Sacrificios; he told me he'd seen a copy of the latter, and had been mystified about its origin until that very day.)

Inevitably, I soon began to find at site after site in Petén great trenches dug into tall pyramids in search of tombs, and smaller ones dug every three or four yards along *caballos*—the looters' term for long, low mounds. Countless times I've found, strewn on the ground near the entrance of such trenches, heaps of broken vessels removed from tombs and discarded as unsaleable, but clearly representing in some cases losses of potentially valuable art and information. I found at one site, for example, that *wecheros* (diggers looking for vases)[12] had dug a trench at one end of a low stairway, cutting through its side and destroying the Early Classic modeled and painted stucco figures on it. These men could also be dangerous, for on one occasion, while visiting the ruins of El Zotz, just west of Tikal, I looked down on the South Plaza from higher ground

32.5 My roll-out photo of the British Museum's "Fenton Vase"
(taken around 1966)—the first of its kind.

on its north side, and thought I saw the roofless skeleton of a champa among the scrub vegetation, but on closer inspection it proved to be a watchtower built by looters for an armed sentinel whose function would be to knock off unwanted visitors, such as archaeologists.

So in the face of the terrible damage caused by widespread market-driven digging, one can only lament—for what else can one do?—that these precious objects could not have been brought to light in an orderly and less destructive manner. The truth is that poverty at the pickax level, and greed at the entrepreneurial, have been relentless engines of destruction, impossible to control.

Like a few other fellow-warriors in my profession, I've sometimes tried to cause trouble for traders in looted antiquities, and also for unprincipled collectors, which is a harder task. In doing so, I've been surprised at finding how different in background and style were two of the most active New York City dealers.

32.6 A looter's dump of ceramics at Río Azul.

André Emmerich, of Swiss origin and now retired from business, used to woo his customers with velvety smooth encomia of his treasures, whereas Ed Merrin, whose speech frankly proclaims his Brooklyn origins, would find it difficult to couch his aesthetic judgments in any but the simplest terms. His pre-Columbian department used to be on the floor above the family jewelry store on Madison Avenue, where umbrellas were also for sale, and high turnover rather than quality appeared to be the goal. But he certainly acquired some useful connections, for the so-called Hauberg stela (of unsolved provenance) passed through his hands, as did the carved wooden lintel that I was able to show had been wrenched out of the great temple at El Zotz, damaging it seriously. He also provided a considerable proportion of Josué Saénz's treasures. And in recent years he's had a different and possibly more profitable connection, a partnership with Asher Edelman, a man well known on Wall Street.[13]

In recent years, though, he and his son, now partners, have run into trouble. This is not directly connected with the origin of their merchandise—apart from the risks the Merrins presumably ran in smuggling it in—but instead from having breached a "cost-plus" agreement with a very wealthy customer who had agreed to pay a commission of 10 percent for pre-Columbian merchandise—but in fact was charged between two and four times as much.

I never took on Merrin as an adversary, but I could hardly avoid challenging Emmerich. He and the Perls Gallery must have sold to Peter G. Wray a large part of his huge collection. Wray had married Gay Firestone and then purchased large cattle ranches in Arizona and New Mexico, only to see his fortune collapse in 1984 when the price of beef plummeted. Facing serious financial problems and the break-up of his marriage, he was forced to sell his best pre-Columbian pieces. These were put on display at the two galleries from which he'd bought them—though at neither of the showings was it openly stated that the pieces were for sale.

An especially intriguing object was a remarkable stone mask (of fuchsite) rumored to have come from the ruins of Río Azul. It was reliably reported that a hieroglyphic inscription engraved on the inside disclosed its origin, but examination of that text had deliberately been made impossible. In his catalog, though, André Emmerich smoothly assured us that "these well known works have carefully documented provenances dating their presence in this country back for many years. They are all objects which have long been studied by scholars, and in most cases widely published."

But really, that was too much! I protested to him by mail:

> *"Long studied by scholars"*—surely not true of most pieces. Indeed, I would say that to most scholars the very existence of many of these pieces had been unknown. *"Carefully documented provenances"*—indeed? As far as I know there is only one item, or rather, pair of items, numbers 32 and 33, with a known provenance, and funnily enough this is not mentioned in your catalog, but in case you don't know, these panels were cut from Stela 8 at Dos Pilas, Guatemala. *"Widely published and in this country for several years?"*

32.7 *Fragment three and a half inches wide of a carved cedarwood bowl found in a looters' camp at Río Azul.*

I listed how many had been published by decades. In sum, twenty-one had been published and thirty-three never had been. My letter was then forwarded to Wray's lawyers; I replied; and the lawyers came back this time with a threat that "if Mr. Wray encounters any difficulty in the orderly marketing of his collection as a result of the defamatory accusations you have persisted in circulating, we will take all appropriate legal action [etc., etc.]."

The correspondence petered out, but I happened to mention it to the redoubtable Charlie Koczka, of the art fraud department of the New York office of U.S. Customs. He told me that a Chilean dealer of notorious reputation had shown an "Olmec jade mask" (quite likely to have been the one exhibited) to Michael Coe's former student, David Joralemon, who recommended Wray to purchase it, and Wray was said to have written a check for $150,000 for it.

But Wray's finances must have suffered a more serious collapse than I had imagined, for he had lost not only his wife, but also his house, was driving a small Honda, and had used his collection as collateral for a $5.38 million loan from the London-based J. Henry Schroeder Bank. But although this may be difficult to believe, the bank had never inventoried the valuables that were delivered to the Sofia Warehouse in New York's Upper West Side.

Then, one morning Charlie invited me to a rendezvous at a coffeehouse near Columbus Circle, where we were joined by John J. Raffa (special agent, U.S. Customs Service), Joe Wolf (U.S. Customs Service, Laredo), and Sharon Pierce (assistant U.S. attorney, Department of Justice, Austin, Texas). We entered Sofia's huge and ancient red brick building and were joined there by two young men from Schroeder's Bank who'd brought the keys to the two vaults holding those treasures. We climbed the iron stairway, our footsteps echoing through the vast interior, and at last the iron doors were unlocked to reveal their contents.

What a shock awaited us! There were numerous Shipibo jars, collected by Wray on an expedition he had once organized, a few Maya vessels of little value, Moché pieces, miscellaneous Mexican material, Guatemalan textiles, a box of stirrups (some possibly of silver), a considerable number of books on pre-Columbian and Latin American art, and a few pieces of Spanish Colonial furniture.

The U.S. attorney from Austin expressed her annoyance at having been lied to by Wray's henchman. As to Wray himself, they said, he evidently suffered amnesia about the mask, having no recollection of buying it.

Charlie was unable to invite me to accompany them on their next visit, which was to Joralemon's apartment. He was at home, but (as I was told later) refused to talk without his lawyer being present. Some months later, Sharon Pierce told me that Joralemon was offered immunity from prosecution in exchange for information. He told them that the Río Azul mask had been sold not long before to a private collector, Bernabé Müller, of Switzerland, so it was out of their jurisdiction. (This man was connected with "Art und Antiquitäten" of Zurich.) All the stuff we saw in the warehouse was eventually sold, but those Maya pots? They could hardly give them away! So the bank "took a bath."

The story of David Joralemon is sad indeed. In the 1970s, while a graduate student at Yale, he wrote some seminal studies of Olmec art, but then he wandered off into a different world of private collections, such as the William O'Boyle collection of figurines, of which he had become curator.[14] It was valued by Silberman at $1.8 million (but for a tenth of that by Robert Sonin) and insured by Chubbs. (David Joralemon's mother worked for the Chubbs, who had sent David and his brother to college). There was a staged burglary, and O'Boyle's secretary was shot in the head six months later. This was a complicated story, and I am certainly not suggesting that Joralemon was implicated in this latter aspect of it. But the unfortunate woman's death does point up the none-too-savory nature of that coterie.

33.1 Trudging towards La Pasadita with the tumpline.
Photo by Eric von Euw.

CHAPTER 33

La Pasadita

While working at Yaxchilan in 1970, I heard an interesting story from Luis de la Cruz (a member of the site's guardian family). He told me that some seven years earlier he had caught sight of men with mules appearing out of the bush on the opposite bank of the river, the mules having been hired, as he later discovered, by a Spanish doctor from Palenque. The men then unloaded the mules' cargo of sculptured stone panels, concealed them under jungle trash, and departed.

The de la Cruz family and others thought they had probably come from ruins at La Pasadita, a lagoon some way in from the river on the Guatemalan side (if so, the mules must have been brought down from Tenosique, as none would have been available on the Guatemalan side, for in those days the land downriver was entirely unpopulated). In any case, the panels remained there for several days before men returned with a boat to take them to Agua Azul, presumably to be flown out from its landing field.

All I could learn about La Pasadita was that it had been discovered by a chiclero named Pedro Martínez, who would speak of it but apparently never showed it to anyone. Then one day Martínez was caught in a whirlpool in the river, his cayuco overturned, and he drowned, dragged down by his boots, pistol, and ammunition belt. The ruins, however, were soon rediscovered, the lintels were wrenched out, and their carved surfaces sawed off to lighten them.

On returning to Yaxchilan in September 1970, I brought with me a photomosaic map of the La Pasadita area and showed it to Miguel de la Cruz. He was able to identify the lagoon, which from Yaxchilan lay only fifteen kilometers north in a straight line. The trail to Tenosique, Miguel said, passed close to it and was normally open, although blocked just then as a recent storm had thrown down many trees. I persuaded him to go off next day with his son-in-law, Juan, to reopen the trail, but during the night heavy rain fell. Juan was willing to start, but neither Miguel nor any of his three men were, out of concern that their wet machetes might slip, with consequent injury to themselves. Finally, however, they did go, on the understanding that they'd stop if rain began again. (Attempting travel in August or September had been something of a gamble, because the drier interlude in the rainy season that often occurs just then can't be relied on.)

Now, however, the sun was shining; but even so it was two days before the men had cleared the trail as far as a *bañadero*, where we could camp if necessary, and then continue clearing the trail ahead of us from there. (A bañadero is a muddy depression where wild pigs wallow.) When Don Miguel returned, he told me they had reopened over a league of the trail, but he, at least, was unwilling to continue. It was *un camino muy feo—muy feísimo, feísimo* (a most dreadful trail!).

There ensued the usual negotiations, and it was arranged that Ricardo—another of Don Miguel's sons—would take me to La Pasadita. (Miguel had ten children, a poor showing compared with his brother's fifteen, all from the same wife). But Ricardo, who had recently walked to Tenosique by another route to fetch a girl and had flown back the previous day, had unfortunately just come down with a terrible fever—though I couldn't help suspecting that he'd simply changed his mind, notorious liar that he was. Instead, however, his brother Jacinto would come, and we recruited another man, Fidel; then, having crossed the river in two cayucos, we nosed into an inconspicuous creek to unload our stuff.

For lack of mules, we would be obliged to carry everything ourselves. To carry my bolsa ahulada, containing hammock, mosquito net, sleeping bag, etc., more easily, I cut a strip of bark from a *mahagua* tree to serve as a *mecapal*, or tumpline, as this bark has a smooth inner surface that doesn't irritate the skin. I would also be carrying my aluminum camera case. We set off, and after some time passed a bañadero named Patastal (for two *pataste* trees that were growing there—these being trees related to *cacao*, the source of chocolate, although their fruit hangs from branches rather than from the tree trunk). Then we reached a campsite called Los Gringos.

There, close to the edge of the aguada, I found two bottles of almost black glass, with deeply dimpled bottoms. One bottle was broken, the other intact, so I took the latter back with me to Cambridge, and there was told that it dates from the nineteenth century. So I feel quite sure that they had lain there ever since Désiré Charnay, the French writer and explorer, drank the wine they contained and cast them away. (As he himself mentions the large quantity of wine from Bordeaux and Aragon that he had brought with him, I feel sure those were bottles were his.)

On hearing, in 1871, rumors of the existence of unexplored ruins along the Usumacinta, Charnay had set off from Tenosique with a staff of fourteen men to lay claim to its discovery. He could well have passed through Los Gringos, and it's just conceivable that this name commemorated his overnight stay there, even after the passage of more than a century (though I'm not at all sure that the word *gringo* was already in use then). And then on reaching the river he discovered, much to his chagrin, that Alfred Maudslay had arrived at the ruins two days earlier, coming from the opposite direction.

We set off on September 14 and reached the lagoon of La Pasadita—none too soon from my point of view, for the neck muscles that keep the tumpline-loaded head from wobbling had, in my case, never before been called upon for such heavy duty.

The lagoon has a diameter of perhaps 250 yards, and lies within a horseshoe of high ground. Jacinto had been told that the ruins lay to the east of the lagoon, and we spent the whole of the next day searching for them. The terrain there is quite broken, with chunks of high ground almost isolated by their vertical rock faces. We also found a chasm reminiscent of the one at Aguateca, although not as deep, but with similar natural bridges of rock. We did find two mounds that had been excavated, but our target eluded us, and next day we returned to Yaxchilan.

On my return to Yaxchilan, late in May of the following year, José and Ulíses de la Cruz, nephews of Miguel and Juan, happened to arrive, and told me they did know the ruins. It would be uncharitable to speculate about the possible involvement of these two lads in the removal of the lintels (although their reputations were not entirely without blemish) and perhaps they were too young to have been involved in the theft, but they did indeed know their way to the building from which the lintels had been removed.

As José soon told me, he'd had, on various occasions, had diverse parts of his anatomy in the jaws of a jaguar, a crocodile, and a jabalí, fortunately escaping each time without serious injury; but understandably he was nervous when boars were about, and kept an eye out for trees easy to climb in case of attack. So on finding a *manada* (herd) of about two hundred jabalí ahead of us, their jaws snapping with a sound suggestive of steel traps, Ulíses, as a tease, began barking like a dog to provoke them—even as his brother! Well, naturally, José was not the only one keeping an extra sharp lookout for climbable trees, for I certainly was.

Owing to the brothers' exceptional knowledge of plants, I was treated during this trip to the best nature ramble of my jungle experience. We ate *chichicaste*, a fruit the size of a small plum, with a regular pattern of dark warts, and white flesh having a texture and fresh taste resembling cashew fruit, only more astringent. The resin, however, sticks the lips together (and since then I have sometimes regretted not having a chichicaste on hand to offer some relentless windbag). Then we tasted water from the roots of *copo* (a fig), and also from these vines: *guayamaco, cobanillo, cruz blanco* (all nearly tasteless), and *cruz colorado*. They couldn't find *parra* (said to be free of taste), or *mandongo* (said to have a flowery perfume).

By chance we came upon a faisán (*Crax rubra*) with chicks, which hid among leaves whilst the mother strutted about very close to us, making hiccuping noises, and twice, a long, drawn-out descending cry like that of a coyote. Near La Pasadita we again came upon an extraordinary number of jabalí, in several troops, grunting and clashing jaws—very *bravo*. And for good measure we also passed right under a large party of howler monkeys.

With only a little scouting we found the hill of the ruins, which was about fifty meters high, with vertical rock faces at two levels on its western side. Of the small group of mounds on top, only one remained standing; the others had collapsed long ago, and their remains had been dug into heavily by looters. Even the standing building didn't look as if it would remain upright much longer, since the removal of lintels had left the vaulted roof with little support at the front, while the outward thrust of the vault had already caused the back wall to incline outward, away from a partition wall. So I was not surprised (though sorry, of course) on hearing not much later that the building had at last collapsed.

This building was unusual in having two doorways in its façade, rather than one or three, but it had another at its west end. The lintels from all three doorways had been wrenched out and lay nearby, their carved undersides having been sawn off neatly. The chamber at its east end exhibited another unusual feature, for it was subdivided by a partition wall reaching up only to the level of the vault-spring. But the truly remarkable feature of this building was the almost complete coverage of the walls and vaulted ceiling of the central room with wall paintings—though these were now in very poor condition.

As we had come only lightly laden—just for a quick look—we marched back next morning to our starting point opposite Yaxchilan.

Buildings embellished with extensive mural paintings are rare in Maya ruins. The three-room building at Bonampak with its interior walls almost completely covered with paintings is unique, but at other sites, such as San Bartolo, Chichén Itzá, and Tulum, mural paintings have survived from periods ranging from the early Preclassic period to the Postclassic. But the distinction of having the painted area extend from the walls up into the vaulted roof is one shared only by Bonampak and La Pasadita.

33.2 *La Pasadita: area of mural in situ depicting bust of man*
(nose and eyes at right of green "earflare").

The murals at La Pasadita, although in very poor condition, were still of considerable interest, and I felt that no time should be lost in returning to obtain some record of them. Then it occurred to me that an attempt to remove a sample of the murals would not be unethical, even at the risk of bungling the attempt, in view of the building's clearly imminent collapse.

When back in Cambridge I read, or re-read, some literature on techniques used in Italy for removing frescoes, and bought the appropriate supplies. These amounted to a small spray gun, polyvinyl acetate solutions, Japanese mulberry paper, a length of calico, and animal glue. In Guatemala, I bought filament tape and a few hand tools (including a little "Surform" plane), and finally, two pieces of chipboard cut to 1.25 meters square. With these and the usual camping supplies, I arrived at Sayaxché in early February 1972, and having rounded up a boat, boatman, outboard motor, and two other men, embarked for Yaxchilan. We spent the night at Altar de Sacrificios in the sad remains of the old Peabody camp there, and arrived at Yaxchilan next day.

I sent for Aurelio de la Cruz, and while awaiting his arrival, did a little more of the almost endless task of recording inscriptions at the ruins. When Aurelio arrived, I asked him, with his cousin and one of my boys, to go off and reopen a shorter trail to La Pasadita that Aurelio knew of, one that starts downriver from below the mouth of the Arroyo Anaité, and then at Lechugal joins the trail we had followed on our previous visit. They came back the same day, having cleared it without trouble—apart from the fact that one of the men had been lunged at by a very poisonous snake, a chalpate (*Bothrops nummifera*). Fortunately, it just caught his trouser leg and no more. So we all set off and reached the lagoon without incident.

Having inspected the best-preserved areas of painting, I came to the conclusion that none was large enough to warrant the removal of an area as large as the chipboard panels we'd brought, so I had the panels cut in half. Another factor in this decision was the obvious difficulty of transporting such large and rather heavy pieces of the stucco layer, sandwiched between chipboard for its protection. Such a large one would have to be slung from a pole borne on two men's shoulders, a very awkward load on a rough trail. So then I marked out on the wall two rectangles of that size for removal, and washed their surfaces to remove green mold—although, as I realized later, I failed to do this as thoroughly as I might have. When they were dry, I sprayed them with 10 percent PVA (polyvinyl acetate) in alcohol. This had the effect of making the lime deposit more transparent, so I also sprayed some other areas that I intended only to photograph.

The next day, I sprayed on one more coat, and when it was dry, brushed two coats of the heavier 20 percent PVA—and then another on the following day. Then I stretched the mulberry paper across both areas with adhesive tape, and brushed animal glue across them. When the glue proved to be very slow in drying, we built a fire in the chamber, which worked wonders, and we were able to apply a second layer of paper and one of cloth.

That evening, the men complained of small meals, but it was their own fault there were no beans; I had told them to put beans on the fire at lunchtime, and they hadn't done so. Here, a packet of instant hashed brown potatoes, given me years earlier by my colleague David Pendergast, served as a quick and delicious supplement.

Next morning, the glue was tacky again from the humidity, so another fire was lit. Now I cut grooves in the plaster outlining the areas to be removed, using a keyhole saw and a serrated kitchen knife, first to cut down to the masonry, and then to open this cut into a V-shaped groove. Another layer of cloth was then applied.

The next step was to put two forked poles and a crosspiece, or beam, up against the wall, with the crosspiece some ten inches above the top of the areas to be removed. The two layers of cloth were trimmed around those areas, and filament tape was pressed well into the upper part of the cloth, passed tightly over the crosspiece and down to it again—several of these being applied. In this way the detached stucco would remain hanging from the crosspiece once the stucco had been detached from the wall.

We detached the smaller piece first, using a specialized instrument to insert upwards from below, in order to separate the stucco from the masonry—this, an instrument commonly called a machete. With the men pulling the upper edge of the cloth and stucco a little away from the wall, I slid the chipboard up from below until the stucco rectangle was laying flat and painted side up on the chipboard; then I cut the filament tapes. Board and stucco were then taken outside, another board placed over it, and the sandwich turned over; then I set to work with the "Surform" plane, smoothing down projecting peaks of stucco until the whole was essentially flat, although many valleys (corresponding to projecting stones in the masonry) remained. The first rectangle of chipboard was placed on this once more, and the sandwich strapped tightly together with filament tape, ready for carriage next day by mecapal.

The other panel gave more trouble. Try as I might, I could *not* get the machete to pass right across, behind the otherwise freely hanging piece; there were stones obstructing. Eventually I realized that before being stuccoed, two small stones had been projecting from the wall. In order to economize in stucco (as I was forced to conclude), these two stones were left projecting, and then ground down level with the stucco surface, so that in those two small areas the paint was applied to stone rather than stucco. It was impossible, then, to avoid leaving two small lacunae in the painting.

I brought the two panels to the Museo Nacional de Arqueología y Etnología in Guatemala City. After a little more planing with the Surform, to further flatten the surfaces,

I filled up the hollows with plaster of Paris and planed those patches flat when dry. Then, on both pieces, I smeared epoxy over the stucco and lowered onto each of them a steel panel manufactured for office furnishing. Once the epoxy had set, I turned the panels over and poured hot, but not boiling, water over them, to soften the glue. The cloth could then be removed, and also the Japanese tissue, and while swabbing with more hot water, removed the last traces of glue.

33.3 La Pasadita mural, remounted in Guatemala City.

Finally, most of the PVA was removed by swabbing with alcohol, but I did give both panels a thin spray-coating of PVA for protection.

Some years later, I received a letter from the Belgian archaeologist Martine Fettweiss, who was inquiring how she could get to La Pasadita to record the murals. She had already done yeoman work recording every scrap of mural painting she could find in the Maya area, and I welcomed her offer to record these, too, since my photographs were far from providing an adequate record.

She would be coming with her French husband, Jacques-Henri Viennot, so I invited my brother Robin to come over from England to join this little expedition. Choosing to take the quickest route to Yaxchilan, we flew in by light plane from Tenosique, and there, luckily found both a boat and a guide willing to go with us to the disembarkation point near the Anaité rapids. Martine's backpack was heavily loaded with rolls of transparent plastic, which she would be using for tracing the murals, and much more, while we carried food supplies and very inadequate camping gear. Since palms suitable for constructing shelters are almost nonexistent near La Pasadita, the rapid construction of *champas arrimadas* (palm frond lean-tos) was impossible, so we just prayed for fine weather.

Our prayers went unanswered. Rain came down hard, and all of us were soaked that night. We lay shivering in our hammocks, trying to adjust our skimpy plastic sheets more effectively to channel the flow of water away from our bodies.

Martine scarcely complained, and by day seemed fearless as she worked in that temple, spending hours in it. From the very first I had been nervous about its dangers: I could see no reason why any of the vault stones should remain in place, other than being used to doing so. From the interstices between them, long, thin roots reached down to the floor, which would serve as trip wires if trodden on or bumped against, to bring stone slabs crashing down. While she worked, I busied myself with mapping the hill upon which the building stood, and poking about in the remains of another structure that formerly faced it, in the hope of finding in the rubble the sawn slabs of other lintels cut by the looters, but I found nothing of that kind, perhaps because everything had been so badly disturbed.

It was not difficult to locate the eventual resting places of two of the plundered lintels—or rather, the carved surfaces cut from them, for they were in public museums in Berlin and Leyden. The third, from the east doorway, is also in Holland, in a private collection, but its owner is uncooperative. The style of Lintels 1 and 2 is quite similar to that of Yaxchilan, and the inscriptions show that La Pasadita was a dependency of that great city.

Then I began to wonder whether the panel, or lintel, found by Dana and Ginger Lamb and illustrated in their book *Quest for the Lost City* might also have come from this site, and perhaps another, now in the Museum of Primitive Art in New York (which later merged into the Metropolitan Museum). I couldn't be sure of this, although one feature of the Lamb panel—a curtain drawn up above the scene—is found also in a panel at Piedras Negras, not far away to the north. But some years later, as decipherment progressed, it became clear that the "Lamb site" lay within the polity of Yaxchilan.

The enterprising Lambs had set out from California in about 1941 to look for the "Lost City"—but where they'd heard or read of such a thing is not divulged. In their story, it supposedly lay somewhere near Mexico's boundary with Guatemala. The Lambs claim in their book to have possessed just ten dollars and sixteen cents, plus an undisclosed sum in a camera bag—and also a Model T Ford as a picturesque accessory. But according to their interesting account, the engine expires, and they hitch it to two mules for traction. When a wheel collapses they abandon both car and mules and press on to Tuxtla Gutierrez, in Chiapas, where the need of a plane to search for the Lost City becomes apparent. As their financial resources have increased somehow to about 240 pesos, Dana considers buying a plane he has seen at the airport. It lacks wings, but fortunately some wings are available, though coming from a different make of plane. The owner tells him he can have both fuselage and wings for free, so all that's necessary now is hard work by Dana, Ginger, and a mechanic to adapt the wings to the foreign body and overhaul the engine.

Next, they prepare an airfield farther east, at Comitán, closer to the Lost City. By now, a little warning flag has gone up in my mind; but then I thought, perhaps an aged aunt had died opportunely, leaving them money, and they hadn't wanted to congratulate themselves in print over Auntie's demise.

Having somehow identified their goal from the air, they commence an arduous over-land trek to inspect it from close at hand. In this enterprise, Dana's knowledge of jungle survival technology proves a lifesaver. Among other interesting tips for those contemplating passage through a jungle, one learns (from the film made of this famous expedition) that sandals are the recommended footwear for such forests.

So the Lambs proceed (and here I am in the British Museum Library, taking notes all the time), but then they are faced by barrier cliffs, "seldom exceeding 1,500 feet high." The film shows Dana spread-eagled perilously on a vertical rock face in a daring attempt to master it. But fortune favors them, for soon they find a cave, and this turns out to be a natural tunnel under this barrier. Using pine torches, they make their way through it, and out again on the other side.

Luck and good judgment bring them at last to the Lost City, and a photo shows Dana, standing in a doorway of one of its masonry buildings. And there they discover a fine panel, broken in two but otherwise well preserved. The two halves were photographed and undoubtedly are genuine. The gods, however, are angry at this intrusion by mortals, and send down rains—heavy and unceasing rains. The waters rise, until Dana and Ginger find themselves marooned on the high ground of the Lost City, which has now become an island. An awkward predicament indeed, but not beyond the abilities of this couple to resolve. They find a suitable tree and in no time Dana has made a beautiful dugout canoe.[1]

The tale is, of course, ridiculous, but how can we explain the lintel? For convenience, its origin is referred to as either the "Lamb Site" or "Laschtunich," the name the Lambs themselves thought up, with its oddly Germanic orthography. Its location has long been a mystery, for the Lambs were vague, and in fact deceptive, about the location of their "lost city." But thinking that with the passage of time Dana might now be willing to reveal its true location, I paid him a visit—Ginger by then having passed to happier hunting grounds. He was living in a sprawling ranch-type house in Hillsboro, New Mexico, with his second wife, Maria Fellin, a friendly Mexican lady. We chatted amicably, and I told him I was sure that his reluctance to indicate the site's location was due to fear of looters finding the place. But now that the lintel had, in fact, been removed and was in Mexico City, surely there could no longer be any reason to conceal its original location. Saying which, I unfolded a map I'd brought. Dana's hand swept slowly over it, and settled on the area south of the Río Lacantún known as the Zona Marquéz de Comillas. This was certainly another evasion, since there's no description in the book of Dana making yet another dugout canoe in order to cross the Lacantún, a major river, nor of crossing it on his reconnaissance flights.

Very generously, he did lend me three sequent strips of 35 mm negatives containing his photographs of the two halves of one lintel, so that I could make good prints from them. Recognizable landmarks in these photos reveal that they were taken while the Lambs, after finding the lintel, were traveling upriver to Yaxchilan where Dana was photographed standing in a doorway of the "Lost City." The photo was reproduced as such in their book, but in fact this doorway is plainly recognizable as the one that a Carnegie Institution photograph, taken in 1929, shows supporting Yaxchilan's Lintel 29 (as it still does). The lintel they found was therefore almost certainly downstream, and not far from Yaxchilan, as suggested by the sequence of images on the negatives.

Alfred Tozzer, the great Harvard Mayanist, had a conversation with Lamb (apparently in 1954, the last year of his life), and was told by him that the lintels had not in fact been found on the Mexican side of the river. When Tozzer asked him what had been the reason for this deception, he explained that neither of them had Guatemalan tourist cards—scarcely necessary for that uninhabited region!

It was not until much later that I learned that the Lambs had offered to engage in counterintelligence work for the FBI along the Pacific coast of Mexico and Guatemala during World War II. But by 2 December 1942 a bureau memorandum reveals that "the Lambs have submitted no information of value regarding Axis activities. . . . When the Lambs were in Washington during March and April of 1942, they exhibited a motion picture of the 'Lost City of Mayapan' [*sic*], supposedly taken in Mexico. . . . Subsequently it was learned that they had sold this motion picture to the Rockefeller Committee, and that the Committee had determined that portions of the picture were faked. . . . Special Agent Hollman has reported that he observed among the possessions of the Lambs a contract with the Rockefeller Committee whereby this motion picture was sold to that organization for $2,400."

The Lambs were then planning a six- or eight-month assignment down the coast of Mexico, across the Isthmus of Tehuantepec, through the Yucatán Peninsula, and then up the east coast of Mexico—a venture somewhat resembling the investigations carried out by archaeologists of the Carnegie Institution for the Navy Department, the aim of which had been detection of secret German submarine bases that the Germans might be building in Central America.

For this, the Lambs advised that they would need new equipment: their existing truck was worn out, and they would need an outboard motor, a metal locator, and a radio direction-finder. They were given fifteen hundred dollars for the instruments and a further thousand for a truck; but when they reported that the price of trucks had gone up to seventeen hundred, the bureau dug in its heels.

Their employment was to end on 28 October 1943, but a week later Lamb told the FBI that he had been trying constantly to get in touch with the president, and although they had not yet succeeded, they had met Nelson Rockefeller, who "desired to employ the Lambs for certain work in Mexico." The letter ends by declaring that "*there is no possibility* the Bureau will need the services of the Lambs in future." A handwritten note in the margin applying to the underlined words reads "Absolutely *No*."

Perhaps it is significant that Rockefeller did obtain a beautiful carved lintel that clearly came from the Laschtunich/La Pasadita area, the first from that area to have entered a museum. This found a place in Rockefeller's Museum of Primitive Art, the contents of which would later be merged, as previously mentioned, into the Metropolitan Museum.

It seemed to me unlikely that the buildings on that small, steep-sided hillock, and the one other we found, constituted the entire site of La Pasadita. Others must surely exist, either standing or ruinous, and they, too, might well be situated upon similar outcroppings. Several years later, then, I made inquiries in San Benito for someone who might know that area well, and a man locally known as "Mexicano" (though he was Guatemalan) presented himself. So with him and my loyal guide and friend Anatolio López, we drove off by Land Rover down the recently completed road to Bethel, a settlement on the banks of the Usumacinta some 15 kilometers upriver from Yaxchilan.[2]

Bethel had been established as a cooperative settlement in the mid-1960s, but by this time, guerrilla insurgency and military countermeasures had created a tense situation along the river, and a military base had been established right in the center of this *cooperativa*. Nevertheless, we thought it might still be possible to reach La Pasadita. Mexicano suggested that he go off alone from Bethel on a reconnaissance, and in the meantime Anatolio and I could check out a rumored site containing a carved lintel only a few hours' walk away in the opposite direction. I was all in favor of that, having no enthusiasm for going on an extremely long walk with doubtful prospects of reaching our destination.

So Anatolio and I set out with a local guide to that other site, which lay near a lagoon that Teobert Maler once visited, Bolonchac. And indeed, there was a carved lintel there—very badly weathered, but clearly in Yaxchilan style. Later, I would discover that by a strange coincidence my colleague David Stuart had visited the same site three weeks earlier and had named it "Las Palmas."

Back in Bethel, we anxiously awaited the return of Mexicano, for he had once acted as guide to the military, and would therefore be a target for guerrilla revenge if recognized. So we were relieved to see him return, but with discouraging news. On the trail to La Pasadita he had been stopped by sentinels. Fortunately they didn't recognize him, warning him instead in quite friendly fashion, "Hey, amigo, you'd better not come this way," or something of the kind. Later, an army officer told me that the guerrillas actually had a camp at the lagoon; and many years later, Stephen Houston, of the Brigham Young University project at Piedras Negras, when hoping to visit La Pasadita, was warned of the danger of land mines along the trails.

In 1983 I received an interesting letter from the now-deceased David Bathurst, then head of the New York branch of Christie's, the auctioneers. He was writing to tell me that a lawyer in Portland, Maine, had inquired, as executor of an estate, whether Christie's would be interested in selling a collection of Maya sculptured panels. The panels had been bought by a man named William Palmer, who had inherited a fortune based on steel and took to spending much of it on sculpture of this kind. Then he invested heavily in Bar Harbor Airlines, and when it failed he went bankrupt, and later died. To settle his debt, the collection had to be sold.[3]

Now, I had managed to persuade David, two years earlier, not to handle any more pre-Columbian material, so his reply to the lawyer had been politely negative; but he did suggest that he get in touch with me as a person knowledgeable about such material—and passed on to me the photocopies he'd been sent, some of which were strongly suggestive of La Pasadita, and one was the Lamb panel! (It seems likely that many of these were the ones Luis de la Cruz had described to me as having spent some days hidden under trash, across the river from Yaxchilan.)

When I telephoned the lawyer, John A. Mitchell, he told me that the panels were in a safe-deposit warehouse in Zurich. Well, I replied, I would be delighted to help him, but of course I'd have to inspect the panels before being able to authenticate them, or provide valuations (not that I had the slightest intention of providing either of those services). Could he make the necessary arrangements? Yes, but he warned me that the warehouse charged very high fees for taking the crated panels down by forklift truck and opening them. Oh, no problem, I replied airily—though all too well aware that there would indeed be a serious problem in paying such fees.

Time passed, and I heard nothing more. I telephoned his office: Mr. Mitchell was tied up. I called again, and this time he was out of town, and after two more calls it became obvious that the unavailability of Mr. Mitchell was intentional. I imagine that after contacting me, he may have consulted a dealer such as Ed Merrin, who, clapping hand to forehead, would have exclaimed: "Oh, no—that man is *poison!*"

Not all of those panels could be attributed stylistically or epigraphically to the area between Yaxchilan and Piedras Negras. One of them was identified by my colleague David Stuart (whose memory bank of images is extraordinary) as being the missing half of Monument 83 at Toniná, Chiapas. So in preparing one of the *Corpus* volumes devoted to Toniná sculpture I was, of course, unable to obtain an actual photograph of this piece for publication, and therefore had to make do with the poor photocopy David Bathurst had forwarded to me. But several of those panels or lintels could indeed have come from a single site in the La Pasadita area, known for convenience by epigraphers as "Site R."

Then in May 2004, I was invited by the Los Angeles Adventurers Foundation to a viewing of the Lambs' film. This had been distributed nationally by RKO in the mid-1950s, but had not been shown again since then. It did explain some passages in the book that I had found puzzling. For example, we see Dana attempting to scale the "barrier cliffs" that were supposed to have blocked their way. No such feature exists anywhere between Comitán and the Usumacinta River, but anyone familiar with the vertical walls of the Río Grijalva's canyon near Chiapa de Corzo, a town they must have passed through on their way to Comitán, would have recognized them in the movie. So the barrier cliffs were invented simply to make use of that footage and add one more spurious hazard to their adventures. (The FBI's charge of faking may have referred to this.)

CHAPTER 34

Toniná

Aflag day in my early wanderings in Mexico was my first visit, in 1959, to Na Bolom, the home in San Cristóbal of the aging Danish archaeologist Frans Blom (Don Pancho) and his wife Trudi (whom I spoke of in Chapters 10 and 11). It was on that initial visit that Don Pancho told me about the first ruined city he had ever examined in any detail; this was Toniná, and he strongly encouraged me to visit that site myself. It was near Ocosingo, a small town lying some forty miles northeast of San Cristóbal as the crow flies, but he warned me that getting there would be quite difficult.

The few roads then existing in central Chiapas ran in valleys between mountain ranges, but none of them went in the direction of Ocosingo, so I had to take a bus heading southeast to Comitán (rather than northeast), and there engage the services of an old Jeep's owner-driver. After seven hours of bouncing over rough roads, stopping to open cattle gates, and struggling through mud, this doughty driver deposited me, somewhat bruised, in Ocosingo, a quiet and pleasant town near a stream in a wide and beautiful valley. From the town, the ruins themselves could not be distinguished, but their direction was pointed out to me, and next morning I set out on foot.

It was cool at first, under a cloudless sky, but after two or three hours' walking I began to feel hot and thirsty. Then the small bottle of water I carried ran dry. But at last, after nearly eight hours of walking—and fortunate reorientation by the solitary person I met on the path—I reached the modest ranch-house of Don José Cruz, the site's caretaker, by which time I was quite exhausted, and thirstier than I'd ever been. His kindly spouse produced a large pitcher of lemonade, eight smallish glasses of which I proceeded to drain in succession. And there I was to enjoy their simple hospitality for two nights.

The ancient city of Toniná, which was founded on a south-facing flank of the Ocosingo Valley, is unique in several respects. It consists almost entirely of closely packed structures of no great size, standing on a series of terraces built up on that sloping terrain. The lowermost terrace, or plaza, supports a single large temple, together with a large ball court and another smaller one. In spite of the irregular topography, the buildings and terraces all face about twenty degrees west of south.

We owe the first illustrated description of Toniná to a French explorer, Guillaume Dupaix, who visited the site in 1808; then came John Lloyd Stephens and Frederick Catherwood, who published their brief account of it in 1841. Thereafter, several interested travelers mention it; but it remained for Frans Blom and Oliver La Farge to make the first professional report, published by Tulane University in 1929.

One other visitor of uncertain identity also deserves mention. He is thought to have been Ephraim G. Squier, an American antiquarian and engineer, most of whose activities were centered on lower Central America; but he is regarded as the person most likely to have undertaken, in the 1860s, the tremendous task of transporting from Toniná to the Museo Nacional in Mexico City a carved limestone monolith weighing about two tons.

No other serious attention would be paid to this site until 1972, when the Mission Archéologique et Ethnologique Française au Mexique began a thorough study of both the ruins and the surrounding region; most unfortunately, their permit allowed excavations only in the peripheral areas. The Mission Française then invited me and my Corpus Program colleague at the time, Peter Mathews, to record and publish all the inscribed monuments then known. This we did, filling Volume 6 with them. But most of these pieces were considerably eroded, having lain for centuries on the ground, exposed to the elements.

Then in 1978, a long-term program of excavation and restoration at Toniná was inaugurated by INAH. Juan Yadeún Angulo was appointed as the project's director, and work under his direction would continue for twenty-five years, and sporadically still does. Much of this, I believe, was supported by a very generous private donor, and before long some wonderful sculpture began to emerge, much of it in pristine condition, although most of the pieces had been broken deliberately in antiquity—another aspect of Toniná's singularity.

As a consequence of this long-term project at the ruins, and of recent improvements to the highway running from Palenque to San Cristóbal via Ocosingo, hotel owners in that town began to see the ruins as a likely magnet for tourism and established a

"Friends of the Ruins Society," hoping to raise money to build a better museum. In this they were joined by Armando Cruz, the son of my generous host of two decades earlier, who by then was owner of the ranch.[1] I was there at the time, and naturally attended the society's first public event, a Grand Rodeo, its posters heralding the appearance in person of "Don Pancho, el Charro Francés."

Ocosingo already possessed an adequate rodeo arena, or lienzo, for in this region of countless small ranches there was no shortage of aficionados. When the time came, Don Pancho, a man of about fifty, clad in a rather ugly black jacket embroidered with endless orange loops and spirals, made his entry into the ring amid great applause, and then exhibited a few feats of horsemanship. He was able to get his steed to make a complete turn on the spot, and then to go a few steps backward. Advancing now to the edge of the ring, he was given a microphone. The band struck up, and Don Pancho belted out numerous rancheros with powerful lungs and in thoroughly professional style, amid wild cheering. I met him later and found him a delightful person, François Gouygou by name. He was a herpetologist with a special interest in crocodiles, based at a reptile zoo somewhere north of Marseilles.

Early in 1992, I went to INAH's offices in Mexico to see if I could obtain permission to record some of the monuments discovered by Yadeún, in return for a promise to supply photographs and drawings for his use. And there in the director's office I found, to my surprise, Roberto García Moll as its new incumbent; and he, in answer to my request, surprised me again by expressing doubt that Yadeún would ever publish his finds properly, and in view of this, he would have a permit prepared for me forthwith.

So in March I visited Toniná to see how work was progressing, and the first novelty I saw was the temporary museum. This was a quaint but rather charming group of four tile-roofed adobe buildings built in a square forming a tiny court, following a common Maya plan. Their walls were painted in colors appropriate for the four Maya world-directions. At the time, only one of the buildings was in service as a museum, and its façade was decorated with Yadeún's representation of Maya cosmology, or in his words, the tetra-espacio-temporalidad of various sites, these being dated in an unfamiliar chronology, "A.K." and "D.K." (but perhaps they signify Antes and Después de K.). If "K" was a person, then hints suggested that his or her birth might have occurred in about 650 A.D. Rather mysterious, but it seemed possible that K might stand for Kukulkán, the Maya Culture Hero. (I had imagined his place in history to be more nebulous, or purely legendary).

The wall on the other side of the entrance was embellished by a dazzling diagram of mystic significance: a vortex of lozenges containing the site plans of well-known Maya cities. Variants of this are reproduced in both the books Yadeún has produced for popular consumption, one of them being identified (helpfully) as the "Structure of structures of the territories and the discourses of power in movement."

Another of those four buildings had a raised balcony—roofed, open-sided, and obviously used by Yadeún as his office. In it was sitting one of the guards, with a teenage boy who had chosen to stand on the belly of a recumbent statue lying nearby (Monument 150, in our numeration).[2] Glancing at his desk, I couldn't help noticing two large volumes on its shelf, one at either end. The fat red one was *Das Kapital*, and a fat blue one, the *Book of Mormon*. Under the terrace-cum-office was a storage area, and since there was one stone torso that I needed to photograph I asked the guard to open it for me. There were, in fact, several torsos inside, but they were overlaid by various more-or-less stratified layers of junk. What first met the eye was an assortment of rubber boots, umbrellas, old clothing, and the like. Below this, a rusty bicycle,

34.1 Toniná: how to store fragments of ancient polychrome wall painting.

discarded hand-operated mowers, worn-out wheelbarrows, etc; then a stratum of sacks of cement, two of which had burst, disgorging part of their contents on the bottom layer, the stone torsos. With difficulty, I hauled out one of these for its portrait: it reminded me of a Chicago gangster in his cement overcoat, ready to take the plunge.

Then I walked up to the lowermost terrace, or plaza, of the ruins, and observed activity higher up. Suddenly a hooded figure came running down, the hood streaming behind him being an old sugar sack with one corner pushed into the other, in the style of Guatemalan construction workers. This was Yadeún, who confronted me without deigning to greet me, but simply forbad me to draw or photograph any of his discoveries. Then, rather touchingly, he revealed that he hoped to gain a reputation as an illustrator and photographer; but then went on more aggressively to tell me that he did not wish to see his discoveries published in a work bearing my name. On the contrary, *I* would have to publish *his* drawings in the *Corpus*.

"No," he went on, "you cannot draw or photograph my discoveries. We are in a fresh age now, and your age of communism is past!"

"What *can* you mean by that?" I asked, but was not enlightened. "But in any case," I continued, "here is my INAH *oficio*, which authorizes me to draw and photograph any object within the archaeological zone. Perhaps I should tell you that Roberto García Moll told me just to go ahead and publish the sculpture."

"*Hazlo, entonces* (do so, then)," he growled, and slouched away.

Next morning, another confrontation. I asked whether I might see his drawings of Toniná inscriptions, because some of them, perhaps, could be used in the *Corpus*.

"Oh, ja, ja, ja!" (he has a guttural laugh). "You think I'm a beginner? Let me tell you, I'm an artist and sell my work for good prices. And I'm an architect, and have examined a thousand sites, stone by stone, and drawn them. And I have developed my own technique for recording hieroglyphic inscriptions: I show them at 45 degrees!"

I have now seen a few of these, the most remarkable being that of the imposing statue of "Tzots Choj," which makes him look like Bionic Man. But why Yadeún chose to spell this invented name with a "tz" and a "ts" in the same word is one of many mysteries; another is why he falsified the condition and circumstances in which that remarkable statue was found. A yard-high photographic poster in color was issued, showing the figure complete and recumbent in a stone cist—whereas the three component pieces of the statue were actually found widely separated, and if it really *had* been found in a burial cist, this would have been a first in the Maya area.

Here it is perhaps relevant to mention complaints now being expressed in print about the unavailability (or nonexistence?) of information concerning the exact provenience of sculptural fragments from Toniná, and their association with other artifacts.[3]

A prerequisite for doing this would, of course, be numeration of every monument as it was unearthed, but remarkably, nothing of that kind seems to exist. (That found in our *Corpus* volumes was applied *ad hoc*, as a last resort.)

On my next visit, that same site guard, who knew me well from the time I was working with the French, opened up another building in the quadrangle—one that served both as a repository of sculpture fragments and as Yadeún's living quarters until a short time before. As there was a mattress on the floor and an adjoining bathroom, he suggested that I make myself at home, but, oh dear!—before moving in I had to drive to Ocosingo and buy scrubbing brushes, rubber gloves, disinfectant, detergent, a plastic sheet, and a large garbage can. These would solve one problem—after some distasteful labor; but another was not so readily solved, for on the floor and on shelves there were large numbers of sculptural fragments, all of them representing less than half of the original—but largely unaffected by weathering. Then I couldn't help noticing two other things: first, that even quite heavy pieces were piled one on top of another, without even a piece of cardboard between them to prevent mutual abrasion; and also that not one piece that I examined was identified by a number. So much for provenience...

I've heard that Yadeún accuses me of having forced my way into that building by breaking a lock. Admittedly, I did once force a padlock to open a bedchamber at INAH's camp at Yaxchilan, so as to store in it the contents of the collapsed artifact storage shed, but never at Toniná. There had been no need.

Then, some years later, Yadeún built himself a modest house about half a mile away, with a good view of the ruins, and I summoned up courage to pay him a visit. Conversation was polite, but uninteresting. I did ask him, though, why he had painstakingly landscaped his small plot of ground in such an unusual fashion? Oh, he'd made it into a miniature version of the topography of the Olmec site Las Limas, the previous project entrusted to him. It was at this site, of course, that he found a now famous greenstone sculpture of a man holding an infant in his arms—but that is another project of his that languishes unpublished.

Personally, I have been deeply saddened by my experiences at Toniná. I recognize that my own relations with Yadeún have not been conducted in the highest traditions of diplomacy (and here I should emphasize that the Peabody Museum has played no part in them), but I doubt whether blandishments of any kind could have modified Yadeún's modus operandi. But what I'm unable to understand is how INAH's Consejo de Arqueología can have remained oblivious of it for nearly thirty long years—either oblivious or indifferent concerning the relentless destruction of Toniná's prehistory.

For if Yadeún's previous work raised some doubts about his competence and ability to publish his work (as one might suppose), how could INAH then have appointed him to work unsupervised at, of all Maya sites, Toniná? Was nobody in the higher ranks of Conaculta, INAH's parent entity, at all concerned? Some may explain their inaction as helplessness in the face of union power, but I could name at least one of its senior personnel who was removed from his position without much fuss. But in Yadeún's case, I can't help wondering whether a position at Conaculta held by a close relative of his may have protected him in some degree.

As it was obvious from the beginning that Toniná was anything but a run-of-the-mill Maya city—but instead, one known for its singularity—Yadeún's apparent failure to record any data while excavating its central portion simply means there's little chance of gaining any further understanding of what must have been that ceremonial center's exceptionally interesting past.

CHAPTER 35

Harvard University

N ow I found myself confronted by a difficult task. I'd have to raise money to
endow a permanent position for David Stuart—or, should he decline it, for
another of the very few other suitable candidates. Raising those funds would
not, I felt sure, be easy. Harvard's central fund-raising unit, the Development Office,
had steadfastly refused to lift a finger on behalf of the Corpus Program, much less supply the names of possible donors. It may be hard to believe, but one of its functionaries
had the audacity (and, in my view, lack of simple common sense) to ask a Harvard
alumnus, guilty of making a contribution to the Corpus Program, for an explanation
of his conduct—when he'd already given $3.5 million to found a chair in some other
field of study.

Among successive deans of the Faculty of Arts and Sciences, one of them in particular took a decidedly adverse posture regarding the *Corpus*, for in 1977 the holder
of this powerful position enlightened the director of the Peabody Museum with his
opinion that the Maya Corpus Program "had no place" at Harvard—thereby making me wonder how bitterly the University of Chicago's governing body must have
regretted its embrace, more than a century ago, of the far more ambitious Egyptian
Epigraphic Survey.

After all, by the late 1970s, progress in reading Maya texts had made such encouraging headway that this dean, had he taken the trouble to inquire, might have understood that a program of recording previously unknown texts, correcting or amplifying
the available transcripts of others, and then publishing them, would be sure to revive a
long dormant intellectual field. Fields of academic interest do, after all, wax and wane,
as he must have noticed; where, for example, does philology stand just now, and what
has happened to the funding it once had?

No one could doubt that the Peabody Museum, with its superb library and vast photographic archives of Maya material, could become a magnet for graduate students with dreams of taking part in the world's last great decipherment. For here, at the Peabody, were unequaled resources: Teobert Maler's marvelous photographs of Maya inscriptions; those, too, of the Carnegie Institution of Washington's Division of Historical Research; and, of course, the expanding files of the Maya Corpus Program. Nowhere else in the world could one find such abundant data of this kind, and already there were persuasive indications that Maya texts might qualify as a complete writing system, capable of making a full record of the spoken word.

Well, by 2006, there were at last signs of increasing interest in this field on Harvard's part, with a new undergraduate course on Maya epigraphy attracting an enrollment of forty. But in retrospect, one is reminded that if university deans can be blind, so, half a century ago, could a president of the Carnegie Institution of Washington. As I have mentioned, one of the institution's various divisions was that of Historical Research, which incorporated the former Department of Archaeology. This was best known to the public for its excavations in the 1930s at Chichén Itzá, and the excellent restoration work it did there; but basic research was by no means neglected, nor was fieldwork at other Maya sites.

When the Second World War ended, the CIW's field operations restarted at the sprawling remains of Mayapan—another huge Maya metropolis in Yucatán. This site did have architectural remains worthy of restoration (and recently, work has been done there by various institutions), but instead of doing this, Alfred Kidder, director of the Carnegie's Department of Archaeology, perversely—it seemed—elected to waste the archaeologists' time by having them scrabble about among the scant vestiges of ordinary dwellings. That, at least, was the view of the distinguished physicist Vannevar Bush, Carnegie's president in 1956.

Tania Proskouriakoff once described to me a Carnegie Institution meeting at which the heads of its various divisions reported on their recent work to Bush and the Carnegie trustees. When it was the turn of Alfred Kidder, he remarked (wryly, I suppose) that scientists in other fields seemed to work out of a sense of mission and obligation to the public, but as for archaeologists, the truth was that they simply liked to dig. At this, Bush scowled, and made no further mention of that department in his discussions. Tania said that although she saw the writing on the wall, Kidder didn't. (But when the blow fell, Kidder did succeed in blackmailing Bush into providing a small continuing salary for the three younger and less prosperous members—Tania, Ed Shook, and Anna Shepherd—under the threat of denunciation before the Society of American Professors.)

35.1 Conversation with Tania and Harry Pollock on the steps to the Tozzer courtyard, 1976. Photo by Hillel Burger, courtesy of the Peabody Museum, Harvard University.

It was certainly unfortunate that the Carnegie withdrew from archaeology, for the thrust of future archaeological research in Mesoamerica would cover just the field of activity that Kidder had indicated: investigation of house mounds, settlement patterns, small workshops, and the like, rather than monumental architecture.

For the Peabody Museum, however, that ill wind did blow good. As mentioned earlier, the CIW's Department of Archaeology's offices had migrated from Washington, D.C., to Cambridge, and its entire collection of documents, artifacts, sherds, plans, photographs and so forth subsequently became the property of the Peabody Museum. Copyright was not an issue because the Carnegie never deigned to copyright anything, as it had no interest in profit.

Owing to this gift, and the Peabody's own involvement in Maya archaeology from as early as 1887, its photographic archives and other materials of interest to the Corpus Program came to exceed by a large margin those of any other institution. The museum also benefited enormously when several old Carnegie hands found refuge there themselves, namely Harry Pollock, Tatiana Proskouriakoff, and the Smith brothers (Bob and Ledyard), all of whom continued working there productively for many years.

35.2 *Lunch in Maya Corpus office, Room K, with weavers from San Antonio, Aguas Calientes, Guatemala, and Peter Mathews, November 1979.*

Stephen Williams, the museum's director when I joined it, had quickly understood the potential of hieroglyphic inscriptions to illuminate more than a thousand years of what then was still prehistory, as did Harry Pollock, but some needed more persuasion. Our great Bowditch Professor of Mesoamerican Archaeology, the late Gordon R. Willey, confessed, in a note he sent me a few years before he died, that he had been slow in appreciating the Corpus Program's potential contributions to archaeology as a whole, and to Harvard's Department of Anthropology in particular. But neither Gordon nor any other academic or administrator could be seriously reproached for failing to introduce the study of Maya writing into the curriculum in the 1960s, because at that time this script was still far from being legible enough for formal instruction. Nevertheless, he did prevail upon Peter Mathews (then a Corpus colleague of mine) to join him in giving a graduate seminar that touched on inscriptions in general and on our work.

When David Stuart joined me on the Corpus, he made it clear that he had a strong desire to do some teaching. He presented this as a medium-term objective, for in fact there was no possibility of his doing so at once, as he knew. But even if his time and the payment of his salary were to be shared in some agreed proportion between the Corpus Program and the Department of Anthropology, the arrangement would still be unstable.

There was really only one solution: acquisition of sufficient funds to establish an independent position for him. In any case, apart from the question of time spent in teaching, Dave and his family couldn't be expected to rely indefinitely upon uncertain NEH or other short-term grants.

For this problem to be solved I would need to raise at least $1.5 million, or preferably $2 million—but how could this be done, without Harvard's help? The challenge haunted me. Fortunately, a partial solution was found, and the chain of events leading to it is perhaps worth telling, as these could never have been foreseen.

I have described that tragic event at the ruins of La Naya when Pedro Arturo Sierra was shot dead by looters, and I've mentioned the efforts we made to transport a few Maya monuments out of the jungle to safety. These latter operations were funded by "Operación Rescate," an outgrowth of the Asociación Tikal, an ad hoc group consisting mostly of Americans and Europeans living in Guatemala.

The largest contribution to this operation had come from the Plumsock Fund, based in Pennsylvania, and it came through the agency of Chris Lutz, then a doctoral candidate in Latin American history, with a special interest in colonial Central America. It was his stepmother who had established this fund in the late 1950s.

35.3 Evelyn Bartlett emerging from the Concord's cockpit, having had a word with the pilot.

I suppose it was the presence of someone from an American university at the scene of the murder that prompted the U.S. press to report the story, the *Wall Street Journal* doing so on its front page, and mentioning my name. By chance the Lutz family lawyer in Indianapolis saw this and sent the clipping to Chris and his wife Sally, neither of whom knew me—with the unexpected result that when, in August 1971, a baby boy was born to them in Guatemala City, the name they chose for him was Ian.

Then, one Saturday evening in about 1980, I attended a formal dinner given by my friend Robert Pirie and his wife, Dierdre. On my left at their splendid table was a lady named Mrs. Bartlett, who at ninety-one made no secret of her age but certainly didn't show it—either in her conversation or her looks—for she had bright eyes, the most beautiful skin for an old lady, and a broad-minded view of things. Naturally, she engaged in talk first of all with her host, but when the time came for a general switching to our other neighbors at table and she turned to me, I couldn't resist telling her, as an opening gambit, that although she might not know it, she had a young step-great-grandson who was named after me. Explanation was requested, conversation flowed, and I became fascinated by this lively and intelligent woman.

Evelyn Bartlett lived in Massachusetts on the North Shore, where she had a farm, and migrated seasonally to another home in Fort Lauderdale. Born Evelyn Fortune, she had grown up in Indianapolis, and there married Eli Lilly, son of J. K. and grandson of Colonel Eli, founder of the Indianapolis pharmaceutical company. This business prospered, as needs no saying, and following Evelyn's engagement her father had persuaded his friend J. K. to sell him some of the company's otherwise closely held shares for her, as a future member of the family.

The shares went from strength to strength; but the same could not be said of the marriage. Some years later, Evelyn divorced Eli without requesting alimony, but her father firmly resisted attempts by the Lillys to regain possession of the shares. In time, these would be inherited by Evelyn and Eli's only child, a daughter named Evie; but she, unfortunately, would be blessed neither with offspring, nor indeed with a happy life. She married three times, her third husband being Whitey Lutz, the father of Chris Lutz by his first wife.

After divorcing Eli Lilly, Evelyn had married Frederic Bartlett, a Chicago-born widower, and an artist of some note. His first wife had been the daughter of another Chicagoan, Hugh Taylor Birch, who had fled his native city in 1892 out of dread of the huge influx of visitors from the four corners of the earth who would soon be crowding into Chicago to visit the World's Columbian Exposition.

He was to find refuge in a very sparsely populated part of Florida, and there made new friends. But soon he was alarming them by purchasing a tract of uninhabited land near a little-known inlet on the Gulf Coast. This, for sure, was throwing money away! Many years later, though, some of this land would be sold, some given as a park to the town that had sprung up there, and some to a university. About twenty acres were retained, and this land, lying between the coastal road and the Inland Waterway, became what Evelyn called her "little hideaway." (The town, incidentally, was Fort Lauderdale!)

In the mid-1950s, her daughter Evie (later Lutz) had settled at a farm in Pennsylvania named Plumsock, and on setting up a charitable foundation, gave this name to it. Upon her death, direction of the Plumsock Fund became the responsibility of Whitey Lutz's son, Chris, then a doctoral candidate in Latin American history, whose area of special interest was colonial Central America. So it came about that with access to Plumsock funds, Chris was able to arrange the endowment in 1978 of a new organization called CIRMA, its Spanish acronym signifying "Center for Regional Investigations in Mesoamerica." This would be a research center with headquarters in Antigua, Guatemala.

35.4 Mrs. Evelyn Bartlett at her Fort Lauderdale home.

Chris had already become alarmed about the rising wave of depredations by looters, and in view of this, arranged for the Plumsock Fund to contribute about ten thousand dollars to the Asociación Tikal for Operación Rescate. It was a contribution from Associación Tikal that had enabled Eric and me to remove that large Ucanal stela and the smaller ones from El Zapote, and deliver them to the National Museum of Archaeology and Ethnography in Guatemala City. This, as Chris affirms, is why he and Sally, reacting to the newspaper accounts of Pedro's murder and my own fortunate survival, chose for their new baby the name I bear.

As a result of this apparently chance encounter (although it's possible that Bob had arranged the placement at that dinner with some thought), Evelyn invited me to visit her farm, and then to lunch or dinner a few times; and later, as my departure for another season of work in Guatemala drew near, she invited me to drop in at her "hideaway" in Fort Lauderdale on my way south.

The taxi from the airport took me along Ocean Drive, passing a series of huge and brilliantly lit hotels, but then I noticed that farther ahead the roadway was dark. I could only imagine there had been a power outage; but on reaching that area, not only were there no streetlights, but no hotels either—just a chain-link fence with sea grape growing over it. So this was Evelyn's little hideaway, Bonnet House. There, she had orchids, black swans, wild monkeys—and a French chef. But she was a star, and she enjoyed life to the full.[1]

Encouraged by her step-grandson, and obliquely seconded by me, she began to make annual contributions to the Corpus Program, and then one of a million dollars, which, with other money already in hand, was sufficient to create the Bartlett Curatorship for David Stuart. For me, and even more for him, this was an enormous relief, because David, who could have walked into any vacant tenured position years earlier, had held out, partly from wanting to continue working in the building where unequaled archives of Maya inscriptions were at hand, and partly because this position, while allowing him to teach, did not oblige him to teach three courses. So he was able to devote much more time on his researches in decipherment than ever he could have as a professor.

But a few years later David moved on to the University of Texas at Austin, which had made him an offer hard to refuse. We miss him, but I find consolation in the existence now of a larger pool of suitable colleagues than there was when he joined the Corpus Program fifteen years earlier. His departure made necessary some thought about the program's future.

A new director would have to be appointed, and this has now been done. But we still need to secure another endowment for a second worker in this vineyard, or else—even with other epigraphers contributing material for new fascicles, the Corpus Program will not finish its work for fifty years at least.

Clearly, both members of the program will have to be calligraphers—for computer-generated drawings could never replace those drawn by hand; and one of them must be an epigrapher. I do, however, foresee significant changes being made in the operations of the Corpus. For one thing, much less of the immensely time-consuming exploration and mapping of sites now remains to be done, since archaeologists from universities and national anthropological institutes have been working at many sites during the last two decades; they will have mapped many sites—and mapping is now much quicker and easier than it was. In fact, fieldwork of this kind has also become very much easier as travel and communication in the jungles of Petén and southern Campeche have improved beyond all recognition.

Another harbinger of a new era has also arrived: digital photography. This will certainly eliminate the unfortunate proportion of photographic images that in the past have proved upon development to be unsatisfactory. Eric von Euw and I used to use four-by-five-inch cameras with Polaroid film; these had one great advantage: immediate proof of failure or success. But I gave it up because the clumsy camera and tripod made many shots impracticable—such as those one sometimes needs to take while perched on an improvised and shaky platform supported by saplings lashed together.

Such developments give me hope that the hitherto sluggish rate of fascicle production will increase considerably. I also agree with the new director, Barbara Fash, that the time has come for inviting epigraphers at other institutions to submit material for publication in the *Corpus*, so long as it conforms to house style. But drawings of complicated Maya monuments done for publication will, I believe (and trust), always be done by hand. Such a drawing may in extreme cases take fifty hours of work, but I can see no possible alternative.

I've said nothing about my living conditions in Cambridge—for these must have a bearing on anyone's general satisfaction with life. My goal from the beginning had been to find a small apartment within ten minutes' walk of the museum, because, to my mind, owning a car would be an unnecessary extravagance—a car, after all, could easily be hired when needed. But since the Guttman Foundation's stipend was quite generous, I moved into comfortable quarters an easy walk from the museum, only to realize quite soon that paying rent for it during months of absence in the field was too

485

wasteful. I would have to find a smaller one—but then, by a stroke of luck, my problem was solved.

I heard that the art historian W. G. Constable, by then retired as Curator of Paintings at the Boston Museum of Fine Arts, and his wife Olivia, both English, were still living in Cambridge. I had never met them, nor did I have a formal introduction, but brashly visited them on the strength of an encounter that David Crawford had had with "WG" (as he was known) about forty years earlier. As it happened, Olivia was on the lookout for a paying guest, now that she was making regular visits to see her hundred-year-old mother in London—while WG, for his part, was growing old and rather deaf. The presence of someone else in the house would certainly ease her worries while on the other side of the Atlantic.

So I was taken in as a paying guest and given the bedroom that one of their two sons had occupied, both of them having flown the nest several years earlier. I breakfasted with Olivia every morning, and in the evening often met their friends. This delightful arrangement continued for many years, but then WG died, and only a few years later, so did Olivia, leaving a great hole in my Cambridge life.

Fortunately, a fresh opportunity would present itself: young acquaintances who were living in a rented apartment only five minutes' walk from the Peabody Museum were moving out: so I moved in. The motives for their departure were easy to understand, since the condition of this apartment was simply dreadful.

Number 16 Mellen Street had been one-half of a wooden two-unit building. When, or by whom, that half had been converted into three apartments I don't know, but the workmanship of that young man's unfinished alterations in apartment number 1 was amateur, to say the least, and the general condition of the whole quite appalling. One wall of what had been the dining room had never been properly finished; instead, the wooden studs had been spanned with hardboard, and then covered with brown cork tiles, some of which were held in place with glue, others with adhesive tape.

A leak in the bathroom shower had rotted the wooden framework supporting the tiles around the bath at the faucet end—so they, too, were now held in place with adhesive tape. Rainwater crashing from blocked gutters in the roof and splashing up from the metal bulkhead of the basement had rotted a window frame, and even destroyed the interior wall plaster beneath it, leaving a large patch of exposed laths. There were only three wall switches in the whole apartment, one in the kitchen, one in the bathroom, and one in what had originally been the dining room, so that on entering after dark I had to grope around, feeling for a desk lamp and its little rotary switch without knocking it over. With only a thin carpet on the floor of the living room, the entrance door, which opened inward, grounded at forty-five degrees . . . but it would be tedious to enumerate all of the apartment's shortcomings.

The house belonged to Harvard Real Estate—as does most of the housing within a wide radius around the university. This is a company owned by Harvard University, but fiscally isolated from the university proper in order to preserve the latter's non-profit-making status. How, then, could such appalling deterioration have occurred? Undoubtedly, one important factor had been the City of Cambridge's rent-control ordinance—the abolition of which was then regarded as imminent.

I hadn't been living there long before I found, on returning one evening, that a large portion of the ceiling had collapsed on the chair in which I usually sat in the evening while reading. I called HRE to report this, and a man came round to assess the problem, bringing with him an instrument to test my bedroom ceiling (this was a broomstick: you push it gently up to the ceiling, then push harder, and if it yields, then the ceiling is hanging like a hammock, and ready to crash—as this and other ceiling had been).

"We'll have these ceilings replaced expeditiously," I was told, "but it will cost you two thousand dollars."

"What! Cost *me*? Surely this is maintenance?"

"No, it's an improvement!"

Too late, it crossed my mind that perhaps I should have inquired whether, if the floor had collapsed, replacement of that, too, would also count as an improvement?

And on the topic of floors, the one in the kitchen merits description, for just in front of the sink, the linoleum had been worn right through, as had two of the layers of plywood beneath it. Of course I had to remove all of the lino, but before putting down new flooring, I mixed a pint of epoxy, and poured it into the depression, thereby obtaining a flat surface upon which to lay new flooring.

Then I became aware that the electrical wiring was so ancient as to be danger-ous, while also noticing that both the three-pin outlets mounted on baseboards were in homemade aluminum boxes. Opening them, I found that in neither of them had the third pin been grounded! I brought this astonishing and dangerous anomaly to the attention of HRE, and was assured that they would send around electricians expedi-tiously to rewire the whole apartment.

"But of course, this will cost you about eight thousand dollars."

"*What*! You can't be serious. Cost *me*?"

"Oh, don't worry, this can be paid over a period of ten years, but of course you will be paying interest at 15 percent on the unpaid portion of the charges."

I could scarcely believe I was hearing such a claim. Who could ever imagine that a unit of an otherwise respectable university would engage in usury—in the accepted modern sense of demanding an exorbitant and unconscionable interest rate? And how, in the first place, could these rack-rent landlords have even considered charging the tenant for such a basic and necessary repair?

But now I was in a quandary. Either I'd have to move out, and perhaps find myself living farther away from the museum (and therefore less inclined to return to work after supper, especially in winter)—or else submit to extortion.

There was, however, a third way. I could rewire the apartment myself. To do so would, I felt sure, violate the rules, but I couldn't let matters stand as they were—and if I simply gave up the tenancy, the next inhabitant would be equally endangered, physically and financially! So, once I had begun, I didn't confine my work to replacing the old and dangerous wiring; I expanded it, even going so far as to install a light switch inside the front door—surely a novelty in such a slum!

Of course, the electricity company's policy of agreeing to cut the current at the external circuit breaker only at the request of a qualified electrician is eminently sensible, so the fact that the juice remained on while I was at work did add a little spice to the operation, but all went well. The work certainly cost me a lot of time and a lot of wriggling under floors, and quite a lot of money, but nothing like that eight thousand dollars plus interest (which if paid over ten years in installments would have added between five and six thousand to the bill).

Just for the experience, I decided to use the BX wiring system, which has the insulated wires run through flexible metal conduits—a system much more difficult to install, and much more expensive, but it is the Rolls-Royce of wiring. Installing this was a challenge, but on inviting a qualified electrician to inspect my work when finished, I was pleased by his assessment that it was "as good as it possibly could be." And in case anyone doubted that I had really rewired the whole apartment myself, I soldered all the connections in the wiring, as proof!

Gradually my improvements and redecorating made the apartment quite satisfactory, and more to my taste—more "homey" than any other would be (a bit shabby here and there, but if you've been brought up in an ancient house, that seems like home!) But with the end of rent control, HRE immediately began raising the rent, and soon I would find myself paying the same rent as my neighbors in other units of the building, on a basis of square footage—but these had been completely renovated, with oak trim, walls moved, entirely new kitchens and bathrooms, etc.

When I complained to HRE (or Harvard Housing, as it's now called), I was told that each unit was always thoroughly cleaned out and inspected before a new tenant moved in. Well, the falsity of this claim would shine forth when I happened to move a small bookcase that I had placed, soon after moving in, to cover an area beneath a recess in a wall (resulting from the later construction of a stairway in the other half of the building)—and what did I find there?

Two cards seven inches square, one heavily imprinted with the word "COAL," in black, and the other with "ICE from Fresh Pond" in red. These, I need hardly explain, take one back to the 1920s, when householders lacked gas stoves and refrigerators—nor would they, in that depressed area, have had telephones for ordering more of what were then essential commodities. Instead, they had to rely on dealers roaming the streets on their horse-drawn wagons, while scanning kitchen windows for any cards displayed there of just the kind I had found.

Really, I am ashamed of Harvard Real Estate—and its managers should themselves feel deep shame. In all the years I had that apartment, the only money spent on it by Harvard, in my recollection, was the installation of a smoke detector, and in the kitchen, a new refrigerator and gas stove. Meanwhile, another task awaited me every fall: cleaning the leaves from the gutters. The roof spanning both halves of the building was flat and covered with sheet-rubber. This had a general tilt toward my side of the building, so that by late November leaves had blocked the gutters and down-pipes on my side, causing the water to cascade noisily onto the metal bulkhead of the basement. So the task of clearing those gutters fell to me, as the tenant most affected. Access by stairway was not possible without going through the third-floor apartment—an approach not always available—so it was much simpler to climb a vertical outside ladder of iron. Then one day I noticed that one of the two bolts attaching the top of the vertical ladder to the building's wooden siding had pulled out from the half-rotten wood...

Enough said...

CHAPTER 36

Recent Discoveries

Among the treasures of Maya sculpture that began to appear in American and European collections in the 1960s, one group of small tablets attracted special attention. They were beautifully carved, consistent in style, of the same grayish stone—and had come to rest in New York City, Chicago, Zurich, Paris, Portland (Maine), and elsewhere. Their provenience, however, was a complete mystery. While some were all-glyphic, others depicted ballgame players in action. The largest dimension of any of them was about twenty inches, and each had been reduced to a thickness of between one and a half and three inches. My erstwhile colleague Peter Mathews, the first to study these as a group, provided a temporary name for their phantom source: "Site Q"—for "query."[1]

While studying the tablets themselves, now widely dispersed in collections, I noticed another trait they had in common, and that was the method employed for reducing their weight, for this was unique in my experience. Inspection of their backs revealed that in each of them a circular saw had been used to cut in from all four edges toward the center. The saw had evidently been hand held, and of too small a radius to cut through more than about 45 percent of the tablet's lesser dimension, so that after the sawing, a narrow neck of uncut stone had remained in the center of each. This, presumably, would then have been snapped by no more than a tap with a rubber mallet on one border of the tablet.

But then, as decipherment progressed and personal names began to be identified in hieroglyphic texts, the origin of these tablets became even more mysterious, for none of the names of personages found in them appeared in texts from known sites. Finding their source now became a great challenge.

I bore this in mind in the course of my travels. One clue that initially seemed promising was the excellent quality of the stone, for at first sight, this would rule out large areas of the Maya lowlands as their source; but then the well-attested hauling of tremendously heavy shafts of stone from distant quarries to Calakmul (where the local stone is of wretched quality) made this consideration worthless.

In the course of more than forty seasons in Petén, I've naturally met and chatted with large numbers of people familiar with those forests, and from them heard many stories of uncertain reliability about ruins, caves, smugglers, good men and bad, mysterious natural phenomena, and suchlike topics of interest. Chains of acquaintances have also formed that seemed at first sight unlikely to be important; but because useful information has sometimes come my way through such links, I've tried to take note of them. As people say, "contingency is all," and here is an example of its workings.

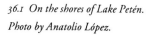

36.1 On the shores of Lake Petén.
Photo by Anatolio López.

Standing one day on the shore of Laguna Petén-Itza in San Andrés, near my little house, I noticed a group of young tourists leaving in a launch. On asking who they might be, I was told they had just returned from visiting the ruins of El Perú, traveling "chiclero fashion"—that is, on foot with pack mules, hammocks, locally made rubberized bags for their sleeping gear, etc. Led by a young man with a French accent, they had a decidedly New Age look and aroma about them.

A year passed, and once again I was on the foreshore at San Andrés, waiting for a boat to San Benito. Having waited long enough under a hot sun to develop a thirst, I retreated to a nearby bar for a cold beer, and who should serve me but the same young Frenchman. He told me his name, Santiago Billi, and when I asked how he had managed to have his tourist visa extended for a whole year or more, he told me that he'd entered Guatemala from Mexico by coming up the Río San Pedro, but the official at the border had failed to put a stamp in his passport requiring him to report to an immigration office within thirty days. So he just stayed.

On meeting him again a year later, this time in Antigua, Guatemala, he told me that he had, at long last, been obliged to leave the country; but on returning to his parents' home in Paris and telling them about this, they exclaimed, "Really, didn't you know that you were *born* in Guatemala?"

He didn't; but now at least he was back in Petén as a Guatemalan resident, and currently employed by Conservation International to search for nesting pairs of macaws along the upper reaches of the Río San Pedro and its tributaries. (Macaws were already dangerously near extinction owing to widespread theft of their nestlings, for these, when full grown, had—woefully—become essential items in the furnishing of high-suburban homes.)

Then on 15 February 1997, I noted in my journal: "Today I ran into Santiago Billi again, who tells me he has found a large site with cut-up stelae, north of the Río Chocop at a place called Lo Veremos." (The Chocop rises about fifteen miles north of Paso Caballos, flows west, then turns south to empty into the San Pedro.) Then I noted, "Could this be Site Q? There's a good chance."

Santiago and I agreed that we couldn't schedule a visit to this site before Easter, in my case because I was to spend Easter week with friends at Punta Pájaros in Quintana Roo. So I called Jim Nations, of Conservation International, and we resolved to make the trip in mid-May. Jim then began studying the latest radar mapping of that general area and thought he could distinguish a Maya sacbe, or causeway, leading from a small lagoon perhaps near Lo Veremos.

The guide that Santiago found us for this trip was a Carmelita man named Carlos Catalán, a man with considerable presence, and a very fast talker. Tall and thin, with a long face, a narrow hawk-like nose and close-cropped hair, he emanated strength and authority. He opened the conversation with the same questions (I imagine) that he put to tourist groups, such as how we proposed to purify the drinking water.

"Drink it straight out of the lake," I replied in macho style, and taking the initiative managed to learn more about his history. Born in Guatemala City, he'd become hot-headed in the turbulent sixties. When his family moved to Carmelita, Carlos was soon earning his living by hunting jaguars and alligators, and also digging ruins—but suddenly he became "green," and opposed all the activities in which he had formerly been engaged.

He agreed to come with us, but wanted to know the names of our party. When I mentioned Anatolio López he stiffened—not, as I soon learned, that he distrusted him; rather, he was trying to restrict information about places of interest in the Carmelita area to local guides; otherwise, he said, tour guides from Flores would be bringing tourists in, and on leaving would have benefited the Carmelita economy only to the extent of a few Cokes. I was able to assure him that Anatolio played no part in the tourist industry.

Now I had to find a four-wheel-drive vehicle large enough for all of us (as Jim Nations, a colleague of his Tom Seever, and David Stuart would also be coming)—plus equipment and supplies, and after touring the rental agencies had to settle for a twin-cab Mitsubishi, doing so reluctantly, as it had very poor clearance.

Next morning, we set off early, and made good time to Carmelita, and then headed off west down a fairly difficult track, with some desvios (bypasses cut round fallen trees). One of these resulted in a tire being punctured by the cut stem of a sapling, and only then did I realize, to my embarrassment and shame, that I hadn't inspected the tires before leaving—but then, the whole trip had of necessity been organized hastily. Now I saw that these tires were of just a few ply, and suitable only for cruising California boulevards. The spare was also a disgrace, a retread worn almost smooth and beginning to peel.

On reaching the end of the track at a spot named Nuevo León, two horses (one with a foal) were awaiting us by prior arrangement. Some sorting and repacking of boxes was called for, and while doing this we noticed that another tire was losing pressure, putting us in a position that might seem hopeless. *How* I blamed myself for not having brought my electric tire inflator. But miraculously a solution was at hand. One of the men rolled the two wheels, one after the other, to a nearby camp of shateros, who readily agreed to take the wheels to Flores for repair and inflation on their next trip to deliver their produce. But who could have imagined that such a service would be available deep in the forest? And all they charged was two dollars!

Next morning we walked in to Lo Veremos in about three hours, and found a good camping spot at the edge of the lake. Soon after settling in, David and I went off to look at a stela fragment lying near our camp, and in no time David became very excited, for here was the name of a ruler named Jaguar-Paw-Smoke who is also mentioned in the Art Institute of Chicago's Site Q panel. So perhaps, at long last, we had found Site Q!

After a morning of walking around the ruins, I became worried that this site might be too small and unimportant to be the source of those extraordinary panels, even though two stelae and four sculptured altars had also come to light—one of the latter bearing a very long text, but unfortunately too weathered to be more than partially legible. The site was certainly modest in size, consisting mainly of one large plaza, with a sizeable acropolis in its northwest corner, a row of five small and apparently identical temples to the southeast, and one outlying group. A search for mounds farther out was unsuccessful. As for the acropolis, this had been so thoroughly dug up that it was impossible to form any idea of the buildings it had once supported, but the heavy digging at its top did suggest that the looters had found treasures there of some kind.

36.2 At La Corona with David Stuart and Anatolio López. Photo courtesy of D. Stuart.

It was true that with the eye of faith one could see where a flight of steps might have ascended the long mound forming the west side of the plaza (bearing in mind that the set of stones may have been part of a stairway), while in its vicinity there were a few small and more or less rectangular plaques of fine-grained gray stone. On returning to Flores, Dave lamented that he had not thought to bring one of these out as a specimen to compare microscopically with one from a Site Q tablet. And then, we thought the name bestowed on this place by chicleros, "Lo Veremos" ("We'll see"), was scarcely adequate, even if prophetic, so Dave renamed it "La Corona," because one of our men had described the row of five little pyramids as resembling a crown.[2]

Word that a Site Q personal name had been found on a monument still in situ spread rapidly, and within a few months a British documentary film producer, Chris Ledger of Granite Productions, let me know that he would be taking a camera crew into La Corona in August to make a program about the discovery. On meeting him in London in June, I advised him emphatically that the rains of July would make the track quite impassable for vehicles. But he was not to be deterred: their departure date was immutable because the film's airing was firmly set for November.

I was far from wishing to discourage him, of course, for he might save us a lot of trouble by bringing back one of those little plain tablets as a sample of local stone to compare with one from a sculptured Site Q tablet. Under these circumstances, the only advice I could give was to get in touch with Bernie Mittelstaedt, who lives near San Andrés and specializes in taking tourists to places in Petén that are impossible to reach by car without four-wheel drive, high clearance, and a winch. To this end he seems to have explored a large number of old logging trocopasses, perhaps also plotting their course by Global Positioning System.

Well, the mules carrying Granite's camping gear and foodstuffs did get through, by dint of heroic struggles, and Bernie succeeded in transporting Chris and the camera crew to the site. They brought back a stone sample as requested, and Dave managed to persuade the director of the University of Maine's Art Gallery, where a Site Q tablet is preserved, to provide him with a chip taken from its back. Then the two specimens were sent to a geologist at the University of Manchester and, gratifyingly, the results were sufficiently similar to confirm, at least tentatively, that La Corona is the fabled Site Q.[3]

The tragic aspect of this story is that a few months later Carlos Catalán was murdered, for motives unknown.

Just after I'd come back from Guatemala late in May 1997, Bill Saturno, who had recently gained a Harvard Ph.D. in archaeology, also returned, having spent a few months wandering about in Petén as a Corpus associate in search of sites with inscribed monuments. He was bursting to tell us about his experiences. At some point, he had been told of a site with large mounds situated not far north of Xultun (a huge, well-known, and heavily looted Maya metropolis that lies a little more than halfway between Tikal and the northwest corner of Petén).

This site would be difficult to reach quickly, so Bill engaged Bernie Mittelstaedt's services. They reached Xultun, and then, after a grueling walk getting lost on the trail in torrid heat (made worse by scarcity of drinking water), they reached the site, and made their way round the tall pyramid. Disappointingly, no discernible architectural features remained, but the entrance to a large tunnel made by looters could not be overlooked. Entering it to seek relief from the heat, they found it continued for a considerable distance in a zigzag but apparently fruitless search for tombs.

Then, quite close to the entrance, Bill noticed, in sweeping his flashlight about, that the looters' tunneling had disclosed a patch of mural painting, still quite well preserved. It measured no more than about thirty inches wide, but its quality was extraordinary, and stylistically of very early date.

Bill hurried back to Cambridge, and every Mayanist shown his photograph of the mural was astonished. There was, however, some concern that difficulties with the Guatemalan authorities might ensue. Nonarchaeologists are at liberty to wander where they will; but for archaeologists the situation is different. Strictly speaking, prior permission is required before one wanders about in an unguarded ruined city.

Having decided that we should come clean as soon as possible, I flew down to Guatemala City with Bill just two days later. At Patrimonio Cultural, the organization that has replaced the former Instituto de Antropología é Historia, the director was a man who had only recently taken up that position. Having previously been in charge of the National Archives, he couldn't be expected to have a wide knowledge of his new domain, but he agreed to see us, and in our talk I emphasized the importance of establishing guards at the site—to forestall a possible return of looters who might be planning to remove that small but exquisite patch of mural painting.

Next, I was hoping to speak with the director of Monumentos Prehispánicos, of the archaeology division of Patrimonio Cultural. This was Nora López, an archaeologist I had never met; but I was told she had broken her Achilles tendon, had undergone surgery, and was laid up at home.

When called by telephone, she kindly invited me to come and see her. I explained the situation, and told her what we'd like to do, namely, open a track for four-wheel-drive vehicles to those ruins without felling any substantial trees; build a small camp for guards near the temple concerned; and block up the tunnel mouth—this, for three reasons: to make it rather more difficult for looters to enter; to kill off the large bats that now inhabited the extensive network of tunnels; and to stabilize the relative humidity. Then I asked her,

"How do you suggest that I should set about obtaining permission to do all this?"

"Just go and do it, that's all," she replied.

Well, this was the most astonishing snap decision by a government official that I've ever heard—but I couldn't help reflecting that her answer might have been different if I'd come from a museum known for accepting donations of looted artifacts.

Bill returned to Cambridge next day, and thereafter Anatolio and I then engaged a young man from San Andrés, and the three of us drove off, first to Uaxactún, and then down a seemingly endless logging track to the ruins of Xultun. We parked the car and set out on foot for San Bartolo. Bill had lent me his pocket GPS, which had the coordinates of the site in its memory under the code BTL (for "Bartolo"), and this, if punched in, would indicate the actual distance and bearing of the site at that moment. But I'd failed to ask him how to operate the thing, and was therefore at a loss, for it resembled not at all my early-model instrument, and had no alpha-numeric keys. What a debacle! So I sat down and punched the buttons blindly and despairingly for an age, like the proverbial monkey trying to write a Shakespeare sonnet. Then suddenly that crucial information popped up, and we resumed our march. Of course, I had to go through this same humiliating and time-wasting procedure a few more times before reaching our goal.

On completing our inspection, we started back, taking a somewhat different route, which Anatolio thought would be shorter. But in fact it led us through a dried-up bajo of an unusual kind, consisting of little grassy islets a yard or more across, separated by deep gullies that during the rainy season would be filled with water. We had to leap from one to another, making progress slow and exhausting—until Anatolio admitted that his decision had been a mistake, and we backtracked. (For Anatolio, a misjudgment of this kind was extremely unusual.)

It was a really hot day in May, the hottest month in Petén. I had brought a water canteen but hadn't filled it completely. Anatolio and the young lad had brought even less water, so I had given them some of mine. I had also neglected to bring salt tablets. We plodded on, and I began to feel extremely weary.

"Anatolio," I called out, "I'm exhausted. I must rest for five minutes."

Ten minutes later, I resumed the march, not feeling refreshed at all, and after another ten minutes I called out,

"Look, I'm too tired to go any farther. So go on, you two, and take my water canteen. Fill it up from the gallon bottle in the car. And put some salt in it from our box of food supplies. I'll wait for you here."

I lay down, eying with interest the occasional vulture circling overhead. Time passed, and the sun went down. On our way out, Anatolio had not used his machete to mark our track, leaving instead a *camino tronchado*—that is, a track marked only by doubling stalks over, preferably those of a plant with very large leaves with silvery undersides that show up well. So I did wonder whether he or the lad would, as it grew dark, have some difficulty in following the path we had taken.

But no, this young man from San Andrés (whose name I'm sorry to have forgotten) did return—alone, for Anatolio was also feeling exhausted. Then I learned how difficult it is at night to follow someone in the bush who is lighting the way with a very small flashlight; and it's no less difficult if you try walking in front.

36.3 At San Bartolo with Bill Saturno. Photo by Horacio
Martínez, courtesy of the San Bartolo Project.

Finally, on reaching the car, all we had to do was drive seventy-five miles back to San Andrés, half of it along a truckpath. I was gritting my teeth to fight off sleep long before arriving.

The next few days were hectic with shopping and then transporting our purchases to the temporary camping spot we had chosen for the guards. This was close to an aguada and to the beginning of the path we had taken to the ruins. (Later, the guards would open a vehicle track leading to a permanent campsite close to the ruins.) We brought in a 250-liter plastic water butt, large amounts of food supplies, kerosene lamps, plastic sheeting for roofing the short-term camp, a first-aid kit, a horse and its pack-saddle, girth, and halter—these, to serve the guards permanently as means of transport for bringing in food supplies purchased in Uaxactún—and much else besides. All these goods had to be transported a considerable distance along a bad road in numerous trips.

36.4 My good friend Douglas Pilling, with the background décor he had arranged, at my investiture of the Order of the Quetzal. Photo courtesy of the Guatemalan Consulate.

A week later, with this done, I took an early morning flight to Boston, hoping to arrive in time to change into evening clothes and reach the annual dinner of the David Rockefeller Center for Latin American Studies during the cocktail hour, for I was hoping I might find there some wealthy Latin American Committee member interested in supporting our new, and as yet unfunded, program at San Bartolo. As the plane was late, I had to shower and change in five minutes; failed to get a taxi; ran and walked, ran and walked—and arrived panting and exhausted, at the great hall of the Harvard Business School, five minutes before the hour when everyone would be taking their seats at table. I looked around desperately—and then spotted a name tag bearing a name well known in Guatemalan business. Abruptly, I confronted him, and did in fact succeed in obtaining our first contribution!

This little effort marked the end of my involvement in the San Bartolo program, for Bill Saturno would require no other help from me. But it has been exciting to follow the revelation of an entire wall of the "mural annex" that the lords of this realm had added at the back of their pyramid. These miraculously preserved paintings depict lively scenes from Maya creation myths. They are masterpieces of design and execution, far surpassing anything previously seen. A further surprise is their date, for this is now placed no later than the second century B.C., or even earlier, thus adding weight to evidence coming from other recent discoveries that tend to push the beginning of the Classic Period back by least two hundred years.

Bill has pursued this work with outstanding energy and skill in the face of huge practical problems. The north wall of the mural (a band about thirteen and a half feet deep) remains intact, plus a short stretch on the adjoining east wall, and the entirety (thirty-one feet) of the adjoining west wall, for the remainder of that annex was destroyed prior to construction of a later enlargement of the temple. (Interestingly, steps were taken by the ancient Maya during this enlargement to protect the single surviving wall-length stretch of mural.)

Because the mural could only be made accessible by tunneling, recording it has been difficult and dangerous. Bill has overcome this and other problems with great skill and energy, as has Heather Hurst, the artist he engaged to make a scrupulously accurate copy of the mural in watercolors. This she has done in the cramped space of a tunnel, ever-mindful, I'm sure, of the possibility that stones set in fill containing no mortar, just above her head, might fall at any moment. This work of hers has been recognized by a well-deserved MacArthur Foundation Fellowship.

Since then, excavation at San Bartolo has uncovered a wall-painted inscription in another part of the same structure. At first sight it resembles the earliest Maya script and cannot yet be read. Radiocarbon dating of wood associated with it suggests a date of about 200 to 300 B.C., putting it at least two centuries earlier than those found at El Baúl and other sites in southeastern Guatemala, previously the earliest known. To date, dozens of other painted texts, remnants of the once extensive wall painting that graced San Bartolo's architecture from the third to first century B.C., have been recovered from continuing excavations. Just as the recording and publication of the corpus of carved texts paved the way for the more complete decipherment of Classic Maya script, perhaps these painted fragments will someday assist in extending our literacy into the era when Maya civilization was just forming.

Epilogue

By William (Bill) Saturno

Despite Ian's early assistance at San Bartolo, planning the path of the four-wheel-drive track, and organizing the initial security of the site, it wasn't until a visit in the spring of 2004 that he was able to sit and enjoy the excavated murals.

After we completed the excavation of the murals, droves of important visitors, Guatemalan captains of industry, foreign ambassadors, and government representatives including then Vice President Stein and President Berger, descended on San Bartolo's diminutive jungle helipad to see the murals firsthand. So many helicopters visited the site that spring that the sound of the whirling blades that had once been an unofficial alarm to drop everything and come running became reduced to just one more forest noise to be ignored in the face of other more pressing labors.

One important visitor, however, arrived by land, having hitched a ride with our weekly supply truck from the village of Uaxactún thirty-five miles (fifty-six kilometers) away. In Uaxactún, the San Bartolo Project driver had heard word of a gentleman who had arrived earlier in the day and rather than impose upon the local hotel had hung his hammock in our bodega to wait for the next vehicle going in to San Bartolo. Finding the man in the midst of a nap, the driver went about his errands, returning after a time to find him patiently pouring over the *Times*. Of course the man was none other than Ian Graham, and after four hours bouncing through the dense forest, the intrepid Maya explorer emerged from the mud-covered pickup.

My wife, Jaime, who had been keeping an informal record of visitors' first words after seeing the murals, informed Ian that the most recent three visitors all uttered the same one-word obscenity, expressing their level of tongue-tied awe. Ian responded, "I am an Englishman, and very unlikely to say that. At best you might get a 'jolly good.'"

As we entered the cramped tunnel, Ian's eyes welled up with tears as he sat silently, taking in the masterpiece. Eventually he uttered quietly, "This is the greatest, really, the greatest find." When he came out Jaime asked if the paintings rated the "jolly good" he had alluded to. He responded with a casual shake of his head followed with great enthusiasm by, "No, they're positively ripping!"

Notes

CHAPTER 1

1. I hadn't understood at all the virulence of my grandmother's contempt for this dismal section of society until I found in our archives the letter she sent my sister Lilias upon learning that she, at the age of about nineteen, had been working at a summer camp in the country for children from one of London's most miserable East End districts. I was deeply shocked by her diatribe—and was not at all surprised that Lilias found it necessary to ask her father to answer it for her. Poor man: this letter must have been the most difficult he ever had to write.

I believe Lilias never returned to Cirencester, but had instead abundant support from our paternal aunt, Lady Helen Graham, known in the family as Aunt Nelly. She, unmarried and notable for a strong social conscience, became president of the British branch of the YWCA. While Lilias, after doing social work in Glasgow's worst and most hazardous slums, the Gorbals, and then in other parts of the world, eventually inherited Braendam, Aunt Nelly's small farm and comfortable farmhouse near Glasgow. She sold the farm, and with the proceeds enlarged and converted the house into a holiday home for very poor Glasgow families, providing a place where children could become acquainted with animals they'd never seen close-up, and "Mum" could give her legs a rest and Dad be cajoled into outdoor activities such as sawing firewood. (Braendam's mission continues to this day with the support and guidance of a French Protestant organization, ATD Fourth World, and the Lilias Graham Trust.)

2. For the *Morning Post*'s *Upstairs-Downstairs* function, see W. F. Deedes, *Dear Bill* (London, 1997).

3. The mansion, Cirencester Park, is textbook Tory, with the formal entrance accessible through a courtyard directly from a street, while the other side looks out on a park seven miles long, thereby expressing bonds with people of both town and country. (Petworth House is the other classic example of this politically expressive layout.)

4. *Hodge and His Masters*, by Richard Jefferies (1880), chapter 13. Elsewhere, in many

passages, Jefferies showed socialist leanings, suggesting that "the hopes of the English Socialists are chiefly founded upon Hodge [i.e., the agricultural laborer]. Only through him could they get at the 'privileged classes,'" (quoted in Looker and Porteous, 1965, *Richard Jefferies, Man of the Fields*, p. 134). But in his chapter on "Fleeceborough," Jefferies wrote: "Farmers have long discovered that it is best to rent under a very large [land-]owner. . . . A very large owner can be, and is, more liberal. . . . A reserve of wealth has, too, steadily accumulated in the family coffers, which, in exceptional years, tides the owner over with little or no appreciable inconvenience." Was he thinking of our grandfather?

5. As ownership of racing stables was not considered proper for duchesses, my father's grandmother employed the nom de chasse of "Mr. Manton." She remains a legend in the history of the turf.

6. On the very day before the flight, Kipling was elected president of the league at its meeting in Folkestone for a conference on "Safety Devices for Airmen." Kipling is quoted as saying, "If five years ago they had met to discuss those questions, they would have been turned out by the police! Probably in five years' time they would meet to discuss something even more wonderful. A new world is opening up before us."

7. Constructed at Moisson, near Paris, by the Compagnie Pierre et Paul Lebaudy, the airship was 338 feet long and 39 feet in diameter, and contained three ballonets. Two Panhard engines of 135 horsepower turned propellers of 16 feet 5 inches diameter in opposite directions at 360 rpm. The *Morning Post*'s rival, the *Times*, reported seven events of aeronautical interest

that day, but interestingly refrained from mentioning this flight!

8. A dashing aeronaut, since he is reported to have invented a parachute forming part of a balloon. With it, Capazza made forty ascents, reaching on one occasion fifteen thousand feet, whereupon the balloon burst (as intended, perhaps?) and reportedly it took him an hour to float down to earth.

9. Uncle Allen (Apsley): In the First World War he served in the Near East, and again in the Second. One of his sons suspected that he may have been engaged in clandestine work in the latter conflict. His accidental death can't be attributed to that, but it would be difficult to find another explanation for the visit made by King Ibn Saud to my Aunt Viola, his widow, at Cirencester in January 1947. A dinner was given for him, presumably attended by particularly well-chosen guests, at the end of which the ladies were just starting to troop out—to leave the gentlemen to enjoy their port, as was then the custom—when suddenly the king stood up, knocking his chair over backward, and made a dash for the door. Nobody had instructed my aunt that according to Saudi etiquette the king had to lead his table companions from the room at their head!

10. Parnall Elf: Now in the Shuttleworth Collection, near Bedford, this plane is maintained in airworthy condition, but disappointingly the management flatly refused to offer me a flight in it. Pressed for a reason, they explained that two of the three Elves ever manufactured had crashed in flames, in both cases because the fuel pump had caught fire. As this was mounted at the rear of the engine and close to the passenger's feet, I could see the

logic of their refusal. But a feature that I hadn't noticed before was this plane's folding wings, which halved the size of hangar it would need. The origin of this pioneering feature must have been the Admiralty contract given to Parnall for a floatplane that could be carried by a submarine and launched from it by catapult. For a 1931 photo of it taking off in this way, see Dollfus and Bouché, 1942, p. 452.

11. Speech at the Albert Hall. See the *Church Times*, July 19, 1935, pp. 64, 65.

CHAPTER 2

1. From my mother's diary for 6 August 1934:

> Yesterday morning when my Communion ought to have made me "more than ordinarily gentle and gracious," as St. Francis de Sales says, I made my opinion about something too evident and, I am afraid, hurt my Alastair. Resolution: To try never to speak in a critical way about Alastair's choice of a housemaster for Ian at Winchester.

2. My grandfather edited a selection of letters written by our Gordon-Lennox ancestors, among them the four girls featured in Stella Tillyard's book *The Aristocrats*. The printing of these letters was a task he himself undertook in movable type while at Pinbury, and had them bound by Sangorsky.

3. R. A. Watson-Watt, J. F. Hurd, L. H. Bainbridge Bell, *Applications of the Cathode Ray Oscillograph in Radio Research* (London: H. M. Stationery Office, 1933).

4. See Stuart Piggot, William Stukeley: *An Eighteenth-Century Antiquary* (New York: Thames and Hudson, 1985), p. 30. See also Arthur B. Cook, *The Rise and Progress of Classical Archaeology* (Cambridge, 1931), p. 21.

5. "Wilks" once showed me a photo of the mobile wireless transmitter and receiver that he made for the Boy Scouts in his Essex parish in, I believe, 1907. Mounted on a pair of bicycle wheels like a barrow, this equipment's success must have been a remarkable achievement in the age of spark transmitters and receivers dependent on "coherers."

6. See Karl S. Pearson and A. E. Morant, "The Wilkinson Head of Oliver Cromwell and Its Relationship to Busts, Masks and Printed Portraits," *Biometrica* 26 (1934): 269–378. See also Rick Jones, "The Strange Tale of Cromwell's Head," *The Spectator*, March 24, 1990, 18, 19.

7. See Tom Reilly, *Cromwell, an Honourable Enemy* (Dublin: Brandon, 1999).

CHAPTER 3

1. The barber's shop has long gone, and since radical alterations were carried out, the only reminder of its existence are two hefty bronze brackets that once supported a glass cylinder containing his large traditional barber's pole.

2. In stating his law of miracles, Littlewood begins with a precise definition of them, and follows this with a statement that in any normal person's life, miracles happen at a rate of about one per month. On what was this based? During the hours we are awake, noticeable occurrences happen at a rate of about one per second, or about thirty thousand each day, or a million a month. Among these, noticeably unusual or memorable events may be only one-in-a-million—so we shouldn't be surprised at

their occurrence about once a month . . .[3]. Fortunately for my purposes, the HMV catalog then included a record consisting of a pure tone sliding at constant volume from the highest pitch audible down to the lowest. With this, any unevenness of response could be detected.

3. A small coil attached to the needle and lying between the magnet's poles generated the pickup's electrical output, and this unit (needle and coil) was mounted on a pivoted arm sprung to provide the light pressure needed to keep the needle in the groove while faithfully following its wiggles. One further complication was called for: the necessity of insuring that on lowering the pickup onto the record the needle was vertical. For this purpose, a slender handle projecting from the front of the pickup was provided for bearing its weight when off the record. So as long as the weight of the pickup was borne by this hinged handle, the coil-and-needle unit remained retracted until the pickup had been lowered onto the record. Release of this handle allowed the needle to descend vertically onto the record.

4. Rosa Lewis, a person so extraordinary, has naturally been the subject of many entertaining anecdotes and published descriptions. Perhaps the best is found in Humphrey Carpenter's *The Brideshead Generation* (London: Houghton Mifflin, 1989).

CHAPTER 4

1. Shipping bombs. A warning that one of my colleagues told me he had seen on a crate of bombs: "The bombs in this crate are packed in a different manner from that formerly used. Compared with the old method, the bombs are now packed upside-down, and the crate must therefore be opened at the bottom. To prevent confusion, the bottom has been labeled 'Top.'"

2. An urgent goal for the U.S. Air Force in the western Pacific was development of a technique for bombing Japanese battleships at sea. Anti-aircraft fire from the ship itself ruled out low-level attacks, while high-altitude bombing, despite the Norden bombsight, was found to be useless. Then at TRE, I heard about research on the pigeon bomb program—which might seem mythical, but I believe it was undertaken seriously. When a battleship was spotted, a pigeon specially trained to peck at any spot on an otherwise blank surface would be put into a compartment close to the nose of a bomb, standing on a ground-glass plate. When the bomb was released, a lens in the nose would cast an image of the ocean on the glass plate, and the pigeon would then peck, as trained, at the battleship's image, while a harness round its neck actuated servo mechanisms controlling the bomb's tail fins. Here, then, was the first smart bomb! (But how, I wonder, would a pigeon be trained to keep its head during the preliminary stage of weightlessness?)

3. For Haltere research, see J. W. S. Pringle, "The gyroscopic mechanism of the halteres of Diptera," *Philosophical Transactions of the Royal Society of London. Series B*, vol. 233, no. 602 (1948): 347–383.

4. German Radar: An exhibit that I didn't look at closely enough was a Würzburg early warning set. A friend of mine and veteran at TRE, the late Ted Cooke-Yarborough, told me of two details that he noticed with interest. Not only did it bear an engraved plate revealing its year of manufacture as 1938, but, significantly, there was provision for it to be operated

on 80, 120, 160, or 220 volts A.C. Those were voltages of the public electricity supply in various regions of France at that time—before a national grid was organized. So here were two surprises: astonishingly early German progress in decimeter radar, and proof that an invasion of France had been foreseen by Nazi military planners long before September 1939.

5. The Graham Navigator: Unknown to me at the time, a conceptually similar, although far more sophisticated, "spider's web" or distance-and-bearing navigation system was in fact under development at TRE just then, and was announced at that first PICAO meeting (though never brought into use).

CHAPTER 7

1. Fortunately, the National Gallery's Giorgione had been cleaned before a Giorgione exhibition was mounted in Glasgow. (It's hard to resist mentioning that when walking by the gallery one day, I heard a Glaswegian ask his companion, "Giargie One? Whü's thaat?"

2. Microbalance: Described in *Microchemica Acta*, Heft 6, 1954.

3. Wit was not lacking in those circles. The quickest flash of it that I remember came from Ed, Lord Stanley of Alderley. Following the marriage of Princess Elisabeth and Prince Philip (Admiral Lord Mountbatten's son), someone seated with me at a breakfast table read from a newspaper a proclamation to the effect that any second-generation or later descendant of the royal newlyweds, who for lack of a princely or ducal title would need a surname, was to bear that of "Mountbatten-Windsor." Quick as lightning, Ed blurted out, "Oh no, that's not right, it should be

Windsor-Cassel!" This was a reference to Lady Mountbatten's grandfather, Sir Ernest Cassel. He and his brother, Sir Felix, were Jews from Cologne who settled in England and made colossal fortunes in banking and industry. Sir Ernest, who died in the early 1920s, had within three years of his death made two donations for charitable purposes amounting to three-quarters of a million pounds, equivalent to about forty million of today's pounds. But perhaps Prince Philip's inheritance from his great-grandfather, even after taxes, could if really necessary help with the maintenance of Windsor Castle.

4. See *Splendours of the East: Temples, Tombs, Palaces and Fortresses of Asia* (1965), edited by Mortimer Wheeler; *Great Palaces* (1964), edited by Sacheverell Sitwell; and *Great Houses* (1968), edited by Nigel Nicolson (all published by George Weidenfeld and Nicolson, Ltd., London).

5. See A. V. Cotton in *Ballet Today*, March 1956.

CHAPTER 8

1. Letter to the *New York Times* from R. H. Westover, Chairman, SS *United States* Foundation, January 12, 2004.

2. See Wilfred Sheed, *The World of Charles Addams* (New York: Knopf, 1991).

CHAPTER 10

1. In 1910, R. E. Merwin photographed a graffito "Pedro Montanes, 1752" on a wall in ruins now known as La Blanca (Peabody Museum Photo Archives). Then I found a possible reference to this colonial farm or ranch in the Guatemalan Archivos de la Nación,

(Exp. 677, Leg. 33, A3.3). It's entitled "Acta acerca de la venta de cierta cantidad de ganado perteneciente a la Hacienda del Rey, situado en el Petén. Año 1775." It reports possession of 1,344 pesos realized from this hacienda, called San Felipe, and it requests instructions, because rains had made the forest impassable and rivers full.

One cannot be sure, however, that this was the same Hacienda del Rey, for an anonymous (undated, but probably eighteenth-century) map in the British Museum, "Plano de los tres Rios de Balys Nuevo y Hondo," marks the "Estancia del Rey" too far south, but of course no map of that area made in those days could possibly be accurate.

CHAPTER 11

1. Gary H. Gossen has made a brilliant study of this festival—one of great complexity, layered with contradictory elements of religious and political dualism. See "The Chamula Festival of Games: Native Macroanalysis and Song, Commentary in a Maya Carnival," published in *Symbol and Meaning beyond the Closed Community* (Gary H. Gossen, ed.) in *Studies in Culture and Society*, vol. 1, (Albany: Institute of Mesoamerican Studies, State University of New York, 1986).

2. In the published account (S. G. Morley, *The Inscriptions of Petén*, vol. 2, pp. 301–9), Stela 1 is shown erroneously at the east end of the stairway.

3. For Nathan Milstein, see Chapter 9.

CHAPTER 12

1. Born Natasha Zahalkaha in Prostejov, in what was then Bohemia.

2. Ilya Chamberlain. Tired of his career as a young violin prodigy, Ilya studied philosophy at the Sorbonne. Returning to music, he became a conductor, and spent two years as assistant conductor at La Scala di Milano—until Mussolini ordered conductors to wear fascist uniform. He continued his career with apparent success in other countries, including the United States, only to abandon this career because, in his own words, he considered himself mediocre and despised mediocrity. Then he established an art gallery specializing in paintings and lithographs, mounting exhibitions of Mexican work in New Orleans, Washington, D.C., and other cities. When last I saw him, he was planning to build a gallery in Cozumel, in Maya style (see the Mexico newspaper *Excelsior*, June 11, 1961).

His little hotel burned down in a fire supposedly set by the owner of the other hotel on the island, but where he then went I never discovered. Thirty years would pass before I visited Cozumel again, and then I could find no one who could tell me anything more about the Chamberlains.

CHAPTER 13

1. Chicleros who tapped trees only up to the first branch were known dismissively as *tronqueros*.

2. See David Adamson, *The Ruins of Time* (London: Allen and Unwyn, 1975).

3. *Dermatobia hominis*, native to Mexico, Central America, and South America.

CHAPTER 15

1. In about 1969, I was given copies of four beautifully printed map sheets covering most of

northern Petén (16°30'N to 17°50'N between 89°00'W and 91°00'W). They were prepared in Rotterdam by photo-interpreters of Royal Dutch/Shell Oil Company using aerial photographic coverage carried out for them in 1937, at a time when Shell had some kind of provisional concession for northern Petén. Two other sheets, not in my possession, extended the coverage to longitude 88°00'. There is abundant marking of dips and strikes and other geological features, but the extraordinary diligence of the interpreters is revealed by their marking Group H at Tikal, which by a strange coincidence was discovered on the ground in the same year by Edwin Shook of the Carnegie Institution's 20th Expedition; and at Mirador, about a dozen of the mounds are shown. How I wish I had had these maps earlier!

2. Laboriously, I had to match up features from pairs of photographs taken on successive lines of flight, working towards the south, until I came to Carmelita.

3. Many years later, two different hand-drawn maps showing the network of these camps came into my hands. They seem to date from the 1930s or '40s, and while neither of them shows any close relationship with cartographic reality, they are interesting because they show that the names bestowed on campsites have generally been quite durable.

4. Those I could remember seeing were at Yaxhá and Uaxactún—the latter described by Oliver Ricketson in his 1937 publication, *Uaxactún, Guatemala Group E, 1926–31*, Carnegie Institution of Washington, Publication 477, Washington, D.C.

5. Adolfo Molina Orantes. He had been the lawyer for the Carnegie Institution of Washington's Guatemalan projects, and was later his country's foreign minister. He was burned to death in the Spanish Embassy in Guatemala when a Molotov cocktail was thrown by a visiting dissident.

CHAPTER 16

1. Reprinted in part from Ian Graham, "Incredible Journey," *Saga Magazine* (June 2002), 48–54.

2. Dr. J. Collis Brown's Chlorodyne, a "patent medicine" known worldwide and first concocted in 1848, was widely advertised in England until at least the 1970s. Its principal ingredients were extract of opium (10 percent morphine), codeine, chloroform, and alcohol (normal dose: five drops). The label quoted an extract from Cassel's *History of the Boer War*: "Gaunter and gaunter grew the soldiers of the Queen. Hunger and sickness played havoc with those fine regiments. But somehow the Royal Army Medical Corps managed to patch the men up with Chlorodyne and quinine."

I have in fact used it on myself and a few others to good effect!

CHAPTER 17

1. G. L. Vinson: "Two important recent archaeological discoveries in Esso Concessions, Guatemala," *Exploration Newsletter* (March 1960), Standard Oil Company (N.J.), New York City. The other site he reported was Tamarindito.

2. It sounds like a good Maya term, but I believe it's just a corruption of "shoulder bag."

CHAPTER 19

1. See James B. Porter, "The Maya Hieroglyph Hoax in the U.S.A.: Phoneticism and

Lounsbury," *Estudios de Cultura Maya* 20 (1999): 131–45.

CHAPTER 20

1. "In July, 1891, when I was traveling on the Río de la Pasión and in the neighborhood of a small Lacandón settlement, I was unwilling to miss the favorable opportunity of obtaining an insight into the ways and doings of this curious little tribe. At the logging camp 'La Unión' of Jamet and Sastré, I embarked in a small rowboat and was rowed to the lake of Itzan, two leagues distant, on whose shores is the small Lacandón village of the same name, peopled by a few families." Karl Sapper, "Ein Besuch bei den Oestlichen Lacandonen," in *Das Ausland* 45 (1891): 892–895.

So it is just possible these Lacandóns stemmed from that settlement, for when the men died and their widows went to Naha, across the Usumacinta, they were rejected as having no kinship in anyone's recollection. But of whether they tried again at Lacanja, the other large Lacandón settlement, I can't say.

2. Sally Christie Notebook entry for 17 May 1970 (Archives of the University Museum, University of Pennsylvania).

3. The less interesting basal panel of the Fort Worth stela was left untouched at the site, but I have reunited it photographically.

CHAPTER 21

1. See Rafael Morales Fernández, "Recuento de Operación Rescate de Monumentos Precolumbinos de Guatemala," *U'tzib* 3, no. 5 (2003): 1–25, Guatemala. But note: there are two small errors on pp. 1 and 2, for in fact nothing had been removed from Machaquilá before

we took four stelae out by helicopter; and they were not flown out hanging from the helicopter, but loaded inside its fuselage. See also articles in the same journal by Karl Herbert Mayer and Bárbara Arroyo.

CHAPTER 22

1. "Arts Mayas du Guatemala," 1968.

CHAPTER 23

1. Linton Satterthwaite, *Concepts and Structures of Maya Calendrical Arithmetics*, (Philadelphia: University Museum, University of Pennsylvania, 1947).

2. See Ian Graham, "Tesoros Arqueológicos del Petén al Extranjero," *El Imparcial*, 17 Julio 1965.

3. See Walter Sullivan, "Jungle Search Is Planned to Break Maya Code," *New York Times*, 4 October 1969.

CHAPTER 26

1. The Yaxchilan visitors' book was destroyed in the 1960s in a fire at Miguel de la Cruz's house, but in 1959 there had been only about thirty signatures in it.

CHAPTER 30

1. I've been told that a passing archaeologist did pick up sherds of Sotuta ware from one of these Sound and Light trenches—sherds of the greatest interest because they indicate an occupation of Uxmal for an unknown duration by people from Chichén Itzá. These have not been mentioned in print, so far as I know.

2. I witnessed the awkward consequence of the failure by César Saénz to notice in time a *descanso* (landing) some five or six steps below

the level that his new stairway had already reached, as he had to dismantle those steps and construct that landing before continuing hectically onward and upward. Another comment: visitors can hardly fail to wonder how one side of that pyramid appears 100 percent intact, even provided with built-in recesses for floodlights, while the other sides show no vestige whatever of masonry facing!

3. When lintels of reinforced concrete were installed in the Monjas, replacing those of decayed wood, the sand used appears not to have had the salt washed out of it properly, judging by the rusting and swelling of the reinforcing rods, causing the concrete to split away. Encouragingly, these have recently been replaced by lintels of chicosapote wood, the appropriate variety.

4. During the clearing of the ball court, fragments of a serpent molding were found, but in this case the opportunity of resetting them as shown in a drawing by Waldeck was missed.

5. Some of the information given here on the restoration of Uxmal is based on Daniel Schávelzohn, *La Conservación del Patrimonio Cultural en América Latina: Restauración de Edificios Prehispánicos* (Buenos Aires: UBA Facultad de Arquitectura, Diseño y Urbanismo, 1990).

6. Carlos R. Margaín, "Las 'reconstrucciones' en arqueología," in *Homenaje a Don Alfonso Caso*.

CHAPTER 31

1. The Guatemalan Air Force had just one of these unusual machines, the tailplane of which was supported by booms extending backward from its two engines, making it possible to load the cargo through its vast rear door. Unfairly, its short fuselage gave rise to its nickname, the Flying Coffin. Normally, passengers were never taken on this plane, but one day, because of some urgent need to reach Flores after Aviateca's morning DC-3 flight had left, I did obtain a ride in it. There were just two places where I could sit: either on the hood of the principal item in the hold, a Jeep (the fuselage being too narrow to allow its doors to be opened), or else on crates containing cans of lubricating oil that were lashed down behind. This would have been a much windier perch because, for convenience, the large rear door of the fuselage had been discarded. All went well until we were approaching Petén, when one of the engines lost power and the plane began to lose altitude. To lessen our rate of descent, the pilot ordered the crates of oil to be thrown out—and we carried on for a while. But then, reluctantly, orders were given for the Jeep to go, too. Its lashings were cut, the pilot put the stick forward to gain speed, shouted at me to hold on tight, and then pulled the nose up sharply. Adios, Jeep!—but we did reach Flores safely.

I wonder if anyone, making his way through southern Petén, has ever encountered a jeep mysteriously lodged in the branches of some great tree. Or nose-down in a swamp?

2. For Sactankiki, see Teobert Maler, "Explorations of the Upper Usumacinta," *Memoirs*, vol. 4, no. 1, 27, Peabody Museum, Harvard University, 1908.

3. Graham, I: "Federico Arthés y la presencia de Guatemala en la Exposicion Mundial Colombina de Chicago (1896)," *Anales de la Academia de Geografía e Historia* 47, no. 45 (1991): 71–77.

CHAPTER 32

1. Unfortunately, my opposition to the antiquities trade led Natasha to remove my name from her list of friends. The last time I saw her was at a Sotheby's sale where her husband, Jacques, was bidding for some immensely expensive Maya incensarios and other items on behalf of Emilio Ascárraga for the Televisa Collection in Mexico. Entries in the catalog for the pieces they wanted were marked "s/l" (sin límites). Natasha died in May 1998 at eighty-six years of age.

2. See "The Case of the Peripatetic 13th-Century Mayan Calendar Book," *New York Times*, December 13, 1977, 45.

3. El Naranjo ranch, on the Río San Pedro, is in fact less than that as the crow flies, but separated by the trackless Sierra del Lacandón range. Another victim of Delfino Suarez at Piedras Negras was Stela 35, which ended up in a museum in Cologne—or rather, its upper half did, for the lower half has disappeared. When I told the museum's curator, a Dr. Boltz, of my disappointment at the museum's complicity in the destruction of hieroglyphic texts, she replied, memorably, "Oh, you know, there are already quite enough hieroglyphs for anyone to work on!"

4. His book, *Découvertes chez les Maya* (Paris, 1968; issued in English as *Mayan Enigma*, New York City, 1971), describes some of his activities at Dos Pilas.

5. See also her "United States Cultural Property Legislation: Observations of a Combatant," *International Journal of Cultural Property* 7, no. 1 (1998), Oxford, England.

6. See *The International Trade in Art* (University of Chicago Press, 1981) and his excellent

summary of the matter in *The Stanford Law Review* 34, no. 2 (January 1982).

7. See John Dorfman, "Getting Their Hands Dirty? Archaeologists and the Looting Trade," *Lingua Franca* (May/June 1998).

8. See Peter T. Furst and Michael D. Coe, "Ritual Enemas," *Natural History* 86, no. 3 (March 1977): 88–91.

9. See Dicey Taylor, "Problems of Narrative Scenes on Classic Maya Vases," in *Falsifications and Misconstructions of Pre-Columbian Art*, pp. 107–124 (Washington, D.C.: Dumbarton Oaks, 1982).

10. See S. Houston and D. Stuart, "The Way Glyph: Evidence for 'Co-essences' among the Classic Maya," *Research Reports on Ancient Maya Writing*, no. 30 (Washington, D.C.: Center for Maya Research, 1989).

11. Named for its former owner, who gave it to the British Museum. For Fenton, see Graham, *Alfred Maudslay and the Maya*, 248 and 268.

12. This term, used in Petén for looters, derives from another species that digs for a living, the agouti, a tailless rodent known as *wech* in 'Kekchi (and in Mexico as *tepezcuintli*). Because their flesh is delicious (and I must confess to having often partaken of it, with pleasure), they are hunted by chicleros and other denizens of the jungle, using dogs to flush them from their lairs among the roots of trees.

13. See "The Takeover Artist Takes Over the Arts," *Manhattan, Inc* (June 1989). More recently, on 2 March 2005, Merrin and his son were indicted by federal prosecutors (*New York Times*, the next day) for inflating by several million dollars their expenses in obtaining pre-Columbian artifacts under an agreement with

two art collectors; this stipulated a commission of between 10 and 20 percent. It was interesting to learn that the collectors were billed for no less than $63 million.

14. See *The Daily News*, March 20, 1987, 5, and *New York Times* items on May 22, August 25, and October 13, 1987.

CHAPTER 33

1. The Lambs describe Río Verde as an old chicle camp on the banks of the Usumacinta, inhabited by an unfriendly and disgusting man they call Don "Natcho." This description is almost certainly based on Agua Azul, an old lumber camp on the Mexican bank of the river, and I suspect that this man was modeled—in just one respect—on Don José Rivera, its by no means inhospitable encargado when I was there a decade later. After serving the Lambs an unpalatable meal, "Don Natcho reached for a tumbler of water, filled his mouth, rinsed the liquid around and then spat it upon the floor. Ginger turned pale under her tan."

My recollection of Don José is that after serving the simple but adequate meal that was all one would expect, he removed his partial set of false teeth, took a mouthful of water, flushed it from side to side, and spat it on the earthen floor, before replacing the teeth. (Of course, Don "Natcho," as described by the Lambs, was too much of a backwoodsman to have had dentures.)

2. In this cooperative, the profit motive swelled up in the breasts of the Protestant members of the community, and they split off to set up a new colony at El Retalteco with a different economic philosophy. When I visited this settlement some years later (the gender of its name indicating a pueblo rather than a cooperativa), guerrilla activity was rampant, and some cooperatives had been dissolved because of it. But at El Retalteco I found zigzag defensive walls of botán (trunks of corozo palms) encircling the village and man-traps dug in the paths leading to it— and in true Vietnam fashion, holes drilled in trees at sharp turns in the path, with sharpened spikes of some hardwood driven into them, upon which it was hoped that nighttime aggressors being pursued would impale themselves. The little stream flowing through it had been dammed, and a notice warned of fines for anyone found washing clothes above the dam. I can only imagine that some North American missionary had suggested all these measures. The streets, too, had hedges of hibiscus, trained into archways over the entrances to house yards—an astonishing sight.

3. Later I would learn that Palmer had bought eighty percent of his collection from Josué Saénz and Merrin, with the small panels coming from the Mexican dealer Sosa; also that when they were eventually sent to Europe, they were shipped initially to Panama, to obscure their source. Their present location is unknown.

CHAPTER 34

1. Sadly, one of the first actions of the Zapatista movement was directed at Rancho Toniná, in the course of which Armando was murdered.

2. Examining it later that day I noticed that a fragment representing the figure's lower right leg was detached, so while unobserved I epoxyed it in place. Unfortunately I lacked the courage to do the same for a substantial area

of sculptured background immediately to the right of the figure's head, for this had split off the shaft and was now lying loosely in place—and now of course is missing. Fortunately I did at least take one photograph of the whole monument while that fragment was in place.

3. See Bryan R. Just, "Modifications of Ancient Maya Sculpture," *RES* 48 (Autumn 2005): 75n, Peabody Museum, Harvard University.

CHAPTER 35

1. To help celebrate in Massachusetts her one-hundredth birthday, she invited a hundred friends to a sit-down luncheon at her farm, where her old friend Dillon Ripley, the great secretary of the Smithsonian Institution, lauded her as being, herself, a great institution. Then she took three of her friends to London on the Concorde for two days of visiting gardens and palaces by helicopter—gardens being her passion. And four years later, she took a short solo ride on an African elephant.

CHAPTER 36

1. See Angela M. H. Schuster, "The Search for Site Q," *Archaeology* (September/October 1997): 42–45.

2. See Ian Graham, "Mission to La Corona," *Archaeology* (September/October 1997): 46.

3. See John Dorfman and Andrew L. Slayman, "Maverick Mayanist," *Archaeology* (September/October 1997): 50–60.

Bibliography

Adamson, David. *The Ruins of Time*. London: Allen & Unwyn, 1975.

Arroyo, Bárbara. "Anotaciones Adicionales a la Labor de Rafael Morales y Operación Rescate." *U'tzib* 3, no. 5 (2003): 26–30.

Bator, Paul M. *The International Trade in Art*. Chicago: University of Chicago Press, 1981.

———. "An Essay on the International Trade in Art." *The Stanford Law Review* 34, no. 2 (January 1982): 275–384.

Carpenter, Humphrey. *The Brideshead Generation*. London: Houghton Mifflin, 1989.

Coggins, Clemency. "United States Cultural Property Legislation: Observations of a Combatant." *International Journal of Cultural Property* 7, no. 1 (1998). Oxford, England.

Cook, Arthur Bernard. The Rise and Progress of Classical Archaeology, with special reference to the University of Cambridge, an inaugural lecture. Cambridge: The University Press.

Deedes, W. F. *Dear Bill: A Memoir*. London: Pan Books, 1998.

Del Rio, Marcela. "Ilya Chamberlain y la Pintura en Cozumel." *Excelsior*, June 11, 1961.

Dollfus, Charles, and Henri Bouché. *Histoire de l'Aeronautique*. Paris: L'Illustration, 1942.

Dorfman, John. "Getting Their Hands Dirty? Archaeologists and the Looting Trade." *Lingua Franca* (May/June 1998). http://linguafranca.mirror.theinfo.org/9805/dorfman2.html

Dorfman, John, and Andrew L. Slayman. "Maverick Mayanist." *Archaeology* (September/October 1997): 50–60.

Furst, Peter T., and Michael D. Coe. "Ritual Enemas." *Natural History* 86, no. 3 (March 1977): 88–91.

Gossen, Gary H. "The Chamula Festival of Games: Native Macroanalysis and Song, Commentary in a Maya Carnival." In *Symbol and Meaning beyond the Closed Community: Essays in Mesoamerican*

Ideas, edited by Gary H. Gossen, 227–67. Albany: Institute of Mesoamerican Studies, State University of New York, 1986.

Graham, Ian. "Construction of a robust torsion microbalance." *Microchimica Acta* 42, no. 6 (1954): 746–49.

———. "Tesoros Arqueológicos del Petén al Extrajero." *El Imparcial*, 17 Julio 1965.

———. "Federico Arthés y la presencia de Guatemala en la Exposicion Mundial Colombina de Chicago (1896)." *Anales de la Academia de Geografía e Historia* 47, no. 45 (1991): 71–77.

———. "Mission to La Corona." *Archaeology* (September/October 1997): 46.

———. *Alfred Maudslay and the Maya*. London: British Museum Press, 2002.

———. "Incredible Journey." *Saga Magazine* (June 2002): 48–54.

Graham, Muriel Bathurst. Speech at the Albert Hall, *Church Times*, July 19, 1935, 64–65.

Houston, S., and D. Stuart. "The Way Glyph: Evidence for 'Co-essences' among the Classic Maya." *Research Reports on Ancient Maya Writing*, no. 30. Washington, D.C.: Center for Maya Research, 1989.

Ivanoff, Pierre. *Découvertes chez les Maya* (Paris, 1968; issued in English as *Mayan Enigma*, New York City, 1971).

Jefferies, Richard. *Hodge and His Masters*. London: Smith, Elder, & Co., 1880.

Johnston, Laurie. "The Case of the Peripatetic 13th-Century Mayan Calendar Book." *New York Times*, December 13, 1977, 45.

Jones, Rick. "The Strange Tale of Cromwell's Head." *The Spectator*, March 24, 1990, 18–19.

Just, Bryan R. "Modifications of Ancient Maya Sculpture." *RES* 48 (Autumn 2005): 69–82. Peabody Museum, Harvard University.

Kennedy, Randy. "Two Dealers in Pre-Columbian Art Are Indicted." *New York Times*, March 3, 2005.

Looker, Samuel J., and Crichton Porteous. *Richard Jefferies, Man of the Fields*. London: John Baker, 1965.

Maler, Teobert. "Explorations of the Upper Usumacinta." *Memoirs*, vol. 4, no. 1, 25–28. Peabody Museum, Harvard University, 1908.

Mayer, Karl Herbert. "Monumentos trasladados y Destruidos de Narajo, Petén Guatemala." *U'tzib* 3, no. 5 (2003): 15–25.

Morales Fernández, Rafael. "Recuento de Operación Rescate de Monumentos Precolumbinos de Guatemala." *U'tzib* 3, no. 5 (2003): 1–14.

Morley, S. G. *The Inscriptions of Petén*, vol. 2. Publication No. 437, Washington, D.C.: Carnegie Institute of Washington, 1938.

Pearson, Karl S., and A. E. Morant. "The Wilkinson Head of Oliver Cromwell and Its Relationship to Busts, Masks and Printed Portraits." *Biometrica* 26 (1934): 269–378.

Piggot, Stuart. *William Stukeley: An Eighteenth-Century Antiquary*. New York: Thames and Hudson, 1985.

Porter, James B. "The Maya Hieroglyph Hoax in the U.S.A." *Estudios de Cultura Maya* 20 (1999): 131–45.

Pringle, J. W. S. "The gyroscopic mechanism of the halteres of Diptera." *Philosophical*

Transactions of the Royal Society of London. Series B, vol. 233, no. 602 (1948): 347–83.

Reilly, Tom. *Cromwell: An Honourable Enemy.* Dublin: Brandon, 1999.

Ricketson, Oliver. *Uaxactun, Guatemala Group E, 1926–31.* Publication 477. Washington, D.C.: Carnegie Institution of Washington, 1937.

Sapper, Karl. "Ein Besuch bei den Oestlichen Lacandonen." *Das Ausland* 45 (1891): 892–95.

Satterthwaite, Linton. *Concepts and Structures of Maya Calendrical Arithmetics.* Philadelphia: University Museum, University of Pennsylvania, 1947.

Schávelzon, Daniel. *La Conservación del Patrimonio Cultural en América Latina: Restauración de Edificios Prehispánicos.* Buenos Aires: UBA Facultad de Arquitectura, Diseño y Urbanismo, 1990.

Schuster, Angela M. H. "The Search for Site Q." *Archaeology* (September/October 1997): 42–45.

Sheed, Wilfred. *The World of Charles Addams.* New York: Knopf, 1991.

Sullivan, Walter. "Jungle Search Is Planned to Break Maya Code." *New York Times,* October 4, 1969.

Taylor, Dicey. "Problems of Narrative Scenes on Classic Maya Vases." In *Falsifications and Misconstructions of Pre-Columbian Art,* 107–124. Washington, D.C.: Dumbarton Oaks, 1982.

Tillyard, Stella. *Aristocrats.* London: Vintage, 1995.

Vinson, G. L. "Two important recent archaeological discoveries in Esso Concessions, Guatemala." *Exploration Newsletter* (March 1960). Standard Oil Company (N.J.), New York City.

Watson-Watt, R. A., J. F. Hurd, and L. H. Bainbridge Bell. *Applications of the Cathode Ray Oscillograph in Radio Research.* London: H. M. Stationery Office, 1933.

Index

looting at, 355–56; mapping of, 355; Stela 1 at, 356–57; Stelae 3, 4, and 5 at, 357; stelae photographs/drawings at, 355

El Zotz, ruins of, 446–47, 448

EMI (record label), 54

Emmerich, André, 437, 448, 449–50

Emmett, Eric, 30

Enoch Soames (Beerbohm), 72

epigraphy. *See* drawings, of Maya monuments; inscriptions, Maya

Erikson, Ernest, 170

Escalante brothers, 250

Esso Oil, 249

Estrada-Belli, Francisco, 422, 423

Europe, importation of plundered antiquities into, 310–11

Expedition (magazine), 264

exploration: aerial photos for, 223–24, 453, 511n2; clothing for, 177, 198–99, 209, 264; GVT for, 225; plotting for, 224–25, 227; supplies for, 195–96, 227; typical day of, 201–4

Fahsen, Federico, 361

Fairchild Packet, 421, 513n1

faisán (bird), 134, 139, 201, 202, 252, 262–63, 425, 456

Fallabón. *See* Melchor de Mencos

Faraday, Michael, 83

FBI. *See* Federal Bureau of Investigation

Feather, N., 42

Federal Bureau of Investigation (FBI), 392, 437–38, 464

Fell, Johnny Brown, 436–37

Fenton vase, 445–46, *447*, 514n11. *See also* British Museum

fer-de-lance (snake), 204

Fernández, Pilar, 282

Ferranti, Sebastian Ziani de, 58

Festival of Games, 145–46, *147–49*, 510n1. *See also* Chamula, town of

Fettweiss, Martine, 461

Firestone, Gay, 449

Firewalk. *See* Chamula, town of

Fisk, T., *272*

flea traps, 202

flora/fauna, in Department of Petén, 146, 162, 265, 331–32, *332*, 356, 456

Flores, Lisandro, 167

Flores, town of: access to, 137, 193–94; airport at, 195; amenities in, 196, *197*; Graham, I., in, 135, 137; hospital in, 204–5; Hotel Cambranes in, 196, *197*;

preservation of, 137; road link from, to Tikal, 195, 213; tourism in, 193–94

Folkens Museum of Ethnography, 170

Fonssegrives, Lisa, 107

Ford Foundation, 349, 398

Förstemann, Ernst, 283–84

Fosburgh, Jim, 108–9

Fosburgh, Minny, 108–9

Francis, John, 92

Franklin, John, 85, 105–6

Franklin, R. E., 369

Freud, Lucian, 90

Freund, Gerald, 399

Friends of the Ruins Society. *See* Toniná, ruins of

Furst, Peter, 445

FYDEP (Petén development organization), 318, 320, 326, 357, 428

Gabor, Eva, 108

Galeani, Celestino, 72

García, Rufino, 368

García, Valentín, 303

García Moll, Roberto, 371, 376, 377–78, 417, 471

García-Pimentel, Carmen, 117

García-Pimentel, Luis, 117

Gastone, Gian, 70

Gatling, John, 213, 214, 249, 258

Gazzaniga, Giuseppe, 107

Gelman, Jacques, 178–79, 514n1

Gelman, Natasha, 163, 177–85, *185*, 188, 429, 510n1, 514n1

Genius Award. *See* John D. and Catherine T. MacArthur Foundation

Genovés, Santiago, 279

Georges-Picot, Nadia, 163, 177–79, 181–82, 185

Georges-Picot, Nina, 162–64, 177–78

Ghika, Niko, 116

Gibbon (Quennell), 71

Gide, André, 72

Gimpel, René, 315

Girólamo da Firenze, 64

Giorgione da Castelfranco, 84, 509n1

Glanville, Bartholemew, 78

glyphs. *See* hieroglyphs, Maya

Godman, Frederick D., 290

Godoy, Julio, 139–40

Godoy Hotel, 218, 326

Goldwater hospital, 103

Gomes, Patrisio, 228, *228*

Gonzalez, Norberto, 417

Goodrich, Jane, 109

Gouygou, François, 471

GPS. *See* Graham's Positioning System

GPS navigation, 224, 274, 498

graffiti: at Calakmul, 388, *388*; at La Blanca, 509n1; by Moore, L., 388, *388*; at Yaxhá, 139, 388, *388*

Graham, Alastair, 6–8, 10, 22, 23, 25, 26, 28–29, 31, 507n1

Graham, Ian: in Acapulco, 177–78; Acton conversation with, 71–73; aerial radar testing by, 54–56, 508n1; at Balcarres, 77–79, 85; at Birr Castle, 68–70; at Bonampak, 178–79, *180–84*, 181–82, 185; camera of, 93–94, *94*; compass use by, 224–25; at Covent Garden, *95–96*, 95–97; demobilization of, 60–61; Dipole Moment Machine by, 65; drawings by, 10, 23, 172, *220*, 221, 267–68, 298, 340, 355, *378–79*, 485; in Dublin, 62–63; Dublin social life for, 66–69; electronics for, 42–43, 508n3; experimentation by, 56–57; financial resources for, 292, 316, 341–43, 346, 362, 397–403, 485; to Fleet Air Arm, 51; in Florence, 70–71; GPS by, 224–25; Graham Navigator by, 59–60, 509n5; GVT by, 225; at Haigh Hall, 49–50, 76–78; at Harvard, 80, 86; with hepatitis, 345; at HMS *Ariel*, 48, 49, 51; on HMS *Superb*, 51; house for, 174; inheritance by, 254; at International Congress of Americanists, 280–81; in Istanbul, 73; in jail, 120, 424–27; with king/queen, 34–36; Kipling letter by, *13*; at Lake Petén, *492*; near La Pasadita, *452*; as Leading Radio Mechanic, 51; London social life for, 88–91, 95–96; MacArthur "Prize Fellowship" for, 397–403; Maler exhibition by, 348; at Malvern, 52–60; maps by, 234; at Monte Albán, 128; musical talents of, 64–65; at National Gallery, 81–87; for National Geographic Society, 419; in navy, 45, 47–60; in New York, 99–111; Order of Quetzal for, 500; Orient Express by, 73; at Peabody Museum, 359–65, *364*, *479*; photography by, 4, 30–31, 93–97, 105–9, *115*, 116, *123*, 128, 130–31, 132–33, 135, *137–38*, *140*, *142*, *144*, *147–58*, 160, *161*, 162, *163*, *165*, *171*, 172–73, 178, *180–85*, 185, 189, 191, *197*, *203*, *205–6*, *208*, *211*, *214*, 215, 220–21, *221*, 234, 254, 261, 270–71, 292, 296, 303, 305, 306, 338–39, 341, 344–46, 355, 368, 381, 383–84, 413, 422, 432, 441, 445–46, 458, 461, 472–73, 485 (*see also* photography); photos of, *4, 7, 88, 108, 114, 122, 169, 189, 251, 273, 284, 319, 364, 376, 378, 393, 394, 440, 452, 479, 480, 492, 495, 499, 500, 501*; publications by, 233; on *Queen Mary*, 124; radar training for, 48–49; report by, 234; Rolls Royce of, 87, 88–89, 99–100, *118*, 236; scientific apparatus by, 65, 84–85, 86–87, 234, 445–46; at Seibal, 135, 268, *269*, *272*, 272–74, *274*; self-photo by, *189*; as Senior Prefect, 34; at Shikar Club, 90–91; social life of, 75–76; *Splendours of the East* photos by, 270–71; on SS *Atalanti*, 190; with Stein, S., *108*; story by, 9; in Texas, 113–14, *114*; topographical notations by, 225; at TRE, 51–60; at Tulum, 187; on *United States*, 99; Von Euw as assistant to, 363, 401, 411; at Walthamstow Technical College, 48; workshop practice for, 26–27, 36

Graham, James, 37–38

Graham, John, 167, 283

Graham, Lilias, *7*, 8–9, 29, 505n1

Graham, Margaret, 9

Graham, Meriel Bathurst, 4, 6–8, *10*, 10–11, 14, *18*, 18–19, 22, 36, 507n1

Graham, Robin, 8, 461

Graham Navigator, 59–60, 509n5

Graham's Positioning System (GPS), 224–25

Graham's Victualing Tables (GVT), 225

Gramophone Company. *See* EMI

Granite Productions, 496

Great Palaces, 95

Great Royal Palaces (Graham, I.), 254

Great War. *See* World War I

Greene, Merle, 367

Gregg, John Allen Fitzgerald, 61–62

Grey, James, 91

Grolier Club, exhibition at, 430–31

Guardia Rural, at Paso, 295

Guatemala City, hospital in, 204–5

Guerra, José, 436

guerrillas, activity by, 320, 368, 436, 465, 515n2

Guillén, Carmen, 226, 232

Güiro, camp at, 234

Guttman Foundation. *See* Maya Corpus Program; Stella and Charles Guttman Foundation

Guzmán, Oscar, 140, 163, 166, 329

GVT. *See* Graham's Victualing Tables

Hacienda Hotel, 345, 406, 409

Haigh Hall, 49–50, 76–78

Hairs, Joya, 166

Hamet Mahogany Company, 327, 331, 422

hammock, 49, 143, 162, 179, 181–82, 187, 195, 198–99, 200, 202, 279, 295, 302, 370

Hardy, G. H., 41

Harrison, Rex, 19–20

Harvard Real Estate (HRE), 487–89

Masefield, John, 25
Mathews, Peter, 311, 401, 470, 480, *480*, 491
Matos Moctezuma, Eduardo, 417
Mauchlay, John W., 57–58
Maudslay, Alfred, 128, 290–91, 338, 384–86, 455
May, Morton D., 315–16
Maya, the: bark-fiber paper codex of, 430–31; Berlin and, 287; books on, 118; building technology of, 416–17; calendar of, 344, 364; carnival ceremonies of, 145; cosmology of, 471; creation stories of, 445; decipherment of, 283–85, 339–40, 343, 442, 484, 491; de Landa and, 284; Dresden Codex for, 284; emblem glyphs for, 287; Förstemann and, 283–84; hieroglyphs of, 217, 233, 280–81, 283–85, *284*, 286, *286*, 287–92, *288*, 339–40, 343, 430–31, 442, 445, 484, 491; housing plan for, 471; Itzá language of, 166; as Kekchi, 172, 233, 251, 279, 329, 333, 433, 514n12; Knorozov and, 283, *284*, 285, 289–90; Kukulkán of, 471; as Lacandón, 129, 141, 179, *180*, 182, *182–83*, 298, 512n1; Madrid Codex by, 281; main sign for, 287; of the Maya, 217, 233; mistakes concerning, 291; names as, 287, 289, 491; on Petén pottery, 445; Proskouriakoff and, 287–89, *288*; research on, 127; Schellhas and, 283–84; Seler and, 283; as syllabic, 285; Thompson, J. E. S., and, 280–81, 286, *286*, *288*, 292, 341, 344, 367, 407, 438, 445; as Tzeltal, 129, 145, 153; as Tzotzil, 129, 145–46, *147–49*; worship by, 158, 160; as Yucatec, 284. *See also* archaeology, Petén; hieroglyphs, Maya; mapping/plotting; *specific sites*
Maya Corpus Program: Bartlett funding of, 484; coding system for, 343; Copán and, 344; to curtail looting, 344; design/content of, 343–45; endowment for, 484, 485; funding for, 402–3, 477; Harvard University and, 402–3, 477; initiation of, 346–47; Kress Foundation funding for, 365; looting of ruins and, 344; MacArthur Prize Fellowship for, 397–403; Maudslay and, 384; Maya weavers at, *480*; Naranjo site of, 345; NEH and donor funding for, 362–63, 397, 400, 402; operations of, 485; at Peabody Museum, 359–65, 478, 479, *479–80*; pilot study for, 316, 341–46; printing of, 365; production rate for, 485; Stuart, D. S., at, 401–2; tax on, 412–13; on Toniná, 466; Uxmal site of, 345, 411; Von Euw and, 349, 363
Mayalum (hotel), 186–87
Mayapan, ruins of, 478
May's Department Store, Maya stela at, 315–16

Mazariegos, Miguel, 310–11
McClintock, Barbara, 399
Mechel, Carl, 173, 356
media: magazine as, 71, 72, 111, 121, 264, 388, 392; newspapers as, 5, 15–16, 17, 68, 121–22, *122*, 206, 226–27, 267, 298, 309, 326, 389, 392, 442, 482, 506nn6–7; *Pathé News* as, 17; *U.S. v. Hollinshead et al.* in, 438
Melchor de Mencos, 218, 318, 345, 421, 424–25; monument storage at, 318
Memoirs of an Aesthete (Acton), 70
Menashe, Samuel, 190
Menassalian, A., 288
Mercer, Henry Chapman, 279
Merrin, Edward, 441, 448–49, 466, 514n13, 515n3
Merwin, Raymond E., 358, 422–23. *See also* Peabody Museum
Messel, Oliver, 68
Metropolitan Museum, 179, 326, 389, 390, 464
Metropolitan Opera House, 107
Meucci, Antonio, 100
Mexico: ban on antiquities trade in, 430, 431; crossing into, 4, 115, *115*; importation of plundered antiquities into, 310, 429, 431, 448, 515n3
Mexikon, Aktuelle Informationen un Studien zu Mesoamerika (journal), 440
Miami Herald Sunday Magazine (newspaper), 392
Middle American Research Institute, 128–29, 267, 342. *See also* Tulane University
Miller, Lloyd, 250
Millington-Drake, Teddy, 116
Mills, John, 83
Milstein, Nathan, 130, 175
Minneapolis Institute of Arts, 432
Mirador Project. *See* Brigham Young University
Mission Archéologique et Ethnologique Française au Mexique, 470
Mitchell, John A., 466
Mitla, ruins of, 128
Mittelstaedt, Bernie, 496
molds, monument: of latex, 164, 254, 255, 261, 339; of papier-mâché, 339
Molina Montes, Augusto, 417
Molina Orantes, Adolfo "Fito," 167, 232, 427, 511n5
monkey, spider/howler, 146, 162, 207, 265, 331–32, *332*, 456, 484
Montalbán, Trinidad, 163–64
Monte Albán, ruins of, 128
Montenegro, Méndez, 326
Montevecchi, Liliane, 123–24

Montrose, James, 6, 7, 37–38, 66
monument, Maya, storage of, 318
Monumentos Prehispánicos, 497. *See also* Patrimonio Cultural
Monument to the Unknown Looter, 309
Moore, George, 72
Moore, Henry, 116
Moore, Lee, 387–95, *388, 393–94*
Morales Fernández, Rafael "Rafa," 216, 316, 318, 321
Morant, G. M., 37
Moreno, Mario. *See* Cantinflas
Morfín, Manuel, 138
Morley, Sylvanus G., 118, 249, 289, 291, 339–40, 437. *See also* Carnegie Institution of Washington
Morning Post (newspaper), 5, 15–16, 17, 506nn6–7
Morrow, Elizabeth, 63–64
Morrow, Michael, 63–64
Morton, Coco, 121–22, 124, 271
Morton, Jane, 121–22, 124, 271
Motul Maya (dictionary), 212, 232–33
mule: for chicle industry, 250; fording rivers with, 262, *263*; for freight, 250, 251, 255, *257*, 275, 345; *ramón* for, 138, 202, 228; as runaway, 257–58, 260; travel by, 134, 136–37, 138, 194, 196, 199–201, 211, 215, 219, 228, 250
Müller, Bernabé, 451
murals, Maya: at Chichén Itzá, 456; La Pasadita, 456, *457*, 458–61, *460*; Maya painting of, 456, *457*, 458, 497; photography of, 497, *499*; removal of, 458–59; at San Bartolo, 456, *499*, 501–3; at Tulum, 456; at Xultun, 497
Murray's Guide to Paris, 382
Museo de América, 281
Museo Nacional (Mexico City), 470
Museo Nacional de Arqueología y Etnografía (Guatemala), 216, 316, 441, 459–60, 484
Museum of Primitive Art (New York). *See* Metropolitan Museum
music, Elizabethan, 63–64
Musica Reservata (musical group), 65
Mysterious Maya (Stuart, Gene; Stuart, George), 169

Naachtún, ruins of, 227
Na Bolom, 128–29, 145, 162, 469
Nakbe, ruins of, 232–33
Naranjo, ruins of: aguada at, *317*; Graham, I., at, 138–39, 316–20; inscriptions at, 315; K'ak' Tiliw Chaan Chahk at, 442; location of, 316; looting at, 296, 298, 316, 318–20, 433–35, 513n3; mapping of, 297, 345; monument removal from, 316, 318;

Stela 4 at, 320; Stela 8 at, 315–16; Stela 28 at, 320; Stela 35 at, 320; Stela 41 at, 318; Stella and Charles Guttman Foundation proposal and, 345
NASA. *See* National Aeronautics and Space Administration
National Aeronautics and Space Administration (NASA), 234
National Airship, The, 15–17, *16,* 506n7
National Arts Collection Fund, 50
National Center of Afro-American Artists, 400–401
National Endowment for the Humanities (NEH), 362
National Gallery (Britain): Crawford, D., at, 50; Graham, I., at, 81–87; Wiggins Collection at, 84
National Gallery of Art (Australia), 381
National Geographic Society, 419
National Institute of Anthropology and History (Guatemala). *See* Instituto Nacional de Antropología e Historia (Guatemala)
National Museum of Anthropology (Mexico), 340
National Museum of Anthropology and Ethnography (Guatemala), 321
National Museum of Archaeology and Ethnography (Guatemala), 316, 331
National Portrait Gallery (London), 386
Nations, Jim, 493
Naylor, Douglas, 61
NEH. *See* National Endowment for the Humanities
Neikrug, Marjorie, 437
newspaper: *Boston Globe* as, 442; *Daily Telegraph* as, 206; *Illustrated London News* as, 267; *El Imparcial* as, 298, 326; *Los Angeles Times* as, 121–22, *122*; *Miami Herald Sunday Magazine* as, 392; *Morning Post* as, 5, 15–16, 17, 506nn6–7; *New York Times* as, 389; *Sunday Beacon-Journal* as, 226–27; *Sunday Times* as, 68; *The Times* as, 5; *Wall Street Journal* as, 482; *Washington Post* as, 309
New Yorker, The (magazine), 388
New York Times (newspaper), 389
Noble, Leila, 116
Nohoch Ek, ruins of, 442
Norman, Dorothy, 116
Nottebohm, Karl-Heinz, 433
Nuffield Foundation, 82
Nuñez de Rodas, Edna, 333

OAS. *See* Organization of American States
Ocoltún. *See* La Florida, ruins of
O espíritu da América prehispánica: 3,000 años de cultura (exhibition), 439–40, *440*

O'Failoin, Sean, 72
Oklahoma (musical), 90
Olmedo, Dolores "Lola," 312–13
O'Mahony, Eioan "The Pope," 66–68
Operación Rescate, 321, 481, 484
Order of the Quetzal, *361, 500*
Organization of American States (OAS), 420
O'Sullivan, Sean, 67

Pabst Lumber Co., 113–14, 177
Palenque, ruins at: Berlin at, 287; crypt at, 287; Graham, I., at, 129, 143; inscriptions at, 284, 287; Temple of Cross at, 284; Temple of Inscriptions at, 287; Temple of Sun at, 289
Palmer, William, 465–66, 515n3
Palmer collection, 436
Paredes, Pablo, 251, *251*, 254
Parents' National Educational Union (PNEU), 11–12, 18
Parnall Elf, 17, 506n10
Parsons, William, 68–69
Paso Caballos, 293, 300
Pathé News, 17
Patrimonio Cultural, 497
Patterson, Leonardo, 381, 437, 439
Peabody Museum: at Altar de Sacrificios, 167, 232, 268, *272*, 274, 275, 283, 458; archival Maya photographs at, 422, 478; CIW archives at, 478, 479; Graham, I., at, 359–65, *364, 479*; library of, 478; Maler photographs at, 290, 362, 478; Maya Corpus Program at, 359–65, 478, 479, *479–80*; Merwin with, 358, 422–23; projects by, 167, 211, 254, 268–69, *288*, 289, 290, 308, 309, 316, 342–43, 347; at Seibal, *272*, 274, 275, 340, 370; Smith, L. with, 167, 170, 173, 232, 254, 272, *273*, 280–81, 324, 340, 362, 479; Visiting Committee of, 443–44; Willey with, 268, 272, *272*, 274, 275, 280–81, 324, 340, 343, 362, 403, 480; Williams, S., with, 343, 347, 391, 420, 442, 480
Pears, Peter, 91–93
Pearson, Billy, 438
Pearson, Karl, 37
Pech, Pedro, 374
Peer Gynt (play), 76–77
Pendergast, David, 439, 459
Penn, Irving, 106–7
Pepe (mule driver), 199–203
Pepper, David, 65
Pepys, Samuel, 37
Perfect Schoolgirl, The (album), 8–9

Perls Gallery, 449
Petén, Department of: aviation within, 193–94; chicle in, 138, 139, 179, 193–95, 202, 208–9, 224, 226, 233, 249–50, 252, 293–95, 302, 311, 331, 337, 422, 431, 510n1, 515n1; Esso Oil in, 249; flora/fauna in, 146, 162, 265, 331–32, *332*, 356, 456; forests of, 193–94; geologists in, 331; logging in, 138, 193, 329, 331, 332–33, 345, 349, 350, 363, 367, 422, 428, 431, 436, 496, 498, 512n1; oil/gas concessions in, 133–34, 213, 218, 249, 250, 260, 271, 384, 445, 510n1; roads within, 193; Royal Dutch/Shell Oil in, 271, 384, 445, 510n1; settlement in, 194; Signal Oil in, 250; Sohio in, 134–35, 218; storm damage in, *257*, 331; Sun Oil in, 213; Tikal in, 132, 137, 193; Union Oil in, 133–34, 250, 260
photography: as aerial, 218, 223–26, 229, 232–34, 413, 420, 453, 510n1, 511n2; of Aguateca, *140, 165*; from Altar de Sacrificios, 445, *446*; Auricon Super 1200 for, 290; from balloon, 109; Bell and Howell Filmo 16-mm movie camera for, 160; by Catherwood, 413; by CIW, 342–43, 362, 368, 478; development of, 290; digital camera for, 485; by Graham, I., 4, 30–31, 93–97, 105–9, *115*, 116, *123*, 128, 130–31, 132–33, 135, *137–38, 140, 142, 144, 147–58*, 160, *161*, 162, *163, 165, 171*, 172–73, 178, *180–85*, 185, 189, 191, *197, 203, 205–6, 208*, 211, *214*, 215, 220–21, *221*, 234, 254, 261, 270–71, 292, 296, 303, 305, 306, 338–39, 341, 344–46, 355, 368, 381, 383–84, 413, 422, 432, 441, 445–46, 458, 461, 472–73, 485; of Graham, I., *4, 7, 88, 108, 114, 122, 169, 189*, 251, *273, 284, 319, 364, 376, 378, 393, 394, 440, 452, 479, 480, 492, 495, 499, 500, 501*; of Graham, I., drawings, *220*, 268; Hasselblad 1000 for, 130–31, 132; by Ivanoff, 433; of La Amelia, 170, *171*; Leica for, 130–31, 132; Maler and, 290, 478; Maudslay and, 290; for Maya Corpus Project, 344–46, 478; by Merwin, 413, 509n1; of murals, 497, *499*; in Peabody archives, 422, 478–79; of Petén archaeological sites, 118, 128, 133, 135, *137, 140, 142*, 143, 162, *165*, 168, *169*, 170, *171*, 172–73, 178, 189, 191, 211, 215, 220–21, 223–24, 227, 234, 261, 268, 290–92, 296, 298, 303, 305–6, 316, 338–42, 349, 355, 362, 363–64, 368, 378, 381, 385, 388, 413–14, 420, 422–23, 432, 441, 445–46, 453, 458, 461, 463, 466, *472*, 472–73, *499*, 511n2, 512n3, 515n2; as photomosaic, 453; roll-outs for, 445–46; stereo-viewer for, 234; by Tippett, 434; at Uxmal, 345
photomosaic, 453. *See also* photography
PICAO. *See* Provisional International Civil Aviation Organization

Picture Post (magazine), 72

Piedras Negras, ruins of: Brigham Young University at, 465; inscriptions at, 431; looting at, 367–68, 431, *434*, 513n3; Maler at, 431; Proskouriakoff and, 287–89, *288*; Stela 2 at, 432; Stela 3 at, 431; Stela 35 at, 514n3; Stuart, D. S., at, 401–2; University of Pennsylvania at, 288–89, 343–44

Pierce, Sharon, 450–51

Pilling, Douglas, *500*

Pirie, Dierdre, 402, 482

Pirie, Robert, 402, 482

plotting. *See* mapping/plotting

Plumsock Fund, 481, 483

PNEU. *See* Parents' National Educational Union

Pollock, Harry, 170, 280–81, 362, *479*, 480

polymerization, 84

Poptún: Kaibiles at, 320; stela fragments in, 318

Pratt, Ruthie, 99–100, 308, 437

Pre-Columbian Art Act (1972), 440

Present Laughter (Coward), 108

Preziosi, Amadeo, 382–84

Preziosi, Donald, 384

primitive art. *See* antiquities

Pringle, John, 56–57

processions, Easter, 216

Proskouriakoff, Tatiana, 287–89, 342, 349, 359–62, *360–61*, 478, *479*

Provisional International Civil Aviation Organization (PICAO), 59, 509n5

Puche, Serra, 413

Purcell, Henry, 93

Putnam, F. W., 423

Queen Elizabeth (liner), 99

Queen Mary (liner), 124

Quennell, Peter, 71

Quest for the Lost City (Lamb, D.; Lamb, G.), 127, 462

Quiriguá, ruins of, 132, 385

Quixchán, Felipe, 370

radar: AI as, 58; ASV Mark II as, 48–49; Rebecca Mark IV as, 53, 55, 59

Radio Petén, 421

RAF. *See* Royal Air Force

Raffa, John J., 450–51

Rambagh Palace, 235, 236

ramón, for mules/horses, 138, 202, 228, 260, 349

Ramonal, camp of, 200–204

Rancho Santa Amelia, 326–27

Randall, John, 59

Ranneft, Johan Everhard Meijer, 341

Rassiga, Everett, 311, 388–89, 391, 430

rattlesnake, *206*, 206–7

Rawlins, Ian, 82–83, 84

Raxujá, 134, 277–80, *279*

Ray, Johnny, 109

Reagan, Ronald, 308

Rebecca Mark IV, 53, 55, 59

Recursos Hidráulicos, 173

Reina, Ben, 166

Reinhold, Robert, 389–90

religious festivals. *See* carnivals/religious festivals

remittance men, 129–30

Rendall, Montagu John, 21

restoration, practice of: at Bonampak by UNESCO, 185; at Chichén Itzá, 418; at Dos Pilas, *169*, 169–70; funding of, 417; after looting, 318, 320; role of tourism in, 417; UNESCO's Venice Charter and, 417; at Uxmal, 413–15

Reyes Porras, Jorge Mario, 421

rey/reina (king/queen), 275

Richardson, F., 288

Richardson, Ralph, 76

Ricketson, Oliver, 511n4

Río Azul, ruins of: Adams, R., at, 167, 204–5, 214, 217; Emmerich's stone mask from, 449; illness at, 217; inscriptions at, 214–16, *216*, 448; looting at, 217, *449*

Río de la Pasión, 133, 140, 170

Río Machaquilá, 251

Río San Pedro, 293, *294*

Rittenour, Glenn, 437

Rivera, Diego, 179, *185*, 312

Rivera, José, 141

River House, 107, *108*

RMS *Queen Elisabeth*, 174–75

RNR. *See* Royal Naval Reserve

Road and Track (magazine), 121

Road to Oxiana, The (Byron), 238

Roamin' in the Gloamin (Lauder), 6

Robinson Lumber Company, 436

Robson, Geoff, 51

Rockefeller, Nelson, 464

Rogers, William D., 342

roll-outs, technique of, 445–46. *See also* photography

Rolls-Royce Phantom II, 235–45, *237*, *238*, *245*

roof, Maya, as vaulted, 253, 416–17, 456

Roosevelt, Archibald, 308

Roosevelt, Selwa "Lucky," 308

Rosse, Ann, 68–69

Standard Oil of Ohio (Sohio), 134–35, 218

Stein, Gertrude, 72

Stein, Susan, 107, *108*, 123

Stella and Charles Guttman Foundation, 316, 341–43, 346, 362, 485. *See also* Maya Corpus Program

Stephens, John Lloyd, 127, 187, 411, 470

stereo-viewer, 225, 234. *See also* photography

St. Louis Art Museum, 316

Stokes, John, 311

Stuart, David S., 217, 339, 401, 432, 445, 465, 466, 477, 480–81, 484, 494, *495*

Stuart, Gene, 169

Stuart, George, 169

Stuart-Wortley, Diana, 43–45

Suarez, Delfino, 431–32, 514n3

Sunday Beacon-Journal (newspaper), 226–27

Sunday Times (newspaper), 68

Sun Oil, 249

surveying: Breed and Mosmer's manual for, 271, 272, 273; chaining for, 273; compass for, 224–25; Hunting Aero Survey Company for, 223; transit for, 272, 273, 411; of Uxmal, 411–12

sweat bees (insect), *169*

Tamarindito, ruins of: drawing of stela at, 324; Graham, I., drawings of, 324; helicopter pad at, 323–24; location of, 323; mapping of, 323; Paris exhibition from, 323–24; Shoran station at, 323; stela at, 323–24

Taylor, Dicey, 445

TCD. *See* Trinity College, Dublin

Telecommunications Research Establishment (TRE), 51–60

Tenejapa, town of: blessing of seeds in, 158; carnival of, 156–58, *156–59*; carnival DVD of, 160; horseback trip to, 153–54, *153–54*; photo of, 155; tourism at, 160; Tzeltal Maya at, 153; worship at, 158, 160

Tepoztlan, temple of, 118

Tercero, Ismael, 349, 354

Thompson, E. H., 211

Thompson, Florence, 292

Thompson, J. Eric S., 280–81, 286, *286*, *288*, 292, 341, 344, 367, 407, 445. *See also* Carnegie Institution of Washington

Thompson, J. J., 41

Thoren, Virginia, 105

Thorndyke, Sybil, 76

Thurman, Uma, 111

Tichenor, Bridget, 116

Tikal, ruins of: Asociación Tikal for, 216, 316; Coe, W. R., at, 137, 267–68, 340, 442; in Department of Petén, 132, 137, 193; Graham, I., at, 132, 137; Group H at, 510n1; Jaguar Inn at, 207; road link from, to Flores, 195, 213; in Tikal National Park, 333; tourism for, 137, 193; University of Pennsylvania at, 137, 340, 343–44; Von Euw at, 349, 354

Tikal, storage facilities at, 321

Tikal National Park, 333

Tillyard, Stella, 25, 507n2

Times, The (newspaper), 5, 506n7

Timon of Athens (Shakespeare), 77

Tin Research Council, 85

Tintal: chicle camp of, 233; as "Z" site, 233, 234

Tippett, C. J., 433–35

Tippett, Elizabeth, 433–35

Toniná, ruins of: Corpus volume 6 on, 466, 473, 474; Dupaix at, 470; Friends of the Ruins Society for, 470–71; Graham, I., photos of, 471–72, *472*; housing at, 471, 474; INAH at, 470, 473, 474–75; looting at, 466; Mission Archéologique et Ethnologique Française au Mexique study of, 470; monolith from, 470; Monument 83 at, 466; Monument 150 at, 472, 515n2; prehistory of, 474–75; provenience of fragments from, 473–74; topography of, 470; tourism at, 117, 470–71; Yadeún at, 470

tortillas, making of, 195–96, 198, 199, 201, 202–3, 204, 228, 251, 300

tourism: at Birr Castle, 69; at Chamula, 145; at Chinajá, 134–35; in Flores, 193–94; in Matamoros, 115; at Monte Albán, 128; role of, in restoration, 417; at Tenejapa, 160; at Tikal, 137, 193; at Toniná, 117, 470–71

Tourtellot, Gair, 273

Tozzer, Alfred, 464

transportation: on Aviateca, 133, 139, 164, 194, 196–98, 223, 226; by canoe, 127, 137, 143, 166, 167, *182*, 196, 218, 219, *294*, 295, 326, 327–28, *327–28*, 369, 370, 463; by helicopter, 250, *322*, 323–24, 328–30, 355–57, 419–20, 484; by horse, 179, 181, 185, 251, 494, 500; by mule, 134, 136–37, 138, 194, 196, 199–201, 211, 215, 219, 228, 250, 251, 255, *257*, 345; by plane, *301*; plotting of, 224–25, 227; via TACA, 439

TRE. *See* Telecommunications Research Establishment

Tres Islas, ruins of: dig at, 172–73; Graham, I., drawings/photographs at, 172; Mechel and, 173, 356; Stela 1 at, 173; Stela 2 at, 173

Trik, Aubrey, 167, 232